Readings in Economics

EDITED BY

PAUL A. SAMUELSON

Professor of Economics, Massachusetts Institute of Technology

JOHN R. COLEMAN

*Dean, Division of Humanities and Social Sciences and Professor of Economics
Carnegie Institute of Technology*

ROBERT L. BISHOP

Professor of Economics, Massachusetts Institute of Technology

PHILLIP SAUNDERS

*Assistant Professor of Economics and Industrial Administration
Carnegie Institute of Technology*

READINGS IN ECONOMICS

Fourth Edition

McGRAW-HILL BOOK COMPANY
NEW YORK   SAN FRANCISCO   TORONTO   LONDON

III

READINGS IN ECONOMICS

PREFACE

This Fourth Edition of the *Readings in Economics* is a sweeping revision of the earlier versions. Only eleven of the selections from the Third Edition, published in 1958, are carried over here. There are a number of reasons why so many new selections elbowed aside some of the older items:

New problems have come into the spotlight for the prime attention of economists and citizens (see, for example, Readings 11, 18–19, 34, 38, 44–45, 55–56, 58–60, 62–69, 75–79).

The number of available readings that meet high standards for economic content and for readability has increased sharply (see such new items as Readings 4, 6, 12–13, 22–23, 31, 37, 41–43, 46–48, 61, 70–72, 76, 80).

The case for presenting alternative policy positions on key economic issues seems to us to be still more compelling as a way of sharpening the analytical thought of the participants in a democratic society (see Readings 15, 24–25, 44–45, 52, 58–60, 63–64, 67–68, 70–71).

The urgency of reminding readers again and again that most interesting economic problems cross and re-cross the lines between economics and the other social sciences has led to a number of choices of an interdisciplinary nature (see Readings 9, 10, 34, 37, 48, 53, 57, 65–67, 76, 80).

We have designed the book around the assumption that learning proceeds most effectively when the reader crosses over the same ground several times, but with greater depth in each crossing. Thus Reading 1 tells much about economics as a whole; the items immediately following begin to sketch in some of the key details. Reading 27 represents a second overview and prepares the reader for the more systematic analysis which is to follow. Readings 61–72 provide fruitful case materials where the economic tools developed earlier may be applied to a range of timely problems. And Reading 80 pulls together many concepts in a final overview of where we stand in the American economy. That final selection could be read with profit by any intelligent and curious American; it can be read with the greatest profit, however, by someone who has already looked at the workings of the economy in successively deeper ways.

Within the bounds set by this assumption, however, there is some arbitrariness in the ordering of the materials. They may usefully supplement any of the standard textbooks in introductory economics. They may be read by an interested layman who, without immediate reference to a standard textbook, wants to see what issues economists are most concerned about these days and wants the exercise of developing his own analytical judgments on some of those issues. Or they may provide a valuable supplement to Learning Resources Institute's 160-film television course,

The American Economy, with which one of the editors was associated as National Teacher and another as a member of the Advisory Committee; a number of selections closely parallel the outline of that course.

We have sought to keep many of the great figures in economic thought—Smith, Ricardo, Malthus, Böhm-Bawerk, Schumpeter—in the *Readings,* not as mere names but as spokesmen with a point of view or of analysis that remains fresh to today's readers. We include some other writers who may be surprised at their presence in the company of formal economists; but they seemed to us, by virtue of their skillful reporting or of their espousal of a policy position, to offer unusually rich material for discussion.

Each item has been edited. We have (1) shortened most items, (2) supplied connecting phrases where this shortening required them, (3) provided new titles and subtitles, and (4) prepared introductory notes and questions to make each reading more valuable. The usual reminders of an editor's touch are missing here, in the interests of smoother reading. But the original source is always identified for the serious reader. The responsibility for this editing is, of course, ours alone.

For this edition, most of the selections and the editing were done by Professors Coleman and Saunders. But they were in consultation throughout the project with Professors Samuelson and Bishop.

Those teachers who used earlier editions of this book and who told us what they liked and did not like will find many of their thoughts reflected in this new edition. So too the instructing staffs at the two institutions where we teach, Massachusetts Institute of Technology and Carnegie Institute of Technology, will find some of their tried and tested favorites among these selections. Mrs. Anne Ramey, Mrs. Mary Haber, and Mrs. Francis Gibson of Carnegie Tech have made a contribution that, well beyond routine typing, represented patience and independent thought in preparing the manuscript. To all of these critics and assistants, and above all to the authors and publishers who let us use their materials so freely, our sincere thanks. And to our readers, some share of the pleasure we felt in putting together many of our favorite readings in elementary economics.

P. A. S.
J. R. C.
R. L. B.
P. S.

CONTENTS

Part 1

THE ECONOMIC FRAMEWORK

The world of economics is all about us, affecting much that we do and think and are. If we are to understand it, as we must for its survival and ours, we need to look at it on several levels.

This first reading gives a broad overview of the "what" and the "why" of the study of economics. It is itself an example of a reading that can easily be skimmed for the general line of reasoning, or on another level, it can more profitably be read with care to pick up the subtler points that will form the basis for so much of the material that is to follow. In economics, as in other demanding disciplines, what seems obvious may turn out to be complex and challenging on closer inspection.

Ben W. Lewis, a professor of economics at Oberlin College, has long been interested in the teaching of economics to college and high school students.

Questions to Guide the Reading

Would an underdeveloped economy define the "economic problem" in the same way that the United States might?

How can it be argued that as rich a society as ours is an economy of scarcity?

How might economic illiteracy hurt our capacity to use our limited resources wisely?

THE STUDY OF ECONOMICS
Ben W. Lewis

The case for economics in the schools is made of the same stuff as the case for democracy itself. The logic is inexorable, and its import in today's situation is alarming. Democracy—and this we have on the very highest authority—means government by the people. But the affairs of government, in large and increasing measure, are economic affairs. To be sure, they have political and other overtones; but no one who casts his glance even casually over the range of matters with which modern governments have to deal will doubt that these matters are economic in substance or in effect. Look for a moment: money, credit, commerce, corporations, tariffs, quotas, foreign aid, development, monopoly, fair trade, farm support, small business, oil prorates, highways, rails, communications, private power, public power, inflation, employment, management-labor relations, distribution of income, education, health, public debt—and taxes.

The relationship between government and economics is reciprocal. Somehow—and almost whether we will it or not—our economics classes are invaded by the Securities Exchange Commis-sion, the Interstate Commerce Commission, the Communications Commission, the Power Commission, the Trade Commission, the Tariff Commission, the Economic Cooperation Administration, the Monetary Fund, the World Bank, the Labor Board, the Federal Reserve, the Treasury, the Labor, Commerce, Agriculture, and Interior Departments, the Social Security Agency, the TVA, Bonneville, the Army Engineers, the Budget Bureau, the Social Security Agency, the Council of Economic Advisers—and the current incarnation of the Hoover Commission.

The simple business of living in the United States in our age calls increasingly upon men to participate actively with other men in the gigantic undertaking of collective governmental decision making on a vast array of complex economic problems and issues. It is demanded of these men that they have economic understanding. The stakes, to put the matter bluntly, are the survival of democracy and human freedom. Freedom will not remain if democracy expires, and democracy will not last beyond the day when it fails to discharge the political-economic tasks

From Ben W. Lewis, "Economic Understanding: Why and What," *American Economic Review*, May, 1957, pp. 653–670. Reprinted with kind permission of the author and editor.

which we ask it to perform. Remember, democracy is government of and by the people, and the capacity of the people to perform will set the level of performance which it is possible for democracy to attain.

Freedom and democracy are abstract concepts, but the matter of their preservation is concrete and immediate. This is our democracy, and we are "the people" on whose economic understanding and economic sense the outcome of our epic adventure in self-government rests.

It will not have escaped notice that in making the case for extending and deepening economics in the schools, I have resisted the temptation to speak of the need of each individual in our highly specialized and interdependent economy for knowledge and skills which will help him to operate more effectively as a buyer and seller of goods and services. Men need to know about credit facilities and practices, installment buying, insurance, tax forms, social security provisions, and a host of other matters in order to move intelligently in making and enjoying their living. But information about these matters is not to be accepted as economics, or in lieu of economics. Such information may come to the student as a by-product of his study of economics, and it is often both possible and productive to employ topics of this kind as a vehicle for developing economic understanding. It may be that many of these things should be taught for their own sake in the schools, if this does not mean too much time and resources diverted from more important work. But the call for more and better economics in the schools does not derive from the need for formal instruction in whether to buy or rent a home or the conditions under which term-insurance is to be preferred to an annuity. A man may be very shrewd in his personal dealings in these matters and still be sadly deficient in economic understanding.

Before setting out my understanding of the shape and nature of economic understanding, let me first clear the ground with a set of negatives. Economic understanding does not consist in the accumulation of a stock of economic information or of an array of useful economic facts. It does not consist of the possession of a "Do-it-yourself" kit of answers to public economic problems or of a package of rules of sound thinking for solving these problems. Nor does it consist of skills or precepts to be employed in the conduct of economic transactions. Economics makes use of all these things, but we are talking here about economic *understanding,* and "understanding" means *understanding.* Understanding is concerned with

"why." Its interest in "what" is strictly ancillary to its interest in "why."

I believe economic understanding is to be gained through an understanding of the central core of economics that dominates all economic situations and issues—"The Economic Problem" faced by all societies of men who live and make their living together. We have economic systems or economies because we are confronted by "The Economic Problem"; economies, all economies irrespective of characteristics or qualities, are fashioned, molded and maintained solely because this problem exists. To understand "The Economic Problem" is to know the purpose and functions of economic systems, and thus to have a clear unmistakable point of reference, a firm home base, from which to proceed in considering any and all questions of economic public policy. I do not claim eternal and universal economic salvation as the reward for such understanding, but I do not hesitate to say that, in its absence, only confusion can prevail.

"The Economic Problem," let us be reminded, is simply: What disposition shall society make of its limited human and natural resources in light of the unlimited needs and desires which these resources can be used to satisfy? This is the most important concept in economics, whether regard be had for economics as a formal study or for what it has to contribute at the school level to general education.

Let me elaborate this thesis. But, first another precautionary negative before I am accused of treating you solely to a bill of thawed-out economic ideas chipped out of our nineteenth-century deep-freeze, and of ignoring the shattering impact upon our thinking of today's dynamic flows, growth modeling, and equation splitting. "The Economic Problem" is not confined to static division; it does not reflect an assumption that produce is fixed in amount and that economic alternatives relate only to kinds and direction. The problem is, what use shall be made of our resources? And I offer "use" to you as a dynamic concept which confronts us with choices bearing on fullness and growth as well as with choices of kind—with questions of "how much" and "how quickly" as well as with questions of "what?"

"The Economic Problem" emerges from two basic, interrelated conditions—(1) man's unlimited desires for goods in the aggregate and (2) the limited human and natural resources available to society for the production of goods in the aggregate.

Mankind has unlimited desires for goods in

the aggregate. Each one of us wants at least a minimum of material goods and services to satisfy his basic needs—such things, for example, as food, shelter, household furnishings, clothing, medical services, and so forth. But each of us desires much more than this basic minimum of essentials. Each would like more, and more varieties, of all of these things and many things in addition. The fact is that if each of us did not have to restrain himself by some notion of what he could afford, his individual desires or wants would run on endlessly. In the aggregate, such limitless desires, multiplied in volume by the number of individuals who inhabit the world, go far beyond anything that society can ever dream of actually satisfying from its limited resources.

Society's human and natural resources available for the production of goods in the aggregate are limited. The goods and services with which we satisfy our desires do not grow in limitless quantities upon limitless trees; they do not appear out of nowhere when we rub a magic lamp or utter a "secret word." Goods must be produced (even those few that do "grow on trees" have to be picked—or picked up and prepared for use). Production requires the use of human resources (labor) and natural resources (land, water, ores, minerals, fuels, etc.), together with techniques and methods for organizing and combining and processing these resources. And we know that, basically, these resources are scarce relative to human needs and desires. Despite our marvelous advances in technology and despite the fact that our standard of material living has on the average risen markedly over the centuries, we can never produce such an abundance of goods that everyone in the world can have all he wants of everything, with lots left over.

Let there be no confusion on this point. Occasionally in our society we are confronted by so-called "surpluses" of particular products (the "butter surplus," the "potato surplus," for example, or the "surplus of used automobiles"). These represent supplies of particular goods in excess of the amounts which buyers with purchasing power at a particular time and place are willing to buy at prevailing prices. In an economic sense they represent particular overproduction in relation to effective demand for particular goods—misproduction or malproduction, or a use or allocation of society's resources of which society, by its market calculus, indicates it does not approve. In the world as we know it, "too many" potatoes means "too few" of other things; it can never mean "too much of everything." Break-

downs in society's institutional arrangements for bringing goods and desires together are not to be interpreted as evidence of society's power to produce without limit. By the same token, we must not be misled by terms and phrases which suggest contradictions where none exist. Specifically, there is no contradiction between an "economy of scarcity" and an "economy of plenty," where "scarcity" is understood as a condition of economizing and "plenty" is understood as its goal.

The reason we bother to manage or economize our resources is simply that, since they are limited in supply relative to the uses to which we would like to put them—that is, since in an economic sense they are "scarce"—it makes a difference to us how they are used. The degree and manner and direction of their use and the disposition of the product resulting from their use have, of sheer necessity, been a primary, basic concern of all societies through the ages. This is what the study of "economizing," or economics as a social science, is about. It is *all* that economics is about.

Presumably any society will want its scarce resources to be "fully" employed (particularly its labor resources), and so used that their power to produce is great and expanding, and that the "right" goods are produced in the "right" amounts and, in each case, by using the "best" combinations of resources. Any society will be concerned, too, that the goods which are produced from its scarce resources are divided fairly among its members.

But the use of such terms as "fully," "right," "best," "fairly," etc., in defining the disposition to be made of resources suggests that alternative uses are possible and that society is faced with the never-ending problem of making millions of continuous and simultaneous decisions in the management or economizing of its resources. Surely we want our resources to be used fully and in the right and best way, but how full is fully? Exactly which ways are right and best and fair? We must remember, too, that society's answers to some of the questions may condition and set limits on its answers to other questions: a decision to promote technological advance *may* make employment less stable, a decision to divide the aggregate product more evenly among everyone *may* have an adverse effect upon the total amount produced, and public policies designed to bring about full employment *may* also promote productive inefficiency and aggravated inequities as an undesired consequence. Nonetheless, answers must be provided by society to "The Economic Problem" faced by men who want to live in harmony and well-being in a world where not everyone can have all he wants of the goods and services that make up his material living.

Thus it is that all societies of men who make their living together must inevitably establish and maintain (or acquiesce in) an economic system or economy—a set of man-made arrangements to provide answers to the all-important economic questions which make up the over-all economic problem: How fully shall our limited resources be used? How shall our resources be organized and combined? Who shall produce how much of what? To whom and in what amounts shall the resulting product be divided among the members of society?

It is the job of the economic system (any economic system) to make the decisions and turn out the answers that society wants, whatever they may be, to these questions; and economics as a discipline is a study of "The Economic Problem" in all its parts, and of the institutional arrangements which men have devised to grind out the necessary answers to the questions which it poses.

The data and materials, the concepts and the "principles" with which the study of economics is concerned and the problems to which it attends all stem from and bear on this central problem: How do we and how might we dispose of the resources upon which the level and quality of our material life depend? This is "The Economic Problem." All other economic problems and issues—for example, the farm problem, the labor-management problem, the problem of taxation, the inflation problem, the problem of full employment, the antitrust problem—are simply partial manifestations of it in particular quarters and under particular conditions and can be dealt with effectively only in conscious relation to the central problem—the *core* of economics. This should be the starting point of our economics teaching, and its destination. Between the starting point and the terminus, students should become familiar with the significant features of our own mid-twentieth century economy with its ever changing combinations of individual markets and collective governmental economic activities and processes. They should become aware of its rationale and of how it has come to be what it now is and of how it contrasts with earlier and other economic systems. They need to know something of the structure and operations of our major economic institutions and the mechanics of income determination, resource guidance, and income distribution. They should experience the

centering of issues and the marshaling and weighing of considerations involved in the determination of policy in one or two areas of public economic policy. But all of this—systems, processes, institutions, mechanics, policy problems—I repeat, all of this should be tied constantly to the core of economics—"The Economic Problem" —and related at every turn to the purposes for which men build economic systems because that problem exists.

A person who possesses economic understanding will relate his consideration of public economic issues, easily and purposively, to the central core—to the starting point, to home base. He will have a sense of the interrelationship of economic phenomena and problems—the "oneness" of the economy—the tie-in between each sector of the economy and the whole and between the economy and himself.

He will know his "way around" and his "way home" in the economy. He will face such choices as those between alternative satisfactions, between present and future goods, between alternative methods of production, between production and leisure, between stability and security and innovation and progress, and between economizing by the market and economizing by government, under whatever conditions and guises these choices may appear, with awareness and a balanced sense of consequences.

He will know that products come from production and will have an appreciation of the contribution made by diverse groups to the totality of production.

Familiarity with the mechanics of economics will not blind him to the reality that the operating forces in any political economy are human. He will know that economic life involves, essentially, the rational living together of human beings—a constant adjustment and readjustment in economic matters comparable to, indeed a part of, the constant adjustment and readjustment that characterize the total business of living together. He will realize that these adjustments frequently bring discomfort, even pain, to those established (vested) interests that are required to adjust, but that failure of one group to adjust may mean privation for other groups and stagnation for the economy as a whole. And he will relate this to situations in which his own interest lies in resistance to change (tariff, price supports, "fair trade," "featherbedding") as well as to those in which his own interest would be served by the adjustment of others.

He will distinguish between areas where "scientific" economic answers are possible, areas where such answers are impossible because necessary information or data are absent, and areas where only value judgments are called for and possible. He will realize it is not the function of economics to provide answers to ethical or value problems but, rather, to help to define and identify such problems and to place them in sharper focus.

Finally, his realization that, in the very nature of the case, economic problems permit of very few "right" answers will be one measure of the

depth of his economic understanding—and the realization will fill him with a sense not of futility but of purpose. It will point up for him his personal role in the political economy in which he lives.

This is what economic understanding can mean. This is what we would like to have for all of our people as members of a free, democratic society. We will never have all of it for everyone, but we cannot afford to seek and work for less.

READING 2

Population comes into the study of economics both as a demand factor (man as consumer) and as a supply factor (man as producer). In the former context, the one with which this reading and the next are concerned, we look at people's needs for food, clothing, shelter, and eventually, all the luxuries that lie beyond. More people mean more demand for goods and services. In the latter context, we look at the capacities of men, by virtue of their health, their education, and their attitudes, to produce the desired goods and services in increasing volume. More people mean more workers.

Here we meet the man and ideas that led Thomas Carlyle to put the persistent stigma of "the dismal science" on economics. The Reverend Thomas Robert Malthus (1766–1834) was a distinguished member of the classical school in economics. Despite his other contributions to the growing science of economics, his fame today rests principally on his gloomy analysis of population. He argues in this passage that, in the absence of moral restraint, population must forever tend to outstrip the available means of subsistence. This analysis, which has not seemed very relevant to the American scene, is now coming back into the world spotlight for reasons developed in the next reading.

Questions to Guide the Reading

If a man is thought of in cold economic terms as both a new mouth to be fed and a new resource for production, why should we be concerned with overpopulation?

How has the United States been able to escape the dire consequences of the Malthusian doctrine?

POPULATION GROWTH AND POVERTY
Thomas R. Malthus

In an inquiry concerning the improvement of society, the mode of conducting the subject which naturally presents itself, is,

1. To investigate the causes that have hitherto impeded the progress of mankind towards happiness; and,

2. To examine the probability of the total or partial removal of these causes in future.

The principal object of the present essay is to examine the effects of one great cause intimately united with the very nature of man; which, though it has been constantly and power-

From T. R. Malthus, *An Essay on the Principle of Population* (Reeves and Turner, London, 1878), 8th edition.

fully operating since the commencement of society, has been little noticed by the writers who have treated this subject. The facts which establish the existence of this cause have, indeed, been repeatedly stated and acknowledged; but its natural and necessary effects have been almost totally overlooked; though probably among these effects may be reckoned a very considerable portion of that vice and misery, and of that unequal distribution of the bounties of nature, which it has been the unceasing object of the enlightened philanthropist in all ages to correct.

The cause to which I allude, is the constant tendency in all animated life to increase beyond the nourishment prepared for it.

It is observed by Dr. Franklin, that there is no bound to the prolific nature of plants or animals, but what is made by their crowding and interfering with each other's means of subsistence. Were the face of the earth, he says, vacant of other plants, it might be gradually sowed and overspread with one kind only, as for instance with fennel: and were it empty of other inhabitants, it might in a few ages be replenished from one nation only, as for instance with Englishmen.

This is incontrovertibly true. Through the animal and vegetable kingdoms Nature has scattered the seeds of life abroad with the most profuse and liberal hand; but has been comparatively sparing in the room and the nourishment necessary to rear them. The germs of existence contained in this earth, if they could freely develop themselves, would fill millions of worlds in the course of a few thousand years. Necessity, that imperious, all-pervading law of nature, restrains them within the prescribed bounds. The race of plants and the race of animals shrink under this great restrictive law; and man cannot by any efforts of reason escape from it.

Population has this constant tendency to increase beyond the means of subsistence, and it is kept to its necessary level by these causes. The subject will, perhaps, be seen in a clearer light, if we endeavour to ascertain what would be the natural increase of population, if left to exert itself with perfect freedom; and what might be expected to be the rate of increase in the productions of the earth, under the most favourable circumstances of human industry.

The potential rate of increase of population.
It will be allowed that no country has hitherto been known, where the manners were so pure and simple, and the means of subsistence so abundant, that no check whatever has existed to early marriages from the difficulty of providing for a family, and that no waste of the human species has been occasioned by vicious customs, by towns, by unhealthy occupations, or too severe labour. Consequently in no state that we have yet known, has the power of population been left to exert itself with perfect freedom.

In the northern states of America, where the means of subsistence have been more ample, the manners of the people more pure, and the checks to early marriages fewer, than in any of the modern states of Europe, the population has been found to double itself, for above a century and a half successively, in less than twenty-five years. In the back settlements, where the sole employment is agriculture, and vicious customs and unwholesome occupations are little known, the population has been found to double itself in fifteen years. Even this extraordinary rate of increase is probably short of the utmost power of population. Sir William Petty supposes a doubling possible in so short a time as ten years.

But, to be perfectly sure that we are far within the truth, we will take the slowest of these rates of increase, a rate in which all concurring testimonies agree, and which has been repeatedly ascertained to be from procreation only.

It may safely be pronounced, therefore, that population, when unchecked, goes on doubling itself every twenty-five years, or increases in a geometrical ratio.

The potential rate of increase of food production.
The rate according to which the productions of the earth may be supposed to increase, it will not be so easy to determine. Of this, however, we may be perfectly certain, that the ratio of their increase in a limited territory must be of a totally different nature from the ratio of the increase of population A thousand millions are just as easily doubled every twenty-five years by the power of population as a thousand. But the food to support the increase from the greater number will by no means be obtained with the same facility. Man is necessarily confined in room. When acre has been added to acre till all the fertile land is occupied, the yearly increase of food must depend upon the melioration of the land already in possession. This is a fund, which, from the nature of all soils, instead of increasing, must be gradually diminishing. But population, could it be supplied with food, would go on with unexhausted vigour; and the increase of one period would furnish the power of a greater increase the next, and this without any limit.

From the accounts we have of China and Japan, it may be fairly doubted, whether the best-directed efforts of human industry could double the produce of these countries even once in any number of years. There are many parts of the globe, indeed, hitherto uncultivated, and almost unoccupied; but even in new colonies, a geometrical ratio increases with such extraordinary rapidity, that the advantage could not last long. If the United States of America continue increasing, which they certainly will do, though not with the same rapidity as formerly, the Indians will be driven further and further back into the country, till the whole race is ultimately exterminated, and the territory is incapable of further extension.

The science of agriculture has been much studied in England and Scotland; and there is still a great portion of uncultivated land in these countries. Let us consider at what rate the produce of this island might be supposed to increase under circumstances the most favourable to improvement.

If it be allowed that by the best possible policy, and great encouragements to agriculture, the average produce of the island could be doubled in the first twenty-five years, it will be allowing, probably, a greater increase than could with reason be expected.

In the next twenty-five years, it is impossible to suppose that the produce could be quadrupled. It would be contrary to all our knowledge of the properties of land. It must be evident to those who have the slightest acquaintance with agricultural subjects, that in proportion as cultivation extended, the additions that could yearly be made to the former average produce must be gradually and regularly diminishing. That we may be the better able to compare the increase of population and food, let us make a supposition, which, without pretending to accuracy, is clearly more favourable to the power of production in the earth, than any experience we have had of its qualities will warrant.

Let us suppose that the yearly additions which might be made to the former average produce, instead of decreasing, which they certainly would do, were to remain the same; and that the produce of this island might be increased every twenty-five years, by a quantity equal to what it at present produces. The most enthusiastic speculator cannot suppose a greater increase than this. In a few centuries it would make every acre of land in the island like a garden.

It may be fairly pronounced, therefore, that, considering the present average state of the earth, the means of subsistence, under circumstances the most favourable to human industry, could not possibly be made to increase faster than in an arithmetical ratio.

The potential rates of increase of population and food compared. The necessary effects of these two different rates of increase, when brought together, will be very striking. Let us call the population of this island eleven millions; and suppose the present produce equal to the easy support of such a number. In the first twenty-five years the population would be twenty-two millions, and the food being also doubled, the means of subsistence would be equal to this increase. In the next twenty-five years, the population would be forty-four millions, and the means of subsistence only equal to the support of thirty-three millions. In the next period the population would be eighty-eight millions, and the means of subsistence just equal to the support of half that number. And, at the conclusion of the first century, the population would be a hundred and seventy-six millions, and the means of subsistence only equal to the support of fifty-five millions, leaving a population of a hundred and twenty-one million totally unprovided for.

Taking the whole earth, instead of this island, emigration would of course be excluded; and, supposing the present population equal to a thousand millions, the human species would increase as the numbers 1, 2, 4, 8, 16, 32, 64, 128, 256, and subsistence as 1, 2, 3, 4, 5, 6, 7, 8, 9. In two centuries the population would be to the means of subsistence as 256 to 9; in three centuries as 4096 to 13 and in two thousand years the difference would be almost incalculable.

In this supposition no limits whatever are placed to the produce of the earth. It may increase for ever and be greater than any assignable quantity; yet still the power of population being in every period so much superior, the increase of the human species can only be kept down to the level of the means of subsistence by the constant operation of the strong law of necessity, acting as a check upon the greater power.

Of the general checks to population, and the mode of their operation

The ultimate check to population appears then to be a want of food, arising necessarily from the different ratios according to which population and food increase. But this ultimate check is never the immediate check, except in cases of actual famine.

The immediate check may be stated to consist in all those customs, and all those diseases, which seem to be generated by a scarcity of the means of subsistence; and all those causes, independent of this scarcity, whether of a moral or physical nature, which tend prematurely to weaken and destroy the human frame.

These checks to population, which are constantly operating with more or less force in every society, and keep down the number to the level of the means of subsistence, may be classed under two general heads—(i) the preventive, and (ii) the positive checks.

The preventive and positive checks described.

(i) The preventive check, as far as it is voluntary, is peculiar to man, and arises from that distinctive superiority in his reasoning faculties, which enables him to calculate distant consequences. The checks to the indefinite increase of plants and irrational animals are all either positive, or, if preventive, involuntary. But man cannot look around him, and see the distress which frequently presses upon those who have large families; he cannot contemplate his present possessions or earnings, which he now nearly consumes himself, and calculate the amount of each share, when with very little addition they must be divided, perhaps, among seven or eight, without feeling a doubt whether, if he follow the bent of his inclinations, he may be able to support the offspring which he will probably bring into the world. In a state of equality, if such can exist, this would be the simple question. In the present state of society other considerations occur. Will he not lower his rank in life, and be obliged to give up in great measure his former habits? Does any mode of employment present itself by which he may reasonably hope to maintain a family? Will he not at any rate subject himself to greater difficulties, and more severe labour, than in his single state? Will he not be unable to transmit to his children the same advantages of education and improvement that he had himself possessed? Does he even feel secure that, should he have a large family, his utmost exertions can save them from rags and squalid poverty, and their consequent degradation in the community? And may he not be reduced to the grating necessity of forefeiting his independence, and of being obliged to the sparing hand of Charity for support?

These considerations are calculated to prevent, and certainly do prevent, a great number of persons in all civilised nations from pursuing the dictate of nature in an early attachment to one woman.

If this restraint do not produce vice, it is undoubtedly the least evil that can arise from the principle of population. Considered as a restraint on a strong natural inclination, it must be allowed to produce a certain degree of temporary unhappiness; but evidently slight, compared with the evils which result from any of the other checks to population; and merely of the same nature as many other sacrifices of temporary to permanent gratification, which it is the business of a moral agent continually to make.

When this restraint produces vice, the evils which follow are but too conspicuous. A promiscuous intercourse to such a degree as to prevent the birth of children, seems to lower, in the most marked manner, the dignity of human nature. It cannot be without its effect on men, and nothing can be more obvious than its tendency to degrade the female character, and to destroy all its most amiable and distinguishing characteristics. Add to which, that among those unfortunate females, with which all great towns abound, more real distress and aggravated misery are, perhaps, to be found, than in any other department of human life.

When a general corruption of morals, with regard to the sex, pervades all the classes of society, its effects must necessarily be, to poison the springs of domestic happiness, to weaken conjugal and parental affection, and to lessen the united exertions and ardour of parents in the care and education of their children:—effects which cannot take place without a decided diminution of the general happiness and virtue of the society; particularly as the necessity of art in the accomplishment and conduct of intrigues, and in the concealment of their consequences necessarily leads to many other vices.

(ii) The positive checks to population are extremely various, and include every cause, whether arising from vice or misery, which in any degree contributes to shorten the natural duration of human life. Under this head, therefore, may be enumerated all unwholesome occupations, severe labour and exposure to the seasons, extreme poverty, bad nursing of children, great towns, excesses of all kinds, the whole train of common diseases and epidemics, wars, plague, and famine.

On examining these obstacles to the increase of population which I have classed under the heads of preventive and positive checks, it will appear that they are all resolvable into moral restraint, vice, and misery.

Of the preventive checks, the restraint from marriage which is not followed by irregular gratifications may properly be termed moral restraint.

Promiscuous intercourse, unnatural passions, violations of the marriage bed, and improper arts to conceal the consequences of irregular connexions, are preventive checks that clearly come under the head of vice.

Of the positive checks, those which appear to arise unavoidably from the laws of nature, may be called exclusively misery; and those which we obviously bring upon ourselves, such as wars, excesses, and many others which it would be in our power to avoid, are of a mixed nature. They are brought upon us by vice, and their consequences are misery.

The mode of operation of preventive and positive checks. The sum of all these preventive and positive checks, taken together, forms the immediate check to population. In every country some of these checks are, with more or less force, in constant operation; yet, notwithstanding their general prevalence, there are few states in which there is not a constant effort in the population to increase beyond the means of subsistence. This constant effort as constantly tends to subject the lower classes of society to distress, and to prevent any great permanent melioration of their condition.

These effects seem to be produced in the following manner. The constant effort towards population, which is found to act even in the most vicious societies, increases the number of people before the means of subsistence are increased. The food, therefore, which before supported eleven millions, must now be divided among eleven millions and a half. The poor consequently must live much worse, and many of them be reduced to severe distress. The number of labourers also being above the proportion of work in the market, the price of labour must tend to fall, while the price of provisions would at the same time tend to rise. The labourer therefore must do more work, to earn the same as he did before. During this season of distress the discouragements to marriage and the difficulty of rearing a family are so great, that the progress of population is retarded. In the mean time, the cheapness of labour, the plenty of labourers, and the necessity of an increased industry among them, encourage cultivators to employ more labour upon their land, to turn up fresh soil, and to manure and improve more completely what is already in tillage, till ultimately the

means of subsistence may become in the same proportion to the population, as at the period from which we set out. The situation of the labourer being then again tolerably comfortable, the restraints to population are in some degree loosened; and, after a short period, the same retrograde and progressive movements, with respect to happiness, are repeated.

One principal reason why this oscillation has been less remarked, and less decidedly confirmed by experience than might naturally be expected, is, that the histories of mankind which we possess are, in general, histories only of the higher classes. We have not many accounts that can be depended upon, of the manners and customs of that part of mankind, where these retrograde and progressive movements chiefly take place.

A circumstance which contributed to conceal this oscillation from common view, is the difference between the nominal and real price of labour. It very rarely happens that the nominal price of labour universally falls; but we well know that it frequently remains the same, while the nominal price of provisions has been gradually rising. An increased number of labourers receiving the same money-wages will necessarily, by their competition, increase the money-price of corn. This is, in fact, a real fall in the price of labour; and, during this period, the condition of the lower classes of the community must be gradually growing worse. But the farmers and capitalists are growing rich from the real cheapness of labour, and thus the wages of labour, and consequently the condition of the lower classes of society might have progressive and retrograde movements, though the price of labour might never nominally fall.

But without attempting to establish these progressive and retrograde movements in different countries, which would evidently require more minute histories than we possess, and which the progress of civilisation naturally tends to counteract, the following propositions are intended to be proved: —

1. Population is necessarily limited by the means of subsistence.

2. Population invariably increases where the means of subsistence increase, unless prevented by some very powerful and obvious checks.

3. These checks, and the checks which repress the superior power of population, and keep its effects on a level with the means of subsistence, are all resolvable into moral restraint, vice and misery.

READING 3

To many living in the relative affluence of contemporary America, Malthus's gloomy predictions in the previous reading may seem remote and badly outdated. One does not have to look far away, however, to find that these predictions are all too relevant in describing the grim realities of much of today's world. Our own national interest as well as a broader concern for mankind in general compels us to ask the question: Can the underdeveloped economies bring their rapidly rising populations under control and advance their levels of living, or must they see hard-won economic gains eaten up in keeping more and more people alive at subsistence levels?

The Committee on Science and Public Policy of the National Academy of Sciences has studied both past and present population trends in various parts of the world in an attempt to put the current world population problem in the proper perspective. As a result of this study, they conclude that an expanded program of research and publicity to promote the effective voluntary control of family size is now an urgent item of world business.

Questions to Guide the Reading

Why should the technically advanced nations of the world concern themselves with the population problems of the less developed countries?

Is there any reason to believe that the less developed countries of today will not follow the population patterns exhibited by the economically developed countries as they move increasingly into industrialization and urbanization?

THE GROWTH OF WORLD POPULATION
National Academy of Sciences

All nations are committed to achieving a higher standard of living for their people—adequate food, good health, literacy, education, and gainful employment. These are the goals of millions now living in privation. An important barrier to the achievement of these goals is the current rate of population growth. The present world population is likely to double in the next 35 years, producing a population of six billion by the year 2000. If the same rate of growth continues, there will be 12 billion people on earth in 70 years and over 25 billion by the year 2070. Such rapid population growth, which is out of proportion to present and prospective rates of increase in economic development, imposes a heavy burden on all efforts to improve human welfare. Moreover, since we live in an interconnected world, it is an international problem from which no one can escape.

In our judgment, this problem can be suc-

cessfully attacked by developing new methods of fertility regulation, and implementing programs of voluntary family planning widely and rapidly throughout the world. Although only a few nations have made any concerted efforts in this direction, responsible groups in the social, economic, and scientific communities of many countries have become increasingly aware of the problem and the need for intelligent and forthright action. We recommend that these groups now join in a common effort to disseminate present knowledge on population problems, family planning, and related bio-medical matters, and to initiate programs of research that will advance our knowledge in these fields.

In pursuit of these objectives, many different kinds of institutions in the United States, both public and private, have important contributions to make. Other than the search for lasting peace, no problem is more urgent.

From *The Growth of World Population* (National Academy of Sciences, Washington, D.C., 1963), pp. 1–38. Reprinted with kind permission of the publisher.

The growth of world population

The population of the world, now somewhat in excess of three billion persons, is growing at about two per cent a year, or faster than at any other period in man's history. While there has been a steady increase of population growth during the past two or three centuries, it has been especially rapid during the past 20 years. To appreciate the pace of population growth we should recall that world population doubled in about 1,700 years from the time of Christ until the middle of the 17th century; it doubled again in about 200 years, doubled again in less than 100, and, if the current *rate* of population increase were to remain constant, would double every 35 years. Moreover, this rate is still increasing.

To be sure, the rate of increase cannot continue to grow much further. Even if the death rate were to fall to zero, at the present level of human reproduction the growth rate would not be much in excess of three and one-half per cent per year, and the time required for world population to double would not fall much below 20 years.

Although the current two per cent a year does not sound like an extraordinary rate of increase, a few simple calculations demonstrate that such a rate of increase in human population could not possibly continue for more than a few hundred years. Had this rate existed from the time of Christ to now, the world population would have increased in this period by a factor of about 7×10^{16}; in other words, there would be about 20 million individuals in place of each person now alive, or 100 people to each square foot. If the present world population should continue to increase at its present rate of two per cent per year, then, within two centuries, there will be more than 150 billion people. Calculations of this sort demonstrate without question not only that the current continued increase in the rate of population growth must cease but also this long-term prognosis: *Either the birth rate of the world must come down or the death rate must go back up.*

Population growth in different parts of the world

The rates of population growth are not the same, of course, in all parts of the world. Among the industrialized countries, Japan and most of the countries of Europe are now growing rela-tively slowly—doubling their populations in 50 to 100 years. Another group of industrialized countries—the United States, the Soviet Union, Australia, New Zealand, Canada, and Argentina—are doubling their populations in 30 to 40 years, approximately the world average. The pre-industrial, low-income, and less-developed areas of the world, with two thirds of the world's population—including Asia (except Japan and the Asiatic part of the Soviet Union), the south-western Pacific islands (principally the Philippines and Indonesia), Africa (with the exception of European minorities), the Caribbean Islands, and Latin America (with the exception of Argentina and Uruguay)—are growing at rates ranging from moderate to very fast. Annual growth rates in all these areas range from one and one-half to three and one-half per cent, doubling in 20 to 40 years.

The rates of population growth of the various countries of the world are, with few exceptions, simply the differences between their birth rates and death rates. International migration is a negligible factor in rates of growth today. Thus, one can understand the varying rates of population growth of different parts of the world by understanding what underlies their respective birth and death rates.

The reduction of fertility and mortality in western Europe since 1800

A brief, over-simplified history of the course of birth and death rates in western Europe since about 1800 not only provides a frame of reference for understanding the current birth and death rates in Europe, but also casts some light on the present situation and prospects in other parts of the world. A simplified picture of the population history of a typical western European country is shown in Figure 1. The jagged interval in the early death rate and the recent birth rate is intended to indicate that all the rates are subject to substantial annual variation. The birth rate in 1800 was about 35 per 1,000 population and the average number of children ever born to women reaching age 45 was about five. The death rate in 1800 averaged 25 to 30 per 1,000 population although, as indicated, it was subject to variation because of episodic plagues, epidemics, and crop failures. The average expectation of life at birth was 35 years or less. The current birth rate in western European countries is 14 to 20 per 1,000 population with an average of two to three children born to a

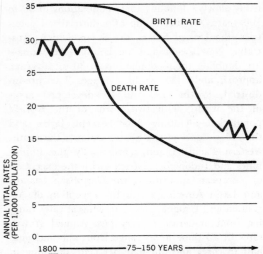

Fig. 1 Schematic presentation of birth and death rates in western Europe after 1800. (The time span varies roughly from 75 to 150 years.)

woman by the end of childbearing. The death rate is 7 to 11 per 1,000 population per year, and the expectation of life at birth is about 70 years. The death rate declined, starting in the late 18th or early 19th century, partly because of better transport and communication, wider markets, and greater productivity, but more directly because of the development of sanitation and, later, modern medicine. These developments, part of the changes in the whole complex of modern civilization, involved scientific and technological advances in many areas, specifically in public health, medicine, agriculture, and industry. The immediate cause of the decline in the birth rate was the increased deliberate control of fertility within marriage. The only important exception to this statement relates to Ireland, where the decline in the birth rate was brought about by an increase of several years in the age at marriage combined with an increase of 10 to 15 per cent in the proportion of people remaining single. The average age at marriage rose to 28 and more than a fourth of Irish women remained unmarried at age 45. In other countries, however, such social changes have had either insignificant or favorable effects on the birth rate. In these countries—England, Wales, Scotland, Scandinavia, the Low Countries, Germany, Switzerland, Austria, and France —the birth rate went down because of the practice of contraception among married couples. It is certain that there was no decline in the re-

productive capacity; in fact, with improved health, the contrary is likely.

Only a minor fraction of the decline in western European fertility can be ascribed to the invention of modern techniques of contraception. In the first place, very substantial declines in some European countries antedated the invention and mass manufacture of contraceptive devices. Second, we know from surveys that as recently as just before World War II more than half of the couples in Great Britain practicing birth control were practicing withdrawal, or *coitus interruptus.* There is similar direct evidence for other European countries.

In this instance, the decline in fertility was not the result of technical innovations in contraception, but of the decision of married couples to resort to folk methods known for centuries. Thus we must explain the decline in the western European birth rates in terms of why people were willing to modify their sexual behavior in order to have fewer children. Such changes in attitude were doubtless a part of a whole set of profound social and economic changes that accompanied the industrialization and modernization of western Europe. Among the factors underlying this particular change in attitude was a change in the economic consequences of childbearing. In a preindustrial, agrarian society children start helping with chores at an early age; they do not remain in a dependent status during a long period of education. They provide the principal form of support for the parents in their old age, and, with high mortality, many children must be born to ensure that some will survive to take care of their parents. On the other hand, in an urban, industrialized society, children are less of an economic asset and more of an economic burden.

Among the social factors that might account for the change in attitude is the decline in the importance of the family as an economic unit that has accompanied the industrialization and modernization of Europe. In an industrialized economy, the family is no longer the unit of production and individuals come to be judged by what they do rather than who they are. Children leave home to seek jobs and parents no longer count on support by their children in their old age. As this kind of modernization continues, public education, which is essential to the production of a literate labor force, is extended to women, and thus the traditional subordinate role of women is modified. Since the burden of child care falls primarily on women, their rise in status is probably an important element in the development of an attitude favoring the deliberate limitation of family size. Finally, the social and economic changes characteristic of industrialization and modernization of a country are accompanied by and reinforce a rise of secularism, pragmatism, and rationalism in place of custom and tradition. Since modernization of a nation involves extension of deliberate human control over an increasing range of the environment, it is not surprising that people living in an economy undergoing industrialization should extend the notion of deliberate and rational control to the question of whether or not birth should result from their sexual activities.

As the simplified representation in Figure 1 indicates, the birth rate in western Europe usually began its descent after the death rate had already fallen substantially. (France is a partial exception. The decline in French births began late in the 18th century and the downward courses of the birth and death rates during the 19th century were more or less parallel.) In general, the death rate appears to be affected more immediately and automatically by industrialization. One may surmise that the birth rate responds more slowly because its reduction requires changes in more deeply seated customs. There is in most societies a consensus in favor of improving health and reducing the incidence of premature death. There is no such consensus for changes in attitudes and behavior needed to reduce the birth rate.

Declining fertility and mortality in other industrialized areas

The pattern of declining mortality and fertility that we have described for western Europe fits not only the western European countries upon which it is based but also, with suitable adjustment in the initial birth and death rates and in the time scale, eastern and southern Europe (with the exception of Albania), the Soviet Union, Japan, the United States, Australia, Canada, Argentina, and New Zealand. In short, every country that has changed from a predominantly rural agrarian society to a predominantly industrial urban society and has extended public education to near-universality, at least at the primary school level, has had a major reduction in birth and death rates of the sort depicted in Figure 1.

The jagged line describing the variable current birth rate represents in some instances—notably the United States—a major recovery in the birth rate from its low point. It must be remembered, however, that this recovery has not been caused by a reversion to uncontrolled family size. In the United States, for example, one can scarcely imagine that married couples have forgotten how to employ the contraceptive techniques that reduced the birth rates to a level of mere replacement just before World War II. We know, in fact, that more couples are skilled in the use of contraception today than ever before. (Nevertheless, effective methods of controlling family size are still unknown and unused by many couples even in the United States.) The recent increase in the birth rate has been the result largely of earlier and more nearly universal marriage, the virtual disappearance of childless and one-child families, and a voluntary choice of two, three, or four children by a vast majority of American couples. There has been no general return to the very large family of pre-industrial times, although some segments of our society still produce many unwanted children.

Population trends in less-developed countries

We turn now to a comparison of the present situation in the less-developed areas with the demographic circumstances in western Europe prior to the industrial revolution. Figure 2 presents the trends of birth and death rates in the less-developed areas in a rough schematic way similar to that employed in Figure 1. There are several important differences between the circumstances in today's less-developed areas and those in pre-industrial Europe. Note first that the birth rate in the less-developed areas is higher than it was in pre-industrial western Europe. This difference results from the fact that in many less-developed countries almost all women at age 35 have married, and at an average age substantially less than in 18th century Europe. Second, many of the less-developed areas of the world today are much more densely populated than was western Europe at the beginning of the industrial revolution. Moreover, there are few remaining areas comparable to North and South America into which a growing population could move and which could provide rapidly expanding markets. Finally, and most significantly, the death rate in the less-developed

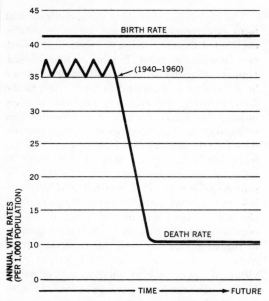

Fig. 2 Schematic presentation of birth and death rates in less-developed countries, mid-20th century. (The steep drop in the death rate from approximately 35 per thousand began at times varying roughly between 1940 and 1960 from country to country.)

areas is dropping very rapidly—a decline that looks almost vertical compared to the gradual decline in western Europe—and without regard to economic change.

The precipitous decline in the death rate that is occurring in the low-income countries of the world is a consequence of the development and application of low-cost public health techniques. Unlike the countries of western Europe, the less-developed areas have not had to wait for the slow gradual development of medical science, nor have they had to await the possibly more rapid but still difficult process of constructing major sanitary engineering works and the build-up of a large inventory of expensive hospitals, public health services, and highly trained doctors. Instead, the less-developed areas have been able to import low-cost measures of controlling disease, measures developed for the most part in the highly industrialized countries. The use of residual insecticides to provide effective protection against malaria at a cost of no more than 25 cents per capita per annum is an outstanding example. Other innovations include antibiotics and chemotherapy, and low-cost ways of providing safe water supplies and adequate environmental sanitation in villages that in most other

ways remain relatively untouched by modernization. The death rate in Ceylon was cut in half in less than a decade, and declines approaching this in rapidity are almost commonplace.

The result of a precipitous decline in mortality while the birth rate remains essentially unchanged is, of course, a very rapid acceleration in population growth, reaching rates of three to three and one-half per cent. Mexico's population, for example, has grown in recent years at a rate of approximately three and one-half per cent a year. This extreme rate is undoubtedly due to temporary factors and would stabilize at not more than three per cent. But even at three per cent per year, two centuries would see the population of Mexico grow to about 13.5 billion people. Two centuries is a long time, however. Might we not expect that long before 200 years had passed the population of Mexico would have responded to modernization, as did the population of western Europe, by reducing the birth rate? A positive answer might suggest that organized educational efforts to reduce the birth rate are not necessary. But there is a more immediate problem demanding solution in much less than two centuries: Is the current demographic situation in the less-developed countries impeding the process of modernization itself? If so, a course of action that would directly accelerate the decline in fertility becomes an important part of the whole development effort which is directed toward improving the quality of each individual's life.

Population trends and the economic development of pre-industrial countries

The combination of high birth rates and low or rapidly declining death rates now found in the less-developed countries implies two different characteristics of the population that have important implications for the pace of their economic development. One important characteristic is rapid growth, which is the immediate consequence of the large and often growing difference between birth and death rates; the other is the heavy burden of child dependency which results from a high birth rate whether death rates are high or low. A reduced death rate has only a slight effect on the proportion of children in the population, and this effect is in a rather surprising direction. The kinds of mortality reduction that have actually occurred in the world have the effect, if fertility remains unchanged, of reducing rather than increasing the average age of the population.

Mortality reduction produces this effect because the largest increases occur in the survival of infants; thus, although the reduction in mortality increases the number of old persons, it increases the number of children even more. The result is that the high fertility found in low-income countries produces a proportion of children under fifteen of 40 to 45 per cent of the total population, compared to 25 per cent or less in most of the industrialized countries.

What do these characteristics of rapid growth and very large proportions of children imply about the capacity to achieve rapid industrialization? It must be noted that it is probably technically possible in every less-developed area to increase national output at rates even more rapid than the very rapid rates of population increase we have discussed, at least for a few years. The reason at least slight increases in per capita income appear feasible is that the low-income countries can import industrial and agricultural technology as well as medical technology. Briefly, the realistic question in the short run does not seem to be whether some increases in per capita income are possible while the population grows rapidly, but rather whether rapid population growth is a major deterrent to a *rapid* and *continuing* increase in per capita income.

A specific example will clarify this point. If the birth rate in India is not reduced, its population will probably double in the next 25 or 30 years, increasing from about 450 million to about 900 million. Agricultural experts consider it feasible within achievable limits of capital investment to accomplish a doubling of Indian agricultural output within the next 20 to 25 years. In the same period the output of the non-agricultural part of the Indian economy probably would be slightly more than doubled if the birth rate remained unchanged. For a generation at least, then, India's economic output probably can stay ahead of its maximum rate of population increase. This bare excess over the increase in population, however, is scarcely a satisfactory outcome of India's struggle to achieve economic betterment. The real question is: Could India and the other less-developed areas of the world do substantially better if their birth rates and thus their population growth rates were reduced? Economic analysis clearly indicates that the answer is yes. Any growth of population adds to the rate of increase of national output that must be achieved in order to increase per capita by any given amount.

To double per capita output in 30 years requires an annual increase in per capita output of 2.3 per cent; if population growth is three per cent a year, then the annual increase in national output must be raised to 5.3 per cent to achieve the desired level of economic growth. In either instance an economy, to grow, must divert effort and resources from producing for current consumption to the enhancement of future productivity. In other words, to grow faster an economy must raise its level of net investment. Net investment is investment in factories, roads, irrigation networks, and fertilizer plants, and also in education and training. The low-income countries find it difficult to mobilize resources for these purposes for three reasons: The pressure to use all available resources for current consumption is great; rapid population growth adds very substantially to the investment targets that must be met to achieve any given rate of increase in material well-being; and the very high proportions of children that result from high fertility demand that a larger portion of national output must be used to support a very large number of non-earning dependents. These dependents create pressure to produce for immediate consumption only. In individual terms, the family with a large number of children finds it more difficult to save, and a government that tries to finance development expenditures out of taxes can expect less support from a population with many children. Moreover, rapid population growth and a heavy burden of child dependency divert investment funds to less productive uses—that is, less productive in the long run. To achieve a given level of literacy in a population much more must be spent on schools. In an expanding population of large families, construction effort must go into housing rather than into factories or power plants.

Thus the combination of continued high fertility and greatly reduced mortality in the less-developed countries raises the levels of investment required while impairing the capacity of the economy to achieve high levels of investment. Economists have estimated that a gradual reduction in the rate of childbearing, totaling 50 per cent in 30 years, would add about 40 per cent to the income per consumer that could be achieved by the end of that time.

To recapitulate, a short-term increase in per capita income may be possible in most less-developed areas, even if the fertility rate is not reduced. Nevertheless, even in the short run, progress will be much faster and more certain if the birth rate falls. In the longer run, economic progress will eventually be stopped and reversed unless the birth rate declines or the death rate increases. Economic progress will be slower and more doubtful if less-developed areas wait for the supposedly inevitable impact of modernization on the birth rate. They run the risk that rapid population growth and adverse age distribution would themselves prevent the achievement of the very modernization they count on to bring the birth rate down.

Conclusion

This brief statement of population problems indicates the pervasive and depressive effect that uncontrolled growth of population can have on many aspects of human welfare. Nearly all our economic, social, and political problems become more difficult to solve in the face of uncontrolled population growth. It is clear that even in the wealthier nations many individuals and families experience misery and unhappiness because of the birth of unwanted children. The desirability of limiting family size is now fairly generally, though not universally, recognized, particularly among the better-educated and culturally advanced segments of the population in many countries.

Effective voluntary control of family size essentially depends upon the successful interaction of two variables: level or intensity of motivation and the availability and utility of procedures. When motivation is high and sustained, difficult procedures for controlling fertility can be used successfully, but when motivation is weak and erratic, simple procedures that impose few demands are essential. Quite obviously any comprehensive program for solving population problems must work with both these variables, must seek to enhance motivation and also to improve procedures for voluntary control of fertility.

A broadly based effort to develop clearer understanding of the physiology and biochemistry of the reproductive process is a primary requirement. Work in this area can be effectively strengthened by expansion and coordination of the activities of the few existing laboratories now devoted to basic problems of human reproduction.

There is a parallel need—no less important—for extensive, systematic application of new basic knowledge in the development of new techniques, procedures, devices, and medically active compounds for the regulation of fertility. Inherent in this requirement is the necessity for assurance of safety in techniques and procedures, and freedom from undesirable side-effects from compounds and treatments.

These objectives require extensive studies in chemistry, physiology, and biochemistry, with large animal colonies and clinical facilities for large-scale animal and, subsequently, human tests.

Field surveys and experiments must be enlarged, and new projects of this kind undertaken on a continuing basis in many more parts of the world, making effective use of growing bio-medical knowledge and newly developed devices, techniques, and compounds. The objectives of these projects should be two-fold: (1) to determine the advantages and disadvantages of various techniques, procedures, and devices, and (2) to determine the degree and scope of their acceptability in various societies, cultures, and economies. To reach the objective, the means must be provided and they must be accepted and used.

We believe that the implementation of the recommendation in this report will lead to substantial increases in our effective knowledge and will also encourage the use of this increased knowledge in a successful attack on the many problems of rapid and uncontrolled population growth.

READING 4

As both population and our level of living continue to rise, increasing demands will be placed on all our resources, including natural resources. No other men on earth are using up resources in anything like the quantity per capita that Americans are. This raises the practical question: Will our supply of natural resources be adequate for the future?

Joseph L. Fisher, president of Resources for the Future, Inc., offers an informed economist's answer to these questions by reviewing past trends in natural resource use and projecting these trends to the year 2000 and beyond. He stresses the extent to which tendencies toward shortage can be checked by the development of new sources of supply, the use of substitute materials, increased imports, and greater efficiency in the use of materials. Yet the outlook for the next few decades appears to be mixed, with the need for some resources likely to be particularly pressing; and even if there is no immediate fear of running out of natural resources, we are still confronted with the challenge of managing our resources more effectively and economizing in their use. To these ends, Fisher offers several policy suggestions.

Questions to Guide the Reading

Under what conditions might an increasing reliance on foreign imports for basic resources weaken the United States' long-run economic position? Under what conditions might such a policy strengthen our position? Is the import picture likely to change substantially as rising population and more rapid industrialization cause new demands for raw materials elsewhere in the world?

To what extent should citizens in New England, the Midwest, or the South be concerned with the possibility of a water shortage in some Western state?

Where does responsibility rest for taking adequate cognizance of our future resource needs and of the impact of those needs on today's resource usage?

OUR RESOURCE SITUATION AND OUTLOOK
Joseph L. Fisher

In a restless world in which one finds only a few islands of economic well-being and complacency, in a precarious world in which nations and individuals must maintain their poise on the knife edge between war and peace, in a technologic world in which new devices pile up high in front of man's capacity to control and use them wisely, in an ambitious and greedy world in which compassion and thought for the other nation, for the other person, is often forgotten—in this kind of world the problems of public policy and individual responsibility are of awful magnitude.

Two-thirds of the people of the world now live not too far from the edge of existence. Some of the others, many of them living here in the United States, are very well off indeed. The differences are striking. People in the wealthiest countries consume nearly twice as many calories of food per person per day as those in the poorest countries. Life expectancy at birth ranges among the nations from over seventy years to about thirty. Per capita real income varies from more than $2000 per person in the United States last year to less than $100 per person in such countries as Burma, Haiti, India, and much of Africa. Energy consumed per person in the richest coun-

tries runs 25 to 30 times as much as in the poorest countries. Economic development has become a problem for every country and for all people, and each must be concerned with the development of the others as well as itself.

But this same world can be characterized differently. It is also a world of hope, promise, and opportunity, with high potentiality always within sight if not within immediate grasp. As many observers have recently pointed out, hundreds of millions of people in those parts of the world less developed economically have awakened to economic possibilities. Their expectations are rising and they are on the move.

Part of the challenge of the future for us in this highly favored country will be through far-sighted and generous public policy to offer in a dignified way all appropriate encouragement and aid to those in less-developed regions in their massive but often fumbling effort to advance themselves in material welfare. We must help them find their own boot straps so they may pull. Each individual in this country shares in the responsibility of understanding these great social and economic forces that are moving in the world and helping to shape public policy

From Joseph L. Fisher, "Our Resource Situation and Outlook: Public Policy and Individual Responsibility," *Proceedings, First Southwest Seminar in Public Responsibility* (University of Oklahoma, Norman, Okla., April, 1960), pp. 12–21. Reprinted with kind permission of the author and publisher.

which will guide these forces in the ways of peace and cooperation. Indiscriminate and large financial aid by itself surely will not do the job.

I shall turn now to a very brief review of the situation and outlook in this country regarding natural resources and raw materials. Resource problems are by no means the whole of our national problems, but they are an important part; resources of land, water, and minerals do form the basis for our elaborate structure of agriculture and industry. The possession of basic resources or the ability to import them or products derived from them, plus the ability to manage and process them, constitutes a most important element of both material welfare and national strength.

In recent years there has been much speculation about the adequacy of natural resources in this country to support a rapidly increasing population at higher and higher levels of living. Many questions arise: Shall we run out of sawtimber, fresh water, oil, or some metal? Or will the costs of obtaining these increase sharply to the extent that economic growth generally will be checked? What will happen if new scientific and technologic developments do not come along in time to furnish us with substitutes? These are important questions not easy to answer but which should be addressed thoughtfully.

An important clue to whether resources are running out in the sense of becoming more costly can be found by examining the historical trends. Consumption of agricultural, timber, and mineral resources has increased greatly over the past century in this country. Per capita consumption likewise has increased, though less rapidly than total consumption. Between 1870 and 1954 the per capita consumption of agricultural products increased nearly 40 per cent, timber products decreased by about one-fourth, and mineral products increased 8 to 9 times.

Consumption of the various resources and raw materials by and large has not been increasing as fast as total national output of goods and services. Between 1870 and 1954 agricultural products as a per cent of national production has dropped from 27 to 8, and timber products from 4 to less than 1. On the other hand, minerals increased from 1.5 in 1870 to nearly 5 in 1920 and then fell away to 3.3 in 1954. These statistics do not mean that natural resources have become less important or necessary in any basic sense; they indicate that other elements of national production have grown faster, such as the provision of processed goods of many sorts and services.

In many respects the best single indicator of our changing resource situation is provided by the historical record of resource prices expressed in constant dollars, as related to prices generally. Viewed in this way, the price of all resource commodities in relation to the general level of all prices went up by slightly less than 20 per cent from the 1870's to the 1950's. Looking inside this aggregate of statistics, it may be observed that relative agricultural prices rose during this period by a little more than 20 per cent, timber prices by a very large 370 per cent, while mineral prices remained unchanged. Within each category specific products behaved in widely different manner; for example, the price of natural gas relative to all wholesale prices fell considerably from 1900 to 1948 and has been rising sharply since then. This price picture may be broadly interpreted by saying that tendencies toward increasing costs such as having to go deeper and into leaner ores for minerals have more or less been counter-balanced by technological improvements of many sorts. The record of prices over many decades, therefore, does not show any clear tendency for resources as a whole to become much scarcer in the economic sense in this country.

To be sure the United States has had to rely increasingly on imports of resource materials, and this indicates that we have prevented major general price rises partly by drawing upon cheaper supplies elsewhere in the world. We are considerably less self-sufficient in many products, epecially the mineral products, than we used to be. In fact, since World War II we have shifted from being a net exporter to a net importer of crude oil, which we now import to the extent of about 16 per cent of domestic consumption. Since the war, also, we have stepped up our imports of iron ore from a very small percentage to some 20 or more per cent. For many of the metals, we have long been an importer, but the per cent has been increasing sharply in the last decade or so.

Employment in basic resource industries such as agriculture, forestry, and mining, while still substantial, has dropped greatly as a per cent of total employment. In 1870 slightly more than half of total employment was in the resource industries. Today this has fallen away almost to 10 per cent. Most of the drop, of course, has come in agricultural employment and is associated with mechanization and very rapid in-

Table 1 Resource Trends in the United States, 1870–1954

	1870	1880	1890	1900	1910	1920	1930	1940	1950	1954
Consumption of resources (1947–49=100)	17	23	30	41	53	62	68	86	103	110
Agriculture	19	27	32	43	54	63	70	92	100	108
Timber products	—	50.0*	73.6†	113.3	121.7	102.2	81.0	87.4	113.0	113.7
Minerals	3.0	6.4	12.9	19.7	37.9	52.4	60.5	73.4	108.8	116.8
Per capita resource consumption (1954)	174	191	195	221	237	238	226	266	279	279
Agriculture	125	138	132	147	152	152	148	179	171	172
Timber products	11‡	12*	14†	18	16	12.0	7.9	8.0	9.0	8.5
Minerals	8.72	14.8	23.8	30.1	47.6	57.1	56.9	64.4	83.1	83.4
Output of resources (as % GNP, 1954 prices)	36	32	29	27	22	21	17	16	13	12
Agriculture	27	25	21	19	15	14	11	10	8	8
Timber products	4.0	3.7	3.9	3.9	2.8	2.0	1.2	1.0	.77	.69
Minerals	1.5	2.0	2.8	3.4	4.2	4.9	4.3	4.1	3.6	3.3
Price of resources (deflated by BLS general wholesale index, 1947–49=100)	78	66	66	68	76	83	85	78	96	90
Agriculture	69	69	68	68	83	78	82	72	92	82
Timber products	26.6	29.3	35.9	39.7	40.6	62.1	53.8	70.5	108.5	104.2
Minerals	119	66.4	64.7	72.9	64.2	105	98.4	97.7	103	107
Net resource imports (1947–49=100)	− 31	− 75	− 77	−107	− 69	− 56	16	294	76	88
Agriculture	−148	−394	−371	−495	−285	−310	−113	482	120	96
Timber products	—	7.8	− 1.9	− 27.7	− 28.0	8.0	− 5.0	35.2	204.6	177.2
Minerals§	− 1.2	—	—	− 6.3	− 14.2	8.4	24.2	266.7	51.6	75.5
Employment in resource industries as per cent of total employment	51.2	51.9	45.4	40.5	33.9	28.5	25.2	21.4	14.6	11.8
Agriculture	49.9	49.5	42.3	36.9	30.4	25.2	22.6	19.0	12.5	10.1
Timber products	.2	.3	.4	.4	.4	.4	.3	.3	.3	¶
Minerals	1.5	1.8	2.4	2.9	2.9	2.7	2.1	1.9	1.6	1.2

* 1879 nearest year.
† 1889 nearest year.
‡ 1869 nearest year.
§ Including gold (of which there were large movements in some years).
¶ Not available.

SOURCE: Neal Potter and Francis Christy, Jr., "U.S. Natural Resources Statistics, 1870–1955," Resources for the Future, Inc., preliminary draft.

creases in yields, especially during the last 20 to 25 years and with the slower rate of growth of agriculture as compared to other elements in the national economy.

These trends are summarized in Table 1 and are drawn from a statistical study of resources in the U.S. economy now being prepared in Resources for the Future under the title, U.S. Natural Resources Statistics, 1870–1955.

It is risky to predict what things will be like in 1980 and 2000 in the American economy and its resources components. One can't be sure whether population will go on increasing the way it has in the past. Productivity could be half again as large as it has been during recent years, or it could be less than it has been. One doesn't know whether the work week will continue to shorten as it has during the past or whether it will hold steady at around 40 hours a week in manufacturing and 45 in agriculture. All of these taken together—increase in population and employment, change in the work week, and productivity expressed in terms of output per man-hour yield—total national product.

Even if one cannot be sure of the future, there are some well defined trends that seem likely to continue. Population in 1959 was 177 million; by 2000 it probably will have risen to somewhere between 258 and 433 million, with a medium and most likely estimate at 331 million. Employment may well double from about 65.7 million in 1959 to a medium estimate of 132 million in 2000. The work week will probably continue to decline so that in 2000 it may be a little over 36 hours in agriculture and about 35 hours in private nonagricultural employment. Output for the economy overall, averaged for many decades past, has been increasing at around 3 per cent each year. For the next 40 years this may be lifted somewhat to about 3.6 per cent a year, somewhat above this in agriculture, somewhat below in the rest of the economy. Here the range can be quite large, all the way from less than 3 per cent to more than 4 per cent. Taking into account the effect of these several factors, one can project a total gross national product in the middle estimate of $2140 billion in the year 2000, nearly 4½ times the $484 billion produced in 1959. In per capita terms the increase will be from $2730 to about $6470. The range for GNP will be from a low of $1630 billion to a high of $3210 billion, and there will be a corresponding range for GNP per capita. These estimates are presented in Table 2.

Associated with an economy which may grow to this general dimension will be increased re-

Table 2   Range of Estimates of Gross National Product and Underlying Factors—1959, 1980, and 2000

	1959	1980			2000		
		Low	Medium	High	Low	Medium	High
Population (million persons)	177	226	245	279	268	331	433
Civilian labor force (millions)	69.3	93	99	108	116	138	173
Civilian employment (millions)	65.7	88	95	105	110	132	168
Average hours per week:							
Agricultural employment	45.2	36.3	40.2	45.6	29.6	36.3	45.6
Private non-agricultural employment	40.6	34.2	37.4	40.5	29.2	34.8	40.5
Productivity (percent yearly increase in output per man-hour):*							
Agricultural	5.2†	3.8	4.2	4.8	3.6	4.2	4.9
Private non-agricultural	1.9	1.7	2.3	3.2	1.7	2.5	3.6
Gross National Product (billions 1959 dollars)	484	933	1,030	1,220	1,630	2,140	3,210
Gross National Product per capita (1959 dollars)	2,730	4,130	4,200	4,370	6,080	6,470	7,410

* 1959 column—1959 increase over 1958; 1980 columns—average yearly increases 1959 to 1980; 2000 columns—average yearly increases 1980 to 2000.

† Long term average.

SOURCE: Estimates taken from work in progress by Resources for the Future and should be regarded as tentative only.

quirements for many kinds of raw materials. These increases are difficult to trace for specific items since one can see only dimly the effects of new technologies, changes in demand, and possibilities for new sources of supplies perhaps in other parts of the world. The ranges become quite large. For example, the projections of demand for aluminum 40 years from now have to embrace an extremely wide range of possibilities. Expansion of present uses of this light, durable, corrosion-resistant metal, plus new uses and adaptations, may continue at a rapid rate, although some slowing down seems inevitable. Widespread use of aluminum for automobile engine blocks, exterior building panels, roofing and wrapping foil, plus possible new uses altogether, could result in a 40-fold increase for aluminum by 2000. On the other hand, less favorable technologic developments in aluminum, combined with more favorable changes in materials competitive with aluminum might limit the increase in demand to only, say 4 times what it is now. A middle-range estimate would indicate about a 12-fold increase in demand.

Middle range estimates of the increase in U.S. requirements by 2000 compared to recent levels for a number of selected key materials may be indicated: for timber, about a 3-fold increase; for wheat about 60 per cent; for feed grains about 55 per cent; for cotton 75 to 80 per cent; for oil about 3¾ times; for coal about 2½ times; for iron ore nearly 2 times; for copper about 5 to 6 times; and for fresh water withdrawals about 2½ times. For many of these, especially the minerals, the range between high and low requirements for 2000 is quite great, although not as great as for aluminum. These estimates and those in Table 2 are taken from another study in progress at Resources for the Future covering all natural resources and raw materials, provisionally entitled "Resources in the American Future."

The adequacy of the domestic resource base to meet these and other demands is mixed. For some such as water it is adequate, assuming fairly large investments in new supplies, prevention or abatement of pollution, recycling for industrial uses, and conservation generally—although the problems will be difficult in certain parts of the country. For others domestic sources probably are inadequate now and may become increasingly so in the future. Many of the metals are in this category. A more precise answer to questions of adequacy hinges on technologic and economic events yet to unfold.

In answering the question of adequacy of resources for economic growth one must include foreign sources as well as domestic. As has been pointed out, this country already imports large amounts of crude oil, iron ore, wood pulp, and other basic items. Trends in comparative costs of production for many raw materials will probably increasingly favor other parts of the world. Whether policy accommodates or resists these trends will be important in determining whether the U.S. economy will be supplied with lower or higher cost materials. Some restraint on growth therefore may arise from this source, but it need not.

The most promising way of avoiding possible resource shortage is through the development of plentiful and cheap supplies of substitute materials. Substitution in the broad sense of the term is a pervading characteristic of modern U.S. economy. Distinctions between specific materials are becoming more and more blurred. This is beginning to be true even between whole categories of materials. This means that a shortage of a particular item is not likely to check general economic growth, at least over an extended period of time. Temporary embarrassment may be acute, a short run thrust toward inflation may result, for a time a disproportionate share of effort may have to be devoted to overcoming or bypassing the roadblock, but in a rich, diverse economy such as that of the United States, it is hard to believe that shortage of any particular raw material will greatly restrain growth, at least through the remainder of the century.

Engineers are very ingenious in figuring out ways to reuse formerly wasted materials and to redesign products and manufacturing processes so as to use less of any material that is becoming scarce. Consumers of end products usually are ready to shift their allegiance to substitutes in response to price advantages; for example, they will be willing to accept oil, natural gas, coal, or electricity (produced by coal, gas, water power or atomic power) as a source of heat in the home, depending upon the price and quality of the service. The chemical industry has become incredibly ingenious in creating new products altogether by rearrangements of atoms and molecules. Plastics, synthetic rubber, and new fertilizers may be mentioned.

This cursory examination of historical trends in resource industries, and the equally cursory look ahead to 2000, do not reveal significant danger of general resource shortage in this country, although sharp supply difficulties undoubtedly will appear for particular raw materials at particular times and in particular industries and places. The contrast between this general conclusion for the United States and for many other countries of the world undoubtedly is sharp. The people of this country must be mindful of this contrast and take it into account in the improvement of our foreign economic policies.

Looking beyond 2000 into the Twenty-first Century, it becomes most difficult to see at all clearly. The picture can be outlined more satisfactorily perhaps by the biologist and the technologist than by the economist. One view of this more distant future is the neo-Malthusian one of more and more people filling up the earth and pressing harder and harder on the means of subsistence, leading eventually to a cessation of economic growth and to lower levels of living.

A second view is that the continued and enriched flow of discoveries and inventions, followed by widespread application, will enable not only this country but the world generally to keep ahead of the explosive growth in population which is in store and which may well see a more than doubling of world population in the last four decades of this century from something less than 3 billion people now to 6 or 7 billion in 2000. There is some evidence that in agriculture, for example, if the best techniques now applied anywhere in the world were applied everywhere, there would be a good deal more food per capita for the 6 or 7 billion people in 2000 than there is now. It appears likely that there is enough oil in the Middle East and the Sahara and other parts of the world to support a greatly expanded industrial economy everywhere in the world. Iron ore is available in rich deposits in northern South America, in Canada, and in other places, some of them probably yet to be discovered, and exists in even more plentiful amounts at lower concentrations. The possibilities for conservation of fresh water, for pollution abatement, and for recycling water are great, while clearly on the horizon is the desalting of brackish water.

Beyond this, into the Twenty-first Century and perhaps beyond, are yet other possibilities including desalinization of sea water, the use of algae for food production, weather modification on a wide geographic scale, the truly widespread application of nuclear energy which will probably begin to become important during the last two decades of this century, further advances in automation and communications, and the recovery of the numerous metals from granite and from the ocean. On these and numerous other possibilities, one will simply have to wait and see, but with some confidence that at least a few of them will work out with diligent attention to research and development.

A third view and one which I prefer to the neo-Malthusian view or the confidence-in-technology view is that, whether one of these views is taken or neither of them, we should strive for increasing control over the key factors in the population-resource problem. Without placing this in the center of our attention, we condemn ourselves to drift either with population trends or technology. The critical variables seem to be the birth rate, the distribution of population within and among countries, the amount and kind of emphasis placed on science and technology in their many aspects, and a willingness to experiment with new instruments of control—or if you prefer a less harsh term than control, with new policies for guiding and influencing the flow of events. Success along these lines could greatly alter our prospects and enhance our effectiveness in adjusting to problems of the Twenty-first Century.

In somewhat more specific terms, much will hinge on our system of education and training, on providing for enough growth-producing investments at home and in the less-developed parts of the world, on enlarging the scope of world trade, and on sharing scientific and technologic advances among the countries. Much also will hinge on adequate conservation of basic natural resources, by which I mean the sustained and increased yield of the renewal resources, the economic extraction, processing, use and reuse of the non-renewables, and the incessant search for cheaper substitutes for costlier materials. Public policies and private actions which favor these objectives will be to the good.

Much will depend also on whether a greater degree of population planning can be achieved on some basis acceptable to groups that now have conflicting views on the matter.

If one adopts this third view that we should aim toward greater control over the major variables, through the development of better policy, then what directions should our activity take? To begin with, we should undertake systematic appraisals of trends in population, resources, economic activities, and so on, so that emerging problems may be foreseen and plans made for meeting them. Economists, to speak only of my own profession, are now reaching out with disciplined techniques of projection for several decades ahead, trying to portray what the future may be like if different forces which they try to specify precisely continue to act. The view of 2000 which I presented earlier is in this newer tradition among economists.

Much attention will have to be given to education in its many phases since this is the surest way to promote scientific and technologic advance, as well as more general understanding of the requirements for action to deal with future problems.

The effort to make materials of all sorts available at lowest cost, from raw materials to finished goods, will have to be incessant, and will have to be world-wide in scope. Beyond this will have to be the enlargement of the international community of nations with a freer flow of investment, people, and ideas.

Attention will have to be given to the imperatives of national defense, probably for many years to come. This will involve the most excruciating kinds of decisions in which the relations between U.S. defense and world peace will have to be balanced.

Perhaps most difficult of all, there will have to be increased willingness to alter the institutional framework of government and business and of economic systems, as the problems and possibilities change. This will have to be done prudently, not recklessly. These are the general directions for public policy in the future, for natural resources as well as in other fields.

Let me mention now a few specific policy directions in the field of natural resources. In water use, it is now becoming quite evident that through much of the western part of the country the allocation of water to industrial and even recreation uses will be more efficient than allocation to irrigation agriculture. A forthcoming study in which some additional water supply in the state of New Mexico is appraised in terms of its effect on state income indicates that the value of the water for municipal and industrial use may be more than 50 times as great as for agricultural use, while it may be some 4 or 5 times as valuable for recreational use. This study, under the direction of Nathaniel Wollman, was aided by a grant from Resources for the Future, and will soon be published by the University of New Mexico Press. Present law governing water allocation, as well as present business thinking, must be given the most critical re-examination.

Agricultural policy in this country, as many have pointed out, is a tangle of inconsistencies. Crop surpluses at home are more than matched by deficits in many other countries. Efforts to reduce production at home and raise incomes have been put together in an assortment of policies and programs which defy sensible administration. New policy directions would have to incorporate some elements of existing policies with some new ones. Price support programs in the face of surplus production and too many people on the farm will have to give way in favor of much more vigorous efforts to encourage movement of people out of agriculture and into industry and services and reallocation of much farmland, such as dry wheat lands, to other uses. The soil bank idea with the retirement of full farms from production of surplus crops in areas not now suited to agriculture probably needs further elaboration and application. Efforts to find industrial use for agricultural products can be expanded as can efforts to establish industry in rural areas and small towns. There is no long-term future for price supports except in the larger context of efforts to help people move out of agriculture and efforts to retire marginal land to other uses. The seeds of this new direction are already contained in some of our agricultural and farm programs, but they need nourishing and developing.

In the minerals field the direction of policy should be toward a planned adjustment of the higher cost segment of the U.S. mineral industries to a long-range outlook which points to increased imports of many items. There has to be an orderly retreat from the untenable position of special indirect subsidies in the mineral industries, except when the case is absolutely clear that these are needed for defense or to ameliorate the human and social effects of economic disadvantages. Short-term subsidies may be acceptable and even desirable, but only when combined with efforts to encourage the contraction of high cost parts of the industry and the resettlement of labor and capital in more profitable lines. To this extent the mineral problem is basically similar to that of agriculture.

In outdoor recreation, one of the most rapidly growing industries in the country, estimates of demand twenty and forty years from now are unbelievably high. There will have to be most vigorous efforts made if this growth in demand is to be satisfied or even half-satisfied. Recreation land will have to be acquired by the several levels of government, especially state government. Technical aid and financial aid have to be provided by the federal government and probably by state governments. Experiments will have to be made to interest additional private owners of potential recreation land and water to develop their holdings for recreation, perhaps as only one of several uses of the holding.

This is no more than a sampling of some of the new emphases and directions for policy in the resource field if we are to meet the visible problems ahead. In concluding, let me turn now briefly to a discussion of the individual's responsibility in all of this. First, of course, it is to keep himself informed about the trends, the problems that lie ahead, and the possibilities for dealing with them.

Second, and closely related to the first, the individual must maintain a flexible and open mind regarding solutions to the new problems. He must be willing to experiment himself and to allow his government to experiment with new policies and new institutional adjustments. Already most people accept this proposition for science and technology, but this willingness to experiment now needs to be extended broadly to the economic and social areas.

Third, he needs to enlarge his horizon in time, in space, in society, and in ideas. He must look to 1980 and 2000 and beyond into the Twenty-first Century. He must consider broadly his state, his region, his country, and his world. He must be concerned about his fellow men on the farms, in the labor unions, in the white collar jobs, in the professions, and in public service everywhere in the world—in India, Ghana, Poland, Cuba, the Soviet Union, Japan, everywhere. He must be willing to consider new ideas of all sorts and to appraise them on their merits, rejecting those that do violence to basic, tested, widely shared ethical principles, but examining all others with a hopeful attitude.

In resource matters the individual's responsibility stems from his broad political and social responsibilities, but may be stated in more specific terms. He must strive to conserve resources and use them wisely. Paradoxically this involves knowing when not to waste time and effort in saving things that won't be needed, as well as knowing when to spend time and effort to save things. The individual must understand the main elements of the resource issues on which he has an opportunity to influence decisions. In the Southwest I suppose this means trying to understand and reach a position regarding farm price supports and the soil bank, the benefits and costs of various possible uses of water, the "best" level of oil imports, the degree and kind of regulation of the natural gas industry, the kind of research that should be carried on through or stimulated by government, and the way in which localities, states, and the federal government should share in various resource programs, such as soil conservation, water pollution abatement, and reforestation.

The individual should take an active part in the shaping of resource policy through appropriate political means. These include voting, of course, but also through his business association, farm organization, labor union, or professional group—especially through statewide organizations such as this committee of 100 on the Twenty-first Century. Finally he has the responsibility of balancing his own private views, interests, and actions with those of others, including, let it be noted, his own children and grandchildren.

None of this is easy. To discharge these responsibilities with increasing effectiveness and inner satisfaction will require an immense educational effort ranging from self-education through voluntary adult programs to the schools and universities. But it can ultimately produce better policy and a closer approach to those broad national aims toward which most of us wish to strive. In addition to being of vast importance, the effort is intellectually challenging and will strengthen our democracy in a most profound and far reaching manner.

READING 5

Widespread agreement could quickly be found for the proposition that we need much capital to sustain and improve our high standard of living in the United States. But what is implied in this approval?

To the economist, "capital" is a word with too many popular meanings. It requires a quite specific meaning if it is to convey a concept with analytical significance in understanding how our economy operates. This definition is found in using the word to refer to either (1) man-made factors of production or (2) goods that have been produced by the economic system not to satisfy present consumption but to aid in further production. In this sense, a nation's stock of *real capital* consists of the improved land, buildings, equipment, and inventories that are used to produce other goods and services. So defined, capital can come into existence only by diverting some of today's scarce resources from the production of "final" goods for present consumption to the production of "intermediate" goods for use in further production. Why would a society choose to follow such an "indirect" or "roundabout" way of satisfying its wants? And why do some societies rely more on capital intensive productive processes than other societies?

The Austrian economist Eugen von Böhm-Bawerk (1851–1914) is best known for his writings on capital and interest. Here he describes how and why capital intensive or "roundabout" methods of production work to man's advantage.

Questions to Guide the Reading

How do other popular uses of the word "capital" relate to the definition employed here?

If capital intensive or roundabout methods of production yield greater results than direct methods, why do we not immediately adopt the most roundabout or the most indirect methods of production available?

CAPITAL AND ROUNDABOUT PRODUCTION
Eugen von Böhm-Bawerk

The end and aim of all production is the making of things with which to satisfy our wants; that is to say, the making of goods for immediate consumption, or Consumption Goods. We combine our own natural powers and natural powers of the external world in such a way that, under natural law, the desired material good must come into existence. But this is a very general description indeed of the matter, and looking at it closer there comes in sight an important distinction which we have not as yet considered. It has reference to the distance which lies between the expenditure of human labour in the combined production and the appearance of the desired good. We either put forth our labour just before the goal is reached, or we, intentionally, take a roundabout way. That is to say, we may put forth our labour in such a way that it at once completes the circle of conditions necessary for the emergence of the desired good, and thus the existence of the good *immediately* follows the expenditure of the labour; or we may associate our labour first with the more remote causes of good,

with the object of obtaining, not the desired good itself, but a proximate cause of the good; which cause, again, must be associated with other suitable materials and powers, till, finally,—perhaps through a considerable number of intermediate members,—the finished good, the instrument of human satisfaction, is obtained.

The nature and importance of this distinction will be best seen from a few examples. A peasant requires drinking water. The spring is some distance from his house. There are various ways in which he may supply his daily wants. First, he may go to the spring each time he is thirsty, and drink out of his hollowed hand. This is the most direct way; satisfaction follows immediately on exertion. But it is an inconvenient way, for our peasant has to take his way to the well as often as he is thirsty. And it is an insufficient way, for he can never collect and store any great quantity such as he requires for various other purposes. Second, he may take a log of wood, hollow it out into a kind of pail, and carry his day's supply from the spring to his cottage. The advantage is

From Eugen von Böhm-Bawerk, *Positive Theory of Capital* (1891).

obvious, but it necessitates a roundabout way of considerable length. The man must spend, perhaps, a day in cutting out the pail; before doing so he must have felled a tree in the forest; to do this, again, he must have made an axe, and so on. But there is still a third way; instead of felling one tree he fells a number of trees, splits and hollows them, lays them end for end, and so constructs a runnel or rhone which brings a full head of water to his cottage. Here, obviously, between the expenditure of the labour and the obtaining of the water we have a very roundabout way, but, then, the result is ever so much greater. Our peasant need no longer take his weary way from house to well with the heavy pail on his shoulder, and yet he has a constant and full supply of the freshest water at his very door.

Another example. I require stone for building a house. There is a rich vein of excellent sandstone in a neighbouring hill. How is it to be got out? First, I may work the loose stones back and forward with my bare fingers, and break off what can be broken off. This is the most direct, but also the least productive way. Second, I may take a piece of iron, make a hammer and chisel out of it, and use them on the hard stone—a roundabout way, which, of course, leads to a very much better result than the former. Third method—Having a hammer and chisel I use them to drill a hole in the rock; next I turn my attention to procuring charcoal, sulphur, and nitre, and mixing them in a powder, then I pour the powder into the hole, and the explosion that follows splits the stone into convenient pieces—still more of a roundabout way, but one which, as experience shows, is as much superior to the second way in result as the second was to the first.

The lesson to be drawn from these examples is obvious. It is—that a greater result is obtained by producing goods in roundabout ways than by producing them directly. Where a good can be produced in either way, we have the fact that, by the indirect way, a greater product can be got with equal labour, or the same product with less labour. But, beyond this, the superiority of the indirect way manifests itself in being the only way in which certain goods can be obtained.

That roundabout methods lead to greater results than direct methods is one of the most important and fundamental propositions in the whole theory of production. It must be emphatically stated that the only basis of this proposition is the experience of practical life. Economic theory does not and cannot show *a priori* that it must be so; but the unanimous experience of all the technique of production says that it is so. And this is sufficient; all the more that the facts of experience which tell us this are commonplace and familiar to everybody. But *why* is it so?

In the last resort all our productive efforts amount to shiftings and combinations of matter. We must know how to bring together the right forms of matter at the right moment, in order that from those associated forces the desired result, the product wanted, may follow. But, as we saw, the natural forms of matter are often so infinitely large, often so infinitely fine, that human hands are too weak or too coarse to control them. We are as powerless to overcome the cohesion of the wall of rock when we want building stone as we are, from carbon, nitrogen, hydrogen, oxygen, phosphor, potash, etc., to put together a single grain of wheat. But there are other powers which can easily do what is denied to us, and these are the powers of nature. There are natural powers which far exceed the possibilities of human power in greatness, and there are other natural powers in the microscopic world which can make combinations that put our clumsy fingers to shame. If we can succeed in making those forces our allies in the work of production, the limits of human possibility will be infinitely extended. And this we have done.

The condition of our success is, that we are able to control the materials on which the power that helps us depends, more easily than the materials which are to be transformed into the desired good. Happily this condition can be very often complied with. Our weak yielding hand cannot overcome the cohesion of the rock, but the hard wedge of iron can; the wedge and the hammer to drive it we can happily master with little trouble. We cannot gather the atoms of phosphorus and potash out of the ground, and the atoms of carbon and oxygen out of the atmospheric air, and put them together in the shape of the corn or wheat; but the organic chemical powers of the seed can put this magical process in motion, while we on our part can very easily bury the seed in the place of its secret working, the bosom of the earth. Often, of course, we are not able directly to master the form of matter on which the friendly power depends, but in the same way as we would like it to help us, do we help ourselves against it; we try to secure the alliance of a second natural power which brings the form of matter that bears the first power under our control. We wish to bring the well water into the house. Wooden rhones would force it to obey our will, and take the path we prescribe, but our hands have not the power to make the forest trees into rhones. We have not far to look, however, for an expedient. We ask the help of a second ally in the axe and the gouge; their assistance gives us the rhones; then the rhones bring us the water. And what in this illustration is done through the mediation of two or three members may be done, with equal or greater result, through five, ten, or twenty members. Just as we control and guide the immediate matter of which the good is composed by one friendly power, and that power by a second, so can we control and guide the second by a third, the third by a fourth, this, again, by a fifth, and so on,—always going back to more remote causes of the final result—till in the series we come at last to one cause which we can control conveniently by our own natural powers. This is the true im-

portance which attaches to our entering on round-about ways of production, and this is the reason of the result associated with them: every round-about way means the enlisting in our service of a power which is stronger or more cunning than the human hand; every extension of the round-about way means an addition to the powers which enter into the service of man, and the shifting of some portion of the burden of production from the scarce and costly labour of human beings to the prodigal powers of nature.

The kind of production which works in these wise circuitous methods is nothing else than what economists call Capitalist Production, as opposed to that production which goes directly at its object. And Capital is nothing but the complex of intermediate products which appear on the several stages of the roundabout journey.

READING 6

At the heart of our economy, organizing the bulk of our resources in response to the demands of the market place, are American entrepreneurs and business firms. Every year thousands of new businesses are started—437,000 in 1961; and every year thousands are discontinued—398,000 in 1961.

In the automobile industry alone, there have been more than 1,500 manufacturers producing over 3,000 makes of cars and trucks since the dawn of the industry. Some turned out only experimental models which never got to the show-rooms. Others were industry giants for a while before their stars burned out. A few—very few—have managed to stay alive in an industry which turned out as many as 7 million cars in a single year. Indeed, the recent demise of the Studebaker Corporation, one of the oldest vehicle manufacturers in the nation, cuts to four the number of major U.S. automobile producers. What determines which firms survive and which do not in today's markets?

Robert Sheehan of *Fortune* magazine attempts to answer this question by examining the organization and operations of the General Motors Corporation, the dominant firm in this industry and a classic example of sustained corporate success. Sheehan's story is an effective introduction to the classic look at pricing and competition which will come in Part 3 of the readings.

Questions to Guide the Reading

How can a firm as large as General Motors maintain effective management control over such a sprawling empire, which includes a large amount of nonautomotive business as well as some 136 different basic auto styles?

Is there, or should there be, any limit to how large a firm can grow in our economy?

What might be some of the advantages and disadvantages of dividing General Motors into several smaller independent companies: (1) for purposes of internal management effectiveness? (2) for purposes of increasing competition in the auto industry? (3) for purposes of preventing "bigness" as such?

HOW GENERAL MOTORS DID IT
Robert Sheehan

Among U.S. industrial companies, General Motors Corp., of course, is the perennial leader in sales and earnings, but the figures it came up with in 1962—sales of $14,640,241,000, profits after taxes of $1,459,077,000—were of a magnitude to benumb the mind. Never in history has a private corporation made so much money. Once before, in the record car year of 1955, G.M. broke the billion-dollar barrier in earnings with a net of $1,189,477,000. Apart from G.M., only the vast A.T.&T. network is in the range (the utility's profits were $1,432,952,000 in 1962). Indeed, most journalists and analysts, in an attempt to make the G.M. figures understandable, compared them not with the results of other corporations—they simply didn't relate vividly enough—but with the statistics of various countries around the world. Thus readers have been informed that G.M.'s sales topped the national budget of France, that its net income was roughly equal to the national income of Ireland, that G.M.'s employees, together with their families, out-number the population of New Zealand.

Admiration of those awesome figures is accompanied by recurrent rumblings in Washington and elsewhere that General Motors is "too big." The Justice Department, for one, keeps a team of eight antitrust attorneys busy pondering and probing G.M. Thus far, most of the antitrust court action has been aimed at the company's peripheral or non-automotive activities, though "peripheral" is a pretty weak word in this instance. G.M.'s "other" businesses—in diesel locomotives, earthmoving equipment, aircraft engines, Frigidaire, etc.—added up to something just short of $1.9 billion in sales in 1962. If G.M. didn't sell the public a single car, truck, automotive part or accessory, it would still rank eighteenth in size among U.S. industrial companies.

It is the company's preponderant position in the U.S. passenger-car market, however, that raises the most controversial questions. The atmosphere becomes tense whenever G.M.'s penetration of the domestic car market approaches or exceeds the 50 percent mark. It is probably no coincidence that when the company first went over the mark, in 1954–55, it was promptly called down to Washington for a session with the late Senator Joseph C. O'Mahoney and the Sub-committee on Antitrust and Monopoly. In 1962, after a considerable lull, G.M. sales ran to 51.9 percent of car registrations. And for the first quarter of 1963, G.M.'s share of the market, as measured by factory sales, was 56 percent (the highest recorded share was Ford's 61.6 percent in 1921).

Inevitably, such a record sharpens the debate about the significance of G.M.'s size and power. But before such questions can even be reasonably discussed, it is essential to understand how G.M. achieved its success. It is a fact of business life, of course, that when the demand in any industry expands rapidly—as it did in the auto industry in 1962—certain advantages naturally accrue to the largest, front-running company. General Motors has the largest ownership—i.e., G.M. cars on the road—to draw on, and the largest number of retail outlets, or dealers. Assuming other things to be equal, G.M. could be expected to enjoy a somewhat greater leverage in a strong car year. But this is not the whole story by any means. For this has been not only a growing market; it was a changing market characterized by a whole new rash of consumer preferences. The past few years have been a time of challenge, and of extraordinary opportunity for all the car companies to break out of their historic patterns and forage vigorously for conquest sales. It was a competitive free-for-all, and the way things turned out, it simply must be concluded that General Motors prejudged the market considerably more accurately than anybody else, adjusted more nimbly to the sudden changes in consumer tastes, maintained an edge in the quality and styling of its products, and sold them as hard as it knew how—and it does know how.

Size, in short, is not the answer to G.M.'s glittering success in the car market, nor for that matter in other markets. What is? Many earnest and able attempts have been made to explain this matter, and many theories new and old have been advanced.

"It is organization that has done it," some say, and once again eighty-eight-year-old Alfred P. Sloan Jr., now honorary chairman of G.M., is being justly canonized for the system he conceived, back in the early Twenties, of "decentralized operations and responsibilities with co-

From Robert Sheehan, "How General Motors Did It," *Fortune*, June, 1963, pp. 97 ff. Reprinted with kind permission of the author and publisher. Copyright, 1963, Time Inc.

ordinated control," for which read, "Give a man a clear-cut job and let him do it." Unquestionably, it is due to the Sloan system that huge General Motors is able to remain so wonderfully lithe. Here is a balance of two apparently conflicting concepts—centralization and decentralization—that preserves the best elements of both. On the one hand, it permits the maximum exercise of initiative by the relatively autonomous division managers, thus fostering, throughout the units of G.M., all the beastly aggressiveness you would expect of a small, hungry company. On the other hand, the system provides, through the subtle ministrations of the G.M. governing committees and general staff, the centralized planning, policy direction, specialized services—and all the considerable economies that go with them—so necessary to a large-scale enterprise.

"It is G.M.'s depth of management that has done it," others say. MEN

The top 700 executives have worked with and around each other for most of their business lives—the average length of service with the company is twenty-five years. No group of executives is more handsomely paid (of the ten highest-paid executives in the U.S. in 1961, eight were G.M. men), and thanks to the company's combination bonus-and-stock-option plan, it is probable that a very high percentage of the personal estate of each is in G.M. stock. They don't have to be wheedled to work hard.

"The people in G.M.," says Chairman Frederic G. Donner, "add up to the greatest single asset G.M. has," and he believes that his most important single responsibility as chairman is to see that he has the right people in the right jobs and good men coming up under them. Yet in another context Donner remarks, "G.M. people are ordinary folks," and this also is true. From a tour of the G.M. executive phalanx, one comes away vastly impressed by the solid competence of every man jack of them—it is difficult to conceive of a surface-slick pretender even penetrating, let alone surviving in, this realistic assembly. On the other hand, they certainly do not dazzle, nor man for man exhibit any patent superiority over their opposite numbers in industry. But one can say of G.M., as a Victorian sage once said of the House of Commons: "It has more sense than everyone in it." G.M.'s corporate or collective judgment—and it lives by collective judgments—adds up to something far sounder and more sensitive than the individual judgments of any or all of its executives.

The fact is that all these things—organization,

depth of management, and just the ordinary people of G.M.—do serve to explain in part at least its record. But this article is less concerned with the universals of G.M.'s structure and philosophy than with the particulars of its accomplishments and more specifically with the hard-nosed facts of the company's conquest of the booming U.S. car market of 1962–63; for if these particulars are known, the universals will fall into perspective. The U.S. passenger-car business is the heart and pulse of the G.M. operation. In 1962 it represented an estimated 65 percent of G.M.'s total dollar sales, or a cool $9.5 billion and, as noted, G.M. is still far out in front in 1963.

In explaining its commanding position, it is significant that though many forecasters grossly underestimated the size of the 1962–63 auto market, G.M. did not. In the fall of 1961, Fred Donner was estimating a 7,200,000 car year for 1962. Ford thought the figure would be around 6,750,000, and other estimates were lower still. The final tally was 7,092,079. As early as August of 1962, Chevrolet's General Manager Semon E. Knudsen was forecasting an equally good market for 1963, but it was the critics' consensus that, in the light of history, it was most unlikely that the auto industry could put two such years together "back to back." Some suggested that sales-minded General Motors was being consciously overoptimistic (it overestimated the 1961 market, for instance). But G.M.'s Executive Vice President James E. Goodman says, "We believed our forecasts and we were prepared. If you based all your plans on history, you would find some new history in the making, and part of that new history could be that you weren't prepared for the change."

Perhaps the difference was that G.M. had a little more confidence in the general U.S. economy than some other people did. Given a stable economy, and a reasonably good figure for consumers' disposable income, there was no mistaking the forces at work that augured for a sharp rise in unit auto sales in 1962, 1963, and beyond. The most compelling factor, as everyone now realizes, was the prospective steep rise in replacement sales as measured by the scrappage rate. As cars purchased in the large-volume years of 1954, 1955, 1956 began to approach their eighth birthday—the age of heavy scrappage—a big bulge in replacement sales was inevitable. At the low point in the auto market in early 1961, the annual scrappage rate was 4,800,000 units. It has since increased by more than 200,000 units a year, and for 1963 General Motors estimates the replacement demand at 5,200,000 cars. Thus only 1,800,000 "growth" sales will be needed to roll up a seven-million-car year. The forces stimulating these additional sales are several. A major one is that the wartime population explosion is now getting into family formation. Not only are new households forming at the rate of around one million per year, but there is a relative increase also in the number of families with sufficient income to buy a new car. There is, moreover, this interesting fact about the millions of war babies now coming into the auto market at eighteen to twenty-two: they have been heavy buyers of used cars, and a tremendous factor in sustaining the strength of the used-car market, which is, in turn, a powerful stimulus to new-car buying. Finally, there has been a continuation of suburban growth, and with it an acceleration in the number of two-, three-, and four-car families.

In view of all this, it is not surprising that all U.S. companies increased their unit sales in 1962. Ford was up 9.2 percent; Chrysler, 5.6 percent; American Motors, 14.1 percent; Studebaker, 7.9 percent. But only General Motors, up 32.1 percent in units, increased its penetration, a rise of nearly five and a half points to 51.9 percent. Ford fell two points to 26.3 percent; Chrysler a point to 9.6 percent; and American Motors was fractionally off at 6.1 percent. Now, of course, there were almost as many factors, of one degree of importance or another, involved in this outcome as there were cars produced. It is possible, however, to describe rather briefly and explicitly the *anatomy*, at least, of G.M.'s triumphant increase in penetration over its competitors. The bare bones of the story are as follows:

Since about 1959, the great new dynamic in the market had been the small car. (And for simplicity's sake, let's call it—as the customers do—the "compact" car, ignoring for the moment such industry subclassifications as *small economy, intermediate, medium-priced small,* etc.) In 1958 the imported small cars, plus American Motors' Ramblers, took 10.8 percent of the total U.S. car market. When the U.S. Big Three began building compacts in 1959, the share of this class of car rose to 18.6 percent, then soared to 31 percent in 1960, and to 38.6 percent in 1961. This was a new ball game, and for the competitors, obviously, a critical test of over-all strategy and all-round skills. For this was not simply a slugging match of compact vs. compact and may the better car win. More important, in a sense, than the quality and attractiveness of the product itself were such considerations as the timing of the introduction of each particular car, its impact on the vital used-car market, and the degree of its incursion on the sales of the corporation's own line of standard-sized cars.

Indeed, if one regarded the competition as strictly a horse race among compacts, G.M., in the early stages, looked astonishingly laggard. In the fall of 1959, G.M. entered the field with the Chevrolet Division's Corvair, a novel, highly specialized little car with an aluminum rear engine. At the same time, Ford introduced the Falcon, a conventionally built small economy car, and early in 1960, the Comet, a slightly larger sister compact, which was marketed by the Lincoln-Mercury Division. Chrysler Corp.'s compact entry was the Plymouth Division's Valiant, and later the Dodge Division's Lancer. In calendar 1960, sales of compacts in the U.S. divided as follows:

Ford	29.9 percent
Rambler	20.7
Imports	20.4
G.M.	13.5
Chrysler	10.3
Studebaker	5.2

In 1961, Ford led again with 30.6 percent of the compacts sold. But G.M., now strengthened by the introduction of its three "B-O-P" compacts—Buick Special, Oldsmobile F-85, and Pontiac Tempest—boosted its compact penetration to 27.6 percent. Chrysler dropped off to an 8.1 percent share.

Meanwhile, hearken to what was happening to the G.M.-Ford competition in the low-price, standard-size car field. In 1959 the standard Ford and the standard Chevrolet had fought to a neck-and-neck finish, each of them taking a fraction over 22 percent of the total car market. But in 1960, while the Ford compacts were mopping up the small-car field, the standard Ford's share of the total car market fell precipitously to 13.5 percent. The standard Chevrolet, in contrast, held firm at 22 percent. In 1961 the standard Ford's decline was substantialy checked—it fell a little less than a point to 12.7 percent. The standard Chevrolet was off a point to 21 percent of the market.

Now the stage is set for G.M.'s decisive breakaway, across the board, in booming 1962. In the small-car field, which rose to almost 42 percent of the total market, Ford had added the Fairlane, a so-called "intermediate" car placed between the Falcon and the lowest-priced standard Ford, and the Meteor, which fitted in between the Comet and the lowest-priced Mercury. With this added punch, Ford increased its share of the compact market to 31.4 percent. This was not good enough, however, to fend off G.M. First of all, G.M. had a hot new compact in the Chevy II, a conventionally built car that squarely opposed Ford's Falcon. Second, it had sharply jacked up Corvair sales by adding the sporty, bucket-seat Monza model to the Corvair line. Finally, all the B.O.P. compacts registered some gains in penetration, and G.M. swept past Ford to capture 35 percent of the compact business.

While this was going on, Ford again lost out in its race with Chevrolet. The sales of the successful new Fairlane, like the Falcon before it, seemingly ate into the sales of the standard Ford, which fell from 12.7 to 10.1 percent of the total market. The standard Chevrolet, despite the great forward thrust of the G.M. compacts, held doggedly to 20 percent of the total car market.

Deep are the roots

From this outline it is logical to deduce that G.M.'s ultimate success was rooted in the fact that (1) it so timed and positioned its small cars as to achieve a maximum amount of "plus" business from the new lines, while at the same time (2) it worked very aggressively to strengthen its position in the standard-size cars. No other company had a comparable balance and spread when the turn in the market came.

All of which would seem to prove, prima facie, that it was superior planning that "did it" for G.M., though it is not to be doubted that in some areas G.M. simply fattened on the mistakes and misfortunes of its competitors, and that at least one triumph—the Corvair Monza—was a stroke of sheer luck. But at least we know that what we are looking at in the current G.M. showcase is not something that was conceived today, or yesterday, nor is it something that can be traced to any single dramatic circumstance or any one hero-type man. The story goes back through many years and involves many people. In the main, however, G.M.'s current success is based on decisions made no later than the fall of 1958.

Start of the cycle

As it happens, this is the point in time when the current management team of Frederic G. Donner as chairman and chief executive officer and John F. Gordon as president took over the leadership from retiring president and chief executive officer Harlow H. Curtice. This was a significant rearrangement of the power lines: it transferred the top executive authority from the president in Detroit back to the chairman in New York. But the change in command was only coincidental to the changes in essential strategy and product planning that were evolving in G.M. at the time.

It is worth recalling, however, that the skies were far from sunny at the start of the Donner-Gordon regime. The economy was severely depressed in 1958; G.M. had to report a 22 percent decline in its domestic car and truck production that year and a drop in earnings of 25 percent. What's more, the public mood was distressingly scornful of Detroit and all its works. Writers were writing vitriolic pieces about the "insolent chariots" and the "two-tone jukeboxes on wheels," and everyone was asking why Detroit couldn't make a small, simple, sensible car like the foreign cars that were selling so well in the U.S. Against these attacks G.M. stood stonily silent or else responded with that irritating blandness that is so often characteristic of the corporation's reaction to criticism. "You take out quality much faster than you can take out cost," G.M. executives would solemnly explain. Or, again, "We have yet to find a way to make a small car larger and more comfortable."

But all the time executives were saying these things they were in fact working behind the scenes to de-emphasize the bulk and blatancy of their standard cars and to develop a line of compact cars. By 1958 the Corvair was already designed, prototyped, and practically tooled up for production. G.M.'s inscrutability went beyond security reasons, though everybody in Detroit guards against, and practices, espionage. There was serious doubt and extended debate throughout the company in the years 1957–59 as to just what the small-car market was going to be worth, and as to what kind of U.S. small car would be most acceptable. Though it dutifully consumer-researched the market, G.M. is not overly trustful of such surveys on an untried product, and never uses them as gospel. Furthermore, G.M. had the most to lose, of all companies, if there was a mass defection from large to small cars. It had to be prepared for the eventuality, but it wasn't of a mind to lead the stampede. It certainly didn't intend to do it with the Corvair.

Cole's car

The Corvair was aborning before there was a known market for a small car, and its biography tells a lot about the pliability of G.M.'s renowned "system." It was the brainchild of

Edward N. Cole, now group executive in charge of all car and truck divisions. Cole first began fooling around with the rear-engine concept, more or less as an academic exercise, when he was chief engineer of Cadillac back in 1946. In 1952 he was made chief engineer of Chevrolet, where his first major task was to design a new lightweight V-8 engine for the all-new 1955 passenger car that was such a smashing success; shortly afterward, Cole was promoted to general manager of the huge Chevrolet Division. Through it all, Cole persisted in the development of his rear-engine idea, and of a car that was now shaping up in his mind as a sort of American Volkswagen. He reached over to G.M.'s Vauxhall Division in Great Britain for the services of its star engineer, Maurice Olley, and made him chief of research and development for Chevrolet. Under Cole's eye, Olley purchased a variety of little foreign cars, tore them down, ran costs, and explored new manufacturing processes.

All this work was carried on without so much as a do-you-mind to anybody in the G.M. hierarchy. A G.M. division manager works under a broad yearly budget with allocations for advertising, engineering, research, and so on, and is not questioned on the things he may choose to do within those limits. What he *is* called to account for is the last line on his profit-and-loss report, and the position of his products in the market. If he has been spending excessively on futures, to the neglect of his salable merchandise, it will show up there. Cole and Chevrolet, needless to say, had no worries on that score. With Corvair, Cole even had the G.M. styling staff secretly working on possible configurations for several years before there was any "official" awareness, at the committee level, of the project. It was not until the fall of 1957 that Cole formally displayed first the clay mock-up and then the camouflaged test model to President Curtice, who liked what he saw and threw it open to the engineering policy group for discussion.

This group—and other policy groups like it— is another heritage from Alfred P. Sloan. Aware that his grand design for the company might in time harden into a stultifying bureaucracy, Sloan encouraged the formation of informal groups, the membership of which cut across lines of authority, to review and project plans and policies in such particular categories as engineering, distribution, overseas operations, etc. Under Donner, the engineering policy group has become, in effect, the spadeworking subcommittee of the G.M. executive committee in the area of auto-

motive programs. Though the chief of staff for engineering is chairman of the group, the staff heads of research, manufacturing, styling, and distribution are also members, as are all nine members of the executive committee. The meetings, held regularly once a month, are long and frequently controversial. Thus, when the executive committee later sits to decide on policy, it doesn't have to engage in the tedious review of written reports, or in a lot of feckless discussion. The problem is already in focus and the decision is made promptly.

It was the consensus of the engineering policy group, and of the governing committees, back in 1957–58, that G.M.'s first move in the small-car field should be to compete directly with the foreign imports. The Corvair, being more European than American in concept, seemed to be the vehicle to do it. What's more, it was ready. So it was approved, and laid down early in 1958.

When the Corvair first hit the market it was far from a success, except in the backhanded sense that it did not cannibalize its Chevrolet big brothers to any visible extent. It was deliberately designed not to, of course, and in that respect it represented a plus for G.M. But it would be naive to think that General Motors anticipated, or accepted without gall, the extent to which Ford's Falcon exceeded the Corvair in sales. From the time they left the post, Falcon was outselling Corvair by nearly two to one (the actual numbers in calendar year 1960 were Falcon 451,158, Corvair 229,525). No doubt the Falcon was taking some sales from the standard Ford, but it was also clear that the Falcon was satisfying a segment of the market—people in search of low-cost family transportation—that the cute little Corvair package, with its smaller interior dimensions, was unable to reach. General Motors moved awfully fast to plug that gap with the introduction, in the fall of 1961, of the Chevy II compact.

Chevrolet engineering had long since been working on the development of a lighter-weight cast-iron engine, a lighter-weight power-glide transmission, and on single-plate springs as a substitution for multiplate springs. So much was on the shelf that the Chevy II, begun in the winter of 1959–60, was on the pilot line by June 1, 1961, and into production in August, 1961.

By now G.M. was fully alive to the new character of the market, with its marked emphasis on variety, and in an unusual move for a new car, Chevy II was brought out in a complete line of models—sedan, coupe, hard-top, convertible, and station wagon. In 1962 it captured 5 percent of the total market with sales of 343,693 units, and it stood off the Falcon, which dropped three points in penetration.

So Chevrolet likes to think its new cars were perfectly timed: that Corvair helped stem the foreign tide, then went on to find its own niche; that Chevy II, brought out in an expanding market, filled the needs of buyers shopping for a second car, or for a good used car, of which there was a shortage in 1962; and therefore that neither of its compacts, in contrast to the Ford experience, hurt its standard-size car. At Ford Motor Co., however, it is not conceded that there was anything wrong with the company's small-car strategy. The tendency in Dearborn, rather, is to attribute the decline of the standard Ford's penetration to a styling failure in the 1960 car— it had a sloping front end that bothered buyers inordinately—and to an insufficiency of models and of change, which has since been redressed.

Whether Chevrolet outwitted Ford or not in the small-car maneuvering, there is no question that its concomitant effort to keep the standard Chevrolet at peak quality and style is what won the over-all competition. For several years running the resale value of a regular Chevrolet, across the line, has been around $100 higher than that of a used Ford or Plymouth. This, above all, has accounted for Chevrolet's relative invulnerability to the low-priced, small-car competition. And so long as this trade-in advantage obtains, there is a great mass of Chevrolet owners that will not defect, including, notably, the big company fleet buyers and the rental outfits, like Hertz and Avis.

The little Bopeeps

About the time the Corvair was finalized in the spring of 1958, work was begun on the medium-priced Buick-Oldsmobile-Pontiac small-car concept. The idea for this class of car was developed in the central planning groups, and the central engineering staff, then headed by Charles A. Chayne, was assigned the task of performing the preliminary aluminum-engine work and the development of lightweight components. Central engineering ultimately built several prototypes, then turned the program over to the divisions so that each could build its own distinctive car. To coordinate the B-O-P program, a special group was set up consisting of the general manager, chief engineer, and chief financial officer of each division involved. They met once a month

for two years. Their responsibility was to see that, without sacrifice of the performance and individuality of the cars, everything was being done to effect the greatest possible economies in costs through the sharing of common parts.

Pontiac's malady at the time was a peculiar one. There was nothing outstandingly wrong with the car in any single respect. It simply seemed to have been drained of its personality—it was a "nothing" type car, competitors were saying. It was low man on the B-O-P totem pole, and sixth in the industry rankings. Knudsen set out to recast Pontiac for more youthful tastes. "You can sell older people a young car," he said, "but you can't sell young people an older car." To help him do it, he brought in a number of younger men from other divisions of the company.

Tuning up the Tempest

One of Pontiac's aims was to maintain a lower price position on its compact, as against the Buick and Oldsmobile compacts. Pontiac felt that the Buick V-8 aluminum engine, designed for use in the other compacts, was too expensive. Accordingly, its engineers set to work developing a four-cylinder iron engine for the Tempest: they simply cut their standard V-8 engine in half, bored four holes in it instead of eight, and were able to use the same assembly line. A four-cylinder engine, however, has always been stigmatized by a certain roughness, and something had to be done about that. Pontiac's advance design group had already developed a rear transmission, for use in the big cars, and it now came up with a new flexible torsional drive. These two features, in the words of Pete Estes, "made a lady out of the four-cylinder engine." In case competitors started reviving the old slurs against the four-cylinder, however, the Tempest offered a V-8 engine as an option.

Sales of the Tempest have been satisfactory, rather than sensational, running to just short of 140,000 units last year. But most important, they have been 80 percent plus business. And for the Pontiac Division, taken as a whole, its success has, indeed, been sensational. Pontiac sold over 528,000 units in calendar 1962, an increase of 42 percent over the previous year, and first-quarter sales in 1963 were running 20 percent ahead of 1962. Behind this rise is a little story which shows that G.M. is not infallible, though quick to adjust. In laying down its 1961 model-year standard-size cars, Pontiac listened to what it now regards as a siren song: that the public was yearning for shorter, simpler cars. Sitting today as Chevrolet's manager, Bunkie Knudsen wryly recalls that when he was Pontiac's manager, "I pulled back Pontiac's wheelbase three inches, and sweated out 1961 with the same wheelbase as Chevrolet, 119 inches. When you give 6,800 Chevrolet dealers a talking point like that to use against you, believe me, you sweat blood." But the next year Pontiac returned to a longer wheelbase, and made a special effort to improve the appeal of its top-of-the-line Bonneville series of luxury cars. Where once the Bonneville was merely window dressing for the Pontiac line, and accounted for less than 6 percent of the division's standard-size car sales, it rose to 27 percent of such sales in 1962.

Buick bounds back

As with Pontiac, both the Buick and the Oldsmobile divisions managed to launch their compacts without harm to the sales of their standard-size cars, though in each case the story has its unique twist. The dramatic ups and downs in Buick's history are indicative of both (*a*) the great deeds a G.M. division can do on the strength of its own initiative, and (*b*) how necessary it is to have the help of the central staff when things go wrong. The Buick experience suggests that in G.M., in the last analysis, the strength of the wolf is the pack, and perhaps it offers a hint of what could happen if, by government order, a division was sheared off from the corporation and made to shift for itself.

In the days when Curtice was running the division, Buick rose from near-failure to the fourth-ranking position in the industry. In 1955, Buick sold 737,859 units, more than any car in its price range ever sold before or since. From there, sales declined headlong to only 245,508 in 1959. One of the troubles was that when Curtice and a number of his top aides moved on to the G.M. executive suite in Detroit, Buick's management was denuded in depth. Buick cars were plagued by mechanical troubles and styling blunders, and of Buick's fine dealer force, nearly half were operating in the red. By 1959 the worried G.M. hierarchy decided it had to intervene. It put in a new team at Buick, headed by burly Edward Dumas Rollert as general manager.

Rollert had handled a number of trouble-shooting assignments for G.M., including, in 1951, the organization of the company's first "dual-purpose" assembly plant at Kansas City, which simultaneously turned out automobiles and jet fighter-bombers. In taking over Buick in May of 1959 there was little that Rollert could do about the basic design and look of the Buick that would show up before 1962. But he did effect an almost immediate transformation in the mechanical quality of the cars. Drawing on his experience in jet-aircraft production, Rollert thoroughly revised Buick's testing and reliability procedures all along the line. And once the quality of the cars was re-established, Buick, through its energetic new general sales manager, Roland Withers, embarked on a comprehensive program of selling the dealers on Buick's new virtues, and of retraining them, from the ground up, in service and sales techniques.

And when the new compact, called the Special after an old Buick favorite, came along in the fall of 1960, it gave a big lift to many a Buick dealer. It developed into the best-seller of all the B-O-P compacts, especially after it began offering, as an option to its aluminum V-8 engine, a new iron V-6 that was about $100 cheaper. The Special now runs to 35 percent of the Buick Division's output, but 73 percent of it is plus business and sales of the regular cars in the Buick line have gone ahead handsomely. In 1962, Buick sold 400,267 cars, an increase of 37.7 percent over 1961. The comeback of Buick has been a big factor in G.M.'s share-of-market triumph.

The show behind the scenes

Thus far, in tracing G.M.'s success, we have been looking mainly at those plain-to-see elements that have been basic to the company's superior competitive thrust—its high marks in over-all market strategy, product selection, and styling. And needless to say, for its final thrust, G.M.'s success depends on its great strength in distribution and sales. It has long been pretty much beyond dispute that G.M. has not only the largest but the financially strongest and most effective dealer organization in the industry. These are the elements, in any given year, that sell automobiles.

But behind all this is, first of all, a vast internal business in parts and accessories that is of itself one of the largest manufacturing complexes in the U.S. Supervised by one of G.M.'s ablest administrators, Group Vice President Roger M. Kyes, this complex includes AC Spark Plug, Delco-Remy, Delco Radio, Harrison Radiator, Hyatt Bearings, Detroit Transmission, and six other divisions. Their products are basic to the structure and performance of all G.M. cars and, of course, through the internal economies effected, this whole operation is a vital factor in G.M.'s profit performance. And in addition to supplying G.M. car divisions with original and replacement parts, this group sells well over $1 billion in parts to the independent aftermarket.

One has to go behind the scenes, also, to see what G.M. is doing to keep its cars sold, which is largely a question of quality, and to keep these hordes of cars coming off the line at the right time, the right place, and in a fantastic number of expressly ordered combinations of color, equipment, and trim. Underlying and sustaining General Motors' remarkable record of sales and profits is its performance in these two areas: the job it does on reliability control; the job it does on scheduling and logistics.

It is rather striking that at a time when its cars are selling with such effortless ease G.M. should be straining so hard to improve quality. Of course, now that the whole industry has extended its new-car warranties to two years everybody is quality-conscious. But this is not the principal motivation. At G.M. it is simply recognized that, the replacement factor being what it is, repeat sales are terribly important. G.M. believes it is the quality of the car, beyond all other factors, that enhances its trade-in value. If that value turns down in any one year, as in the case of the 1960 Ford, it may take several years to turn it back up.

Building in reliability

G.M. has always rigorously carried on physical inspection and has long engaged in quality control, which is a statistical or sampling approach to inspection. But these practices, as Oldsmobile's Jack Wolfram puts it, are essentially police actions that catch mistakes after they have been committed. The big pitch at G.M. now is the preventive concept of "systems reliability control," adapted from the military and introduced throughout the divisions some four years ago. Each division has a well-staffed reliability department, which usually works independently of the inspection and quality-control forces. The director of reliability reports to the general manager. Reliability's job is not to check the work against the blueprints, but to begin with a study of the initial design of each component, determine all probabilities, and see that the utmost reliability is engineered into the product at the design stage. Reliability then follows through with the same kind of study of the manufacturing

stage, and after that it runs a series of reliability tests on the product prototypes that are the equivalent of a year's operation.

Among other records or near-records broken by G.M. in 1962 was its percentage of net income to sales. At a neat 10 cents on the dollar, it was the company's highest profit-to-sales ratio in a dozen years. It is a characteristic of the automobile industry, where such a high proportion of the costs are fixed costs, for the profits to rise sharply in a high-volume year after the breakeven point has been passed. But General Motors had something more than that going for it in 1962. Partly because of its accurate forecast of what the total market would be, and partly because the rise in sales, though spectacular, was remarkably steady, G.M. was able to avoid peaks and valleys in its production scheduling. The fact that the company did not have to go through the usual process of putting on extra workers, then laying them off, saved substantial sums in supplemental unemployment benefits required under the union contract. The even flow of its line rate also had a beneficial effect on quality. When an assembly-line rate is increased from forty to forty-three cars per hour, it not only means an addition of 100 people on the line but it changes the job content of every man on the line, and workers have a tendency to be less productive and to make more mistakes.

Nevertheless, the proliferation of models, options, and varieties of color and trim has enormously complicated G.M.'s problems in logistics and inventory control. There are now a total of 136 models of passenger cars offered by G.M. compared with eighty-five models eight years ago. But that doesn't begin to suggest the problem—the options on engines alone run to almost unbelievable figures. The standard Chevrolet, for instance, has four basic engine options, and with the different carburetor combinations offered, the number of engines is, in effect, raised to twelve. But when the power requirements of all the optional equipment are taken into consideration, it means that Chevrolet has to be prepared to furnish no fewer than 106 varieties of power plants for its standard-size passenger cars alone.

Yet Chevrolet delivered over two million cars in 1962, with an actual reduction, in the averages throughout the year, of dealers' stocks on hand. Where it used to take about four weeks to deliver a Chevrolet on a sold order, the time has now been cut to an average of sixteen days from the date of the order to the date of delivery anywhere in the U.S. This flexibility has been achieved largely by virtue of the computer. Chevrolet production, procurement, and sales reports are now on a complete electronic data-processing system. In the past, schedules were reviewed and revised on the basis of the dealers' ten-day reports. Today the dealer reports his sales daily to the zone office, and the complete information is fed into the EDP equipment for instant transmission to Detroit. Thus Knudsen, his sales manager, and his manufacturing manager do not have to wait ten days to know what is going on in the market. Changing customer preferences in models, options, color, and styles can be instantly sized up, and the production schedules and the mix can be adjusted within a week's time. Chevrolet manufactures on the replacement theory rather than on order. If the rate of depletion on red trim, say—or any other buyers' choice—is faster than originally projected in the schedules, the factory immediately starts replacing at the higher rate. It is by such techniques that G.M. has been able to adjust so rapidly to the public's rapidly changing tastes.

Sunlight and shadow

In the U.S., G.M. is, by all measurable standards, a mighty impressive monument to the American economic system. But the monument casts a shadow—a giant shadow of the giant's sheer success. Has G.M. now grown so big as to threaten the health of the very system that made its success possible?

The pending government antitrust actions against G.M. are a somewhat mixed bag of suits principally aimed at G.M.'s non-automotive activities, although one of them challenges G.M.'s bus business, and another relates to the distribution of Chevrolet cars. The suits now total five:

A criminal suit charging the company with unfairly using its power as the largest railroad shipper to capture over 80 percent of the diesel-locomotive market. A related civil suit seeks divestiture of the Electro-Motive Division that builds the locomotives.

A civil suit charging the company with incipient monopoly in the off-highway, earthmoving-equipment field, and seeking to nullify G.M.'s acquisition, back in 1953, of the Euclid Road Machinery Co.

A civil suit alleging that G.M. monopolizes 80 percent of the sales of city- and intercity-type buses.

In a criminal suit a federal judge in Los Angeles, in March, 1963, entered a judgment of acquittal to charges that G.M. had conspired to prevent its dealers from selling new Chevrolets through discount houses. G.M. still faces a related civil suit, however, in which the government seeks injunctive relief.

Finally, since 1959, a federal grand jury in New York, fortified by voluminous documents subpoenaed from G.M., has been conducting a broad investigation of possible violations of the antitrust laws in the automotive industry.

The billion-dollar question

Of the pending lawsuits Chairman Donner simply says: "We expect to defend them one by one. We happen to think that what we've been doing is the right thing to do in a competitive market. We have done nothing to be ashamed of." This is straightforward reaction to the specific charges, but the ultimate question of G.M.'s size will continue to be a matter of debate. Indeed, what the business world is forever wondering about is whether, one fine day, the government will go for the big one—a frontal attack on G.M.'s size, its better-than-50 percent share of the U.S. passenger-car market, and perhaps, after the pattern of the diesel-locomotive case, ask for the divestiture of a major car division, such as Chevrolet.

All this is pure speculation, of course, and is not based on anything the Department of Justice has publicly said, and certainly not on anything strange or circuitous that General Motors has done. As far as the passenger-car business is concerned, the questions raised by G.M.'s spectacular success appear to be concerned not so much with behavior as with structure, not with business morality but with economic philosophy, not with practice but with theory. Is bigness, of itself, bad? Should power be dismantled because of its capabilities for uncommitted abuses? These are legitimate questions that jurists and economists have wrestled with in the past, and they will continue to do so as long as the American economic system endures. Discussion of these abstract problems, however, should never get too far away from what a company did or did not do to achieve its success and eminence.

This report on what G.M. has accomplished of recent years at least makes plain that it has in its way served the consumer. G.M. never offered him more choice or better quality, and all at prices that have remained virtually unchanged since the fall of 1958. These prices, moreover, were certainly free of collusion, discrimination, exclusive deals, or below-cost subsidies. To be sure, G.M. was hard on the competition—all of it—but did it "oppress" any competitor? There's a difference. The best answer to that comes from a high executive of a rival auto company. "They beat us last year," he said, "on product and not with monopolistic power plays. If G.M. is going to be cut down to size, we want to be the party that does it."

READING 7

The previous reading told of a well-established firm that has long stayed on the top of a huge industry. This one tells a different story of success: the spectacular use of a newcomer in one of the growth industries of the 1960s, the electronic data-processing field. Its purpose is not to tell a typical story of new corporations, for the Control Data Corporation is obviously far from typical. Instead, its usefulness is to show that the economy still has such dynamic changes taking place in it and to illustrate that this one path to success required far more research and development expenditures than was true of most great corporations of the past.

This article from *Business Week* magazine is again a vital background piece for the market discussions which are to follow later in the readings.

Questions to Guide the Reading

What were the principal factors accounting for Control Data's rise? Are those same factors applicable in a large number of additional situations?

How important is it to the economy that there continue to be such opportunities for major new businesses to thrust ahead? What can public policy do to enhance the likelihood that such opportunities will continue to exist in the future?

THE RISE OF CONTROL DATA CORPORATION
Business Week

COMPANIES

SMALL, SMART, SHARP

Against computer giants such as IBM, six-year-old Control Data Corp. is growing swiftly by picking its jobs and refusing to battle the big ones head-on.

When you're small fry in a sea of hungry sharks, and the waters around you are filled with giants who can demolish you with a flick of their tail, one way to survive is to be a pilot fish. By swimming below and just behind the jaws of the biggest shark in the school, you will eke out a fair living on the morsels the big one misses. But you will have to be fast and agile to avoid being caught and destroyed by those powerful jaws above you.

From "Small, Smart, Sharp," *Business Week*, May 25, 1963, pp. 154 ff. Reprinted with kind permission of the publisher.

Six years ago, a group of engineers led by William C. Norris left the Univac Div. of Sperry Rand to start a new data processing equipment company in Minneapolis. They called it Control Data Corp., and they were very small fry indeed in a sea of very big fish.

In the waters in which they launched themselves, International Business Machines Corp. was the biggest and fiercest fish of all; powerful Univac was angry; Minneapolis-Honeywell, General Electric, and RCA had billion-dollar smiles and shiny teeth; Philco was sharpening its bite; National Cash Register, Monroe Calculating Machine Co., and Burroughs Corp. were gliding along with the power of strong marketing organizations; and Bendix was swimming ahead on its engineering talent.

Where to start

Almost all these big fish had decided to tackle IBM in its own pond--business data processing— because that's where their market research (and IBM's sales) showed that 90% or more of sales would be. Few, in 1957, realized how much a frontal assault on IBM would cost. Today, almost all have yet to see a profit.

Control Data Corp. had less than two-thirds of a million dollars to spend getting started, and a direct attack on IBM was impossible to contemplate. So CDC decided to build a computer that would operate, roughly, on the standards that IBM, the industry's leader, was creating for data processing equipment. In the six years since that decision was made, CDC has grown to a $50-million operation with 3,200 employees and has shown profits since its second year.

The computer CDC designed was a large-scale scientific model, and it was one of the earliest to be transistorized. Norris and his engineers planned to sell it with few accessories. The customers CDC wanted were strictly professionals who would not need all the hand-holding most new computer customers require. That kind of help IBM was well equipped to give, but the cost of it was reflected in rental rates.

Engineering talent

In 1957, the number of experienced computer users who would want the kind of equipment and service CDC planned to offer was small. Few gave the new Minneapolis company much chance to survive. But the group was not without business savvy. It consisted of scientists and engineers who believed they could make a good electronic computer to sell at a rock-bottom price. Most were computer pioneers. They had formed a company to make computers once before—in 1946—called Engineering Research Associates. And in Norris, they had a man who combined the precise planning of a Navy officer with the steady hand of a touch engineer.

Now 51, sinewy and graying, Norris is an electrical engineering graduate of Nebraska University. He was a sales engineer for Westinghouse X-ray Div. before World War II. In the Navy he did research on fire control, rose to commander, and became Director of a Naval Communications Section.

Engineering Research Associates was formed by a group of naval officers who had served with Norris; he became its vice-president of operations. In 1952, ERA was sold by its backers to Remington Rand, which also had purchased the Eckert-Mauchly Computer Corp., designer of Univac. With that change, Norris became vice-president of Remington's ERA Div. In 1955, he was appointed vice-president and general manager of Sperry Rand Corp.'s Univac Div.

Looking back on it now, Norris calls the ERA-Remington Rand merger a "tremendous mismatch." The rapid turnover of top executives at Remington Rand made long-range planning most difficult, he says.

"We sat there with a tremendous technological and sales lead and watched IBM pass us as if we were standing still," he recalls. "When Remington Rand started breaking up the Univac Div. part by part, I left."

Austere setting

With Norris went a group of eight engineers, and CDC was born. The group went to work in rented quarters in an old paper warehouse across the street from the Minneapolis Star and Tribune plant. They put up temporary partitions of plasterboard, which even now are still unpainted. Board meetings were held in a closet-sized room with a chipped washbasin on the wall. But this was the setting for the manufacture of one of the most modern of all possible products —solid state transistorized computers.

Picking prospects

There were enough customers with odd problems in mathematical analysis to get CDC started. So the company began its existence as the pilot fish lives—not trying to compete for the big lush mouthfuls, the business data processing jobs. It let the big sharks fight while it nibbled away at the scientific computer applications and established a good beachhead in the Atomic Energy Commission and the Defense Dept.

CDC picked its prospects carefully. "We can't afford to spend much on unsuccessful proposals," says James G. Miles, vice-president of marketing. He estimates it costs competitors around $20,000 to study a customer's needs and mount a serious sales effort. By selective selling, and by shooting for the jobs where the odds are in its favor, CDC has landed two-thirds of the customers it has submitted serious proposals to, Miles says.

The hard years

In its second year, CDC showed its first earnings—around $280,000. But they were hard years. The company started with 300 shareholders who put up $600,000 at $1 a share. At first, it had no plans to make large computers, but its first product, the $1.4 million 1604 computer, turned out that way. Before it even landed its first order in June, 1958, CDC acquired another company, Cedar Engineering, Inc. to get some manufacturing business. The deal almost sank them. Cedar took about $500,000 in working capital, and salaries were cut in half to conserve cash. After CDC got its first order for a 1604 system, Allstate Insurance purchased $350,000 worth of 6% preferred stock to aid in financing.

In six years the company has come along so fast that its top executives still find it hard to believe that the new, severely modern suburban headquarters of the company really is theirs. And they watch with the pride of parenthood the quarterly reports that document a rapidly increasing sales and earnings volume—from a $200,000 loss in 1958 to the $41-million sales and $1.5-million earnings in the fiscal year that ended in July, 1962. In the first nine months of fiscal 1963, sales totaled $38.5-million, with earnings of $1.7-million.

To Norris, the company's growth rate seems perfectly normal. "We're right on schedule," he says.

New and bigger

While making money, the company has managed to keep new products coming along, too. Within a few weeks it plans to ship the first of a new series of large-scale computers called the 3600. At an average system cost of $2.5-million each, the 3600 has five times the performance of CDC's basic 1604-A, and—at the present time—is the largest commercially available computer in the world. And at CDC's Advanced Development Laboratory, in Chippewa Falls, Wis., work is progressing on what the company is convinced will be the largest and most powerful computer ever built.

Called the 6600, the new giant will have five times the problem-solving capacity of the 3600. It is scheduled to go to the Lawrence Radiation Laboratory in Livermore, Calif., in 1964. The AEC contracted to pay $5.5-million for the super computer, and CDC will incorporate it into its commercial line if demand warrants. But, realistically, no one at the company expects mobs of customers to be breaking down the door for this one.

Scientific market

Why should a small company like CDC undertake to build bigger and bigger computers rather than smaller ones that are easier to put together? The answer is one of the basic keys to CDC's strategy. The company's main stamping ground is the scientific community. And scientists keep needing bigger and bigger machines to solve increasingly difficult problems in physics and space technology. Also, quite simply, CDC can make more money on the big jobs.

"You have to have customer engineers near every computer you sell," says George S. Hanson, sales executive. "With a small computer in an isolated location, that would cost you money. But you can afford to assign people to live with a big machine no matter where it is for as long as it is there."

Sales vs. rentals

Competing computer makers tend to downgrade CDC's performance in earnings by pointing out that the company has been able to show profits because it has sold most of its machines, rather than renting them, has a high proportion of government sales (about 70%), has been shy on providing programming aids, and has not developed its own peripheral equipment. Two years ago, that evaluation was quite true. Now it isn't.

At present, about 75% of the small computers—and 50% of the large—are rentals. And although the company is not yet strong on so-called "applied programming," it does supply a full set of automatic programming aids. One of these is FORTRAN, the IBM algebraic language compiler that permits a scientist to program a computer in an English and algebraic notation rather than the detailed instructions of binary numbers.

Separate divisions

Because up to two-thirds of the total cost of equipment in any data processing system is in the peripheral machinery, such as tape and card readers, magnetic tape transports, and random access memory systems, CDC is developing its own proprietary lines in all these devices. It has set up a separate Peripheral Equipment Div. and plans to make every type of accessory it will need by 1965. As it did with its first products, CDC is concentrating on engineering and design in its new division. Its manufacturing consists almost wholly of assembly and testing. As a result, about half of its employees are in the so-called "professionally exempt" category, and nearly half of these are engineers. There are relatively few unskilled workers in the company.

Part of the company's appetite for skilled manpower was satisfied last month when CDC purchased Bendix Corp.'s Computer Div. It kept about 400 Bendix employees, most in sales and service engineering. CDC has been extremely tough in deciding what engineering projects under way at Bendix were to be continued or stopped. This led to rumors that CDC was not going to service the Bendix computers now in existence.

The company has been trying desperately to spike such talk. It considers Bendix customers a concentrated source of future sales. Norris says both engineering and programming projects for the Bendix G-15 and G-20 systems will continue.

However, as in any situation where employees feel they have had their company sold out from under them, there undoubtedly will be larger morale problems and organizational difficulties from absorbing Bendix than CDC, as a small company, has yet had to face in its previous acquisitions.

The pattern of swift growth set in the first year of the company's life has continued. CDC acquired Control Corp. in 1960 to give it know-how and market access in oil, gas, and water distribution systems. A year ago it established a joint venture with Holley Carburetor Co. to manufacture printers. In 1962, it formed Meis-con Corp. after acquiring Meisner Engineers, a bankrupt Chicago civil engineering firm that used computers for engineering design. And, in 1963, it made another acquisition, a Dutch instruments manufacturer, Electro-Fact, N. V. Computer control systems eventually will pick up information directly from instruments, so CDC feels it is important to have knowledge in that field. The Netherlands plant also will give Control Data a manufacturing facility in the Common Market to supplement its sales offices in Switzerland, Scandinavia, West Germany, and France.

Planning the plan

All this surely is going to bring more and more management problems for CDC. But Norris, almost a fanatical long-range planner (every department has to keep a five-year plan and update it three times a year), has plans for that, too. He is deliberately pushing more and more autonomy on his division heads. Not surprisingly, the emerging corporate structure resembles IBM.

Norris is unworried by the possibility that swift technological change may upset his long-range planning. "Technological change is one of the easier things to plan for," he says. But he does not feel that CDC is large enough yet to engage in basic research. Nevertheless, CDC's kind of research would be considered fairly basic in most other, less scientifically finicky industries.

While Norris won't reveal details of what is inside the five-inch-thick-looseleaf binder that contains the corporation's master five-year plan, he will provide a general outline of the company's future. He deflects the question of whether CDC will make a major effort in business data processing by a flat statement that 45% of total computer sales will be for industrial and scientific use—a prediction few in the industry agree with at the moment.

"We aren't going to overtake IBM," he says, "but there is a very big market in our specialties, and we plan to continue to penetrate the industrial field. We'll probably slide into business data processing gradually, since there never has been much difference between the equipment."

But as CDC moves through the changing plans in the big five-year book, attempting to stay fast and agile while growing, one thing is quite certain: A company that started out as a pilot fish is getting to look more like a shark.

READING 8

How important are stockholders in today's economy? They are certainly numerous (over 17 million in 1962) and they nominally own America's corporations, yet most of them have little desire to thrust themselves into the complex decisions necessary for the smooth functioning of the businesses which they own. Even if they had the desire—and the ability—to function actively as owners, many might feel frustrated by the sheer number of stockholders and number of shares that would be a prerequisite to a decisive voice in company policy.

Increasingly, then, the role for today's stockholders is a passive one. If they are dissatisfied they are more likely to shift their funds than to take direct action within the corporation concerned. In varying degrees, the effective control of many corporations thus is in the hands of professional managers. These men, who ordinarily hold only a small part of the outstanding stock, can usually keep themselves in office as long as they keep a majority of the stockholders reasonably happy.

Nevertheless, once a year the stockholders of every corporation have a right to attend an annual meeting where the affairs of the company are discussed and a few important matters of policy may theoretically be voted upon.

The late Burton Crane, a business writer for the *New York Times*, discusses some current issues in the conduct of these annual meetings.

Questions to Guide the Reading

Is the separation of ownership and management in most American corporations efficient? Is it democratic, and should it be?

What are some areas where a conflict of interest might arise between the owners of a modern corporation and its hired professional managers? How effective is the annual meeting of shareholders as a device for resolving these possible conflicts? What alternatives are available?

TODAY'S STOCKHOLDERS' MEETINGS
Burton Crane

From mid-March through mid-June, some 3,300 publicly owned companies will go through the tragicomedy known as the annual meeting of shareholders.

Once again the sentimentalist who "hasn't missed a meeting in forty years" will take the floor to send best wishes to the president's wife.

Once again, in all probability, some realist will decline to make unanimous a vote of confidence in the officers who have been gaily sending the company into bankruptcy.

Once again there will be complaints about the free lunches. These will cover their edibility and, perhaps, their absence.

And once again there will be discussions of serious concern not only to this particular company but to all companies.

Not a town meeting

The annual company meeting has often been compared to the New England town meeting. It is not any such thing. It is not even especially democratic, because shareholders vote share by share rather than poll by poll. The more shares, the more votes. It is even less democratic than it might be because investment over the last twenty years or so has become thoroughly institutionalized.

From Burton Crane, "Although Votes Are Not Equal, Small Holders Play a Big Role," *New York Times*, Sunday, March 18, 1962. Reprinted with permission of Mrs. Crane and the publisher.

Pension funds, banks with trusteed accounts and investment companies customarily vote automatically for the present management. Only when a scandal or a real fight for control has broken into the open does any of them even bother to think about the problem.

Then what purpose does a company meeting serve? Why shouldn't management be allowed to go its own way, raising its own salaries, voting itself bonuses and forgetting the downcast eyes and modest bearing that employees are supposed to owe their bosses?

The modern corporate set-up is not much more than 75 years old. Before that, except for a few canals and railroads and Western Union Telegraph, the owners of corporations generally ran them. Gradually, as corporations grew too complex for one-man rule or as some bosses grew too rich to be bothered, the non-owner executive was called in. This was the management revolution, about which business magazines have piped so many pulsing paeans.

This went pretty far. Until the Securities Acts were passed in the early Nineteen Thirties the lack of shareholder control over the corporations they owned was positively British. Proxies sometimes ran for years and years. The Securities and Exchange Commission stopped that, insisting that they run for one year or one meeting only. It insisted that proxy statements be mailed out except for companies in which another company or a family group held better than 50 per cent control.

This was the beginning of what might be called a counter-revolution. Groups of small shareholders—actually, the majority shares of most corporations are owned by small shareholders—began to get together to attend annual meetings, to ask for more information, to assert some of the rights to which they felt themselves entitled as owners.

The group's leaders

Leaders of the counter-revolutionary group are unquestionably Lewis D. Gilbert, who was so completely ignored at the Consolidated Gas annual meeting in 1932 that he never quite recovered; his brother, John J. Gilbert; Mrs. Wilma D. Soss, president of the Federation of Women Shareholders in American Business, Inc.; and Mrs. Evelyn Yvonne Davis. Lewis Gilbert is independently wealthy and has made this crusade his life work.

For years Lewis Gilbert was a noisy annoyance

to company managements, and newspapers, as a rule, treated him as a figure of fun, the comic relief at many a company meeting.

But as he and other protesters continued their campaigns the attitude of the press began to change. Reporters assigned to the meetings found themselves more and more in agreement with the points raised. Moreover, a Gilbert appearance often made an otherwise deadly annual meeting almost bearable. Many managements then—and some managements still—try to make their meetings as boring as possible.

Over this same period advertising men were inventing a street—they called it Madison Avenue —and public relations consultants were springing full-armed from the heads of Ivy Lee and Carl Byoir. The public relations men took over the counter-counter-revolution.

Dragged into the open with their sins upon them once each year, some corporation executives decided to make a virtue of the ordeal. They began making their meetings pleasanter, with free lunches, movies, scientific demonstrations and occasionally, the introduction of new products.

The SEC more than occasionally took notice of the complaints of dissidents and took action through its rules. So did the New York Stock Exchange. For example, it has ruled that all listed companies—even though exempted by the SEC—must solicit proxies by the end of 1962. It forced Johnson & Johnson to knuckle down to this rule. It struck Cannon Mills from the list when it refused to comply.

The big stock exchange houses also have been bringing pressure on the corporations, but quietly, without publicity. Especially when engaging in underwritings, they are insistent that the companies volunteer more and more information.

Member firms cannot, of course, vote stock held by them in Street names if there is any controversy whatever mentioned on the proxy ballot. The shareholder of record must do the voting, on a ballot signed by the brokerage house of record. The broker is not allowed to volunteer any information in disputed matters. He may, however, vote his own stock as he wishes.

Some issues listed

Here are a few of the issues that are sure to arise in the days ahead. Many of them already are posed as questions on proxy ballots. For example, Lewis D. Gilbert has been campaigning for:

The end of the stagger system for electing directors, which prevents a management from being ousted from control in a single year.

The election of auditors, on the principle that the auditors should be responsible to the owners, rather than to the employees.

Annual meetings in more convenient locations, including rotation of meetings. Last year the Olin-Mathiesen Chemical Corporation held a meeting in Saltville, Va., with a population of 2,800. Only two directors attended. Even the president didn't make it.

Mandatory cumulative voting rights. This would allow important minority groups to have at least some representation on boards of directors. Cumulative voting is now required in twenty-three states.

Pre-emptive rights for shareholders. Some companies do not require that shareholders have the first right to buy new securities in proportion to their holdings.

Mrs. Soss says that the Gilbert brothers have had a habit of working for a limited number of objectives and hammering them home by repetition. The group that she heads is a little more venturesome and inventive.

A battle is on now for a secret ballot. Many employees are also shareholders. Could they vote their proxies against the management slate of directors or against a management proposal with-out jeopardizing their jobs? Mrs. Soss and her group fought for eight years to get a secret ballot proposal on the American Telephone and Telegraph Company proxy ballot. It was defeated last year but is being reintroduced.

More than a quarter of the shares of Sears, Roebuck & Co. are owned by Sears, Roebuck employees through their pension fund and profit-sharing plan. This was administered by a five-man committee, on which management had three representatives. The committee voted the stock—naturally for the management side of any argument.

The Federation of Women Shareholders claims credit for introducing the idea of the pass-through vote. The Sears employees in the profit-sharing plan are now able to vote a confidential ballot, expressing their own ideas. When American Motors proposed its profit-sharing plan without a pass-through vote, Mrs. Soss and her group objected and the stock exchange required its inclusion. Mrs. Soss says:

"We believe in a people's capitalism as an answer to communism. There cannot be a people's capitalism without wide ownership by small shareholders. There can be no people's capitalism without corporate democracy."

And corporate democracy seems to be difficult without spokesmen who know General Robert's rules of order and carry portable squawkboxes to get the floor when there aren't enough microphones.

READING 9

As implied in the previous reading, the more complex the business world becomes, the more firms have to rely upon specialized professional talent for their desired results. An interesting question to ask early in the study of economics is whether or not this discipline has much to contribute to the running of the business firms that are so critical in our system.

Sidney S. Alexander, professor of industrial management at the Massachusetts Institute of Technology and a long-time consultant in industry, discusses what economics can and cannot contribute toward the successful conduct of a business enterprise.

Questions to Guide the Reading

What contribution would a deeper understanding of how our economy operates make to the American businessman? Would a businessman who had studied economics or hired a professional economist be more likely to make good profits than one who had not?

In what types of firms and in what types of business decisions are professional economists likely to be most valuable? In which are they likely to be least valuable?

ECONOMICS AND BUSINESS PLANNING
Sidney S. Alexander

What can economics contribute to the conduct of a business enterprise? To this question there is a simple and obvious answer: Economics is the study of the fundamentals governing business, and it stands in the same relationship to the practice of business as knowledge of physical laws and facts to the practice of engineering.

But this proposition, like so many others that are simple and obvious, is just not true. There is no economic handbook, comparable to an engineering handbook, such that a skilled practitioner can consult the appropriate table and find the answer to his practical problem. It may be true, in some sense, that economics is to business as physics is to engineering, but the relationship must be more obscure and possibly more profound than the direct application of scientific study to the solution of the practical problem. As an analogy, I might ask you to consider how useful Einstein's theory of relativity would have been in helping you to get your automobile engine started when it had failed—purely an exercise in applied physics.

The tools and the modes of thought of economics are clearly not the tools of business practice. They can, however, be useful in the practice of business, and it is my purpose to indicate how. But the application is neither simple nor direct.

An economist friend of mine, exploring job opportunities in the motion picture business, was told by a movie tycoon: "If I had an economist on my staff I wouldn't know what to do with him." It is my impression that the heads of some of our greatest corporations who have hired economists have not known what to do with them either. Nor did the economists have a clear idea of what they were to do. Yet, I think a notable contribution is being made by economists to the businesses which they serve, and the full potentialities have not yet been realized. In this, as in so many other human affairs, what can be done is worked out by facing up to the problems as they emerge rather than by the construction of an orderly and complete blueprint in advance.

Economics can be divided into three broad subjects: *macroeconomics,* national income and all that; *microeconomics,* supply and demand and all that; and *descriptive economics,* all that. The great name in macroeconomics is Keynes, in microeconomics, Marshall, in descriptive economics, the National Bureau of Economic Research.

The coat of arms of macroeconomics is the rising curve of expenditure as a function of income intersecting the forty-five degree line of the equality of expenditure and income. The motto: Saving Equals Investment. The coat of arms of microeconomics is the ancient and honorable supply and demand curves crossed in a field. The motto: Supply Equals Demand. Descriptive economics can best be broken down into two branches, statistical and institutional, and the statistical, in turn, into two types: statistical methods, or applied calculus, and statistical practice, or applied arithmetic. Their respective coats of arms are white and black balls in an urn and a chart of the Bureau of Labor Statistics index of the cost of living. The other branch of descriptive economics, the institutional, has a coat of arms in the style of an old civic mural, with panels showing scenes from industry, agriculture, commerce, and government.

Each of these broad fields of economics has its own contribution to make to business. Macroeconomics is useful principally in the short-run forecasting of aggregate business activity, microeconomics in long-run planning and in profit-maximizing. Descriptive economics, which lends practical content to what would otherwise be barren theory, is useful both in relating the firm to its environment and in long-run planning.

Short-term forecasting

The most obvious contribution that economics can make to the conduct of a business is in short-term forecasting of the business cycle. The study of the business cycle is clearly recognized as the special province of economists, and it was in their role of analysts of the current and prospective state of business that economists were first hired in private business. The large metropolitan banks were among the first to recognize the contribution that economists can make to the analysis of

From Sidney S. Alexander, "Economics and Business Planning," *Economics and the Policy Makers: Brookings Lectures, 1958–59* (The Brookings Institution, Washington, D.C., 1959), pp. 1–26.

business prospects—for somebody else. Some 30 years ago the characteristic job of a bank economist was the publication of a monthly letter on business conditions to be made available to the bank's customers. Internal consumption was not prohibited but there is no evidence that it was widely indulged in. Economists, by and large, were not directly involved in the business conduct of the banks at that time. The large downtown New York banks often had huge pillars in front of their buildings, but the pillars did not really support the roof. They also had economists inside, but the economists did not help guide portfolio policies. The pillars remain, or in more recent structures, their prestige value is served by large expanses of glass, but the economist's role has changed. Undoubtedly, this change is a consequence of the development of a more specialized professional approach to the analysis of aggregate business activity, largely a combination of Keynesian theory with the empirical work on the national accounts pioneered by the National Bureau of Economic Research and further developed by the Department of Commerce.

At any rate, the first thing that is usually expected of an economist in business is the short-run forecasting of business conditions, the application of macroeconomics to current problems. This sometimes takes the form of a disembodied general appraisal of business conditions circulated within the top management, but it is frequently also embodied in the budgeting procedure. For most large corporations the periodic short-term budgets start off from the assumptions of business conditions forecast by the economist. The individual divisions, on those assumptions, then prepare their own forecasts of total sales of their products for the entire industry, and the company's share of the industry's sales. The economist then reviews the divisions' forecasts for their consistency with his own forecasts for the economy and for the industry.

In this review function, the economist depends not only on his skill in macroeconomic analysis, but also on his training and experience in descriptive economics, particularly in empirical statistics. That is, the economist serves not only as the forecaster of general economic conditions, but as the window upon the world for the company. In the latter capacity, he depends upon specialized skill in the interpretation of industry statistics as well as specialized analysis of the consequences of emerging developments. The tool of analysis corresponding to this function has no concise name, but proceeds from the tradition of empirical research in economics. An economist is by no means the only one who could extract information and predictions useful to the firm from statistics and general economic developments external to the direct experience of the corporation. But he is certainly more nearly fitted than one not trained in economics, and the responsibility will usually fall to an economist if the corporation employs one.

What are the economic tools of analysis for forecasting general business conditions? The most pretentious tool is the elaborate econometric model. But neither in business nor in government has this tool been utilized extensively in a practical way. These models do indeed have great promise, but the promise still lies in the future. Less comprehensive or less systematically organized techniques are those in principal use at present.

A second tool is that of the economic indicators, time series useful in predicting levels of economic activity. Some of these indicators are like Ambrose Bierce's definition of a barometer—an ingenious instrument that tells you the sort of weather you are having. But some of them do have forecasting value. The work of Geoffrey Moore at the National Bureau of Economic Research, based upon the earlier work of Arthur F. Burns and Wesley C. Mitchell, suggests that certain economic time series, called the leading series, characteristically reach their cyclical turning points well ahead of the turning points of the general business cycle. My own investigation of these leading series as forecasters suggests that while they do in fact lead turning points of the business cycle with a lead averaging about six months, the length of lead is highly variable.

Even worse, these leading series frequently yield false leads. They often show turning points when the business cycle does not. Just how frequently they yield false leads depends upon the extent to which they are smoothed. The more they are smoothed the fewer false leads they indicate, but smoothing also cuts down the length of their lead. Their predictive power can roughly be summarized, so far as my studies are concerned, by the observation that the leading series can, with a given degree of reliability, signal business cycle turning points some four months ahead, on the average, of the Federal Reserve index of industrial production's signal of equal reliability. This four-month average lead is, of course, subject to a good deal of variation.

Essentially, these series lead because they are sensitive to the rate of change of business activity. When an upswing slows down, they turn down. A slowdown of an upswing frequently does precede a business cycle downturn. In such cases the leading series yield true leads. But it frequently happens that an upswing renews its vigor after a short lull. In such cases the leading series yield false leads. While the frequency of false leads and the high variability in the length of true leads limits the forecasting value of the leading series, that value is still considerable.

By far the most common method of forecasting in business, as in government, is the lost horse method. The name is based on the old prescription for finding a lost horse. You go where the horse was last seen and ask, "Where would I go next if I were a horse?" This technique is, in particular, applied within the framework of the Keynesian analysis. According to that analysis, the gross national product is determined by the aggregate level of expenditure, part of which is itself geared closely to the level of the gross national product, while the remainder has a more nearly autonomous variation. The lost horse technique then is applied to the autonomous elements such as investment in plant and equipment, government expenditure, exports, and the autonomous component of consumption expenditure.

While this method is operated within the theoretical framework of the Keynesian analysis, its application at critical points is an art rather than a science. It requires the identification of the areas where autonomous variation in expenditures can be expected, and the quantitative estimation of these autonomous variations. Of course, government expenditure is one of the most important of the autonomous components and the amateur can be separated from the professional practitioner of the lost horse method according to whether the forecaster relies on the budget estimates or makes his own independently. For, in spite of the fact that the budgetary expenditures and receipts are officially estimated by the government, the errors in forecasts of the governmental sector are among the most important errors in actual practice in forecasting levels of aggregate economic activity. This process is far from perfect and is still beset with difficulties.

While the lost horse method is undoubtedly the one in most general use by economists both in government and in business, second place among economists and first place among businessmen is certainly occupied by the persistence method, the so-called naive model. Even in meteorology, I am told, one of the best predictions of tomorrow's weather is that it will be the same as today's, outside of New England. Possibly meteorology has passed beyond this point, but there is some question whether economics has. The chief economist of one of our largest corporations tells me that when his short-term forecast actually has to be committed to paper a very high respect is paid to the likelihood that economic conditions will continue to move in the direction in which they have most recently been moving.

Two sorts of persistence models should be distinguished. The first is persistence of level, the second, persistence of change. The first says that next year's business will be about the same as this year's, the second, that next year's rate of change will be about the same as this year's. The persistence of change assumption is the more popular, at least among economists.

Let us not be too scornful of the persistence assumption. In at least one thorough test of econometric models of forecasting the persistence models were used as a basis for comparison, and they certainly were not outclassed. But the great flaw in the persistence method is that it cannot predict a turning point. It is like Napoleon's drummer boy who knew very well how to beat a charge but had never learned how to beat a retreat. Yet in short-term forecasting, the prediction of turning points is the very heart of the problem.

While complaints are often made of the unpredictability of economic affairs, it can be argued that there is actually a great deal of predictability. Thus a persistence type estimate of the Federal Reserve Index three months hence as equal to this month's index plus two thirds of the change over the past three months will explain about 94 per cent of the variance of the FRB Index in the postwar period. But that hardly qualifies as a prediction. What we are really interested in is reducing the remaining errors. What is simply predictable is taken for granted, only what is as yet unpredictable is regarded as worthy of prediction. That is why the persistence models may be taken as the base line from which the value of other forecasting techniques can be measured.

Also similar to a technique used in meteorology is the specific analogy method. If you can find days in the past when the weather maps strongly resemble today's map you can expect tomorrow's weather to be about the same as followed those previous examples. Similarly, the economic prospects for the immediate future may be forecast on the basis of what happened the last time things shaped up as they are now shaping up. This technique, in economics, is subject to the limitation that the number of recorded business cycle configurations is infinitely smaller than the number of recorded weather maps. Consequently, the specific analogy method is used principally at times of great structural change such as the onset of war or its termination. At such times it may be helpful to inquire what happened the last time that a similar event occurred.

Another forecasting technique, more frequently used by noneconomists than economists, is the periodicity method. In its extreme form this implies a uniformly timed succession of ups and downs of the business cycle. Its forecasts are based on time alone, or on the time since the last turning point. While this notion of rigid periodicity is generally scorned by economists as in the witch doctor stage, nevertheless, in the postwar period when a downswing approaches twelve months, or an upswing approaches three years in duration, it is reasonable to look closely for signs of a turning point.

The coexistence of dubious methods of short-term forecasting with the more respectable ones does reflect the limited claims that can be made for the best of the methods in present use, the lost horse technique. The tools of short-term economic forecasting may not be very sharp, but they are useful nonetheless. They are most useful in the hands of an artist; they cannot be applied mechanically, which means that they tell only part of the story. The remainder depends on the judgment and insight of the economist, bred by familiarity with the workings of the economy, but not yet reducible to a scientific technique. The economist can bring to this process a theoretical structure for conditional forecasts, the governing conditions being the actual variations of the autonomous expenditures.

While conditional forecasts are useful for government and for monetary authorities who have power to alter some of the basic conditions, they are not of interest to business men who require unconditional forecasts. In order to convert a conditional forecast to an unconditional one, the governing conditions must be estimated. This is where the art of finding the lost horse comes in. The forecaster must use his best judgment, based on his familiarity with the current data and his intuitive "feel" for the workings of the economy, in estimating the governing conditions.

Long-term planning

While the most obvious task of the economist in the large corporation is short-run forecasting, his most valuable contribution, it seems to me, is in long-run planning. To some extent, this is a consequence of the greater amenability of long-run developments to economic forecasting techniques. While it is often quite hard to estimate whether the fourth quarter of next year will have a gross national product higher or lower than the fourth quarter of this year, it can quite reliably be estimated that the gross national product ten years from now will be some 35 per cent higher than it was this year.

The persistence method of forecasting, which works only indifferently well in the short run and misses all the turning points altogether, works very well in the long run, at least for aggregate output. Of course, the persistence method cannot be so appropriately applied to the components of the gross national product as to the aggregate. Individual industries wax and wane, and the firms within them are traditionally likened to the trees of the forest. But the other techniques applicable to the estimates of long-run developments will usually be found to be simpler than those applicable to the short-run. Asymptotic solutions are frequently possible even when general solutions are beyond our power. In more homely language, you can often say where you are going to end up without knowing exactly how you are going to get there and when.

Even though long-run developments are both more important and more easily appraised than short-run, the short-run problems get the lion's share of attention in business, as in government. The businessman, deeply immersed in the day-to-day affairs of the business, never has the time and very rarely has the temperament for study of the long run. His experience in meeting urgent problems of the moment tends to emphasize, in his thinking, the short-run factors at the expense of obscuring the underlying long-run factors. The flow of information to him is from everyday experience of circumstances as they are. Long-run problems require projection into circumstances as they will become or can be made to become. Consequently there is a real opportunity for a valuable contribution by the economist in bringing long-run considerations to bear on a firm's decisions.

It would be a false statement of the role that economic thinking can play to say that if you have a long-run problem you should get an economist to work on it. Much more important, if you have an economist working on your problems he is more likely to look to their long-run aspects—if he is a good economist. Even for an economist, however, once he is injected into a business situation, the temptation is strong to get into the urgent problems of the day and to neglect the long-run aspects.

The major contribution that an economic mode of thought in particular, or a scientific mode of thought in general, can make to the analysis of business problems, and those of government too, is the reduction of the problems to rational study, the transfer of as much as possible out of the field of the intuitively and implicitly appraised to that of the rationally and explicitly appraised.

Many of the critical decisions of long-run planning are once in a decade decisions, some are once in a lifetime. It can hardly be expected that anyone could handle such problems on the basis of his own personal experience. There should be no wonder that this sort of analysis is a field for specialization. Those skills most important for the businessman—skills in negotiation, in execution, and in administration—are not usually associated with the sort of introspective analysis appropriate for the projection into an "as if" world of the future. But the economist is a specialist in the analysis of the "as if." As one author has stated, "Economic analysis is a substitute for the sixth sense of businessmen." The sixth sense probably does better in sensing the short-run situation, but not as well in sensing the long-run. Even when the businessman himself would be highly skilled at making such a study, the doctrine of comparative advantage suggests that it may be more advantageous to turn the study over to a specialist in analysis while the businessman concentrates on problems of administration and execution.

The characteristic long-run problem of the business enterprise is what business should it be in and on what scale. This is the principal content of business planning, and it centers on capital budgeting.

How does one actually go about making projections of future developments which can serve as the basis for long-run planning? Once again, the lost horse method is the dominant technique, but in a different and less well-defined framework. Microanalysis does not furnish as neat a combination of theory with descriptive statistical categories as is available in macroeconomics in the relationship of the Keynesian theory with the national accounts. In the short-term analysis, one need merely run down the categories of the national accounts to make sure one has included the relevant categories. In long-term projection of sub-aggregates the elements of the analysis cannot be so clearly identified in advance. Like the famous recipe for rabbit stew, which begins "catch a rabbit," a long-run projection must begin with the identification of the relevant variables. The second step is the estimation of the direction and extent of their variation.

The principal claim of the economist to expertise in long-run projection of business situations must be based on his feeling for the relevant variables. Lawyers are sometimes said to be experts in relevance, but that claim can probably be made by all scientific workers as well. Only recently has it been recognized in the natural sciences that the so-called scientific method describes the process of demonstration rather than discovery. Discovery depends on insight and belief—in the tradition of Columbus, not of Euclid. Even in pure mathematics, one generation makes the great discoveries and the next cleans up the proofs. So, too, in the much humbler field of applied business analysis, there is great room for insight and intuition informed by experience and by perception of the relevant facts.

Macroeconomics helps only in the first step, the estimation of the level of aggregate economic activity over the period for which the plans are being made. The next steps are to determine the movement of the output of the particular industry relative to aggregate business activity, and beyond that the change in the share of the firm within the industry, and how that will depend on what the firm does. Here a combination of microeconomics and descriptive economics comes to the fore.

I recently asked an economic consultant, studying whether his client should abandon operations in a particular geographical area or should build a whole new organization there, why the client could not perform the analysis for himself. The reply was that he wouldn't know where to begin. This very simply sums up the position of the economist as a specialist in knowing where to begin, and hopefully, where to go from there, in the analysis of a projected situation.

What is required is skill in appraising an analytical problem, in identifying the relevant variables, and in using empirical techniques to estimate them and theoretical analysis to integrate the estimates into a picture of possible future developments under assumed conditions. This, of course, is a rough description of the requirements for successful empirical research in any discipline. The skills are not restricted to economists, and, indeed, others than economists, natural scientists in particular, now offer consultation services in the analysis of long-run problems for business firms. It is quite interesting to see how much economics they are rediscovering in the process.

An economist may be permitted to believe, however, that a person trained in economics, and more particularly, experienced in economic research, can appraise these problems from a somewhat richer background, relative to the needs of the problem, than can one trained in other disciplines.

A more fundamental claim that can be made by the economist for special competence in the long-run analysis of business problems is that of familiarity with the general context of these problems and insight into the nature of the relationships. Plato was fond of arguing that the horse trainer is the one most likely to be well informed of the nature of horses, and the musician of the nature of music. This familiarity with the nature of the process is principally the contribution of descriptive economics, both institutional and statistical.

The great contribution that the economist can play is to bring into explicit consideration the pattern of long-run factors that should be kept in mind both as the background for short-run decisions and the substance of long-run decisions. This is the nugget of truth in the claims, sometimes extravagant, for the benefits of long-range planning. Long-range planning does bring into open discussion the problems of the long run that might otherwise go by default. It imposes upon the corporation the task of consciously facing up to the problems of the long run, of bringing the background into the picture instead of pushing it out of sight.

If an outsider is to make a constructive contribution, critical or otherwise, to the conduct of a firm's long-run planning, he must be skilled in the art of analysis of long-run business problems. While this skill is by no means confined to economists, training and experience in economic analysis and research is certainly one of the best bases from which to approach a problem of business from outside the business itself. The economist cannot hope to have the same familiarity with the internal facts of the business as those who have spent a lifetime in it. He must substitute for knowledge of the particular facts a knowledge of the general configuration of business relationships, so that he can readily learn the relevant facts and fit them into an analytic framework designed to appraise the long-run consequences of any given decision.

The contribution of the outsider is not only that of criticism based on a broader perspective. There is also the opportunity, indeed the necessity, of asking the questions that should be asked but aren't. Sometimes they are unasked for lack of time or skill on the part of those intimately engaged in the business, but sometimes the inquiry is suppressed for fear of what will be found out, just as some people can't find time to visit the doctor or dentist. Once these questions are raised, however, they do require explicit consideration of what was previously taken for granted, the starting point on the road to improvement.

This process may be illustrated by the simple example of the adoption of punch card methods of accounting. In order to convert an accounting system to a punch card installation, the whole system has to be re-examined and the question asked about each element, "What is its purpose?" As a result, activities which have been carried on for a long time without specific justification other than custom are brought before the bar of utility. The new system is likely to be superior to the old, not only because of the advantages of machine over hand methods of computation, but also because of the rationalization of the process, which is an incident of the new installation. Of the two elements, the second is usually the more valuable.

Conclusion

Having made strong claims for what economics can do for business, I feel it appropriate, in closing, to ask whether it is, in fact, likely to do what it can do. For the successful application of economics to business a great deal of judgment is required. Economics can help to form the judgments, but the judgments, to be sound, must also take into account the context of facts from which economic theory habitually abstracts. The frequent complaint that economic analysis is too theoretical to be useful in practice is usually based on the belief that abstraction has been made from some of the fundamental facts. Economics can be valuable in business only to the extent that it comes to grips with the facts of the situation, making allowance in particular for those considerations that are left out of the theoretical formulations. There is a type of business consultant who tries to apply "the book" to the particular problem in hand. Usually the book does not fit. There are others who come with an open mind, guided by theoretical principles but adapting them to the facts as they find them. These are the ones who may be aided to superior insights by their training and experience in economics.

The most important problems of business are problems of adjustment to uncertainties. In this context the economist in business does well to adopt as his motto the old proverb, "In the land of the blind, the one-eyed man is king."

Part 2

THE LEVEL OF JOBS, INCOMES, PRICES, AND PRODUCTION

Only 35 million of the Americans living today (less than 20 per cent of the present population) were twenty years of age or older when the Great Depression of the 1930s began. Yet the tragic events of this decade have left a profound legacy for all Americans—even the vast majority "too young to remember the depression." The story is too big and the impact too great to make it safe for Americans to remain ignorant of what it meant to be in the labor market in the 1930s.

No other depression in our history matched this one for severity or length. At its depths as many as one of four Americans able and willing to work could find no jobs, but no statistics can convey the full despair and the human misery that marked these years for millions of proud and ambitious Americans. Coming at the end of a decade of buoyant optimism during the 1920s, the Great Depression shook many men's faith in the possibility of a self-regulating economy operating at high levels of employment and prosperity. It was the era of the 1930s that gave rise to so much of the debate, which grows as the years pass, on the appropriate role of government policy in promoting economic stability.

David A. Shannon, associate professor of history at the University of Wisconsin, has made an intensive search through the contemporary documents of this period to tell the story in terms of the human beings who lived through it.

In the following three excerpts from Shannon's lively book, Karl de Schweinitz tells a Senate committee of poverty in the city of Philadelphia after local relief funds had been completely exhausted in the spring of 1932, Remley J. Glass describes the plight of the farmers in the corn belt for the readers of *Harper's* magazine, and Oscar Ameringer describes a baffling paradox for a House Congressional Committee—the paradox of agricultural produce going to waste for want of a profitable market at the same time that millions of Americans were without food.

Questions to Guide the Reading

What light do these readings shed on the rise of new economic institutions in the 1930s? To what extent do those institutions—labor unions, agricultural aid programs, and social security, for example—still bear the imprint of the depression in their policies?

What were the main lessons derived from the economic experiences of the 1930s? Are these lessons ones that can be learned and applied without reliving through such a crisis?

A. CITY POVERTY: PHILADELPHIA*
Karl de Schweinitz

MR. DE SCHWEINITZ: When I appeared before the Subcommittee last December, I stated that there were 238,000 persons out of work in Philadelphia and that we estimated unemployment in the city in ordinary times to be between 40,000 and 50,000. There are now 298,000 persons out of work. In other words, whereas in December our employment was a little less than

From David A. Shannon, *The Great Depression* (Prentice-Hall, Inc., Englewood Cliffs, New Jersey, 1960), pp. 19–28, 45–48. Reprinted with kind permission of the editor and publisher. The original sources are indicated below as each excerpt is introduced.

* Karl de Schweinitz in Federal Cooperation in Unemployment Relief, Hearings before a Subcommittee of the Committee on Manufacturers, United States Senate, 72nd Cong., 1 sess., on S. 4592 (Washington: Government Printing Office, 1932), pp. 20–26. Reproduced in Shannon, pp. 45–48.

five times what one might call normal unemployment, today it is six times normal unemployment.

In December I told you that 43,000 families were receiving relief. Today 55,000 families are receiving relief.

In December our per family grant was $4.39 per week per family. It is now $4.23 per family. Of this $4.23 per family, about $3.93 is an allowance for food. This is about two-thirds of the amount needed to provide a health-maintaining diet. . . . I want to tell you about an experience we had in Philadelphia when our private funds were exhausted and before public funds became available.

On April 11 [1932] we mailed to families the last food orders which they received from private funds. It was not until April 22 that the giving of aid to families from public funds began, so that there was a period of about 11 days when many families received nothing. We have received reports from workers as to how these families managed. The material I am about to give you is typical, although it is based on a small sample. We made an intensive study of 91 families to find out what happened when the food orders stopped.

In a little less than 9 per cent of these families there were pregnant mothers and in a little more than one-third of the families children of nursing age.

This is how some of these families managed.

One woman said she borrowed 50 cents from a friend and bought stale bread for 3½ cents per loaf, and that is all they had for eleven days except for one or two meals.

With the last food order another woman received she bought dried vegetables and canned goods. With this she made a soup and whenever the members of the family felt hungry they just ate some of the soup.

Here is a family of a pregnant mother and three children. They had only two meals a day and managed by having breakfast about 11 o'clock in the morning and then advancing the time of their evening meal. Breakfast consisted of cocoa, and bread and butter; the evening meal of canned soup.

One woman went along the docks and picked up vegetables that fell from the wagons. Sometimes the fish vendors gave her fish at the end of the day. On two different occasions this family was without food for a day and a half.

One family had nothing the day the food order stopped until 9 o'clock at night. Then the mother went to a friend's house and begged for a loaf of bread. This woman finally got two days' work at 75 cents a day. She bought a little meat and made a stew from vegetables picked up which they cooked over again every day to prevent its spoiling.

Another family's food consisted of potatoes, rice, bread, and coffee, and for a period of a day and a half they had no food at all.

SENATOR COSTIGAN: Are the cases you are citing typical or extreme?

MR. DE SCHWEINITZ: They are typical. I could tell you about many others, but while tragic it would become monotonous, and a few will illustrate the situation as well as many.

Here is another family which for two days had nothing to eat but bread, and during most of the rest of the time they had only two meals a day. Their meals consisted of bread and coffee for breakfast, and bread and raw or cooked carrots for dinner.

The gas company was careful not to turn off gas in a great many of these families, so in some instances food could be cooked.

Another family did not have food for two days. Then the husband went out and gathered dandelions and the family lived on them.

Here is another family which for two and a half days went without food.

Still another family thinking to get as much as possible with their last food order bought potatoes and for 11 days lived only on them. . . .

I should also like to say that when we talk to people who ask about unemployment they say, "Well, people manage to get along somehow or other don't they? You do not have very many people who really drop dead of starvation." That is perfectly true. Actually, death from starvation is not a frequent occurrence. You do not often hear about casualties of that sort. This is because people live in just the way that I have described. They live on inadequacies, and because they live on inadequacies the thing does not become dramatic and we do not hear about it. Yet the cost in human suffering is just as great as if they starved to death overnight.

SENATOR COSTIGAN: What you say is not only shockingly true but Senator Copeland, of New York, has recently reported cases of known starvation this past winter.

MR. DE SCHWEINITZ: The hospitals have had definite cases of starvation. . . .

A great many people raise the question as to whether the unemployed are a good-for-nothing lot and are out of work because of their own fault. They are not. We have definite studies to show that they had had long and good work records and that they are active, earnest human beings. All they want is a job.

SENATOR WAGNER: No really intelligent person asserts that today.

MR. DE SCHWEINITZ: No intelligent person, no; but lots of persons raise that question.

SENATOR WAGNER: I said intelligent persons.

MR. DE SCHWEINITZ: Yes; we are agreed on that.

I want to repeat that to-day the unemployed are upstanding, intelligent, earnest, capable people, but if we put the children in these families under a period of malnutrition such as they are going through to-day, what sort of people are we going to have 20 years from now, and what will we say at that time about them?

What kind of working people will they be if we continue treating them as we are treating them now? . . .

SENATOR COSTIGAN: One other question, Mr. de Schweinitz. Are World War veterans among the recipients of your relief?

MR. DE SCHWEINITZ: Oh, yes; a great many.

SENATOR COSTIGAN: They are suffering with the rest?

MR. DE SCHWEINITZ: There is no distinction. We have all creeds, all groups, all races; everybody is suffering together.

In Philadelphia, in large areas, no rent is being paid at all, and the landlords, the small landlords, are suffering terribly in a great many instances and sometimes by reason of their own losses they have been obliged to come to us for help.

B. RURAL POVERTY: IOWA*
Remley J. Glass

My home county may well be considered a fair example of Iowa and the Corn Belt. It is one of the ninety-nine counties of Iowa and similar to those throughout the Middle West. Its condition and problems are typical of the entire Corn Belt. Organized before the Civil War, its early citizenry was purely American pioneer stock which successfully withstood the attacks of Indians and the vicissitudes of border existence. To this nucleus have been added a considerable group of Irish immigrants who are centered in two or three southern townships, and a larger portion of Scandinavians who constitute the majority in five or six northern townships. The manufacturing industries in our county seat have brought groups of laborers from the south of Europe, while Mexico likewise has furnished its full quota. Two railroads first came through this county in the late sixties, and other lines were built to tap its agricultural and manufacturing resources as late as the beginning of the present century.

The wheat and corn of pioneer farming gave place in part to hogs, beef cattle, and dairy herds, and the development of sugar beets added to its prosperity. The county seat, with the establishment of large manufacturing industries, assumed an almost metropolitan air with com-

fortable homes and a contented people. Railroads radiating from the town made it the trading and jobbing center of a considerable area. A conservative prosperity was ours.

During the year after the great debacle of 1929 the flood of foreclosure actions did not reach any great peak, but in the years 1931 and 1932 the tidal wave was upon us. Insurance companies and large investors had not as yet realized (and in some instances do not yet realize) that, with the low price of farm commodities and the gradual exhaustion of savings and reserves, the formerly safe and sane investments in farm mortgages could not be worked out, taxes and interest could not be paid, and liquidation could not be made. With an utter disregard of the possibilities of payment or refinancing, the large loan companies plunged ahead to make the Iowa farmer pay his loans in full or turn over the real estate to the mortgage holder. Deficiency judgments and the resultant receiverships were the clubs they used to make the honest but indigent farm owners yield immediate possession of the farms.

Men who had sunk every dollar they possessed in the purchase, upkeep, and improvement of their home places were turned out with small amounts of personal property as their

---

* Remley J. Glass, "Gentlemen, the Corn Belt!" *Harper's*, CLXVII (July, 1933), pp. 200–206. Reproduced in Shannon, pp. 19–26.

only assets. Landowners who had regarded farm land as the ultimate in safety, after using their outside resources in vain attempts to hold their lands, saw these assets go under the sheriff's hammer on the courthouse steps.

During the two-year period of 1931–32, in this formerly prosperous Iowa county, twelve and a half per cent of the farms went under the hammer, and almost twenty-five per cent of the mortgaged farm real estate was foreclosed. And the conditions in my home county have been substantially duplicated in every one of the ninety-nine counties of Iowa and in those of the surrounding States.

We lawyers of the Corn Belt have had to develop a new type of practice, for in pre-war days foreclosure litigation amounted to but a small part of the general practice. In these years of the depression almost one-third of the cases filed have to do with this situation. Our courts are clogged with such matters.

To one who for years has been a standpatter, both financially and politically, the gradual change to near-radicalism, both in himself and in those formerly conservative property owners for whom his firm has done business down the years, is almost incomprehensible, but none the less alarming. Friends and clients of years' standing have lost inherited competencies which had been increased by their own conservative management. Not only their profits, but their principal has been wiped out. The conservative investments in real estate which we Middle Westerners have for years considered the best possible have become not only not an asset, but a liability, with the possibility of deficiency judgments, that bane of mortgage debtors, staring us in the face. Not only have the luxuries and comforts of life been taken from us, but the necessaries are not secure.

Men and women who have lived industrious, comfortable, and contented lives have faced bravely the loss of luxuries and comforts, but there is a decided change in their attitude toward the financial and economic powers that be when conditions take away their homes and imperil the continued existence of their families.

The interests of insurance companies and outside corporations in Iowa real estate have resulted in a form of absentee ownership never before dreamed of. Large numbers of farms held by these outside interests are administered by men who do not have sympathetic appreciation of local conditions, and of the friendly relations which have been traditional between Corn Belt landlord and tenant.

From a lawyer's point of view, one of the most serious effects of the economic crisis lies in the rapid and permanent disintegration of established estates throughout the Corn Belt. Families of moderate means as well as those of considerable fortunes who have been clients of my particular office for three or four generations in many instances have lost their savings, their investments, and their homes; while their business, which for many years has been a continuous source of income, has become merely an additional responsibility as we strive to protect them from foreclosures, judicial receivership, deficiency judgments, and probably bankruptcy.

Thank heaven, most country lawyers feel this responsibility to their old clients, and strive just as diligently to protect their clients' rights under present conditions as they did in the golden days before the depression. Every time, however, when I am called to defend a foreclosure action filed against some client or friend, it is forced on my mind that an estate accumulated through years of effort has not merely changed hands but has vanished into thin air.

As I sit here my mind turns to one after another of the prominent landowning families of this country who have lost their fortunes, not as a result of extravagance or carelessness, but because of conditions beyond their control, and which were not envisaged by the most farsighted.

Just after the Civil War one Johnson Burke came to our Iowa county from New York State, bringing with him what in those days was considered a comfortable fortune. His white hair, long beard, and patriarchal appearance resulted in his being termed Grandfather Burke; and as the years passed and Johnson the Second assumed that same patriarchal appearance, the founder of the family became Great Grandfather Johnson Burke to all of us. His New York shrewdness enabled him to buy tax titles and purchase farms at advantageous prices until he and his family were the leading landowners in the county. As the years passed he left his square-built frame house on the bank of the creek and spent his time in Long Beach, that second Capital of Iowa, in California.

The second generation did not get along so amicably, and extensive and expensive litigation was brought to determine the rights of the active head of the second generation and his brothers and sisters. As a young lawyer, I sat in the courtroom and listened intently to the long list of farms owned by Great Grandfather Burke and the estimates of their value which even in those pre-inflation days went into seven figures. Finally a settlement was made whereby Johnson the Second took over most of the Iowa real estate, paying off the other heirs in cash, mortgages being placed on the lands in order to make the settlements. In the long noonings we lawyers chatting in the courthouse commended the wisdom of young Johnson in the advantageous values at which he took in the farms.

Years passed and Johnson the Second grew feeble with oncoming age and the worries of rent collection and interest payments, and the third generation furnished the head of the family. Values of mortgaged land kept going down. Interest, general taxes, and special assessments for drainage projects whereby more land might be brought under cultivation to produce a greater surplus took a larger and larger share of the once ample income from this estate. Tax sales and foreclosures, judgments, and receiverships have followed in rapid succession until now most of the fertile acres which this family once owned are handled by a trustee who is waging a losing battle to save something from the wreckage. Mind you, the last generation did nothing which had not been considered good business by the preceding generations. Their management was sound, their loans were conservative. And yet their all is gone. This is but one of dozens of instances of more or less prominence in my home community.

The old maxim of three generations between shirt sleeves and shirt sleeves is finding a new meaning out here in the Corn Belt, when the return to very limited means in a formerly prosperous population is the result not of high living and spending, but of high taxes, high dollars, and radically reduced income from the sale of basic products.

Take, if you please, what seems to me to have been a typical case of the tenant farmer, one Johannes Schmidt, a client of mine. Johannes was descended from farming stock in Germany, came to this country as a boy, became a citizen, went over seas in the 88th Division, and on his return married the daughter of a retired farmer. He rented one hundred and twenty acres from his father-in-law and one hundred and sixty acres from the town banker. His live stock and equipment, purchased in the early twenties, were well bought, for his judgment was good, and the next eight years marked a gradual increase in his live stock and reductions in his bank indebtedness. During these years two youngsters came to the young couple and all seemed rosy.

In the year 1931 a drought in this part of the Corn Belt practically eliminated his crops, while what little he did raise was insufficient to pay his rent, and he went into 1932 with increased indebtedness for feed, back taxes, and back rent. While the crops in 1932 were wonderful and justified the statement that the Middle West is the market basket of the world, prices were so low as not to pay the cost of seed and labor in production without regard to taxes and rent.

Times were hard and the reverberations of October, 1929, had definitely reached the Corn Belt. The county-seat bank which held Johannes' paper was in hard shape. Much of its reserve had been invested in bonds recommended by Eastern bankers upon which default of interest and principal had occurred. When the bottom dropped out of the bond market the banking departments and examiners insisted upon immediate collection of slow farm loans, as liquidity was the watchword of bank examiners in the years 1929 to 1932. When Johannes sought to renew his bank loan, payment or else security on all his personal property was demanded without regard to the needs of wife and family. Prices of farm products had fallen to almost nothing, oats were ten cents a bushel, corn twelve cents per bushel, while hogs, the chief cash crop in the Corn Belt, were selling at less than two and one half cents a pound. In the fall of 1932 a wagon load of oats would not pay for a pair of shoes; a truck load of hogs, which in other days would have paid all a tenant's cash rent, did not then pay the interest on a thousand dollars.

This man Schmidt had struggled and contrived as long as possible under the prodding of landlord and banker, and as a last resort came to see me about bankruptcy. We talked it over and with regret reached the conclusion it was the only road for him to take. He did not have even enough cash on hand to pay the thirty-dollars filing fee which I had to send to the Federal Court but finally borrowed it from his brother-in-law. The time of hearing came, and he and his wife and children sat before the Referee in Bankruptcy, while the banker and the landlord struggled over priorities of liens and rights to crops and cattle. When the day was over this family went out from the office the owner of an old team of horses, a wagon, a couple of cows and five hogs, together with their few sticks of furniture and no place to go.

George Warner, aged seventy-four, who had for years operated one hundred and sixty acres in the northeast corner of the county and in the early boom days had purchased an additional quarter section, is typical of hundreds in the Corn Belt. He had retired and with his wife was living comfortably in his square white house in town a few blocks from my home. Sober, industrious, pillars of the church and active in good works, he and his wife may well be considered typical retired farmers. Their three boys wanted to get started in business after they were graduated from high school, and George, to finance their endeavors, put a mortgage, reasonable in amount, on his two places. Last fall a son out of a job brought his family and came home to live with the old people. The tenants on the farms could not pay their rent, and George could not pay his interest and taxes. George's land was sold at tax sale and a foreclosure action was brought against the farms by the insurance company which held the mortgage. I did the best I could for him in the settlement, but to escape a deficiency judgment he surrendered the places beginning on March 1st of this year, and a few days ago I saw a mortgage recorded on his home in town. As he told me of it, the next day, tears came to his eyes and his lips trembled, and he and I both thought of the years he had spent in building up that estate and making those acres bear fruit abundantly. Like another Job, he murmured "The Lord gave and the Lord hath taken away"; but I wondered if it was proper to place the responsibility for the breakdown of a faulty human economic system on the shoulders of the Lord.

When my friend George passes over Jordan and I have to turn over to his wife the little that is left in accordance with the terms of his will drawn in more prosperous days, I presume I shall send his widow a receipted bill for services rendered during many years, and gaze again on the wreckage of a ruined estate.

I have represented bankrupt farmers and holders of claims for rent, notes, and mortgages against such farmers in dozens of bankruptcy hearings and court actions, and the most discouraging, disheartening experiences of my legal life have occurred when men of middle age, with families, go out of the bankruptcy court with furniture, team of horses and a wagon, and a little stock as all that is left from twenty-five years of work, to try once more—not to build up an estate—for that is usually impossible—but to provide clothing and food and shelter for the wife and children. And the powers that be seem to demand that these not only accept this situation but shall like it.

C. POVERTY AND PLENTY: AGRICULTURE*
Oscar Ameringer

During the last three months I have visited, as I have said, some 20 States of this wonderfully rich and beautiful country. Here are some of the things I heard and saw: In the State of Washington I was told that the forest fires raging in that region all summer and fall were caused by unemployed timber workers and bankrupt farmers in an endeavor to earn a few honest dollars as fire fighters. The last thing I saw on the night I left Seattle was numbers of women searching for scraps of food in the refuse piles of the principal market of that city. A number of Montana citizens told me of thousands of bushels of wheat left in the fields uncut on account of its low price that hardly paid for the harvesting. In Oregon I saw thousands of bushels of apples rotting in the orchards. Only absolute flawless apples were still salable, at from 40 to 50 cents a box containing 200 apples. At the same time, there are millions of children who, on account of the poverty of their parents, will not eat one apple this winter.

While I was in Oregon the Portland Oregonian bemoaned the fact that thousands of ewes were killed by the sheep raisers because they did not bring enough in the market to pay the freight on them. And while Oregon sheep raisers fed mutton to the buzzards, I saw men picking for meat scraps in the garbage cans in the cities of New York and Chicago. I talked to one man in a restaurant in Chicago. He told me of his experience in raising sheep. He said that he had killed 3,000 sheep this fall and thrown them down the canyon, because it cost $1.10 to ship a sheep, and then he would get less than a dollar for it. He said that he could

* Oscar Ameringer in Unemployment in the United States, Hearings before a Subcommittee of the Committee on Labor, House of Representatives, 72nd Cong., 1 sess., on H.R. 206, H.R. 6011, H.R. 8088 (Washington: Government Printing Office, 1932), pp. 98–99. Reproduced in Shannon, pp. 26–28.

not afford to feed the sheep, and he would not let them starve, so he just cut their throats and threw them down the canyon.

The roads of the West and Southwest teem with hungry hitchhikers. The camp fires of the homeless are seen along every railroad·track. I saw men, women, and children walking over the hard roads. Most of them were tenant farmers who had lost their all in the late slump in wheat and cotton. Between Clarksville and Russellville, Ark., I picked up a family. The woman was hugging a dead chicken under a ragged coat. When I asked her where she had procured the fowl, first she told me she had found it dead in the road, and then added in grim humor, "They promised me a chicken in the pot, and now I got mine."

In Oklahoma, Texas, Arkansas, and Louisiana I saw untold bales of cotton rotting in the fields because the cotton pickers could not keep body and soul together on 35 cents paid for picking 100 pounds. The farmers cooperatives who loaned the money to the planters to make the crops allowed the planters $5 a bale. That means 1,500 pounds of seed cotton for the picking of it, which was in the neighborhood of 35 cents a pound. A good picker can pick about 200 pounds of cotton a day so that the 70 cents would not provide enough pork and beans to keep the picker in the fields, so that there is fine staple cotton rotting down there by the hundreds and thousands of tons.

As a result of this appalling overproduction on the one side and the staggering underconsumption on the other side, 70 per cent of the farmers of Oklahoma were unable to pay the interests on their mortgages. Last week one of the largest and oldest mortgage companies in that State went into the hands of the receiver. In that and other States we have now the interesting spectacle of farmers losing their farms by foreclosure and mortgage companies losing their recouped holdings by tax sales.

The farmers are being pauperized by the poverty of industrial populations and the industrial populations are being pauperized by the poverty of the farmers. Neither has the money to buy the product of the other, hence we have overproduction and underconsumption at the same time and in the same country.

READING 11

Once again, in the early 1960s the United States is baffled by unemployment. The numbers involved are small alongside those who were jobless in the 1930s; but our tolerance for this waste is also less today.

A certain amount of unemployment is always with us, even in the best of times. Men may differ about what this "normal" rate of unemployment is, and some will question particular aspects of our measuring techniques; nevertheless, recent years have seen an increasing concern with "long-term" "hard-core," or "structural," unemployment—even in the face of our generally sustained post-World War II prosperity. With a rapidly increasing number of young persons reaching working age, and with a dynamic technology constantly altering our employment structure, these problems will remain high on our agenda in the years ahead.

In the spring of 1963, *Newsweek* made a brief survey of the problem of contemporary unemployment and told the story through the use of six case studies. Even though it is a far cry from being the 1930s all over again, it is still an important story in a wealthy and proud nation.

Questions to Guide the Reading

In what respects are the lessons from the contemporary unemployment different from those of the unemployment of the 1930s? Are there respects in which today's joblessness poses a more difficult problem?

What are the most important factors in determining whether or not unemployment becomes an increasingly serious problem during the next ten years?

TODAY'S UNEMPLOYMENT
Newsweek

Poverty in the midst of plenty—that is the bitter, baffling anomaly of unemployment in the United States today.

Americans unquestionably earn more, spend more, and enjoy more material wealth than any other people in the history of the world, and the figures keep going up. Yet within these glittering statistics lies a bitter paradox: 4.9 million people are jobless; on a seasonally adjusted basis, 6.1 per cent of the labor force is unemployed.

At least one in every five persons in the U.S. labor force, what's more, will be unemployed at some time this year. At least another 2.6 million workers will be restricted to part-time employment because a full-time job is unavailable. At least one in every eleven workers in the nation's 30 biggest cities will continue to tramp the streets in search of a job that isn't there. And nowhere will the paradox be more pronounced than in the hard core of unemployment, where there will be at least 5 million persons jobless for fifteen weeks and quite probably more, about half of them the breadwinners in their families.

All this adds up to what President Kennedy calls "our No. 1 economic problem"—and the problem has been growing steadily worse. After the first postwar slump of 1948–49, the nation's unemployment rate fell to 2.7 per cent in the recovery that accompanied the Korean War (compared with the 3 per cent level that U.S. government economists consider "full employment"). Then came the recession of 1953–54, followed by an upturn during which joblessness never fell below 4.2 per cent. The unemployment floor has moved progressively higher in the succeeding recessions. In fact, the nation hasn't achieved what the Administration now calls the "interim goal" toward full employment—4 per cent jobless—during any single month since 1957; the nation has suffered five years of what Labor Secretary W. Willard Wirtz calls "intolerably high" unemployment. Causes of the problem:

The economy hasn't been growing nearly fast enough. The U.S. growth rate since 1957 has averaged only 3 per cent a year vs. 5 per cent for Western Europe (though, of course, Europe started with a greater potential for expansion—a lower over-all economy and war devastation to be repaired).

New workers have swelled the labor force by 21 per cent since World War II vs. a 17 per cent increase in jobs. And the work force is increasing more rapidly now. Two years ago, 2.6 million Americans reached the age of 18; two years from now, the number reaching that age will be 3.8 million.

Automation is eliminating an estimated 1.5 million jobs a year.

Through the rose-colored glasses of the affluent masses, however, the unemployed are almost invisible. "Much of the unemployment is scattered," says Wirtz, "and many who are without jobs are not in a desperate state. This is part of the problem of getting people to care about it."

Furthermore, there are many who challenge the figures—even though a panel of academic experts last year studied the government's unemployment surveys and pronounced them valid in concept and execution. The president of a big Chicago department store, for one, questions the accuracy of unemployment data; he would like to see a "qualitative analysis" to show how many of the jobless are in fact employable.

Some Americans are, indeed, fatalistic about joblessness. A successful San Francisco importer says: "Chronic unemployment has been with us in the past. It is with us now. . . . Unemployment is going to stay, and we are going to have to live with it."

Other Americans believe the unemployed are shiftless. A hard nosed business man in West Virginia says: "Cut off their relief payments and they'll have to go to work. . . . Give them a deadline, and then nothing more."

In truth, unemployment is not as bad as it once was. One need look no further for a striking comparison than the Great Depression of the '30s—when 12.8 million workers, fully 25 per cent of the labor force, were unemployed. Unable to pay rent, unable to meet their mortgage payments, millions of Americans were evicted. Whole families lived—and died—in tarpaper shacks and tin-lined caves and scavenged for food. Many, who could not beg or borrow enough to feed their hungry children, stole what they could. Many others turned their children out to fend for themselves. Before the worst was over,

From *Newsweek*, April 1, 1963, pp. 58 ff. Reprinted with kind permission of the publisher.

violence and unrest swept the land, and there was open talk of revolution.

The times, and man's humanity toward man, have changed. Thanks to unemployment compensation, supplemental unemployment benefits, aid to dependent children, relief payments, and other public and private aid programs, the unemployed today are housed, clothed, and fed far better than ever before—not comfortably, but in most cases at least adequately. It is symbolic of the new era that a man may apportion part of his relief check toward a mortgage payment on his house, rather than lose it; that under the government's new food-stamp plan, he not only gets better food, but he no longer has to stand in line, pitiful and ragged, for his monthly dole of "molly-grub"—Federal surplus-food commodities such as yellow meal, powdered milk, and peanut butter. If a man sells pencils on a Pittsburgh street corner, or panhandles on New York's Madison Avenue, or cadges drinks in a Chicago bar, chances are he has done it for years, through good times and bad. In Hollywood's unemployment office, sultry-eyed starlets and Japanese dancing girls applying for benefits, along with bewhiskered actors and shorts-clad beach bums, can make the visit for the conventionally unemployed almost pleasant.

But one thing remains unchanged: the bleak despair and the unending hopelessness of the millions of willing workers cast on the industrial slag heap. By latest government count, there are 2.2 million workers unemployed so long that they have exhausted all their unemployment compensation benefits—and the figure is growing by 40,000 a week. There are uncounted millions more who have been forced into involuntary retirement for lack of work, who have failed to qualify for unemployment compensation, or who have never worked at all. The brunt of the burden falls on those least able to bear it—the young and the old, the Negro, the man with outmoded skills or no skills at all, the man living in a depressed area, and the unskilled woman, either widowed, divorced, or deserted, who must toil to support herself and her children. Theirs is what Labor Secretary Wirtz called "the human tragedy of life without opportunity." Worse still is the gnawing fear of permanent uselessness—the fear of millions that they will still be on the no-help-wanted list when the nation's economy moves on to new record heights. From the major categories of America's unemployed, here are six case histories:

Alfred Michel, 54, of West Mifflin, Pa., is a gap-toothed, broken-nosed steelworker who hasn't worked in three years and who will probably never work again. Like a third of the long-term unemployed, he is too old. ("When jobs are tight," says Wirtz, "the day a man over 45 loses his job is the day he became 'old.' ") Despite his 37 years in the mills, Michel was furloughed when United States Steel closed its outmoded and inefficient open-hearth plant at Clairton, near Pittsburgh, and he was placed in U.S. Steel's huge "labor pool" to await reassignment. He is still waiting.

Nor is he alone in his predicament. There are currently 100,000 steelworkers drawing supplemental unemployment benefits (up to 65 per cent of base pay); there are many more, like Michel, who have long since exhausted such benefits. His sole subsistence is a relief check for $78.10 every two weeks, out of which he must pay $54 a month on the house into which he has sunk his life's savings. At the moment, he is a year behind in his payments.

Were there only Michel and his wife, he wouldn't complain. But though he has raised five children on his laborer's pay, he still has two daughters to go, one 14 years old and the other 16.

"I don't mind so much," Michel says, his voice choked with emotion, "but it's the girls. They're growing up. They want to go to dances and parties and things. They need pretty dresses and things so they don't feel ashamed, so they don't feel different from other people. But I can't give it to them. I can't give them nothing."

Does he feel bitter? "No," he says, yet he adds quietly, like a child: "But they did away with my plant. They ought to get me a new plant."

Anthony Rocha, 17, of Atlanta, Ga., is a small, slight youngster who exudes a nail-chewing nervousness; he is a high-school dropout; he has never had a real job. Of average intelligence, but two years behind his class because of illness and accidents, Rocha quit Atlanta's Fulton High School two weeks before Christmas while in the ninth grade, against his parents' wishes.

Dressed in a white shirt and tan, tight-legged trousers, lounging on a couch in his modest home, he tried to explain why. "Some people find an interest in school, but I just didn't. [So] me and a friend of mine decided we would just quit and get us a job. I didn't realize it would be so hard to find one. I've tried to get jobs at service stations, a bakery, and all the grocery stores out here, but there just aren't any jobs for a person like me."

There were other reasons, of course, for his leaving school. Anthony's step-father, who never finished high school himself, is a warehouse stockman who earns only $62.50 a week, with which he must support a family of five.

"All I wanted to know when I quit school," adds Rocha, "was that I could support myself and stop mooching on my mother and father. I realize now I definitely made a mistake."

But the wisdom came too late, as it frequently does. That's the main reason there are more than 500,000 unemployed teen-agers in the U.S. today, more than 10 per cent of the unemployed. These figures are even more chilling in view of Labor Department predictions that of the 26 million youngsters who will enter the work force during the 1960s, 7.5 million will be high-school dropouts, ill-equipped for space-age work. "What can a kid do about unemployment," asks Wirtz, "pick up his phone and call his congressman?"

Buster Taylor is 57, he has a minimal education ("I can print pretty fair"), and he has little to offer an employer but a strong and willing back. But his worst handicap is the fact that he is a Negro in Chicago, a city where Negroes account for 13 per cent of the work force but make up a full 40 per cent of the unemployed.

According to the National Association for the Advancement of Colored People, the same is roughly true in Detroit, Philadelphia, and St. Louis, and to a lesser degree in Los Angeles and New York. While these estimates are impossible to check, the Labor Department last week placed the nationwide unemployment rate among Negroes at 13.3 per cent, more than twice the national average. "For the white, it's a mild recession," asserts Herbert Hill, forceful labor secretary of the NAACP. "For the Negro, it's a full-blown depression." Hill's answer: a double-barreled attack on discrimination in company hiring policies and in trade-union hiring-hall policies and apprentice-training programs. But for a fellow like David Blackshear, a 34-year-old New York textile examiner, jobless since September, Hill's attack is meaningless. "I don't think it's prejudice," says Blackshear. "The garment industry is just stagnant."

Nor is Hill's solution enough to Buster Taylor. Taylor and his wife, Laura, came out of rural Mississippi in the early '40s. Lucky at first, Taylor found a steady job in a meat-packing plant, then served his time in the service, and returned to civilian life as the operator of a fork-lift truck for the same firm. Like some 30,000 other packinghouse workers, he was automated out of his job. Although he quickly found employment in a nearby produce market, driving a truck and hauling 100-pound sacks of potatoes, his workweek eventually dwindled from five to four days, then three, then—two months ago—nothing. And because he worked on a day-to-day basis on his last job, Taylor is ineligible for unemployment compensation.

How have he and his wife survived? On Mrs. Taylor's $24-a-week unemployment compensation, a "windfall" from her brief period of employment as a sorter last year with a Chicago feather wholesaler, plus an occasional visit to the market where Taylor used to work. "They give me some of the potatoes or lettuce they can't use," Taylor explains, "and that keeps us from starving. But you can't get meat like that. And it doesn't put any oil in the burner."

Antonio Moreno of Visalia, Calif., has worked at his trade since he was 15 years old. Now he is 61, the father of eleven children, and he has only one remaining ambition in life: "I want a full-time job and to be paid a just wage for my labor." But because he is a migrant farm worker, Antonio Moreno hasn't a chance of achieving that ambition. Indeed, he is lucky to work at all.

Things have changed little for the migrant farm worker since John Steinbeck chronicled their frightful estate in "The Grapes of Wrath." He may benefit from workmen's compensation, limited disability insurance, and improved housing. But to most migrant farm workers, these mean little. The reason is simply that there never has been sufficient work to provide a decent year-round living. And with automation edging its way into the fruitful lands of the southern San Joaquin Valley, the work for the Antonio Morenos becomes less and less.

In lush Tulare County, for example, there were 25,000 seasonal jobs for 25,000 farm workers four years ago; last year there were only 17,000 jobs. The other 8,000 had been replaced by gigantic, ponderous mechanical cotton pickers, 15 feet tall, 8 feet wide, and 10 feet long, each capable of picking more cotton a day than 30 to 50 men, depending on the terrain. With similar automatic equipment cutting a wide swath through the South and Southwest, one in every five migrant farm workers is, in effect, permanently unemployed.

Moreno, slight and stooped, his face the color of tanned leather, recalls that he was once assured at least four to five months' work in the cotton fields. "Now, maybe, I get one month," he adds. "And then I can only pick where the machines can't go, in the mud, in the weeds, where the crop is poor."

Still, Moreno is one of the lucky ones. He has a four-room house that he built with makeshift skills and makeshift materials on a lot that he bought for $200. And with pooled earnings of about $2,000 a year, he has managed to keep his whole family together.

To keep his family together over the next two years, however, will take a minor miracle. Moreno had to borrow $346 from the Visalia finance company to meet emergency medical payments and other pressing money needs. Since he already owed $477, he was forced to mortgage his house, its furnishings, and his lot for a total of $1,032, including $207 in carrying charges. Net result: he must pay $43 a month for the next 24 months, a fantastic amount for a migrant farm worker.

Mrs. Florence Almeida, 40, of New Bedford, Mass., is petite, blond, and pretty. If she would smile, she would be very pretty, but she finds little to smile about these days. She is a widow with three children and she hasn't got a job.

By some standards, Mrs. Almeida is well provided for; she receives $111 a month in aid to dependent children and $75 a month as the widow of a veteran. But with $48 monthly to pay on her 1959 Plymouth and the expense of a growing family, she has to work to live, and since Christmas, the living has been anything but easy.

A $1.75-an-hour presser in a garment factory, she was furloughed "temporarily" just before the holiday; called back early this month, she was furloughed permanently after a week's work.

At times, Mrs. Almeida seems resigned to it. "I'm not a worrier by nature and I accept things," she states matter-of-factly. "I think about leaving New Bedford, but the living here is so nice and I'm settled." In the next breath, however, she adds: "But if I didn't have security at home, I don't know where I'd look for it. I don't know where I'd find work."

Thomas Pastellak of Scranton, Pa., is a handsome, black-haired, 26-year-old with the cut of an Ivy Leaguer. He quit school after the ninth grade to help support his mother (his father had vanished); nonetheless, he is an articulate, well-read person. One of the first to sign up for an electronics course under the Manpower Develop-

ment and Training Act (MDTA), he graduated near the head of his class. That was Dec. 4, and he still hasn't found a job.

Pastellak lives in a depressed area.

Theoretically, MDTA courses are designed to train men for existing job opportunities within the communities in which the classes are conducted. Unfortunately, in their effort to rush an electronics program into being, Scranton school officials misgauged the market. Of the first eleven electronics graduates, only two have found employment utilizing their new-found skills. Dr. Richard F. McNichols, superintendent of Scranton schools, now admits that in Scranton, a depressed area for a decade, "the job potential just isn't there." And wherever else Pastellak has gone in search of a job—in other Pennsylvania cities, in New Jersey, and in New York—the jobs available in electronics have been either committed to local residents or demand a knowledge and training far beyond any MDTA program.

To Pastellak the problem is deeply personal and intimate. He wants to marry. "I met a girl here in Scranton three years ago," he says. "When I was a seaman on the Great Lakes, I realized then that it was no life for a married man. I gave her a ring in 1961 and came home to stay. I haven't had a steady job since. We were supposed to have been married last year, but how can you get married without a job?"

By government definition, a depressed area like Scranton is one of "substantial and persistent unemployment." By statistical analysis, it is one where unemployment is at least 6 per cent and has been 50 per cent higher than the national average for three of the four preceding years, or 75 per cent higher for two of three years, or twice the average for one of the two preceding years. In hard fact, a depressed area is one largely impervious to the benefits of even a booming economy; it is a running trough of poverty in the sea of plenty. And though the major depressed areas are in the highly industrialized Northeast, the problem is far from isolated. In March, 1963, there were no fewer than eighteen "major" depressed areas, 103 "smaller" areas, and 454 "very small" areas—a blight that stretches from Alabama to Washington, from New York to California.

A depressed area, what's more, gets caught in a vicious circle. As unemployment rises, savings dip, retail sales fall, new industry tends to shy away, and there are still fewer jobs. The inevitable result is a grim, gray hopelessness for people like Pastellak—people that America's $500 billion-plus economy may have left behind.

Foremost sufferer of this economic disaster is unquestionably the nation's "coal-bin" — the anthracite-bituminous mining region that starts near Scranton in the Appalachians of Pennsylvania, generally follows the mountain range down through West Virginia and eastern Kentucky, and picks up again in the Central States mining region of southern Illinois. The culprit is "mechanization." In 1950, it took 415,582 miners to extract 516 million tons of coal from the earth; in 1962, working with giant bits, automatic coal-loaders, and automatic tipples, a mere 136,500 miners extracted 243 million tons of coal. After a recent visit to the area around Welch, Davy, and Gary, W. Va., Labor Secretary Wirtz commented: "If you could take every American through [such depressed communities as these] just for five minutes, we wouldn't have to worry about fiscal or economic policies, because it would arouse a feeling, a realization, that something has to be done and done fast." A longtime resident of the job-blighted West Virginia area recently added a touching postscript. She said: "Why like I told a friend of mine, we feel just like we are all alone on a lonely island here."

For the young, the resolute, and the strong, there is only one solution: migration. From the coal fields of eastern Kentucky, some 500,000 persons have moved in the past 10 years. The same pattern holds true in the dying Mesabi Iron Range of Minnesota, where nearly one in every five workers is unemployed and young people are very scarce. And in the Deep South, save for Florida (which led the nation in growth), emigration during the 1950–60 period drained millions of people from the land, most of them Negroes heading for the industrialized North. Of those left behind, many can be found in clusters any morning of the week along the main thoroughfare of Atlanta and virtually any city in the South, waiting and hoping that someone will hire them for a day's work.

Fearful of a 7 per cent unemployment rate by 1967 if present trends persist, the Administration feels it can no longer wait. President Kennedy made that clear in his Manpower Report to Congress early in April, 1963. "Greater employment opportunities, and a work force ever more capable of making use of such opportunities—these are among the foremost domestic needs of the nation. We must meet them. Ours

is a rich nation, but not inexhaustibly so." The President's formula:

Tax reductions and reforms designed to "generate larger markets, additional investment, and more job opportunities."

A Youth Employment Act for "stimulating and tapping the potential of unemployed youngsters."

Expansion of educational opportunities for all citizens.

Strengthening of the unemployment insurance system.

Extended minimum-wage protection for workers not now covered.

But these are, for the most part, long-range remedies, some of which may never clear Congress—certainly not without major revisions and changes. For the moment then, the main hope of the long-term unemployed, the depressed areas, and the dormant regions of the land, lies in the government's $900 million public-works program and $435 million retraining program, administered through the Area Redevelopment Act of 1960 and the Manpower Development and Training Act of last year.

One day early this month, to dramatize the government's helping hand, Mrs. Lyndon B. Johnson turned over a ladylike spadeful of mud at ground-breaking ceremonies for a new $69,000 library in St. Albans, W. Va. The construction eventually will benefit hundreds of townspeople. And $15 million worth of other make-work projects are under way in West Virginia.

Public works are at best a partial solution to unemployment, and to some communities may be no help at all. The mayor of Welch, W. Va., is not enthusiastic about a proposed multimillion-dollar Federal-State-local sewer project. He wonders whether Welch can afford its share of the expenses, which may run to 50 per cent, and he doubts there are enough local skilled workers for the job; thus most of the money might go to out-of-towners.

Of more hope to the onetime hopeless are the Federal programs to train the unemployed, primarily in woodworking, metalworking, hospital, stenographic and clerical skills. (Students are paid modest "salaries," approximately equal to local unemployment benefits.) In Connecticut, for example, some 90 per cent of those who have completed such training programs have been placed in well-paying jobs in their new skills. Even in West Virginia, where the job potential is probably as low as anywhere in the nation, 635 of the 1,027 people who have completed retraining courses found steady employment—a 61.8 per cent average.

The transformation in those who have been placed in new jobs is remarkable. Russell Smarr of Mingo County, W. Va., at 40 aged far beyond his years, used to earn $25.96 a day in the mines, plus overtime. Two years of unemployment, however, brought him to a machineshop course in Belle, W. Va., and he got a job as a machinist last year in a nearby FMC Corp. plant. He started at $2.08 an hour, now earns $2.43 an hour. Interviewed on the job, he smiled at a question that to him was ridiculous and wiped a greasy hand across his cheek. "I'm not making what I made in the mines," he said, "but I'd never go back. I've got a trade now—and I think this training business is one of the best things that's ever happened around here."

Joe Schley, 24, of Milwaukee, his wife eight months pregnant, earns $80 a week as a welder. The Army veteran says "We were really worried about having enough money for the baby, but everything is going to be all right."

Equally important, morale perks up even before a student graduates into a job. The appreciation of wiry, blue-eyed Pat Parsons, 37, unemployed and for all practical purposes unemployable before he enrolled in a Birmingham, Ala., class for welders last fall, typifies the spirit. Parsons and his wife will have to scrimp a full year while he completes the course; and yet he says: "It's hard as hell, but I don't have any regrets. I'm thankful for the opportunity to learn a trade, and I know I'm going to make it when I get out."

Many, if not most, of the nation's leading businessmen—men like Henry Ford II of the Ford Motor Co., Roger Blough of U.S. Steel, and Ralph J. Cordiner of General Electric—are convinced that the educational process, in the classroom or on the job, is the only logical way to solve the problem of workers displaced by automation and other forms of technological progress. Only through the acquisition of the needed skills for the future, they maintain, can workmen hope to find fulfillment in the operation or maintenance of automatic machines and computers that can turn out a finished engine block every 45 seconds; that can roll a 19-ton bar of steel into a sheet of steel one-tenth of an inch thick with no human help at all; that can store millions of bits of information and deliver in an hour a design for a new plant that a platoon of architects couldn't match in a year.

Most businessmen agree with Ford, Blough, and Cordiner that, whatever the short-run pains of automation, the nation will benefit in the long run.

Organized labor also recognizes that automation is inevitable and may be ultimately beneficial, and that it may even lead to new and better jobs by introducing products and services that do not now exist. But can anyone, in labor, management, or government, say with any degree of certainty that there will be enough jobs for all?

READING 12

Given the fact that each of the relatively mild post-World War II recessions has left an increased amount of unemployment in its wake, Robert Nathan, a leading consulting economist of Washington, D.C., argues that the nation needs newer and bolder economic policies than those which have been employed to date.

This article is illustrative of one approach to unemployment, an approach characterized as "liberal" on the political spectrum and involving a bigger role for governmental and private planning than we have heretofore known.

Questions to Guide the Reading

How adequately do the proposals here take into account the costs as well as the gains of any course of action? Would implementation of the proposals threaten our ability to achieve economic goals other than full employment?

If, as Nathan suggests, apathy and resignation characterize many of our public approaches to unemployment, why is this?

THE ROAD TO FULL EMPLOYMENT
Robert R. Nathan

Continued pursuit of the economic policies of the past several years offers little prospect that the United States is on the threshold of achieving, let alone maintaining, relatively full employment. There is still an absence of the policies and the implementation needed to bring about more vigorous growth, lower levels of unemployment, and assurance that the postwar pattern of recessions will not persist.

The postwar record

The performance of the American economy since the end of World War II has been generally superior to our earlier record, particularly with respect to major business cycle fluctuations. The four postwar recessions have been of short duration and moderate severity compared to past experience. The built-in stabilizing influence of unemployment compensation, of the social security system, of the enlarged level of public expenditures, and of the responsiveness of our tax structure has played a more important role in moderating cyclical fluctuations than have discretionary fiscal policies. We have done better because of policies adopted before, during, and immediately after World War II than because of what we have done in the past dozen years or so.

There can be no absolute guarantee against a serious business contraction, but there is good reason to anticipate that major depressions will never again bring the degrees of wasted resources and human hardships which the nation experienced again and again in the past. Clearly, however, we have not done nearly well enough, and there are no firm indications that we are on the verge of full employment. Vigorous expansion is less likely than continued stagnation or even a decline.

Perhaps it is the improved postwar performance itself which is the major political obstacle and which makes so elusive those economic policies needed for achieving growth and full employment. The fact that there has not been a major depression since the end of World War II and that there has not been widespread suffering largely explains why there has not been strong public pressure upon the executive and legislative branches of the federal government for better performance. However, absence of a popular demand for constructive policies is no reason for our leaders to be complacent.

In the context of the environment in which we live, our postwar record is far from satisfactory. The ideological competition which prevails throughout the world today surely demands nothing less than the best possible functioning of our free enterprise system. Recurring recessions, idle manpower and other wasted resources, and a low rate of growth will hardly induce the uncommitted and new nations to imitate our free enterprise system. Even more important, the tremendous unsatisfied needs of our own people and huge security and foreign economic aid requirements all are reasons for a relentless effort to use our resources more fully and efficiently.

Why haven't we done better? Partly, it is fear of inflation; partly, it is fear of balance of payments difficulties; partly, it is fear of a rising national debt; and probably, most importantly, it is apathy and resignation.

There are still many policy makers and economists who have serious doubts whether full employment can be attained and maintained without inflation and without further weakening our foreign exchange position. There are others who believe that accelerated technological changes, the shifting composition of production patterns, and the existence of numerous distressed areas in our economy are factors so disruptive and so complex as to make high levels of employment impossible without severe inflation and increased government regulation and regimentation. Fortunately, there are others who are convinced that relatively fuller employment can be achieved without the damaging consequences of inflation, weakening of the dollar, and more government control; they are against fighting inflation and gold outflow with economic contraction and unemployment. The fears of inflation and payment imbalances and regimentation stem, in considerable degree, from failures in leadership and in economic statesmanship.

Specific policies have neither been proposed nor enacted which are adequate to deal with our persistent unemployment and lagging growth.

From Robert R. Nathan, "The Road to Full Employment," *Industrial Relations*, Vol. 2, No. 1, October, 1962, pp. 29–38. Reprinted with kind permission of the author and publisher.

Dangers in deflationary policies

Certainly, we must seek to prevent inflation. We must strive to bring our international payments into better balance with receipts and to halt the outflow of gold. On these objectives there can be no serious disagreement. The real issue is whether we fight inflation and the adverse balance of payments situation by deflationary and contractionist measures or whether we pursue specific policies or controls to prevent inflation and to strengthen our balance of payments posture, while at the same time striving for greater growth and fuller employment. Unless we take a strong and unequivocal position that the answer to inflation and to adverse balance of payments developments does not lie in a contractionist policy, we will not enjoy sustained high levels of employment and a high rate of economic growth. If we pursue price stability and a stronger dollar through the drying-out process, we are likely to have far more idle resources and the dollar may become weaker rather than stronger.

When inflation is attributable to excess aggregate demand, it is appropriate and necessary to pursue tight monetary and fiscal policies. But if inflation is due to other factors, such as administered prices or sudden shifts in demand or upward cost pressures, we should seek to correct these developments by specific measures. There is little point in flooding a city in order to extinguish one or even a few fires that have broken out. Of course, it is not simple to identify the causes of price increases or to evolve effective remedies. But that does not justify taking the seemingly easy, but terribly costly, path of contracting the level of economic activity. A stagnant economy and growing unemployment could well lead to a greater loss of economic freedom over time than might be entailed in fighting the identifiable forces of inflation by selective policies and devices, such as specific credit controls, wage and price guidelines, more flexible taxation instruments, more vigorous antimonopoly measures, and the like.

Similarly, we must not seek the solution to our balance of payments difficulties by trying to lower prices through more unemployment and more idle productive capacity. Our highly favorable trade balance does not suggest that we have priced ourselves out of world markets and that we need deflation at home to preserve the soundness of the dollar abroad. Rather, the payments deficit is attributable to defense, aid, and foreign investment. It would be fine if our trade balance could be increased to support these outflows, but the price is far too great if we pursue the deflationary route.

We have greatly reduced the impact of foreign aid on the gold reserve by severely curtailing offshore procurement of goods and services furnished through aid programs. This was distasteful to many of us, but it is better to deny offshore procurement than to eliminate foreign aid or to deflate our economy. We are taking steps to cut drastically the impact of defense spending abroad on our balance of payments, and this is much better than purposefully creating unemployment at home. We should remove incentives to investing abroad in developed countries that have accumulated foreign exchange and gold reserves. It may even be necessary to place restrictions on foreign investments by Americans. This is not a desirable measure, but it is better than deflating and contracting the economy of the United States.

The deficiency of aggregate demand

An analysis of economic trends and relationships over the past decade leads to the conclusion that aggregate demand has tended to be persistently and probably increasingly inadequate. Even during the investment boom of 1955 and 1956 we did not experience reasonably full employment. That investment spurt was not sustained because there was inadequate aggregate demand to utilize the new capacity. There has been idle capacity in many industries ever since 1957. It seems clear that steps must be taken to increase aggregate demand if we are to achieve a higher rate of growth, full employment, and high levels of investment expenditures.

The problem is clearly not one of inadequate savings or of an unfavorable environment for investment. The most favorable environment for investment is an expanding market which creates the need for more productive capacity. The lack of adequate aggregate demand has been the principal dampening influence on investment. Recent economic policies have tended to aggravate this problem of inadequate total demand.

Our over-all tax system has become relatively less progressive since the end of World War II. Many changes have contributed to this tendency, but the most important have been the increase in state and local taxes relative to federal taxes and the change in depreciation provisions in 1954.

States and localities depend primarily on sales and property taxes. These revenues fall relatively more heavily on the middle and low income groups than on the higher income recipients. Federal revenues are derived largely from corporate and personal income taxes. The federal income tax falls relatively more heavily on higher income groups. This shift in tax incidence has certainly tended to dampen the increase in consumption expenditures that is needed to assure adequate markets for an expanding economy.

Of major significance was the change in federal tax provisions for depreciation in 1954. The new law permitted accelerated amortization through liberalized methods of computing depreciation. This change served as a significant stimulus to industrial and building investment. It was no doubt an important factor in the very marked rise in plant and equipment and other construction expenditures in 1955 and 1956. Simultaneously, it contributed to a sharp rise in gross savings of corporations. The increase in plant and equipment expenditures, largely attributable to the more liberal depreciation allowances, resulted in a pronounced rise in capacity. But the boom in investment did not persist, because we did not act to bring about the increase in demand which would make relatively fuller use of this capacity.

The Administration has proposed the investment credit as a stimulus. This could bring a sharp rise in plant and equipment expenditures, but expectations of tax reform could modify the impact. The real question is whether the resulting higher rate of investment will persist. This in turn depends on whether our policies will be geared to create the demand needed to keep our expanding capacity at work and induce more investment.

Further changes in depreciation regulations have been announced by the Administration, and these should also serve to stimulate investment. But again it is important to recognize that such measures may make for greater instability. There is a serious question whether the higher level of investment induced by such devices will continue unless steps are taken to assure higher levels of consumption and of public investment.

Wage-price and tax policies

Another area of government policy which may pose serious economic consequences is the wage-price field. The Administration is seeking to influence wage negotiations and price determinations in an effort to halt further inflation. The end objective of price stability is commendable. Wage increases which are persistently larger than increases in productivity can contribute to higher costs and rising prices. On the other hand, restraint on wage increases can bring about a shift in income distribution away from labor income to profits, putting a dampening effect on consumer expenditures. This would certainly make more difficult the achievement and maintenance of full employment. It is desirable and essential to fight inflation selectively rather than by general deflation, but the pursuit of price stability through wage restraint must be undertaken with care and discrimination if the result of economic stagnation is to be avoided.

Profitability of business is an inherent and essential ingredient of the effective functioning of our free enterprise system. Adequate incentives are essential for investment and expansion. Yet, we must not lose sight of the fact that lowering of corporate tax rates is an important incentive only when business is profitable. Lower corporate tax rates on a lower level of profits can yield lower after-tax earnings and be less stimulating to investment than higher corporate tax rates on a much higher level of corporate profits. Tax rates are important, but the prospect of a vigorous and growing market is the major stimulant to investment.

No economic policies are ever all white or all black and this has been true of all administrations in Washington. However, it does appear that the Kennedy Administration is relying as much if not more on business incentives relative to fiscal policy than was the Eisenhower Administration. The Kennedy Administration appears to be moving through tax and wage-price policies more and more along the business incentive route than toward assuring the needed expansion of aggregate demand.

Most business economists are strong advocates of the incentive route. They are confident that with more attractive incentives, business will invest more money and this will bring a sufficient rise in aggregate demand to support further increases in investment on a sustained basis. They believe that more public investment is not required and that special efforts to increase consumption expenditures are not needed. Our history of booms and busts when corporate and personal income tax rates were very low hardly supports this confidence. Investment outlays in plant and equipment and in inventories have always been the most volatile elements in the expenditure area.

If the stimulus to investment through the incentive route does not bring sustained full employment, then the government will have to engage in more public investment and deficit-financing to assure an adequate level of total demand. Unfortunately, many who follow this line of thought are unwilling to urge more government investment or government deficits even when clearly needed, because of the political environment.

Policies for full employment

We should seek to contribute to economic growth and stability through a variety of policies and not to rely exclusively on public investment or deficit financing. We should favor progressive taxation to stimulate consumption expenditures, although we must recognize the need to keep tax rates within the range which will not destroy incentives to work and invest. We should be concerned about the income distribution effects of taxation and other policies from the points of view both of incentives and of aggregate demand. To the degree that such measures do not bring full employment, we should pursue over-all fiscal policies to maintain aggregate demand at the level necessary for full employment.

There are tremendous unsatisfied needs for public investment and public services in the areas of health, education, urban redevelopment, mass transit, flood control, water supply, highways, and the like. There are huge deficiencies in private consumption, especially among the tens of millions of families and individuals in the low income categories who are not sharing in our affluence. There is a great need to modernize our industries. There are distressed areas all over the country that need rehabilitation. The potential certainly exists for markedly expanding aggregate demand for decades and generations ahead. Government policies must be designed to activate that demand, consistent with the fuller use of our manpower and other resources.

There is a strong likelihood that greater growth and less frequent and milder recessions will be achieved only through a substantial increase in the public debt. Whether this will be politically feasible depends on how important full employment and growth are to the American people. When unemployment varies between 5 and 7 per cent, the number of individuals who suffer severe hardship is rather limited. The proportion of families which suffer from total unemployment is even smaller. Those who are unemployed are probably the least articulate of our citizens. Certainly, they are the least organized. The persistence of the low income problem is a reflection of the fact that these less fortunate persons, who have been largely by-passed by our prosperity, cannot forcefully make themselves heard.

Unless the President and his top officials and congressional leaders provide the needed leadership, public demand will not be likely to bring about the kinds of policies that are needed for full employment and faster growth. Public frustration might lead to changes in the political content of the Congress and ultimately in the party in control of the White House, but without executive leadership the prospects will not be favorable for the needed policies and legislation to improve our economic performance.

The Administration must recognize the need for an expansionist fiscal policy or forego the full employment goal. It should implement such a policy through a variety of techniques. Certainly, a substantial tax cut with heavy concentration on the lower and middle income groups would be highly stimulating. Perhaps the setting up of various public authorities to engage in investment in self-liquidating public projects could be done in a manner which would keep these investment outlays outside the normal government budget and the borrowing outside the federal debt figures. Another technique might be the development of more government guarantee and credit insurance programs, which would stimulate private investment in essential projects without a corresponding rise in the national debt.

In terms of resource use, it would be preferable to fulfill more of the pressing needs for public investment and public services than to reduce taxes. These needs should take priority over a rising level of luxury consumption. Certainly they should be satisfied rather than allowing idle resources to accumulate wastefully. The challenge in the effort to achieve more needed public investment is to establish financial arrangements which will avoid a rising national debt, and thus prevent the nervous breakdowns which a rising debt would bring to the more conservative elements in the country.

The prospects of getting an expansionist fiscal policy through a sizable tax reduction are no doubt more favorable than through a substantial and prompt increase in public investment. Tax cuts can take hold more quickly. For cyclical purposes, temporary increases or reductions in the lowest tax bracket rates can contribute greatly to stability. But for growth and full employment, spontaneous response is not the most urgent factor. What is needed is public investment rather than tax cuts.

If a reduction in federal taxes is to be made, consideration should be given to transferring the benefits to state and local governments through some such device as a credit against federal income tax liability for state income tax payments. Such a move would improve the capacity of state and local governments to supply essential local facilities and services. Certainly, however, if political circumstances dictate that the only feasible approach to an expansionist fiscal policy is through a general tax cut, then let us have one promptly and sizably so that full employment can be achieved and the rate of growth accelerated and a recession avoided.

We need to strengthen our unemployment insurance system so that coverage is extended, and especially so that benefits bear a more reasonable relationship to prevailing wage rates. We need to raise social security benefits so that they are more in line with prevailing levels of income. These measures would help expand consumer expenditures and improve the effectiveness of automatic stabilizers.

We need to develop inducements which would help modernize American industry and thereby make it more competitive in world markets and more able to fulfill domestic needs. In effect, we need to formulate both patterns and levels of governmental revenues and expenditures which would give us the needed levels of total demand for full employment without inflation.

Considerable progress is being made in assisting economic development in the distressed communi-ties around the country. Full employment will make the distressed area problem more manageable, and, in turn, successful efforts to help specific areas will make the pursuit of full employment more fruitful. But even if we achieve full employment, we will continue to need training, relocation assistance, and aids for distressed communities.

The need for over-all goals and plans

Specific decisions on taxes, deficits or surpluses, social security, distressed area assistance, farm price supports, and a thousand and one other important policies must be made almost continually. What is most important is that these decisions be made in the context of over-all goals and plans. For far too long and among far too many of our otherwise responsible citzens, the word "planning" has been a nasty word. It is too often confused with governmental regimentation and even with socialism and communism. We need and can have more and better planning and still preserve the fundamental freedoms of an enterprise system. In fact, our free enterprise system can best be preserved and made healthier and, in many ways, freer if we think and plan ahead and formulate our monetary, credit, fiscal, and other policies in the framework of better-defined goals and basic economic plans. Only with better and more planning are we likely to speed our rate of growth, achieve full employment, enjoy greater stability, and demonstrate the great virtues of our free and competitive enterprise system.

READING 13

Here is still another approach to the persistent unemployment that marked the early 1960s. Herbert Stein, research director of the Committee for Economic Development, sees the problem more in terms of freedom lost through unemployment than of production lost. And he insists on asking questions about inflation at the same time that we talk of reducing the burden of unemployment.

This approach ends up with a less direct role for government than Nathan proposed in the previous reading. But it still involves government to a far greater extent than we knew in the pre-Depression years. Even the proposals to beat inflation by strengthening the forces of competition in labor markets would lead to a new sphere of law and public action. Stein argues that these new directions for governmental policy are preferable to the most widely discussed alternatives for reducing unemployment.

Questions to Guide the Reading

To what extent is Stein's emphasis on the labor market consistent or inconsistent with Nathan's emphasis, in the previous reading, on aggregate demand as the focal point for an effective full-employment policy?

Has our experience to date with moral suasion and wage-price guidelines supported Stein's analysis of the implications of such policies? Can we have the more competitive labor markets for which he pleads without seriously curbing the essential functions of unions?

REDUCING UNEMPLOYMENT—WITH OR WITHOUT INFLATION
Herbert Stein

One still encounters people who refer to the "Full Employment Act of 1946." Of course, there is no such Act. A bill with this title was considered in Congress, but it was not enacted. Instead Congress enacted the Employment Act of 1946.

The adoption of an "Employment Act" rather than a "Full Employment Act" was significant. In arriving at this decision, Congress recognized that "full employment," meaning zero unemployment, was impossible. More important, the change in the title of the Act, together with its language and the discussion surrounding its enactment, implied that there could be no absolute goal, to be achieved at all costs and by any methods. The import of the Act was that low unemployment was a valuable goal, to be pursued by all means that did not cost more than the benefits of the resulting reduction of unemployment were worth. This was all that Congress could sensibly say, and it is the policy of the United States.

We cannot, therefore, look at the fact of unemployment and conclude that we have failed to carry out our national policy. Neither can we conclude that there has been a failure because unemployment has exceeded 4 per cent. The use of 4 per cent as a standard or target implies that there are means of holding unemployment to 4 per cent that do not cost more than they are worth. This may be so. But no amount of restating 4 per cent as a goal will move such a proposition from the realm of question to the realm of fact. We can test the reasonableness of the 4 per cent goal by evaluating the policies required to achieve it, but we cannot test the policies in

terms of whether or not they achieve the 4 per cent goal.

We do not have, could not have, and would not want a "full employment" policy. What one should discuss is whether we have the policy that gives us the most employment, at least unemployment, we can have without excessive cost, relative to the benefits. This can be answered only by attempting to specify a superior alternative to the policy we have, or have had. The answer will in any case have to be subjective. The benefits of higher employment and the costs of getting it cannot be converted into quantities of a single homogeneous value—like billions of dollars of national income—that can be objectively compared with each other. The costs may come in such forms as distributional and moral consequences of inflation, weakening of union power, increasing government intervention in labor and product markets, and international psychological effects of weakened confidence in the U.S. dollar, for example. In the end we can only hope to specify a little more satisfactorily the varied costs of different policies; the choice will have to be made in the political process.

Why unemployment matters

What is it about unemployment that makes its reduction an important objective? This question is worth asking because the answer helps to define what unemployment is and also suggests the kinds of values that must be considered in balancing the costs and benefits of reducing unemployment.

From Herbert Stein, "Reducing Unemployment—With or Without Inflation," *Industrial Relations*, Vol. 2, No. 1, October, 1962, pp. 15–27. Reprinted with kind permission of the author and publisher.

Essentially we are concerned about unemployment because it reflects an impairment of a basic freedom. As the Council of Economic Advisers put it, "mature individuals should be able to choose for themselves how they spend their time, as between gainful employment, housework, leisure and education." In more cold-blooded language, we believe that freedom to dispose of property is a basic freedom, and the property most people have to dispose of is their labor. Unemployment is a condition in which people are not free to dispose of their property as they wish.

That it is the loss of freedom rather than the loss of production that concerns us is clear from our attitude to the unemployment of one million workers as compared with the absence of many million potential workers from the labor force. We do not consider it a major objective of national policy to increase the size of the labor force, even though that might add more to national output than a reduction of unemployment.

We are concerned with the loss of income of the unemployed as well as with their loss of freedom. And yet, if we think of lifetime incomes, unemployment is probably a less important cause of poverty than many others that are not regarded as such urgent problems.

The freedom to work has, of course, one major qualification. A person who wants employment at the salary of a reigning movie star is not deprived of freedom if he is unable to find it—unless he is a reigning movie star prevented from finding employment by a black list or some such device. Freedom to work is freedom of an individual to work for a wage equal to the value of his product. This is the only kind of freedom to work that could be consistently available to all. Everyone cannot work for a wage exceeding the value of his product. Freedom to work is freedom of contract, that is, the freedom of two parties to enter a mutually acceptable agreement for the employment of one by the other.

What unemployment is

If we define unemployment as inability to find work at a wage equal to the value of the worker's product, the unemployed would include some people not covered in our available statistics and exclude some people who are covered. There are some people who have jobs and are therefore not counted as unemployed, but they are unable to find work at wages equal to the value of their products. Take the following

hypothetical case: a worker in Pittsburgh wishes employment in a steel mill at $3 an hour. The steel mill could sell his product at a price that would cover the costs if it employed him at $3 an hour. However, the employer has a labor contract which requires him to pay $4 an hour, and at this wage the employer cannot afford to hire him. So the worker finds employment in a supermarket at $1.50 an hour. He is not counted as unemployed, although his freedom to work at a wage equal to the value of his product has been abridged. On the other hand, a person who seeks, and is qualified for, work in a supermarket and cannot find a job is counted as unemployed.

Now it will be said that the second situation is much more serious than the first, and this is probably correct in general. But it need not always be so. The worker who is employed in the supermarket instead of the steel mill may be a married man with three children and the one who can't find work may be a high-school boy on vacation. This does not minimize the problem of those who have no jobs. It only suggests that there is another problem. Its significance for this paper is that some policies that would help solve the problem of the jobless would not help solve the problem of those with the wrong job, while some other policies might help to solve both.

On the other hand, there are undoubtedly some people counted as unemployed who do not want to work for a wage equal to the value of their product. We do not know how many there are. When a sample of the population is surveyed to discover how many are unemployed, the jobless are not asked at what wage they are willing to work. And, even if they were, we would not be much closer to knowing whether they are willing to work for the value of their product. Probably most people seeking jobs would be willing to work for their past wages, so that excessive wage demands on the part of individuals would be found mainly among those whose productivity had significantly declined. Such declines might be due to seasonal fluctuations, changes in the geographical and occupational structure of the demand for labor, and the aging of individual workers. It is not suggested here that the cases in which jobless people are willing to work only for a wage in excess of the value of their product constitute a large fraction of the number counted as unemployed. The whole point is probably significant chiefly in thinking about measures to reduce unemployment by raising the productivity of jobless people.

Causes of unemployment

Why should a person who is willing to work for a wage equal to the value of his product be unable to find a job? The important reasons fall into four general categories.

1. The worker and the employer who would be willing to hire him may each be ignorant of the other's existence and location.

2. Bringing the worker and the job together may involve costs, of geographical movement and of training, that neither may be able to bear. To say that the worker is willing to work for a wage equal to the value of his product implies that he is willing to work for that wage net of the costs of moving and training. But the worker may have too little capital to cover these costs himself, and our financial institutions are not adapted to lending on the job prospects of unemployed workers. The prospective employer may be unwilling to bear these costs because he cannot be sure that the worker will perform effectively and stay with him.

3. Even though the worker may be able freely to set the money wage at which he will work, his real wage may be too high in terms of the willingness of employers to hire him. This implies that the relationship between wage movements and price movements is such that, whatever money wages are, real wages will be too high to permit the employment of more workers.

4. The unemployed worker may be unable freely to set the money wage at which he can be employed and may therefore be unable to specify a wage at which someone would be willing to hire him.

Little will be said here about the first two points—lack of job information and costs of movement and training. Undoubtedly these are real causes of unemployment. How important they are and whether their importance is increasing we do not know, and we could hardly know without a program to cure the causes. Experts seem to be agreed, with confirmation from foreign experience, that government programs can be devised to reduce unemployment by improving information and financing movement and retraining. Up to some point these programs would be worth their cost in the simple sense that the addition to national income would exceed the budgetary cost. At least part of the budgetary cost could be recouped through tax payments by the workers who benefit. The pro-

gram would be anti-inflationary, since it would increase the effective supply of labor where the demand is greatest. The adoption of the Manpower Development and Training Act in early 1962 was an important step in this direction. Certainly our tardiness in this field has represented a failure to carry out a high employment policy worth its cost.

In the thirties a great deal of effort was devoted to showing that the third cause of unemployment listed above could be a real cause. The essential point was that a decline of money wage rates might bring about a decline of equal proportion in money expenditures for goods and services. If this happened prices would fall as much as wage rates with no increase in output or employment. Real wage rates would not have fallen, and there would be no incentive to hire more workers.

This whole argument is of little relevance for explaining unemployment today. First, money wages do not decline with unemployment at the rates we have experienced in the postwar period. Secondly, it is extremely unlikely that a decline of money wage rates under present conditions would cause a decline of equal or larger proportions in money expenditures and prices and thus fail to increase employment. Third, and most important, whether money expenditures would actually decline if money wages declined would depend on the government's monetary and fiscal policy. There is every reason to think that government policy could and would prevent any substantial or continued decline of money expenditures if wage rates declined. The government is not able to prevent completely all fluctuations of total money expenditures, and it may have some inhibitions about raising total money expenditures at a rapid rate. But it would have neither great difficulties nor inhibitions about preventing a persistent decline of money expenditures. In fact, there have been only two year-to-year declines of total money expenditures in the postwar period, 1948 to 1949 and 1953 to 1954, and neither was as large as one per cent.

The cause of unemployment that is most relevant today and most difficult to deal with is the fourth listed above—the inability of the jobless person to set the money wage at which he will work. Even though a jobless person may be willing to work and someone may be willing to hire him at a money wage below the prevailing rate, he may be unable to offer his services below the prevailing rate. It is sometimes said—or used to be said—that if employment could be increased by a decline of money wage rates, and money wage rates do not in fact decline, the jobless are not involuntarily unemployed. But this involves a confusion about who sets and maintains the wage rates. The jobless do not insist upon wage rates at which they cannot be employed. Employers and employed workers, in formal or informal agreement, and in some sectors the government, set wage rates at which jobseekers are excluded from employment. As far as the jobless are concerned, their unemployment is involuntary.

Why are wage rates set at levels at which people seeking work cannot be employed? We used to discuss this question in terms of reasons for the failure of wage rates to decline when there is unemployment. All kinds of institutional rigidities—wage contracts, minimum wage laws, the desire of employers to maintain morale of their workers, and sheer sluggishness of adjustment—could be adduced as explanations.

Accepting as a fact of life that wage rates do not fall, an employment policy could be formulated with a simple piece of arithmetic as follows:

The number of employed workers (N) times their annual compensation per worker (W) equals the total compensation of employees.

Total compensation of employees equals a rather stable fraction (K) of total expenditures for goods and services (GNP).

Then the total number of employed workers equals a fraction (K) of GNP divided by the annual compensation per worker.

$$N = \frac{K(GNP)}{W}$$

If it is desirable to raise employment by any given percentage, this can be done without requiring wage rates to fall by raising GNP by the same percentage. For example, if the number of people wishing work rises by one per cent per annum, employment could be provided for them without any decline of wage rates by a one per cent annual increase of GNP.

However, our problem today is neither to explain why wage rates don't fall in the presence of unemployment nor to devise a policy to contend with the fact that they don't. For example, from 1957 to 1961 the labor force—the number of people at work or seeking work—increased by 5 per cent. If our problem were simply that wages don't fall, it would have been possible to employ the additional members of the labor force by a 5 per cent increase in GNP. In fact, GNP increased by 18 per cent, but employment increased by only about 2.5 per cent and unem-

ployment increased from 4.3 per cent to 6.7 per cent of the labor force. Compensation per employed worker rose by about 16 per cent.

People were kept from finding jobs because the prevailing wages at which they were permitted to be employed *rose so rapidly* that it was not worthwhile to employ them even though total demand for goods—total GNP—rose at 4.5 per cent per annum. This is the fact we must explain and with which policy must contend. To explain why wage rates rose by 4 per cent per annum despite the presence of many people willing to work without any wage increase is difficult—much more difficult than to explain why wage rates don't fall in the presence of unemployment. Probably an answer would have to be compounded out of the following elements.

1. The high expectations regarding the size of annual wage increases—a legacy of the period of low unemployment and rapid inflation after the war.

2. The general acceptance of wage increases equal to the average rise of productivity plus the cost of living as a standard—commonly interpreted as a minimum—to be met regardless of the amount of unemployment.

3. The desire of labor union leaders to deliver more, in the form of compensation per employed union member, than the workers could have expected without the union.

4. The power of strong unions to get a substantial part of their demands, which are influenced by the foregoing factors.

5. The tendency of employers, even when not facing strong unions, to give wage increases more or less matching the general expectations, either to preserve employee morale or for some other reason.

6. The competitive bidding up of wages in the occupations or areas where labor shortages appear despite the average rate of unemployment.

7. The tendency of wage rates not to fall, even in areas or occupations of exceptionally large unemployment.

Unfortunately we do not know the relative weights of these factors, and of others that may have been omitted, or the extent to which they will continue to exert their influence in the future. Yet such knowledge is important in determining what policies are available, what their costs will be, and whether they can succeed.

Several possible views of the situation are listed here.

Probably the most optimistic view is that the rate of increase in money wages in the past few years was a delayed reaction to the earlier post-war experience of labor shortages and rapid inflation. If this view is correct, the annual rate of money wage increase can be expected to decline as time passes, if we meanwhile follow a restrictive policy that prevents the resurgence of inflationary expectations. This restrictive policy might cause more unemployment for a period than would otherwise be necessary, but this would be the price paid for making higher employment possible later without inflation, or even with inflation.

Another possible view is that the recent rate of wage increase, amounting to about 4 per cent a year in average hourly compensation, is fixed by institutional factors. It will not be reduced even if an unemployment rate of 5 or 6 per cent persists and will not be increased by a reduction of the unemployment rate to, say, 4 per cent. If this is the case, we can get lower unemployment without more rapid wage increases and more rapid inflation by stimulating a greater increase in demand. A more restrictive policy would not result in less inflation but only in less employment. Under these conditions, more employment costs nothing in terms of inflation.

A third, less optimistic view, is that the rate of wage increase has been held down in the past four or five years by unemployment averaging around 6 per cent. If unemployment were 4 per cent, the rate of wage increase would be more rapid—say 6 per cent per annum—although no one knows what the figure really would be. This rate would be stable. Thus there is some rate of increase in money demand that will keep the unemployment rate stable at, say, 4 per cent, with a rate of inflation that is stable but higher than in the previous case.

A frightening view of our situation is that the rate of wage increase at, say, 4 per cent unemployment is not stable but explosive. Suppose that now, after several years of price increases averaging 1.5 per cent per annum, we were to achieve a 4 per cent unemployment rate with an average wage increase of 6 per cent per annum. This might be accompanied by price increases of 3.5 per cent per annum rather than 1.5 per cent. This would raise the rate of wage increase at high employment, which would raise the rate of price increase (inflation), and so on. If we assume that the rate of annual wage increase at high employment will equal the annual rate of increase of output per worker, plus the

rate of price increase in the past year, plus a little bit more, high employment will require an accelerating rate of inflation without limit. The ultimate conclusion of this view is that high employment is literally impossible.

These more extreme extrapolations of our present condition will not happen. We will not have either continuously accelerating inflation or continuously rising unemployment. Why not? There seem to be three possible reasons.

1. "Money illusion" may be strong and persistent. A system of wage determination that generates average wage increases of more than 2 per cent per annum at high employment when prices are stable and more than 4 per cent when prices are rising 2 per cent a year will, if this view is correct, not generate wage increases of more than, say, 12 per cent when prices are rising 10 per cent. Actually, there is no good reason to think this will be the case if inflation continues and is recognized. This is a weak reed.

2. Something, presumably the government, will intervene to change the wage-determination process. This intervention might take the form of changes in the structure of collective bargaining, government wage-price control, and moral suasion.

3. The basic condition that is being extrapolated to produce the final conclusion of infinite inflation may not exist. That is, the wage system may not generate wage increases exceeding productivity gains plus the past rate of price increase. In this case, annual wage increases of 12 per cent with annual price increases of 10 per cent would be a stable situation (assuming annual productivity gains of 2 per cent). But so also would annual wage increases of 2 per cent with annual price increases of zero be a stable situation.

Do we know a better policy?

Can one devise, out of these uncertainties and possibilities, a better policy than we have had? It has been suggested above that improvements might be made in two respects—a better supply of information about job opportunities and the financing of movement and training. The remainder of this paper concentrates on the more critical area of policies regarding the rate of growth of total money expenditures and the determination of wage rates.

The policy we have had can be characterized as consisting of two parts:

a) A combination of monetary and fiscal policies producing a rise of total money expenditures too slow to produce the maximum employment that would have been possible during the past four or five years and not so slow as to prevent price increases. This has turned out to mean an average annual increase of 4.5 per cent in money expenditures, an average annual increase of 1.5 per cent in the price level of all goods and services,[1] and an average unemployment rate of around 6 per cent.

b) Exhortation and moral suasion directed toward restraint in wage increases.

Conclusions about the possibility of doing better than this will depend in large part on attitudes towards inflation, the present international financial system, and direct government controls over wages and prices. The attitudes that underlie this paper should be exposed at this point.

It is not clear that inflation of 1, 2, or 3 per cent per annum, which is not expected to continue and which it is the policy of government to stop, has adverse effects on the level or growth of production, although there are some effects on the distribution of real income which are difficult to appraise. But it is doubtful how long such an inflation can continue without becoming expected. It seems particularly unlikely that the government could pursue a policy which produced inflation or inevitably resulted in inflation without creating the firm expectation of inflation. This would be true even if the government tried to conceal its policy, which would be immoral.

An economy in which steady inflation of *x* per cent per annum was confidently expected would largely behave like an economy in which zero inflation was expected, once it had become adjusted to the inflation. But we start with innumerable institutions and arrangements predicted on the expectation of no inflation—even after 20 years of inflation. Adjustment to the expectation of inflation would be expensive and disruptive. And in the end it would be pointless, since the economy would behave as it would without inflation.

This does not mean that we cannot have some inflation without serious costs. Obviously we have had it. But permanent inflation cannot be the policy of the government.

The argument against inflation is often buttressed these days by reference to our international financial position. It is said that if inflation continues, and even more if it increases, the continued or increased balance of payments deficit and loss of gold will put the United States in an untenable position.

This argument opens up an area of discussion too large for treatment in this paper. However, a point of view may be briefly indicated. The problem divides into two parts. First, is it probable that any policy likely to be desirable in terms of domestic considerations alone will create difficulties that cannot be managed within the confines of the existing international financial system? On this question expert opinion is divided. The second and more fundamental question is whether the international financial system could, if necessary, be reformed so that it would not require the United States or any other large segment of the free world to follow policies which would be undesirable on domestic grounds alone. The answer to this is almost certainly affirmative. Therefore, it will not be maintained here that U.S. domestic policy should be substantially and persistently constrained by balance of payments considerations, although some adaptation to these considerations does have to be made in the form and timing of policy.

Finally, the range of alternative policies available for consideration depends very much on attitudes towards direct government price and wage controls. In my opinion such controls are a serious evil, to be invoked only in an emergency —in wartime, for instance. They are an evil for the same reason that unemployment is an evil, because they restrict freedom. It is not sensible to restrict the freedom of everyone to contract for the sale of his products or labor in order to provide the jobless with the freedom to sell their labor. Rejection of direct controls in peacetime is standard doctrine in the United States. The only question relates to "soft" controls—moral suasion—and involves whether they are controls at all or would probably lead to controls.

This set of preferences does not provide the basis for a confident criticism of recent policy as inadequate. We would almost certainly have had more employment if money GNP had risen more rapidly after 1957. But we would also almost certainly have had more inflation. The question is sometimes asked how much more inflation we would have had from 1957 to 1961 if unemployment had been 4 per cent rather than 6 per cent, and whether avoiding that much inflation was worth the extra unemployment. One can only have hunches about the first part of this question.

---

[1] As measured by the price index used for deflating the Gross National Product, rather than the consumer price index.

But the second part poses the wrong issue. For, the extra unemployment of 1957–1961 may very well have prevented not only more serious inflation during that period but also subsequent inflation "forever after," and thus may have created the basis for high employment in the future.

The only goal at which we can logically and consistently aim is high employment with no inflation. To get there we had to go through a transition period in which the rate of inflation subsided. During this transition, wage-increase expectations and employers' calculations of the wage increases they could pass on were tempered by experience with unemployment and slack sales. Thus some period of excessive unemployment was probably inevitable, and it would be hard to maintain that no price in unemployment would be worth paying.

Still, the question may be raised whether we have been paying too much. In one sense we probably have. Although total money GNP rose by 4.5 per cent per annum from 1957 to 1961 and will probably have risen by 5 per cent per annum from 1957 to 1962, this increase was not steady. There were declines in 1958 and 1961. Although the declines were small, we would have had more employment with very little more inflation if these declines had been prevented or moderated. This would not have been easy, but stabilization of the government's own activities would have helped. Big swings in the size of the surplus that would have been yielded at high employment and in the rate of expansion of the money supply could have been avoided.

Aside from the question of the steadiness of the rate of growth, the 4.5 or 5 per cent per annum rise of money GNP since 1957 seems to me difficult to criticize as inadequate. But I believe it is important that the present recovery should carry through to higher levels of business activity and employment than we reached in 1960. This is simply because, after five years in which unemployment has averaged about 6 per cent, continued unemployment is more serious than it was earlier. The costs of unemployment cumulate in effects on the long-term unemployed, on investors' expectations, and on political vulnerability to ill-considered "cures." Also, we can better afford a temporary increase in the rate of inflation after five years of rather moderate inflation and dampened expectations than we could earlier. Therefore, we now need, within a general policy of long-term restraint on inflation, to allow or stimulate the economy to rise to a substantially higher level of activity and employment.

The transition to a state of high employment and zero inflation will be eased and quickened if we can moderate the forces making for excessive wage increases. This presumably is the motivation behind the efforts of the Eisenhower and Kennedy Administrations to rally voluntary support behind a set of guidelines to wage and price behavior. Yet this method, if effective at all, contains a number of defects and dangers.

1. The guidelines focus attention on the general proposition that if prices are stable, wages should rise at the rate of increase of national average output per man hour. Although numerous appropriate exceptions are always stated, the general proposition is the only one that can be translated into a precise number and the only one that is likely to have much influence. This will have an adverse effect on the adjustment of relative wage rates, an adjustment which is essential to solving problems of structural unemployment as well as the problems of workers who are unemployed in the sense that they don't have the jobs in which their production and earnings would be highest.

2. Moral suasion is a force which enlists the pressure of public opinion, and possibly other sanctions at the disposal of government, in support of a pattern of conduct prescribed by government. This form of control is not made more palatable by the fact that it operates without legal standards and without opportunity for judicial review.

3. Social responsibility and vulnerability to the force of moral suasion are not evenly distributed around the economy. The addition of this randomly distributed influence to the other factors determining wage rates will worsen the pattern of relative wage increases in different industries and occupations.

4. There is a danger of sliding from moral suasion to general statutory controls as a way of correcting the unevenness and uncertainties of the voluntary method.

The approach to the problem that is most consistent with the freedom of all workers to find the jobs in which they would have the highest earnings is to strengthen the force of competition in labor markets. This approach immediately raises the question of the power of labor unions. We don't know how important this question is from the standpoint of the long-run possibility of keeping the number of jobless people low. Less than 30 per cent of non-agricultural employees are in unions, not all of which are strong. Although the effect of strong unions may be to reduce employment opportunities in the labor markets where they operate, possibly sufficient employment opportunities may be found elsewhere. But even if this should be true, problems would remain. The effect of the strong unions would still be to keep some workers from finding the jobs which they would prefer and at which someone would be willing to hire them. It is doubtful whether we can encourage or condone in principle a situation which would obviously be intolerable if it were more widespread—a situation in which the employed workers in a labor market, represented by a single union, determine in negotiation with their employers the conditions on which any others may be employed there.

Prescription in this field is, of course, difficult, partly because unions serve valuable social, economic, and political functions for which we should be willing to pay a price. As usual we would like to have the valuable functions at a lower price. Unfortunately, the discussion has been dominated by people who either did not see the value or did not see the price, and this has not been constructive. Still there are steps that could be taken, if the problem were recognized. We should not expect to establish perfect competition in labor markets, any more than the antitrust laws have done so in product markets. We should expect that measures designed to strengthen competition will sometimes unfortunately strike down innocent and beneficial arrangements and practices. But it should be possible to alter the course of history to some degree in a desirable direction.

I do not mean to end on a note which suggests that the solution of grave problems depends upon measures that are intellectually impossible to prescribe and politically impossible to achieve. By reasonable standards of performance, we have not been doing badly in maintaining high employment. We could have done better in the recent past and can do better in the future. We have a great deal to learn, as economists and citizens, but looking at what we have done, rather than at what we have sometimes said, provides grounds for confidence about our capacity to learn.

READING 14   LIVING WITH INFLATION: THREE CASE STUDIES

Inflation, which means a general rise in the price level, may be mild or severe. The United States has not experienced what most observers would call a severe inflation for many years. Yet the widespread concern over price rises of better than 2 per cent per annum in the 1950s suggests that the fears of runaway inflation may have a powerful grip on American thought.

Certainly the stories of what much more rapid inflations have done to creditors and debtors, to different groups of income receivers, and to political and social institutions in other times and places deserve our careful attention. How do men accommodate themselves to periods of unrestrained price rises? And what is left in the wake of such periods?

Here are three case reports on severe inflations. Frank D. Graham, former professor of economics at Princeton University, describes the burdens placed upon the German society by one of the most spectacular inflations in history—the post-World War I German inflation of 1919–1923. Eugene M. Lerner, of New York University, describes the inflation in the American Confederacy during the Civil War.

Internal monetary reform and a revised plan for German reparations (the Dawes Plan, adopted in 1924) finally halted the German inflation, and military defeat finally ended the Confederacy's monetary problems, but the case of Chile offers the unusual experience of a nation struggling decade after decade with substantial price increases almost constantly eroding the purchasing power of the currency. Yet this prolonged inflation has not developed into the type of galloping hyperinflation that has wrought havoc in other countries. This puzzling experience is described by Joseph Grunwald, director of the Institute of Economic Research of the University of Chile, Santiago.

Questions to Guide the Reading

What common characteristics are there in the three inflations described?

What lessons are there for the United States today in these case studies?

A. GERMANY, 1919–1923*
Frank D. Graham

Germany, in common with other warring countries, departed from the gold standard at the outbreak of hostilities in 1914. On November 20, 1923, the German paper mark, after having fallen to an infinitesimal fraction of its former value, was made redeemable in the newly introduced rentenmark at a trillion to one. The rentenmark, after a short but honorable existence during which its gold value remained substantially stable at that of the original gold mark, was supplanted by the present [1930] standard reichsmark.

The regime of inconvertible and depreciating paper money thus ran for a little less than a decade. The progress of depreciation was, however, very unevenly distributed over these ten years. During most of the war-period the exchange value of the mark did not fall greatly from par with the dollar and if, when the issue of the conflict was no longer in doubt, it sank heavily, it was still quoted in December 1918 at more than twelve American cents. During the peace negotiations, however, German exchange continued to fall fast. This downward movement persisted till February 1920 when the descent was checked at just a shade below one cent per mark, that is, at about 1/24 of its pre-war value. A quick recovery then set in which carried the rate to nearly 3¢ in May. Though there was some reaction from this figure relative stability at a level of from 1½ to 2¢ was attained in June. By early 1920 the period of immediate adjustment to post-war conditions may therefore be considered to have been completed. Not until September 1921 did the value of the mark again fall below one American cent and as late as June 1922 it still sold for about ⅓ of a cent. From then onward the decline was vertiginous till the final collapse in November 1923. At the latter date forty-two billion (42,000,000,000) marks were worth but a single American cent.

Without a complete ouster of the currency concerned, no corresponding depreciation appears in the long and varied annals of monetary history. Never before had a paper money fallen at so rapid a rate over such an extended period.

While the payments of cash reparations in 1921 undoubtedly played an important part in promoting the decline in the currency, and while the sanctions imposed on Germany in 1923 led to the ultimate collapse, this is, of course, by no means the whole story. Reparations gravely affected public finances but the fiscal difficulties were far from being solely due to this cause. It is true that, if a more soundly conceived and executed reparations policy had been adopted by the creditor Powers, inflation of the currency might perhaps have been stayed by the vigorous measures of reform of the public finances initiated in Germany in 1920. But inflation had none the less proceeded far before any cash reparations whatever had been paid and it was accelerated after they had been entirely suspended. Its roots went back into the early war period and it was, in many German quarters, nurtured rather than repressed. The war administration had looked with a much too friendly eye on inflationary policies. The initial impetus thus given was never checked and long after the war was over the Reichsbank was entirely too pliable in its attitude toward both governmental and private borrowing.

The attitude of the Reichsbank was but one aspect of a fairly general complacency toward currency depreciation. The burden of the great internal government debt, piled up during and immediately after the war, meant exceedingly high taxes unless it should be lightened by a decline in the value of the counters in which it was expressed. Though currency depreciation meant confiscation of the property of holders of the government debt it was the line of least

* From Frank D. Graham, *Exchange, Prices and Production in Hyper-Inflation Germany, 1920–1923* (Princeton University Press, Princeton, New Jersey, 1930), pp. 1–14. Reprinted with kind permission of the publisher.

Table 1 Treasury Bills Discounted by the Reich, Issues of Paper Currency, Index of Wholesale Prices, and Index of Dollar Exchange Rates Against Paper Marks: 1919–1923 (*Value figures in millions of marks*)

End of Month	Total Amount of Treasury Bills Discounted by the Reich*	Total Issues of Paper Currency (Except Emergency Currency)†	Index of Wholesale Prices† 1913 = 1	Index of Dollar Exchange Rates in Berlin‡ 1913 = 1
1919 Dec.	86,400	50,065	8.03	11.14
1920 June	113,200	68,154	13.82	9.17
Dec.	152,800	81,387	14.40	17.48
1921 June	185,100	84,556	13.66	17.90
Dec.	247,100	122,497	34.87	43.83
1922 June	295,200	180,169	70.30	89.21
July	308,000	202,626	100.59	159.60
Aug.	331,600	252,212	192.00	410.91
Sept.	451,100	331,876	287.00	393.04
Oct.	603,800	484,685	566.00	1,071.94
Nov.	839,100	769,500	1,154.00	1,822.30
Dec.	1,495,200	1,295,228	1,475.00	1,750.83
1923 Jan.	2,081,800	1,999,600	3,286.00	11,672.00
Feb.	3,588,000	3,536,300	5,257.00	5,407.00
Mar.	6,601,300	5,542,900	4,827.00	4,996.00
April	8,442,300	6,581,200	5,738.00	7,099.00
May	10,275,000	8,609,700	9,034.00	16,556.00
June	22,019,800	17,340,500	24,618.00	36,803.00
July	57,848,900	43,813,500	183,510.00	262,030.00
Aug.	1,196,294,700	668,702,600	1,695,109.00	2,454,000.00
Sept.	46,716,616,400	28,244,405,800	36,223,771.00	38,113,000.00
Oct.	6,907,511,102,800	2,504,955,700,000	18,700,000,000.00	17,270,129,000.00
Nov.	191,580,465,422,100	400,338,326,400,000	1,422,900,000,000.00	1,000,000,000,000.00
Dec.	1,232,679,853,100	496,585,345,900,000	1,200,400,000,000.00	1,000,000,000,000.00

* Practically all government borrowing after 1919 was in the form of discounted Treasury bills. The figure for November 1923 is as of the 15th of that month.

† In the index number of wholesale prices from December 1919 to December 1922 inclusive, the figures represent monthly averages. From January to June, 1923, statistics are available for specific days three times a month, and from July to December, 1923, weekly. The figures in the table are for the latest available date in each month.

‡ The December 1919 figure for the index number of exchange rates is a monthly average. All other figures for this index are end-of-month quotations.

SOURCES OF DATA: (1) *Zahlen zur Geldentwertung in Deutschland 1914 bis 1923*; Statistisches Reichsamt, Verlag von Reimar Hobbing, Berlin, 1925, pp. 6–10, 16–18, 46–7. (2) *Germany's Economy, Currency and Finance*, Zentral-Verlag G.m.b.H., Berlin, 1924, p. 63.

THE LEVEL OF JOBS, INCOMES, PRICES, AND PRODUCTION 83

resistance for the Treasury and was thus not unwelcome in official circles. The policy of inflation had, in addition, powerful support from influential private quarters.

Inflation was therefore combated but half-heartedly at best. Though several of the administrations of the years 1920 to 1923 made valiant attempts to arrest its progress they could not summon the sustained powers necessary to success. It may well be doubted whether a stable standard could in any case have been set up while immense reparations debts were plaguing the situation. But this must remain an open question. So long as wealth and income were being merely transferred by the decline in the value of the monetary unit and not, as a sum, diminished, so long as scapegoats could be found to assume the burdens and yield of their substance to those who knew how to profit from the situation, projects of reform were treated cavalierly. It was only when enterprisers, instead of surely profiting from inflation as they long did, were suddenly plunged into a sea of uncertainties, only when business activity passed from the stage of exhilaration to panic, only when resistance to a further assumption of losses on the part of the public at large became general, that influential opinion veered to a conviction of the necessity of restoring a stable standard. The pass to which matters had then come is shown in Table 1.

The masses of the urban population were living from hand to mouth, nay, had nothing in their hands but worthless bits of paper which the farmers would no longer accept in exchange for grain. Food riots were general. Political dissolution was in imminent prospect and armed revolt had already raised its head. Affairs were indeed so black that it is clear, in retrospect, that they actually facilitated the reform by imbuing the people with the resolution of despair.

Inflation had shaken the social structure to its roots. The changes of status which it caused were profound. No such shifting of property rights, in time of peace, had ever before taken place. Great numbers of families of long established wealth and position were reduced to beggary at the very time that new or additional fortunes of staggering magnitude were being accumulated. The old middle class wellnigh disappeared and a new group came into prominence. There was less change in the condition of the masses—they had not so much to lose—but the wiping out of savings, insurance, and pensions pressed heavily upon the worker even if his losses did not parallel those of some of the better-to-do social classes.

The drama, and particularly the tragedy, of the time have left an indelible impression of the evils of inflation on the minds of the generation which lived through it. The most striking effects were in the realm of the distribution of wealth rather than in production but there were periods, principally in the final stages of depreciation, when the great majority of the population was in extreme want and perhaps even more distressing uncertainty. When prices were rising hourly by leaps and bounds, when the purchasing power of present and prospective receipts of money was vanishing before it could be spent, or would even be acquired, the population of a so highly specialized exchange society as Germany, was subjected to a wellnigh intolerable strain.

B. THE AMERICAN CONFEDERACY, 1861–1865*
Eugene M. Lerner

The worst inflation in American history since Revolutionary times plagued the South during the Civil War. For thirty-one consecutive months, from October, 1861, to March, 1864, the Confederate commodity price index rose at the average rate of 10 per cent per month. In April, 1865, when Lee surrendered and the Civil War ended, the index was ninety-two times its prewar base. Like all people living through rapid inflation, southerners directed their invective against the instrumentality through which the increase in prices occurred. They exhorted, threatened, vilified, and enacted legislation to regulate and control businessmen and farmers who sold goods at more than "fair" prices. Their Congress declared the capable Secretary of the Treasury,

* From Eugene M. Lerner, "Inflation in the Confederacy, 1861–1865," in Milton Friedman (ed.), *Studies in the Quantity Theory of Money* (University of Chicago Press, Chicago, Ill., 1956), pp. 163–175. Reprinted with kind permission of the author and publisher.

Table 1   General Price Index of the Eastern
Section of the Confederacy
(*First four months of 1861 = 100*)

Month	Year				
	1861	1862	1863	1864	1865
January	101	193	762	2,801	5,824
February	99	211	900	2,947	6,427
March	101	236	1,051	4,128	8,336
April	101	281	1,178	4,470	9,211
May	109	278	1,279	4,575	...
June	109	331	1,308	4,198	...
July	111	380	1,326	4,094	...
August	120	419	1,428	4,097	...
September	128	493	1,617	4,279	...
October	136	526	1,879	4,001	...
November	161	624	2,236	4,029	...
December	172	686	2,464	4,285	...

Christopher G. Memminger, unfit for public office; but prices continued to rise. Memminger resigned, but his successor was no more successful at stopping the rise of prices.

The general commodity price index of the Confederacy (Table 1) increased steadily from the outbreak of war in April, 1861, until May, 1864. In response to a currency reform enacted in February, 1864, prices stopped rising and, indeed, fell slightly until November. In December, 1864, the price index started to climb again and continued to rise sharply until the war's end.

The rapid rise in prices after the outbreak of war reduced the real value of Confederate notes. Lenders refused to extend credit unless they were repaid in gold, leather, or some other commodity, and creditors refused to accept payment for obligations incurred before the war. A client wrote J. D. Davidson, an attorney in Lexington, Virginia, that "some time about the 1st of the present month, Mr. Jack Jordan again came to me when I refused to take the money [for his debt] owing to the condition of the currency." The creditor wanted Davidson to prevent the debtor from repaying his obligation. In the North, where the inflation was not nearly so severe, William McCormick wrote his brother Cyrus, then in England, that events reminded him of Dr. Witherspoon's allusion to the time when "creditors were seen running away from their debtors and their debtors pursued them in triumph and paid them without mercy."

As early as 1862 some southern firms stopped selling their products for currency alone, and customers were forced to offer commodities as well as notes to buy things. Manufacturers were compelled to pay part of their employees' salaries in commodities. One complained that "money will buy little or nothing here, and unless I can find some means of getting food for my workmen, I fear I shall lose them."

In the North the McCormicks protected themselves from the continuous rise in prices by purchasing durable goods and real estate. William McCormick "felt that paper money kept on deposit was unwise . . . and bought nearly 3,000 tons of pig iron," a supply large enough to last the firm two years. The McCormicks bought paints, nails, lead, and lumber in such quantities that storage space had to be enlarged. Land and property were bought with a minimum down payment and a maximum mortgage "to have a place to put our depreciated notes if [the inflation] gets worse."

Many southerners protected their wealth in the same manner, but were accused of speculation and burned in effigy. The Confederate Congress, trying to "get" the speculators, enacted a tax law allowing property bought before January 1, 1862, to be assessed at its 1860 value. Property bought after January 1, 1862, was to be assessed at its purchase price.

The continuous and rapid rise in prices caused Secretary Memminger to write in December, 1863, that "the continuance of the notes as a circulating medium to their present extent involves the ruin of public and private credit, and will deprive the government of the means of defending the lives and property of its citizens." Some program to effectively reduce the stock of money was imperative.

On February 17, 1864, the Confederate Congress enacted a currency reform. All existing currency and call certificates except one-, two-, and five-dollar bills could be converted, dollar for dollar, into 4 per cent bonds until April 1, 1864. The notes still outstanding on April 1 were to be exchanged for new issues at the rate of three for two. With this one law, one-third of the South's cash was erased.

In anticipation of the currency reform southerners tried to reduce their cash balances and drove up prices more sharply than at any time since the war began. In the single month between February 15 and March 15, 1864, the price index increased 23 per cent. In medieval times the crown debased coins in periods of falling prices and restored the specie content in periods of rising prices. Such policies "gave surprising stability to prices in the long run," but Professor

Hamilton indicated that they may have "intensified short term instability." The attempt of the Confederacy to stabilize prices through a well-publicized currency reform had just that effect.

In May, 1864, the currency reform took hold, and the stock of money was reduced. Dramatically, the general price index dropped. This price decline took place in spite of invading Union armies, the impending military defeat, the reduction in foreign trade, the disorganized government, and the low morale of the Confederate army. Reducing the stocks of money had a more significant effect on prices than these powerful forces.

Taxes, however, were still uncollectible, bonds unsalable, and the government expenditures continued large. The printing press was again resorted to, and by December, 1864, prices began to rise. They continued rising until the end of the war.

Like all people who live through prolonged and rapid price rises, southerners came to realize that the only way to avoid the tax of inflation was to reduce their cash holdings. Some resorted to limited forms of barter and refused to accept cash alone for their products. Others adopted more stable currencies, such as northern greenbacks, or made their notes payable in commodities. Durable goods, land, precious metals, and jewelry were kept as ultimate reserves instead of notes or deposits. As velocity increased, prices rose still higher and the real value of cash balances declined.

Taxing through printing money was as appealing to the Confederate government as it was to the Continental Congress in earlier years of American history and to so many governments since that time. What is remarkable is that so large a fraction of the southern war effort could, in fact, be financed by currency issue. It betokens the enormous importance that people attach to having a currency, even a depreciating one, and the great amount of real resources they are willing to pay for it.

C. TWENTIETH CENTURY CHILE*
Joseph Grunwald

There is some evidence that Chile's price inflation started as far back as the late 1870's. Since the beginning of the official consumer price index in 1928, there have been only about four years, but not consecutive ones, during which it may be said that relative price stability existed.

Chile's very severe depression of the 1930's and the influence of the war years of the forties brought a very erratic pattern of price movements during those two decades. On the average, the yearly price increase was roughly 10 per cent during the thirties and 20 per cent during the forties. The inflation rate increased somewhat during the first years of the fifties, but in the middle of 1953 a price explosion took place which brought the yearly inflation rate to over 80 per cent by 1955. With the 1956 anti-inflation program the inflation rate dropped to 38 per cent in 1956 and 17 per cent in 1957. Price increases were higher in 1958 and 1959, reaching about 35 per cent annually, but since the end of 1959 a relative stability has been attained.

Inflation became a way of life and was institutionalized into the legal and socio-economic structure of the country, each sector of the economy constructing its own defense apparatus.

The wage and salary sectors achieved the right to legal wage readjustments in some relation to the cost-of-living index. These income adjustments applied not only to wages and salaries but also to pensions, retirement and other social security incomes. The other mechanism for the salaried classes was price control and subsidized imports of certain basic consumer items.

The self-employed and profit-earning groups defended themselves first through anticipating the inflation by increasing their prices even before the annual wage adjustments came around, and following this up by further price increases after the wage adjustments were given. Second, the credit mechanism also served as an inflation defense for the more substantial businesses. Increases in costs due to wage adjustments and price increases of raw materials were readily ab-

* From Joseph Grunwald, "The 'Structuralist' School of Price Stabilization and Economic Development: The Chilean Case," in Albert O. Hirschman (ed.), *Latin American Issues* (The Twentieth Century Fund, New York, 1961), pp. 91–101. Reprinted with kind permission of the publisher.

sorbed through relatively easy access to credit for the privileged groups, while for others credit was sharply rationed or unavailable.

The government sector defended itself against inflation through the printing press. It is clear that deficit spending became unavoidable as government revenues were based upon the previous period's assessments compared to current pricing for government expenditures.

Nearly all of the sectors of the community hedged through the building up of inventories. This applied also to consumer groups, who bought consumer goods for storage rather than for use.

It is not surprising that this inflation spirit developed a finesse and cleverness in handling the pressures of price increases in all sectors. Although most of the defense mechanisms employed were in themselves quite inflationary, there is little doubt that they brought a certain self-confidence to the community which helped to stave off panic.

The curious aspect of Chile's inflation history of close to a century is that the country never experienced runaway inflation. One would think that, once a country reaches such high rates of price increases as Chile did, hyperinflation would follow almost automatically. There is no satisfactory answer to this. The fact is that not enough money was printed for hyperinflation to develop. But if the forces that made the authorities "print money" were so strong as to maintain a 20 or more per cent yearly inflation for many years, what stopped those forces from compelling a snowballing monetary expansion? Probably the social pressures were not strong enough, and perhaps public confidence was greater than is generally thought. But if among the factors of hyperinflation is public panic, then the defense mechanisms which the Chilean community has built up over the years have helped to avoid it—no matter how inflationary these mechanisms may be in themselves.

READING 15   DEBATE ON CREEPING INFLATION

The American record in the 1950s was one of moderate or "creeping" inflation. The impact of this was widely and emotionally discussed throughout the decade, but the concern reached a peak when prices continued to rise even in the midst of a mild recession in 1958. Was this a portent of inevitable inflation even when jobs were scarce? Did it mean that more severe inflation must follow as soon as employment picked up once again? And what difference did inflation make?

Creeping inflation's critics were numerous. Its defenders were rarer. One of the most articulate defenders was the late Sumner H. Slichter, professor of economics at Harvard University. His view that a modest amount of inflation was both inevitable and healthy in any economy committed to high levels of employment and growth attracted considerable attention, and drew forth the rebuttal by Jules Backman, professor of economics at New York University, which begins on page 90. The main issue with which they are concerned was somewhat eclipsed in the early 1960s by the stability of prices which appeared to stem from too high a rate of unemployment. But an economy that seeks a way back to a point near full employment will have to ask itself once again: Can we have stable prices too?

Questions to Guide the Reading

Have there been significant changes in the American economy in the 1960s to lend greater weight to one side or the other in this debate on inflation?

How adequately might Americans be able to protect themselves against a steady inflation that hovered around 2 per cent per annum? How adequate are the assurances that inflation will not be likely to go much beyond that point in the near future?

A. THE CASE FOR CREEPING INFLATION*
Sumner H. Slichter

The principal economic issue dividing the American people today is the issue of growth of the economy vs. stability of the price level. Mr. Eisenhower has declared that a stable price level "is an indispensable condition for achieving vigorous and continuing economic growth" and has placed strong emphasis on the prevention of inflation in his State of the Union message, his budget message, and his economic report.

His critics accuse him of discouraging growth in order to stabilize the price level. The A.F.L.-C.I.O. Economic Policy Committee has charged that Mr. Eisenhower's program is "a sure-fire prescription for stagnation." The Joint Congressional Economic Committee, under the chairmanship of Senator Paul H. Douglas of Illinois, is about to start hearings on the problem of reconciling full employment, an "adequate" rate of growth and price stability.

Is it true, as Mr. Eisenhower says, that there is no conflict between vigorous economic growth and a stable price level? Or must permanent inflation be accepted as a necessary condition to maximum growth? And if maximum growth entails creeping inflation, what will be the consequences for the economy? Will the United States price itself out of world markets? Will confidence in the dollar be undermined and will there be a disastrous flight from the dollar with creeping inflation developing into a gallop? Will creeping inflation produce great suffering among recipients of fixed incomes? Or are the consequences of creeping inflation greatly exaggerated?

The inflation of the 1950's in the United States has been caused by a mixture of strong demand for goods and a strong upward push of costs, but the principal reason the price level has increased and slow inflation must be expected to continue more or less indefinitely is the strong tendency for labor costs to rise faster than output per man-hour. During the past ten years, for example, hourly compensation of employes in private industry outside agriculture has risen more than twice as fast as output per man-hour.

The unions explain this by asserting that wages were simply chasing prices up, but the

facts refute the claims of the union spokesmen. In *every one* of the past ten years the percentage rise in the hourly compensation of workers exceeded the percentage rise in the consumer price index. Furthermore, in nine out of the past ten years, the rise in hourly compensation of workers exceeded the rise in the wholesale prices of finished goods. Wages were not chasing prices up; on the contrary, prices were chasing wages, and were falling behind each year.

The tendency for wages to outrun output per man-hour is bound to occur in an economy of private enterprise and powerful trade unions whenever the demand for goods is strong—that is, whenever the conditions are favorable for rapid growth. Wages could be prevented from outrunning output per man-hour if the bargaining power of unions were weakened and the bargaining power of employers strengthened by the maintenance of a fairly high rate of unemployment.

Some members of the Board of Governors of the Federal Reserve System, some members of the Council of Economic Advisers and some private economists have proposed that tight credit policies be used to create the amount of unemployment necessary to keep wages from rising faster than productivity and to keep the price level steady. The amount of unemployment needed would vary with the phase of the business cycle, the vigor of foreign competition and the year-to-year fluctuation in the size of crops, but recent experience indicates that an unemployment rate of 5 to 8 per cent would be required.

Fostering unemployment in order to keep wages from outrunning productivity, however, would mean retarding the growth of the economy. Hence the conflict between maximum growth and stable prices is real—the community must decide which it prefers. There is little doubt which way the decision will go because the loss to the community from a retarded rate of growth would increase at a compound rate and would soon become intolerably burdensome. Suppose that the economy, which is capable of increasing its productive capacity at the rate of 4 per cent a year, were held to a growth of only

* From Sumner H. Slichter, "Argument for 'Creeping' Inflation," *New York Times Magazine*, March 8, 1959. Reprinted with kind permission of the publisher.

2 per cent a year in order to keep the price level steady. At the end of ten years the economy would have a productive capacity more than 26 percentage points less than it would have had at the greater rate of growth.

What about the long run effects of creeping inflation? Would not creeping inflation bring frequent recessions, so that in the long run more real growth would be achieved under a stable price level? There is no doubt that rapid growth entails the risk of recession, but the occasional recessions that accompany a high rate of growth need not be severe. Much progress has been made in building up resistance of the economy to contraction. The recession of 1958 illustrates this progress. The drop in business investment and the liquidation of inventories were moderately severe, but personal income and retail sales remained remarkably steady. As a result, the recession was both mild and short. In view of the growing capacity of the economy to resist contraction, one must reject the view that a stable price level is a necessary condition to the maximum rate of growth.

Are not changes possible in our institutions, policies, or business practices that would enable us to avoid creeping inflation and at the same time realize our maximum growth potential? There are many changes that would diminish the tendency for prices to rise, but none of them would assure that unions would not push up wages faster than industry could raise output per man-hour in the strong sellers' markets that would characterize a rapidly growing economy.

The possibility of price and wage controls may be dismissed, partly because the people would not tolerate controls in time of peace and partly because controls are easily evaded by changing the quality of goods and by introducing substitute goods. Strong public hostility to excessive union wage claims will have some effect on wages, but not much. Union members expect their officers to get all that they can for the members and would displace officers whom they suspected of failing to represent them faithfully. Union members, however, are not immune to public opinion, and strong public hostility to excessive demands will tend to weaken by a small amount the upward pressure of unions on wages.

What about the possibility of curbing the power of the trade unions by organization on the part of employers, by depriving unions of some of their present privileges and immunities, or by imposing new restrictions on unions? More organization among employers would help, but too much should not be expected from it. The employers are organized for dealing with unions in the steel industry, the coal industry, the railroad industry, and at the local level in many of the building trades, but in none of these industries have employers been able to prevent wages from outrunning output per man-hour.

Depriving unions of some of their present extraordinary privileges, such as the use of coercive picketing to force people to join or the conscription of neutrals in labor disputes, would remove some glaring injustices, but would have little effect upon the bargaining power of most unions. Breaking up some of the large unions, as has been suggested by George Romney and others, would have consequences that are hard to predict. Unions would lose some of their present ability to support strikes by some members while other members work and pay special assessments into a strike fund. Nevertheless, the new unions might drive hard bargains. There would be rivalries among them and each would have a strong desire to make a good showing.

Thus, if there were three or four unions in the automobile industry, each might feel a strong urge to make a better settlement than any of the others. Hence, breaking up the unions might increase their militancy and make reasonable settlements with them more difficult.

But whatever the possible results of the breaking up of unions, that step is not going to be taken. The American workers want their unions, and any effort to destroy or seriously weaken organized labor would cause the workers to rally to the support of the unions and make them stronger and more aggressive than ever.

The most promising methods of checking the tendency of rising labor costs to push up prices are new methods of management that enlist the ingenuity and imagination of the men at the machines and benches in reducing the ratio of labor costs to income from sales. Experience in more than a score of plants shows that amazing things begin to happen when workers share in a plant-wide bonus, based upon their success in narrowing the ratio of labor costs to income from sales, and are given good opportunities to discuss their ideas regularly with management. The common interest that everyone in the plant has in reducing labor costs produces an almost startling degree of teamwork and cooperation.

The new methods of management were introduced a few years ago by the late Joseph Scanlon, and his work is being carried out by his followers. But a generation or more will probably be required to spread the new methods throughout industry and adapt them to enterprises of various sizes and kinds. Eventually American industry will drastically modify its methods of handling labor and draw on the great capacity of rank and file workers to contribute to improvements in technology. The new methods of management may or may not be adequate to prevent wages from outrunning productivity, but they hold more promise for checking rising labor costs than any device that has yet been developed.

If a generation or so will be required for new methods of management to check the rise in labor costs, what will happen in the meantime? Fears that the United States will be priced out of world markets are far-fetched. Prices in most other important industrial countries have been rising in recent years even faster than in the United States. Between 1950 and 1957, for example, the increase in the index of wholesale prices in Britain was more than twice as large as in the United States. In Sweden and Norway it was more than three times as large, in France almost three times as large, in West Germany almost twice as large, in Austria four times as large.

No one knows, of course, whether prices in other industrial countries will continue to rise faster than in the United States. Since the principal industrial countries are in competition with one another and since they all are more or less subject to the same influences (such as powerful trade unions and an insistent popular demand for social services that precludes important reductions in taxes), all of the industrial countries are likely to experience about the same movement of the price level.

The competitive position of the United States is very strong, especially in manufacturing. This is indicated by the fact that our exports of finished manufactures are nearly three times as large as our imports. But if important industrial countries were to succeed in underselling us on a broad scale, that would not be a calamity for us. On the contrary, it would help us check inflation by stiffening the resistance of American employers to union demands and by encouraging employers to cut prices.

Also ill-founded are fears that creeping inflation will precipitate a flight from the dollar and that creeping inflation will sooner or later become a gallop. Every country in Europe has had creeping inflation during the past ten years. The idea has become pretty well accepted that a continued drop in the purchasing power of money is to be expected. And yet in virtually all countries the rise in prices between 1953 and 1957 was considerably less than in the period 1948 to 1953.

As for a general flight from the dollar, the practical question arises: "Where is the money to go?" Other currencies have limited attractiveness because almost any country one might name has economic and political problems as formidable as those confronting the United States. Flight into commodities is not satisfactory because the future price of each commodity depends upon specific market conditions (supply, demand, competition of substitutes) far more than on what happens to the general price level. Some shifting of investment is bound to occur and already has occurred, but the process tends to limit itself.

For example, if the price level is expected to rise 2 per cent a year, a good bond yielding nominally 5 per cent has a true yield of 3 per cent. Such a bond may be as attractive as a stock that has been bid up so that it yields only 2.5 per cent.

Our conclusion is that there is no immediate prospect that conflict can be avoided in advanced industrial countries between the desire for the maximum possible economic growth on the one hand and a stable price level on the other hand. This conflict is created by the rise of the relatively new institution of collective bargaining which is too well established and produces too many important benefits to be disturbed simply because it produces creeping inflation.

But the prospect that we shall be living under creeping inflation does call for various common sense adaptations and adjustments. Efforts should be made to speed the adoption of the new methods of management that automatically reward workers for helping reduce the ratio of labor costs to sales income. Pension plans, including the Federal old-age and survivors' insurance plan, should be adapted to creeping inflation. This means that they should either be fitted with escalator clauses or revised every now and then to compensate for the rise in the price level.

People should review their investment policies and should not hold long-term bonds or other long-term fixed-income investments unless the yield is sufficient to compensate them for the probable annual loss in purchasing power. Long-term wage contracts should contain escalator clauses. But in general, people should realize that living under creeping inflation in the future will not be essentially different from living under creeping inflation in the past—in fact, prices will probably rise considerably less in the next ten years than in the past ten.

Most important of all, people should realize that the alternative to creeping inflation is a fairly substantial amount of chronic unemployment. The problems of creeping inflation are a small price to pay for avoiding the much greater problems of unemployment and a rate of growth that falls far short of our potential.

B. THE CASE AGAINST CREEPING INFLATION*
Jules Backman

There is a general agreement that economic growth is indispensable for a strong America. However, there has been considerable public debate about the ideal rate of growth and how to achieve it.

One school of thought asserts that "an inescapable cost" of a desirable rate of growth is creeping inflation. It holds that the alternatives are "creeping inflation and economic growth" or "price stability and unemployment." In this way, creeping inflation is given "respectability by association," while price stability is subject to "guilt by association."

The second school of thought holds not only that we can have both a desirable rate of growth and stable prices, but that we can maintain our growth only by keeping prices stable.

Creeping inflation refers to a price rise of 2 per cent or 3 per cent a year. Prof. Sumner Slichter, one of the exponents of the first school, states that this type of "slow inflation must be expected to continue more or less indefinitely." Such an annual rate of increase does not seem to be very large, but an annual rise of 2 per cent will wipe out half of the purchasing power of the dollar in thirty-five years, and a 3 per cent rate will result in a similar reduction in less than twenty-five. This is the simple arithmetic of creeping inflation.

Nevertheless, apologists for creeping inflation argue that it is unavoidable if we are to achieve the rate of economic growth which is necessary to enable us to attain our aspirations at home and to meet the threat from Russia. They explain that it is inevitable because labor costs rise more rapidly than output per man-hour. According to this argument, trade unions are so powerful that these excessive increases in wages and other labor costs could be stopped only by stringent governmental monetary and fiscal controls. The result of such curbs would be large-scale unemployment, which would limit economic growth. We are told that we must, therefore, accept creeping inflation as a lesser evil.

There is no disagreement concerning objectives between the creeping inflationists and those who are opposed. We are agreed that our goal is a maximum achievable rate of economic growth. We are agreed that unemployment is undesirable and exacts a high social cost. We are agreed that inflation—creeping or any other kind—is not desirable as a way of life. We disagree as to the means by which we may achieve our goals. The creeping inflationists say that we cannot achieve all three goals, that we must choose among them. The anti-creeping inflationists say we can achieve growth, a minimum level of unemployment *and* price stability.

The arguments against creeping inflation may be summarized as follows: (1) it slows long-term economic growth; (2) it makes recessions worse; (3) it hurts fixed-income groups and savers; (4) not everyone can be protected against it by "escalator clauses"; (5) it leads to galloping inflation; (6) it is not inevitable in an expanding economy.

(1) Creeping inflation slows long-term economic growth

There is general agreement that to meet the threat of the expanding Russian economy our own economy must continue to grow as rapidly

* From Jules Backman, "The Case Against Creeping Inflation," *New York Times Magazine*, May 3, 1959. Reprinted with kind permission of the author and publisher.

as possible. Some say we must step up our rate of growth to about 5 per cent a year as compared with our long-term record of about 3 per cent. While the difference between 3 per cent and 5 per cent appears to be small, it becomes enormous with the passage of time. With a growth rate of 3 per cent, total output of goods and services in our economy increases fourfold in about fifty years. With a 5 per cent rate of increase, on the other hand, total output in a half century would be more than ten times as large as it is at present.

Everyone is in favor of the highest possible rate of economic growth. But there are practical limits to expansion which must be faced. When we exceed these limits the pressures for inflation become intensified. President Eisenhower properly has pointed out that a stable price level is "an indispensable condition" for achieving the maximum growth rate in the long run.

History does not support the assumption that economic growth must be accompanied by rising prices. Economic growth has occurred in many periods of stable or declining prices. Two such major periods in the nineteenth century—the Eighteen Twenties and Eighteen Thirties and the last third of the century—were periods of declining prices. During the Nineteen Twenties, when prices remained relatively stable, national output rose about 4 per cent a year. On the other hand, from 1955 to 1957, when prices crept upward almost 3 per cent a year, national output rose less than 2 per cent annually.

Two major factors have contributed to economic growth in this country: higher productivity and an expanding population. Two-thirds of our 3 per cent annual rate of growth has been accounted for by rising output per man-hour, about one-third by increasing population. Increases in productivity, therefore, provide the key to future economic growth. Output per man-hour is affected by many factors but the most important has been the investment in new machines and equipment. The magnitude of such investments depends upon the level of savings. Savings will be discouraged by creeping inflation, and thus long-term economic growth will be stultified.

Confronted by creeping inflation, savers are more interested in speculating—to protect themselves against losses in purchasing power—than in providing capital for industry. There is ample evidence of this tendency in the rampant specu-

lation now taking place in stocks. If inflation should continue to be a threat, more and more persons would try to protect themselves in this manner. The result would be a speculative binge which would ultimately collapse. Such a development could only act to retard economic growth.

To stimulate economic growth it is necessary to create an environment in which savings will be encouraged and business will be willing to convert those savings into new plant and equipment. Price stability encourages savings, while tax incentives could be used to induce new investments. This is the road to greater economic growth.

Creeping inflation also interferes with business planning. When protection against price rises becomes a dominant factor, business men are not likely to plan boldly for expansion. One result is an adverse impact on job creation.

(2) Creeping inflation makes recessions worse

It is true that fear of higher prices may give a temporary stimulus to the economy. But this development induces speculation in inventories. Eventually, the inventories become burdensome, then the economy experiences a setback. The 1948–49 downturn properly has been described as an inventory recession. Inventory liquidation also was significant in the 1953–54 and 1957–58 recessions.

When protection against tomorrow's higher costs becomes a major factor in industry decisions to expand capacity today, the net result tends to be overexpansion—followed by a sharp decline in new investment in plant and equipment. The current lag in the capital goods industries reflects the aftermath of the overexpansion of 1955–57. Thus, creeping inflation means more cyclical unemployment. It is not an alternative to unemployment; it is a significant cause of unemployment. And it is little solace to those who become unemployed that they may have received overtime pay during the boom.

We normally anticipate that there will be 2.5 to 3 million workers unemployed even when the economy is operating at full speed. This frictional unemployment usually is short-term, representing individuals changing jobs or seasonally unemployed (as in the construction, apparel or retail trades). Therefore, when we have a total of 4.3 million unemployed, our real problem is how to create about 1.5 million jobs. The economic cost of unemployment must be measured in terms of this smaller figure.

The hardships attending unemployment should not be minimized. The price in terms of broken homes, loss of self-respect, loss of national output, and related developments is a heavy one indeed. This is why every effort must be directed to adopting the proper policies to reduce unemployment.

Creeping inflation exacts a double toll: first, a loss in the buying power of our money; second, added unemployment. It carries a high price tag.

(3) Creeping inflation hurts fixed-income groups and savers

Persons with fixed or relatively fixed incomes —those who live on proceeds of life-insurance policies, pensioners, those who work for non-profit organizations, government employes and bondholders—are hardest hit by any cut in the purchasing power of money. Ask the pensioner who planned his retirement twenty years ago how he gets along today with the dollars that buy less than half of what they bought then.

With an increasing number of senior citizens in our population, and with the growth of private pension plans, this is a matter of serious national concern. The hardships experienced by these persons can be just as tragic as those suffered by the unemployed.

In addition, families with savings accounts, United States Saving Bonds and other types of savings find their purchasing power steadily eroding. These various forms of savings aggregate about $400 billions. Every increase of 1 per cent in the price level, therefore, wipes out $4 billions in purchasing power.

This problem cannot be evaluated in terms of one-year or two-year results. As we noted earlier, creeping inflation could cut the total value of savings in half within twenty-five to thirty-five years. This is a heavy cost and cannot be ignored.

Nor can workers escape the adverse effects of creeping inflation. Higher prices cut the purchasing power of wages and benefits received under security programs. The part of a wage increase which is excessive is taken away—in whole or in part—by price inflation. Reduced profits mean reduced incentives to invest in new plant and equipment; one result is fewer job opportunities. And unemployment, which thus may attend excessive labor-cost increases, means that those who hold their jobs obtain part of their higher real earnings at the expense of those who lose their job or who fail to obtain jobs.

(4) Not everybody can be protected against creeping inflation by "escalator clauses"

It is significant that not even the apologists for creeping inflation regard it as something to be encouraged. Rather, we are told it is an evil which must be tolerated and to which adjustment must be made. One suggestion is that "escalator clauses," such as those now contained in many union contracts, might be extended to pensioners, insurance beneficiaries, bondholders and the like. This proposal acknowledges the ill effects of inflation, but suggests that the burden could be neutralized.

But not everybody can ride the escalator. It is the height of folly to imagine that we can inflate without some groups paying the price.

Professor Slichter has suggested that under the conditions of creeping inflation people "should not hold long-term bonds or other long-term fixed-income investment unless the yield is sufficient to compensate them for the probable annual loss in purchasing power." What would happen to our financial system if bondholders should attempt to liquidate their investments en masse? The basic weakness of the apology for creeping inflation is reflected in the recognition of the problem in this area.

(5) Creeping inflation leads to galloping inflation

Psychology plays an important role in economic decisions. As the purchasing power of money steadily erodes, more and more persons will seek to protect themselves against future price rises. The resulting flight from money into goods would accelerate the rate of increase in prices. Creeping inflation could then become galloping inflation, and finally runaway inflation.

It is true that such a development would require support from monetary and fiscal inflation. But that this support would be forthcoming seems probable as long as we persist in tolerating wage inflation and insist upon full employment.

(6) Creeping inflation is not inevitable in an expanding economy

Many factors are at work today to raise or hold up prices. They include the agricultural support program, the high level of Federal, state and local government spending, the increases in various sales and excise taxes, featherbedding and make-work rules, controls affecting imports and the steady expansion in private debt.

The primary cause of creeping inflation, however, as Professor Slichter has pointed out, is wage inflation—labor costs rising faster than output per man-hour. When wage inflation abates, price inflation also is moderated. It is noteworthy that, despite business recovery in the past year, consumer prices have remained stable and wholesale prices have risen only fractionally. This temporary stability reflects the likelihood that output per man-hour has risen more rapidly than the long-term rate (a typical recovery performance), and that, as a result, wage inflation has been at a minimum — perhaps even nonexistent — for the economy as a whole during this period.

The basic problem, then, is to counteract wage inflation. Two factors make this difficult. One is the national objective to maintain full employment, the other is the growth of powerful labor unions.

The full-employment policy makes it difficult to impose those stringent monetary and fiscal checks to rising prices which would create deflation and unemployment. The national concern over unemployment has assured union leaders that their wage policies will be underwritten by new inflationary measures when necessary. In other words, full-employment policies have increased the bargaining strength of the unions.

The problem of wage inflation could be ameliorated if union leaders and the workers they represent accepted the fact that our average standard of living cannot rise faster than national productivity. Only as we produce more can we obtain more goods and services, or more leisure, or some combination of both.

However, since it is the job of union leaders to get as much for their members as fast as they can, there is little point in criticizing them for taking full advantage of the present situation.

We can make more progress by taking action on two fronts:

First, the power of the unions must be curbed. There is little agreement on how this may be accomplished. Some students of the problem have suggested applying the antitrust laws to limit unions' monopoly power. Others have proposed more drastic remedies, such as limiting the power to strike, or curbing the size of unions.

Each of these proposals involves serious difficulties which must be carefully evaluated. Possibly some other solution will be forthcoming. However, unless some means is found to curb excessive union power and its abuse, this source of pressure for creeping inflation will continue.

Second, the Employment Act of 1946 should be amended to include the goal of stabilizing the purchasing power of the dollar as well as the goal of maintaining high-level employment. This would provide a guide against which to measure proposed policies. It would not mean wage or price controls. Individual prices would continue to fluctuate as at present but public policy would have as one objective the prevention of marked changes in the general price level.

Uncertainty would be substituted for the present certainty that inflationary wage increases will be supported by governmental actions. The new element of uncertainty might impose some restraint upon unions. It might also make industry less willing to grant excessive wage increases because it would make their recovery through higher prices less certain.

One important caution must be noted. There is no magic in a stable price level. Stability of prices during the Nineteen Twenties did not prevent the most catastrophic depression in modern history. Stability of prices from 1952 to early 1956 did not prevent the 1954 recession—or the 1955–1957 boom. General price stability may conceal important disparities in price relationships or in cost-price relationships which in turn upset the effective functioning of the economy. In other words, general price stability is not a cure-all for the problem of the business cycle.

Nevertheless, if these limitations are kept in mind, the inclusion of the goal of price stability in the Employment Act will focus national attention on inflation and its causes. The public will be made aware of the dangers that are inherent in monetary and fiscal inflation with their impact upon total demand, wage inflation with its impact on costs, and other policies which act to raise or hold up prices. And, certainly, full awareness of the sources—and evils—of creeping inflation is an indispensable step in mobilizing public opinion against inflationary policies.

READING 16

The debate in the previous article touched a wide range of the issues involved in moderate increases in the price level. Now it is necessary to look at some of these issues more intensively and to try to set the inflation into a more comprehensive framework of analysis.

Charles L. Schultze, of the Indiana University, has been prominent among the economists studying inflation at close range. He finds that neither the "demand-pull" nor the "cost-push" view of inflation offers a satisfactory explanation for the inflation of the 1950s. He offers a theory of "demand-shift" inflation which directs our attention to particular segments of the economy rather than to overall costs or demand factors. The policy implications of this analysis indicate that anti-inflationary monetary and fiscal policy must take into account the composition as well as the level of total demand. The full flavor of these latter implications will be sharper once the later readings on fiscal and monetary policy have been covered. This article serves as a prelude for what is to come.

Questions to Guide the Reading

What support or rebuttal does this article offer for the arguments of Slichter and Backman in the previous reading? What are the chief unresolved issues raised by all three authors?

How well equipped are our political instruments to implement, and our private economic institutions to live with, any of the policy proposals offered here for dealing with renewed inflation?

EXPLAINING AND TREATING CREEPING INFLATION
Charles L. Schultze

The domestc economic policy of the United States during the last years of the 1950's has been dominated by the fear of inflation. Concern about gradually rising prices has perhaps been the most important single factor, not only in determining monetary policy, but also in restraining the magnitude of governmental expenditures for defense, school construction, natural resources development, and indeed for almost the entire range of government programs except road-building. While the general price indexes have been relatively stable in recent months, and unemployment has been hovering about the 5 per cent mark, the federal budget for fiscal 1961 and the monetary policies of the Federal Reserve System are clearly premised on the belief that continued restraint of aggregate spending is called for by the existence of underlying inflationary forces.

"Demand-pull" theories

The object of monetary and budget restraints is to limit the growth of aggregate expenditures in the economy. To the extent that a general rise in the price level stems from an excessive growth in total expenditures relative to the economy's output capacity, such restrictions, insofar as they remove the excess growth in expenditures, can control the price increases without at the same time reducing output and employment.

Traditional economic theory recognizes such an excess of total spending as the prime, indeed as the only, cause of inflation. If, in spite of monetary and budget restraints, prices continue to rise, this simply demonstrates that the restraints are not severe enough to accomplish their object. Central bankers throughout the world may generally be counted on to hold this

From Charles L. Schultze, "Creeping Inflation—Causes and Consequences," *Business Horizons* (Indiana University, Bloomington), Summer, 1960, pp. 65–77. Reprinted with kind permission of the author and publisher.

traditional view of the inflationary process. Their discussions of inflation tend to inveigh heavily against "profligacy," "excesses," and "overspending"; public virtue is equated with a "sound" currency, and policy proposals are couched in terms of stern warnings against the immorality of nations' trying to spend more than they produce.

"Cost-push" theories

A competing explanation of recent creeping inflation is the "cost-push" hypothesis. It maintains that inflation can and does arise in the absence of excess total spending. The most common version of this new inflation thesis attributes general price increases to autonomous upward advances in wage rates, mainly in union-organized industries. This particular variant of the cost-push hypothesis has been adopted by many business organizations and by individual businessmen in their speeches and other public statements.

The concept of cost-push inflation not only fits in with the over-all philosophy of most business organizations, but it confirms the experience of many a businessman who first sees inflation when he confronts it in the form of higher costs. Even if these higher costs result from an excess demand for labor arising out of excess total spending in the economy, the time sequence of the businessman's own experience makes a cost-push theory seem eminently reasonable.

Not surprisingly, a rival version of the cost-push theory has been adopted by union leaders and by many spokesmen for the liberal left—the villain of the piece is not organized labor but the market power of big business. Advances in "administered" prices, justified by neither increases in demand nor increases in costs, have been the initiating and sustaining factor in the price-wage spiral.

Policy implications

Both variants of the cost-push theory lead to a common conclusion. Since wages and prices tend to be set in partial independence of the state of the market, moderate monetary and fiscal restraints cannot halt inflation. Rather, by restricting the level of monetary expenditures in the face of independently rising prices and wages, such restraints lead to unemployment and idle industrial capacity.

Here again, two schools of thought may be discerned. The first believes that it would be disastrous for the government to validate the rising prices and wages. Monetary and fiscal restraints are called for even if they do lead to greater unemployment and excess capacity. Somewhat in the spirit of a parental "this hurts me more than it does you," advocates of an austere monetary policy would chastise "anti-social" price and wage behavior—first in the hope of limiting the extent of the current misbehavior, and second in the belief that continued punishment would eventually inculcate more socially desirable behavior on the part of the wayward unions (or monopolies, as the case may be).

The other school of thought places much greater priority on full employment and rapid economic growth than on absolute price stability. Such critics of current monetary and fiscal policies feel that, since the basic cause of the inflation is not excess spending, a relaxation of current restrictive policies would result in little additional price increase but would achieve significant gains in real output. Many of them would further advocate various forms of mild wage and price controls as a final resort. In any event, they would not sacrifice a higher level or rate of growth in national output in an attempt to stabilize a slowly rising price level.

Alternative hypothesis

A careful analysis of recent inflationary processes is a prerequisite to the formulation of monetary and fiscal policy. Even those who are not particularly concerned about the failure to contain a slowly rising price level are vitally interested in achieving other economic goals. And the use of general monetary and fiscal policies for anti-inflationary purposes will have widely different implications for the attainment of such goals as full employment and rapid economic growth, depending upon what one assumes to be the particular nature of the inflationary process.

Price and wage rigidities. A detailed examination of the economy during the past five years appears to indicate that neither of the two prevalent theories of the inflationary process can satisfactorily explain the events of that period. Boiled down to its essentials, the debate between the demand-pull and cost-push theories centers on the sensitivity of price and wage decision-making to the state of the market for goods and for labor. If prices and wages are flexible in response to changes in the demand for goods and labor, then inflation cannot proceed in the absence of excessively rising total demand. This does not mean that cost increases would not accompany inflation. Rather, the demand-pull explanation implies that costs would not rise without the prior and continuing stimulus of rising demands for factors of production. If, on the other hand, price and wage decisions are not closely tied to the state of the market, the general price level can increase despite the absence of an excessive growth in the over-all demand for goods and labor.

No one would deny, of course, that there is some level of unemployment and excess capacity that would halt the advance in wages and prices. But the central contention of the cost-push theorists is that wage and price decisions in an economy operating at or close to full employment are not sufficiently influenced by *moderate* changes in market conditions.

In fact, however, wages and prices in the modern American economy cannot be characterized simply by whether or not they are sensitive or insensitive to the state of market demand. *One of the major features of prices and wages is that they are substantially more sensitive to increases in demand than they are to decreases.* Price competition and downward price flexibility are still significant characteristics of some important areas of the economy—agricultural products and many other crude materials being the major examples. But in a very large part of the economy, prices are "sticky"; they do not decline readily in the face of growing excess capacity.

The reasons for this downward rigidity are manifold. To some extent, rigidity is due to the market power exercised by the small number of giant firms that dominate many American industries. In part, it is a natural consequence of the fact that pricing decisions are made in an atmosphere of uncertainty about the future. Once we abandon the textbook world in which business firms, with known or certainly expected cost and revenue curves, continually price to maximize short-run profits, we must recognize that the maintenance of prices during periods of excess capacity is not an irrational act.

There is a large and growing body of economic literature that discusses the problem of downward price rigidity and the propensity of firms to pay more attention to costs than to demand, particularly in a situation of declining demand. It is not the purpose of this essay to summarize that literature. Let us rather note the fact as a matter of common experience and analyze its consequences.

Downward rigidity is even stronger in the case of wage rates. During all of the years between 1900 and 1960, there were only five in which the average of manufacturing wage rates was lower than in the preceding year. If, as a guide, we set 4 per cent unemployment as a rough but convenient division, with higher unemployment ratios labor scarcity, and if we specify $2\frac{1}{2}$ per cent as the average annual wage increase consistent with stable unit labor costs ($2\frac{1}{2}$ per cent is the average annual gain in productivity), we find that of the thirty-four years in which wage increases were greater than $2\frac{1}{2}$ per cent, seventeen were years of labor surplus and seventeen were years of labor scarcity. In no case did wage rates decline when unemployment was less than 7 per cent of the labor force. And in all of the years in which wages did decline, consumer prices were also substantially lower than in the preceding year. Conversely, there were ten years in which wages rose while unemployment was above 6 per cent. The downward rigidity of wage rates in the face of declining demand for labor is not, therefore, a new phenomenon, nor is it traceable solely to the existence of organized labor. Whatever one's belief with respect to the power of unions to raise wages, however, there is little doubt that they have strengthened the already existing floor under wage rates.

If prices and wages are relatively insensitive to declines in demand but do respond to increases in demand, then a rise in the general price level can occur in the absence of either an over-all excess of demand or an autonomous upward push of wages. *In any situation characterized by a marked shift in the composition of demands, prices and wages will tend to rise in the sectors experiencing increased demands and will not fall, or certainly not by a corresponding amount, in the sectors facing declining demands.* As a consequence, the average level of prices will rise. The process of resource allocation, in other words, does not simply realign the relative position of individual prices and wages. Rather, in a world in which prices and wages are sticky downward, attempts to effect a rapid change in the allocation of resources tend to raise the whole price level.

The spread of cost increases. The inflationary consequences of a substantial shift in the composition of demands is not confined merely to this averaging process. Rapidly rising demands for the products of particular industries transmit their impact to the rest of the economy through their influence on the prices of materials and the wages of labor. Crude material prices are normally quite flexible and are unlikely to increase significantly in the absence of an over-all increase in demand. Prices of intermediate materials, supplies, and components, however, are predominantly more cost-determined and fairly rigid downward. Prices of those materials chiefly consumed by industries with rapidly rising demands advance, since a sharp increase in the demand for the final product will usually (though not inevitably) imply a rise in the demand for specialized materials. On the other hand, prices of materials and supplies chiefly consumed by industries with declining demands do not fall unless the demand deficiency is very large. Industries that use both types of materials confront an increase in the composite cost of their raw materials, even though such industries are not themselves experiencing increases in demand.

An even more important mechanism by which cost increases are propagated throughout the economy is the spread of wage, salary, and other cost increases from industries with rising demand and high profits to industries with declining demand and falling profits. As prices and production rise in some sectors of the economy, profits in those sectors tend to advance sharply. The rising profits generate higher costs. Unions have an increasingly lush target at which to aim, and management more of a tendency to pay what the unions want rather than suffer the consequences during a particularly profitable period. Perhaps equally as important, the fear of potential new rivals, attracted by the higher profits, often induces firms to utilize a part of their increasing profits for upgrading products, for elaborate research and development projects, for stepped-up advertising campaigns, *et hoc genus omne.*

The cost increases in industries with growing production and profits filter out through the rest of the economy. The pressure on specialized engineering and scientific resources is felt in all of industry. The nonprice competition initiated by increased research and development and by product upgrading in high-profit industries forces firms in other industries to incur at least some of the same cost outlays. Moreover, firms in industries with stable or declining demand find themselves having to pay wage increases, even though their demand for labor is not rising. It is not that they fear an immediate loss of their work

force if wage increases are not granted—indeed, we have postulated a situation in which there is no over-all shortage of labor. However, firms faced with periodic fluctuations in the demand for their product cannot afford to acquire the reputation of being low-wage firms—otherwise they might sacrifice easy access to the labor market during periods of rising demand. Further, an increasingly unfavorable wage differential is a marvelously effective way in which to insure declining labor efficiency.

Industries in which there is substantial concentration of market power in the hands of a small number of firms are more likely to be subject to the spread of cost increases than are competitive industries. This is so because firms with significant market power are much more likely to pass along a large part of the increased costs in the form of higher prices. Hence, they are less prone to "get their backs up" over demands for wage advances and other upward cost tendencies during periods of slack demand than are firms in more competitive industries. A rise in steel wages is much more likely to be imitated in the automobile industry than in the apparel industry, given the same conditions of demand in both cases.

For all of these reasons, the pattern of wage increases set in the rapidly expanding industries is likely to spread, in a modified fashion to be sure, throughout the rest of the economy. During the 1955–1957 boom, for example, the average wage increase in the five most rapidly expanding manufacturing industries was 9½ per cent. The average increase in the five least rapidly expanding industries was 9 per cent. Yet output expanded by an average of 12 per cent, and production-worker employment by 2 per cent in the former group of industries; while output and employment declined by 6 and 9 per cent respectively in the latter group. The same tendency for wage increases in slowly expanding industries to match those in rapidly expanding industries has also been noted in most of the countries of Western Europe.

Effects of market structure. The tendency for rising profits in oligopolistic firms to be dissipated in rising wage rates, even when the demand for labor is not excessive, has been strikingly illustrated in a recent study by Harold Levinson published by the Joint Economic Commitee of the U.S. Congress. Relative changes in wages among the nineteen manufacturing industry groups were studied year by year during the

1947–58 period and related to changes in other economic variables. In no year was there a significant relationship between changes in employment and changes in wage rates. During years of rapidly rising total demand (mainly the years between 1947 and 1951, with the exception of 1949), there was no significant relationship between the magnitude of changes in wage rates on the one hand and the level of profits and the degree of market concentration on the other. However, in recession years and in almost all of the years since 1952, there was a significant positive relationship between wage rates and the latter two factors.

Further evidence of the link between market structure and inflation was the finding that, in years of rapidly rising total demand, there was no significant relationship between relative changes in prices and relative changes in unit costs among manufacturing industries, while, during the last five years, the relationship between changes in prices and changes in costs was significant. Conversely, the margins between prices and costs, as reflected in profit ratios, were significantly related to the degree of market concentration during recent years but were not so related during the earlier post-war years in which total monetary demand was rising very rapidly.

"Classical" inflation. The fact that a shift in the composition of demands can itself generate a

rise in the general level of prices does not, of course, explain all inflations. The really major inflations have clearly been the results of an over-all excess of monetary demands. The rise in prices during and immediately after World War II and the largest part of the price advances during the Korean conflict were a response to an excess of aggregate demand. And in such situations, monetary and fiscal actions designed to restrict total demand are appropriate policy measures. But the rise in the price level that began in 1955 and continued through 1958 cannot be explained by a rise in total spending that pressed upon the nation's capacity to produce.

A detailed examination of the 1955–58 period is beyond the scope of this article—a brief summary, however, may indicate the process by which a rise in the general price level can occur quite independently of an over-all excess of demand.

The anatomy of recent inflation

During 1955, the economy recovered swiftly from the recession of 1954. Expenditures and output in all of the major volatile sectors of the economy advanced rapidly. After late 1955, however, a change in the nature of the advance took place. While the demand for business plant and equipment continued to increase at a very rapid pace, housing construction and automobile sales fell sharply from the peaks reached in 1955.

Table 1   Rates of Change in Gross National Product and Major Components
(*Percentage changes expressed as annual rates*)

Period	Gross National Product	Business Fixed Investment*	Residential Construc-tion	National Security	Automobile Purchases†	Other Gross National Product
1Q, 1947—4Q, 1948	10.1	17.1	32.2	−3.9	22.8	9.1
4Q, 1948—4Q, 1949	−3.3	−19.7	12.3	7.4	5.0	−4.2
4Q, 1949—1Q, 1951	19.0	24.8	23.5	69.5	36.8	14.6
1Q, 1951—3Q, 1952	6.2	3.8	−6.2	62.6	−25.5	3.5
3Q, 1952—2Q, 1953	8.4	13.3	12.5	9.8	89.0	4.4
2Q, 1953—3Q, 1954	−1.4	1.0	10.3	−17.4	−19.0	1.2
3Q, 1954—3Q, 1955	11.4	13.8	19.6	−2.0	63.0	10.4
3Q, 1955—2Q, 1957	5.5	11.2	−5.8	8.3	−7.4	6.2
2Q, 1957—2Q, 1958	−1.8	−16.1	0	1.3	−34.0	1.1

* Purchases of producers' durable equipment (excluding passenger vehicles) and nonresidential construction.
† Purchases of automobiles by consumers and business, plus the change in inventories of auto manufacturers and dealers.
SOURCE: Basic data from *U.S. Income and Output* and various issues of *Survey of Current Business*.

Total expenditures on gross national product increased by slightly over 5 per cent per year during the two years from mid-1955 to mid-1957, before the recession set in. Instead of the 3½ to 4 per cent annual growth in real output, which should normally accompany such a rise in expenditures, output rose by only 1½ per cent. Capacity rose substantially faster than output so that, throughout the period, excess capacity in most industries was rising.

Table I shows the changes in the major categories of gross national expenditures during significant subperiods of the postwar years. The fact that some categories of expenditures rise and fall more rapidly than the total is, of course, a familiar phenomenon during recessions and recoveries. But in recent years this divergence of expenditure pattern has led to inflationary pressures.

During the 1955–57 period of slowly rising output and growing excess capacity, industrial wholesale prices rose by about 9 per cent. But the increase was not uniform in all industries. Price rises were generally largest among industries with the largest increases in output, and smallest among industries with the smallest increases in output. However, even in industries with declining output, prices on the average also rose. Price-output relationships in the steel and automobile industries were out of line with those of other industries—prices rose substantially further, relative to output, than the average relationship exhibited by other industries. The capital goods industries experienced a price rise of about 17 per cent over the two-year period and accounted for most of the output gain. The average price rise for all other industries (excluding steel and automobiles) was about 6 per cent, despite the fact that their combined output declined in the face of growing production capacity. If we include steel and autos among these "other" industries, the average price increase was 8 per cent.

The price-output relationships during this period appear to conform the hypothesis outlined above. In the capital goods and associated industries, both demands and prices increased rapidly. The rising demands in these areas were balanced by falling demands elsewhere; yet prices did not decline in most industries with falling demand. Indeed, cost increases, stemming at least in part from the rise of demands and profits in the capital goods industries, led to moderate price advances in industries with declining demands and growing excess capacity.

Table 2 Changes in Prices and Cost in Manufacturing Industries (*Changes in percentage points*)

Price or Cost Item	1947–57	1955–57
Price of value added:*	39.4	9.6
Unit wage cost	12.9	2.9
Unit salary cost	13.3	5.6
Unit gross margin:	10.2	−1.2
Depreciation	(5.2)	(1.0)
Profits and interest	(5.0)	(−2.2)
Unit indirect taxes†	2.9	1.3

* The "price of value added" is the price of final products minus the unit cost of materials purchased from manufacturing firms.
† "Indirect" taxes include sales, property, and all other business taxes except those levied on income.

SOURCE: Charles L. Schultze, *Prices, Costs and Output for the Postwar Decade* (Committee for Economic Development, Washington, 1960), Table 7.

The rise in fixed costs. Another important characteristic of the period was the fact that the greatest part of the rise in costs stemmed not from wage costs but from overhead costs—depreciation and salaries. Throughout the postwar period, there has been a widespread substitution of white-collar workers for direct production labor. Seventy per cent of the rise in private nonfarm employment during the decade between 1947 and 1957 represented increased employment of overhead-type labor. Between 1955 and 1957, over 80 per cent of the employment rise was in this category. The trend in manufacturing has been even sharper. All of the postwar increase in manufacturing employment has been overhead employment. In fact, between mid-1955 and mid-1957, employment of production workers declined while that of overhead personnel increased. These facts are reflected in Table 2, which represents data on the breakdown of unit costs in manufacturing.

Of the 9.6 per cent point increase in the price of manufacturing output[1] between 1955 and 1957, 5.6 percentage points were contributed by the rise in salary costs alone. The substitution of salaried overhead labor for hourly rated production labor is, of course, not in itself inflationary.

[1] The "price" of manufacturing output is the average price per unit of manufacturing products minus the cost per unit of raw materials purchased from nonmanufacturing firms. It measures the contribution of the manufacturing sector to the final price of the product.

However, such a substitution does tend to raise the proportion of relatively fixed costs in total costs. During the period after late 1955 when producers were expanding plant and equipment rapidly and increasing their staffs of professional, technical, clerical, and similar personnel, the failure of output to rise in the face of these rising fixed-cost outlays led to a sharp increase in unit costs. The evidence suggests that at least a part of the rising fixed costs was passed along via higher prices. Instead of pricing on the basis of cost calculations adjusted to the level of output in anticipation of which the overhead costs were incurred, prices were set on the basis of costs calculated at actual output rates, which fell increasingly short of anticipated output in many industries.

The relationship of costs and prices in manufacturing during the three postwar recessions seems to confirm this finding. Despite falling demand and growing excess capacity, the price of output in manufacturing rose in each recession, although by a smaller amount than unit costs. Most of the increases in costs were accounted for by rising overhead costs per unit, not by rising wage costs. This phenomenon was common to all three recessions; the reason why product prices fell during the 1949 recession and increased in 1954 and 1958 is to be found in the behavior of agricultural prices, rather than in sharply different price-cost behavior in the manufacturing sector itself.

The rising proportion of fixed costs to total costs has resulted in an increased sensitivity of productivity and unit costs to changes in output. During the 1955 to 1957 period, those industries with the largest output gains generally tended to have the largest productivity gains. A similar relationship between output gains and productivity gains has also been noted during other periods. Because of this relationship, restraints on aggregate demand that reduce output rather than simply eliminate an excess of demand over capacity may, for certain ranges of output, increase costs rather than reduce them. In other words, under certain circumstances, productivity-decreasing effects of demand restraints may be larger than any accompanying reductions in factor prices.

Policy implications

General monetary and fiscal controls. As weapons for combating inflation, general monetary and fiscal controls are supposed to achieve their objective by reducing or moderating the rate of increase in aggregate monetary demand to a level or rate of growth that matches the output potential of the economy. From the standpoint of inflation control, traditional theory tells us that it makes little difference on what sectors of the economy the controls initially impinge. If prices and wages are flexible in both directions, inflation cannot occur without an over-all excess of monetary demand. Hence, even if monetary and fiscal pressure should have a larger impact on one area of the economy than on another, relative prices will shift about, and resources will flow from one industry to another, but over-all stability will be maintained. Further, insofar as the differential sensitivity of various sectors to changes in monetary policy does not arise from imperfections in the money and capital markets, there is no "inequity" in the differential impact. This sensitivity merely reflects the fact that certain sectors are unwilling to pay the price for obtaining funds in a capital market that is not swollen by additions to the supply of money.

In the case of fiscal policy, it is admittedly difficult to conceive of changes in expenditures and, more pertinently, in taxes that would be completely neutral in their effects on the economy. Nevertheless, in traditional theory, the principle is still valid; to the extent that it is concerned with restraining inflation, fiscal policy should seek to restrain aggregate demand; differential impacts on various sectors of the economy are regarded as effects to be avoided as much as possible.

Once we abandon the neoclassical concept of a highly competitive and symmetrically flexible price system busily shuttling resources back and forth, the evaluation of general monetary and fiscal controls must be modified. The institutional facts of life in the modern American economy include: (1) downward rigidity of prices and wages; (2) highly cost-oriented pricing in many industries; (3) tendency for cost increases to spread out from industries with rapid growth in demand, productivity, and profits to other "less fortunate" industries; and (4) a changing structure of costs in the direction of more fixed costs relative to variable costs.

Under these circumstances, a rapid shift in the composition of demands can lead to a mild advance in the general price level even after excessive total spending has been eliminated. Any attempt to contain such an inflation by reducing total spending still further will lead to unemployment, and possibly a slower long-term rate of growth. General restraints of a moderate nature may have little success in reducing the rate of price increase. This is not to say, of course, that there is no role for general monetary and fiscal policy, any more than the fact that penicillin does not cure migraine headaches implies that penicillin is of no value in treating other types of maladies. But, if it is to be useful rather than harmful, the remedy must be suited to the disease.

Some alternative policies. If we grant the fact that the resource allocation process can itself lead to a slow rise in the price level, there are five possible attitudes that might reasonably be adopted.

1. Repress aggregate demand by whatever amount is needed to remove the inflation. There is always some level of unemployment and excess capacity sufficiently large to "break" wage and price rigidities. Indeed, the great depressions of the past performed this surgical function. One of the reasons why creeping inflation seems to be a recent phenomenon is that, in the past, massive doses of unemployment broke the "ratchet" under the price level.

2. Use monetary and fiscal controls as effectively as possible to eliminate aggregate excess demand. If prices still continue to rise, then adopt the advice of the ancient Oriental sage— "relax and enjoy it." Do not sacrifice full employment for the sake of restraining an inflation that amounts to only a few per cent per year. Moreover, the full utilization of capacity may itself keep productivity growing at its potential, which in turn may lift some of the pressure for cost and price increases.

3. Supplement general fiscal and monetary controls with qualitative credit controls and specific tax measures designed to infringe only on sectors with rapidly rising demands. In other words, attempt to moderate the rapid shifts in the composition of demands that are a chief factor in creeping inflation.

4. Intensify antitrust efforts in an attempt to make prices and wages more sensitive to changes in market conditions. This approach, in contrast to the third approach, would try to bring about in the economy those conditions under which the traditional inflation theory would apply. With prices and wages flexible in a downward as well as an upward direction, only an aggregate excess of demand could lead to inflation.

5. Institute direct wage and price controls. Various proposals have been offered along this line, from the mild suggestion of fact-finding boards to the full panoply of wage and price controls established by the OPA in World War II.

Selective monetary and fiscal controls and stronger doses of antitrust medicine would both represent attempts to reduce the incompatibility between the goals of full employment and price stability. Before abandoning the hope of achieving a simultaneous fulfillment of both goals, as alternatives 1 and 2 above imply, or before turning to direct wage and price controls, the possibilities of moderating creeping inflation by other means clearly deserves exploration. The remainder of this article will be devoted to a brief summary of the advantages and disadvantages of selective monetary and fiscal controls in the context of creeping inflation. (The decision to concentrate on an evaluation of these policy weapons arises solely from a lack of space and out of deference to the limited qualifications of the author to discuss the potential effectiveness of antitrust policy. It should not be taken as a judgment against the usefulness of more stringent antitrust policies.)

Selective credit and fiscal controls. No brief summary could hope to do justice to the complex issues raised by selective monetary and fiscal controls. The recent Federal Reserve Board study of consumer credit controls alone ran to five volumes and then reached no firm conclusions. Rather, what might prove useful is a consideration of the problem of selective controls in the context of an inflation arising out of shifts in resource allocation. In the past, such controls have usually been discussed either in terms of their impact on *aggregate* monetary demand or in terms of achieving a permanent shift in resource allocation toward a more "desirable" pattern. Our discussion of creeping inflation suggests a third criterion for evaluating selective controls —can they prevent the excessively rapid shifts in the composition of demands that lead to inflation, and, if they can, are the results worth the price paid to achieve them?

It was pointed out earlier that the success of general monetary controls in restraining inflation would not depend on the evenness of their impact on the various sectors of the economy, so long as prices and wages were flexible in both directions and resources could be fairly easily transferred from industry to industry. Once we postulate downward rigidity of prices and wages, however, the shift in expenditures occasioned by the uneven impact of monetary controls becomes a matter of concern.

Under such circumstances, even if general monetary restraints impinged evenly on all sectors of the economy, they could not meet the major inflationary problem without holding down the growth in output. If, on the other hand, general monetary controls were systematically uneven in their impact, it would only be a coincidence if they had their main effect on the sectors generating the inflation.

The three major and highly volatile sectors of the economy over which it seems possible to exercise some form of selective control, without at the same time venturing into direct governmental regulation of individual spending, are (1) consumer purchases of durable goods (particularly automobiles); (2) residential construction; and (3) business purchases of plant and equipment. During the 1955 to 1957 period, for example, it was the combination of rapidly rising plant and equipment expenditures and declining expenditures on residential construction and automobiles that gave us the phenomenon of a rise in the general price level unaccompanied by excessive aggregate demand.

Installment and mortgage credit. Selective controls over mortgage and consumer installment credit have been used on a number of occasions in the United States. A similar, though modified, influence on housing expenditures is exercised by the FHA and VA mortgage regulations on down payments and maturities. By regulating minimum down payments and maximum maturities on loans, such controls can influence both the magnitude and timing of expenditures on residential construction and consumer durable goods. During periods in which upward pressure on the price level was being exerted by a rapid increase in the demand for one or both of these categories of goods, reduction of maximum allowable maturities and an increase in minimum down payments could be expected to reduce demand pressures without directly reducing the demand for other categories of goods. Indeed, a reduction in the flow of funds used to finance housing and autos should increase the availability of credit to other sectors of the economy. Conversely, during periods of slackening demand for autos and housing, it would be possible, by relaxing selective

credit controls, to stimulate expenditures for such goods without weakening the monetary or fiscal restraints applied to the rest of the economy.

Residential construction and consumer installment credit are quite different in terms of their sensitivity to *general* credit controls. Mortgage credit appears to be quite susceptible, after a moderate time lag, to a general tightening of credit. In part, this sensitivity stems from the existence of a maximum nominal interest rate imposed by statute on FHA and VA mortgages. When the general level of interest rates increases, the ceiling on FHA and VA mortgage rates induces lenders to switch part of their limited supply of funds to more lucrative types of securities. Even without interest ceilings, however, institutional rigidities in the mortgage market would probably make mortgage credit more sensitive to general controls than most other sectors of the economy. Because of this sensitivity, residential construction outlays have tended, in recent years at least, to behave in a countercyclical manner, rising during recession and early recovery (easy money) and falling during later prosperity years (tight money). Consumer installment credit on the other hand is less sensitive to general credit controls.

On the whole, the fairly extensive experience in this country with selective credit controls has been quite satisfactory in terms of administrative feasibility and economic effectiveness. As the official reply of the Board of Governors of the Federal Reserve expressed it (in answer to a Joint Economic Committee questionnaire), "The comparatively favorable experience of the Federal Reserve System in administering selective regulation in the areas of stock market credit, consumer credit, and real estate credit is unique. . . ." Although the Board, in its 1957 study of consumer credit control, took a more neutral position, there is little in the study to indicate that such controls would be administratively unfeasible or economically ineffective.

Plant and equipment expenditures. Unlike the case with consumer installment credit and real estate mortgages, we have had little experience in this country in trying to control directly the volume of business expenditures on plant and equipment. During World War II and the Korean conflict, a combination of excess-profits taxes and accelerated depreciation allowances was used to channel investment goods into defense or defense-related industries. However, the purpose of selective regulation in the circumstances we have been discussing would not be to influence the direction of business investment spending, but rather to moderate its fluctuations by techniques that do not directly impinge on other areas of expenditure.

There are several possible indirect measures that might be utilized to influence the volume of business capital outlays without imposing general restraints on the entire economy. Variable depreciation allowances for tax purposes have been suggested as such a measure. Frequent variation of allowable depreciation rates, however, might lead to substantial accounting and enforcement problems. More important from the standpoint of this discussion, there is serious question about the effectiveness of moderate changes in allowable depreciation rates. One investigation of the liberalized depreciation provisions introduced by the 1954 revision of the tax code concluded that the investment stimulus from such provisions would be quite limited. For reasonable rates of discount, the excess of the present worth of liberalized depreciation over the old straight-line depreciation turns out to be quite small. For medium to high discount rates, moreover, the difference in depreciation was found to discriminate in favor of short-lived assets.

While there is no firm agreement on the subject, most statistical investigations have found that, under normal conditions, the magnitude of the flow of internally generated funds is one of the most important determinants of business investment. Varying depreciation allowances would affect the flow of funds to a firm only after the investment had been made. Furthermore, the time lags in question would overlap, so that funds would often be increasing from a liberalizing action taken in the past just when new circumstances dictated restrictions.

The Swedish government has developed a system of selectively influencing the volume of investment that seems to avoid many of the problems associated with variable depreciation allowances. In essence, it works as follows: Firms are allowed to deposit a certain proportion of their tax liabilities with the central bank. In turn, when the government wishes to stimulate investment, these reserves, in whole or in part, are released to the firms for investment purposes. In addition, a tax credit equal to a small percentage (now set at 10 per cent) of the investment outlay may also be claimed. These provisions allow the firm, at the discretion of the government, to amortize its investment immediately for tax purposes, and to receive the funds at once without waiting until the investment is completed. This does not *guarantee* that the funds will be used to raise the level of investment above what it would have been. Nevertheless, it does provide both a powerful incentive and a source of funds for investment outlays. The additional investment allowance is an added incentive.

By raising the corporate tax rate during periods in which substantial excess demands for capital goods threaten price stability, and at the same time allowing firms to reserve certain of their tax payments for future investment purposes, fluctuations in investment outlays might be moderated without applying restrictive measures to the rest of the economy.

Conclusion

Because of the downward rigidity of wages and prices and the tendency for costs to rise whenever profits increase, a sharp change in the composition of demands or a difference in rates of growth in productivity among different industries can lead to a rise in the general level of prices. In the modern American economy, creeping inflation can, therefore, occur even though the over-all demand for goods does not exceed total supply.

General monetary and fiscal controls cannot eliminate such an inflation without keeping the economy significantly below its output potential. On the other hand, monetary and fiscal policies that do not restrain over-all demand, but impinge only on the sectors where demand is excessive, may limit inflationary forces during a period of creeping inflation. Counter-inflationary monetary and fiscal policy, in other words, must take into account the composition as well as the level of total demand. Had investment demand risen more slowly between 1955 and 1957, and automobile and housing demand more evenly over the 1954 to 1957 period, we would have experienced a larger rise in output and a smaller increase in prices than that which actually occurred.

In the last few pages, we have suggested the possibility of using selective monetary and fiscal policies to combat creeping inflation. Even should such selective controls prove administratively feasible and economically effective, there is a major question that remains to be answered before their use could be recommended: Do we wish to check the dynamism of the economy by moderating the shifts in demand between various sectors of the economy? In other words, how much are we willing to pay for slowing down the rate of price increases in a manner that does not jeopardize full-employment objectives?

We are seldom faced with a policy question whose resolution does not involve balancing potential gains against potential costs. We can either attempt to alter the composition of demand by using selective monetary and fiscal policy or we can accept the moderate price increases that take place. This is the choice, so long as we wish to maintain full employment. We cannot solve the problems—indeed we shall do positive harm—by attempting to cure creeping inflation with strong doses of general monetary and fiscal medicine.

READING 17

Earlier and later readings in this section illustrate the complexity of the problems of keeping *total demand* in balance with *productive capacity* in a manner that avoids unemployment and inflation. In recent years, however, we have become concerned with still another measure of aggregate economic performance—the *growth* of productive capacity itself.

The roots of this new concern are many. Our new interest in the growth of the world's underdeveloped economies has led to new curiosity about that same growth process at home. Our involvement in the cold war with the Communist economies has forced us to ask how well we are doing in using our resources within the context of free choices. Our changing definition of urgent unfinished business at home—adjusting to automation, to a swelling labor force, to surging expectations of minority groups, to transfers of still more labor out of agriculture, and to more imports from Europe and Japan—brings us again and again to a realization that rapid growth in jobs is essential to our well-being.

How much the economy has accomplished in growth is often forgotten. The American economy of the 1960s is startlingly different from what it was just a short time ago. These next pages provide a number of ways in which we can stand back and see what we have done in the twentieth century. No one index by itself serves to tell the whole story: it takes measures of total product, per capita product, labor, and capital to see even the bare outlines of growth. Beyond that, a measure of unemployment among workers plays its part by highlighting the extent to which, in the midst of marked increases in our well-being, we still fell short of using what resources were available.

The Committee for Economic Development, which prepared the charts and commentary on these next pages, is a group of business leaders and educators organized to promote the study and understanding of current economic policy problems.

Questions to Guide the Reading

What are the strengths and weaknesses in the use of Gross National Product as an overall measure of an economy's record?

Which of the trends sketched out in these charts are likely to continue in the foreseeable future, and which are likely to change significantly from the path of the past?

A LOOK AT THE GROWTH RECORD

Committee for Economic Development

GROWTH OF GROSS NATIONAL PRODUCT

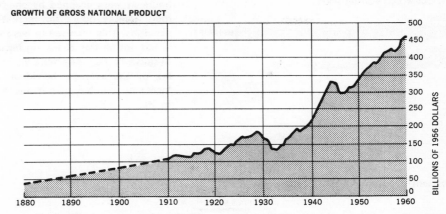

Fig. 1   Total production of goods and services was 14 times as large in 1960 as it was in 1880. The rise took place at an average rate of 3 per cent a year, and on the average total production doubled almost every twenty years. The growth was irregular: the sawtooth movement upward reflects business cycles—booms followed by recessions and depressions—which occurred during the period. Prior to 1910 these up-and-down fluctuations do not show on the chart because before then data were plotted only every tenth year. The growth is shown in terms of an unchanged dollar.

GROSS NATIONAL PRODUCT PER PERSON (in 1956 dollars)

Fig. 2   Because population more than tripled over the period, the rise in product-per-person was naturally less than the rise in total product. The product-per-person in 1960 was four times as much as in 1880. This covered not only the income-earners but everybody in the population, from day-old infants to nonagenarians.

DISPOSABLE INCOME (in 1956 dollars)

PER PERSON

PER FAMILY

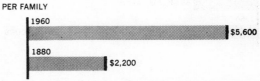

Fig. 3   Disposable income per person—what is left for each individual to spend or save after payment of all taxes—more than tripled over the period. This increase is smaller than the quadrupling of product per person due to the fact that taxes per person became higher on the average. Disposable income per family also rose, but not by the same percentage because the number of persons per family has declined.

From *Economic Growth in the United States: Its Past and Future* (Committee for Economic Development, New York, 1958), pp. 27–36. Charts updated to 1960. Reprinted with kind permission of the publisher.

AVERAGE WEEKLY WORKING HOURS

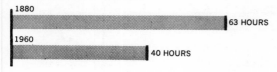

1880
63 HOURS

1960
40 HOURS

Fig. 4 An accompaniment to economic growth of great social importance has been the increase in leisure. From 1880 to 1960, average weekly hours at work dropped by one-third, leaving far more waking hours for recreational and other activities. This increase in leisure also shows up —but not on this chart—in fewer years of work, because of the many more years spent in schooling by the average individual, and the greatly increased number of persons who retire earlier in life.

GROWTH IN POPULATION AND LABOR FORCE

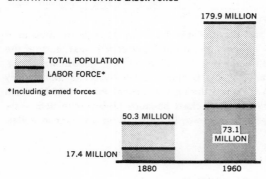

179.9 MILLION

TOTAL POPULATION
LABOR FORCE*

*Including armed forces

50.3 MILLION

73.1 MILLION

17.4 MILLION

1880   1960

Fig. 5 One of the major factors in the growth of total production over the period was the fact that population much more than tripled, and the size of the labor force more than quadrupled— the latter from 17,400,000 to 73,100,000 persons. The number of women included in the labor force grew in this same period from 2.6 million to 23.6 million.

TOTAL MAN–HOURS WORKED

1880
55 BILLION HOURS

1960
145 BILLION HOURS

Fig. 6 As a result of the much larger labor force a greater amount of work could be done in the society, measured by hours. The total man-hours of persons at work rose from 55 billion hours in 1880 to 145 billion hours in 1960. This was in spite of a marked drop in the average number of hours worked by everybody.

GROWTH IN OUTPUT PER MAN-HOUR

1880

1960

Fig. 7 Our society now produces five times as much in each hour worked as it did in 1880. This central development in the panorama of growth was made possible by many interacting factors: advancing technology, an increasing quantity of capital goods, improvements in the skills of labor and of business management, larger markets, increasing specialization—all operating within a society of great mobility and having political, economic and social institutions favorable to growth.

HORSEPOWER PER PRODUCTION WORKER IN MANUFACTURING

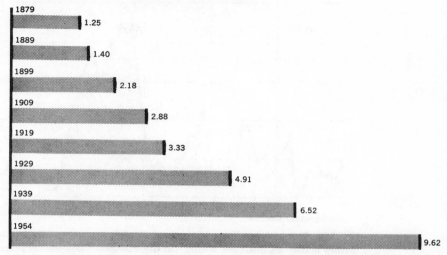

1879   1.25
1889   1.40
1899   2.18
1909   2.88
1919   3.33
1929   4.91
1939   6.52
1954   9.62

Fig. 8   High among the causes explaining ever-rising output per man-hour has been the increase in the amount of capital goods standing behind the average worker. One indication of the increase in capital is the steady advance in the horsepower available in manufacturing establishments for each production worker employed. All kinds of capital goods, however, including those provided by governmental investment, have assisted in raising output-per-man-hour.

CHANGES IN EMPLOYMENT BY INDUSTRY GROUPS

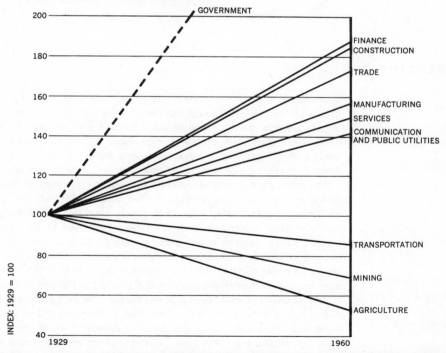

Fig. 9   This chart shows the changes that took place from 1929 to 1960 in the pattern of employment in this country. Indirectly, also, it suggests the mobility, both of labor and of capital resources, that has been a continuing characteristic feature of American economic growth.

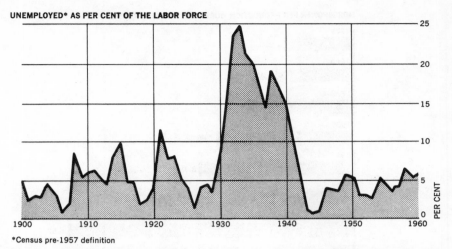

UNEMPLOYED* AS PER CENT OF THE LABOR FORCE

*Census pre-1957 definition

Fig. 10 This chart reflects the influence of the recurrent fluctuations in economic history known as business cycles. On the economic side depressions have meant the waste of resources that could have been used to produce goods for current consumption and for investment to make possible further growth. On the human side it has meant demoralization for those who could not find jobs. Deep depressions are one of the hazards we must avoid if we are to provide conditions conducive to healthy economic growth in the future. Even in prosperous years, some people are temporarily out of work because they are changing jobs or just entering the labor force, or because of readjustments in individual businesses.

READING 18

Given the spectacular achievements of the American economy in the past, where do we go from here? Having attained the highest standard of living in the world, should we now devote more of our attention and energies to less material concerns than continued economic expansion? Or do the increasing pressures of today's world call for an ever-improving economic performance in the United States? These are not easy questions to answer, for an individual or for a nation.

The difficulty begins when we first talk about measuring economic performance. There are at least two yardsticks that might be used: the yardstick of what we have done compared with what others have done, and the yardstick of what we have done compared with what we would like to do. Given the fact that human wants, even in a rich society such as ours, appear to be insatiable, the second yardstick imposes the tougher measure. Yet recent economic developments in other parts of the world seem to indicate that the former yardstick may also impose a sterner measure in the future than it has in the past.

The strength of this reading is not that it tells us how to answer the questions about our growth goals, but rather that it sharpens those questions for us. It forces us to put the *costs* of growth alongside the *gains* of growth. And it sketches in sharp outline the "why" type of inquiry that must precede wise choices. The authors are two economists. Herbert Stein is the research director for the Committee for Economic Development, and Edward F. Denison is a senior member of the research staff of The Brookings Institution.

Questions to Guide the Reading

How is it possible in a decentralized, private enterprise economy to formulate an overall growth goal and to translate that goal into an action program? How might a determination by Americans to promote greater domestic growth make itself felt?

Does greater growth inevitably mean a larger role for government in the economy? How can we construct a balance sheet of gains and costs in any such enlarged role?

WHY GROWTH?
Herbert Stein and Edward F. Denison

The American economy works well. It produces the highest income per capita ever known, and a rate of growth that raises real income per capita by half from one generation to the next. This income, and its increase, are widely distributed. Economic advance has produced a revolutionary reduction in the hours and burdens of work. Americans have great freedom to use their resources and incomes as they choose. The system is highly responsive to the demands of the people, producing with exceptional efficiency, inventiveness and adaptability the particular goods and services for which a private or public demand is expressed. Unemployment remains a problem, but one so reduced in magnitude since the 1930's as to be qualitatively different.

America and the civilization to which it belongs stand at an historic turning point. They confront a critical danger and inspiring opportunities. The danger is indicated by the phrase "cold war." Among the opportunities are to help the billion people of the underdeveloped world realize their aspirations, to reduce nationalist and racialist limitations upon man's freedom and horizons, and to push back the frontiers of human knowledge in many directions. Neither avoidance of the danger nor realization of the opportunities *requires* that the American economy work better, although better economic performance would make both objectives easier to attain. Insofar as movement toward these more important goals depends upon the availability of economic resources, the American economy as it is and is likely to be can provide them. It would be tragic

if the United States should fall prey to the danger or fail to grasp the opportunities because of preoccupation with the idea that it is not rich enough and needs to become richer faster.

Having said this, we can turn to the question of improving the performance of the American economy. We confine our discussion to the relation between the production we can expect from the economy, if it operates near its capacity, and our "needs."

From 1929 to 1957 the total production of goods and services in the United States increased at an average rate of 2.93 per cent per annum. We estimate that if unemployment is kept to about 4 per cent of the labor force, the annual rate of growth from 1957 to 1970 would be 3.27 per cent, and from 1957 to 1980 would be 3.24 per cent. At the estimated rate of growth the Gross National Product would be about $709 billion in 1970 and $972 billion in 1980.

This estimate of future growth assumes that no special measures are taken to accelerate growth other than the reduction of unemployment. It is based on an analysis of the probable contribution to growth that will be made by several factors—the number, hours of work, educational attainment and age-sex composition of the labor force, the stock of capital, the increase of knowledge, and others. It assumes, among other things, that the 1970 labor force will be about 19 per cent larger, and average annual full-time working hours about 5 per cent shorter, than in 1960; that the educational attainment of the labor force will increase sharply; that the capital

From Herbert Stein and Edward F. Denison, "High Employment and Growth in the American Economy," *Goals for Americans* (Prentice-Hall, Inc., Englewood Cliffs, N.J., 1960), pp. 163–190. Reprinted with kind permission of the authors and publisher.

stock will grow at about the rate indicated by past ratios of saving to national product under prosperous conditions.

Some of these assumptions may turn out to be incorrect. Any estimates of the future may be wrong. We offer ours only as the most reasonable basis we know for considering any policy problems to which an estimate of future growth may be relevant.

The most obvious question to ask about the projected rate of growth is: Will it be enough? In one sense of course the answer is No. The growth of production is the source from which desires for goods and services are satisfied. These desires appear limitless. However fast production may grow, some desires wll be left unsatisfied, and many will wish that growth were faster.

However, the rate of growth will not be increased by wishing. Steps will have to be taken to increase it. By and large these steps will involve some cost to someone—otherwise we could assume that they would already have been taken. (Remember that we are discussing the problem of raising the rate of growth above that which would otherwise result at high employment—whatever that rate may be.) The question then is not whether faster growth is desirable but whether it is sufficiently desirable to justify any particular step that might be taken to achieve it.

This question may be concretely illustrated as follows. We estimate that if annual hours of work were to remain at their 1957 level, rather than to decline at the rate we project, our annual rate of growth from 1957 to 1970 would be 3.6 per cent instead of 3.3 per cent. Faster growth is a good thing and reduction of hours of work is a good thing. The question is whether increasing the rate of growth is more important than reducing hours of work. Similar questions can be asked about increasing immigration, or employment of women, or expenditures for education, or taxes for public investment, or tax changes to promote private investment, or expenditures for research.

When the question is put in this way it becomes obvious that the authors of this paper cannot responsibly pretend to answer it. We can try to illuminate the benefits of more rapid growth and indicate the costs of achieving it. But whether the benefits are worth the costs can be answered only by those affected or by those making the decisions. The costs and benefits are not reducible to any common terms that permit their objective measurement and comparison. In the end the decision will have to reflect subjective judgments, and insofar as they are collective decisions they

will have to reflect some consensus of subjective judgments.

Whether a collective decision about the rate of growth should be made, through government, is in our opinion a real and serious question. The alternative view is that the desirable rate of growth and the correct means to achieve it are those that would emerge from private decisions. These would inevitably be affected by the action of government in discharging its important functions. But these functions do not include the explicit determination of the rate of growth. We believe that there is much to be said for this position, and we trust that it will receive due weight in public discussion of growth. We do not examine this position here only because it seems more fruitful to use our limited space to indicate what choices are available in the economic system if collective choices are to be made.

How much is growth worth?

If our economy grows at the rate we project, 3.3 per cent per annum, total output (Gross National Product) will be about $710 billion in 1970. If it grows at 4 per cent per annum, GNP in 1970 will be about $780 billion. The value of the higher rate of growth is $70 billion of output in 1970 and corresponding amounts in other years.

How much is this $70 billion worth? Obviously, the answer will depend upon what the $70 billion consists of and what wants it satisfies. If it includes critical defense expenditures, the caloric intake necessary for sustaining the population, the capital assistance that would set the underdeveloped world on the road to growth, then the $70 billion will be of the utmost importance. But anyone can think of possible uses of $70 billion that would be of little importance.

One can conceive of all possible uses of output being ranked in an endless descending series from the most important to the less important, to those of no importance at all, to those of negative value. Ideally, with $710 billion of GNP we would go down from the top of this list through the $710 billion most important uses. If we had another $70 billion of GNP we would take the next most important $70 billion of uses, all of which would be less valuable than any of the first $710 billion. The value of the additional $70 billion would be much less than 10 per cent of the value of the first $710 billion.

It may be that the actual American selection of uses of output does not conform to this pattern. Possibly we select more or less at random from the most important, less important, and unimportant uses. In this case the additional $70 billion of output might be as valuable, dollar for dollar, as the first $710 billion.

There might even be a systematic bias in the process, which causes the less important needs to be satisfied before the more important. If so, the needs satisfied by the additional $70 billion of output would be much more important, on the average, than those satisfied by the first $710 billion.

The importance of more rapid growth depends critically upon how well we allocate our output among our needs. This simply means that if we can count on devoting our expected output to satisfying our most urgent needs, additional output will be only as valuable as the satisfaction of our less urgent needs.

As the authors see it, the key current question about the allocation of output relates to the division between private and public uses. There may be limits upon the amount of public expenditure that keep critical public needs from being met, even though much less important private needs are met. Suppose, for example, that we cannot or will not spend more than 20 per cent of the gross national product for public purposes. If the gross national product in 1970 is $710 billion we can have only $142 billion of public expenditures, even though this may leave unmet many public needs more important than the needs satisfied by some of the $568 billion of private expenditures. The value of raising the GNP would then lie in the additional public expenditures it would permit.

It should be understood that in this paper we have made no evaluation of the need for additional public expenditure. Here we are concerned only to explore the implications for economic growth on the hypothesis that a very large increase of public expenditure is necessary.

There are two main possibilities to be considered. One is that we cannot raise tax rates above their present levels, at least without serious effects upon economic growth. The other is that we *will* not raise tax rates. In either case the yield of the existing tax rates sets a limit to public expenditure, and the only way to raise that expenditure would be to increase the yield of the existing tax rates by increasing the rate of economic growth.

Granted a willingness to raise tax rates, it must be recognized that certain patterns of tax increase might tend to retard the rate of growth.

But substantial additions to revenue can be obtained without such an effect. This might involve some combination of (a) increases in the beginning rate of individual income tax (b) a broadening of the income tax base by reduction of exemptions and exclusions and (c) increased taxation of consumption. Such taxation would be burdensome, but this burden is simply that which is implicit in any decision to sacrifice private consumption for public expenditures.

Whether higher public expenditures financed by higher taxes will retard the rate of economic growth depends not only on the character of the taxes but also on the character of the expenditures. If the expenditure increase is heavily weighted with public investment, research, education, and defense programs with a large research content, and if the taxation impinges almost entirely on private consumption, the net effect may be a higher rate of growth.

The argument to this point may be summarized as follows: if the national product is wisely used, the contribution of a higher rate of economic growth would be the satisfaction of less critical needs, not of the most critical needs. But the less critical needs are still worth satisfying, and should not be disregarded. They motivate a large part of the work done in this country.

If this country does not allocate its output to the most important uses, it cannot be sure that any specified rate of growth or level of output will satisfy its critical needs. In this case there are two possibilities. One is to increase the rate of growth, which would probably increase the likelihood that important needs would be met. The other is to become more intelligent in recognizing and responding to vital needs. The latter is essential whatever is done about the former. If we are not wise in the use of our resources, we cannot expect the abundance of our resources always to compensate.

The competition of Soviet growth

Up to this point we have been discussing the value of more rapid growth as a means of satisfying private or public needs for goods and services. In the present state of the world, rapid growth of the American economy may have an additional value.

Let us postulate this situation. The Soviet economy is now growing at a percentage rate higher than ours. If this should continue, the absolute annual growth of the Soviet economy will overtake our growth (it may already have done so). Although there are strong reasons to believe that the Soviet Union will be unable to maintain a growth rate faster than ours once it has achieved a comparable level of technical efficiency, let us nonetheless assume that it will do so. Suppose further that, despite this, the United States is able to maintain an adequate military establishment, provide for necessary public services and sustain a rate of growth of private income that is satisfactory to the American people individually. Would we then regard our rate of growth as adequate?

This is an extremely difficult question to answer. It requires us to project our imaginations into a totally new economic, political and psychological situation. We, our allies, neutral nations, and the Soviet bloc are all deeply affected by the vision of the United States as by far the world's richest and economically strongest country. It is hard to conceive a world in which this would not be true.

But it seems possible that a change to a situation in which the Soviet economy is generally recognized to be growing faster than ours, not only in percentages but also absolutely, not in spurts but steadily, and is approaching ours in total size, could have profound consequences. It could greatly strengthen the confidence of the Russians in their own system, increase the attraction of the Communist system for the independent, underdeveloped countries, worry our allies about their reliance upon us, and weaken our own morale.

These consequences might not follow. Certainly they are paradoxical on their face. They imply that in order to increase the attraction of our system to populations with average per capita incomes of $100 we, with per capita incomes of $2,000, must become still richer faster. They imply that even though we fully discharge our real obligations to our allies, they will lose confidence in us because we do not choose to raise our personal consumption more rapidly. They imply that the rest of the world will not evaluate us by the standards we choose for ourselves but will compel us to be measured by standards made in Moscow.

Moreover no one really knows what the standards are in the production race upon which world opinion is said to hinge. We do not know whether the Soviet GNP is now one-third of ours or two-thirds of ours, because the composition of their GNP is so different from ours. And it is not clear whether the race is in GNP at all, or in steel production, or in butter consumption per capita. Each side presumably wants to race on its own track and to persuade the world that it is the right track. The outcome may depend as much on the persuasion as on the running.

Nevertheless the possibility described cannot be ignored. Accelerating our pace in the production race is probably a positive factor for our national security. How important a factor it is, the authors cannot pretend to say. This is a question the American people will have to decide on the advice of people more expert than we in the politics and psychology of the cold war. If they should decide that it is important, this would, in our opinion, be the strongest reason for a collective decision to increase the rate of growth.

The costs of accelerating growth must still be considered. We do not do *everything* that might promote our national security. Especially, we want to promote our national security in the most efficient way. Somehow we must judge whether a cost of x spent in accelerating growth will yield more in national security than the same cost spent for weapons, or for foreign aid, or for space exploration, or for education, or for reducing racial discrimination, or for tempering nationalism, or for many other things that affect our military, political and psychological position in the cold war.

How might we grow?

On the basis of our estimates, the national product could be raised one per cent above what it would otherwise be in 1970, which would add .1 per cent to the annual growth rate over the next ten years, by any one of the following means:

Double the rate of net immigration during the next decade; or

Curtail by about one-third the reduction that might otherwise be expected in standard annual working hours; or

Reduce by one-eighth the loss of labor resulting from illness, accidents, seasonal fluctuations, excess labor in agriculture, illegal activities, concentrated long-term unemployment, and labor disputes; or

Raise the proportion of gross national product devoted to net investment 1.1 percentage points above what it would otherwise be throughout the next ten years.

This result might also be achieved by an assault

on obstacles to the most effective use of resources and on immobility; by an even greater increase in research outlays than is now in prospect; by more effective allocation and organization of the research effort; or by narrowing the gap between the average level of techniques and the best known. The yield from these has not been quantified, but we believe that the effort required to add 1 per cent to the 1970 national product through any of these channels would be major, not trivial.

Increase in education is a major source of long-term growth, but it is already too late to raise 1970 output by lengthening the education of those now attending school.

We of course cannot estimate the effort that the American people might be willing to undertake to increase the rate of growth by these means. Without an extraordinary concerted effort, however, we doubt that the effect would be "big," if by "big" is meant the order of magnitude suggested by an increase from 3 per cent to 4 per cent, or from 4 per cent to 5 per cent. This is not a surprising conclusion. There is no reason to expect an increase in growth out of proportion to the increase in the forces that produce growth. An increase from 3 per cent to 4 per cent is an increase of one-third; an increase from 3 per cent to 5 per cent is an increase of two-thirds. The authors would not accept this criterion of bigness. We consider differences much smaller than this important and, if achieved by means that are worth their cost, well worth seeking.

Economic growth is a good thing, and it is tempting to elevate any good thing to the state of a goal of national policy. The main point of our paper is that the establishment of such a goal is wise only if the benefits of the "good thing" are worth its costs. We have neither invented nor discovered the costs. In fact, we suppose that consciousness of these costs has weighed in the decisions not to undertake the measures that might have given us more rapid growth in the past.

In closing, the authors repeat what was said at the outset. We do not, in this paper, attempt to decide what the public attitude toward the rate of growth should be. This is a question that the people must decide, referring to the kinds of considerations discussed here but also in the end expressing their own values, their own views of what is worth what.

READING 19

The general factors underlying a nation's growth rate are easy enough to list. But to make some specific judgments on the separate contributions of these factors in the past or, more so, in the future requires a brave man. Yet even the roughest of quantitative measures are necessary preludes to studying the gains and costs of any new proposal, as suggested by Stein and Denison in the previous reading.

Here Robert M. Solow, professor of economics at Massachusetts Institute of Technology, pulls together much of the current thinking on the "real" or supply side of economic growth. This side tells us what we might accomplish, but growth requires a demand for the products of the higher growth rate as much as it does a supply of those products. The paper, then, must be read as addressing itself to one key issue (growth of capacity), while leaving another (growth of demand) to be dealt with in the fiscal and monetary articles which follow this section.

Questions to Guide the Reading

What are the principal policy choices that might flow from an acceptance of the Solow estimates on the relative importance of the various factors contributing to our growth record to date?

How important to the American economy are the differences between the "three percenters" and "four percenters" in the debate on growth?

SOURCES AND OUTLOOK FOR GROWTH
Robert M. Solow

To me, economic growth means the expansion of the economy's potential output, its capacity to produce. What is produced in a particular quarter or year or decade cannot for long exceed the economy's normal potential or capacity. But it may well fall short, if the level of demand is insufficient to buy what the economy is capable of producing.

If we concentrate on economic growth as the growth of capacity to produce rather than the growth of demand, which is an important but separate problem, the foundation of any broad view must evaluate the major determinants of potential output and productivity in an economy, the chances of influencing them and the effectiveness of changes in the determinants on capacity output itself.

Determinants of potential output

Everyone is in broad agreement about the nature of the major determinants of potential output, but there is some disagreement about their relative influence, and recent research has led to some revision of earlier opinions. The main sources of potential output we can name pretty clearly:

1. The first determinant is the number of people available for employment; the number of hours they wish to work; and the level and distribution of skills, education, health and attitudes toward work. I suppose one ought to include managerial and entrepreneurial knowledge and ability as a special kind of labor, or perhaps it deserves a heading to itself.

2. The second broad and important determinant is the size of the existing stock of capital goods and its distribution by age, by industry and by location.

3. The third important determinant is the level of technology. Here one must distinguish between the extent of technological knowledge and the degree to which it can be made effective, because that may depend in large part on the age distribution of the existing capital stock. There is a sense in which the whole civilized world shares the discoveries of modern science and engineering on an equal basis, but an economy saddled with an antiquated stock of capital may be unable to use what in principle it knows.

4. The fourth determinant, I would say, is the terms on which the economy has access to natural resources, whether through domestic production or through imports.

5. The fifth determinant is the efficiency with which resources are allocated to different economic ends; the extent of monopolistic or other barriers to the movement of capital and labor from low productivity to high productivity uses; and the degree of resistance to the introduction of new technology.

If these are the basic determinants of potential output, then the growth of productive capacity is largely limited by the rate at which the basic determinants can be expanded and improved. That, in turn, depends upon the ease with which these determinants themselves can be influenced by conscious policy or fortuitous events, and upon the sensitivity of potential output to changes in the determinants themselves.

Opinions about this have changed drastically over the last century, and even over the last dozen years. The classical economists believed that the ultimate limit to economic growth was given by the finite availability of natural resources. It has always been a source of wonder to me how such intelligent and perceptive men, writing at a time when the industrial revolution had clearly taken secure hold on England, could so underestimate the power of technological progress in offsetting the effects of diminishing returns. Maybe this is a high standard to apply. We still occasionally read dire predictions that we are about to run out of natural resources.

Technology and resource scarcity

The truth is, of course, that as certain raw materials become physically scarce, it becomes more expensive to extract them from nature; but this tendency is offset partly by technical progress, partly by investment in improved methods and

From Robert M. Solow, "Economic Growth and Residential Housing," in *Conference on Savings and Residential Financing, 1962 Proceedings* (United States Savings and Loan League, Chicago, 1962), pp. 120–139. Reprinted with kind permission of the author and publisher.

management, partly by increased reliance on imports and partly by the substitution of cheap raw materials for expensive ones. Even these "partly's" may not add up to the whole. If the offsets are not fully effective, resources can be obtained at somewhat higher cost by digging deeper, using leaner ores, conserving wastes and using heavier equipment. The necessity of devoting more labor and capital to extractive industry is indeed equivalent to a net decline in the productivity of the economy as a whole; but it certainly does not set, as far as we can see, an absolute limit to the growth of the economy.

One way of measuring the effects of resource scarcity is by looking at the long-term trend of raw materials prices relative to finished product prices in general. When one does so, one finds that all raw materials are now about 25% more expensive relative to finished products than they were at the turn of the century, but only 5% more expensive than they were in 1925–1959. More interesting than this very gentle tendency toward increased real cost of raw materials is the wide variety of behavior exhibited by different classes of raw materials. Lumber products have indeed increased rapidly in relative price, almost doubling since 1925–1929, and almost tripling since the turn of the century. This is the way Ricardo presumably expected all raw materials to behave. But there actually may have been some tendency for this trend to moderate in recent years. Mineral construction materials, on the other hand, are cheaper relative to finished goods in general than they were at the turn of the century, though not quite as cheap as they were just before 1914. In any case, the only sound conclusion is that there is much less to natural resource scarcity than meets the eye.

We are a long way from having reliable quantitative answers to the kind of question I am now discussing, but about some gross facts I think we can be fairly confident. I believe, for instance, that it would now be generally accepted that earlier thinking on this subject substantially underestimated the influence of improving the quality of human resources on the economy's capacity to produce.

Educational level and income

This is a particularly tricky area in which to make quantitative inferences, mainly because of the difficulty of imputing observed differences in income at different educational levels in part to differences in native ability and in part to edu-

cation itself. But if one takes Edward Denison's recent estimates as a fair example, he attributes some 40% of the average annual growth between 1929 and 1957 in national income per person employed to the effects of education in improving the quality of the average man-hour of work. Between 1909 and 1929, he estimates the contribution of education to have been only about a quarter of the annual growth rate in productivity. Notice that this estimate excludes the contribution of education to the advance of knowledge itself.

In other words, had the educational level of the labor force remained stationary where it was in 1929, national income per person employed would have risen not at an average annual rate of 1.6%, as it did between 1929 and 1957, but at something less than 1.0% per year. That is a big difference.

The other big revaluation that has taken place in recent years has to do with the relative importance of capital investment and technical change. The older economists seemed to think of increases in output per man-hour (of constant quality, though they did not often mention that) as being primarily or exclusively a matter of the deepening of capital, of increased capital per worker. Within the last 10 years, research done by Schmookler, Abramovitz, Kendrick and others, including myself, seemed to show that this was not the case. An explanation of the macroeconomic facts appeared to require the conclusion that observed increases in output per man-hour over a 50-year period had only little to do with the increase in capital per worker. The bulk of the explanation, between 85% and 90%, had to come from other sources such as labor quality, technological progress and the like.

Capital investment and economic growth

This downgrading of fixed investment as a source of growth had genuine policy implications. Calculations based on these ideas suggested that substantial rates of growth were obtainable with little or no net investment, and that any visible acceleration of growth through the stimulation of capital formation would require fantastic amounts of investment—although people sometimes forget that with net investment only about half of gross, a 10% increase in the rate of gross investment means in the short run a 20% increase in the rate of net investment.

I finally came to think that this undervaluation, or downgrading, of the importance of capital investment was really a little implausible and that all reasoning like that, including my own, overlooked the fact that at least some technological progress requires being embodied in newly designed types of fixed capital before it becomes effective in production. Investment thus serves the purpose not only of adding to the stock of capital per worker, but also of improving its quality, of carrying new technology into operation.

You could easily devise numerical examples that would convince you that this could make a real difference in the story. When account is taken of "embodied" inventions, the kind of inventions that need new kinds of capital to become effective, then a surge in the rate of capital formation will have bigger effects on potential output than the simple notion of "residual" productivity increase would lead one to expect.

Some rough econometric estimates I once made seem to me to give a plausible figure for the size of the investment effort needed to support a somewhat higher growth rate over the next 10 years. For example, a growth rate of 4% annually in potential GNP between 1960 and 1970, which means a growth rate of some 4½% in realized GNP if 1970, unlike 1960, is a year of full utilization, would require investment in plant and equipment of roughly 11% of GNP as compared with about 9% in the last few years and slightly higher than we had in 1955–1957. This is on the assumption that all technical changes need to be embodied in new fixed capital.

One of the troubles with this whole line of thought is that it is just about impossible to make aggregate data tell anything about the extent to which innovations are of the embodied kind and the extent to which they are disembodied. Denison simply assumes it is half and half, and comes to the conclusion that between 1929 and 1957 less than 10% of the annual growth rate of national income per person employed can be imputed to the increase in reproducible capital per employee, while over a third of the annual growth rate of productivity in the same period can be attributed to the advance of knowledge. My casual guess would be that more than half of technical progress is the embodied kind, but I do not know how to find out.

Capital stock: size, age distribution

The extra "oomph" one gets from investment in this new view comes from the fact that a burst of investment changes not only the size of the capital stock, but also its age distribution. Lowering the average age of the capital stock gives a productivity bonus. But it is not easy to change the average age of a long-lived stock. An increase in plant and equipment investment relative to GNP will eventually move the age distribution of capital as far as it is ever going to move it, and then it will not move it any further. Then the average age remains stationary and the higher growth rate lapses back to what it was when the investment quota was lower, relative to GNP. Output will be forever at a higher level, but the very long-run growth rate will not change. But over a 10- or 20-year period, the change in the investment quota might make a substantial difference.

I might conclude this section by remarking that we probably know least about the contribution to economic growth that could be made by more efficient allocation of resources, the costs of monopoly, restriction and immobility. In some areas—agriculture, perhaps—the costs may be great, and therefore the growth advantage, temporary of course, from removing the restriction may be correspondingly great. But not much is known about the economic costs of monopoly and similar sources or malallocation.

I have been dealing at a fairly general level with the trends in ideas about economic growth. When one comes to specific projections of the prospects for economic growth in the United States over the next decade, it turns out that there are at least two schools of thought. They might be described as the three-percenters and the four-percenters. The five-percenter is a dying race.

Three-percenters vs. four-percenters

The most important three-percenter is Edward Denison, whose monumental work I have already cited. Denison estimates that in the absence of a massive policy effort to raise the rate of growth—and the elements of that effort need only be mentioned to scare the pants off you—potential output will grow at something like 3.3% a year over the next decade. Note that this growth rate refers to potential output, not realized output. If, as the evidence seems to suggest, real GNP in 1960 fell 5% or 6% below potential, then the path from 1960 to full employment in 1970 would rise at about 3.8% or 3.9% a year on the average.

The four-percenters are represented by the National Planning Association, the Council of

Economic Advisers and apparently John F. Kennedy. They estimate that a moderate policy program favoring economic growth could make potential output rise at something like 4% a year between 1960 and 1970—perhaps even a little faster. And if the path to 1970 winds up at full employment, the actual annual growth rate could exceed 4½%.

No one has yet tried to trace back the difference between the two schools of thought to critical hypotheses or evaluations, and I think it is worth doing. Maybe we ought to begin by laying out the assumptions the two schools hold in common. One would suppose that both schools of thought would at least begin from one piece of common ground: the rate of growth in the past. But even there one finds a vague but important difference in view.

The long-term rate of growth of potential GNP in the United States from 1929 to 1960, or even from 1909 to 1960, is about 3% a year. The three-percenters tend to start from that figure and ask where one might find grounds to hope for an acceleration. But the 15 years since the end of the Second World War have already seen a substantial acceleration beyond 3%. Between 1947 and 1960, actual GNP rose at an average rate of 3½%, and rough allowance for the slack existing in 1960 can raise the postwar rate of growth of potential output to 4%. Some of that extraordinarily rapid growth was undoubtedly a consequence of unrepeatable factors: the war itself, and the long depression that preceded it. Even so, the Council of Economic Advisers has estimated that since 1954 or 1955, by which time the legacy of war and depression had probably run its course, potential GNP has been increasing at some 3½% a year.

The four-percenters tend to start from the more recent record, and this explains in part their more optimistic conclusions. But one cannot decide the issue on such grounds. There is no general law of economics or nature which tells you whether the last 50 years or the last 15 years provide a better guide to the next 10 years. No analogies about tails wagging dogs or dogs wagging tails have any explanatory power, because the economy, whatever it is, is probably not a dog. You have to look closer.

Labor force and hours worked

The least controversial element in projections of economic growth for the 1960s is the labor force and the trend of annual hours worked. The three-percenters and the four-percenters are in rough agreement that the labor force will grow at an annual rate of about 1¾% between 1960 and 1970, substantially faster than the 1.3% annual rate recorded between 1947 and 1960. As usual, part of this growth in potential employment will be offset by a continuation of the trend toward shorter hours. The fairly universal conclusion is that annual man-hours at full employment will rise at about 1¼% a year to 1970, compared with ¾ of 1% from 1947 to 1960. This already gives us a leg up toward faster growth of aggregate output during the coming decade. But what actually happens depends, of course, on the path of output per man-hour, and that is the nub of the difference between the two schools of thought.

Between 1947 and 1960, potential GNP per man-hour rose at an annual rate of 3.2% a year— 3.8% between 1947 and 1954, and 2.6% between 1954 and 1960. If productivity rises between 1960 and 1970 at the same rate as it did from 1954 to 1960, potential GNP will grow at an annual rate of 3.8% a year in the coming decade. If productivity rises somewhat faster than it did between 1954 and 1960, but slightly less fast than between 1947 and 1960, and considerably slower than between 1947 and 1954—say, at 3% a year or thereabouts—then potential GNP can rise at 4% a year between now and 1970. To bring about this acceleration will cost something, perhaps an increase in the plant and equipment share in GNP from the 9.5% of 1954–1960 (even with 1955–1957) toward the 11.2% of 1947–1954. Indeed, the four-percenters project for 1960 to 1970 a growth in the stock of capital of about 3½% a year, about the rate achieved from 1947 to 1960, and a bit faster than 1954–1960.

The three-percenters, on the other hand, project a rise in output per man-hour at only about 2% a year, roughly the rate observed in the 1929–1960 period, and considerably slower than the postwar, or even the 1954–1960, rate. Correspondingly, Denison, for example, projects capital stock growth at 2.5% a year rather than 3.5%, faster than 1929–1957 (1.9% a year including the Great Depression) but slower than anything observed in the postwar period.

Sources of differences of opinion

To sum up the gross difference of opinion: Starting from the same projection for employment and hours, the four-percenters estimate productivity to rise at a rate of about 0.7% or 0.8% a year faster than the three-percenters do, and this makes the difference between 3.3% and 4.0% in the annual rate of growth of GNP.

Can we track down this difference to more specific hypotheses? We can. The seven-tenths of a point in the growth rate can be accounted for in this way:

a. The one percentage point difference in the estimated rate of growth of capital accounts for about 0.20 to 0.25 point in the rate of growth of GNP.

b. Denison estimates pure technological change to proceed at an annual rate of about 0.2 point below that of the postwar period, and this accounts for about the same difference in the rate of growth of GNP. Optimists expect no such deceleration, and some even hope for a slight increase.

c. The pessimistic projections have investment in education contributing 0.1 point less to productivity growth than in the recent past.

d. By a complicated bit of guesswork, Denison estimates that a much smaller part of the expected decline in hours worked will be offset by automatic improvement in productivity resulting from lessened fatigue and the like; this is enough to account for 0.2 percentage point in the growth of productivity and of output.

I have time for only a few cursory comments on these ultimate components of the difference between a 3% and a 4% growth of potential.

a. There can be no doubt that some part of the postwar spurt of fixed investment was a "make-up" phenomenon, and the rate of growth of the capital stock has slowed visibly in recent years. But the weakness of fixed investment is both cause and effect of the slack that has developed in the economy since 1956, and that slack is remediable by policy.

Even so, the problem should not be blinked. If there is anything to the law of diminishing returns, then extra growth of output through the deepening of capital can be bought only at the expense of a lower profit rate on capital. It is the combined job of fiscal and monetary policy to sweeten that profit rate a little at the margin and to make a somewhat lower profit rate more acceptable by lowering the return on assets alternative to real capital. There might then be difficulties on the side of saving, and this might call

for additional policy measures or be taken as a sign that economic growth is not a highly valued social goal.

b. On the rate of pure technological progress, nobody is in a position to speak with authority. There has certainly been an immense increase in research and development expenditure in the postwar period, much of it financed by the federal government and concentrated on industries connected with defense. Whether those outlays have already borne fruit or whether there is more to come, it is difficult to say. But there is perhaps a case for believing that federal policy could contribute to the acceleration of economic growth by an effort to spread into purely civilian industries the kind of technological pressure that seems to have had major results in electronics and space technology.

c. It may be that as time goes on, given the finite number of days in the year, the all but universal diffusion of primary and secondary education, and human impatience, there is an inevitable retardation in the rate at which the quality of the labor force can be improved through education. The unevenness of educational quality from state to state suggests that perhaps something can be done there to pick up the 0.1 point on the growth rate that Denison loses. I am not competent to judge.

d. On this point I think Denison is not so much vulnerable as unconvincing. His assumption is that as late as 1929, when the average employee worked about 2,500 hours a year (between 48 and 49 hours a week), any small reduction in the hours of work was fully compensated by a corresponding increase in productivity because of diminished fatigue, better attentiveness and the like. By 1957, on the other hand, when the average employee worked about 2,050 hours a year, or just about 40 hours a week, he assumes that a further slight reduction in hours was offset to the extent of 40% by the same forces. Extrapolation leads to the conclusion that further reduction in hours will be only about 20% offset and, therefore, more damaging to output.

That some such process is at work is surely true, but Denison himself emphasizes how little is known about the exact relationship. I cannot bring myself to believe that as recently as 1929 the marginal product of an additional hour worked was negative, and I suspect that those European countries which still have a workweek close to 48 hours would be surprised to learn that they could add to output by working less.

Moreover, the reduction in average hours since

1929 has been much sharper in the diminishing agricultural work force than in industry. The average workweek in manufacturing was 44 hours in 1929. It does not matter so much exactly what the degree of offset was in 1929. If the change in the offset was more gradual than Denison suggests, his conclusion would not be so pessimistic.

I conclude that when it is tracked down to its origin, the difference between the three-percenters and the four-percenters is not solidly based. That does not say who is right, but it does suggest the possibility that economic policy need not turn our society on its ear to elicit a growth of potential output near to 4% a year.

Full employment and economic growth

Here I would like to say something about the relation between full employment and economic growth as goals of policy. Does an aggressive full employment policy also stimulate economic growth or retard it?

There are a number of subquestions here which need to be disentangled. The view has recently been expressed in the United Kingdom that some decrease in the average pressure of demand on resources, accompanied by a small increase in the unemployment rate, would be desirable for several reasons and could be engineered without any deterioration in the growth rate and perhaps with some improvement.

I am not sufficiently well acquainted with conditions in the United Kingdom to hold a strong opinion on this subject, but I do not find this view wholly implausible. For one thing, continuous full employment may tend to generate inflationary pressure on prices (whether originating in labor markets or product markets) and recurrent balance-of-payments crises, which require that the upward march of demand be halted frequently.

In turn, the necessary restriction of demand, either through credit tightness or tax policy, may for one reason or another fall heavily on fixed investment. I can easily imagine that this chain of events could make it true that a little extra slack could be engineered without ultimately reducing the growth rate, and perhaps even help it over a decent interval of time.

Secondly, it is often said that a perpetually tight economy builds up immobilities, barriers to the adoption of new technology and resistance to competition. This may be so. It has been so long since the American economy operated with that

degree of tightness, that I have no fresh observations to report. What I have observed in the United States is the reverse phenomenon. Too much slack in an economy can build up the same kinds of pressures against innovation, against technological advance, against the mobility of labor and capital from declining to advancing sectors of the economy. In the United States, at least, one even observes an ebb and flow of sentiment for a shortening of the workweek with the business cycle, which relates not to any real preferences for leisure as against income but to a feeling that there is simply not enough employment to go around without a decrease in weekly hours.

Other examples are not hard to find. The movement of labor out of agriculture, for instance, is clearly intimately related to labor market conditions in industry. When urban unemployment is low, the rate of migration out of agriculture is high, and vice versa. Of course the rate of migration is also sensitive to the market for agricultural products. When farmers are doing well, as during the Korean war, even a tight demand for labor in industry will not pull up the migration rate. But that does not contradict my observations.

To take another example, the recent report of a presidentially appointed commission to study work rules on the railroads showed a majority, including all the public members, agreeing that there is altogether too much featherbedding, too much stultification of technical progress by clinging to antiquated work rules. Such commissions usually try hard, too hard, to be neutral, so the finding is almost certainly true. Now, even in a full-employment economy, an elite occupational group would probably cling to its quasi-rents, but I do not believe the resistance to change would be so great if the demand for labor in the economy at large were considerably higher.

Growth and economic efficiency

Even if I am right and the American economy loses some efficiency because the level of demand is too low, it might still be true that other economies lose some efficiency because the pressure of demand is too high. There might indeed, from this point of view, be an optimal degree of tightness. I am only concerned to say that the United States is clearly on the slack side of that. There exists no conflict on these grounds between the goals of full, or at least fuller, employment and rapid growth.

This position that—to quote a recent Report of

the Council of Economic Advisers—"a full employment economy can achieve more rapid growth than an economy alternating between boom and recession; for that reason effective stabilization policy is the first step toward a policy of economic growth" has been attacked as theoretically weak and even anti-Schumpeterian. I suppose it is the latter, but not the former.

Joseph Schumpeter argued that the business cycle is the way in which a capitalistic economy makes progress. Eliminate or damp the business cycle, and you slow down the rate of progress. More specifically, of course, Schumpeter had a theory of the bunching of technical innovations. The depression is a way of shaking the unsuccessful or obsolete ones out of the system. Anyone who believes this doctrine believes in strong medicine. The business cycle Schumpeter was thinking of, which is supposed to be necessary for capitalist progress, was not the minor postwar business cycle, but the deeper 10-year major cycle of the 19th century and the prewar years. If that is necessary for economic growth, then the almost world-wide acceleration of growth during the last 15 years becomes very difficult to explain.

Short business cycle and economic growth

Indeed, even the belief that the short business cycle is an indispensable midwife for economic growth is hard to maintain in the face of the postwar history of western European countries. Most of them have experienced faster productivity growth than we have; most of them have shown a sharper acceleration of their prewar trends; and all of them have maintained a consistently tighter pressure of demand and a consistently lower unemployment rate than we have, even allowing for differences in definition and statistical practice.

I have been arguing that steady full employment need not prejudice the growth of potential output. It is a more difficult question whether steady full employment might itself increase the rate of growth. This is once again largely a question of the rate of investment. Despite the fact that plant and equipment spending falls off in recession and rises in recovery, it is logically possible that wiping out the business cycle might not increase the average rate of investment relative to aggregate output. It might be that over a complete business cycle we get all the investment we would get even if the business cycle were not there, only we get it concentrated in periods of high employment, filling in the holes left by periods of low employment.

If, for example, investment were governed simply by the acceleration principle, this would be the case. Nobody can say for sure what the true state of affairs is. I am inclined to believe that the main effect of high-level stability on the volume of investment would be a reduction in the riskiness of investment. It seems plausible that one of the reasons businesses seem to demand a high expected rate of return on new projects is to compensate for the risk of inadequate markets.

The confident expectation of full employment by reducing that risk would probably make for a somewhat lower acceptable average rate of return. In my neoclassical view, that is an important part of the battle to generate higher capacity through the deepening of capital, for, apart from the effects of technical progress, each successive increment to productivity bought in this way involves diminished profitability. If I am right on this, an aggressive full-employment policy would elicit more investment averaged over a cycle than we now have, and this would contribute to economic growth. This argument also suggests that an important part of a fiscal policy designed to add to growth through investment might be an extension of income averaging for tax purposes, more complete loss offsets for corporations and, in this way, some socialization of risk.

READING 20

It took America a long time to getting around to creating a central bank for bankers. But, while the Federal Reserve System which emerged in 1913 was a product of delays and compromises, it went on to assume a far bigger place in the economy than its founders could have imagined. Some of its roles—clearing house for checks, and bank supervisor, for example—could equally well be fulfilled elsewhere in the financial world. But its influence on the nation's money supply is big and basic. By expanding or contracting the member banks' reserves, the "Fed" seeks to make money either more available and cheaper, or less available and dearer for loans to industry or consumers.

Exactly how effective these deliberate changes in the money supply are is a subject on which economists will differ—and on which the next readings will focus. But there is little disagreement on the proposition that the members of the Fed's Board of Governors are among the economy's more important decision makers in influencing the levels of jobs, incomes, prices, and domestic gold stocks. How then does the Fed work? Who has influence on its decisions, and how is that influence employed?

Charles R. Whittlesey, professor of finance and economics at the University of Pennsylvania, describes some of the changes in the operation of the system since its inception fifty years ago, and provides an essential part of the structural background for the recommendations which follow in the later readings.

Questions to Guide the Reading

Does the System, as described in this reading, provide (1) adequate power for the key men to implement their policy decisions and (2) adequate checks against possible abuse of that power?

How well does the System function in raising critical monetary questions for review and in bringing expert knowledge and judgment to bear on those questions?

POWER AND INFLUENCE IN THE "FED"
Charles R. Whittlesey

Legislation authorising the establishment of the Federal Reserve System was enacted in 1913 and operations began just a few weeks after the start of the First World War. As its first half century draws to a close the System is a very different institution from what was contemplated by its founders. It is not too much to say that but for its ability to adapt to changing needs and conditions, the Federal Reserve System would be as out of date as was the National Banking System whose accumulated shortcomings the Federal Reserve Act was designed to remedy.

Many of the changes in the Federal Reserve have been common to central banks generally. New mechanical techniques have been developed, new objectives recognised, and new instruments of policy adopted. The forms taken are not necessarily the same as abroad: there is less use of selective instruments and directives, for example; and the co-ordination of open market operations by a system-wide Federal Open Market Committee acting through the New York Federal

Reserve Bank is an ingenious American improvisation. Developments such as these are part of everyday knowledge.

In addition, there have been important administrative changes, some of which are hardly recognised outside the System itself. Partly as a consequence of these changes, proposals have been advanced which promise to be the subject of continuing controversy and conceivably of far-reaching actions. The purpose of the following discussion is to call attention to the more significant of the changes and to examine certain proposed reforms.

Concentration of power in the chairman of the Board of Governors

In testimony before the Senate Finance Committee a number of years ago Marriner Eccles declared that the Federal Reserve System is run by seven men. By this he meant the seven members of the Board of Governors. Mr. Eccles, it

From Charles R. Whittlesey, "Power and Influence in the Federal Reserve System," *Economica*, Vol. XXX, No. 117, February, 1963. Reprinted with kind permission of the author and publisher.

will be remembered, was the prominent Utah banker who came to the Board early in the Roosevelt Administration and was its chairman for a dozen years before, during, and after the Second World War. It was during his administration that legislation was passed making the Board of Governors the centre of power for the System.

A few days after Eccles appeared, the present Chairman, William McChesney Martin, Jr., testified before the same committee that the number of those running the system should be put at not seven but 127. This total comprises the seven Governors, presidents of the 12 Reserve banks and nine directors from each of the Reserve banks. Neither of these figures is particularly significant, a fact which both men, of course, fully realised: quite different (in some cases negligible) degrees of authority are exercised by different individuals within the seven-member group; and most of the 127 have little actual power while there are others outside this total whose influence is very considerable. These observations will become clear as we proceed.

Anyone familiar with the history of the Federal Reserve System is well aware of the dominant influence exercised by Mr. Eccles during his incumbency as Chairman of the Board of Governors, and more recently by Mr. Martin. There is relatively little disposition inside or outside the System to question either Mr. Martin's abilities or his intentions, although there are a good many who would challenge some of the policies for which he has stood. But there are widespread misgivings as to the wisdom of allowing a situation to continue in which one man is able to exert such dominating authority as he now holds over so important an instrument of government and economic life as the central bank.

The power resting in the hands of the Chairman is primarily traceable to three sources. In the first place, he is likely to have a decisive part in appointments to the Board of Governors and to the two top administrative posts in each of the regional Reserve banks. Secondly, he is the spokesman for the System in official relations at the highest levels. This means that he appears frequently before committees of Congress and is well known personally to leaders there. He meets at regular weekly intervals with the Secretary of the Treasury; and he may find the President turning to him for counsel and aid, as seems to have been done frequently by both Eisenhower and Kennedy.

Finally, the Chairman is in a position to influence the decisions of the Federal Open Market Committee (F.O.M.C.), the body which sets policy for the regulation of credit. Regulation of credit is the principal basis of Federal Reserve control over economic activity. In this relationship, therefore, the influence of the Chairman transcends the Federal Reserve System and extends to the economy as a whole. (The manner in which the F.O.M.C. operates, giving the Chairman such great influence, will be described presently.)

In addition, the power wielded by the Chairman is greatly influenced by the personal qualities of the man. This was true of Mr. Eccles and it is notably true in the case of Mr. Martin. As the son of an early president of the St. Louis Federal Reserve Bank, Mr. Martin has a lifelong knowledge of and devotion to the Federal Reserve System. His sincerity and public spiritedness combined with unusual personal charm have greatly impressed the political leaders with whom he comes into almost daily contact. These qualities have been similarly helpful in his dealings with other central bankers and with representatives of foreign governments, as well as in his relations with businessmen and the general public. Moreover, they strengthen his position, as does the prestige derived from these other associations, with his colleagues on the Board and throughout the Federal Reserve System. All this is combined with a unique singleness of purpose, persuasiveness, and patience.

It is with good reason, then, that a recent study by two former Federal Reserve staff members, now professors at leading universities, places the Chairman at the top of a descending series of what they term the "nodes of power" in the Federal Reserve System. Such a listing fails, however, to suggest how much greater the power of the Chairman is than that of any of the other "nodes." Nor does it bring out clearly enough that the power now held by the Chairman probably resides less in the office than in the particular individual occupying the office. The listing is as follows:

1. Chairman of the Board of Governors.
2. Other Governors.
3. Staff of the Board, particularly the senior advisers.
4. Federal Open Market Committee.
5. Trading desk of the Federal Reserve Bank of New York.

6. President of the Federal Reserve Bank of New York.

7. Other Reserve bank presidents.

8. Boards of directors of the regional Federal Reserve banks.

9. System-wide committees, standing and *ad hoc*.

10. Federal Advisory Council.

The listing given is offered as the personal evaluation of the authors (who base their judgment on knowledge gained as Reserve bank employees) and is to be accepted as such. It would probably be challenged at a number of points, e.g., that the other Governors are placed too high and the presidents of the Reserve Banks including New York too low on the scale. Admittedly the listing is as of the present moment: there have been times when the head of the New York Federal Reserve Bank would have stood at the top. No informed person would deny, however, the dominant position currently held by Mr. Martin. This is the point that matters. Rather than concern ourselves with other details it is appropriate to turn now to two other significant changes of the past decade—which are reflected, it may be noted, in the above listing.

Transformation of the Federal Open Market Committee

The necessity of co-ordinating the System's open market operations as an instrument of credit control, which was not contemplated in the original Federal Reserve Act, led to the creation of an informal open market committee in the early 1920's. It was given legal status, with prescribed form and procedures, by the Banking Act of 1933. Under the leadership of Chairman Martin, changes have now been introduced in the conduct of the Committee which constitute a landmark in the history of the Federal Reserve System.

Formerly, decisions relating to open market operations were delegated to a sub-committee. The full committee, which met only four times a year, often did little more than ratify actions taken by the sub-committee, though occasionally major policy action was undertaken. This procedure has now been changed. The sub-committee was abolished in 1955 and the F.O.M.C. meets every three weeks to decide on policy matters. The meetings are attended by the Board of Governors and the presidents of all twelve Reserve

banks, as well as a considerable number of staff officers.

The conduct of the meetings, though informal, follows a clearly established routine. After other preliminaries, an analysis of business and financial conditions is presented by senior staff members. Each of the governors and presidents is then expected to offer his views, the order of the participation alternating from meeting to meeting. At the end the Chairman speaks. His remarks may take the form of a summary giving a consensus of the opinions and recommendations of the rest of the group. Where judgments are divided he may tip the scales for one side or the other. And sometimes, if he feels strongly on a particular issue, he will make a case for his position whether or not it conforms to that of others. Members are given an opportunity to comment on the Chairman's remarks, and the precise wording of the final directive to the Account Manager is specifically voted upon.

The Account Manager, an officer of the New York Federal Reserve Bank whose duty it is to carry out the open market policies laid down by the Committee, is asked if the wishes of the committee are clear to him. He ordinarily says that they are. It is reasonable to suppose that the views of the Chairman as presented at the end of the session contribute strongly to the impressions formed by the Account Manager. In carrying out for the next three weeks the directives laid down in this manner there is not only considerable latitude but also the simple necessity, in the face of developing conditions, for the Account Manager to exercise his own judgment. It is here that the influence of the trading desk of the New York bank becomes apparent.

Two consequences of the change in procedures of the F.O.M.C. are clear from what has been said. One is the way in which it contributes to the power of the Chairman. The other is the resulting influence exercised by the trading desk. A third effect is less obvious but not necessarily less important. This is the contribution which the method of conducting the Committee has made toward unifying the System and raising the quality of administration.

The full and frequent meetings of the Committee afford access throughout the System to knowledge as to what goes on at the top, and why. The representatives of every bank participate along with those of all the other banks. The presidents are brought into direct personal contact every three weeks with members of the Board and with one another. The result has been to promote friendly relations and high morale. The unifying tendencies extend to all parts of the System, a fact of considerable importance in view of its decentralised regional structure.

The attention devoted to an airing of all aspects of central banking problems at the tri-weekly meetings serves both an educational and a leavening purpose. Officials at the periphery of the System are in a position to be as fully informed as those at the center. In particular, the best thinking available in the System is openly brought to a focus. Weaknesses as well as strengths in thinking and leadership among the highest officials of the System are exposed to the view of others. It is noteworthy that significant changes have been gradually taking place in the composition of top management of the Reserve banks. These shifts have been in the direction of a greater role for the highly trained professional who has made a career of central banking. This development would seem to be partly, at least, a product of the changed procedures of the F.O.M.C.

Without question, the changed character of the Committee's proceedings has raised the level of central banking in the United States. The question remains, however, as to whether it has not at the same time introduced certain dangers. One of these is the possibility that it may tend toward undue conformity in thinking on central banking and other matters of public policy. Another is that it may enable the Chairman to wield undue influence. Confidence in Mr. Martin and the fact that among the presidents and governors are men of ability and courage tend to moderate the apparent seriousness of these dangers. But they cannot be said to remove them, either for the present or for the future.

Rising influence of economists

It is significant that the listing of power groups given above places members of the economics staff just below the Chairman and the Board of Governors. This would have seemed incredible only a few years ago. Yet even this, as will be seen, does not fully measure the increase that has taken place in the influence of professional economists.

As a matter of history, economists have played a not unimportant role from the beginnings of the System. The original legislation establishing the Federal Reserve System was drafted under the guidance of H. Parker Willis, then of Wash-

ington and Lee and later of Columbia. W. W. Stewart and E. A. Goldenweiser, both former professors of economics, were instrumental in building up what has become one of the foremost statistical and research organisations of the world. Adolph Miller, a member of the Board from 1916 to 1931, Allan Sproul, long the head of the Federal Reserve Bank of New York, and Alfred H. Williams, president of the Philadelphia Federal Reserve Bank from 1941 to 1958, all were professional economists. But the ascendancy of the economist group—in terms of number involved, importance of positions held, and influence exerted—dates from the decade of the 'fifties and seems to be largely attributable to Chairman Martin.

The most striking, though not necessarily the most significant, manifestation of the rise of economists has been their appointment to topmost administrative positions. By 1961, the presidents of six of the twelve Federal Reserve banks were professional economists, all but one of them holders of the Ph.D. degree. Trained economists were also conspicuous at the vice-presidential level. As far as the Federal Reserve is concerned, a background in economics now seems to provide better credentials than experience in law or banking for the responsibilities of a central banker.

The academic influence is to be observed elsewhere in the system. Two members of the Board of Governors are former deans, one a specialist in labour and the other in agricultural economics. Educators, most of them trained as economists, are also prominent among the directors of the Reserve banks. By way of contrast, a listing of Reserve Bank directors made in 1925 failed to disclose a single director as coming from academic circles.

The major contribution of the economics profession to central banking in the United States, however, is in terms of information and ideas rather than personnel. In the first place, research activities of the economics staff of the Board and the banks are responsible for the assembling and processing of data upon which policies are based. Economics staffs throughout the System prepare an elaborate array of statistical and other information for use at F.O.M.C. meetings and at other times. Secondly, the economists are to be regarded as having been the principal source of thinking on central bank policy. Many of the distinctive features of Federal Reserve policy in recent years are believed to have originated with the economics group. These include the so-called "bills-only" policy for confining open market operations almost exclusively to Treasury bills, the tight money policy of the Eisenhower period, and the opposition to selective instruments of credit control other than margin requirements. Issues involved in problems such as these are highly technical. It is no reflection on the Chairman and other members of the Board to suggest that they have neither the time nor the talent to originate policies such as these. As the chief spokesman for the Federal Reserve, Mr. Martin is officially identified with all major policy moves. Moreover, he has been an extraordinarily effective exponent of the measures in Congress and before the general public. But the presumption is that the ideas themselves come from the advisers, that the Chairman consults with them and is converted to the views which they present, and then, as happens with converts, often becomes their most zealous advocate.

Some of the measures espoused have been highly controversial. The bills-only policy and at times the tight money policy were criticised by many economists. Even within the System disagreement over particular policies is said to have been so strong as to have caused the resignation of certain high officials and staff members. Monetary economists might be disposed to question the wisdom of stands taken by System economists, but few would dispute their influence.

There are other aspects of the role of System economists which are less controversial. The important role of Board economists in meetings of the F.O.M.C. has already been noted. A senior economist and often other members of a bank's economics staff are called upon to brief the president before these meetings. At Chairman Martin's express invitation, one economist from each Reserve bank attends the meetings. In some cases he may later report on what took place to the group that helped with the briefing. A bank's senior economist and perhaps other members of the staff can be expected to know considerably more about, and generally speaking to have considerably greater influence on, major policy decisions than any of the directors.

Conversion of the meetings of the F.O.M.C. into a forum for the discussion of central banking problems and policies as noted earlier has meant that these sessions take on somewhat the character of graduate seminars. Attendance of senior economists from the Board and the banks, even though they do not actually participate, lends a professional atmosphere. It also means that those charged with the formulation and execution of Federal Reserve policy are exposed to personal contact with the experts inside and outside the meetings. The appointment of such experts to senior executive positions is one manifestation of the impact which these associations have made on the System. And this in turn means that increasingly it becomes difficult to differentiate, so far as qualifications are concerned, between the economist group and the management group. Finally, it is to be supposed that the number of economists holding high administrative positions facilitates the flow of ideas between the two groups.

READING 21

How well is our monetary system working? An independent businessmen's organization, the Committee for Economic Development, set up a Commission on Money and Credit in 1957 to take a searching look at America's financial institutions. The distinguished members of the commission spoke for themselves and not necessarily for C.E.D. itself; they included presidents and board chairmen of large corporations and banks, three labor leaders, a top farm spokesman, lawyers, and two educators. Frazer B. Wilde of the Connecticut General Life Insurance Company was chairman of the study group.

The commission's report appeared in 1961. Its key place in economic literature is due not so much to the novelty of its analysis or proposals as to the consensus represented on some critical issues. Controversy about monetary policy continues, as the next two readings suggest; but there is also a substantial body of ideas that have come into widespread acceptance about what changes in the money supply can and cannot contribute to the pursuit of our economic goals.

This reading is a small part of a condensation of the commission's report prepared for broad distribution.

Questions to Guide the Reading

How well do the commission's recommendations for structural changes in the Fed relate to the introductory statement on national economic goals? Are there still better ways of changing the Fed to meet those goals?

The previous reading raised questions about the adequacy of the power in the Fed and of checks on that power. Does the commission's report help to answer those questions in an effective way?

MONEY AND MONETARY POLICY
Commission on Money and Credit

In the course of its examination of the U.S. monetary and credit system, the Commission has studied the role of the Federal Reserve System and the effectiveness of its control measures.

From these examinations several recommendations for structural and institutional changes have emerged. For the most part, these recommendations propose either structural and institutional changes that will contribute to the more effective functioning of the economy or propose broad guides for specific policy decisions. The Commission has tried to avoid specific policy prescriptions for particular problems. It has tried to confine its recommendations and suggestions for change only to situations where the present structure has not worked well. It has avoided recommendations for change merely for the sake of change or merely to achieve a more logically consistent structure. The recommendations do not call for the wholesale overhaul of our financial structure. They consist of many small changes which frequently affect evolving trends.

The recommendations are based on the fundamental assumption that the economy will continue to be largely a private enterprise economy. This form of economic organization, with its stimulus to individual initiative, has been a key element in explaining our outstanding record of economic growth and national well being and is well suited to perform effectively in the years ahead. The Commission believes, however, that both private enterprise and government have major and complementary roles to play in achieving national objectives, and that neither one nor the other can do the whole job.

The Commission recognizes clearly the limitations of what a study such as this can accomplish. We do not live in a perfect world, and neither the Commission nor anyone else can prescribe mechanisms, structures, and policy guides which will guarantee the ideal attainment of national objectives. We can and should strive for a significant improvement in performance, and the Commission believes that the changes suggested will contribute toward that improvement.

National economic goals

The Commission has reached certain major conclusions relating to the three major economic goals of economic growth, full employment, and price stability.

Although not satisfied with recent rates of growth, the Commission does not recommend the establishment of any specific rate of growth as a target in itself. However, using available estimates as a guide, it finds that it is reasonable to assume a growth rate of real Gross National Product of somewhere between 3½ and 4½ per cent per year in the 1960's, if the United States can succeed in maintaining the level of aggregate demand necessary to assure low level unemployment.

As a target for monetary, credit, and fiscal measures, low level unemployment has been defined as being somewhere near the point where the number of unfilled job vacancies is about the same as the number of unemployed. In such circumstances there will still be substantial unemployment as well as unfilled vacancies, but both difficulties can be eased by other, non-credit measures specifically designed to improve the functioning of the labor market.

As to price stability, the Commission finds that, even without special action to eliminate or offset the inflationary biases in the economy, a more

From "Money and Credit: Their Influence on Jobs, Prices and Growth," *New York Times*, June 25, 1961, Special Section XI. Reprinted with kind permission of the Committee for Economic Development.

satisfactory record of smaller price increases than in the period since 1952 should be attainable. National policy clearly should be to avoid even mild increases in the price level, as long as the cost in terms of other equally vital objectives is not excessive.

Since it is deeply concerned with the role of all government agencies involved in originating or executing economic policies, the Commission would place greater responsibility in the office of the President for the proper, continuing, and effective coordination of money and credit instruments necessary to achieve the national economic goals. It would seek to coordinate the Federal Reserve System more closely with the Government's economic policies, in accordance with the mandates of the Employment Act of 1946. The Commission also seeks a greater degree of centralization for the Federal Reserve System.

The Commission's recommendations for the private sector of the economy are aimed largely at policies designed to stimulate the forces of enterprise and competition by relaxing the restraints imposed by over-restrictive government regulations. Here it would eliminate specific controls that distort the working of the market mechanism, and thus create an environment conducive to growth.

For the private banking and non-banking institutions its recommendations are aimed at increasing, through a lessening of restrictions and controls, the availability of credit in the hope of thus releasing capital to stimulate economic growth.

Monetary policy

Control over conditions governing the quantity of money is inevitable in a modern industrial society. As the nation has adopted more positive economic goals, it has become interested in whether monetary control can be used flexibly to influence the behavior of expenditures, output, employment, and prices. Clearly it can, but monetary adjustments alone cannot ensure attainment of these goals. On the other hand, the lack of an appropriate monetary policy can frustrate their accomplishment.

Changes in the degree of restraint or ease in monetary policy have an effect on the total flow of expenditures and in turn on output, employment, and prices. Because the link between the initial actions taken by the Federal Reserve to influence bank reserves and these variables is general, pervasive, and indirect, and because no attempt is made by the monetary authority to allocate credit among specific users, this approach to monetary policy is frequently referred to as general monetary control.

Monetary control. The concept underlying general monetary control is relatively straightforward. Monetary restraint reduces the availability of credit and increases its cost; and these retard the flow of expenditures, employment, income, and output. Monetary ease in general has the opposite effects on credit, and thus encourages an expansion in these flows.

The Federal Reserve System exercises general monetary control through the use of three major instruments. These are: (1) The power to set the level of required reserves that member banks must hold; (2) engagement in open market operations, which alter the volume of actual reserve balances available to banks; and (3) changes in the terms under which banks may replenish a deficiency in required reserves by borrowing from Federal Reserve banks. All three instruments of policy, and open market operations in particular, directly affect the net reserve position of member banks. They also have direct impacts on other economic variables.

A change in monetary policy may take the form of positive actions, such as open market sales, increases in required reserve ratios, or changes in discount policy. But a shift to a restrictive policy often takes the form of failing to increase reserves in the face of a rising demand for credit.

The Federal Reserve authority may attempt to restrain economic activity by engaging in open market sales of Treasury bills. These sales influence at least six distinguishable elements in the economy: net bank reserves are reduced; the money supply falls; the price of government securities tends to decline and yields to rise; the money value of total assets tends to fall; the over-all liquidity of financial portfolios is reduced; and the ability and willingness of banks to lend is reduced.

With interest rates higher, some individuals and businesses reduce their demand deposits on which they earn nothing and purchase securities or shift to interest bearing thrift deposits. The demand deposits are made available to other individuals and businesses who wish to increase their expenditures, or to financial institutions which make loans to individuals and businesses who want to borrow to increase their outlays. Thus, even though the money supply has not expanded, the mobilization of idle balances will finance more expenditures, and the velocity of money is increased. But this does not mean that a restrictive monetary policy is fully offset.

Monetary restraint causes a reduction in the willingness and ability of nearly all institutional lenders to meet all the credit demands made on them. While it is difficult to make any precise assessment of the volume of loans refused during recent tight money episodes, it appears to have been substantial.

Monetary restraint also affects the desire of the public to spend, through the changes it brings about in the rate of interest and in the market value of income-yielding assets, and the liquidity of the public's wealth holdings.

In general, the sensitivity of demand for real assets to a change in interest rates and credit terms depends on the relative importance of interest charges in the total cost. Interest is a large element of cost in most home purchases and the demand for housing shows marked sensitivity to changes in mortgage interest rates and credit terms—expanding significantly during periods of easy money and contracting sharply when money is tightened.

Borrowing by state and local governments for capital expenditures also tended to increase when credit has been easy, to decrease when credit conditions became tight.

Changes in policy. The studies of the actual behavior of business investment and interest rates have not reliably isolated the effect of monetary policy from shifts in other determinants of investment. The evidence, however, indicates that some kinds of investment are sensitive to changes in interest costs.

The evidence on consumer expenditures other than for residential construction indicates that changes in credit terms have some slight direct effect.

Changes in monetary policy have other less direct effects on the rate of expenditures than through their effect on the cost and availability of credit. The very announcement or recognition of a change in monetary policy may contribute to changes in attitudes and expectations as to the future rate of growth of demand, sales, income, and profits and the future level of prices. These attitude changes may have a substantial effect on investment expenditures since a direct restraint in state and local construction, residential construction, and some categories of business investment will reduce the flow of new orders to a wide range of businesses. Moreover, job uncertainty for employees may also increase, and consumers may become less willing to incur new indebtedness, and curtail consumer durable purchases.

A policy of monetary ease to stimulate an expansion of expenditures operates through the same processes as a restrictive policy but in the reverse direction. An expansive policy would tend to increase the net reserve position of member banks, to increase the prices and reduce the yields on Treasury securities, to improve the liquidity of banks and other lending institutions, to enhance the wealth position of all holders of financial assets, and to increase the money supply. These changes, however, may not be as effective in stimulating economic activity as the reverse measures can be in restraining it.

Combination of effects. The changes in the degree of monetary restraint or ease appropriate to the conduct of countercyclical policy does not have a controlling impact on any specific sector of expenditure, but the pervasive and cumulative combination of a number of small effects is sufficient to make flexible monetary policy a useful instrument of stabilization policy.

It is true that a policy of monetary restriction has sometimes been carried on for too long, and that at other times the expansions of bank reserves or reduction in reserve requirements in a recession has created problems in controlling the ensuing upswing. These weaknesses reflect, not inherent defects of monetary management, but rather the inadequacy of the techniques employed and the criteria used for the timing of the changes in monetary policy. However, certain measures can be taken to speed up the effects of monetary policy.

Monetary restraint on the upswing will be more effective if idle cash in the hands of the public can be held to a minimum, if excess bank liquidity at the start of the upswing is minimal, and if the Federal Reserve and Treasury, taken together, work to increase the long-term federal debt in the hands of the public. The effectiveness of monetary policy on the downswing will be increased if the Treasury and Federal Reserve take direct action to reduce long-term as well as short-term interest rates. If excessive liquidity positions of banks, other lending institutions, and the public are not allowed to develop, and if the Federal Reserve and the Treasury take direct action to speed the adjustment process of long-term as well as short-term interest rates, the impact of monetary policy should be felt sooner.

The Commission does not advocate placing sole reliance on monetary policy for stabilization purposes. Because of its reversibility and the possibility of changing policy by small steps, monetary policy can be used in precisely the circumstances when discretionary fiscal policy changes should not be used because the need for so powerful an instrument is not yet clear. In summary, the Commission believes that especially when monetary policy is used in conjunction with other stabilization measures, it is a valuable and effective instrument of stabilization policy.

Long-run monetary policy. Countercyclical monetary policy is concerned with timing net injections or withdrawals of bank reserves so that they will best dampen fluctuations in the level of economic activity. Long-run monetary policies must provide a monetary climate consonant with an adequate and sustainable rate of growth and over-all price stability. This climate should permit the banking system to expand its loans and investments and hence the supply of money at a rate commensurate with the economy's underlying growth potential. Since the quantity of money needed to permit economic growth will depend on a variety of elements, particularly changes in the stock of money substitutes, the money supply need not increase at the same rate as the increase in the economy's growth potential.

The Commission urges that the average rate of growth of the money supply should be consistent with the continued maintenance of high employment at stable prices and adequate economic growth, but we recognize that, in accordance with particular circumstances, it may be appropriate for the money supply to grow more or less rapidly than the output of the economy at high employment.

Instrument of control. The Commission concludes that open-market operations should be the normal or usual instrument of general monetary policy. Instead of relying on a "bills-only" policy, the Federal Reserve should, when domestic or international conditions warrant, influence directly the structure as well as the level of interest rates in pursuit of contracyclical monetary policies and should deal in securities of varied maturities. This recommendation does not mean a return to a pegged structure of prices and yields for government securities. And the normal use of open-market operations in bills to carry out technical and seasonal changes in bank reserves is appropriate.

The Commission concludes that the discount facility is still of considerable value in our banking system, and that it should be retained as an ultimate source of temporary credit.

Clearly the intent of the Federal Reserve Board is to have discount administration relatively homogeneous among the twelve Federal Reserve Banks, and the Commission urges continued efforts to assure uniform standards of discounting practice. Uniform standards, of course, mean that like circumstances result in like treatment, at the same time permitting differences in practice where regional differences in economic conditions or needs so require.

Discount rates are now set for each Federal Reserve Bank by vote of its board of directors subject to the review and approval of the Federal Reserve Board. However, credit markets have become essentially national in character and the possibility of utilizing differential regional discount rate policies is negligible. Regional differences in discount rates would be ineffective in view of the active market for federal funds and Treasury bills. Under these circumstances a national discount rate policy is appropriate to correspond with a national open-market policy.

Reserve requirements. While changes in reserve requirements are a powerful instrument of credit control, they are awkward and cumbersome in comparison with open-market operations, and present difficult problems of adjustment for many medium and small banks. The Commission believes that the power to change reserve requirements should be used only sparingly and to serve longer-run objectives.

The present general form of fractional reserve requirements against net demand deposits is adequate for the purposes of general monetary policy and the Commission recommends that it be continued.

Reserve requirements for demand deposit for all member banks should be made identical and the classification of banks into country banks and reserve city banks should be eliminated.

The Commission recommends that existing statutory reserve requirements against savings and time deposits be repealed, and that pending repeal of such requirements, those banks and competing thrift institutions subject to them be permitted to hold reserves in the form of either cash or Treasury securities with maturities up to five years.

The reserve base required to support a long-run expansion in the stock of money can be supplied either through open-market operations or through a reduction in required reserve ratios. Which method is used will affect the leverage with which monetary control operates, that is, the multiple by which demand deposits can be increased or decreased for any change in required reserves; net Treasury interest costs; and the level of bank earnings.

The Commission recommends that Congress continue to grant to the Federal Reserve Board a range within which reserve requirements can be set for demand deposits, perhaps from 8 to 18 per cent, so that the Board can adjust the specific level to meet the needs of growth or to meet emergency needs.

Selective controls.   One suggestion frequently made for strengthening the effectiveness of monetary policy is that there should be more use made of selective monetary measures. If selective controls were used, the authorities could alter the terms and conditions on which credit is made available for particular purposes. Now the only selective control available to the Federal Reserve authorities is the power to alter margin requirements on credit granted by any lender—banks and others—for the purpose of purchasing or carrying listed securities.

Proposals for selective controls over other specific uses of credit are usually directed toward controlling volatile sectors of spending, such as spending on consumer durable goods, housing, inventory, accumulation, and industrial plant and equipment.

Whether the Federal Reserve should be granted additional powers to alter the pattern of credit and resource allocation through the exercise of new selective controls is a practical matter. It hinges largely on whether particular types of changes in the composition of spending among broad classes of output not readily affected by general controls can be identified at the time as being so destabilizing as to threaten the achievement of major economic objectives.

Consumer credit.   The Commission is almost evenly divided as to the desirability of granting standby authority to the Federal Reserve Board for consumer credit controls. In the absence of a consensus, no recommendation is made except to urge an investigation of better forms of such controls, which can be administered more effectively if they should be needed.

The arguments for variable controls over the terms of housing mortgages are similar to those for consumer installment credit controls. The

Commission recommends that the terms of housing loans insured or guaranteed under VA and FHA programs be varied in support of the countercyclical and price stabilization policies of the government. These changes would be administered by the VA and FHA. No further power to change credit terms on residential mortgages by the Federal Reserve Board is believed necessary.

The instability of business spending for inventory accumulations and for plant and equipment purchases has contributed significantly to cyclical fluctuations. General monetary controls do not appear to have rapid effects on either, although selective controls might.

No seemingly effective selective control device has yet been devised for affecting these volatile business expenditures. It may well be that controls of such expenditures more effective than general credit measures will be necessary to achieve our major economic objectives, and the Commission suggests that possible methods of influencing inventory and business investment expenditures on a selective basis be investigated by the government.

Span of control.   Because the Federal Reserve authorities do not have direct control over some 8,000 commercial banks which are not members of the System, and because they also have no direct power over non-bank financial institutions the suggestion has frequently been made that the direct reach of Federal Reserve control should be extended to cover both categories of institutions.

The problem presented by non-membership in the Federal Reserve System have long been recognized. The Commission recommends that all insured commercial banks be required to become members of the Federal Reserve System.

The more rapid growth of non-bank financial intermediaries than of commercial banks has focused attention on the question of their significance as a potential offset to monetary policy. Because of their closeness to money, changes in the volume of these near-money assets issued by non-bank financial institutions may have an important effect on the demand for money balances and hence on the velocity of money.

Because the contributions of non-bank financial institutions to cyclical changes in the velocity of money appear to be too small to warrant such an extension, and because their effect on velocity over the long-run can easily be taken into account in regulating the long-run money supply, the Commission recommends that there be no extension of direct Federal Reserve controls over non-bank financial institutions.

Organization of Federal Reserve. The basic questions about the structure of any Federal agency are both administrative and political. The basic issue involved was the "independence" of the Federal Reserve from other parts of the government and from the banking community it both serves and regulates. While accepting basic arguments for independence, the Commission nevertheless finds that the need for better coordination is very important.

From this premise the Commission made several recommendations for changes in the structure of the Federal Reserve System. They are as follows:

The Chairman of the Board and the Vice Chairman of the Federal Reserve should be designated by the President from among the Board's membership to serve a four-year term coterminous with the term of the President of the United States. The Commission felt that this strikes a balance in formal status between tenure at the President's pleasure, which some members of the Commission prefer, and no change, which other members advocate.

The Federal Reserve. The Federal Reserve Board shall consist of five members with overlapping 10-year terms, one expiring each odd year. (Members should be eligible for reappointment.)

The Federal Reserve Board Chairman should be the chief executive officer of the Board, empowered to handle administrative matters.

Occupational qualifications for Board members should be eliminated. Instead, the statute should stipulate that members shall be positively qualified by experience or education, independence, and objectivity. Salaries of top government officials should be sharply increased, and in view of the gravity of their responsibilities Federal Reserve Board members should be compensated at the highest salary level available for appointive offices in the government.

The present statutory Advisory Council should be replaced by an advisory council of 12 members appointed by the Board from nominees presented by the boards of directors of the Reserve Banks. At least 2 nominees should be presented by each bank, not more than one to represent the same sector of the economy, and the Board should make its selection, one from each district, in such a manner as to secure a Council broadly representative of all aspects of the American economy. Council members should serve for 3-year terms, not immediately renewable.

This law should formally constitute the twelve Federal Reserve presidents as a council to meet at least four times a year with the Board.

Open-market policies. Open-market policies should be vested in the Board. In exercising its open-market policy the Board should consult with the Council and twelve Reserve Bank presidents.

The determination of the rediscount rate (the same for all Reserve Banks) should be vested in the Board. In establishing the rate the Boards should consult with the 12 Reserve Bank presidents.

The determination of reserve requirements should continue to be vested in the Board. In determining these requirements the Board should consult with the 12 Federal Reserve Bank presidents.

The present capital stock of the Federal Reserve Banks should be retired. Instead, membership in the System should be evidenced by a membership certificate of $500, the same for each member bank.

The Commission believes that the Federal Reserve should follow the general rule that the public be kept informed with reasonable promptness and detail of the reasons for its major policy decisions and actions.

READING 22

The report of the Commission on Money and Credit, on which the previous reading was based, has already accomplished one of its implicit objectives: stirring up new, searching discussion about our monetary system. One of those who joined in the early discussion is a top expert on the Fed, G. L. Bach, who is Maurice Falk Professor of Economics and Social Relations at Carnegie Institute of Technology.

Here, Professor Bach concentrates not on the vast areas of consensus about money and monetary policy but rather on the questions that remain unsettled even after the commission's work. The compatibility of our economic goals with one another, the continuing uncertainties about lags in money's impact on the economy, the issue of independence in the Fed—all these come under searching examination here. But this reading must be seen as a commentary from within the large community of scholars generally sympathetic to the commission's findings. The next reading represents a quite different approach to the whole subject.

Questions to Guide the Reading

Is the issue of conflicting economic goals at the root of our debate about just what form our monetary institutions, including the Fed, should take today? How might Bach's plea for "careful, dispassionate weighing of the social gains and costs involved in giving up one national goal in order to achieve more of another" be responded to?

The background piece by Whittlesey, the report of the Commission on Money and Credit, and now the Bach article all bear on the independence of the Fed in our economic life. What conclusions emerge most strongly from this discussion about the principle and the procedures that should underlie the relationship among the Fed, our national government, and the private banking community?

MONEY, POLITICS, AND THE "FED"
G. L. Bach

The economics and politics of modern money and credit, with special emphasis on the Federal Reserve System, was the main assignment of the Commission on Money and Credit. The need for such an examination is clear: for since the Federal Reserve was established a half century ago, much has changed—the role of government has mushroomed; the national debt has grown from virtually nothing to nearly $300 billion; the United States has become the world's undisputed economic leader, the one massive international creditor and international banker for the non-communist world.

One looks in vain in the Report presented by the Commission for penetrating new analyses or perspectives on the problems wrought by these changes, or for new policy approaches or machinery in the field of money and credit. Above all, the Commission has not dealt convincingly with the No. 1 dilemma of modern monetary policy—how to encourage high-level employment and rapid growth while repressing inflation. But, notwithstanding these shortcomings, the Commission's recommendations should not be written off by thoughtful Americans. For while they contain little that is new, they are sober and responsible,

and they do raise important questions about the way monetary policy works and how it might work better.

What the Commission has to say about the Federal Reserve, money, and monetary policy can be broadly lumped under four main heads: (a) the goals of Federal Reserve policy; (b) what monetary policy can do; (c) Federal Reserve independence; and (d) Federal Reserve organization and operations.

Economic goals

The Commission begins its Report with a statement on "National Economic Goals." Its position can be summarized as follows:

The Federal Reserve's goals should be part of, and substantially the same as, the goals of general national economic policy.

Reasonable price stability, sustained high levels of employment and production, and an adequate rate of economic growth should be the three main objectives of monetary policy—and these must be achieved within a framework of economic freedom and primary reliance on the

From G. L. Bach, "Economics, Politics and the Fed," *Harvard Business Review*, January–February, 1962. Reprinted with kind permission of the author and publisher.

market mechanism, while recognizing the need for adequate national security measures.

These three goals are roughly of equal importance, and they can be attained simultaneously within the general framework indicated above.

The first two propositions are eminently sensible and widely accepted. But the third is the rub. Are high employment, rapid growth, and stable prices of roughly equal importance? Can they all be attained together? If something must give, what should it be?

Here the Commission, with its objectivity, its generous budget, and its large group of economic researchers, could have done a vital job which apparently went undone. There is strong reason to suppose that we may face painful choices in the future, especially between keeping prices stable and unemployment low. If so, sound policy decisions require a careful weighing of the costs of trading one objective off for the other.

For monetary policy this is especially crucial, because avoidance of inflation has been traditionally the No. 1 goal of central bankers. Maintenance of high-level employment and output has generally been secondary; and, at least until recently, little direct attention has been paid to the encouragement of economic growth. But many, perhaps most, economists today argue that high-level employment and output of wanted goods and services are the fundamental goals—that large-scale unemployment of men and machines is *the* major economic waste. They say that moderate inflation, while undesirable, involves mainly a redistribution of financial claims rather than a diminution of real output of goods and services. In short, it is more important to maximize total output than to quarrel over who gets how much of a smaller total.

These comments are not intended to imply that inflation is unobjectionable. Rather, I wish to stress how little has been accomplished—and, unfortunately, how little the Commission has added—in careful, dispassionate weighing of the social gains and costs involved in giving up some of one national goal in order to achieve more of another.

More attention to these long-range fundamental issues and less day-to-day operating advice on monetary and fiscal policy would have made the Report a more valuable document.

Can we have both high employment and stable prices? The Commission says *yes,* but its discussion leaves me uneasy. *If* we face inflation based on excess income claims, then there is a dilemma that cannot be wished away. That is, if labor unions, business, agriculture, and all the others demand larger incomes in the market place than can be satisfied at high-employment national output, then their higher wage and price demands generate inflation—higher prices, wages, profits, and money incomes generally, rather than more real output. Such inflation cannot go far without more money to support the higher spending and prices; therefore, the Federal Reserve can stop it merely by sitting tight and providing no new bank reserves. But the price of doing so is high— growing unemployment, with falling output and sales, at the higher prices. Then we must choose: stable prices or higher employment and rapid growth.

The Commission proposes modernization of the Congressional mandate to the Federal Reserve, to spell out the goals it urges. The present law is little changed from 1913, when the Fed's main purposes were "to furnish an elastic currency, to afford means of rediscounting commercial paper, and to establish a more effective supervision of banking." These are now routine. The Commission would substitute a mandate parallel to that established for the administrative agencies of the government in the Employment Act of 1946, with reasonable price stability added as a goal, but without specifying any target rate of economic growth. It is hard to disagree with the modernization recommendation, if we agree on what our national goals are.

Role of monetary policy

What can monetary policy do toward achieving these goals? A good deal, the Commission says, but probably not as much as fiscal policy; and monetary policy needs a lot of help in preventing inflation in a world of strong unions, of administered prices, and of restrictions on job mobility.

By and large, the Commission's views are orthodox on money and credit. The Report calls for strong use of the traditional monetary policy weapons, and finds that, in general, the Fed has done a good job in using them. It wants primary emphasis on open market operations (as does just about everybody else); doubts the wisdom of frequent changes in reserve requirements; thinks the rediscount rate bears about the right (minor) amount of emphasis now; and opposes "bills only." On selective controls, it is generally negative except for margin requirements in the stock market; but it could not agree on the control of consumer credit, where about half the members were for re-establishing Federal Reserve stand-by controls, and half against.

There are some technical recommendations offered, notably that reserve requirement differentials on demand deposits be eliminated and reserve requirements be removed on savings and time deposits, as part of a general plea for more equal treatment of commercial banks and other financial intermediaries. Finally, to spread the impact of federal monetary policy and to make its burden more equitable, the Commission recommends that all insured banks be required to become members of the Federal Reserve System, subject to the System's reserve requirements and supervisory standards.

The Commission's Report ranges over the entire area of monetary policy, with a tone that is generally optimistic. A number of points are especially worthy of note.

Lags & uncertainties. Behind the scenes, a battle rages among economic researchers over the precise ways that monetary controls affect private spending and the performance of the economy. There is general agreement that the Federal Reserve can control the quantity of money (demand deposits and currency) within reasonably narrow limits by controlling the volume of excess reserves held by the commercial banks, although it sometimes faces substantial lags in getting the results it wants. But how much and how fast any changes in the supply of money affect national production, employment, and prices is another matter.

One set of research results suggests that the supply of money does indeed dominate the level of economic activity, but that there is a highly uncertain lag—varying generally from six to eighteen months—between Federal Reserve action and the resulting change in economic activity. If this is so, it throws grave doubts on the efficiency of Federal Reserve attempts to mitigate booms and depressions. With such lags current policy changes may have their effect only when the need is past, and may indeed make things worse.

Another main line of research agrees on the importance of money, but suggests that the lag probably is not over six months or so for the main impact of Federal Reserve policy. This, with a little luck in forecasting, is short enough to provide real hope for helpful results. The right timing of monetary ease and restraint is crucial. Alas, the Commission throws no new light on such a fundamental issue.

Another basic, unsettled question is the extent to which money and credit conditions affect the level of business investment in plant, equipment, and inventories. Still another question is their impact on residential construction. Another is how much they influence the spending of state and local governmental units. Investment spending by these three groups plays a central role in business fluctuations. Standard monetary doctrine holds that tighter money checks such investment significantly and promptly, that easy money stimulates it. But modern research leaves the truth in the shadows and, again, the Commission throws no new light.

Controlling "new" inflation. Most of what the Commission says about using tight money to check inflation could have been written a generation ago. For traditional "demand pull" inflation, where inflation comes from excessive total demand, a gradual squeeze on spending by limiting the growth of bank credit, or even contracting it, is the accepted remedy. And there is no reason to suppose that it will not work, if the medicine is applied judiciously. True, an overdose of tight money could send the patient into a relapse of unemployment and recession, but this is the "art" of central banking—to fit the monetary remedy smoothly to the need for it.

The nasty problem arises when the inflation comes from excess income claims—when wages and prices push up in some sectors even though substantial unemployment remains. As was indicated above, monetary restraint can still check the inflation—*if* we are willing to pay the price. Federal Reserve action holding down bank lending and limiting the money supply will sooner or later check rising prices. But, in doing so, it will hold total spending below the level needed to produce high employment and rapid growth at the higher wages and prices set by some economic units, even in the face of unemployment and weak markets elsewhere in the economy. To pin the blame on the troublemaking groups who push up wages and prices too fast is right—but it is not very helpful to the monetary authorities, who can only control the supply of money.

No one knows how important this kind of inflationary pressure will be in the future. The Commission hopes, wishfully, I suspect, that it will not be very important. It emphasizes that other measures can help too—better information on job openings, higher labor mobility, elimination of both union and management barriers to job shifting, antitrust action to encourage price flexibility, and elimination of government policies which support rigid prices. It calls for business and labor statesmanship to avoid unreasonable income demands, and turns its back firmly on direct wage and price controls. All things considered, the Commission suspects that attempts to get unemployment below 4% (or so) of the labor force by expansionary monetary-fiscal policy will bring some inflation. Most economists, I believe, would consider this optimistic indeed; the figure may well be nearer 5% or 6%, and possibly even higher. And this means 4 million or 5 million people unemployed, with a corresponding waste of potential output and an inevitable drag on economic growth.

Businessmen and bankers, therefore, who have a simple answer to the inflation problem—just tell the Federal Reserve to stand firm with tight money—would do well to face up to this dilemma. The Commission has certainly not overemphasized it. The answer is far from easy; neither the Commission nor anyone else has yet come up with a clear answer. This is the greatest challenge to monetary policy today.

Economic growth. Over the past decade Americans, used to being first in everything, have had some uncomfortable facts to face. In economic growth, we are not only not leading the race, but we are back with the also-rans. Both the communists and our Western allies seem to be outdoing us by substantial margins. Could monetary policy help more?

The Commission's Report is sobering. There are no panaceas, though somewhat easier money might have helped a little. The money supply needs to grow fast enough to support a growing total expenditure, but not at any set rate like the much-discussed 3% per year proposed by those who doubt the ability of the Federal Reserve to open and close the money spigot at the right times on a discretionary basis. The Commission seems almost to come to the position that when growth is too slow because of underemployment (as over the past several years), this is evidence of inadequate growth in the money stock. But it doesn't quite say so. Many other observers are more critical, arguing that too-slow monetary growth, due to fear of inflation, has significantly slowed U.S. economic growth since 1955. The old dilemma of how to restrain inflationary pressures (real or feared) and simultaneously to expand employment and growth is found everywhere throughout the volume.

The monetary authorities need the finesse of a tightrope walker. Too little money will hold back spending, investment, and employment—

wasting output and slowing economic growth below otherwise attainable levels. Too much money encourages inflation, without appreciably speeding economic growth. What we need is just the right amount of money, in between underemployment and inflation. Once the Federal Reserve has approximated that and thus minimized the waste of recession, there is little more that monetary policy can do. Easier money —especially lower long-term interest rates—might safely help stimulate investment if we could count on a budget surplus to restrain inflationary total spending, but this is a nice balance indeed to hope for. As a practical matter, it is largely up to fiscal policy, revision of the tax system, more investment in education and scientific research, and a step-up in just plain hard work to push the growth rate up still further.

Through this maze of unsettled but, alas, fundamental disputes underlying monetary policy, the Commission has trodden a careful, middle-of-the-road path. The public or private administrator can never wait for absolute truth. He must act on the best information available to him. The Commission's views represent a fair picture of well-informed professional opinion. Perhaps this is all we could ask.

It is only fair to recognize that the economics profession has not been able to provide the guidance needed through its own research over many years. But, as on the problem of economic goals, the Commission had vast opportunity and large resources. A more fundamental study of the role of money and the foundations of monetary policy would have been of greater long-run value, both in providing a firmer basis for current policy and in showing the gaps in knowledge we need to fill to make better policy decisions in the future.

Issue of independence

In a temperate analysis of governmental operations and Federal Reserve responsibilities, the Commission draws these conclusions:

1. The President must bear the central responsibility for governmental economic policy recommendations and execution.

2. Federal Reserve responsibilities for national economic policy are closely intertwined with those of other government agencies, especially the Executive Office of the President and the Treasury.

3. Federal Reserve independence is now ade-

quately protected, and Federal Reserve influence could be increased by closer participation in governmental policy determination.

4. To the end of closer and more informal working relationships between the Federal Reserve and the White House, the Federal Reserve Board chairman and vice chairman should be designated by the President from among the Board's membership, with four-year terms coterminous with the President's.

5. To improve efficiency and attract more able members, the Federal Reserve Board should be reduced from seven to five members, and all major Federal Reserve monetary powers should be centered in the Board.

6. To improve national economic policy formulation and coordination, the President should establish a cabinet-level "Advisory Board on Economic Growth and Stability," including the chairman of the Federal Reserve Board.

These proposals have been widely criticized by conservatives on the ground that they would undermine the independence of the Federal Reserve. The critics suggest that the "liberals" on the Commission somehow outflanked the "conservatives" in bringing about this stab in the back for financial soundness (a neat trick if indeed it occurred, since two thirds of the twenty Commission members were highly successful businessmen and bankers, only two were labor leaders, and the other five were independent professional men). On such a vital issue of monetary arrangements as this, it is well to take a closer look.

Case for independence. Stated bluntly, the traditional argument for Federal Reserve independence is that, if independent, the Fed will stand against inflation and financial irresponsibility in the government. History tells of many treasuries which have turned to money issue to pay their bills when taxes were inadequate. The modern world's major inflations have all come with large governmental deficits, covered by the issue of new money (currency or bank deposits). While legislatures vote the expenditures, treasuries must pay the bills. Thus, it is argued that treasuries have a predictable inflationary bias, however well-intentioned their secretaries may be. Against this bias, central bankers are alleged to be basically conservative; they can be counted on to look out for the stability of the monetary unit.

Another variant is based on the presumption that the entire political process is inherently in-

flationary. It is always easier for Congress to spend money than to raise taxes; "politicians" are inherently financially irresponsible. Thus, an independent Federal Reserve is needed to call a halt to the overspending tendencies of the politicians, and to the tendency of the politicians to plump too readily for good times for the economy as a whole, even though these good times may generate some inflation.

Lastly, there is an argument that the President, the politician par excellence, is not to be trusted on financial matters, and that an independent Federal Reserve is needed to see that he does not go too far with expansionary, inflationary economic policies.

Meaning of independence. These arguments suggest that we need to examine the meaning of the term "independence." Independence from whom? A Federal Reserve independent of the U.S. Treasury rests squarely on the realistic assessment of history. Treasuries *have* been inflationary in their biases, and we therefore need a powerful agency in governmental economic circles to stand against these inflationary biases when they threaten the soundness of our economic structure.

But Federal Reserve independence from the Congress is hardly meaningful in our governmental system. Congress established the Federal Reserve. It can change it any time it wishes, or call it to account for any of its actions. Federal Reserve officials readily acknowledge their responsibility to Congress—though the Fed need not go to Congress for appropriations to conduct its affairs and though, in practice, Congress, happily, is reluctant to intervene directly in Federal Reserve policy making.

The really difficult question is this: Should, or can, the Federal Reserve be independent from the President? The Constitution clearly allots to the federal government the power to create money and regulate the value thereof. In our society, where bank deposits comprise some 80% of our total money supply and currency only 20%, control over the supply of bank credit *is* control over the volume of money. Federal Reserve officials have consistently recognized the basically governmental nature of their function, though they value the close relationships they have with private bankers.

Furthermore, control over the money supply of the nation is a vital operating responsibility. Monetary policy is inextricably intermingled with fiscal policy and debt management policy, if the nation's economic goals are to be achieved effectively. The President must ultimately be responsible for recommendation and execution of the nation's basic economic policy. This logic leads clearly to the conclusion that the Federal Reserve must work closely with other agencies under the general responsibility of the President for executing national economic policy.

To give an independent Federal Reserve the power to negate the basic policies arrived at by the executive and legislative branches of the federal government would be intolerable for any administration, Republican or Democratic. But independence, looked at practically, is a matter of degree, not of black and white. The real question, thus, is the terms on which the Federal Reserve participates in governmental policy making and execution.

Need for cooperation. To be most effective, the Federal Reserve needs to be in a position to work closely with the other major government agencies responsible for national economic policy —especially the Treasury, the Budget Bureau, and the Council of Economic Advisers. No Federal Reserve chairman has ever claimed that the Board should disregard the debt management problems of the Treasury, or that the government's financial needs should be given no weight.

On the contrary, all major Federal Reserve officials have agreed on the need for close working relationships with the Treasury on monetary, fiscal, and debt policy. The times when the Federal Reserve has been least effective have been the times when it has been most isolated from the President and from effective, coequal working relationships with the Secretary of the Treasury and other high-level government officials. This was substantially the case throughout the much-discussed decade of the 1940's when the Federal Reserve was most subservient to Treasury debt-management needs. Secretaries Morgenthau and Snyder were close personal confidants of Presidents Roosevelt and Truman; but Federal Reserve officials seldom saw either President.

An effective Federal Reserve voice for the stable money point of view can best be assured if the Fed is an active, continuous participant in the day-to-day process of governmental economic policy formation. Seldom indeed does a central bank undertake a major war with the Congress and the Administration in a showdown on economic policy. Federal Reserve participation in policy making will generally be a more effective device for presenting the sound money point of view than will spectacular defiance of the government's policies. Extreme independence is, unfortunately, likely to mean splendid isolation from the decisions that matter.

On balance. The need is for recognized Federal Reserve independence from the Treasury *and* for coequal voice with other major agencies in the economic policy councils of the government. In other words, the need is to maintain a strong and substantially independent voice for a stable-money point of view without placing Federal Reserve officials in an untenably isolated position, where to use their independence involves major intragovernmental conflict and divided national economic policy. Budgetary and monetary matters call for the best efforts of wise men. But we must not fall into the trap of supposing that all wisdom will reside in appointed Federal Reserve officials, rather than in other government officials appointed by the same President and approved by the same Senate. The President, the Secretary of the Treasury, and other high governmental officials also seek to advance the national welfare, as they see it. How best to mesh the judgments and responsibilities of these various public officials is the problem, not simply to set up an independent nongovernmental board with a legal (but seldom practical) power to say *no* to the U.S. Government.

Recommended changes. To improve the coordination of over-all economic policy and to increase the influence of the Federal Reserve while maintaining its special quasi-independent status, the Commission recommends primarily two modest changes:

1. The President should establish a cabinet-level "Advisory Board on Economic Growth and Stability" which would include the chairman of the Federal Reserve Board.
2. The term of office of the chairman (and vice chairman) of the Federal Reserve Board should be made coterminous with that of the President, to eliminate the possibility that a Federal Reserve chairman would be personally unacceptable to a President.

A new President could (as now) immediately appoint one new Board member, and could name him chairman; or he could name a new chairman from among existing Board members. The staggered-term membership of the Board would remain unchanged, except that it would be reduced from seven to five members. While further centralization of System authority in the Board would increase somewhat the President's power over the Fed, overlapping ten-year terms would go far to protect the stability and independence of the Board members from short-run political pressures.

These two recommendations might help substantially to assure effective working relationships between the Fed, the Presidency, and the rest of the administrative branch of the government. To insist that a new President accept a Federal Reserve chairman to whom he objected strongly would probably serve little purpose, and would be more likely to decrease the effectiveness of the Fed than to increase it. As a practical matter, the chairman must represent the System in its most important contacts with the President, as well as with the Treasury and in most cases with Congress. Making the chairmanship coterminous with the President's term, though it might have little importance in most instances, makes practical administrative sense. It is significant that both William M. Martin, the present chairman of the Fed, and Marriner S. Eccles, chairman for longer than any other man and the individual who was most responsible for the restored independence of the Fed in 1951, concur in the recommendation to make the chairmanship coterminous with the President's term.

Appointment by the President of an "Advisory Board on Economic Growth and Stability" would be one device for assuring closer coordination among the governmental agencies (including the Fed) responsible for national economic policy. Whether such a special advisory board would be effective would depend heavily on whether the President wanted to use it. Some such device is obviously necessary. The Commission wisely avoids a recommendation to make such an advisory board mandatory by legislation, while stressing the importance of coordinated national policy formation in which the Federal Reserve has a strong voice.

Critics have labeled these recommendations a stab in the back for Federal Reserve independ-

ence. This appears to be a serious exaggeration. They reflect operating realities, and are modest proposals indeed when viewed in the light of the experience of most other nations, where central banks have been completely subordinated to treasuries or to governments.

Conclusion

Now that the Commission's proposals concerning money and credit are out, what do they amount to in total? What will be their impact on monetary thinking and on legislation and administration?

In sum, the Commission—a group of 20 able, conscientious men—have found that our monetary and credit institutions serve us well, that monetary policy can play a significant role in helping to provide stable economic growth without inflation, and that no sweeping changes are needed in our monetary arrangements. These are encouraging conclusions, though one can wish that the Commission had dug deeper in a search for new insights into our monetary problems.

The Commission suggested no real solutions for our toughest monetary problems, notably how to achieve rapid growth, high employment, and stable prices together, and how to compromise effectively domestic and international monetary requirements. It is easy to criticize the findings. But critics need to face up to the hard job of themselves producing realistic, integrated proposals for improving monetary arrangements and policy. A half century after the first National Monetary Commission led to establishment of the Federal Reserve, finding Commission consensus on so much of modern monetary policy is encouraging. Businessmen and other citizens, along with government officials, will do well to listen to the Commission's analyses and advice. But for them, and especially for professional economists, the challenge to understand better and to devise more imaginative monetary and credit policies remains.

READING 23

The report of the Commission on Money and Credit probably summed up many of the most widely held views about our monetary system. But there are some noted dissenters. One distinguished economist who wants the United States to pursue quite different policies in managing its money supply is Milton Friedman of the University of Chicago.

His reservations in this article touch again and again upon the ability of men to act wisely in the use of discretionary monetary powers. Neither the record nor the logic of the case is compelling evidence, in his view, for relying upon a few men charged with altering the money supply as they think best in meeting new economic conditions.

Questions to Guide the Reading

How might the members of the Commission on Money and Credit be expected to reply to each of Friedman's major points? Are the alternative policies implicitly accepted by the Commission clearly superior to those advocated here?

How helpful are the lessons out of the past, as Friedman describes that past, in assessing what discretionary monetary policy might reasonably be expected to accomplish in the future?

THE CASE FOR MONETARY REFORM
Milton Friedman

The United States has developed a unit fractional reserve banking system. From time to time there had been so-called banking crises and panics; the last one before World War I was the panic of 1907. Those panics arose under circumstances in which, for one reason or another, many people questioned the ability of the banks to convert their deposits into currency.

In a fractional reserve system, if a large number of people try to convert their deposits into currency they cannot succeed in doing so. There are few words in the English language which are greater misnomers than the term "deposits" for those liabilities that are on the bank's books. People think that a deposit means "you go and leave it there." Now, we all know that the money goes in at one window and goes out at another, and that what is deposited is only a small percentage, the so-called fractional reserve. Consequently, if everybody tries to get "his" deposit, he cannot do so.

When doubts arose about banks, people would tend to try to withdraw their deposits. This would have caused widespread bank failures. Such bank failures were prevented by a concerted refusal on the part of the banks to pay currency for deposits, called a suspension of payments. That term is a misnomer, too.

Those of us who remember the banking panic of 1933 are inclined to believe that early banking panics were like the one in 1933. They were

not. In the early banking panics, like 1907, the banks stayed open for business despite a suspension of payments. People continued to make payments and to do business through banks. The only thing changed was that the bank would not hand currency over the counter for deposits. It would transfer checks from one account to another, but checks had to be marked payable only through the clearinghouse. What was called suspension of payments was, in fact, a restriction of convertibility of deposits into currency. The business of the country could continue, and indeed expand, until the panicky fear of bank failures was over and payments could be resumed.

Suspension of payments of this kind was a severe step, but it was a therapeutic measure which prevented the failure of a few banks from leading to the failure of a large number of other banks. However, it was widely believed that this represented a severe and serious defect in the banking system. This led to the establishment of the National Monetary Commission in 1909, and this in turn led to a series of proposals for reform which ultimately ended in the Federal Reserve Act and the establishment of the Reserve System in 1914.

Now, a major purpose in establishing this system, it is quite clear, was to prevent any such banking panic or suspension of payments by the banks to the public.

From Milton Friedman, "A Program for Monetary Stability," in *Conference on Savings and Residential Financing, 1962 Proceedings* (United States Savings and Loan League, Chicago, 1962). Reprinted with kind permission of the author and publisher.

Experience under the Reserve System

The period since 1914, under the Federal Reserve System, is well known, but it is interesting nonetheless to contrast it with the prior period. The interesting thing to ask, I think, is: Comparing the period from 1914 to the present date with the preceding 40 to 50 years, in which case did we have a greater degree of monetary stability?

There is no doubt about the answer. There was a greater degree of monetary stability in the period before the establishment of the Federal Reserve System than in the period after, whether measured by changes in interest rates, instability in the stock of money, instability in prices or instability in economic activity. By any measure I know of, the period after has been more unstable than the one before.

One obvious reason is that there were two world wars after 1914. Those wars would have caused instability under any system. But omit the wars and the answer is still the same. The period since 1914 has been more unstable, in the peacetime years alone, than the period before 1914.

I hasten to add that this is an oversimplification. The great period of instability was the 20 years between the wars, 1919 to 1939. There is no other 20-year period in our history that comes anywhere close to having such great instability. That period contained three major contractions. First there was an inflation from 1919 to 1920, then a severe contraction, then the 1929 to 1933 episode and then the 1937 to 1938 contraction. The period since the end of World War II has not been more unstable than earlier periods, but rather more stable than most.

Greater instability since 1914

Yet, taking as a whole the period since 1914, there is no question that it has been more unstable. Moreover, that period contains the worst banking panic in our history. The 1933 banking panic with its bank holiday, when banks were closed for a week, was incomparably severer and more sweeping than any earlier panic. Whereas the earlier panics came before banks failed and prevented them from failing, the 1933 panic came after the banks had failed and indeed closed the doors of many good banks that were open the day before the panic. The number of banks that opened their doors after the banking holiday in March 1933 was decidedly less than the number that had been open before, and a large fraction of the banks that did not reopen ultimately paid out 100% to their depositors.

So here was a system, established in 1914 for the purpose of preventing banking panics and providing monetary stability, which in practice was associated with the greatest banking panic in U.S. history and a great deal of instability of money.

Is the reason simply that the problems the System had to cope with were severer after the war, so that the earlier system, too, would have had the same problems? I cannot hope to indicate here the reasons I think the answer is in negative, but if you were to examine in detail the successive episodes in the period after 1918, I think you would agree that that is the only conclusion justified by the evidence.

Under the earlier monetary and banking system, imperfect though it was, we would have had less of an inflation in World War I. The wartime inflation would have been there anyway, but the postwar inflation from 1918 to 1920 would not have occurred, which would have eliminated a third of the total inflation. We would not have had the drastic fall in prices in 1920 and 1921, the sharpest fall within a brief period in the whole history of the United States and perhaps of any other country. Prices fell nearly 50%, and two-thirds of the decline came in the six months from August 1920 to February 1921.

The Great Depression

Most important of all, under the earlier system we would not have had the Great Depression of 1929 to 1933. This depression had a traumatic effect upon the thinking of people and their attitude with respect to money and many other matters. It was this event that led to a shift from the belief that money is of the greatest importance to the belief that it is a minor matter which can be left to one side. It was the major event that led to a shift of emphasis from monetary policy to fiscal policy and that produced a widespread expansion in the role of government in the economy after 1933.

It has been widely taken for granted that 1929 to 1933 demonstrated the importance of monetary control. It has been said that here we had a system which was established to prevent such a depression and which had the power, but which in fact did not prevent it. Therefore it was concluded that it must be that money is not very important. I myself think that the episode suggests just the opposite. It suggests that money is so powerful that it needs to be controlled more closely than it was then. If you examine the 1929 to 1933 episode, you will conclude that it was a needless episode. There is no doubt that with the powers then existing in the hands of the System, a very large part of the decline could have been prevented.

I do not mean to be casting blame or suggesting incompetence or lack of will or anything like that. It may be that the ablest, the most intelligent, the most public-spirited men would have made the mistakes that were made at that time. The 1929–1933 period was not one in which the economic depression forced a decline in the stock of money. The decline in the stock of money was a direct consequence of the sequence of bank failures. The banking failures were not important primarily because they involved the failures of financial institutions. They were important because they forced a decline in the stock of money. They forced a decline in the stock of money because the therapeutic device that was earlier available, the device of concerted restriction of convertibility of deposits into currency, was not available because the Reserve System had been established as a lender of last resort. However, the lender of last resort did not perform the function of providing the liquidity in the market that would have enabled the banks to meet their obligations.

At all times the Reserve System had ample power to keep the stock of money from declining. But there is no sign at all of any autonomous easing action on the part of the Reserve System until the spring of 1932, when, faced by great congressional pressure and threats of congressional investigation, the System engaged in open-market operations to the tune of a billion dollars. It stopped two weeks after Congress adjourned. It is literally inconceivable that if the stock of money had stayed constant instead of falling by a third, money income could have fallen by a half or that prices could have fallen by a third. I do not mean to say there would not have been a recession or contraction. It might have been a severe one, but it would have been of a wholly different order of magnitude, and not a catastrophe.

We come to the very important step that was taken: the establishment of the FDIC in 1934, which did prevent banking panics by insuring depositors, thus preventing contagion from spreading as a result of bank failures. In the latter 1930s, the Federal Reserve System was almost entirely passive. The Treasury took over the role of being the money manager.

The Fed's postwar performance

The Federal Reserve did not assume an active role in monetary policy again until after the Treasury-Federal Reserve accord in 1951. The actual performance in the postwar period has been vastly better. This is because the performance has been within a narrower range. We have not moved very vigorously in either direction, but the capacity to make mistakes has not been eliminated.

When we had a contraction in 1957 to 1958, the Federal Reserve System was severely criticized for having maintained what was regarded as a tight money policy for too long, for not reversing itself until late in 1957. It was widely feared that the contraction would be sharp and that the Reserve's hesitancy in reacting to it would make it sharper still. So in early 1958 the System turned around, and in late 1958 there was a very rapid expansion in the stock of money. The increase in the rate of expansion in the stock of money coincided with economic expansion. The recession turned out to be milder than many people expected it to be. The Reserve System, in consequence, must have felt that its own position was rather supported by contrast with that of its critics. It felt that the reason it had had to be so tight from 1956 to 1957 was that it had maintained ease for a very long time before 1955.

This time it decided to have a different policy. The expansion had been under way barely six months when the Reserve System tightened up, early in 1959. The rate of change in the stock of money reached a peak during the summer of that year, and then started going down. I think this clearly was one of the major factors that produced a business cycle peak in 1960 after a very short and brief expansion. That expansion did not run its natural course; it was choked to death early. The steel strike which came at the end of 1959 made it a little difficult to see what was going on, but I think the fact of the matter was that money was tightened up unduly early and that the effect was not felt for something like a year or a year and a half. When it was felt, there was a contraction from 1960 to 1961.

Once again the Reserve System turned around and started to put on a great deal of steam, and again the contraction turned out to be relatively mild, reaching its trough in the spring of 1961. Since then we have been in an expansion, and already there are signs that exactly the same policy is being repeated. Once again we are taking monetary measures, it seems to me, that are likely to spell an early end to this expansion. In this latest episode there is more excuse because of the so-called gold problem. Nonetheless, the main point I want to make is that we again have a series of erratic changes.

In retrospect, it seems perfectly clear that we would have been better off if we had avoided the tightening and the easing and had kept the policy on a steady, even keel instead of shoving one way and then shoving too far the other way.

The lesson I draw from this brief survey of history is that the major problem is how to avoid major mistakes, how to prevent such a concentration of power in a small number of hands that that group can make a major mistake. The great virtue of a decentralized system is that mistakes average out. If one unit does something wrong, it does not have a wide effect. If the power is centralized, there is a great deal of power to do good but, along with it, a great deal of power to do harm. The problem is how to erect a system which will have the effect of reducing the power for harm without unduly reducing the power for good, and which will provide a background of monetary stability.

The problems of monetary reform

That brings me to the problems of monetary reform. These can be classified under three headings: institutional organization of the private banking system; monetary powers of the Federal Reserve and the Treasury; and criteria for controlling the stock of money.

With respect to the institutional organization of the private banking system, we have had extension of governmental control over the private banking system largely because of the intimate relation of banks to the stock of money. Banks have been controlled more closely than other financial institutions for this reason primarily. It recently has been argued extensively, as you know, that the commercial banking system has been declining relative to financial intermediaries such as savings and loan associations, mutual savings banks and so on, that in some way or other the expansion of these intermediaries limits the effectiveness of monetary management and that it would be desirable to extend control by the Federal Reserve to them. I think this whole argument reflects a funda-

mental misconception of wherein the power of the Federal Reserve System lies. The detailed control of banks has almost nothing to do with the essential power of the System. The essential power of the System is the power to determine the total stock of what we call high-powered money—pieces of paper we carry around in our pockets and the reserve balances which the banks hold at the Federal Reserve Banks.

Conceive for a moment a system in which no commercial banks are members of anything called the Federal Reserve System and in which no government agency has any direct control of banks. Let there be no legal reserve requirements for banks at all. Let there be, however, an agency which has an exclusive monopoly of the printing of pieces of paper that can be used for hand-to-hand currency or for vault cash by banks to meet their obligations.

I submit to you that such a system retains all the essential power which the Federal Reserve System now has and that all the rest is trimming. Legal reserve requirements of banks, the ability of the Federal Reserve System to alter these requirements, the requirements that banks keep their reserves as deposits with the Federal Reserve System, the supervision by the Federal Reserve System over day-to-day operations of banks, the clearing of checks by the System—these are all trimmings. You could strip them away and you would not destroy the Reserve System's power.

On the other hand, set up an alternate agency that can print the green paper stuff available for hand-to-hand currency or for vault cash by banks, and the power of the System is destroyed. In consequence, I really think that there is no justification for extending control to financial intermediaries.

Controlling interest on deposits

What we want to do along these lines is to reduce the degree of control which the System exercises over commercial banks. The most obvious way in which the degree of control could be reduced is in minor respects. The present ceilings on interest rates and the present law that makes it illegal to pay interest on demand deposits could and should both be abolished. Their potential for harm has been demonstrated very clearly in recent months.

The prohibition of interest on demand deposits makes for a greater degree of instability in the relationship between demand deposits and time deposits than would otherwise prevail. When interest rates in general go up, the interest rate that commercial banks pay on time deposits tends to go up also, and this tends to increase time deposits in relation to demand deposits. If interest were paid on demand deposits, it could go up, too, and offset the rise in interest on time deposits. Because of the interest ceiling on time deposits, every now and then a still greater degree of instability is introduced into the banking situation because of the arbitrary movement in the fixed price.

In December 1956, the price that banks could pay on time deposits was raised. There was a period, prior to that, of a very slow rise in commercial bank time deposits, and then a very rapid rise. In December 1961, the rate of interest that could be paid by banks was raised again. There has been an extraordinarily rapid rise in time deposits since then, which has made it very difficult to read the monetary figures and to know what they are saying and what is going on.

This instability has nothing to do with the nature of the system. It is introduced entirely by arbitrary regulations of prices; and a very minor, but not negligible, reform would be obtained by either of two devices. The Reserve System could inaugurate one of these on its own. It could set the maximum that the commercial banks could pay on time deposits at 20%; that would keep the regulation from being a source of difficulty. Or, preferably, Congress could pass a law repealing the provision that the banks may not pay interest on demand deposits and repealing any price fixing on time deposits. Either of these would be a minor reform, but worth while.

Banking under 100% reserves

To go much further in reforming the institutional organization of the banking system, it would be necessary to go in the radical direction of eliminating controls over individual banks, in the direction of 100% reserve banking. This move would tend to eliminate all control over the lending and investing activities of banks and would separate out the two functions of banking. On the one hand, we would have banks as depository institutions, safekeeping money and arranging for the services of transferring liabilities by check. They would be 100% reserve banks, pure depository institutions. Their assets would be government liabilities—either pieces of paper or deposits to the credit of the bank on the books of a reserve bank or its equivalent. I would favor the government's paying interest on those liabilities just as it now pays interest on its general government debts. Under a 100% reserve bank, it would be desirable to do this in part because it would provide such banks with an appropriate source of income to enable them to compete on the right level with other banks for funds. Even if we did not go this far, it would be desirable, under present law, to have the government pay interest on its liabilities to commercial banks, namely, on commercial bank demand deposits with the reserve system.

If 100% banking were established, our present banks would be sliced off into other branches operating like small-scale investment trusts. They would be lending and investment agencies in which private individuals would invest funds as they now do in investment trusts and other firms, and these funds would be used to make loans. Such organizations could be completely exempt from the kind of detailed control over financial activities that banks now are subject to.

So much for the institutional organization of the private banking system, which I am skipping over very hastily because I want to turn to matters that perhaps are more important, namely, the monetary powers of the Federal Reserve System and the Treasury.

Supervisory and monetary powers

In addition to its monetary powers, the Federal Reserve System currently has supervisory and examination responsibilities with respect to member banks. In practice, the actual examination is done by an examiner employed by the Comptroller of Currency, by the FDIC or by a state banking commission, so that each bank is not in fact examined by the three agencies that technically have supervisory responsibilities. It seems to me that it would be desirable to go further along these lines. Even if nothing more is done now in the way of extensive reform, supervisory power should be concentrated in one of the other agencies, such as the FDIC, rather than in the Reserve System; and the Reserve System should be relieved of any technical supervisory responsibility and its role legally concentrated on exercising monetary powers.

The more important problem is these monetary powers of the Reserve System. As you know, they consist primarily of three items: (1) the power to change reserve requirements of member banks; (2) the power to rediscount for member banks; and (3) the power to engage in open-market operations.

Of these three powers, the first two are, I

think, inefficient and poorly designed tools of monetary management. In making this judgment, I am assuming that our present system is in all respects unchanged, that the institutional organization of the banking system is what it is and that the criteria for controlling the stock of money are whatever they now are. My purpose in doing this is to separate issues: whatever the criteria are, there remains the question whether present powers are efficient tools for achieving them.

What changes in the present powers of the System would make it more efficient? There seems to be a very strong case for streamlining these powers by eliminating the power of the System to change reserve requirements and to rediscount, and by requiring it to limit its activities to open-market operations. It really is not true that three tools are necessarily better than one, if they can go in opposite directions or if they get in one another's way. That is the case here. To change the metaphor, it is easier to juggle one ball than three.

Suggested changes in present powers

The power to change reserve requirements is a poor tool because it is discontinuous. Changes in reserve requirements tend to be by one percentage point or half a percentage point. If they were by 1/100 of a percentage point it might not be so bad, but a change of 1% in reserves is a very large change. In order to offset the effect, the Reserve System does two things at once. If it makes a one percentage point decrease in reserve requirements with the one hand, with the other hand it pulls out the reserves released; similarly, if it increases the required reserve ratio, it provides additional reserves by open-market operations. This is what it must do if it is going to smooth the effect of reserve requirement change; the offset is never accurate and the whole operation becomes simply an unnecessary source of disturbance. Anything that can be done with reserve requirement changes can be done with open-market operations. Hence, the power to vary reserve requirements ought to be abolished.

So far as rediscounting is concerned, it no longer serves the function of providing a lender of last resort. It was introduced originally for the purpose of enabling banks to have an additional source of liquidity in time of need. That function is now performed indirectly by the FDIC, whose existence helps to prevent banks

from getting into a position where there may be a run on them or, if there is a run on one bank, prevents that run from spreading to other banks.

As a tool of monetary management, rediscounting is unsatisfactory. It tends to lead the Reserve System to do things at times that it has no intention of doing. How tight a particular discount rate is depends on market conditions. Suppose market rates are falling, for whatever reason, as in late 1959, while the Federal Reserve rediscount rate is stable. The same rate then becomes tighter than it was before. The willingness of banks to borrow depends upon the relation between the discount rate and the market rate. If the market rate is high compared to the discount rate, banks have an incentive to borrow. If it is low, they have an incentive to get out of debt to the Reserve Banks, which is the situation now.

The fall of 1959 is a good example. The discount rate was held stable. Market rates moved from a level above the discount rate to below. I am oversimplifying, but the result was that Federal Reserve credit outstanding declined, but not because of any desire on the part of the System to make it decline. The stock of money fell, but not because of any explicit design on the part of the System to make it fall. The System did not deliberately intend to produce a decline in the stock of money from 1959 to 1960; this happened in spite of the System's behavior and, in that particular case, largely because the rediscount rate, being fixed, led to this result. I could give many other examples, but I think this one illustrates my point that the rediscount rate gets the System into trouble.

One way to prevent the discount rate from being a source of trouble would be to fix it at 20%. That would solve the problem. As an alternative, the power of the System to engage in rediscounting could be abolished by law. That would leave available only open-market operations, which are by all odds the most effective way to control the stock of money.

With respect to open-market operations, I should add, however, that there are two agencies now operating. The Federal Reserve and the Treasury both engage in open-market operations.

Role of Treasury in open market

The Treasury's operations illustrate the general principle that the problem is to keep people from making mistakes. The Treasury's debt operations could promote stability, but in fact they have been highly irregular and a source of uncertainty in the market. The best thing to do would be to eliminate that effect. Technically, the best way to do it would be to put all debt management in the hands of the Federal Reserve; it does not make any sense to have two independent agencies in debt management. There would, however, be great political objections to consolidating debt management in the Federal Reserve System.

An alternative that would be just about as good would be to have the Treasury Department adopt a policy that would be stable and predictable. One component of such a policy would be for it to sell no further securities except by auction. To do so it would have to alter the present system of auctioning, which cannot be used in this way for long-term bonds because it is a system in which people pay the price they bid. It is a discriminatory pricing system. The Treasury ought to sell all securities by a method of auction under which all actual purchases are made at the same price. A second component of such a policy would be to reduce the sale of securities to only two kinds or at most a small number of securities, perhaps a very short-term bill and a long-term bond. A third component would be that it should offer them for sale at regular intervals and in stated amounts, so that the public would know six months or a year ahead of time that every week, say, there is going to be an auction for a specified amount of bills and every month for a specified amount of the longer bonds. Further manipulations of the amounts outstanding could be left to the Federal Reserve in connection with its policy for open-market operations.

These changes would provide a streamlined system in which, on the one hand, the Federal Reserve has a simple and efficient tool—open-market operations—and, on the other hand, the Treasury no longer messes up the monetary situation by its erratic debt issues—by its experiments first with one long-term bond and then another, first with advance refunding and then some other "gimmick."

Criteria for controlling the stock of money

What should this streamlined machinery be used for? What should be the criteria for deciding how to change the stock of money?

As I see it, there are only three kinds of criteria for controlling the stock of money.

One is the kind of automatic criterion that is provided by a commodity standard, a gold standard in which we do not have discretionary management of the system but in which the amount of money in the system is determined entirely by external affairs.

I think such a system is neither desirable nor feasible in the United States today. It is not desirable because of the cost involved in getting people to dig up the gold in one part of the world in order to bury it in another part of the world. It is not feasible because we cannot do it on our own; it depends on the willingness of nations all over the world to engage in an international gold standard, and this, I believe, they are not willing to do. It also is not feasible because we are not willing at home to obey its discipline; we are not willing to subordinate domestic stability to the necessities of the external balance of payments.

I should qualify this last statement. Nobody will say he is willing to sacrifice domestic stability to the balance of payments, yet our present policy is one in which we are doing it. Precisely because we are not willing to face the issue clearly, I think we are doing in practice what nobody will say explicitly he is willing to do.

So I do not believe that a "real" gold standard is feasible or possible.

The second alternative is to have discretionary management of money on the part of a group of managers. I have gone to some lengths into our historical record to show the kinds of results discretionary management yields. I do not believe that we have learned so much more than our predecessors that it now is safe to trust these powerful tools in the hands of discretionary managers. The conclusion I have reached on the basis of both the past and recent records is that money is too important to be left to central bankers, if you will permit me to paraphrase Clemenceau.

I come to the conclusion that there is only one other alternative. That is to adopt some kind of rule which will guide our monetary managers, the Reserve System or anybody that controls the stock of money. Many economists have been in favor of the rule that the System be instructed to keep a price level stable. I myself think it is not a good rule. I think the relation between the stock of money and the price level, while close, is too loose, in short intervals and over short periods, for that rule to specify precisely what the Federal Reserve System or any other governmental authorities should do. It still leaves a dispersal of responsibility and the possibility of major mistakes being made.

Steady rate of growth desirable

So I am led to suggest as a rule the simple rule of a steady rate of growth in the stock of money: that the Reserve System be instructed to keep the stock of money growing at a fixed rate, ⅓ of 1% per month or 1/12 of 1% per week or such and such a percentage per day. We instruct it that day after day and week after week it has one thing, and one thing only, to do and that is to keep the stock of money moving at a steady, predictable, defined rate in time.

This is not, under our present System, an easy thing to do. It involves a great many technical difficulties and there will be some deviations from it. If the other changes I suggested were made in the System, it would make the task easier; but even without those changes, it could be done under the present System. While this is by no means necessarily an ideal gadget, it seems, in looking at the record, that it would work pretty well. It would have worked far better, as far as I can see, over the last 50 years than what we actually had, and I think it would continue to work well in the future. I think we do not really know enough under present circumstances to do much better—and this has nothing to do with the particular people who are in control.

I do not believe anybody, including myself, knows enough to do any better. Almost everyone is in favor of countercyclical monetary policy. However, when you ask each one what he means by that policy, you find that Mr. Jones's policy is anathema to Mr. Smith, and Mr. Smith's to Mr. Robinson. In point of fact, there is agreement only on the glittering generalities that the Reserve System should do the right thing in the right way at the right time. There is no agreement on how you know the right time and the right thing to do. The appearance of agreement dissolves, once you put it to the test.

READING 24

The case for government spending and taxing for essential services not readily available otherwise—internal and external security, for example—has seldom been challenged. But, ever since the 1930s, there has been prolonged debate on the extent to which such spending and taxing should be shaped not by needs for specific services but rather by the broad search for an economy operating at high levels of employment without inflation.

The key issues in the debate about fiscal policy for the federal government appear to be these:

1. *Will it work?* Can government effectively alter its spending or taxing at the right time and in the right amount to have the desired effect? What does past experience teach us?

2. *What about the national debt?* Can we afford deficit financing and still avoid inflation? Must we balance the budget every year, over the business cycle, or simply at times of full employment?

3. *Is it compatible with free enterprise?* Does a bigger stabilizing role for government hurt or help the preservation of free economic institutions in today's world?

In this article, Francis M. Bator of the Department of Economics at Massachusetts Institute of Technology states the case for those who find a proper and healthy function of government in the use of fiscal powers to achieve our employment and price goals. His analysis summarizes the interventionists' answers on the debt and inflation questions.

Questions to Guide the Reading

What are the principal difficulties associated with a willingness to use an active fiscal policy of deficits and surpluses? Which of the difficulties are economic in nature and which are political?

If Bator is right in his comments on the impact of our large national debt, why do fears about that debt continue to be so widespread?

THE CASE FOR ACTIVE FISCAL POLICY
Francis M. Bator

I think it safe to infer that most people, if asked their views about the proper rule of conduct for a fiscally responsible government, would answer: "Balance the budget, or, better still, run a surplus and pay off the national debt." In contrast, a very large majority of economists hold that whatever may be the case for balance or imbalance in a particular year, the budget-balance rule is misleading and mischievous, bound to result in gross misallocation of resources.

To be sure, the question of what the level of federal spending and taxing ought to be in a particular year is a matter of legitimate dispute. There is room for technical argument about the exact quantitative effect of budgets on employment, prices, the growth rate, and the like. More important, there would be ground for debate even if economic forecasting were an exact science. Different budgets will have different effects on the balance between private and public use of resources: on the balance between defense and schools, on the one hand, and personal consumables on the other; on consumption today as against investment for consumption in the future; on income distribution—matters which touch on fundamental ethical, social, and political values, about which reasonable men will differ.

The question at issue here, however, is whether the federal budget should be balanced year in and year out as a matter of right. Is budget balance a sound general rule of fiscal conduct?

Anyone who believes, as I do, that it is not—especially if he finds irritating the liturgical quality of the editorial incantations—is tempted to score some debating points. Why, for instance, is annual balance the right rule, not monthly or

weekly balance? Or, if it is the impact of government as a whole that matters, why should the *federal* budget be balanced? Should it not be used to offset surpluses and deficits in state and local budgets? Or—and this is an issue of some importance—why, of the three budgets prepared by the federal government, is the "administrative budget" invariably singled out as the budget to be balanced, considering that it excludes some $25 billion worth of federal trust fund transactions, shows corporate-profit-tax accruals with a half-year lag, and treats loans as though they were expenditures? The difference is not trivial: in the current fiscal year the administration budget is expected to be in the red by $7 billion. The national income accounts budget, which is the most relevant from the point of view of economic impact, will show a deficit of only about $500 million.

But these are debating points. For the true case against balance, one has to probe deeper.

The case against budget balance

The view that budget balance is a bad guide rests on the following series of propositions (stated in their boldest form):

1. Both inflation, a rise in the federal level of prices, and recession, a shortfall in the output of the economy relative to potential output, are bad.

Although it is a question of degree—rapid or sustained inflation and deep or persistent recession are qualitatively more damaging than a slow, intermittent upward creep in prices and short, shallow recessions—the point needs little defense. Inflation results in capricious redistribution of income and wealth, and, in increasing proportion

From Francis M. Bator, "Money and Government," *Atlantic Monthly*, April, 1962. Reprinted with kind permission of the author and publisher.

to its speed, will blunt the efficiency of the price system in allocating resources according to consumers' tastes. Recession, as evidenced by unemployment in excess of 4 percent of the labor force, involves both the personal tragedy of joblessness and the irredeemable waste of valuable goods and services, as reflected in lost wages and profits. As a consequence of the three recessions since 1953, we have squandered, in the form of idle capacity and idle men, some $180 billion worth of potential output, an amount equal to about one third of the economy's total output in 1961. And recession, like inflation, leads to arbitrary and damaging changes in the distribution of income. Although everybody except the smart or lucky speculator loses—profit incomes shrink proportionately more than do wage incomes—a large fraction of the loss in wages and salaries is shouldered by the unemployed.

2. *If we are not to suffer either appreciable price inflation or recession, total demand for goods and services must be kept in close balance with the growing potential of the economy to produce them.*

Total demand for goods and services consists of the sum of personal consumption expenditures, private investment spending for plant, buildings, equipment, and inventory, and government purchases of goods and services.

Potential output is the maximum output the economy is capable of producing at an efficient, businesslike level of operation, with unit costs close to their minima, with plants operating at about 95 percent of rated capacity (not 105 percent), with enough slack to avoid persistent bottlenecks, and with the unemployment rate, which is the best single indicator of slack, at about 3.5 to 4 percent (not 2.9 percent, as in 1953, or 5 to 7 percent, as in 1960–1961).

3. *Although a more or less competitive price-market system, based on private property and the incentive of profit, is a potent device for efficiently mediating the allocation of resources among private uses according to consumers' wants, it is not equipped with an automatic balance wheel which will ensure that total demand will remain in phase with potential output, even if all government budgets are kept in balance and the monetary authorities follow the canons of orthodoxy.*

For circumstantial evidence one has only to skim the economic history of capitalist market economies. But, suggestive as it is, the crude evidence about boom and bust is not conclusive. Many argue, for instance, that the fault has lain entirely in clumsy meddling by muddled governments. And, indeed, one cannot deny that only too often government has been the culprit. There *is* need for better fiscal and monetary performance.

However, the truth that governments have a black record does not imply that if only they went out of business or were restricted to the maintaining of the jails, financed through annually balanced budgets, then the price mechanism would ensure a close match between demand and potential output. There exist powerful built-in forces in a market economy which tend to generate wide, self-aggravating swings in total demand. Even under the most favorable assumptions of perfect competition, with flexible prices and wage rates, the stabilizers built into a wholly private price-market system could only guarantee that no situation of recession or depression—or, with a fixed supply of money, of price inflation—could persist indefinitely. It is not at all certain that they would ensure tolerably prompt correction of either an inflationary or a deflationary gap between total demand and potential output.

In a modern context, with the prevalence of market control in both labor and product markets, there simply do not exist automatic private market forces which will keep fluctuations within tolerable limits. The fiscal and monetary powers of government represent the only effective antibody mechanism we possess.

It must not be thought that the apparent invulnerability to serious depression of the United States economy since the war disproves the point. During every one of the post-war recessions we were saved from much more serious trouble by the stabilizing effect of the decline in tax revenues and the increase in social security spending which automatically follow any decline in incomes and rise in unemployment. In 1958, the automatic deficit provided us with a cushion of the order of $7 billion. It is not pleasant to think about what would have happened if we had obeyed the dictates of ideology and attempted to balance the budget by cutting down on spending, or by raising tax rates as did the government in 1932.

4. *By appropriate variation of taxes, transfer payments, or its own purchases, and by appropriate supplementary use of credit policy, the federal government can substantially limit the swings in total spending and contain within reasonably narrow bounds—narrower than in the recent past—any gap that may occur between total demand and output, on the one hand, and potential output, on the other. In order to do so, how-*

ever, the federal budget must either periodically show a large deficit, as well as, periodically, a surplus; or, if deficits are ruled out of order or kept within narrow limits, the absolute level of the budget (purchases and matching taxes) will have to be varied by enormous amounts.

The crude qualitative facts about the workings of fiscal measures are simple. Raising the level of government purchases will add directly to the flow to total demand. If not offset by taxes, it will give rise also to an equal increase in private incomes, and thereby induce a rise in the private component of total demand. The induced increase in private demand, in turn, will further swell private incomes, and hence cause a still further but smaller rise in private demand. The process of expansion is self-limiting, since on each round of the circular flow of spending → output → income → spending, there will be some leakage into private saving or, unless rates are cut, taxes.

A reduction in taxes or an increase in government transfer payments will not in and of itself add to demand. However, it will raise the level of private after-tax income, and hence induce an increase in private demand. Once again, the first-round increase in private demand will further raise private incomes and cause a still further, smaller rise in private demand. Once again, the process of expansion is self-limiting.

None of this bears any analogy to "pump priming," strictly defined. The notion that a *one-shot* injection of public spending would suffice to ensure a *sustained* change in the level of total demand is no part of modern economics. It takes a sustained change in the level of spending or taxing (to a new plateau) to cause a sustained larger change in the level of total demand. The leverage is due to the induced secondary increase in private demand.

There is no need to labor the mechanics. The fact is that a gap between total demand and potential output can be offset by a change in the level of government purchases or transfer payments of taxes, or by some mutually reinforcing or even partly countervailing blend of all three kinds of action, combined with reinforcing or partially countervailing monetary measures. Moreover, unless the different instruments are used to defeat each other, the initial fiscal change need only be some fraction of the gap. The secondary induced effects on private demand will make up the difference.

Does it follow from all this that to eliminate a deflationary shortfall of demand we must have a deficit, that surpluses are not only a good thing

but have a restraining effect on total demand, and that balanced budgets are neutral?

If so, the case for deficits in recession and surpluses to fight demand inflation would be both strong and clear. However, it is not quite so. Balanced budgets are not neutral, but have an expansionary effect. The effect on total demand, for instance, of a balanced budget with purchases and taxes (less transfers) at an annual rate of $10 billion will be approximately $10 billion per year. The $10 billion worth of pre-tax income generated by production in response to government orders is all siphoned off by the Treasury, and therefore, private after-tax income and hence *private* spending are not affected. But as long as government purchases and taxes remain at $10 billion a year, total demand will be $10 billion higher than if government spending and taxes were zero.

For the same reason, any balanced change in purchases and taxes will cause total demand to change in the same direction and approximately by the same amount. (The economist reader will note that I ignore changes in private spending owing to changes in income distribution, and also the effect on investment of the rate of change in the level of income and of changes in interest rates caused by government finance. Quantitatively, such effects will be too small to alter the qualitative conclusions.)

But if balanced increases in the federal budget will add to total demand, and balanced decreases will compress demand, what remains of the case against balance? Why not do honor to "fiscal responsibility" and fight recessions and inflation by balanced changes in spending taxes?

There are two related reasons. In order to offset a shortfall in total demand by a balanced rise in purchases and taxes, we should have to increase government purchases by approximately the full amount of the shortfall. In general, the smaller the deficit we allow ourselves in recession, the larger will be the increase in government purchases needed to offset a given deficiency in total demand. And the larger the swings in budget levels, the more resources will have to be shifted back and forth between private and government use, for no better cause than that the alternative would be to shift them back and forth from some use into involuntary nonuse.

There is also a second, deeper reason for not accepting the budget-balance rule. Government budgets are not simply a device for securing harmony between total demand and potential supply. The public budget is the principal means for channeling resources to the national defense and to education, public transportation, public health, and basic research. It is also an important means for combating the pockets of primitive poverty in various parts of the country; for helping the old and the sick; and for ensuring, by education, housing, and public health, a greater equality of opportunity for children of equal ability. When we decide on the level of public spending, we are in effect deciding how much of our resources to allocate to these public tasks and how much to leave for private capital formation and the personal consumption of those better able to help themselves.

Inevitably, opinions will differ about what the balance should be. Inevitably, too, the differences must be compromised by means of political procedures operating through our institutions of representative government. But one thing is plain. The choice should not be made in blind response to variations in total private demand, as it would be if we insist on maintaining the budget in balance.

5. If we responsibly follow modern fiscal doctrine, paying no heed to the balanced-budget rule, we can do much better than we have in the past in avoiding both recession and demand inflation. At the same time we shall be free, within broad limits, to strike whatever balance we desire between public goods and private goods and between current consumption and investment for growth, without foreclosing on questions of income distribution and without in any way weakening our reliance on the price-market system for mediating production and exchange according to private profit and, where private goods are concerned, private choice.

The eminent economist Paul Samuelson has called this doctrine the "neo-classical synthesis" because it combines the deep truths of classical economics, which apply to the scarcity-ridden world of full employment, with what we have learned during the past three decades about recessions and depressions—and inflations. It is perhaps the happiest proposition ever spawned by the "dismal science," but it is no daydream. As Samuelson put it, the doctrine "springs from careful use of the best modern analyses of economics that scholars here and abroad have over the years been able to attain."

It is important not to claim too much. Even if we manage our fiscal and monetary instruments with much greater skill and wisdom than we have in the past, many of our economic problems will remain. The modern fiscal doctrine is no cure-

all. But none of the qualifications and refinements which a fuller discussion would require should be used to conceal its central import. Modern democratic governments can, by reasonably sensible exercise of their traditional fiscal and monetary instruments, sharply limit the excesses of boom and bust. Moreover, they can do so without any undesirable increases in government spending, without recourse to any of the paraphernalia of direct controls which would abort the workings of the price system, and without resort to the socialist medicine of nationalization and government production.

Why it is, then, that modern fiscal and monetary doctrine is so disturbing to many people who think of themselves as conservative? Why do they consider radical and dangerous a doctrine through which we can virtually cure the most serious failures of capitalist institutions by treatment no more harsh than, say, appropriate variation of tax rates and of the supply of money?

Much of the explanation lies in the realm of history and social psychology. One wonders, for instance, to what degree the attitude of the older generation of businessmen reflects an instinctive association, no matter how unjustified, of modern fiscal doctrine with the anti-business flavor of the New Deal.

Some of it, however, involves such matters as inflation and the balance of payments, and a misunderstanding of what we can and cannot expect markets to do for us. It is to these that we now turn.

"Where will the money come from?"

The clue to a whole class of objections to deficit spending lies in the perennial question, "Where will the money come from?" It is to evade the issue to point out the obvious—that the government can either borrow money from the public by selling it some IOU's or manufacture money, if not by the printing press, by the more subtle device of borrowing from the central bank. The question is, should it?

Consider the more radical-sounding method—financing of deficits by selling bonds to the Federal Reserve, thereby increasing the amount of money outstanding. Why do most people consider that a dangerous thing to do?

The standard answer, "Inflation," raises a crucial issue of definition. If one chooses to *define* inflation as an increase in the stock of money, then, of course, printing money is tantamount to inflation. But if so, the question, "Why is printing money bad?", remains unanswered, unless one is satisfied with, "Printing money (inflation) is bad because printing money (inflation) is bad."

What people really have in mind, of course, is that printing money will *cause* inflation, defined not as an increase in the money supply but as a rise in the level of prices. There will be "too much money chasing too few goods"—or, more precisely, too much money spending chasing too few goods, and therefore there will have to be a rise in prices and a fall in the value of the currency.

Will it be so? An increase in government spending relative to taxes financed by new or even borrowed money will certainly cause total spending for goods and services to rise. If total spending is thereby made to press against potential output, the effect would indeed be inflationary; there would be a rise in prices. But there is nothing in modern fiscal doctrine which favors increased spending and cutting taxes when total demand is pushing against potential output. The modern prescription is quite the opposite: when demand threatens to outrun potential, contract the supply of money, cut spending, and/or raise taxes (even though the budget is in the black and revenues are rising).

The occasion for cutting taxes relative to spending and expanding the supply of money arises when total demand is substantially less than potential output, and therefore, an increase in total spending is precisely what is wanted in order to draw idle labor and idle plant and machinery into producing useful private or public goods. In other words, the modern prescription calls for the expansion of demand only when the extra spending can be accommodated by drawing idle resources and idle men into useful employment, and when, therefore, the additional demand need not exhaust itself in rising prices.

But will not the increment in money created during recession cause trouble once the economy is approaching full employment? Not if we follow the modern prescription and apply our monetary and fiscal brakes in accordance with the circumstances. When inflation threatens and the need is for keeping total demand in check, the Federal Reserve can supplement restrictive fiscal measures by using open-market operations and its power over the reserve requirements of commercial banks to mop up any excess money and tighten credit.

(To avoid inflation, it would not suffice simply to maintain the supply of money constant. An increase in the money supply is not a necessary condition for inflation to occur, any more than it is a sufficient condition. Total spending for goods and services is not rigidly limited by the stock of money. The rate of turnover of money—the velocity of circulation, so-called—can and does rise, and not a little, during periods of expansion; with bullish prospects for capital gains on securities, and worries about the price level, people will economize on idle cash. Moreover, with a modern fraction-reserve banking system, the central bank has to take action during a boom just to keep the money supply constant. The natural response of our monetary system in the absence of active central-bank policy is to feed any expansion.)

The proper use of taxes

The importance of penetrating the "veil of money" and forcing oneself to think through what the effects of fiscal and monetary measures will be on the demand and supply of real goods and services is perhaps most vividly illustrated by the example of taxes. The economic justification for taxation (as for borrowing) is not, shocking as it may seem, to conserve money by collecting enough of it to finance the government's expenditures. It is, after all, not money that is scarce as an inescapable fact of nature, but goods and services, and the labor and the managerial and technical skills, the machinery, plant, transport facilities, and raw materials needed to produce those goods and services. And if it is goods and services that we care about and want to conserve, then we must employ taxes not to secure balance between the Treasury's income and outgo but rather to bring about such changes in private demand as are necessary to ensure that total private plus public demand will neither exceed potential output, causing inflation, nor fall substantially short of potential output, thereby causing wanton waste of resources.

The point is of central importance: the principal purpose of raising taxes is to compress the level of private demand and thereby release resources from private use—not to finance government. For instance, if President Kennedy's barely balanced administrative budget for fiscal 1963 should turn out to be based on too optimistic a forecast about the rate of expansion of private demand, and if, therefore, revenues during the fiscal year begin to fall short of planned expenditures and the budget begins to show red, then raising tax rates or cutting expenditures in order to eliminate or reduce the deficit would be the wrong thing to do. It would amplify the initial shortfall in total demand; it would shift more resources from private and public use into involuntary idleness. Assuming that it is resources, labor and real capital, that we care about, sensible fiscal policy would call for measures which would make the automatic initial deficit bigger—for increases in spending above the originally planned level and/or a cut in tax rates, as well as easy money.

Conventional fiscal thinking leads to upside-down economics also in regard to inflation. If, during the 1963 fiscal year, total demand—and hence income, output, and employment—should grow much faster than is now anticipated and the administrative budget begins to show a much larger surplus than is now expected, and, most important, if bottlenecks and widespread price pressures begin to appear, then the appropriate fiscal reaction would not be either to spend the windfall of extra revenue or to give it away in tax cuts. The right policy would involve some mixture of tight money, higher tax rates, and cutbacks in spending—that is, making the budgetary surplus larger.

The moral is plain. If we want to use taxes to help balance the economy, we must be prepared to take active measures to make both deficits (in recession) and surpluses (during demand inflation) bigger.

What about the national debt?

From reading the editorial pages of some of our newspapers, one might conclude that among our national pastimes, railing against the national debt belongs somewhere between baseball and sex. Yet the economics of the national debt are both straightforward and undramatic:

1. All the reasons why deficits financed by the printing press are inflationary only when undertaken at the wrong time apply a fortiori to deficits financed by borrowing from the public. (The act of borrowing, taken by itself, tends to depress private spending, in that it will reduce bank reserves, cause interest rates to rise, and lead to generally tighter credit. However, the negative effect on private spending will be much smaller than the positive effect when the government spends the money.)

2. Of all our national concerns, the worry that one of these days the ax will fall and we shall have to pay off the entire national debt is per-

haps the most groundless. To be sure, each day of every week there will be bondholders who will want to be paid off. If so, they can sell their bonds at the going market price if they are legally "marketable," or turn them in if they are not. In this one respect, government bonds are like the bonds of AT&T or any other large private corporation. Of course, in the case of the government, the bonds are secured not by a claim on the profits and assets of a particular corporation but by the fiscal and monetary powers of the United States government. If the government fails to use its fiscal and monetary powers to prevent price inflation, holders of private bonds suffer as well as holders of government bonds.

3. Almost all other analogies between the national debt and private debt or international debt are false. Private debt, or debt owed to foreign governments or individuals, is external. It is owed to others. The national debt is internal. It is owed by Americans to Americans. It does not reflect a claim by others on our resources. There is no external creditor.

4. The total of goods and services available to our children and grandchildren will not be smaller because there will be in existence during their lifetime a national debt, some of which will have been incurred last year or this. They will owe the money to each other. The taxes collected by government from any grandchild Peter to finance interest and repayment will go into the pockets of some grandchild Paul who inherited government bonds. (Anyone who thinks the above reasoning somewhat shady might reflect on the fact that, just as there is no subtraction from the total of goods and services available to us when some of the debt is paid off, there is no net gain of goods and services to a nation and its citizens when the debt is incurred. Increasing the national debt, unlike adding to external debt, does not enable a nation to have more goods and services than it can produce; repaying it, in turn, will not deprive it of any output that it has the resources to produce.)

5. It does not follow that the national debt is without burden. There *is* a deadweight loss involved in the transfer of resources, in the form of interest, from taxpayers in general to bondholders. If, therefore, the national debt were to grow much faster than the GNP, there might be cause for concern. However, the facts are reassuring. The ratio of the publicly held federal debt (including debt held by the Federal Reserve Banks and by state and local governments) to the GNP, which was 45 percent in 1939 and

rose to 118 percent in 1945, has fallen more or less steadily, to 64 percent by 1952 and 46 percent by 1961. Interest charges in 1961 amounted to 1.5 percent of the national income, as against 2.3 percent in 1946.

"It didn't work in the thirties"

Of all the myths which masquerade as solid economic truth, few are more pernicious or false than the proposition that a compensatory fiscal policy was tried during the 1930s and found wanting. The truth is, as anyone who bothers to take a look at the crude quantitative evidence would quickly come to suspect, that it was not tried—at least not until 1940–1942, when it worked like a charm, although then, because of the urgent needs of national defense, we had to overdo it.

The measurement of fiscal impact is a subtle and technical business. It is necessary, for instance, to sort out the discretionary changes which occur when the government changes tax rates or its spending programs from the automatic changes in spending and revenues which occur as a built-in consequence of changes in income and employment. Certainly one cannot tell much by simply looking at deficits. Nonetheless, it is a salutary if slightly misleading fact, in the light of the massive collapse in the level of private demand from $96 billion in 1929 to $48 billion in 1933, that the federal deficit was $2.1 billion in 1931, $1.5 billion in 1932, $1.3 billion in 1933, $2.9 billion in 1934, $3.5 billion in 1936, and $0.2 billion, $2.0 billion, and $2.2 billion, respectively, in 1937, 1938, and 1939. The federal surplus in 1921 was $1.2 billion; the deficit in 1942, $33.2 billion.

Actually, even at a superficial level, the federal performance was rather better than that. If one corrects for the decline in the price level between 1929 and 1933, the federal budget went from a surplus, as measured in 1961 prices, of $2.4 billion in 1929 to deficits of $4.9 billion in 1931, $3.4 billion in 1933, and (a peak) $8.5 billion in 1936. Even in "real" terms, however, federal deficits were dwarfed by the $65 billion drop in the level of private spending between 1929 and 1933, as measured, once again, in 1961 prices.

Whatever doubts the above figures may raise about the proposition that during the Great Depression the federal government engaged in a compensatory fiscal program of the size which modern doctrine would have called for are confirmed by M.I.T. Professor E. Cary Brown's rigorous econometric analysis of the quantitative impact of fiscal policy in the 1930s, "Fiscal Policy in the 'Thirties: A Reappraisal" (*American Economic Review*, December, 1956). Brown demonstrates that

> The federal government's policies were little more than adequate in most years of the 'thirties to offset [the] contractive effects of state and local government . . . the fiscal policy undertaken by all three levels of government was clearly relatively stronger in the 'thirties than in 1929 in only two years—1931 and 1936. . . . The primary failure of fiscal policy to be expansive in this period is attributable to the sharp increase in tax structure enacted at all levels of government. . . . The federal Revenue Act of 1932 virtually doubled full employment tax yields.

It would be easy in the light of present knowledge but unfair to cast all the blame on the Roosevelt Administration. To be sure, there were people who recommended much larger increases in spending, sensing that somehow the old classical rules derived from scarcity were not entirely applicable to a situation where one quarter of the labor force was unemployed and plant and equipment were operating at 50 percent of capacity. Some people even suggested that increased spending need not be accompanied by higher tax rates, that it might be a good idea, rather, to encourage additional private demand by cutting taxes. But it is difficult for a democratic government to violate deeply held rules of "fiscal responsibility," no matter how wrongheaded. Moreover, there simply did not exist, until the very late thirties, a comprehensive doctrine, factually based on a rational analytical structure, which would have proved a defense against the great many who felt that budget deficits were taking the country to perdition.

Cost-push inflation

A rather more sophisticated argument against the modern doctrine than any we have yet considered—more sophisticated in its premise, if not in its conclusion—turns on the phenomenon of inflation during recessions. Since imperfect competition in many labor and product markets can lead to inflationary wage-price bargains and cause many prices to be flexible only in one direction, up, and since many prices are publicly administrated or protected—for example, in transport, power, agriculture—price inflation is not invariably a symptom of demand pressing against potential output. It can occur, as in the 1950s, while markets for both labor and goods are slack.

If the pessimists are right, if labor and management will not exercise restraint at the bargaining table and in setting prices, then no level of total demand will yield both price stability and the full use of our potential. Our monetary and fiscal managers will face a continuing choice between a little faster price creep and a little less output and more unemployment. But whatever line we may wish them to take, the case *for* a sophisticated, flexible, differentiated fiscal and monetary strategy, and *against* the balanced-budget rule, stands. The nastier the winds and the tides, the more dangerous it is to tie down the tiller dead center.

There is an important technical point here. If we manage to achieve an average unemployment rate of 4 to 4.5 percent by ranging between 3 percent during booms and 6 percent during recessions, wage rates and prices will rise less than if we achieve the same 4 percent average with variations running from 2.5 percent to 7 or 8 percent. The rate of increase in wage rates during booms is a function not only of the duration of the boom but also of the amount of excess demand in the labor market. On the other hand, any decline in wage rates that occurs during a recession is only marginally sensitive to the amount of excess supply in the labor market. Having more slack during recessions will not cancel out the effect on wage rates of more excess demand during booms. (In general, when the economy is near full employment, wages and also prices rise more than proportionately as unemployment drops.)

The balance of payments

There remains the argument that we cannot afford deficits because of the balance of payments. Since rapid expansion of demand will suck in imports and, if it triggers a rise in prices, will make our exports less competitive and imports more attractive, there is good reason to set more modest targets than would be the case if the United States were living in isolation and did not have to maintain a large surplus of exports over imports to cover its international obligations and the outflow of private capital. Balance-of-payments and cost-push considerations certainly help to explain the Kennedy fiscal strategy of cautious expansion, of not trying too quickly to close the still substantial gap between demand and potential output.

Once again, however, all this has to do with the setting of more or less modest targets for total demand. And once again it strengthens rather than weakens the case for flexible, variegated use of our fiscal and monetary controls to keep total demand growing at the rate which offers the best compromise between the marginally conflicting requirements, on the one hand, of international balance and domestic price stability, and, on the other, of more output and faster growth.

The argument that a deficit—no matter how benign it may be in terms of the price level and our exports and imports, and how desirable in terms of output, employment, and the profitability of the American market for the foreign investor—is too dangerous to tolerate because of its effects on "world psychology" hardly merits comment. The notion that the international financial community, including the large European central banks, will engage in large-scale dumping of dollars, and thereby precipitate a major financial crisis, simply on account of a deficit in the United States administrative budget is preposterous on its face and hardly consistent with the fact of a $7 billion deficit during the current fiscal year. It does not follow, of course, that there is no need for improved international monetary arrangements to make the dollar and the pound less vulnerable to destabilizing speculation.

Feasibility

What about the charge that economic life is too uncertain and complicated for the fiscal and monetary authorities to know what they are doing?

It would be foolish to assert that to operate an effective stabilization policy following modern doctrine is easy. Forecasting is an art, matters of timing and magnitude are delicate, and the machinery of administration and legislation is cumbersome. We cannot and should not try to eliminate all fluctuations or play it too close. Good fiscal doctrine requires that one leave plenty of room for error.

But, in the main, the view that "It cannot be done" is wrong. There is much more regularity to economic life than most people suspect. Damped by the built-in stabilizers, the economy moves slowly and predictably enough for us to keep adjusting our fiscal and monetary controls according to need—unless, of course, we lock them in place. (People who are concerned that delayed responses will make for perverse policy should give strong support to the President's request for stand-by authority temporarily to vary income-tax rates by up to five percentage points, subject to congressional veto. Such discretionary authority would be a powerful instrument of "preventive action," as Walter Lippmann called it. Anyone who doubts its efficacy—or the feasibility of translating modern monetary and fiscal doctrine into responsible policy—would do well to test his views against the 1962 *Annual Report of the Council of Economic Advisers.*)

Irresponsible government?

There is left, of course, the big question: Can a democratic government be trusted to be responsible? Anyone inclined to think not should keep in mind that to abandon the balance-the-budget rule is not to abandon all constraints on government spending. Any increase in spending which will cause total demand to exceed potential output will cause a sharp rise in prices. The faster the growth in government spending, the less occasion will there be for deficits to stimu-

late private spending, and the more frequent will be the need for surpluses to counter inflation. To claim that relaxing budget balance gives license to government to go on a binge of spending is to assume that the American government will create run-away inflation. Is that likely, given the sensitivity of the electorate to increases in prices? Certainly the stability of the price level during the past year should provide reassurance.

Nevertheless, there is no denying that if we jettison budget balance, we do in effect remove a constraint on government. But is that a sufficient reason for not doing so, for insisting on balance? Surely one must consider what the consequences would be if the restraint is not removed. For make no mistake, the price system, if not supplemented by a fiscal and monetary policy following modern doctrine, provides no protection against large-scale unemployment and rapid inflation. Can we afford such failure? How long would the country remain committed to a capitalist orientation?

READING 25   THE CASE FOR THE BALANCED BUDGET

These two excerpts state the opposing case to the one advanced by Professor Bator in the previous reading. They are written by men with impressive experience in Washington: Maurice Stans was at one time director of the Bureau of the Budget under President Eisenhower, and Harry F. Byrd has been a United States Senator from Virginia since 1933.

Both men are prominently identified with what was for a long time in our history the orthodox view of government's fiscal responsibility. "Balance the budget" has had and still has a firm hold on American thought; its strength was nowhere more evident than in the tax-cut debate of 1963 when even the pro-tax-cut forces in Congress sought assurances that it was really safe to run a deficit deliberately. The roots of the fears and doubts about even temporarily unbalanced budgets are well set out in these excerpts.

Questions to Guide the Reading

Are the policy guides that would flow from Stans and Byrd identical with one another? Might Stans accept a deficit under some circumstances where Byrd would still plead for a balanced budget?

Do these two excerpts offer a satisfactory rebuttal to the Bator position? Is it possible (and likely) that we can have the active fiscal policy for which Bator calls and still manage to avoid the inflation which Stans and Byrd fear as we approach full employment levels?

What would be the implications of steady decreases in the federal budget? Would we then get sufficient expansion of private debts to utilize the growing volume of savings in the economy?

A. THE NEED FOR BALANCED FEDERAL BUDGETS*
Former Budget Director Maurice H. Stans

The federal government should have a balanced budget; its expenditures, especially in times like these, should not exceed its income. Of this I am deeply convinced.

As a matter of fact, I find it difficult to understand why there are still some people who do not seem to agree. Even though I have now been an official of the government almost four years and know by hard experience that there are at least two sides to all public questions, on this one the facts speak eloquently for themselves. And the arguments that are marshalled in opposition to show that a balanced budget is unimportant—or that it can be safely forsaken for lengthy periods of time—certainly seem unsound. It is true that we as a nation have been extremely fortunate in maintaining our fundamental strengths thus far despite the heavy deficit spending of the past thirty years. But we cannot count on being lucky forever; and more and more the consequences of past profligacy are now catching up with us.

Let us look at some of the facts:

1. It is a fact that in 24 of the last 30 years (i.e., up to 1959) the federal government has spent more than it has received.

2. It is a fact that last fiscal year (1958) the federal government had a deficit (12.5 billion dollars) larger than ever before in time of peace.

3. It is a fact that the federal government debt is now 290 billion dollars (in 1959) and that the annual cost of carrying that debt is more than 10 per cent of the budgeted income of the government—and has been going up.

4. It is a fact that our economy is operating at a higher rate of activity than it ever has before and that the standard of living it is producing for all America is far beyond that of any other country in the world.

5. It is a fact that in times of high economic activity there is competition among business, consumers, and government for the productive resources of the country; if government, by indulging in high levels of spending in such times, intensifies that competition, it openly invites inflation.

6. It is a fact that with an unbalanced budget, federal borrowings to raise the money to spend more than income tend to add to the money supply of the country and therefore are inflationary.

7. It is a fact that the purchasing power of the dollar has declined more than 50 per cent in the last twenty years. Today we spend more than $2.00 to get what $1.00 would buy in 1939.

8. And finally, it is a fact that all too often in history inflation has been the undoing of nations, great and small.

True, there are many people who still feel that a bit of inflation is a tolerable, if not a good, thing. I think they fail to see that a bit of inflation is an installment on a lot of inflation—a condition in which nobody can hope to gain.

Those of our citizens who believe that inflation is not undesirable simply overlook the history of nations. Inflation is an insidious threat to the strength of the United States. Unless we succeed in exercising a tighter rein over it than we have been able to up to this point, I am afraid that we will all lose—as individuals, as a nation, and as a people.

In my view, the facts that I have recited clearly demonstrate the need for:

1. Containing federal expenditures within federal income—which means balancing the budget—in fiscal years 1960 and 1961.

2. Establishing the principle of a balanced budget—including some surplus for reduction of the national debt—as a fiscal objective for the prosperous years ahead.

These are the standards on which fiscal integrity for the nation should rest. These are the standards by which the force of inflation induced by reckless fiscal policy can be averted. Yet in 24 of the last 30 years we have not been able to attain them.

Let us look at some of the circumstances which have caused heavy federal spending in the past and have, perhaps, made us insensitive to the dangers of deficits.

Looking back

Over the last three decades the federal government has spent 264 billion dollars more than it has received. The six years in which there was

* From Maurice H. Stans, "The Need for Balanced Federal Budgets," *Annals of the American Academy of Political and Social Science,* 1959. Reprinted with kind permission of the author and publisher.

an excess of income over expense produced negligible surpluses in relation to the deficits of the other years.

We need hardly be reminded of the cause of most of those deficits. In the earlier years it was depression; in the middle years it was war; in recent years it has been war again and then recession.

In the depression years it was not possible to balance the budget; while government services and costs were growing by popular demand, federal revenues declined as a result of economic inactivity. The efforts made to balance the budget by increasing tax rates in 1930 and 1932 and in 1936 and 1938 were apparently self-defeating.

As for the expenditure side of the budget, the decade of the 1930's produced a great deal of talk about "pump-priming" and "compensatory spending"—federal spending which would compensate in poor times for the decline in business and consumer demand and thus lend balance and stability to the economy. The theory was, of course, for the federal government to spend proportionately larger amounts during depression times and proportionately smaller amounts during good times—to suffer deficits in poor years and enjoy surpluses in prosperous years, with the objective of coming out even over the long pull.

Then, in the early 1940's came World War II. During the war years, the federal government's expenditures vastly exceeded its income, and huge further deficits were piled up. In retrospect, most students of wartime economic developments now agree that we did not tax ourselves nearly enough. We did not pay enough of the costs of war out of current income. We created a large debt while suppressing some of its inflationary consequences with direct economic controls, but the suppression was only temporary.

Depression and war, although major factors, were not the only reasons for increased federal expenditures and deficits during the past thirty years. It was more complex than that. In the 1930's the national philosophy of the responsibilities of the federal government underwent a major change. The country's needs for economic growth and social advancement were gradually given increased recognition at the federal level.

The aim of economic growth, of social advancement, and of "compensatory" economic stability became intertwined. Many federal activities of far-reaching implications were established in ways which affected federal expenditures for very long periods of time—if not permanently. Social security, greatly increased support for agriculture, **rural** electrification, aids to home owners and

mortgage institutions, public housing, public power developments like the Tennessee Valley Authority and other multipurpose water resource projects, and public assistance grants are just a few examples. All of them, however, remained as federal programs after World War II. And we were actually fighting in that war before federal spending for work relief could be stopped.

The immediate postwar period was marked by dramatic demobilization. Nevertheless, many of the major costs of war lingered on. The maintenance in the postwar period of even the reduced and relatively modest structure of our Armed Forces was far more costly than anything that existed in the way of the machinery of war prior to 1940. The war also left us with greatly increased expenditure commitments for interest on public debt, for veterans, and for atomic energy. The Marshall Plan and the mutual security program followed in succession. It became obvious next, that the cold war was going to be expensive. Then, with the Korean aggression, it became necessary to rearm and, even after the shooting stopped, the peacetime striking force and defensive machinery we had to maintain continued expenditures at levels that far exceeded in cost anything we had earlier imagined.

Thus, the postwar growth of the budget has been partly in the area of national security, partly deferred costs of World War II, and partly the inheritance of activities and ways of thinking that characterized the depression of the 1930's. We have now learned that many of the programs the federal government initiated in the 1930's were neither temporary nor "compensatory" in character. Moreover, we have not only retained many of them, but we have also greatly expanded them in the postwar period. Since World War II we have seen large increases in federal expenditures for urban renewal, public health, federal aid for airports and highways, new categories and a higher federal share of public assistance grants, aid to schools in federally impacted areas, great liberalization in aid to agriculture, as well as new programs for science, education, and outer space.

The present

What can we conclude from all of this?

It seems to me that in the first place we must recognize that the compensatory theory of federal spending has failed thus far and offers little hope for the future unless we exert a more forceful and courageous determination to control the growth of federal spending. The major spending programs which originated in the depression years have in most cases persisted in the following decades. A work relief project could be turned off when we started to fight a war, but most of the programs established in the 1930's developed characteristics of a far more permanent sort.

An example can be found in the program of the Rural Electrification Administration (REA). This program was started in 1936 when only a minority of farm families enjoyed the benefits of electricity. Today, 95 per cent of our farms receive central station electric service. We have invested 4 billion dollars in this program, at 2 per cent interest. Nonetheless, indications are that future demands for federal funds will be even greater as the REA cooperatives continue to grow.

The startling fact is that three out of four new users currently being added are nonfarm users. About one-half of REA electric power goes to industries, communities, or nonfarm families. The reasonable approach is that rural electric cooperatives should now be able to get some of their financing from other than government sources, especially for nonfarm purposes that compete with taxed private industry. Recognizing this, President Eisenhower last year—and again this year—recommended that legislation be adopted to encourage cooperatives to switch from government to private financing, and his budget recommended a decrease in the funds for government loans. These proposals were not enacted by the Congress.

Inability to turn off expenditures is not all that is wrong with the compensatory theory of the prewar period. Initially, it deals largely with the spending side of the fiscal equation whereas the income side now appears to be playing a more important part. Today—with corporate income tax rates at 52 per cent—any substantial reduction of corporate earnings produces an immediate proportionate and large loss to the federal treasury. Personal income taxes also respond, though less sharply, to a fall in national production and employment. Thus, when times take a turn for the worse, federal revenues decline promptly and substantially.

Couple this with enlarged social obligations in times of recession or depression—unemployment compensation, public assistance, and so on—and you have substantial leverage of a more or less automatic character for the production of federal deficits in times of depressed economic activity. To do more than this—to deliberately step up expenditures still more, for public works and other construction, as was done in 1958—runs

grave risks. There is, first, the risk that an antirecession expenditure program cannot be turned off after the recession, but instead represents a permanent increase in the public sphere at the expense of the private. Second, it is difficult to start programs quickly, so the major impact may come long after the need for the economic stimulation has passed. Both of these risks mean that antirecession actions can well represent an inflationary danger for the postrecession period. The danger is there even if, as some believe, positive governmental intervention is required to counter recessions. It is more grave, however, if—and I believe this was proved true in 1958–59—the economy is vigorous and resilient enough to come out of a temporary recession and to go on through a revival period to new prosperous peaks without any direct financial federal interference.

I think we may conclude that it is inevitable that our nation will be faced with large budgets in the years ahead. This is particularly true for the defense obligations which our country has assumed, for its international undertakings to provide economic and military assistance to other free nations, and as a result of many programs which have been started over the years—major programs for water resource development, agriculture, veterans' benefits, low-cost housing, airways modernization, and space exploration—all these and many others have taken on a permanent quality which makes it clear that federal budgets will be large budgets in our lifetimes.

There is still another conclusion which springs from this short recitation of the history of the last thirty years. It is that the federal government has assumed more and more responsibility for activities which formerly were regarded as being under the jurisdiction of state and local governments. More and more the federal government has assumed responsibility for public assistance, housing, urban renewal, educational aid to areas with federal installations, and many other programs that are now supported by federal grants-in-aid to the states. All this, of course, contributes to the conclusion that these federal programs are not only large at the present time, but have a built-in durability—a staying power with which we must reckon as a fact of life.

I think these thoughts are well summarized in the words of Mr. Allen Sproul, former President of the New York Federal Reserve Bank, who recently said:

Government, in our day, touches upon the economic life of the community in an almost bewildering variety of ways, but its overall influence comes into focus in the consolidated cash budget and, in a subsidiary way, in the management of the public debt. When we abandoned the idea of taxation for revenue only and admitted, as we must, a more important role of Government in economic affairs, we thought up a tidy little scheme called the compensatory budget. This envisaged a cash budget balanced in times of real prosperity, in deficit in times of economic recession and in surplus in times of inflationary boom. What we have got is a budget that may throw up a shaky surplus in times of boom, but that will surely show substantial deficits in times of recession. The bias, over time, is toward deficits, with only wobbly contracyclical tendencies.

Looking ahead

It seems to me that as we move into another decade it will be essential to recognize that unless we have a more positive program for operating our federal government within its income, the forces that have gained such tremendous momentum in the past will perpetuate the tradition of deficits—to the great disadvantage of the country as a whole.

Assuming a continuous, but not uninterrupted, economic growth for the country, accompanied by ever-increasing, but not uninterrupted, growth of federal revenues, we should nevertheless expect that the growth of programs started in the past will have a strong tendency to absorb the expected additional revenues—unless aggressive controls are exercised by an alert administration and a statesmanlike Congress during those years.

On those occasions when the economy recedes from its way of growth, we must expect great leverage to be exerted toward the building up of additional deficits. We must learn to live with recession-induced deficits as a matter of necessity, but we should not take un-needed actions

which mortgage our nation's future with both more debt and an inflationary potential.

Conclusions

It seems to me to follow from these facts and analyses that it should be the policy of the federal government to strive determinedly for a balanced budget at all times, for, clearly, if it does not, the forces at work to upset financial stability will surely prevail as a matter of momentum.

As we move into the next decade we have the lessons of the three past decades to guide us:

1. Federal programs persist and in most cases grow. As demand expands, the programs expand. It is extremely difficult to curtail them. Their growing costs—and a growing economy—must be reckoned with realistically. This means that actions should be taken to reduce or to end them as they accomplish the purposes for which they were initiated (eighteen such proposals were made in President Eisenhower's budget message for the fiscal year 1960).

2. In times of recession, it is important to avoid doing things as temporary expedients which will become longer range programs and create major problems later on. We have plenty of these as carry-overs from earlier days; we should avoid creating new ones for the years ahead.

3. We must, of course, learn to live with deficits when major national emergencies threaten or exist in our country. But we should resolve to create equivalent surpluses later on to offset such deficits.

The lesson is clear. We should pay as we go, and if we are to look for debt reduction or tax reduction on a sound footing—as we should—we must do more than this. We must plan for substantial budgetary surpluses in good years—or we will surely contribute to further dangerous inflation in the years ahead.

B. THE EVILS OF DEFICIT SPENDING[*]
Senator Harry F. Byrd

As I see it, balancing the budget without resorting to legerdemain or unsound bookkeeping methods is certainly in the category of our No. 1 problems.

Beginning with 1792, the first fiscal year of our Federal Government, and through 1916, Federal deficits were casual and usually paid off in succeeding years. In this 124-year period there were

[*] From a speech by Senator Harry F. Byrd reprinted in *Congressional Record*, vol. 101, pt. 4, 84 Congress, 1 Session, May 4, 1955, pp. 5693–5695.

43 deficit years and 81 surplus years. As late as July 1, 1914, the interest-bearing debt was less than $1 billion.

In Andrew Jackson's administration the public debt was paid off in toto, an achievement in which President Jackson expressed great pride.

It can be said for this first 124 years in the life of our Republic we were on a pay-as-you-go basis. In that period I think it can be accurately said that we laid the foundation for our strength today as the greatest nation in all the world.

It is disturbing these days to hear some economists argue the budget should not be balanced and that we should not begin to pay on the debt because, they allege, it will adversely affect business conditions. Have we yielded so far to the blandishments of Federal subsidies and Government support that we have forgotten our Nation is great because of individual effort as contrasted to state paternalism?

Evils of deficit spending

Here are some of the evils of deficit spending: The debt today is the debt incurred by this generation, but tomorrow it will be debt on our children and grandchildren, and it will be for them to pay, both the interest and the principal.

It is possible and in fact probable that before this astronomical debt is paid off, if it ever is, the interest charge will exceed the principal.

Protracted deficit spending means cheapening the dollar. Cheapened money is inflation. Inflation is a dangerous game. It robs creditors, it steals pensions, wages, and fixed income. Once started, it is exceedingly difficult to control. This inflation has been partially checked but the value of the dollar dropped slightly again in the past year. It would not take much to start up this dangerous inflation again.

Public debt is not like private debt. If private debt is not paid off, it can be ended by liquidation, but if public debt is not paid off with taxes, liquidation takes the form of disastrous inflation or national repudiation. Either is destructive of our form of government.

Today the interest on the Federal debt takes more than 10 percent of our total Federal tax revenue. Without the tremendous cost of this debt our annual tax bill could be reduced 10 percent across the board.

Budget reform?

Proposals have been advocated changing our budgetary system. The Secretary of the Treasury

[Mr. Humphrey] has not approved these proposals and I am certain he will not. But there are two budgetary proposals which recur with persistency, and I want to warn you of them.

First, there is the proposal for a cash budget. Those who advocate the cash budget are suggesting that the Government pay its routine bills with savings of the citizens who have entrusted protection of their old age and unemployment to the guardianship of the Federal Government. These trust funds were established from premiums paid by participants in social security, unemployment insurance, bank deposit insurance programs, etc. Not a cent of these funds belongs to the Government.

Second, some are advocating a capital budget which means that so-called capital expenditures should not be considered as current expenditures in the budget.

Those who advocate the so-called capital budget must start out with the fallacious assumption that the Government is in business to make a profit on its citizens. To my knowledge the Federal Government has never made a bona fide profit on any Government operation.

They must assume that debt contracted by a Federal agency is not a debt of the Federal Government and a burden on all of the taxpayers.

I am an old-fashioned person who believes that a debt is a debt just as much in the atomic age as it was in the horse and buggy days.

A capital budget must assume that Government manufacturing plants, such as atomic energy installations, are in commercial production for a profit, and that Government stockpiles are longtime investments for profit instead of precautions against emergencies when they would be completely expendable with no financial return.

Likewise, it must assume that the agriculture surplus program is primarily a long range investment deal instead of a prop for annual farm income to be used when needed on a year-by-year basis.

While the vastness and complexity of the Federal Government of the United States necessarily makes budgeting difficult, the so-called conventional budget currently in use offers the best approach to orderly financing with fullest disclosure.

What is needed for a better fiscal system is fuller disclosure of Federal expenditures and responsibility for them—not less, as inevitably would be the case with so-called cash and capital budgets.

With full disclosure of the Federal expenditure situation, the American people then would have an opportunity to decide whether they wanted to recapture control and bring the rate of spending into balance with the rate of taxing and thus reduce the tremendous Federal debt burden we are now bearing.

A tax cut?

No one favors a reduction of our present burdensome taxes more than I do. I sit on both sides of the table. As an individual, I pay substantial taxes on my business operations. As a member of the Senate Finance Committee I have the opportunity to hear testimony of those who protest exorbitant taxation.

But as anxious as I am as an individual for tax reduction, I am opposed patriotically to tax reduction which requires us to borrow and add to the public debt. It seems to me to be a certain road to financial suicide to continue to reduce taxes and then to borrow the money to make good this loss in revenue.

As things are now shaping up, there will be keen competition between the two political parties for tax reduction. If we reduce expenditures

this is all well and good but, under political pressure, we should not yield to reducing taxes and still further unbalance the budget. Tax reduction should never be made a political football.

To borrow money to reduce taxes is not, in fact, a tax reduction. It is merely a postponement of the collection of taxes as, sooner or later, the taxes thus reduced will have to be paid with interest. There is only one sound way to reduce taxes and that is to reduce spending first.

At home we can get along without Federal usurpation of individual, local, and State responsibilities, and we can get along without Federal competition in business whether it be hotels, furs, rum, clothing, fertilizer, or other things.

The Bible says if thine eye offend thee pluck it out. I say if the Federal Government should not engage in such activities, we should first stop new invasions and then gradually, if not abruptly, eliminate the old intrusions. When we do these things we shall balance the budget, for lower taxes and reduced debt. There will be no further need for trick budgets and debt-ceiling evasions and hiding taxes. The Government will be honest in itself, and honest with the people.

READING 26

The citizen who has worked his way through the debate in the previous readings can be forgiven for saying at this point, "Please just tell me what the record has been—and I'll decide for myself if I want to have the government play a more active role in stabilizing the economy." But his frustrations must continue, for the record is not that clear nor that simple.

This reading is one interpretation of the record that commands much attention because of the qualifications of its authors, President Kennedy's Council of Economic Advisers as of January, 1963: Walter W. Heller of the University of Minnesota and Gardner Ackley of the University of Michigan. This interpretation must be read within the context of a strongly argued position by the Administration for a large tax cut in 1963.

Questions to Guide the Reading

Are the data included here consistent with other hypotheses about the performance of the economy in the years under consideration? Where is the interpretation most convincing? Where does it leave key questions unanswered?

To what extent does the record show increased sophistication by government in the use of its economic powers? Does the record offer a firm basis for believing that large-scale depressions may be a thing of the past and runaway inflation an unlikely part of the future?

THE RECORD ON FISCAL POLICY
Council of Economic Advisers

Government deficits are not a new fiscal experience for Americans. The first part of this chapter reviews several relevant aspects of that experience, and in particular distinguishes two kinds of deficits and their economic effects—deficits that grow passively out of economic recession or inadequate growth, and deficits that grow out of positive fiscal action, such as tax reduction, to invigorate the economy. The perspective is further widened by placing the Federal deficit or surplus in the context of balancing and offsetting deficits and surpluses in the other major sectors of the national economy.

Since deficits increase the national debt, it is important also to appraise that debt in relation to the Nation's wealth and the Nation's income. The national balance sheet allows us to view the Federal debt as one of a set of interrelated assets and liabilities.

Passive fiscal policy and automatic stabilization. Any weakening in private spending will reduce incomes, causing tax revenues to fall and transfer payments to rise. Thus disposable incomes will decline less than pre-tax incomes, and will be partly cushioned against the decline in private demand. In effect, the impact of the decline in private income is shared with the Federal Government, which does not shrink its purchases when its income falls. The greater the extent to which a fall in government revenues cushions the decline in private incomes, the less the flow of spending for output will be curtailed.

Automatic stabilization operates in reverse when private demand increases. Additional income is generated, but part of it is siphoned out of the spending stream in higher tax payments and lower transfers. Disposable incomes therefore rise less than incomes before taxes, and the spending and re-spending is limited and damped.

Thus the tax-and-transfer response narrows fluctuations in income caused by irregularities in the strength of demand. The sharper the response of tax collections to changes in GNP, the stronger the stabilization effect. Although the tax-and-transfer response cannot prevent or reverse a movement in GNP, it can and does limit the extent of cumulative expansions and contractions.

At least with respect to contractions, this is clearly an important service to the economy.

Automatic fiscal stabilizers have made a major contribution in limiting the length and severity of postwar recessions. Each of the four postwar recessions—1948–49, 1953–54, 1957–58, and 1960–61—has been both short and mild. The decline in real GNP from its peak to its trough has ranged from a high of 4.4 percent in 1957–58 to a low of 2.1 percent in 1960–61, and the duration of the recessions has varied from 9 to 13 months. Changes in disposable personal income from quarter to quarter have been much smaller than changes in GNP. Although GNP changes were frequently negative (in each of the postwar recessions), disposable income fell in only one quarter in the entire postwar period. This relative stability of personal disposable income has been mainly due to the automatic fiscal stabilizers, together with the tendency of corporations to maintain their dividends at the expense of retained earnings during recessions. The maintenance of disposable incomes has prevented sharp declines in consumer expenditures. The resulting stability in markets for consumer goods, which constitute by far the largest component of final demand, has prevented any drastic collapse in business investment in fixed capital.

Automatic fiscal stabilizers increase the stability of the economy. Stability is a desirable thing for an economy that is balanced where it wants to be. Thus, an economy operating, on the average, at high levels of output and employment benefits from a tax-and-transfer system highly responsive to changes in output and income, as a cushion against sharp movements of aggregate demand either toward inflation or toward recession.

However, in the present situation—with the American economy laboring for over five years well below its potential rate of output—automatic stabilization becomes an ambiguous blessing. The protection it gives against cumulative downward movements of output and employment is all the more welcome. But its symmetrical "protection" against upward movements becomes an obstacle on the path to full employment, throttling expansion well before full employment is reached.

Under such conditions, high employment can

From *Economic Report of the President, January 1963* (Government Printing Office, Washington, 1963), pp. 66–83.

be restored—as is being proposed under the 1963 tax program—by a reduction in taxes. When this is done the need is not primarily to lessen the responsiveness of tax receipts to changes in GNP. Rather the whole schedule of taxes should be lowered—so that, at any given GNP, taxes siphon off less private purchasing power—while leaving the response of tax receipts to *changes* in GNP about as great as before. To be sure, it is almost impossible to lower taxes without lessening to some degree their sensitivity to changes in GNP. But the purpose of such a change should be to lower the level of taxes—and hence their persistent drag on purchasing power—rather than to reduce their automatic countercyclical response.

Tax cuts to aid recovery. Just as we have had postwar experience with automatic stabilization, we have had experience with active tax cuts which served positively to increase demand. These experiences are of interest in the present context.

In two of the postwar recessions—1948–49 and 1953–54—tax cuts helped to check the decline and to spur the ensuing recovery. Neither of the tax cuts is an example of deliberate countercyclical fiscal action, but both had important expansionary effects which came when they were needed.

Under the Revenue Act of 1948, which was passed by the Congress in April, taxes were reduced by $4.7 billion. While at the time, the tax cut appeared inappropriately timed—few observers were predicting recession—when the recession of 1949 in fact occurred, it turned out to be fortunate that the tax cut had been legislated. The cut was retroactive to January 1, 1948, and as a result refunds were exceptionally large in mid-1949. The upturn began in October 1949. In addition to the tax cut, there was a significant increase in Federal expenditures in late 1948 associated with the introduction of the Marshall Plan. This also helped to mitigate the recession. The economy was further stimulated in the expansion phase by the heavy increases in placement of military orders associated with the Korean War, which began in June 1950. As a result of the tax cut and the increased expenditures, together with the effects of the automatic stabilizers, the recession was short and mild, and the ensuing expansion was strong. By the first quarter of 1951, unemployment had been reduced to 3.5 percent of the labor force.

As a result of the rapid expansion, by the second quarter of 1950, Federal tax liabilities as shown in the national income accounts had risen substantially above the levels that prevailed at the time taxes were cut in the second quarter of 1948.

Taxes also were cut during the recession of 1953–54. Effective January 1, 1954, the excess profits tax was repealed, and personal income tax rates were reduced. Excise taxes were reduced on April 1, and further tax reductions for both individuals and corporations were embodied in the Internal Revenue Code of 1954. These measures are estimated to have reduced Federal revenues by about $6.1 billion (seasonally adjusted annual rate) in the first half of 1954. Further cuts which went into effect later brought the revenue loss on a full-year basis to about $7.4 billion. These cuts in personal and corporate income and excise taxes were partially offset, however, by an increase of about $1.4 billion (annual rate) in OASI contributions, which became effective on January 1, 1954. For the most part, the tax reductions in 1954 were part of a program of tax reform and were not viewed primarily as fiscal policy measures aimed at countering the recession. Yet as a result of the tax cuts that became effective at the beginning of 1954, disposable personal income and personal consumption expenditures turned up in the first quarter, while personal income and GNP were still declining. It is generally agreed that the recession ended in August. Tax reduction, together with an easy monetary policy which made a plentiful supply of funds available to finance a strong expansion of housing and automobile demand, helped to shorten the recession and to invigorate the ensuing expansion which brought unemployment down to 4.2 percent of the labor force by the third quarter of 1955.

As a result of the expansion, by the first quarter of 1955 total Federal tax liabilities, as shown in the national income accounts, had risen significantly above the level that prevailed in the fourth quarter of 1953 before the tax cuts were put into effect.

While the tax cuts of 1954 helped considerably in rescuing the economy from the recession, it should be recognized that had they gone into effect earlier, the recession of 1953–54 might have been completely avoided. Government expenditures (principally defense spending) were cut by nearly $11 billion between mid-1953 and mid-1954. The tax cuts took effect 6 months after expenditures began to fall. As it was, fiscal policy, taken as a whole, was contractionary in this period and was a major cause of the recession. The Federal deficit as shown in the national income and product accounts was $7.0 billion (seasonally adjusted annual rate) in the second quarter of 1953 when the recession began. By the fourth quarter the operation of the automatic stabilizers associated with the decline in economic activity had increased the deficit to $11.8 billion despite significant cuts in expenditures. The deficit dropped to $10.6 billion in the first quarter of 1954, and as a result of sharp cuts in expenditures, to $5.4 billion in the second quarter despite the tax reductions that went into effect in the first half of 1954.

Private scholars who have studied the period have estimated that if the economy had continued to operate at the same rate of unemployment that prevailed in the second quarter of 1953, the budget deficit would have dropped from $7.0 billion in that quarter to $3.8 billion in the fourth quarter of 1953 and would have shifted to a surplus of $3.0 billion by the second quarter of 1954. This represents a shift of $10 billion between the peak of the previous recovery and the trough of the recession. It is an approximate measure of the net contractive effect of active fiscal policy during this period.

Fiscal policy in the 1930's. During the 1930's, America had its longest uninterrupted experience with budget deficits. Their persistence, their relatively large size in comparison with GNP, and their association with an unprecedented unemployment rate (averaging 18.2 percent from 1930–39) have sometimes been interpreted as demonstrating the futility of expansionary fiscal policy.

The 1930's were a tragic period in the Nation's history. The "Great Depression," the causes of which are still not fully diagnosed, produced a tremendous "gap" between actual and potential output—not the 6 percent average of recent years but about 40 percent during much of the period. In such an abnormal situation, it is perhaps too much to expect that fiscal policy alone could have fully offset a prolonged failure of the private economy to generate strong expansionary forces.

But in fact, active fiscal policy was not employed vigorously, consistently, or with proper timing. And whatever constructive impact fiscal policy may have had was largely offset by restrictive monetary policies and by institutional failures—failures that could never again occur because of fundamental changes made during and since the 1930's.

Some conclusions from past experience. Several conclusions emerge from the preceding review.

The automatic stabilization which our present fiscal system provides is a powerful weapon to damp cyclical movements of output and employment. It is one of the factors that has kept the U.S. economy free from major depressions in the postwar period.

The postwar record shows that deliberate tax cuts can have a countercyclical impact, encouraging recovery by stimulating private demand. The experience reviewed above shows how in two cases tax reduction contributed in this manner to recovery from recession. The fact that these tax changes came at times when they helped to check recession and encourage recovery was, however, largely accidental.

The 1948 tax reduction was intended as a permanent one, reflecting the postwar decline of military expenditures. The 1954 tax cuts were also intended as a permanent adjustment to the sharp reductions in government expenditures at the end of the Korean emergency. But a recession will not always coincide with the need for permanent tax reduction. The temporary fluctuations in private demand that are commonly responsible for cyclical movements in business activity thus may call for temporary adjustments in fiscal policy that can be reversed as the need for them recedes.

A weak private economy can generate very large deficits without receiving a positively stimulating effect from those deficits. The large passive deficits of the 1930's provide examples. More recent examples appear in the experience of the past 5 years. Although the administrative budgets presented for the fiscal years 1958–63 foresaw a surplus in every year, averaging $1.4 billion, the actual outcome has been a deficit in all but one of these years, averaging $5.5 billion.

Passive deficits are largest when the economy experiences recession. A recession which would reduce the expected GNP gains in fiscal year 1964 by even $15 billion below what they would otherwise be would add almost $5 billion to the deficit.

The experience of the last few years should make it clear that merely to incur deficits is not an appropriate objective of policy. For it is not the deficits as such that provide stimulus. Only reductions in tax rates or increases in expenditures have an actively stimulating role. The passive deficits which are the product of recession or slack, however, have a valuable cushioning function. Nevertheless, it is an appropriate objective of policy to eliminate the deficits that are the product of a recession or a sluggish economy—because of the human and economic waste that is involved in recessions and slack. The proper objectives of policy are full employment and growth, and recessions and slack are the opposites of these.

It is clear that the deficit which a slack economy or recession produces cannot realistically be eliminated by raising tax rates or by reducing government expenditures. Its source is not excessive spending or tax rates that are too low. The attempt to eliminate a deficit by these means would be largely self-defeating. Such a policy would be disastrous for employment, incomes, profits; the deficit would remain; and the role of the dollar as an international currency would be undermined.

Expenditures that are wasteful or represent improper fields of government action (something which only the public, acting through elected representatives, can determine) should surely be eliminated. But unless taxes were simultaneously reduced by more than expenditures decline, the effect would be contractionary on the economy. The beneficial effect on incentives through lower

tax rates might be more than offset by a net loss in demand. A cut in expenditures reduces market demand directly by the full amount of the cut, while an equal reduction in taxes expands market demand by a smaller amount, because a part of the reduction will be added to personal and business saving.

Deficits that result from recession or slack can be eliminated only by restoring and maintaining a vigorous, rapidly growing economy. If the tax system imposes an excessive drag on the economy—through its effects on purchasing power and on incentives—tax rates may be too high relative to expenditures, even though the budget is in deficit. Thus, tax revision, involving both reduction and reform, can not only provide stimulus for growth and prosperity, but can even, as a result, balance the budget or produce surpluses. Recession and slack generate deficits; prosperity and growth balance budgets.

Tax reduction and the national debt

Tax reduction in 1963 will, as indicated previously, lead to a transitional increase in the budget deficit.

The significance of the public debt—and its increase in 1963—can be best understood by put-

Table 1   Federal Debt and Interest Payments on the Debt, Selected Calendar Years, 1939–62

Item	1939	1946	1950	1955	1960	1962*
	Billions of Dollars					
Federal debt:†						
Total‡	47.6	259.5	256.7	280.8	290.4	304.0
Held by the public§	38.6	205.3	196.7	204.3	207.9	217.6
Interest payments on debt:						
Total debt	1.0	5.0	5.6	6.5	9.3	9.6
Debt held by the public	.8	4.2	4.3	4.8	6.7	6.9
	Percent					
Debt as percent of gross national product:						
Total debt	52.3	123.2	90.2	70.6	57.7	54.9
Debt held by the public	42.4	97.4	69.1	51.4	41.3	39.3
Interest payments on debt as percent of national income:						
Total debt	1.4	2.8	2.3	2.0	2.2	2.1
Debt held by the public	1.1	2.3	1.8	1.5	1.6	1.5

* Preliminary estimates by Council of Economic Advisers.
† Amount outstanding, end of calendar year.
‡ Gross public debt and guaranteed issues held outside the Treasury.
§ Total less amounts held by U.S. Government investment accounts and by Federal Reserve Banks.
SOURCES: Treasury Department, Department of Commerce, and Council of Economic Advisers.

ting the debt in the context of the over-all economy and taking into account the development over time of both the debt and the economy.

World War II led to a $211.9 billion increase in total Federal debt outstanding—from $47.6 billion in December 1939 to $259.5 billion in December 1946, as shown in Table 1. By December 1962, the debt had risen by a further $44.5 billion. Since the war, its size relative to the total economy has declined by more than one-half: the ratio of the debt to GNP was 123 percent at the close of 1946, and at the close of 1962 it was 55 percent. The decline has been fairly steady and has continued in each of the last 2 years. While the absolute size of the debt will again increase during the fiscal year 1963, it will continue to decline relative to GNP: the growth of 1.8 percent in the debt will be less than the expected rise of 4.3 percent in GNP.

The absolute amount of interest payments shown in the administrative budget has risen from $5 billion in the calendar year 1946 to over $9 billion in the calendar year 1962, primarily because of the necessity of refinancing at higher current interest rates debt incurred during World War II. Such payments, however, have declined as a percentage of national income and as a percentage of total Federal expenditures during the postwar period.

Even in the perspective of the GNP, figures for *total* outstanding Federal debt and gross interest payments overstate the debt "problem." The total outstanding debt includes Federal securities held by the U.S. Government investment accounts—such as the social security trust funds—and by the Federal Reserve System. Interest payments on these components of the debt are, in effect, internal transfers of funds within the Federal Government itself and do not involve payments to the public. Moreover, debt held by the government investment accounts and the Federal Reserve does not pose a significant problem of debt management. The economically significant concepts are, accordingly, the publicly held debt, which excludes these components, and Federal interest payments to the public, which excludes interest transfers within the Government.

The publicly held Federal debt was $217.6 billion in December 1962, compared with total outstanding Federal debt of $304.0 billion. In the calendar year 1962, net Federal interest payments to the public were $6.9 billion, compared with the $9.6 billion of interest shown in the administrative budget. From 1946 to 1962, the net

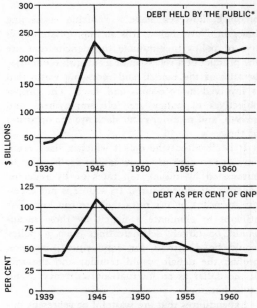

*Total gross public debt and guaranteed issues less amounts held by U. S. Government investment accounts and by federal reserve banks; end of calendar year.

Fig. 1   Federal debt held by the public and its relation to gross national product. Sources: Treasury Department, Department of Commerce, and Council of Economic Advisers.

increase in the publicly held debt was $12.3 billion, compared with the increase of $44.5 billion in the total outstanding Federal debt. (See Table 1 and Figure 1.) Net publicly held debt per capita fell from $1,450 in 1946 to $1,170 in 1962.

Since 1946, State and local governments in the United States have increased their net indebtedness fivefold—from $13.6 billion to $72 billion, or from $96 to $390 per capita. During this same period, total net private debt increased from $154 billion to an estimated $672 billion. Net corporate debt, accounting for one-half of this total, tripled its 1946 level, while individuals and noncorporate business increased their net indebtedness by over fivefold during this period.

Whether the increases in indebtedness in these sectors were wise or foolish depends not on the mere fact of an increase in their debt, but on the purposes achieved and on the future prospects of the individuals or organizations assuming the debt obligations. For the Federal Government, these same guides underlie our judgment as we decide whether an increase in the debt is appropriate. Federal expenditure programs must be rigorously judged on their merits. The decision as to the appropriate method of financing them, however, should be based on the Nation's economic condition, not on the object of the expenditure. In this respect the public debt is unique.

Federal debt and national wealth. Our national wealth consists of real objects which yield direct services to us (such as the family automobile) or enable us to produce more or better goods and services (the machines in a factory). It also includes the amount by which Americans' claims on foreigners exceed foreigners' claims against Americans.

The measured national wealth, together with the skills and efforts of our labor force, constitutes the productive capacity of the American economy, the source of each year's output. In turn, the portion of annual output devoted to net investment equals the yearly addition to our national wealth—in the form of productive equipment, plants, houses, schools, post offices, and so on. The national wealth grows rapidly in prosperous years when investment is high and slowly in years of recession and slack.

If our public debt were owned by foreigners, it would be a deduction from our national wealth and would place a direct burden on our economy by requiring us to export part of our total output to cover interest and amortization. But our public debt is nearly 95 percent internally held. Public debt held by Americans neither directly increases nor directly reduces national wealth. Also, it is not directly related to the asset holdings of the Government—although it may be noted that a recent report of the House Government Operations Committee estimates that the total wealth, including military assets, owned by the U.S. Government, exceeds its debt.

The tax program that is being proposed for enactment this year will bring about an increase in investment, both by raising demand and reducing excess capacity and by increasing incentives and the availability of funds. Thus, it will increase the accumulation of real capital and add to our national wealth.

Under other circumstances, of course, a fiscal policy which involved an increase in the public debt might operate to reduce real investment and retard the growth of national wealth. For example, when employment is high and demand is pressing against capacity, deficit financing of public noninvestment expenditures may contribute to inflation or raise interest rates and thereby depress private capital formation. Changes in national debt, therefore, bear no simple relation to changes in national wealth. An increase in national debt may indirectly spur the growth of wealth under some conditions and stifle it under other conditions.

The burden of the public debt. An understanding of the relation between national debt and national wealth helps to place the problem of debt burden in further perspective. In what respects can it be said that public debt imposes a burden on either present or future generations?

1. As indicated above, the kind of fiscal policies we follow can either increase or decrease the living standards of future generations by affecting the stock of wealth we bequeath to them. But, clearly, the tax program being proposed for enactment in 1963, which encourages both high employment and high capital formation for economic growth, will benefit future generations as well as our own. It will do so even though it results in some increase in the public debt.

2. At full employment, an increase in interest payments on the publicly held Federal debt will ordinarily require higher personal income and corporate profits taxes than would otherwise be necessary in order to prevent inflation. The resulting transfer from taxpayers to interest recipients does not constitute a direct draft on the real resources available to the American people as a whole, but it may impose a burden of a more subtle kind. By dampening incentives, the higher tax rates may reduce total output. How serious such a burden will be depends on the level of tax rates that is needed. In recent years, interest payments to the public by the Federal Government have amounted to less than 2 percent of the national income, as shown in Table 1. Moreover, the ratio of interest payments to national income has declined, and it is this ratio that matters in setting the required level of tax rates. Given the magnitudes of debt change involved in a fiscal policy for high employment, and relating them to the expected growth of our economy, it is likely that the debt burden will continue to decline.

3. A further potential disadvantage of debt service may result from its effects on income distribution. If all the debt were held by one group of investors while taxes were paid by a quite different group, undesirable distributional consequences might result. This, however, is not the case in the United States where debt-holding is fairly widely dispersed and our tax structure

partially offsets the distributional effects of interest transfers.

Today's economic problem is slack, not inflation. Thus, under the present circumstances there is no reason to fear such increases in the public debt as tax reduction may entail. The ratio of interest payments on the debt to national income is small and is likely to fall, not rise. Nor is

there any danger that the increase in the Federal debt will be a burden on future generations. Tax reduction will increase investment, and hence the wealth we will bequeath, not decrease it. The danger is the opposite one. By failing to take expansionary fiscal action, we will keep both consumption and investment depressed, thus hurting not only ourselves, but future generations as well.

Part 3

ON MARKETS AND PRICES

All economies have one problem in common: relatively limited resources to be allocated among the unlimited wants of their people. Indeed an economic system may be viewed as a way in which a society organizes itself to answer certain fundamental questions: WHAT goods and services shall be produced? HOW shall they be produced? FOR WHOM shall they be produced? At the core of the American economic system, there is a much-lauded but little-understood mechanism for answering these questions: the free marketplace.

The late Sumner H. Slichter, professor of economics at Harvard University and a prolific writer on the American economy, here describes how this system relies on the motivations of individual freedom, self-interest, and profit to give it its forward thrust, and how it relies too on the forces of competition to check the accumulation of power in the marketplaces. The picture is a qualified one even at the time of Slichter's writing (1928); it is still more qualified today as we increasingly modify the market mechanisms with one restraint or another. But none of those modifications lets us escape from the necessity of beginning with an understanding of the market system in its purer forms. Society may or may not want to operate in a totally free private-enterprise world; but it must at least know that bench mark if intelligent choices are to be made.

Questions to Guide the Reading

The market mechanism described here was eloquently discussed by an early and towering figure in economics, Adam Smith, in this manner:

> Every individual necessarily labors to render the annual revenue of the society as great as he can. He generally indeed, neither intends to promote the public interest, nor knows how much he is promoting it. . . . he intends only his own security; and by directing that industry in such a manner as its produce may be of the greatest value, he intends only his own gain, and he is in this, as in many other cases, led by an invisible hand to promote an end which was no part of his intention. Nor is it always the worse for the society that it was no part of it. By pursuing his own interest he frequently promotes that of the society more effectually than when he really intends to promote it. I have never known much good done by those who affected to trade for the public good. (*The Wealth of Nations*, Book IV, Chap. II, 1776.)

How does this "invisible-hand" mechanism work in, say, getting resources to move where they are most desired by consumers, or arriving at prices that serve to clear the marketplaces?

What is the nature of the system of values on which such a free-market society might be built? To what extent are these values that might be shared by men in the Soviet Union, or in one of the newly developing countries of Africa?

What is the rationale on which we have chosen in our economy to interfere at some points with the workings of the market system? Have we succeeded in finding what Adam Smith could not find, an effective way of pursuing the public good by direct intervention rather than by the use of the free markets?

FREE PRIVATE ENTERPRISE
Sumner H. Slichter

Possible forms of economic organizations

Every economic system must provide some way of doing three fundamental things: (1) getting goods produced; (2) determining what share each person shall have in the total product; and (3) regulating the consumption of goods, that is, determining who shall consume this good and who that. The manner in which these three basic economic processes are performed stamps the economic system with its most essential characteristics. How does the existing economic order organize and regulate the production, distribution, and consumption of goods?

There are several ways in which these activities *might* be organized and regulated:

1. On the basis of family autonomy. Each family might produce everything which it uses, relying upon others for nothing. In such a society there would be no trade.

2. On a communistic basis. What is produced and what each person does might be determined by the group as a whole and the product might be the property of the group, to be divided in accordance with socially determined rules.

3. On a despotic basis. The things produced and the tasks of each person might be decided by a despot or a despotic class, the product in all or in part being the property of the despot to be shared with the others as he saw fit.

4. On the basis of custom and heredity. Instead of choosing his own work or having it selected for him by the group or a despot, each person might be born into his occupation. He might be expected to do the thing which his father did, and other occupations might be closed to him. Likewise the share of each person in the product and the things which he is permitted or forbidden to consume might also be determined by custom.

All of these methods of organizing and controlling economic activities have been more or less prevalent in the past and, indeed, instances of them still exist. They are not, however, the methods which prevail today in the United States. It may seem a strange way of doing, but we organize industry by, in effect, saying to each individual, "Choose your own occupation. Pro- duce what you like. What you do, to whom you sell, what or from whom you buy, the prices you get or give, are all your own concern. You are free, subject to a few restrictions, to produce whatever you wish regardless of whether or not it is needed, regardless of whether or not too much of it already exists. You are likewise free to refrain from engaging in any occupation no matter how acute may be the shortage of goods or how pressing the need for your help. You are free to buy from whoever is willing to sell and to sell to whoever is willing to buy. You are equally free to refuse to buy or sell whenever you please and for any reason or no reason."

This is what we mean by *free private enterprise*. Under it the government confines itself in the main to the suppression of fraud and violence and to the enforcement of contracts. It does not itself engage in or attempt to guide the course of industry. It pursues a "let alone" or "hands off" policy. Let us now see how, under free enterprise, the three fundamental economic processes of production, distribution, and consumption take place.

How free enterprise organizes production

Why does not a system of freedom, in which each person is at liberty to pursue whatever occupation he pleases and to produce whatever he wishes, result in hopeless chaos? Why do not many essential articles fail to get made and why does not the output of many things far exceed the demand for them? How can we get along without a central directing body to discover how much different things are in demand and to tell each of us what to produce?

To put the problem specifically, how does New York City each day obtain about the quantity of milk that it demands? Of the thousands of people engaged in supplying New York with milk, almost none knows either how much the city consumes or how much is being produced. And yet, despite this ignorance, New York each day receives about the amount of milk that it demands. There is neither a great surplus nor a shortage. Milk does not spoil because there is no one to consume it, and babies do not go without it because too small a supply reaches the city on

From Sumner H. Slichter, *Modern Economic Society* (Henry Holt and Company, Inc., New York, 1928), Chap. III. Reprinted with kind permission of the publisher.

some days. At the same time, other cities in the neighborhood are also receiving their daily supply from the same territory. Each uses a different quantity, yet each receives about the amount it demands.

This comparatively simple case illustrates our problem. What determines the relative quantities of each and everything produced—how much cotton, corn, oats, wheat, or oranges we raise, how much steel, lumber, coal, or cloth we produce? What tells us when to make more and when less of each commodity?

The guide upon which we rely is the profit in making different goods, which, of course, depends upon the prices which they command and the cost of producing them. Suppose, for example, that New York failed to receive enough milk to satisfy the demand. Rather than go without milk or drink less, many people would be willing to pay more. Consequently the price would promptly rise. This would tend to end the shortage. More milk would be shipped to New York and less to other places. This would continue until there was no greater profit in selling milk in New York than elsewhere.

Just as price regulates the distribution of milk between cities, so it also determines the total amount produced in the country as a whole. Failure of the supply to keep pace with the demand would cause the price to rise. The greater profit to be had from the sale of milk would cause farmers to produce more of it. Some farmers, who had been separating their milk and selling the cream to be made into butter, might turn to the sale of whole milk. Others might abandon raising grain, stock, or fruit and enter dairy farming. As the output of milk increased, the price, of course, would drop. This would continue until producing milk was no more attractive than alternative branches of farming. If, furthermore, the demand for milk were to fall off or the supply to increase faster than the demand, farmers, in order to dispose of their supply, would be compelled to lower the price. Milk production would become a less profitable occupation, men would be deterred from entering it, and some of those already engaged in it might be led to abandon it or at least to reduce their output. And this would continue until the price rose and milk production became no less attractive than alternative occupations.

Price also determines in large measure where and how goods are made. Because living in New York City is expensive, it might seem a poor place in which to locate a factory. But the great stream of immigrants who for many years en-tered the country at New York and who were reluctant to undertake a long journey through a strange country provided the city with a bountiful supply of cheap labor. To take advantage of this, many industries, such as the needle trades, grew up in or near the East Side. At one time the Genesee valley in western New York was an important wheat region and Rochester, at the falls of the Genesee, was a great milling center. As the urban population in the East has grown, the greater profits in dairying and in fruit and truck raising have driven wheat raising to the West. The same is true of sheep raising. At one time, New York State contained nearly 5,000,000 sheep; now it has less than one-tenth that number. The growth of urban population has made dairying so profitable that most farmers cannot afford to raise sheep in New York.

Whether goods shall be made by hand or by machinery is often a question of money costs. Shall houses be built of wood or brick? As long as our immense forests were far from exhaustion, wooden houses were the almost universal rule. In Europe, where timber is less plentiful, frame dwellings are the exception. We still use timber to a greater extent than do most countries, but the cost of certain woods, such as white pine, has caused us to use cheaper varieties—Norway pine, hemlock, spruce, Douglas fir. Shall land be farmed intensively or extensively? The English obtain about twice as many bushels of wheat per acre as do the Americans, but we obtain about twice as many bushels per man. The reason is that in England, where land is relatively expensive, it is economized by the use of more labor and less land. Here where labor is expensive in comparison with land, labor is economized by the use of more land and less labor.

How shares in the output of industry are determined

In our highly specialized society, each of us, at the best, contributes to industry's output very few things. One man may produce wheat, another wood, another milk, another cattle, another corn. In fact, most men do not contribute even one complete product. Hundreds of workers combine their efforts to make a suit of clothes, a pair of shoes, an automobile, or a telephone.

Although each individual makes a very specialized contribution to the product of society, each wishes to obtain from that output hundreds of articles. The man who produces only wheat desires flour, butter, sugar, clothing, shoes, hats, magazines, furniture, services of doctors, dentists, lawyers, and much else. If he contributes 2,000 bushels of wheat to society's stock of goods, how much is he entitled to withdraw?

Just as prices determine what things are produced, in what proportions, and by what methods, so, under free enterprise, they also determine the share of each person in the output of industry. If our imaginary wheat grower, who has produced a crop of 2,000 bushels, obtains $1.25 for each bushel, he is thereby enabled to purchase articles valued at $2,500. Just how much this is, will depend upon the price of shoes, hats, sugar, and the various other things which he desires. The next year he may work harder and produce 2,400 bushels. In the meantime, however, the price of wheat may drop to 75 cents a bushel. Hence, despite the fact that he has worked harder and raised more wheat, he has only $1,800 to spend for goods. And if, perchance, prices in general have risen, each of his dollars will buy him less than the year before. In a word, what share a man receives in the product of industry is determined by the prices of what he has to sell quite as much as by how industriously and efficiently he labors.

How consumption is regulated under free enterprise

There are many ways in which we might determine what goods each person shall consume. We might undertake to ascertain the peculiar needs of each and see that he was afforded some special opportunity to obtain the things which would satisfy them. Or we might study the ability of different persons to use goods to the advantage of the rest of us and arrange for men of outstanding ability to receive the things which they require in order to be of greatest service to the community.

To a limited extent, we do regulate consumption upon the basis of either needs or ability to use goods advantageously. Schooling is considered so important that many governments supply a certain amount of it free or below cost. Police and fire protection, parks, playgrounds, and, to some extent, transportation, communication, and insurance are also considered so essential that they are provided by the government. Fellowships and scholarships, awarded to students of special promise, are among the few attempts which we make to place goods within reach of those who can use them to special advantage.

Under a system of free enterprise, however, which permits men to buy whatever they can get on the best terms that they can obtain, neither need nor ability to use goods for the benefit of others necessarily has much to do with determining how goods are consumed. Of far greater importance are the prices of different commodities and the ability of different persons to pay these prices. Goods go to those who are able and willing to pay the most for them—not to those who have the greatest need for them or who will do the greatest good with them.

In some respects, the control of consumption by price and ability to pay works out very satisfactorily. Suppose, for example, that unfavorable weather or blight made it likely that the potato crop would be exceptionally small. It is obvious that we should need to consume potatoes sparingly, making more than customary use of substitutes. If, on the other hand, the outlook were for a large crop, it would be to our interest to use more potatoes than usual. In each case, price produces the desired effect. If the prospects are for a small crop, the higher price induces sparing consumption; if a large crop seems probable, the low price encourages larger consumption. Because skilled labor is scarce, it is desirable that we economize it by using its products sparingly. The high wages of skilled craftsmen make their products expensive and encourage consumers to avoid wasting them. Commodities which can be made only at great risk of accidental or industrial disease should also be used sparingly. In so far as these hazards cause workmen to demand higher wages, they increase the price of the products and limit their consumption.

Although the regulation of consumption by prices usually encourages the economizing of scarce goods, it does so in a manner not altogether satisfactory. If consumption must be reduced this should perhaps be accomplished by those using less who can do so with the smallest inconvenience and sacrifice. As a matter of fact, the well-to-do, who are best supplied, are least induced by higher prices to curtail their purchases. It is the poor, who can least afford to reduce their consumption, who get along with less when the supply falls short. In periods of severe food shortage, such as often occur during war time, the regulation of consumption by ability to pay works such hardship that it is sometimes superseded by a system of rationing.

Some claims on behalf of free enterprise

Since free enterprise is the principal method by which our economic activities are organized and controlled, our study of modern industrial society must very largely consist of an inquiry into how freedom works under present-day conditions—such as machine industry, huge corporations, and science applied to business. But before we proceed further with our analysis, it will be helpful to become familiar in a general way with some of the claims which have been made in behalf of free enterprise. The "obvious and simple system of natural liberty," as Adam Smith called freedom of enterprise, has been regarded as the one and only way in which men might attain the maximum satisfaction of their desires with a minimum outlay of sacrifice. It is true that this extreme view has been accepted by few economists of repute and that since the middle of the last century, it has been increasingly under attack. Nevertheless it has had and still does have a wide acceptance by the general public and by certain schools of politicians, and it is appealed to frequently in political controversies. And even though we no longer spend much time discussing whether or not we can *always* trust free enterprise to regulate economic activity better than any other method, we are frequently compelled to decide whether or not it is the best way of controlling a specific economic activity under specific circumstances. Consequently the claims which have been made on its behalf are still very live issues.

The reasoning in support of the belief that freedom of enterprise is the maximum of satisfaction at the minimum of cost is very simple. Each individual, it is said, is better able than any one else to judge his own interests. If men are at liberty to spend their money as they choose, they will naturally purchase those things that will yield them the most satisfaction. Consequently the very commodities which give consumers the greatest pleasure are the most profitable for business enterprises to produce. Likewise, if men are free to use such methods of production as they wish, they will select those which involve the least cost per unit of output. With the goods which give the greatest gratification being made by the methods which are least costly, it follows, according to the theory, that there will be the maximum surplus of satisfaction over sacrifice.

Some assumptions of the theory of free enterprise

But if this result is to follow, two things would appear to be necessary: (1) goods must go to the consumers who will derive the greatest pleas-ure from them, and (2) the tasks of making goods must be assigned to the workers who can perform them with the least sacrifice for each unit of product. Does freedom of enterprise cause either goods or jobs to be distributed in this manner?

We have already seen that under a system of free enterprise goods tend to get into the hands of those who offer the best prices for them. But how then can they be consumed so as to yield the maximum of satisfaction? Are the people who are willing and able to pay most for goods also those who will derive the most satisfaction from using them? If they are not, it would appear possible to increase the surplus of satisfaction over sacrifice by causing goods to be distributed more in accordance with needs and less in accordance with ability to pay. We have no way of comparing the amount of pleasure which two persons derive from consuming an article. And yet it seems ridiculous to assert that ability to derive satisfaction from goods is proportionate to ability to pay for them. Assume that A and B each wish a pair of shoes. A, who is well-to-do, is willing to pay $12; B, who is poor, will offer only $7. Obviously A will get the shoes. But because he is rich and well supplied with shoes, an additional pair is only a slight convenience to him. B, poor and scantily supplied, has urgent need for another pair. It seems clear that the sum total of satisfaction would be greater if B obtained the shoes, and yet it seems equally clear that under freedom of enterprise they will go to A.

We are no better able to compare the pains suffered by different persons than we are the pleasures which they enjoy. Nevertheless it does not appear probable that freedom of enterprise necessarily causes jobs to be distributed so as to result in a minimum sacrifice for each unit of output—so that, for example, persons who can do heavy work with least fatigue will be given heavy work. Rather jobs tend to go to those who are willing to do the most work for the least money. Now the fact that X is willing to do a job for a dollar a day less than Y does not necessarily mean that X finds the task less onerous or unpleasant than Y. It may simply mean that he needs the money more and is willing to work at a lower rate in order to get it.

In face of the fact that ability to derive pleasure from goods does not appear to correspond to capacity to pay for them and that jobs are not necessarily given to the men who can do them with the least sacrifice for each unit of product, how can it be asserted that industrial liberty results in a maximum of satisfaction over sacrifice? But the exponents of free enterprise are not without a reply. To interfere with liberty in order to bring about a distribution of goods upon the basis of needs rather than ability to pay, or in order to cause jobs to be assigned to those who perform them with least sacrifice, might have the *immediate* effect of increasing the surplus of satisfaction over sacrifice. But this result, it is said, would be short lived. Men have the greatest incentive to improve their efficiency when they are free to compete for any jobs which they desire and to spend their income as they see fit. Were this incentive diminished by distributing jobs to those who could perform them with the least sacrifice and goods to those who would derive the most pleasure from them, output would inevitably decline. What would be gained by a different distribution of goods and jobs would be lost through smaller production.

The significance of competition

But how is it possible for us to trust business enterprises with so much freedom? In other branches of human relations, laws to regulate conduct seem to be quite essential. Why should industry be an exception to this general rule? If we leave business concerns free to make anything they like by any methods which they see fit, what is to prevent them from supplying the public with poorly made or adulterated goods or from using methods that are cheap in terms of dollars but expensive in terms of human sacrifice? Might not the sum total of pleasure be greater and of pain be less if the state enforced certain standards of quality or prohibited the use of certain methods of production?

The theory of free enterprise does not, it is important to emphasize, assert that restraints upon human selfishness are not needed. It simply assumes that they are provided by *competition.* This, according to the theory, is the great regulative force which establishes effective control over economic activities and gives each of us an incentive to observe the interests of others. Thus business establishments are deterred from furnishing adulterated or poorly made goods by the fear that customers may shift their patronage to rivals. Likewise the enterprises which fail to protect their men against accidents or industrial disease or which work them unusually hard, are penalized by the refusal of laborers to work for them except at a higher wage than other employers pay.

The mere existence of competition, however, is not enough. For it to perform satisfactorily the protective function attributed to it, certain very definite conditions must be present.

To begin with, an appreciable proportion of buyers and sellers must be willing to discriminate against those sellers or buyers who ignore, and in favor of those who take account of, the welfare of others. Otherwise, of course, no one has an economic incentive to pay attention to the well-being of his fellows. Assume, for example, that an enterprise pollutes a stream by dumping refuse and chemicals into it. From the standpoint of the firm, this may be an economical method of production. But from the standpoint of the community it is an expensive one because it kills the fish, spoils the stream for bathing, and makes it foul and ill-smelling. But competition will not stop the pollution unless an appreciable number of consumers, wage earners, or investors refuse to deal with the firm which is responsible—that is, unless a substantial number of consumers refuse to buy from it, or wage earners to work for it, or investors to put money into it. But if the enterprise charges no more than its rivals for goods of equal grade, offers equally attractive conditions of employment, and pays as high dividends, who has an interest in discriminating against it? Perhaps the very fact that the enterprise pollutes the stream enables it to offer better terms than its rivals. Or take the case of child labor—another method of production cheap in dollars and cents but expensive in terms of human cost. If the firms which employ children are able, *because of that very fact*, to sell for less or to pay higher wages to adults or higher profits to investors, who is going to discriminate against them? Under these circumstances, does not competition positively encourage the employment of children?

But willingness to discriminate between those who consider the interests of others and those who do not is insufficient. Competition protects consumers against inferior ware only when they know good quality from bad; it protects laborers from unguarded machines only when they know which employers have and which have not guarded their machines. In other words, competition is an efficient protective agency only when buyers or sellers have the information necessary to make intelligent choices. It fails, for example, to protect consumers against milk from tubercular cattle because the ordinary buyer of milk has no way of distinguishing the milk of healthy cows from that of diseased.

The information needed for intelligent choices

may be available, and yet many buyers or sellers may be too ignorant, too careless, too neglectful of their own interests to use it. If, for example, workmen show no disposition to shun plants which are notoriously dangerous or unsanitary, what incentive have employers to improve conditions?

Some issues raised by free enterprise

The whole theory that industrial liberty results in a maximum net satisfaction rests, it will be recalled, upon the assumption that each individual knows his own interests better than any one else and consequently can make his own decisions better than any one can make them for him. Is this true? May not free enterprise fail to yield the greatest possible satisfaction precisely *because* it results in choices which are molded too much by impulse, habit, prejudice, ignorance, or clever sales talk and too little by reflection, investigation of facts, or comparison of alternative opportunities? Under the system of economic freedom, choices are largely a matter of individual decision. This means that they are usually made in a hurry and by amateurs who have little opportunity to obtain expert advice. This situation may not be inevitable, but it exists. And yet millions of individuals, each attempting to decide for himself about the purchase of scores of articles concerning which he knows little, are an easy prey for ingenious selling and advertising experts. It may be true, as the theory of free enterprise asserts, that each individual knows his own desires better than any one else, but of what good is this if he has time to investigate neither what he is buying nor what he might buy, or if he is prevented by a skillful salesman from reflecting very much as to what he really does wish after all? Hence, when we find the United States spending more for tobacco than for education, the explanation may be, not that we desire tobacco more than education, but simply that the facilities for getting people to buy tobacco are more efficient than those for persuading them to pay for education. A representative body which could employ experts to investigate people's needs and desires and to test products might be able to spend a considerable portion of consumers' money with greater satisfaction to them than they could obtain by spending it themselves.

Perhaps the most striking aspect of the theory of free enterprise is its assertion that intervention of the government in economic activities is unnecessary. The theory, as we have said, does not deny that restraints on human selfishness are needed. It simply asserts that we can trust competition to provide them. But closer inquiry reveals that the defenders of free enterprise do not trust competition to do all things. However much they trust it to guard the lives and limbs of workmen against dangerous machinery or to protect consumers against injurious foods, they do not rely upon it to enforce contracts or to prevent fraud. But the same reasoning which is used to prove that the government need not intervene on behalf of wage earners and consumers can be employed to show that laws are not required to guard business men against fraud or breach of contractual obligations. Would not a customer who refused to pay his bills soon experience difficulty in getting dealers to sell to him, and would not an enterprise which violated its contracts find other concerns unwilling to deal with it? Is not the aid of the courts in these matters as superfluous as laws to protect workmen against dangerous machines or consumers against adulterated wares?

This inconsistency in the theory of free enterprise is to be explained by its origin. The theory was invented several hundred years ago to justify the demand of business men for release from oppressive legal restrictions. That the makers of the theory should have had greater faith in the capacity of competition to protect workmen against loss of life or limb than in its capacity to protect business men against bad debts is not surprising. When the rights of business were involved, it seemed quite proper for the government to lend the aid of its courts; only when the interests of consumers or wage earners were at stake did competition become a perfect protective instrument and intervention by the government "paternalistic" and "an unwarranted invasion of private rights."

Because the theory of free enterprise assumes that competition is needed to prevent freedom from being abused, it must also assume that competition is a more economical method of production than monopoly. Otherwise the claim that freedom results in the greatest satisfaction and the least sacrifice could not be correct. In many instances, however, it seems reasonably certain that monopoly is more economical than competition. The clearest cases are the so-called "octopus" industries, such as gas, electric light and power, water, railway, and street railway, which must run wire, pipe, or rails close to each consumer in order to deliver the service. It is the cost of duplicating this part of the plant which makes competition in these industries so uneconomical. In the oil industry, the desire of each landowner to obtain as much of the oil as possible causes him to put down an excessive number of wells along the edge of his property, thus diminishing the pressure under which the oil is held, substantially reducing the quantity which can be recovered, and greatly increasing the cost of getting it. Or consider the wastefulness of competition in distributing milk. With only a few customers in each block, a driver must travel many miles to reach several hundred customers. A study of competitive milk distribution in Rochester, New York, indicated that 2,509 miles of travel were necessary to distribute milk which a monopoly could deliver with 300 miles of travel. Competition required 356 men, 380 horses, and 305 wagons; a monopoly, it was estimated, would need 90 men, 80 horses, and 25 horse-drawn trucks. In most other industries, the case against competition is less clear, but undoubtedly there are many in which monopoly would be more economical.

The exponents of economic freedom answer that, even though monopoly is more economical at any given time, it may be less so in the long run. The search for new and cheaper methods of production needs, it is said, the spur of competition. In other words, competition more than makes up for its wastes by stimulating the development of better techniques.

Although the theory that government intervention in industry is unnecessary presupposes the existence of competition, the very absence of state interference often results in monopoly. This is not surprising. Indeed, it would be strange if business men left at liberty to do as they like, should not frequently combine to exploit the public rather than compete to serve the public. Consequently the government may find itself compelled to intervene either to enforce competition or to regulate monopoly. Either policy, of course, is a departure from the principle of free enterprise.

READING 28

The market system is all about us. We buy and sell, and use money as the medium of exchange, with such ease that we often miss seeing just what functions the market and the exchange medium fulfill for us. Sometimes we need to get an unusual, even artificial perspective on this system in order to understand it. Then perhaps we can come at long last to feel about markets as Monsieur Jourdain came to feel about prose in Molière's *Le Bourgeois Gentilhomme*: "By my faith! for over forty years I've been speaking prose without knowing anything about it."

R. A. Radford found an unusual vantage point from which to view markets in his experiences as a British prisoner of war in Germany during World War II. Here he saw, in microcosm, the emergence of complex markets out of a simple barter system; he saw a medium of exchange, cigarettes, emerge to perform the same functions that less "useful" money performs for us. The very simplicity of the story he tells has made this article a minor classic in economics. To understand its full flavor is to know the world around us better than we knew it before.

Questions to Guide the Reading

Why did a system of exchange develop among the prisoners, and what is the parallel case for exchange in the world outside the prison camp?

What determined how elaborate or simple this prison market system became? What determines the extent to which we develop and use markets in everyday life?

THE ECONOMIC ORGANISATION OF A P.O.W. CAMP
R. A. Radford

Introduction

After allowance has been made for abnormal circumstances, the social institutions, ideas and habits of groups in the outside world are to be found reflected in a Prisoner of War Camp. It is an unusual but a vital society.

One aspect of social organisation is to be found in economic activity, and this, along with other manifestations of a group existence, is to be found in any P.O.W. camp. True, a prisoner is not dependent on his exertions for the provision of the necessaries, or even the luxuries of life, but through his economic activity, the exchange of goods and services, his standard of material comfort is considerably enhanced. And this is a serious matter to the prisoner: he is not "playing at shops" even though the small scale of the transactions and the simple expression of comfort and wants in terms of cigarettes and jam, razor blades and writing paper, make the urgency of those needs difficult to appreciate, even by an ex-prisoner of some three months' standing.

Nevertheless, it cannot be too strongly emphasised that economic activities do not bulk so large in prison society as they do in the larger world. There can be little production; as has been said the prisoner is independent of his exertions for the provision of the necessities and luxuries of life; the emphasis lies in exchange and the media of exchange.

Everyone receives a roughly equal share of essentials; it is by trade that individual preferences are given expression and comfort increased. All at some time, and most people regularly, make exchanges of one sort or another.

Although a P.O.W. camp provides a living example of a simple economy which might be used as an alternative to the Robinson Crusoe economy beloved by the textbooks, and its simplicity renders the demonstration of certain economic hypotheses both amusing and instructive, it is suggested that the principal significance is sociological. True, there is interest in observing the growth of economic institutions and customs in a brand new society, small and simple enough to prevent detail from obscuring the basic pattern and disequilibrium from obscuring the working of the system. But the essential interest lies in the universality and the spontaneity of this economic life; it came into existence not by conscious imitation but as a response to the immediate needs and circumstances. Any similarity between prison organisation and outside organisation arises from similar stimuli evoking similar responses.

The following is as brief an account of the essential data as may render the narrative intelligible. The camps of which the writer had experience were Oflags and consequently the economy was not complicated by payments for work by the detaining power. They consisted normally of between 1,200 and 2,500 people, housed in a number of separate but intercommunicating bungalows, one company of 200 or so to a building. Each company formed a group within the main organisation and inside the company the room and the messing syndicate, a voluntary and spontaneous group who fed together, formed the constituent units.

Between individuals there was active trading in all consumer goods and in some services. Most trading was for food against cigarettes or other foodstuffs, but cigarettes rose from the status of a normal commodity to that of currency. RMk.s existed but had no circulation save for gambling debts, as few articles could be purchased with them from the canteen.

Our supplies consisted of rations provided by the detaining power and (principally) the contents of Red Cross food parcels—tinned milk, jam, butter, biscuits, bully, chocolate, sugar, etc., and cigarettes. So far the supplies to each person were equal and regular. Private parcels of clothing, toilet requisites and cigarettes were also received, and here equality ceased owing to the different numbers despatched and the vagaries of the post. All these articles were the subject of trade and exchange.

The development and organisation of the market

Very soon after capture people realised that it was both undesirable and unnecessary, in view of the limited size and the equality of supplies, to give away or to accept gifts of cigarettes or

From R. A. Radford, "The Economic Organisation of a P.O.W. Camp," *Economica*, Volume XII, 1945. Reprinted with kind permission of the editor.

food. "Goodwill" developed into trading as a more equitable means of maximising individual satisfaction.

We reached a transit camp in Italy about a fortnight after capture and received ¼ of a Red Cross food parcel each a week later. At once exchanges, already established, multiplied in volume. Starting with simple direct barter, such as a non-smoker giving a smoker friend his cigarette issue in exchange for a chocolate ration, more complex exchanges soon became an accepted custom. Stories circulated of a padre who started off round the camp with a tin of cheese and five cigarettes and returned to his bed with a complete parcel in addition to his original cheese and cigarettes; the market was not yet perfect. Within a week or two, as the volume of trade grew, rough scales of exchange values came into existence. Sikhs, who had at first exchanged tinned beef for practically any other foodstuff, began to insist on jam and margarine. It was realised that a tin of jam was worth ½ lb. of margarine plus something else; that a cigarette issue was worth several chocolates issues, and a tin of diced carrots was worth practically nothing.

In this camp we did not visit other bungalows very much and prices varied from place to place; hence the germ of truth in the story of the itinerant priest. By the end of a month, when we reached our permanent camp, there was a lively trade in all commodities and their relative values were well known, and expressed not in terms of one another—one didn't quote bully in terms of sugar—but in terms of cigarettes. The cigarette became the standard of value. In the permanent camp people started by wandering through the bungalows calling their offers—"cheese for seven" (cigarettes)—and the hours after parcel issue were Bedlam. The inconveniences of this system soon led to its replacement by an Exchange and Mart notice board in every bungalow, where under the headings "name," "room number," "wanted" and "offered" sales and wants were advertised. When a deal went through, it was crossed off the board. The public and semi-permanent records of transactions led to cigarette prices being well known and thus tending to equality throughout the camp, although there were always opportunities for an astute trader to make a profit from arbitrage. With this development everyone, including non-smokers, was willing to sell for cigarettes, using them to buy at another time and place. Cigarettes became the normal currency, though, of course, barter was never extinguished.

The unity of the market and the prevalence of a single price varied directly with the general level of organisation and comfort in the camp. A transit camp was always chaotic and uncomfortable: people were overcrowded, no one knew where anyone else was living, and few took the trouble to find out. Organisation was too slender to include an Exchange and Mart board, and private advertisements were the most that appeared. Consequently a transit camp was not one market but many. The price of a tin of salmon is known to have varied by two cigarettes in 20 between one end of a hut and the other. Despite a high level of organisation in Italy, the market was morcellated in this manner at the first transit camp we reached after our removal to Germany in the autumn of 1943. In this camp—Stalag VIIA at Moosburg in Bavaria—there were up to 50,000 prisoners of all nationalities. French, Russians, Italians and Jugo-Slavs were free to move about within the camp; British and Americans were confined to their compounds, although a few cigarettes given to a sentry would always procure permission for one or two men to visit other compounds. The people who first visited the highly organised French trading centre with its stalls and known prices found coffee extract—relatively cheap among the tea-drinking English—commanding a fancy price in biscuits or cigarettes, and some enterprising people made small fortunes that way. (Incidentally we found out later that much of the coffee went "over the wire" and sold for phenomenal prices at black market cafes in Munich: some of the French prisoners were said to have made substantial sums in RMk.s. This was one of the few occasions on which our normally closed economy came into contact with other economic worlds.)

Eventually public opinion grew hostile to these monopoly profits—not everyone could make contact with the French—and trading with them was put on a regulated basis. Each group of beds was given a quota of articles to offer and the transaction was carried out by accredited representatives from the British compound, with monopoly rights. The same method was used for trading with sentries elsewhere, as in this trade secrecy and reasonable prices had a peculiar importance, but as is ever the case with regulated companies, the interloper proved too strong.

The permanent camps in Germany saw the highest level of commercial organisation. In addition to the Exchange and Mart notice boards, a shop was organised as a public utility, controlled by representatives of the Senior British Officer, on a no profit basis. People left their surplus clothing, toilet requisites and food there until they were sold at a fixed price in cigarettes. Only sales in cigarettes were accepted—there was no barter—and there was no higgling. For food at least there were standard prices: clothing is less homogeneous and the price was decided around a norm by the seller and the shop manager in agreement; shirts would average say 80, ranging from 60 to 120 according to quality and age. Of food, the shop carried small stocks for convenience; the capital was provided by a loan from the bulk store of Red Cross cigarettes and repaid by a small commission taken on the first transactions. Thus the cigarette attained its fullest currency status, and the market was almost completely unified.

It is thus to be seen that a market came into existence without labour or production. The B.R.C.S. may be considered as "Nature" of the textbook, and the articles of trade—food, clothing and cigarettes—as free gifts—land of manna. Despite this, and despite a roughly equal distribution of resources, a market came into spontaneous operation, and prices were fixed by the operation of supply and demand. It is difficult to reconcile this fact with the labour theory of value.

Actually there was an embryo labour market. Even when cigarettes were not scarce, there was usually some unlucky person willing to perform services for them. Laundrymen advertised at two cigarettes a garment. Battle-dress was scrubbed and pressed and a pair of trousers lent for the interim period for twelve. A good pastel portrait cost thirty or a tin of "Kam." Odd tailoring and other jobs similarly had their prices.

There were also entrepreneurial services. There was a coffee stall owner who sold tea, coffee or cocoa at two cigarettes a cup, buying his raw materials at market prices and hiring labour to gather fuel and to stoke; he actually enjoyed the services of a chartered accountant at one stage. After a period of great prosperity he overreached himself and failed disastrously for several hundred cigarettes. Such large-scale private enterprise was rare but several middlemen or professional traders existed. The padre in Italy, or the men at Moosburg who opened trading relations with the French, are examples: the more subdivided the market, the less perfect the advertisement of prices, and the less stable the prices, the greater was the scope for these operators. One man capitalised his knowledge of Urdu by buying meat from the Sikhs and selling butter and jam in return: as his operations became better known

more and more people entered this trade, prices in the Indian Wing approximated more nearly to those elsewhere, though to the end a "contact" among the Indians was valuable, as linguistic difficulties prevented the trade from being quite free. Some were specialists in the Indian trade, the food, clothing or even the watch trade. Middlemen traded on their own account or on commission. Price rings and agreements were suspected and the traders certainly co-operated. Nor did they welcome newcomers. Unfortunately, the writer knows little of the workings of these people: public opinion was hostile and the professionals were usually of a retiring disposition.

One trader in food and cigarettes, operating in a period of dearth, enjoyed a high reputation. His capital, carefully saved, was originally about 50 cigarettes, with which he bought rations on issue days and held them until the price rose just before the next issue. He also picked up a little by arbitrage; several times a day he visited every Exchange or Mart notice board and took advantage of every discrepancy between prices of goods offered and wanted. His knowledge of prices, markets and names of those who had received cigarette parcels was phenomenal. By these means he kept himself smoking steadily—his profits—while his capital remained intact.

Sugar was issued on Saturday. About Tuesday two of us used to visit Sam and make a deal; as old customers he would advance as much of the price as he could spare them, and entered the transaction in a book. On Saturday morning he left cocoa tins on our beds for the ration, and picked them up on Saturday afternoon. We were hoping for a calendar at Christmas, but Sam failed too. He was left holding a big black treacle issue when the price fell, and in this weakened state was unable to withstand an unexpected arrival of parcels and the consequent price fluctuations. He paid in full, but from his capital. The next Tuesday, when I paid my usual visit, he was out of business.

Credit entered into many, perhaps into most, transactions, in one form or another. Sam paid in advance as a rule for his purchases of future deliveries of sugar, but many buyers asked for credit, whether the commodity was sold spot or future. Naturally prices varied according to the terms of sale. A treacle ration might be advertised for four cigarettes now or five next week. And in the future market "bread now" was a vastly different thing from "bread Thursday." Bread was issued on Thursday and Monday, four and three days' rations respectively, and by

Wednesday and Sunday night it had risen at least one cigarette per ration, from seven to eight, by supper time. One man always saved a ration to sell then at the peak price: his offer of "bread now" stood out on the board among a number of "bread Monday's" fetching one or two less, or not selling at all—and he always smoked on Sunday night.

The cigarette currency

Although cigarettes as currency exhibited certain peculiarities, they performed all the functions of a metallic currency as a unit of account, as a measure of value and as a store of value, and shared most of its characteristics. They were homogeneous, reasonably durable, and of convenient size for the smallest or, in packets, for the largest transactions. Incidentally, they could be clipped or sweated by rolling them between the fingers so that tobacco fell out.

Cigarettes were also subject to the working of Gresham's Law. Certain brands were more popular than others as smokes, but for currency purposes a cigarette was a cigarette. Consequently buyers used the poorer qualities and the Shop rarely saw the more popular brands: cigarettes such as Churchman's No. 1 were rarely used for trading. At one time cigarettes hand-rolled from pipe tobacco began to circulate. Pipe tobacco was issued in lieu of cigarettes by the Red Cross at a rate of 25 cigarettes to the ounce and this rate was standard in exchanges, but an ounce would produce 30 home-made cigarettes. Naturally, people with machine-made cigarettes broke them down and re-rolled the tobacco, and the real cigarette virtually disappeared from the market. Hand-rolled cigarettes were not homogeneous and prices could no longer be quoted in them with safety: each cigarette was examined before it was accepted and thin ones were rejected, or extra demanded as a make-weight. For a time we suffered all the inconveniences of a debased currency.

Machine-made cigarettes were always universally acceptable, both for what they would buy and for themselves. It was this intrinsic value which gave rise to their principal disadvantage as currency, a disadvantage which exists, but to a far smaller extent in the case of metallic currency;—that is, a strong demand for non-monetary purposes. Consequently our economy was repeatedly subject to deflation and to periods of monetary stringency. While the Red Cross issue of 50 or 25 cigarettes per man per week came in regularly, and while there were fair stocks held, the cigarette currency suited its purpose admirably. But when the issue was interrupted, stocks soon ran out, prices fell, trading declined in volume and became increasingly a matter of barter. This deflationary tendency was periodically offset by the sudden injection of new currency. Private cigarette parcels arrived in a trickle throughout the year, but the big numbers came in quarterly when the Red Cross received its allocation of transport. Several hundred thousand cigarettes might arrive in the space of a fortnight. Prices soared, and then began to fall, slowly at first but with increasing rapidity as stocks ran out, until the next big delivery. Most of our economic troubles could be attributed to this fundamental instability.

Price movements

Many factors affected prices, the strongest and most noticeable being the periodical currency inflation and deflation described in the last paragraphs. The periodicity of this price cycle depended on cigarette and, to a far lesser extent, on food deliveries. At one time in the early days, before any private parcels had arrived and when there were no individual stocks, the weekly issue of cigarettes and food parcels occurred on a Monday. The non-monetary demand for cigarettes was great, and less elastic than the demand for food: consequently prices fluctuated weekly, falling towards Sunday night and rising sharply on Monday morning. Later, when many people held reserves, the weekly issue had no such effect, being too small a portion of the total available. Credit allowed people with no reserves to meet their non-monetary demand over the weekend.

The general price level was affected by other factors. An influx of new prisoners, proverbially hungry, raised it. Heavy air raids in the vicinity of the camp probably increased the non-monetary demand for cigarettes and accentuated deflation. Good and bad war news certainly had its effect, and the general waves of optimism and pessimism which swept the camp were reflected in prices. Before breakfast one morning in March of this year, a rumour of the arrival of parcels and cigarettes was circulated. Within ten minutes I sold a treacle ration, for four cigarettes (hitherto offered in vain for three), and many similar deals went through. By 10 o'clock the rumour was denied, and treacle that day found no more buyers even at two cigarettes.

More interesting than changes in the general price level were changes in the price structure. Changes in the supply of a commodity, in the German ration scale or in the make-up of Red

Cross parcels, would raise the price of one commodity relative to others. Tins of oatmeal, once a rare and much sought after luxury in the parcels, became a commonplace in 1943, and the price fell. In hot weather the demand for cocoa fell, and that for soap rose. A new recipe would be reflected in the price level: the discovery that raisins and sugar could be turned into an alcoholic liquor of remarkable potency reacted permanently on the dried fruit market. The invention of electric immersion heaters run off the power points made tea, a drug on the market in Italy, a certain seller in Germany.

In August, 1944, the supplies of parcels and cigarettes were both halved. Since both sides of the equation were changed in the same degree, changes in prices were not anticipated. But this was not the case: the non-monetary demand for cigarettes was less elastic than the demand for food, and food prices fell a little. More important however were the changes in the price structure. German margarine and jam, hitherto valueless owing to adequate supplies of Canadian butter and marmalade, acquired a new value. Chocolate, popular and a certain seller, and sugar, fell. Bread rose; several standing contracts of bread for cigarettes were broken, especially when the bread ration was reduced a few weeks later.

In February, 1945, the German soldier who drove the ration waggon was found to be willing to exchange loaves of bread at the rate of one loaf for a bar of chocolate. Those in the know began selling bread and buying chocolate, by then almost unsaleable in a period of serious deflation. Bread, at about 40, fell slightly; chocolate rose from 15; the supply of bread was not enough for the two commodities to reach parity, but the tendency was unmistakable.

The substitution of German margarine for Canadian butter when parcels were halved naturally affected their relative values, margarine appreciating at the expense of butter. Similarly, two brands of dried milk, hitherto differing in quality and therefore in price by five cigarettes a tin, came together in price as the wider substitution of the cheaper raised its relative value.

Enough has been cited to show that any change in conditions affected both the general price level and the price structure. It was this latter phenomenon which wrecked our planned economy.

Paper currency—bully marks

Around D-Day, food and cigarettes were plentiful, business was brisk and the camp in an optimistic mood. Consequently the Entertainments Committee felt the moment opportune to launch a restaurant, where food and hot drinks were sold while a band and variety turns performed. Earlier experiments, both public and private, had pointed the way, and the scheme was a great success. Food was bought at market prices to provide the meals and the small profits were devoted to a reserve fund and used to bribe Germans to provide grease paints and other necessities for the camp theatre. Originally meals were sold for cigarettes but this meant that the whole scheme was vulnerable to the periodic deflationary waves, and furthermore heavy smokers were unlikely to attend much. The whole success of the scheme depended on an adequate amount of food being offered for sale in the normal manner.

To increase and facilitate trade, and to stimulate supplies and customers therefore, and secondarily to avoid the worst effects of deflation when it should come, a paper currency was organised by the Restaurant and the Shop. The Shop bought food on behalf of the Restaurant with paper notes and the paper was accepted equally with the cigarettes in the Restaurant or Shop, and passed back to the Shop to purchase more food. The Shop acted as a bank of issue. The paper money was backed 100 per cent. by food; hence its name, the Bully Mark. The BMk. was backed 100 per cent. by food: there could be no over-issues, as is permissible with a normal bank of issue, since the eventual dispersal of the camp and consequent redemption of all BMk.s was anticipated in the near future.

Originally one BMk. was worth one cigarette and for a short time both circulated freely inside and outside the Restaurant. Prices were quoted in BMk.s and cigarettes with equal freedom—and for a short time the BMk. showed signs of replacing the cigarette as currency. The BMk. was tied to food, but not to cigarettes: as it was issued against food, say 45 for a tin of milk and so on, any reduction in the BMk. prices of food would have meant that there were unbacked BMk.s in circulation. But the price of both food and BMk.s could and did fluctuate with the supply of cigarettes.

While the Restaurant flourished, the scheme was a success: the Restaurant bought heavily, all foods were saleable and prices were stable.

In August parcels and cigarettes were halved and the Camp was bombed. The Restaurant closed for a short while and sales of food became difficult. Even when the Restaurant reopened, the food and cigarette shortage became increasingly acute and people were unwilling to convert such valuable goods into paper and to hold them for luxuries like snacks and tea. Less of the right kinds of food for the Restaurant were sold, and the Shop became glutted with dried fruit, chocolate, sugar, etc., which the Restaurant could not buy. The price level and the price structure changed. The BMk. fell to four-fifths of a cigarette and eventually farther still, and it became unacceptable save in the Restaurant. There was a flight from the BMk., no longer convertible into cigarettes or popular foods. The cigarette re-established itself.

But the BMk. was sound! The Restaurant closed in the New Year with a progressive food shortage and the long evenings without lights due to intensified Allied air raids, and the BMk.s could only be spent in the Coffee Bar—relict of the Restaurant—or on the few unpopular foods in the Shop, the owners of which were prepared to accept them. In the end all holders of BMk.s were paid in full, in cups of coffee or in prunes. People who had bought BMk.s for cigarettes or valuable jam or biscuits in their heyday were aggrieved that they should have stood the loss involved in their restricted choice, but they suffered no actual loss of market value.

Price fixing

Along with this scheme came a determined attempt at a planned economy, at price fixing. The Medical Officer had long been anxious to control food sales, for fear of some people selling too much, to the detriment of their health. The deflationary waves and their effects on prices were inconvenient to all and would be dangerous to the Restaurant which had to carry stocks. Furthermore, unless the BMk. was convertible into cigarettes at about par it had little chance of gaining confidence and of succeeding as a currency. As has been explained, the BMk. was tied to food but could not be tied to cigarettes, which fluctuated in value. Hence, while BMk. prices of food were fixed for all time, cigarette prices of food and BMk.s varied.

The Shop, backed by the Senior British Officer, was now in a position to enforce price control both inside and outside its walls. Hitherto a standard price had been fixed for food left for sale in the shop, and prices outside were roughly in conformity with this scale, which was recommended as a "guide" to sellers, but fluctuated a good deal around it. Sales in the Shop at recommended prices were apt to be slow though a good price might be obtained: sales outside could be made more quickly at lower prices. (If sales outside were to be at higher prices, goods were withdrawn from the Shop until the recommended price rose: but the recommended price was sluggish and could not follow the market closely by reason of its very purpose, which was stability.) The Exchange and Mart notice boards came under the control of the Shop: advertisements which exceeded a 5 per cent. departure from the recommended scale were liable to be crossed out by authority: unauthorised sales were discouraged by authority and also by public opinion, strongly in favour of a just and stable price. (Recommended prices were fixed partly from market data, partly on the advice of the M.O.)

At first the recommended scale was a success: the Restaurant, a big buyer, kept prices stable around this level: opinion and the 5 per cent. tolerance helped. But when the price level fell with the August cuts and the price structure changed, the recommended scale was too rigid. Unchanged at first, as no deflation was expected, the scale was tardily lowered, but the prices of goods on the new scale remained in the same relation to one another, owing to the BMk., while on the market the price structure had changed. And the modifying influence of the Restaurant had gone. The scale was moved up and down several times, slowly following the inflationary and deflationary waves, but it was rarely adjusted to changes in the price structure. More and more advertisements were crossed off the board, and black market sales at unauthorised prices increased: eventually public opinion turned against the recommended scale and authority gave up the struggle. In the last few weeks, with unparalleled deflation, prices fell with alarming rapidity, no scales existed, and supply and demand, alone and unmellowed, determined prices.

Public opinion

Public opinion on the subject of trading was vocal if confused and changeable, and generalisations as to its direction are difficult and dangerous. A tiny minority held that all trading was undesirable as it engendered an unsavoury atmosphere; occasional frauds and sharp practices were cited as proof. Certain forms of trading were more generally condemned; trade with the Germans was criticised by many. Red Cross toilet articles, which were in short supply and only issued in cases of actual need, were excluded from trade by law and opinion working in unshakable harmony. At one time, when there had been several cases of malnutrition reported among the more devoted smokers, no trade in German rations was permitted, as the victims became an additional burden on the depleted food reserves of the Hospital. But while certain activities were condemned as anti-social, trade itself was practised, and its utility appreciated, by almost everyone in the camp.

More interesting was opinion on middlemen and prices. Taken as a whole, opinion was hostile to the middleman. His function, and his hard work in bringing buyer and seller together, were ignored; profits were not regarded as a reward for labour, but as the result of sharp practices. Despite the fact that his very existence was proof to the contrary, the middleman was held to be redundant in view of the existence of an official Shop and the Exchange and Mart. Appreciation only came his way when he was willing to advance the price of a sugar ration, or to buy goods spot and carry them against a future sale. In these cases the element of risk was obvious to all, and the convenience of the service was felt to merit some reward. Particularly unpopular was the middleman with an element of monopoly, the man who contacted the ration waggon driver, or the man who utilised his knowledge of Urdu. And middlemen as a group were blamed for reducing prices. Opinion notwithstanding, most people dealt with a middleman, whether consciously or unconsciously, at some time or another.

There was a strong feeling that everything had its "just price" in cigarettes. While the assessment of the just price, which incidentally varied between camps, was impossible of explanation, this price was nevertheless pretty closely known. It can best be defined as the price usually fetched by an article in good times when cigarettes were plentiful. The "just price" changed slowly; it was unaffected by short-term variations in supply, and while opinion might be resigned to departures from the "just price," a strong feeling of resentment persisted. A more satisfactory definition of the "just price" is impossible. Everyone knew what it was, though no one could explain why it should be so.

As soon as prices began to fall with a cigarette shortage, a clamour arose, particularly against those who held reserves and who bought at reduced prices. Sellers at cut prices were criticised and their activities referred to as the black market. In every period of dearth the explosive question of "should non-smokers receive a cigarette ration?" was discussed to profitless length. Unfortunately, it was the non-smoker, or the light smoker with his reserves, along with the hated middleman, who weathered the storm most easily.

The popularity of the price-fixing scheme, and such success as it enjoyed, were undoubtedly the result of this body of opinion. On several occasions the fall of prices was delayed by the general support given to the recommended scale. The onset of deflation was marked by a period of sluggish trade; prices stayed up but no one bought. Then prices fell on the black market, and the volume of trade revived in that quarter. Even when the recommended scale was revised, the volume of trade in the Shop would remain low. Opinion was always overruled by the hard facts of the market.

Curious arguments were advanced to justify price fixing. The recommended prices were in some way related to the calorific values of the foods offered: hence some were overvalued and never sold at these prices. One argument ran as follows:—not everyone has private cigarette parcels: thus, when prices were high and trade good in the summer of 1944, only the lucky rich could buy. This was unfair to the man with few cigarettes. When prices fell in the following winter, prices should be pegged high so that the rich, who had enjoyed life in the summer, should put many cigarettes into circulation. The fact that those who sold to the rich in the summer had also enjoyed life then, and the fact that in the winter there was always someone willing to sell at low prices were ignored. Such arguments were hotly debated each night after the approach of Allied aircraft extinguished all lights at 8 P.M. But prices moved with the supply of cigarettes, and refused to stay fixed in accordance with a theory of ethics.

Conclusion

The economic organisation described was both elaborate and smooth-working in the summer of 1944. Then came the August cuts and deflation. Prices fell, rallied with deliveries of cigarette parcels in September and December, and fell again. In January, 1945, supplies of Red Cross cigarettes ran out: and prices slumped still further: in February the supplies of food parcels were exhausted and the depression became a blizzard. Food, itself scarce, was almost given away in order to meet the non-monetary demand for cigarettes. Laundries ceased to operate, or worked for £s or RMk.s: food and cigarettes sold for fancy prices in £s, hitherto unheard of. The Restaurant was a memory and the BMk. a joke. The Shop was empty and the Exchange and Mart notices were full of unaccepted offers for cigarettes. Barter increased in volume, becoming a larger proportion of a smaller volume of trade. This, the first serious and prolonged food shortage in the writer's experience, caused the price structure to change again, partly because German rations were not easily divisible. A margarine ration gradually sank in value until it exchanged directly for a treacle ration. Sugar slumped sadly. Only bread retained its value. Several thousand cigarettes, the capital of the Shop, were distributed without any noticeable effect. A few fractional parcel and cigarette issues, such as one-sixth of a parcel and twelve cigarettes each, led to monetary price recoveries and feverish trade, especially when they coincided with good news from the Western Front, but the general position remained unaltered.

By April, 1945, chaos had replaced order in the economic sphere: sales were difficult, prices lacked stability. Economics has been defined as the science of distributing limited means among unlimited and competing ends. On 12th April, with the arrival of elements of the 30th U.S. Infantry Division, the ushering in of an age of plenty demonstrated the hypothesis that with infinite means economic organisation and activity would be redundant, as every want could be satisfied without effort.

READING 29

The preceding reading, about a prisoner-of-war camp, looked from an unusual angle at the market mechanisms which surround us in the American economy. It offered a brief study in parallels. A quite different way to deepen our understanding of markets is to see what happens when we do not permit prices to perform their rationing functions.

In wartime, we have sometimes suspended parts of the price system in the interests of avoiding inflation, keeping government costs down, and promoting equity in the distribution of such nonmilitary goods as are available. The case for price controls in wartime is a powerful one, but the complications are mountainous. Interference at one point leads to unforeseen consequences at another point. Once we turn Adam Smith's "invisible hand" into the "visible hand," we see more clearly how the parts of the economy mesh together into the whole as crisis after crisis is brought to the fore.

This brief news story from *Business Week* builds a dramatic link between the price of hogs in Chicago and a shortage of steel in Pittsburgh during World War II.

Questions to Guide the Reading

How do the formal tools of supply-and-demand analysis help to explain the consequences of the corn and hog price ceilings?

In the absence of controls, how would the free market have met the problem of the abnormally high corn-hog price ratio? What would be the advantages and disadvantages in that way of facing the problem?

A GLANCE AT PRICE CONTROLS
Business Week

Army, Navy, and top war production officials all are warning the White House against letting hogs eat so much corn that processors of the grain will lack raw material in 1944 as they have in 1943. Under Secretary of War Robert P. Patterson, Under Secretary of the Navy James Forrestal, and War Production Board Chairman Donald M. Nelson all urge immediate and basic correc-

From "Corn for War," *Business Week*, October 23, 1943. Reprinted with kind permission of the publisher. This item was originally cited in Bela Gold, *Wartime Economic Planning in Agriculture* (Columbia University Press, New York, 1949), pp. 171–172.

tive action in addition to government stockpiling of 50,000,000 bu. of corn to be earmarked for wet and dry processors.

Present effort

The War Food Administration is appealing to farmers to sell corn under its guarantee to pay them any increase in corn ceilings prior to Nov. 30 on corn marketed from Sept. 28 through Oct. 31. A similar guarantee in July yielded 35,000,000 bu. which supplied processors through September. War Food Administration hopes to garner at least an equivalent amount this month.

WPB officials scathingly indict the inflated hog for impeding the war program. They have charts, tables, and text depicting its hampering influence on war industries ranging from adhesives and asbestos to iron ore and petroleum. They charge that WFA correctives to date have been palliatives.

Bill of particulars

Some of the points in WPB's indictment are these:

(1) That because corn isn't moving to deficit feed areas, the shipping of iron ore on the Lakes has been dangerously reduced by priorities to import Canadian wheat for feeding livestock in such dairy areas as the Northeast.

(2) That by pre-empting grain needed for alcohol and rubber production, the hog is compelling the use of tankers for the importation of Caribbean molasses for industrial alcohol whereas these tankers otherwise could have been used for shipping petroleum from Gulf ports.

(3) That by retarding the production of casein, through the excessive feeding of skim milk to hogs, it is necessary to import casein from Argentina for use in the manufacture of adhesives needed in the production of paper, textiles, plastics, V-boxes, prefabricated houses, building materials for defense housing, and paints.

Suggested steps

WPB officials demand a sharp reduction in the production of hogs. This would be accomplished by cutting profits to be made on hogs by (1) upping the ceiling price of corn, or (2) reducing the ceiling price on hogs.

The current corn ceiling is approximately $1.07 a bu., Chicago; the hog price ceiling is $14.75 a cwt., Chicago. This corn-hog ratio of nearly 14 to 1 contrasts with the theoretical break-even point of 10 to 1 or 11 to 1. Wartime peak for the ratio in the Corn Belt was 19.5 to 1 in October last year.

The official goal

To conserve feed, War Food Administrator Marvin Jones is asking hog producers to limit 1944 pig output to 100,000,000 head compared with 125,000,000 in 1943. Officials realize, however, that in view of the record-size 1943 corn crop in principal Corn Belt states, it may be necessary to take action on prices.

READING 30

One of free man's perpetual concerns is checks upon power. In our economy, we look to competition to supply much of the restraining force on power accumulation. Let a man seek to abuse his power in a competitive market by charging too high a price or paying too low a wage, and the impersonal forces of the market will take care of him. But every society, our own included, seeks more than one goal. Thus, protection against monopoly is not enough for us. Sometimes, for example, we seek security even while we pursue progress. It thus becomes important to ask whether a dynamic competitive system can promote security even while it encourages progress.

John Maurice Clark, late professor of economics at Columbia University and one of the foremost figures in American economics, turns to these issues in a brief excerpt from a classic on the free economy.

Questions to Guide the Reading

What are the costs associated with the maintenance of a competitive economy? Can those costs be minimized without detracting from the gains that flow from such competition?

What presuppositions must be made in order to render Clark's "quality competition" beneficial for the consumer?

THE CASE FOR COMPETITION
John Maurice Clark

The chief agency on which defenders of the market economy have relied to keep self-interest within useful bounds and prevent it from becoming oppressive is the system of free competition. Without it free exchange between unequals could still be tyranny and its freedom a sham.

Competition is an outstanding example of an institution that nearly everyone approves, yet almost no one carries his approval through consistently. This is partly a case of the familiar double standard—competition for the other fellow, protection for me—but it is only partly that. It is partly because competition has two opposites: which we may call monopoly and security, postponing for the moment the question what these terms mean. Nearly everyone favors competition as against monopoly, and nearly everyone wants it limited in the interest of security. And hardly anyone pays much attention to the question where one leaves off and the other begins.

Competition is our main safeguard against exploitation. In our sophisticated civilization we dare not trust the terms of exchange to tribal custom and sense of honor, as some primitive peoples can. Under self-interest, people of our advanced stage of culture would naturally incline to give as little and get as much as possible; they would increase their gains by reducing their services, by producing less to sell for more. But competition works the simple miracle whereby each one increases his individual gains by increasing his services rather than reducing them: he makes more by producing more to sell for less.

The question how far this price-reducing pressure goes, and how far it is safe and desirable to have it go, is one of the key questions in the nature and usefulness of competition. Put in other words, it is the question whether competition threatens security, to an extent requiring some kind of protection. On this theme we might imagine a colloquy between prosecution and defense running somewhat in this fashion:

Prosecution. How can everybody get rich by selling for less? That is the way to make everybody poor.

Defense. You get rich by having other people sell to you for less. And if you sell for less yourself, you haven't lost as much as you have gained. The essential thing is that, in trying to gain by selling for less, people produce more, and that extra product remains and is not canceled out. Some individuals may be ruined if they sell for too little—it's up to their common sense to stop short of that. But how can everybody get poor by all producing more?

Prosecution. When prices and wages all go down together in a slump, that seems to make the slump deeper, not lift us out of it. And in ordinary times millions of workers have injured their health and grown prematurely old, farmers have mined their soil and made dust-bowls, and irreplaceable treasures of coal and oil have been criminally wasted.

Defense. I grant you these abuses are serious; the level of competition needs to be protected to prevent that sort of thing. And it ought to be possible to mitigate slumps, so that wages and prices would not be driven down to destructive levels. But if you let people peg their own wages and prices, then you are back in the condition in which they are all trying to get rich by selling for more—which can't make them all rich—and producing less, which ends by making everybody poorer. We may have to set limits on competi-

From John Maurice Clark, *Alternative to Serfdom* (Vintage Books, New York, 1960), pp. 64–67, 73–76, 80–82. Reprinted with kind permission of the publishers and of the copyright holders, the Regents of the University of Michigan.

tion, but we can't afford to abolish it. It stimulates production; and if it is reasonably equal and fair, it safeguards distribution against the building up of privileged classes.

Prosecution. The little man hasn't a fair chance against the big one; and the majority of business enterprises end in failure.

Defense. If the big man wins by efficiency, that is the customer's gain, meaning everybody's. If he wins in other ways, we should try to improve the rules so as to prevent it. If failures simply eliminate the inefficient, that is the price of progress.

This debate could go on for a long while, but perhaps the main points have been made. Returning to our key terms, "security," which has good associations, suggests safeguards for the essential needs of the little man, while "monopoly," which has bad associations, suggests swollen gains for the big man. The accepted view seems to favor the first and oppose the second. But the ends of security may be sought by the methods of monopoly; and the size of an interest is no sure index of whether it is seeking to protect the minimum needs of solvency or is out for all it can get.

What is competition?

The first thing that seems to be needed is to supply a conception of competition that covers different degrees and is not limited to impossible perfection or destructive rigor. The question of desirable degree is a natural second step. Competition is rivalry for economic goods or gain: rivalry that centers in offering the other party a bargain good enough to induce him to deal with you in the face of his free option of dealing with others who are freely offering him the same kind of inducement for the same kind of return. The terms have to be worth your while—that is a bottom limit—and the top limit is set by the other party's freedom to go elsewhere if anyone else offers terms more attractive or more advantageous to him than yours are.

The rivalry may be in buying or selling or working for advancement. It merges into "substitution" where inducements of different kind or quality are offered. But the essential thing is that your gains are limited by the fact that you will lose business to your rivals if you let your offer become less attractive than theirs. Wherever this will happen, there is some competitive force at work. And the force and effectiveness of competition hinges, among other things, on how large and how speedy this transfer of business is, in response to a small inducement. The competitive check is not very effective unless, if your offerings get substantially inferior to your rivals', you will fairly soon lose all or most of your business.

(1) The rivalry has certain general characteristics. Business competitors are under more pressure than monopolists to try to make the largest possible net return, because if they do not, they may not stay in business long. But there are high-cost and low-cost producers, and the low-cost concerns have some margin of discretion in this matter. The efficient production on which their superiority rests is precious, and they will do nothing to endanger it; but in other matters they are free to try experiments with long-run ideas of policy. They do not have to squeeze out the last dollar this year's market will afford. In some cases, where their superiority depends on having gained a lead in the race for improvement in which all are engaged, a ten per cent advantage in cost might be reckoned as equivalent to three or four years' normal progress in productivity, so that it might be lost if the low-cost concern should cease to progress for about that length of time; in other cases, where the superiority is due to location or some other enduring cause, this way of representing it might not be appropriate.

On the other hand, there is nearly always a quota of border-line producers who must better their current record or go out of business, and in some industries there is a fringe who can work only when demand is strong. They must make the most of every short-run possibility. The pressure on these concerns may affect their policies in selling, buying materials, or hiring labor. Competition of employers for labor sustains wages; but where a concern is under strong competitive pressure in the sale of its product, but is less competitive as a hirer of labor—a frequent situation—its competition may force it to squeeze wages down. This is one of the problems that union policy has to meet.

(2) Under competition no one seller can control supply. If he withholds part of his own supply, incidentally to holding his price, others are free to fill the gap.

(3) It is often said that under competition there can be no bargaining, but under the definition here adopted, bargaining is merely limited in scope.

(4) Finally, one neglected feature of competition is the fact that, like most human matters, it is always evolving. The character and force of competitive tactics tend continually to change,

as people learn what to expect of their rivals and try new ways of adjusting themselves to the rivalry. Therefore the character of competition seems to depend partly on how long a given type of competitive contacts has been in operation. Competition may tend to settle down to a sort of stalemate unless fresh areas and types of competitive contact are continually being opened up; for example, by improved transportation bringing new producers into a market, or by the starting of new enterprises or the introduction of new processes or new products. Competition needs to be dynamic; if it gets to obeying fixed and rigid laws, it is already half dead.

Competition in price is sometimes contrasted with competition in quality. The distinction is real, but it would probably be more exact to speak of competition in price where quality is standardized, and competition of sellers offering different qualities, with price as a co-ordinate inducement. "Competition in quality" is real and powerful, and includes on the whole the healthiest forms of competition. If every seller is free to choose whether he will offer a quality close to his rivals' or markedly different, if the buyer is equally free to choose between them, and if this rivalry forces every seller to offer something that will attract free buyers, the rivalry is surely one of the most desirable sorts, and the mere difference in quality cannot in itself lead to monopoly profits.

It may, of course, get into a rut where differences in quality become stabilized, and price-differentials equally stabilized, so that a producer knows that any change in his price will be instantly followed by his rivals, just as may happen where quality is identical. It works best where there is a constant search for innovations that are substantial enough to lead to an alteration in the previous price-differentials.

One kind of innovation that seems particularly likely to be held back is one that greatly increases the durability of a product, all at once. This naturally tends to reduce total demand for the product; and where all the producers are virtually sure to adopt it if one takes the lead, even the leader may soon find his volume of business reduced instead of increased as a result. This is especially likely to happen if the number of producers is small. There might logically be cases in which an improvement of this sort would be more likely to be introduced if one concern held a patent on it than if all could freely copy it and promptly wipe out the first user's gains. This is perhaps the chief defect of quality-competition in practice; and it may be a cloud with a silver lining, as delaying a type of improvement that is especially likely to lead to "technological unemployment."

From this standpoint, the growing fertility of industrial chemistry in turning out an increasing variety of synthetic materials, and the resulting flow of different products, are among the healthiest features of the situation, starting fresh competitive contacts that may serve as an antidote to the tendency of old ones to settle into a rut. Such innovations seem to be coming along so plentifully that we need not be afraid that technical progress will come to a standstill, even if shoemakers fail to adopt the most durable method of making waterproof heels. One of the costs of this progress is the burden of selection it imposes on the customer and the need for technical guidance to aid him in this increasingly difficult task.

READING 31

In few, if any, places are the forces of supply and demand so unrestrained in their effects on prices as in that most volatile, exciting, and perplexing of markets— the stock exchange. Here the ownership of American corporations is constantly in flux. Buyers and sellers of ownership shares, armed with a relatively large amount of information on prevailing market conditions, enter and leave at a rapid enough rate to keep prices forever on the move.

The stock exchange, with its own language and its own ground rules, is at root simply a meeting place for the representatives of buyers and sellers. The results of the buying and selling are clear and fast; they show up on the ticker tapes for all men to see. But the motivations back of that buying and selling are seldom so apparent. Yet part of the understanding of any market is the ability to detect the underlying forces at work. This is necessary even if only to disabuse ourselves of the notion that any one force by itself causes the major changes in buyers' or sellers' behavior.

Henry C. Wallich, professor of economics at Yale University and a former member of President Eisenhower's Council of Economic Advisers, wrote this article at a time in 1957 when wide swings in the stock market were too often assumed to be linked tightly to overall changes in our level of business activity. By illuminating one market so clearly, he helps us go on to the complexities of other markets.

Questions to Guide the Reading

At what points does this analysis find its closest parallels to the market for, say, potatoes? At what points are the forces in the stock exchange closest to being unique?

Why has the stock market been subjected to increasingly close regulation by government and by its own members over the years?

Institutional investors (e.g., big pension trusts) have become an increasingly big force in the stock market. How might this affect stock market behavior?

WHAT MAKES STOCKS GO UP AND DOWN?
Henry C. Wallich

The New York Stock Exchange sometimes goes through violent gyrations, gaining or losing as much as eight billion in a day. In these frantic ups and downs brokers say they do not know whether to weep for their losses or smile because of their commissions.

The headlines when the market drops may make a gloomy accompaniment to the market's hectic tune—of layoffs, cuts in output here and there, weakness in commodity prices. The public reads and wonders whether this is just another case of Wall Street jitters or whether it means something more ominous. Does the action of the stock market signal a depression ahead?

I shall argue that movements of the stock market do not always, and certainly not inevitably, forecast movements in business. Conceivably we may be heading into a depression. But if so it might easily take the market by surprise as it would most of us. And it is entirely possible for the market to take a dive—or to advance—without business following after.

To substantiate these points we shall have to inquire what makes the stock market move—a 200 billion dollar question in terms of the stock listed on the New York Stock Exchange alone, and a great deal more if we take all publicly held stocks in the country together. Fortunately, it is easier to discover what caused the market to move in the past than to predict what it will do in the future. Anyone who knew much about the future of the market would scarcely waste his time informing others. But the record of the market's past performance is engraved so firmly in the minds and pocketbooks of investors that an analysis can readily be made.

The record exhibits a variety of forces that have impelled the market along its seemingly eccentric course. One important factor is the comparative return on stocks and on bonds. Stocks, which pay variable and uncertain dividends, are riskier investments than bonds, with their contractual obligation to pay a fixed interest. The return yielded by stocks, therefore, ought normally to be higher than that from bonds, to compensate the investor for the greater risk. Ever since the war this has been precisely the situation.

From time to time it may happen that stocks

From Henry C. Wallich, "What Makes Stocks Go Up and Down?" *New York Times Magazine*, November 3, 1957. Reprinted with kind permission of the author and publisher.

lose this yield advantage. During the last two years, for instance, many stocks that had risen very high suffered such a fate. In these circumstances some investors find it tempting to switch from stocks to bonds. This naturally tends to push the stock market down. Switching of that sort no doubt was one of the causes behind the recent market decline.

Another potentially powerful lever acting on stock prices is credit. Easy stock market credit added fuel, for example, to the 1929 boom. Margin calls against over-extended borrowers speeded the subsequent collapse, bearing out the old saying that enough easy credit and free advice will ruin anybody.

Since 1934 control over stock market credit has been in the hands of the Federal Reserve Board. The board has tended to play it safe and its regulations have greatly reduced the role of credit as a cause of stock market improvement.

The stock market is sensitive also to taxes—as who is not? Peculiarly enough, taxes sometimes push prices up, not down. President G. Keith Funston of the New York Stock Exchange told a Congressional committee that he suspected the capital gains tax of having this effect. Since the capital gains tax becomes payable when stocks are sold at a profit it discourages selling and so helps to keep up the market. Other taxes, like the late, unlamented excess profits tax, clearly depress stock prices. The removal of the excess profits tax at the end of 1953 no doubt helped to speed the market on its upward surge during the following years.

The course of stock prices shows the traces also of changes in the saving and investing habits of individuals and institutions. Two such changes stand out in recent years. More persons have discovered the joys and sorrows of stock ownership than ever before—more than 8,500,000 of us now own stock. And institutional investors, such as pension funds, mutual funds and insurance companies, have been growing by leaps and bounds and have bought large amounts of stocks. This surge of demand naturally has helped to put stock prices up.

But the flowering of institutional investors has had still another effect. These buyers have concentrated, out of prudence as well as shrewdness, on a relatively small number of blue chips—the big, well-known companies. The description of an institutional portfolio manager as a man who employs a research staff to discover the stocks in the Dow-Jones averages no doubt falls short of perfect justice. But, in effect, that is just what they have been doing. They all bought the same well-known stocks, and partly because they did these stocks went up more than the rest, which, of course, proved that the buyer's judgment was right.

The late Lord Keynes, who made considerable money in the market, likened this sort of thing to a beauty contest in which the judges' task was not to pick the girl they thought prettiest but the girl who would get the most votes. For investors the trick has been to discover what stocks other buyers were bullish on. Institutional investors, during the years 1953–55, were bulls with a strongly developed herd instinct. Their votes went largely to the same stocks, and they were richly rewarded.

On the other side of the coin we must note that institutional buying does lend a certain strength and solidity to the market. Investors live and die, but institutions go on forever. By their nature institutional investors must take a long view, toward the distant peaks and beyond the foothills of near-term ups and downs. They are less easily stampeded than individual market enthusiasts—as professionals they have learned that not every seasonal dip is the beginning of a major depression. The market increasingly is looking to them as a source of stability.

This listing of factors which may move the stock market even in the absence of business changes could be lengthened further. It is already long enough, however, to reach the conclusion that by no means all stock market ups and downs are motivated by current or expected moves in business. They may, and not infrequently do, reflect changes in interest rates, in taxes, in the availability of stock market credit, and in fashions among buyers.

When all this is said and done, however, the fact remains that the ups and downs of business are the most potent levers activating the market. "The market" consists, of course, of the stocks of thousands of companies, big and small, which by no means all move together.

Each company's stock moves according to its particular outlook for profits and dividends, which is shaped, in part at least, by events and conditions inside the company. The quality of the management, the development of new products, the expansion of its plant and equipment determine a good part of a company's progress. But no business is immune to changes in demand and in costs, and these are governed largely by general business conditions. Here is the link that ties together, albeit not very reliably, business conditions and stock market prices.

There can be no doubt that, other things being equal, the market tries to anticipate and reflect the outlook for profits and dividends. That, after all, is the way for investors to make money. The question is how well it succeeds. To be a good forecaster the market must meet two tests. First, it must anticipate the turning points of business as they develop. Second, it must make up its mind how high or low these fluctuations, as well as the longer term trend, are likely to carry.

To catch the turning points, the market must correctly interpret some of the straws in the wind that usually begin to fly before the storm breaks. Investors who are in business themselves sometimes can see trends shaping up early: new orders, the movement of inventories, customers' moods and financial conditions, prices firming or weakening. Statisticians also watch figures, like construction contracts, business failures, new incorporations, hours worked a week, and wholesale prices. These are data that have tended to move in advance of business turns.

The historical record, going back well into the nineteenth century, shows that far more often than not the market has anticipated turns in business correctly. It has been less accurate since the end of the war, however, than it used to be. Let us look at a few pages of history that record notable errors of the market.

In 1929 the market failed to signal the business downturn by several months. It also vastly overestimated reasonable prospects for profits and dividends, as shown by the exorbitantly high ratios of prices to earnings before the crash. Easy availability of credit no doubt was in part responsible.

In 1932 at the bottom of the depression, the market did call the turn well in advance. But it was far too pessimistic about what American business was worth. Never since have stocks sold anywhere near the lows at which some investors seem to have thought them a good sale in 1932.

In 1942 the market remained bearish long after profits and dividends had begun to turn up—both circumstances being due, of course, to the war. In 1946 the market broke sharply, without any obvious reason, in anticipation apparently of a post-war depression that never came.

In 1953 the market correctly signaled a downturn. Then, after business had just begun to slide off, investors seemed to change their minds. The market turned around and took off on a two-year flight that more than doubled the averages. Profits and dividends, after a mild dip, tagged along, but at a far more modest rate. By this performance the market seemed to say that for a number of years stocks had been grossly undervalued.

The historical record points to two conclusions: (1) The market, though often right, has been far from infallible as a forecaster of business trends. (2) The market has had great difficulty in appraising the magnitude of business fluctuations and their effects upon profits and dividends. Many of its vagaries are traceable to this latter failing, which may profitably be examined a little further.

The market's dilemma in trying to find some benchmark of values is quite understandable. To begin with, anyone trying to come up with an answer would have to make up his mind about the very existence of the business cycle. Has it been licked, or is it still with us? If prosperity is going to be more or less permanent, if profits and dividends are to be always higher and higher, stocks obviously are worth much more than if fat and lean years are inter-larded.

In the "New Era" of the nineteen twenties, investors concluded inaccurately that big depressions were a thing of the past. During the years from 1945 to 1953 investors seemed to have been waiting, like Sewell Avery of Montgomery Ward fame, for the "inevitable" post-war depression. During the following years, a new "New Era" seems to have broken out, with a consequent joyous revaluation of all stock values. In the words of Leo Model, an extremely successful judge of values, stocks shifted from a price basis "minus fear" to one "plus hope."

A second dilemma for the market is the value of growth—how much to pay for tomorrow. If a company's profits and dividends were to grow 10 per cent per year on average for the next twenty years, they would reach about seven times their present level. What allowance should today's price make for such prospects of trees growing pretty close to the sky? Investors' opinions on this score seem to have undergone some remarkably optimistic revisions in the last four years—at least prior to the recent drop. In the process many old stock market wheelhorses have suddenly been revealed as growth companies.

It is intriguing to note that this conversion has occurred with scarcely any assist from the national income statistics. Total corporate profits after taxes, which in 1948 had got up to $20,300,-000,000 and in 1950 to $22,100,000,000, failed to rise above $21,000,000,000 in the boom years 1955 and 1956. In terms of constant purchasing power they were unquestionably lower in 1955 and 1956 than in the earlier years. This is hardly a picture of exuberant growth.

The companies covered by Standard and Poor's index did rather better than the national total. Between 1950 and 1956 they managed to raise their earnings from about $1,800,000,000 to $3,000,000,000 a year. (Part of this gain was accounted for by mergers, by changes in the index and probably by conditions created by the Korean War and the excess profits tax.) But this concentration of earnings, with the biggest companies gaining at the expense of the rest, probably has its limits. For the long pull the market as a whole is tied to the growth potential of the Gross National Product and its subdivision, Corporate Profits.

These two sober statistics seem reasonably steady; they are unlikely to run away or go through the roof. If the Gross National Product continues to grow at about 3 per cent a year, or a little more allowing for price increases, as it has done on average in recent years, corporate profits on average probably will be limited to advances roughly of that order. At a 3 per cent rate profits would grow by no more than about 35 per cent in ten years. Many genuine growth companies undoubtedly will perform much better, but the stock market as a whole cannot escape economics.

Finally, the market has to cope with factors almost beyond rational business appraisal, especially the danger of war, political trends and inflation. War means intense business activity, but also restrictions and high taxes. The market has always had a hard time making up its mind about the net balance between these conflicting influences. The stock market consequences of a nuclear war defy all calculation—they would in any case be one of our lesser concerns if that ultimate calamity should strike.

Politics has meant, in recent years, a major change in "climate." Although corporate profits after taxes accounted for a higher share of national income under President Truman than under President Eisenhower many observers credit the great advance beginning in 1953 to the "confidence factor."

Inflation, likewise, has proved a two-edged sword. Against the long inflationary waves since the First World War the stock market has protected its followers very adequately. These past inflations, however, have been predominantly money inflations. What we are facing today is predominantly a labor inflation. Labor is trying to increase its share of the national income at the expense of capital—and the fixed-income groups as innocent bystanders are incidental victims of the battle. If labor succeeds, how will stocks work out as an inflation hedge? Fluctuations in hopes and fears on this score bring fluctuations in stock prices.

Where facts are so hard to come by it is little wonder that some members of Wall Street sometimes seek refuge in rumor and fancy. Wall Streeters speak mostly to other Wall Streeters. Sentiment travels quickly and becomes an independent force.

The market, like the human heart, sometimes has its reasons that the head doesn't know of. When stocks are going up, Wall Street puts on its rose-tinted glasses and finds most of the news good. When they go down, Wall Street begins to look for bad news and will certainly find it. Mole hills of misfortune suddenly loom like mountains. At such times it is not the news that makes the market but the market that makes the news.

It takes only a small minority of investors and traders susceptible to such influences to move the market. If the others sit tight and neither buy nor sell, the market will be dominated by the nervous minority.

The belief I expressed earlier that the market is no sure barometer of future trends receives further support from these observations. In the end, truth and sense will prevail and will force the stock market, that graveyard of prophecies, back into line with fact. But meanwhile the market may have given off some distinctly misleading signals, lending substance to what the Street says is to be found there: "The bears, the bulls and the bum steers."

Despite frailties like these, it is only fair to say that Wall Street is becoming a much more thoughtful and judicious place than it was thirty years ago. The tipster who once infested the market and at times endowed it with a virtual immunity to facts is vanishing. The "insider" who cut a swath through the Street, every inch a bull and spouting omniscience, has become rare.

Their places have been taken by slide-rule-wielding security analysts and investment officers with sharp pencils. Men like Benjamin Graham and Albert Hettinger have shown that scholarly research, if combined with good judgment, can pay off enormously.

Wall Street as a whole, it is true, still lags behind most of American industry in the application of advanced research methods. In part this reflects a scepticism flowing from the well-advertised misfortunes that some economists have suffered in the market in former years. But new methods have been developed meanwhile—sample surveys, advanced statistical techniques, computing machines.

These approaches are not so ambitious as some earlier ones that claimed to forecast the business cycle. Neither will they make sense out of nonsense. But used as aids, not as alternatives, to good judgment they could perhaps render services that Wall Street has not yet fully exploited. As Wall Street progresses in this direction our understanding of the forces that move the stock market should improve and the market itself should become stabler and a better place for the average man's savings.

READING 32

Agriculture comes as close as any industry to fitting the conditions for perfect competition—large numbers of independent sellers, identical products, and relative ease of entry. But a combination of forces has worked to produce "the farm problem" in the United States. Demand for farm products has risen less than proportionately to the rise in consumer incomes. Supply of these products has risen sharply with new technology. The Great Depression worsened the position of many farmers to the point where Federal intervention in this classical case of free markets was widely called for. Now, three decades later, the farm policies of the 1930s are still with us in modified form. Their results—heavy government spending without much evidence that the poorest farmers are helped and huge surpluses of foodstuffs stored at public expense—have baffled and annoyed just about everybody. There are few defenders of the prevailing policies, but there is also little consensus yet on what should be done to make the situation more defensible.

Edward Higbee, professor of land utilization at the University of Rhode Island, provides a penetrating review of where we now stand in the long debate. His plea that our agricultural aid policies be updated to take into account the urbanized way of most Americans' lives adds new fuel to that debate.

Questions to Guide the Reading

Do the factors and forces which led us into strong government intervention in agricultural markets in the 1930s suggest that it will be extremely difficult to retreat from that intervention today?

What are the tests by which we should appraise the appropriateness of any proposed farm policy? Do the cushions provided for some other groups—tariffs, minimum wages, fair-trade laws—provide justification for cushions in agriculture?

WHICH WAY FOR THE FARMERS' MARKETS?
Edward Higbee

Even if we accept the loose definition of a farm used by the Census of Agriculture, there were only 15 million persons living on farms in 1959. Since that year the estimated drop-out rate has averaged 4 per cent a year. Such high mortality gives survivors the jitters. It is no wonder they are agitated and prone to grab in all directions for straws. A lot of people who are in line for elimination do not want to quit farming. They are being squeezed out by a combination of tech-

From Edward Higbee, *Farms and Farmers in an Urban Age* (Twentieth Century Fund, New York, 1963). Reprinted with kind permission of the author and publisher.

nology, economics, and politics which they can do very little to resist if they lack the capital to expand and take full advantage of new techniques, tax loopholes, and government subsidies. Fellow farmers, professional farm spokesmen, professors, journalists, congressmen, bankers, merchants, physicians, labor organizers, and industrialists all have a straw or two of advice to toss to the farmer who is drowning in a sea of surplus crops and surplus wisdom.

As might be expected, farmers do not always take kindly to the advice which is proffered them. When the Committee for Economic Development hit the nation's headlines with its finding that American agriculture would be better off with lower price supports, no acreage controls, and two million fewer farmers, the Farmers Union Grain Terminal Association took radio time to return the compliment. ". . . Perhaps," said the broadcast for the Association, "it would be only fair for farmers to try to . . . make a report on what they'd recommend for corporations. Things, perhaps, like doing away with subsidies to big business, cutting tractor prices by a third, lowering interest rates one-half, unlocking interlocking boards of directors, putting business on the free market so it could be competitive at home and around the world. In other words, if corporation chiefs claim to know what's best for farmers, we're sure farmers have some appropriate suggestions as to what would be good for corporations." The broadcast ended with a question: "What do you think?"

It did not take long for a few thoughts to materialize. In several midwestern towns Ford dealers and Sears, Roebuck stores were picketed by members of the National Farmers Organization because executives of these companies had served on the CED agricultural committee. Oren Lee Staley, national president of the NFO, said the demonstrations were intended to get the companies to repudiate the CED report. Farmers, he implied, had had enough free advice from outsiders to last them a while.

On the other hand the embattled husbandmen seem to be oblivious to the attitudes of a lot of people who are not "corporation executives." Ordinary citizens have grown tired of giving up a portion of their wages to support farm programs that only result in more surpluses and bigger storage bills. Thirty years of subsidized farm surpluses have exhausted the public's tolerance for "temporary" farm relief which seems to have bedded down into a permanent slot in the budget.

Who gets the help?

The day has drawn to a close when farmers could count on broad public support for a program of government spending either to increase their profit margins when they are adequately capitalized or to keep them in full-time agriculture when they are under-capitalized. The fact that most of the help goes to a relatively small percentage of upper-bracket operators who are better off than the majority of taxpayers has hurt the cause of those who are really in a bind. As the farmers' ranks are thinned each year, the subsidies paid to those who remain increase rather than decrease. This fact does not make sense to the ordinary citizen who pays the bill. He would expect that fewer and more substantial farmers would need less help.

It should be emphasized that most agricultural commodities are not on the subsidy list (Table 1); public aid has been concentrated in certain selected segments of agriculture where overproduction is critical. In 1960 five commodities—cotton, wheat, corn, grain sorghums, and dairy products —received 91 per cent of all price support aid, yet they represented only 40 per cent of the value of all farm production. The producers of these commodities, however, are numerous, and they are heavily concentrated in the Lower Middle Class distress group (i.e., farms producing from $2,500 to $10,000 worth of commodities annually).

As much as 85 per cent of all corn is fed to livestock on the farm where it is grown or on farms nearby. Farmers themselves are the primary market for this feed grain. Thus, in this case, the public subsidizes a crop that is used primarily by the growers themselves.

Influence

Despite the decline in the number of farmers and the decline in rural populations, agricultural interests have long managed to maintain their influence in the nation's legislative halls. They have been able to do this because election districts in many cases did not reflect the new patterns of population settlement. Until very recently the rural districts of Maryland were able to elect a majority of the state senate, even though they contained less than 15 per cent of the state's population. Before 1962 one vote in Georgia's least populous county had a value equal to 100 votes in its most populous county. The late Governor Eugene Talmadge of Georgia was so con-

Table 1 Commodity Credit Corporation Expenditures, 1952–61, and Estimated Net Inventories, August, 1962

Commodity	Net Expenditures Fiscal Years 1952–61	Value of Estimated Inventories, August, 1962
Feed grains:		
Corn	4,085.1	712.4
Grain sorghums	1,379.0	713.7
Barley	442.6	26.6
Oats and rye	148.7	12.0
Total, feed and grains	6,055.4	1,464.7
Wheat and flour	9,411.6	2,104.2
Rice	773.7	.2
Other grains	163.6	115.4
Total, grains	16,404.3	3,684.5
Cotton	3,168.6	249.2
Dairy products	2,358.8	348.7
Tobacco	498.4	318.4*
Total of above	22,430.1	4,600.8
Interest and general overhead	2,261.3	. . .
Change in loans held by banks	556.2	. . .
Bartered materials transferred to supplemental stockpile	1,008.8	. . .
Public Law 480 commodities not listed above and related costs not segregated by commodity (transportation estimated)	972.8	. . .
All other	121.5	4.2
Total, CCC	26,238.3	4,605.0

* Represents loans.

SOURCE: *Congressional Record*, August 25, 1962.

temptuous of the urban vote that he once declared he did not bother to campaign in counties where streetcars ran. In 1962 Vermont's state senatorial districts were the same as they had been in 1793 with the result that the Town of Burlington (population 33,000) had one state senator to match one senator from the Town of Victory (population 48). The same story of disproportionate legislative influence in the grip of rural minorities has characterized every state in varying degrees since the time when people in metropolitan areas began to outnumber those in rural districts back in the early 1920s.

Now it appears that the era of strong rural influence at the political pork barrel is near its end. In March, 1962 the U.S. Supreme Court indicated that election districts with greatly differing populations may violate the rights of individual citizens in the more populous districts by diluting the value of their ballots. Since that decision rural districts with small populations but strong legislative powers have begun to pull in their horns.

The increasing antagonism toward farm subsidies on the part of urban taxpayers seems to stem from the fact that Washington's farm spending, which began as a temporary relief appropriation, has become the third largest regular item in the federal budget where it follows defense and interest on the debt. Moreover, the farm program is no longer primarily a relief measure for the distressed, but has become instead an income subsidy device for one of the most progressive segments of the national economy. The financial distress of American agriculture, as it has been publicized in recent years, is largely a fiction

Table 2   Value of Production by Class of Farm, 1959

Value Class (by worth of annual production)	No. of Farms	% of Farms	% of Total Value of Farm Sales
$500,000 +	1,200	1−	4.6
$100,000–$500,000	21,000	1−	12.4
$40,000–$100,000	80,000	2+	14.5
$20,000–$40,000	210,000	6	18.4
$10,000–$20,000	483,000	13	21.9
$2,500–$10,000	1,272,000	34	22.8
Under $2,500	1,641,000	64	5.3

SOURCE: *Census of Agriculture,* 1959, Vol. II.

evolved by lumping statistics and manipulating definitions in such a way as to make it appear that the plight of farmers in the lower brackets is the plight of all.

With 72 per cent of all farm income going to 22 per cent of the census farmers (Table 2) it is fairly obvious that these 22 per cent are the real producers and doing very well. The other 78 per cent of census farmers are no longer agriculturists in the modern sense and are not equipped to survive over the long haul unless drastic measures are taken soon to allocate to those who still have a chance a definite percentage of the market before their present percentage slips even more. Yearly doles will not do the trick; they just prolong the agony. If 78 per cent of all census farmers are doing badly it is not because the city is cheating them or the government is callous. It is because they are economically obsolete. A minority of progressive, high-speed agriculturists have pushed them to the wall and taken over the lion's share of production. The taxpayer is in no position to reverse what business competition has already achieved. There are other more critical social problems than this one calling for public attention—urban unemployment for one. The 0.8 million First Class and Upper Middle Class commercial farmers (i.e. those producing more than $10,000 worth of commodities annually), who produce most of the surpluses and consequently get the biggest government checks, are among the most successful of all American entrepreneurs.

Those farmers who appear most distressed in the census data are helped very little by government programs. The 1.6 million Third Class operators, who are 44 per cent of all census farmers but take in only 5 per cent of all farm income (Table 2), are financially and physically incapable of producing surpluses. Their farms are not big enough, nor are they equipped with the machinery that would make overproduction possible.

Their misery, which in some cases is real but more often contrived, makes all agriculture look sick. By a kind of mathematical editing, which seldom takes into account off-farm incomes that usually exceed farm incomes, these people are made to appear destitute.

The basic conflict

In between the 0.8 million farmers who constitute the prosperous and highly productive upper crust of American agriculture and that mass of 1.6 million part-time yeomen at the bottom, there are 1.3 million Lower Middle Class farmers many of whom are in full-time commercial agriculture and want to stay there. They think they can survive even though their chances are poor because by modern standards they are only semi-employed. They do not seem to realize that their basic trouble is that they have been outflanked in economic competition by other farmers. Many of these Lower Middle Class farmers want to grow bigger. Others, realizing that capital is hard to come by, would like to be frozen in their present positions and figure that tight government controls through allotments could protect them against further encroachment by the hacienda and "adequate" family farms. Their competition argues against such a static, hold-the-line philosophy. It says this would stop technological advance and oblige the consumer to patronize inefficiency—a burden that could become as costly as present government programs.

It is up to the taxpaying public to choose whatever side it wishes in this basic conflict between efficient, well-capitalized farmers and those who are less efficient largely because they lack the capital to apply modern technology. If the public chooses to protect weak farmers by means of stringent government allotments, it will in effect underwrite inefficiency and in the end it might be penalized in the form of higher food prices. The magnitude of this risk is not great, however, since all 2.9 million farmers in the Lower Middle and Third Classes put together now have only 28 per cent of the market. Without government floor prices market levels are likely to be determined chiefly by what the 0.8 million farmers in the First and Upper Middle Classes will accept. As long as these producers, who account for 72 per cent of all production, operate competitively prices will be low.

The cost of food could only become unreasonable if, in addition to government allotments, the public were to continue to grant price supports as it has in the past. The history of price support efforts indicates that they do not shelter the small farmer, but they do stimulate his bigger competitors. They should be discontinued in favor of letting free enterprise determine price. As a concession to the marginal farmer, he should be offered the opinion to accept or reject an official allotment which would preserve for him his present small share of the market. He would not be well off and his lot would not be likely to improve, but he would not be so quickly forced out of business if he wanted to stay under the adverse circumstances he is already familiar with.

The sharp conflict of interests within the agricultural fraternity has become fairly transparent, and it is equally clear that public subsidies have aggravated it. There are three main types of public policy which might be advocated under the circumstances. One solution would be to withdraw all forms of government intervention and let farmers slug it out among themselves in a free market until only the fittest survive. Another solution would be to freeze the *status quo* with tight allotments. A third approach would be some kind of subsidy-sweetened compromise between these two extremes. A spirit of compromise has dominated Congress for the past thirty years. In its solicitude to hurt no farmer's feelings it has advanced and financed programs which have only feinted at the problem but never struck a solid punch. While this approach has been easy on agriculture it has been rough on the taxpayer. Costs to the public have mounted while farmers appear to be more displeased than gratified by the inconclusive results.

The dilemma of the Lower Middle Class

Which way should farmers of the Lower Middle Class turn on farm policy—toward the free market or toward allotment controls? Or should

they get out of agriculture altogether? In public opinion polls these farmers generally say they are opposed to government acreage allotments even with price supports. They still seem to cherish the dream that they will grow and catch up with "adequate" family farms. Yet in secret balloting these underdogs usually play it safe and approve controls.

While polls and ballots are not taken or recorded according to economic class, it is obvious from the small number of husbandmen in the top categories and the large number in the lower income groups that the latter can roll up a substantial majority on any issue put to a vote. Whenever all farmers vote it is the opinion of the low income groups which ultimately tip the scales, for these groups can cast more than two-thirds of the ballots even though they control less than one-third of agriculture's capacity to produce. Big agriculture's lobbies work hard in Congress, principally through the Farm Bureau, to prevent some crucial policy decisions from ever reaching the grass roots ballot box. In 1962 the administration under Secretary Freeman proposed that farmers producing the major surpluses of wheat, feed grains, and dairy products should be given a chance to decide between tight allotments with price supports and a free market without public aid. Only wheat farmers got the chance to vote and they approved the plan by a 68.4 per cent majority.[1]

Political corn

The public has been shaken by the realization that costs of crop programs, instead of diminishing, are on the increase. Instead of solving old problems, commodity programs have created new ones. Although there are only half as many farmers today as there were in the thirties when government aid was first broadly extended, farm appropriations have multiplied many times. As farmers have become fewer, more efficient, and wealthier they have demanded more public aid

[1] EDITORS' NOTE: However, in May, 1963, when wheat farmers were asked to vote on a program for stricter controls with high support prices, they rejected it by a majority of 50,000 in a total count of 1,145,000 voting farmers. The American Farm Bureau had campaigned against the program, pleading instead for an alternative of voluntary land retirement with continuing, but lower support. Secretary of Agriculture Freeman, in fighting for the "strict controls–high support price" program argued that only the poorest land would be taken out of production under the Farm Bureau plan and surpluses would therefore continue.

and gotten it. To the urban mind this does not seem reasonable. On every side the city taxpayer observes an urgent need for local public services which he cannot afford. Yet he sees the federal government spend billions to buy farm produce which it then turns over to those who rent storage facilities.

Among the costliest of all farm programs is the one which supports the prices of livestock feed grains: corn, sorghums, barley, and oats. Since livestock and their products represent more than half the value of all agricultural marketings, it is easy to comprehend the far-reaching influence of the feed grain program—and the fact that Congress faces it with the greatest reluctance and the greatest variety of compromise.

A prevailing opinion among corn belt farmers is that any reduction in feed grain acreages should be voluntary but price supports should be mandatory. Lower Middle Class farmers rightly claim that fixed allotments would prevent them from getting bigger as they would have to do if they were to catch up with the technological revolution. With equal correctness big farmers complain that "controls" would cheat them out of advantages they have gained by being efficient under the free enterprise system. As one Indiana grower told a visitor, "What would appeal to us most would be strong price supports with no controls." Then he added with a grin, "But, of course, we can't have everything." Recognition by the corn-hog farmer that he cannot have everything does not prevent him from trying. He would like corn prices pegged at levels where he can make a profit by feeding grain to the government if he does not feed it to hogs. With equal insistence he objects to what Charles B. Shuman, president of the Farm Bureau, refers to as giving government the "power to club the farmer's brains out."

The Kennedy administration's Food and Agriculture Act of 1962 departed from thirty years of precedent when it recommended that all feed grain farmers either accept strict acreage controls or become ineligible for price supports. When this measure came into the House most corn belt representatives jumped on it with both feet, and they were no small factor in its defeat by a vote of 215 to 205. Having failed in its first attempt to clip this part of the farm budget, the administration was obliged to change its approach. It fell back to what was essentially the Eisenhower-Benson position which the corn belt had torpedoed when the Republicans were in office. Ezra

Taft Benson of Utah guided policy for the Department of Agriculture in those crucial years when the costs of farm price supports made their great leap forward. Those were the days when it became apparent to all that the technological revolution had given farmers a capacity to outproduce the Treasury as long as the government was committed to buy at profitable prices whatever was not consumed.

The key to the Benson program was the level at which the government might have been obliged to support prices. If support prices were high they would stimulate unnecessary production by specialists. If they just covered the costs of production by the most efficient, they might put the Lower Middle Class growers in jeopardy. Benson wanted price levels close to costs of production by the most efficient farmers to dissuade big producers from overloading the government storage bins at the taxpayer's expense. Throughout the eight years Secretary Benson was in office he never received authority from Congress to put government supports down to where he thought they belonged. The average support price of corn during his tenure ranged from a high of $1.62 in 1954 to a low of $1.06 in 1960.

Ezra Taft Benson is generally regarded as having been a failure in office, but it was a failure imposed by Congress, which hog-tied him from the start because of pressures back home. It would be easy to anticipate that under such a program the Lower Middle Class corn-livestock farmer would be at a disadvantage in competition with others who operate on a larger scale with more modern equipment; so they objected. It is also easy to see that with floor prices raised to a level which would keep the Lower Middle Class afloat, the specialists in the upper brackets could have a field day growing surpluses for the public treasury. Since that was a rather tempting prospect they, too, objected. Government stocks of corn rose from 736 million bushels in 1954 to 1,675 million bushels in 1960. In 1961 specialized cash-corn growers in the corn belt averaged 86 bushels per acre. Specialized corn-livestock farmers, who raised corn for their own use, had average yields of 61 to 84 bushels per acre. A 1962 study by the Ohio Agricultural Experiment Station indicates that the costs of corn production in the corn belt of west central Ohio in 1958 were $62.82 per acre for small farms of 50 to 141 acres while they were $55.33 per acre on farms of 364 to 996 acres. These figures indicate that some specialists able to produce 84 bushels per acre can now raise corn for 66 cents a bushel. It is well known that the best technicians are getting average yields of over 100 bushels per acre and so are producing for even less.

When the Eisenhower-Benson plan became the fall-back position of the Kennedy-Freeman administration during the final battles of the 87th Congress, it again encountered opposition from the corn belt. However, the measure squeaked through to the surprise of many. It is scheduled to become operative in 1964 unless the 88th Congress modifies or replaces it. As it read in the autumn of 1962 the Freeman version of the old Benson plan would pay farmers to retire land voluntarily. It would also set the lowest limit for corn support prices at 50 per cent of parity.[2] Translated into cash this would mean a floor of about 80 cents a bushel instead of the $1.20 which has prevailed since 1961. Since the cost of production by the most efficient cash grain growers is around 60 to 70 cents, there is still room for profit, but the margin is so greatly reduced that overplanting would not be likely. Since the idea of parity became popular in the 1930's feed grain production per man-hour has increased more than eight times. This phenomenal increase in agricultural efficiency makes the parity concept obsolete.

The Freeman version of the Benson bill gives the Secretary power to choke off surpluses which Benson never enjoyed. The language of the legislation makes it mandatory that the lowest permissible support prices prevail if the Secretary of Agriculture believes that anything higher would result in additions to government stocks already in storage. If farmers do not want to accept strict allotments without federal subsidies, then to the urban taxpayer this arrangement may be an acceptable alternative.

Republican Karl E. Mundt of South Dakota was prominent among those in the Senate who

[2] Parity was a term widely used in the nineteen twenties and thirties to indicate the price at which a farmer would have to sell a given quantity of farm goods to buy the manufactured articles he could have bought had he made both transactions at the parity date. Parity, of course, was a casualty of the technological revolution in agriculture because that revolution raised efficiency on farms at a far faster rate than efficiency in industry improved. It has made no sense to claim parity for farmers in recent years because their unit costs of production have generally declined while industry, on the other hand, has experienced a general increase in unit costs of production. The term parity is still used, however, as a measuring stick and as a political gimmick.

denounced the new bill as too severe. On September 21, several days before it was enacted into law, he informed his colleagues:

> It seems to me that this legislation, as it comes to us from conference, heralds the collapse of the whole price support concept in agriculture, and provides, in lieu of a fairly satisfactory and rewarding system of price supports, a system of fluctuating price supports, worse by far in their impact on farmers than anything that was ever presented to us by Secretary Benson or the Department of Agriculture. As is well known, Secretary Benson himself was an advocate of flexible price supports. This proposal goes further than the Benson flexible price philosophy, because it not only provides a further flexing of prices downward, but it is tied to an anchor instead of to a star.

Senator Mundt stated what the urban taxpayer had long suspected: that agricultural price supports had been hitched to a star.

Time for decision

The *Wall Street Journal* is not preferred bedtime reading in the corn belt; its point of view is more likely to produce nightmares than sweet dreams. However, this is the way that newspaper looked at agriculture in the late summer of 1962. "The day is approaching, slowly or not," wrote feature columnist Paul Duke, "when Congress will fundamentally alter Federal farm laws . . . days of drift seem numbered." For all its dallying, Congress seems inevitably headed toward accepting the challenges laid down by two successive Secretaries of Agriculture. These challenges of Ezra Taft Benson, Republican, and Orville L. Freeman, Democrat, agreed on just one crucial point: The Government cannot go on forever giving farmers both artificially high prices and freedom to produce. Secretary Benson's proposals essentially aimed at denying them the former. Secretary Freeman's planning basically aims at denying them the latter. Congress, unwilling to accept either harsh prescription, has year after year voted a mishmash—headed neither toward a consistent low-price, free-market agriculture nor toward a tightly regimented high-price farm economy. Yet the course of historic events now makes it practically certain the lawmakers will at last turn down either one road or the other.

In view of a hardening urban attitude toward increasingly heavy outlays for agriculture, farmers in the numerous but depressed Lower Middle

Class will soon have to make up their minds as to whether they want tight controls that will help them keep their present 23 per cent of the market without public aid or whether they want to take their chances in open competition. A fateful decision on this issue cannot be deferred indefinitely. A reluctance to face the choice has characterized the past decade and is reflected in the saying going the rounds among farmers who dislike either alternative—"Benson made a Democrat out of me and now Freeman is turning me back into a Republican."

The basic reason drastic measures must be taken, particularly by the Lower Middle Class, is that if this group of 1.3 million farmers were out of agriculture entirely the remaining farmers in the First and Upper Middle Classes could take care of themselves. The fundamental weakness of the Lower Middle Class, and one that can hardly be remedied at this late stage of technological development, is that it is undercapitalized in an age when farm efficiency calls for a high level of capitalization. Labor income is low. The returns from capital investment are more satisfactory.

The general public should hardly be expected to make up for this deficiency in capital assets through subsidies. If it were, then every unemployed urban citizen might conclude that it is also a public responsibility to set him up in business if he cannot find a job. One of the strangest aspects of public policy at the present time is the highly articulate concern about the low incomes of 1.3 million undercapitalized entrepreneurs in agriculture's Lower Middle Class while other more serious social and economic calamities have befallen the more numerous families of the urban unemployed who have less income and less equity in property. Certainly the democratic way of life is more threatened by growing urban slums than it is by the decline of the undercapitalized family farm, but as yet there is not even a Department of Urban Affairs in the federal government.

READING 33

In a perfectly competitive market, no one producer can have any sizable impact upon the quantities produced or the prices charged. The market is impersonal; Producer A has no occasion to think about what any specific Producer B may do, simply because there are hundreds or even thousands of Bs in the market. But in cases of oligopoly (few sellers), every producer if he is wise will think long and hard about the actions of the remaining few producers. Producer A knows—and sometimes fears—Producer B. The structure of prices in such a market is often a fascinating study in mutual trust and, sometimes, distrust.

One of the landmark cases under the Sherman Antitrust Act resulted in the Supreme Court's order to break up the giant American Tobacco Company in 1911. What emerged thereafter was an industry of few sellers. There has been no evidence of collusion or overt contact among the successor firms to the original American Tobacco Company. But the handful of producers have been keenly aware of one another's presence.

William H. Nicholls, professor of economics at Vanderbilt University, discusses some of the more interesting features of pricing in this industry. The price leadership picture which he draws with such fine detail is an invaluable supplement to textbook discussions of oligopoly.

Questions to Guide the Reading

From the point of view of the consumer, what is gained by having oligopoly and price leadership in the cigarette industry in contrast with the near-monopoly of the pre-1911 era?

What are likely to be the most critical considerations entering into any one cigarette manufacturer's decision to go along with or to hold out against a price change elsewhere in the industry? What then are the preconditions for effective price leadership?

PRICE LEADERSHIP: THE CASE OF THE CIGARETTE INDUSTRY
William H. Nicholls

Evolution is not a force but a process. . . .
John Viscount Morley

This is a summary and appraisal of cigarette price policies since the Tobacco Trust was dissolved by Court action in 1911. After a brief summary of the principal trends in the cigarette market during 1911–50, we try to analyze the process by which present cigarette policy evolved. We shall be primarily concerned with the means by which the uncertainties inherent in the circular interdependence of a non-collusive, oligopolistic market structure were resolved.

A. Principal trends in the cigarette market, 1911–50

The most important single characteristic of the American cigarette market has been the highly dynamic nature of the demand for cigarettes. During 1911–50, cigarette production in the United States increased from 10 to 393 billions and per capita consumption increased nearly twentyfold. Furthermore, these trends were almost wholly uninterrupted, production falling below previous levels only during 1920–21, 1931–33, and 1949. With the demand curve for cigarettes shifting so steadily upward, each of the four major successor firms to the Tobacco Trust (American Tobacco, Reynolds Tobacco, Liggett and Myers, and Lorillard) could, in considerable part, direct large advertising outlays to extending the aggregate market to its own advantage rather than to taking old customers away from its principal rivals. Their combined advertising expenditures not only contributed to the expansion of total cigarette consumption, but, during most of the period, greatly strengthened their position relative to the rest of the industry. Thus, having inherited 80 per cent of the nation's cigarette business from the Trust, the four successor companies had achieved a market position of perhaps 97 per cent by 1925 and controlled 98 per cent as late as 1931 (Table 1). During the 1930's, the development of the first significant independent competition since the dissolution reduced the position of the successor companies to 74 per cent, more than half of their loss being attribu-

table to the rise of lower-priced "economy" brands, which had taken over 15 per cent of the domestic market by 1939. However, by 1950—thanks largely to the virtual disappearance of the economy brands—the successor companies' position had recovered to 82 per cent. The three major brands alone (Lucky Strike, Camel, Chesterfield)—which have always received the bulk of the industry's advertising outlays—increased their relative importance from 82 to 86 per cent during 1925–31, fell back sharply to 66 per cent in 1939, and accounted for 68 per cent by 1950.

Among the four successor firms, the relative distribution of cigarette sales has fluctuated widely since the dissolution (Table 1). The years 1911–25 were characterized by the rise of Reynolds (which had received no cigarette business from the Trust) to a position of dominance (45 per cent in 1923) and the precipitous decline of Lorillard. During 1925–31, American rapidly pushed far into the lead (39 per cent in 1931)—largely at the expense of Reynolds—while Lorillard for the first time showed some vitality. Between 1931 and 1939, all four companies suffered important setbacks, with American showing the greatest loss of relative position, Liggett & Myers the least. While continuing to show a decline in relative position, Reynolds held a slight lead (with 24 per cent) in the latter year. Since 1939, American has again definitely taken over first place (31 per cent in 1950) although Reynolds has also experienced a relative gain.

Since 1927 (with the exception of 1934 and 1944), Liggett & Myers has never ranked higher than third place in the American cigarette market. Even prior to that time, Liggett & Myers followed a conservative, non-aggressive price and advertising policy, with Reynolds largely setting the pace. After 1927, either Reynolds or American took the lead in most basic policy decisions and their relative positions have fluctuated widely over the years, in contrast with Liggett & Myers' more stable market percentage. Throughout most of the period since the dissolution, Lorillard has been of relatively minor importance in the ciga-

From William H. Nicholls, *Price Policies in the Cigarette Industry* (Vanderbilt University Press, Nashville, Tennessee, 1951), Chap. XIII. Reprinted with kind permission of the author and publisher.

Table 1   Summary of Market Positions of Principal Cigarette Companies, Selected Years, 1911–50

| | | | | | | | | Total Sales as Per Cent of U.S. Cigarette Production | | | Total U.S. |
| | | | | | | | | | All | 3 Major | Economy | Production |
Year	Amer.	L.&M.	Rey.	Lor.	4 Co's.	BW	PM	Other	Brands	Brands	(Billions)
1911	37.1	27.8	0	15.3	80.2	...	...	19.8	...	...	10
1925	21.2	32.0	41.6	1.9	96.7	...	...	3.3	82	...	82
1931	39.4	22.7	28.4	7.0	97.6	0.2	0.3	1.9	86	0.3	117
1939	22.7	21.6	23.7	5.7	73.7	10.6	7.0	8.7	66	14.8	181
1950	30.9	18.7	26.9	5.5	82.0	6.1	11.0	1.8	68	0.9	393

rette market, not having produced more than 8 per cent of the nation's cigarettes since well before 1925. Of the five principal independents which grew to significant size during the 1930's, two (Brown & Williamson and Philip Morris) outranked Lorillard by 1939. Since the latter date, Philip Morris has continued to expand its market position considerably but the other principal independents (including Brown & Williamson) have rapidly lost ground.

Since the dissolution, the list prices of the major cigarette brands have been relatively inflexible. During the 38 years 1913–50 inclusive, the price of Camel cigarettes was changed 20 times, exclusive of 5 increases (two of them by amounts greater than the tax) resulting from changes in federal cigarette taxes and one upward adjustment in OPA's cigarette price ceiling not related to a tax increase. The list price of Camels ranged from $4.00 to $8.00 per thousand over this period. Had the tax been constant at its present rate throughout 1913–50, however (and had earlier list prices been increased by exactly the amount of the difference in tax rates), the range would have been narrowed to $6.00–$8.50, the lowest price falling in 1933 and the highest in 1919–21. During 1913–23—before virtually identical list and net prices of the three major brands became the rule—the list price of Camels (adjusted to present tax rates) ranged from $6.25 to $8.50, with 9 price changes not associated with tax increases. During the much longer period of virtual list-price identity 1923–50, however, the range (at present tax rates) was $6.00–$8.00, with only 11 price changes (plus one OPA increase) unrelated to tax increases. Thus, during the 27 years of virtual list-price identity the number of price changes only slightly exceeded that during the earlier 11-year period and the range of prices was somewhat less.

Because of the large and fixed federal cigarette tax, however, even these relatively inflexible list prices have resulted in more flexible net prices

to manufacturers after dealer discounts and tax. Thus, the range in the net price of Camels during 1913–50 was $1.85 (1933) to $4.05 (1919–21). During 1913–23, the range was $2.28–$4.05 and, during 1923–50, $1.85 to $3.56 (1950), or 3.4 cents a package. If one eliminates two special periods of price-cutting—that of 1928–29 within the Big Four and that of 1933–36 directed against independent competition—and the wartime period of price controls, the range in net prices is narrowed to $2.51–$3.56, or 2.1 cents a package, during a total period of 17 years since 1923. These data underline the barriers which the large federal tax has imposed against price competition, the extreme severity of the 1933 price cuts, and the more moderate price policy which the major firms have followed since 1937.

The price history of the three major brands during 1912–23 reflected many of the characteristics which one associates with the concept of competitive price behavior. Diverse price differentials did exist among the three brands as they were introduced, and the timing and extent of changes in prices and discounts varied considerably from one brand to another. While Reynolds' influence on the price policies of its two major competitors was already discernible, the latter companies did sometimes take independent action in price changes. Despite the frequent diversity of list prices among the three brands, discounts were usually adjusted openly or secretly to bring net prices fairly closely in line—a result still consistent with a process of price competition.

When the three major firms moved to virtual list and net price identity in August 1923, however, any resemblance to competitive price behavior disappeared.

Combined net profits of the three major companies grew from 50 to 106 million dollars during 1923–31, a period in which they accounted for 90 per cent or more of total cigarette production. During the same period, their rates of earnings on net worth increased from 15–20 per cent to

17–22 per cent. Their loss of business to independents, and the resulting severe price reductions of 1933, cut their net profits in half and their earnings to 8–13 per cent in that year. By 1940, their net profits had recovered to 73 million dollars and their earnings to 13–17 per cent, despite a continued loss of relative market position. The coming of price controls brought a tremendous increase in their absolute and relative sales but by 1943 had resulted in a reduction in their combined net profits to 57 million dollars (just above their 1933 low) and earnings of 10–13 per cent. With the price increases of 1946–50, their combined profits at last passed the previous peak of 1933, amounting to 108–111 million dollars in 1948–50, when they earned 12–16 per cent on net worth. This rate of earnings approached their 1932–39 average of 13–17 per cent but still fell short of their average earnings of 18–21 per cent during 1924–31. Nonetheless, it is clear that the three major companies have consistently enjoyed earnings well above normal competitive levels and that the effects of potential and actual competition over many years have not been sufficient to eliminate significant amounts of monopoly profits.

B. The process of revising incorrect anticipations under oligopoly

Since 1911, the American cigarette market has been characterized by oligopoly. Because the great bulk (68–91 per cent) of the nation's cigarettes has been produced and sold by three successor firms, no one of them could ignore the influence of its own price decisions upon the sales (hence price policies) of the other firms or, in turn, the influence of their resultant price policies upon its own sales. Even the smallest of the three major firms, Liggett & Myers, recognized this circular interdependence clearly in stating that its cigarette prices depend "to a considerable extent upon what its chief competitors are doing and what they are likely to do in respect of price changes." Such recognition did not spring full-blown from the dissolution decree. But during 1917–23—after the three major brands had been introduced—each of the three firms certainly came to realize that circular interdependence did exist. It then became incumbent upon each firm to try to judge correctly the nature of this interdependence. For, until it knew what assumptions to make as to the extent and timing of any interactions which it might set in motion by a change in its own policies, it could not correctly assess

the probable *ultimate* effects of this change upon its own profits. The simplest way to have eliminated these oligopolistic uncertainties would have been outright merger or formal collusion. But, operating under the shadow of the recent dissolution decree, the successor firms could hardly avail themselves of these alternatives. Hence, a policy of experimentalism—by which the three companies tried out different price differentials and different timings of price changes (and responses to price changes)—was forced upon them.

There is ample evidence in the price history of 1917–23 that the major firms' original anticipations of rival reactions were incorrect. This was especially true during the earlier part of the period when price *increases* were the order of the day. An outstanding example of incorrect anticipations was American's unsuccessful attempt to lead in a price increase in September 1918. It is obvious that American expected its major rivals to follow upward and seriously underestimated the costliness (in loss of sales) of its policy in the event that they failed to do so. Out of this experience, American apparently revised its anticipations of rival reactions, becoming understandably reluctant to initiate price changes thereafter. While Reynolds was less unfortunate in leading price increases during 1918–19 even its success was mixed, with American once following upward all the way, once only in part. In the latter case, Reynolds then cut below American, which (through secret discounts) moved to the same level as Reynolds. Reynolds used similar techniques in following Liggett & Myers' one initial price *increase* only part way, and in following American's single initial price *decrease* by an even larger price cut, in each case thereby establishing the price level to which the original price leader then moved. Obviously, each of these price changes again reflected uncertainty as to what rival reactions would be. But, by its own choice of policies, Reynolds made it clear that a failure to follow its lead completely would result in its returning to lower prices but created a serious doubt as to whether it would itself follow its rivals' leads. While the latter doubts might have led to new conflicts and uncertainties, these were resolved by an increasing willingness of the other firms to concede a position of price leadership to Reynolds.

Uncertainties regarding probable rival reactions to initial price *cuts* were more easily diminished. During the period of price decreases 1921–22, American and Reynolds both discovered that the other would promptly meet price cuts in full,

Table 2   Summary of Price Leadership Among the Three Major Cigarette Companies, 1917–50

Time Period	Company Initiating Price Change	Number of Successful Leads			Number of Unsuccessful Leads		
		Upward	Downward	Total	Upward	Downward	Total
1917–23	Reynolds	2	2	4	0	0	0
	American	0	1	1	1	0	1
	Liggett & Myers	1	0	1	0	0	0
	Uncertain	2	0	2	0	0	0
1924–39	Reynolds	4	1	5	0	0	0
	American	0	2	2	0	0	0
	Liggett & Myers	0	0	0	0	0	0
1940–50 (ex. OPA)	Reynolds	2	0	2	0	0	0
	American	2	0	2	1	0	1
	Liggett & Myers	0	0	0	2	0	2
1917–50 (ex. OPA)	Reynolds	8	3	11	0	0	0
	American	2	3	5	2	0	2
	Liggett & Myers	1	0	1	2	0	2
	Uncertain	2	0	2	0	0	0

thereby making it possible for each to anticipate correctly the other's reaction to a price decrease. Although reluctant to conform with this policy, Liggett & Myers' resistance to price cuts during 1921–22 probably revealed the costliness of such a policy and brought it around to the same point of view. Experience with secret rather than open price differentials was apparently found to be an unsatisfactory technique (probably because they did not remain secret) of increasing sales, being little used after 1919.

The market situation of 1917–23 had all the elements which, according to general theory, would result in a highly unstable or even chaotic outcome. Unquestionably, each of the three major firms was originally extremely uncertain as to the extent and timing of its rival's reactions to a price change. Furthermore, the fact that each firm at times tried to initiate price changes (Table 2) implies that each aspired to a position of price leadership in order that it might set that price which would correspond most closely to its own maximum-profit position. Yet, while there were indeed elements of instability during this period, the impressive fact is the pattern of order which rather quickly emerged. Such an outcome—particularly in view of the fact that there was apparently no formal collusion of any kind—is in itself remarkable and stands in sharp contrast with theoretical predictions of extreme instability. This outcome would suggest that anticipations as to rival reactions, while initially incorrect, can be

gradually revised with experience until they become both correct and compatible. While it is impossible to predict, on purely theoretical grounds, that such revisions will converge or the paths by which convergence may be reached, the concrete fact in the cigarette industry is that they did so.

Although American and Liggett & Myers subordinated their aspirations for price leadership to Reynolds' claims only reluctantly, Reynolds meanwhile enforced its own claims with considerable restraint. As a result of this element of "give and take," price competition (such as there was) was kept within reasonable bounds. And, reluctance and restraint notwithstanding, Reynolds' position of price leadership—particularly in the more uncertain area of price *increases*—was gradually recognized, reinforced by its steadily growing strength in the cigarette market. Once this became true, remaining uncertainties could be (and were in August 1923) easily resolved by standardizing dealer discounts—so that identical list prices automatically produced the identical net prices to manufacturers which had tended to result anyway—and by making responses to changes in the leader's price, whether upward or downward, complete and immediate.

We may conclude that the crucial step in eliminating oligopolistic uncertainty in the cigarette industry was the mutual recognition that one of the three firms was to act as price leader, particularly on price increases. For this step eliminated the problem of a "kinked" demand curve which would otherwise have faced each of the three firms. Such a discontinuous demand curve would result if each oligopolist believed that "rivals will quickly match price reductions but only hesitatingly and incompletely (if at all) follow price increases." Under this pattern of expected behavior, the demand curve for the product of each oligopolist would have a kink at the existing price. The part above the kink would be more elastic, indicating the given firm's loss of business if it should raise its price, other prices remaining unchanged at the old level. The lower part would be more inelastic, showing the given firm's gains of business if its price cuts were at all times matched by its rivals.

American's unsuccessful efforts to bring about a general price increase in 1918 and its experience with matched price cuts during 1921–22 were undoubtedly such as to convince it of the reality of the "kink." Had the other two firms (especially Reynolds) had precisely the same experience, any one of them would have been extremely reluctant to lead in a price increase because of the belief (verified by experience) that the others would not follow upward. Under such circumstances, cigarette prices would have been highly insensitive to changes in cost or demand, hence extremely rigid. Furthermore, unless the existing price was initially at the level which would maximize their joint profits, the final price would also have to be below that level. Thus, the advantages of mutual recognition of one (*any one*) of the oligopolists as price leader become obvious. For, once the price leader (Reynolds) could correctly anticipate that its price increases would be followed, the "kink" in its demand curve disappeared and it could raise prices with impunity. What the other firms lost in initiative was far more than offset by the gains in certainty as to the "rules of the game" on price increases, which made greater joint profits possible.

C. Factors favoring a policy of cigarette-price identity

A striking characteristic of cigarette policies after 1923 was that a policy of price identity (rather than differential prices) among the major brands evolved.

Between August 1923 and May 1951, there was a total of only 15 days on which the list (and net) prices of the three major brands differed because of a rival's delay in responding to an initial price change on one of the brands. At all times (except 1923–28 and 1946–49, when minute price differences of 3–5 cents a thousand existed among them), the three major brands had (apart from what was apparently a small amount of price-shading) absolutely identical list prices, dealer discounts and net prices. The fourth major successor-company brand (Old Gold), while probably never important enough to have upset the common price policy had Lorillard shown more independence, also conformed fully with the policy of price-identity except for a small 10-cent-per-thousand differential during 1928–29. Thus, the prices of the three (or four) brands moved together, either upward or downward, with an almost perfect harmony of amplitude and timing. The same was true for the major standard brands of Philip Morris and Brown & Williamson after 1940, by which time these two independents had successfully established themselves in the standard-brand field.

To be sure, substitution (though imperfect) in consumption established certain narrow limits upon the extent to which price differentials might be profitable. But at least, within these limits, they became possible. Hence, a policy of price identity or price differentials among the several brands became a matter of deliberate choice, based upon expectations of the relative profitability of alternative courses of action. Why, then, was it a policy of price *identity*, and not one of price differentials, which emerged?

First, at the time the three major brands were introduced, there were already certain "customary" retail-price classes (10, 15, and 20 cents a package) which the three companies apparently felt it necessary to respect. These "customary" price classes introduced a very strong element of discreteness into price policies and favored pricing for identical retail prices as compared with so great a minimum price differential as 5 cents. (During the years since 1930, the rapid increase in odd-cents state taxes has effectively destroyed such discreteness in cigarette prices. But, in the early history of the industry, "customary" or "convenient-coin" prices undoubtedly exercised an important influence on cigarette price policies).

Second, the concentration of advertising on the three brands served to set them apart (in the minds of consumers) as a particular class of product differing from non-advertised minor brands. The effect of such advertising was probably such as to diminish the elasticity of demand for the three brands as a class, while tending to break down the imperfections of substitution within the product class. As a consequence, the elasticity of demand for any one of the three brands was probably increased—a result further enhanced by the steadily growing increment of new, unattached smokers. Because of the small number of firms, sensitivity to the prices of rival products was greatly increased, thereby reducing the likelihood that any given firm could successfully maintain a significant price differential below other brands. Again, therefore, a strong tendency toward identical prices would have been expected.

Third, the tendency of consumers to judge quality by price created a further barrier to departures from price identity among the three brands. We have argued that the existence of discrete price classes, with advertising concentrated upon a single price class, encouraged price identity within that class. But it is equally probable that, as they became accustomed to price identity among the major advertised brands, consumers increasingly judged the extent to which the three brands were close substitutes (in terms of quality) by their common price. Because of this perverse psychology created by product differentiation, an unmatched price cut on one major brand might cause consumers to associate the lower price with lower quality—particularly if the lower price forced a significant reduction in the firm's advertising outlays—so that they would remain with (or soon shift back to) the higher-priced brands. While this factor favoring price identity among the major advertised brands can easily be exaggerated, it is noteworthy that the two principal independent brands (Philip Morris, Raleigh) which finally succeeded in attaining volume sales in the standard-brand price class, did so by initially selling in a *higher* price class, lowering their prices only after they had become established. On the other hand, with minor exceptions, none of the economy brands has yet entered the standard-brand price class after becoming established at lower prices, which made significant advertising outlays prohibitive.

Fourth, the growth of cigarette taxes has increasingly diminished the prospect of gains from unmatched price cuts below other brands and favored even unmatched price increases. Since the dissolution, federal, state and local governments have pyramided taxes upon cigarettes. These taxes have almost invariably been specific rather than graduated or *ad valorem*, and have now reached so high a proportion (50 per cent or more) of the retail price as to make even an unmatched price cut (a price differential below

competing brands) of questionable value. Thus—in a state levying a three-cent-per-package cigarette tax in addition to the seven-cent federal tax—suppose that the manufacturer of any one of the major brands of cigarettes had been successful in establishing an unmatched price cut of one cent a package at retail at 1949 prices. To achieve this 5-per cent reduction in the retail price, he would have had to reduce his own final net price by 12 per cent. The effect of present taxes upon the economy-brand manufacturer is even more severe—a 15-per cent reduction in net price would have been required to reduce the retail price by 5 per cent, and an 18-per cent reduction to reduce the retail price by a full cent. Thus, combined cigarette taxes—being so large and unrelated to retail price—have been an increasingly important factor favoring continued price identity.

The effect of these various factors was undoubtedly to strengthen the tendency of oligopolistic competition to result in a policy of price-identity. Given this tendency, absolute price identity was obviously superior to small departures from price identity as a means of eliminating the uncertainties of oligopoly. Even small and variable differences in list prices, discounts and net prices might arouse suspicions that rivals were not living up to the mutually-recognized "rules of the game." Prices and discounts, being the most precisely measurable and most fully publicized variables of market policy, could also be reduced to foolproof "rules" more easily than quality of product (blend, packaging, etc.) and quantity of advertising.

But none of these reasons is enough to explain fully the acceptance of price leadership among the major producers. Why, in particular, were the other firms always willing to follow Reynolds' price *increases*? Because, on balance, they recognized the advantages to themselves in doing so. In most instances, they were "glad to follow" because they "saw the opportunity to make some money," "to reinstate . . . our earnings," or "to increase income." Again, counsel for Liggett & Myers stated it most clearly. "The opportunity to increase sales by not following [was] illusory," since such an action was certain to force "the others . . . to return to the lower figure." Hence, if it is believed that "the higher price will not adversely affect public buying of this type of product, or invite new competition into the field, obviously each has the most natural and legitimate of reasons for following the increase." Even so, why was recognition of a *single* price leader among the dominant firms necessary? The answer lies in the elimination of the kink in the demand curves of the oligopolists. Obviously, no one of the three firms was sufficiently dominant to establish prices to which its rivals would react purely competitively because, individually, they had no influence over price. Rather, their circular interdependence was so great that —unless the kink was eliminated by mutual acceptance of a common leader for price increases —prices might be frozen despite significant increases in costs or demand. If so, it would become impossible to readjust to changing market conditions in such a way as to hope to achieve and maintain a position of maximum joint profits for the dominant group.

Hence, while Reynolds may at times have turned its position as price leader somewhat to its own advantage, its declining market position after 1923 increasingly put upon it the burden of establishing for the group a price policy which rather promptly reflected changing market conditions, if its position of leadership was to be maintained. American's price cuts of 1933 indicate its belief that, at that time, Reynolds had failed to do so since 1931. On the other hand, Reynolds' price increases of 1929, 1934 and 1937 undoubtedly did represent appropriate adjustments to increased demand and costs, enhancing the willingness of the others to follow. Significantly, there is no evidence that, during 1924–39, American even considered leading in a price increase, higher costs or otherwise. And, while frequently justifying its willingness to follow upward on the basis of costs, Liggett & Myers admitted that trends in costs merely determined "whether we followed gladly or whether we followed reluctantly." Even rising costs did not cause Liggett & Myers to give any thought to leading in a price increase because, as "third seller," it did not wish "to take a chance" on doing so. In any case, the high relative importance of selling costs to total costs probably forced the price leader to give his principal attention to changing demand factors rather than to changing production costs.

Since the direction (if not identical amplitude and timing) of all other price increases of 1924–39 might have been expected in terms of changing market conditions, it was the 1931 price increase which provided the acid test for the common price policy. If ever there was a time when a refusal to follow a price increase might have appeared likely to pay off in increased relative sales, it was then. Yet in 1931, as well as at other times, American and Liggett & Myers apparently believed that their retention of the lower price would result only in temporary gains since Reynolds would then restore its price to its previ-

ous lower level, whereas their gains would be permanent if they matched Reynolds' increase. American confirmed this by saying that—in conjunction with a lower price policy on its cigarette substitutes (roll-your-own and pipe tobacco) —it "naturally saw the opportunity to make some money" and "reserve[d] the right to make price changes downward" if its expectations were not fulfilled.

On the other hand, Liggett & Myers officials thought the increase "was a mistake" and "ill-advised." Why, then, did Liggett & Myers follow —especially if it really believed that its current sales position was so weak that it was, for once, "doubtful of its ability to force the [other two] manufacturers . . . to cancel their increases"? Why shouldn't such a doubt have encouraged rather than discouraged an independent price policy? Both American and Liggett & Myers replied that their failure to follow would have given Reynolds a sufficient increment of advertising funds to prevent them from substantially increasing their sales at the lower price. Such an argument is wholly unconvincing and completely inconsistent with their belief in the absolute necessity of fully matching price decreases.

In view of past experience—reinforced by the depressed economic conditions of 1931—it seems absurd to suppose that the failure of either American or Liggett & Myers to follow Reynolds' price increase would not have forced a cancellation of that increase. Hence, the former companies must have believed that the possibility of increased joint profits at the higher common price was sufficiently great to warrant the experiment, while the possible gains from resisting the change were temporary, hence "illusory." By following upward, as Liggett & Myers clearly recognized, each firm ran "the risk of retaliation by consumers, but that retaliation [would], based on price, be visited on all rivals equally. . . . For a manufacturer to suffer with other manufacturers a loss of sales may be unpleasant but it is not fatal; one of the leading sellers will presumably readjust its price as soon as the effects of the excessive price are obvious." Of course, the real risk was that the aggregate elasticity of demand for cigarettes had been underestimated by the price leader— that is, that the "retaliation of consumers" would be *so great* that profits would be diminished rather than increased. It was recognized, however, that —if experience led to a diminution of profits—a joint price reduction could correct the situation.

According to Liggett & Myers, had it refused to follow the 1931 price increase, it would have run the greater risk "of losing [its relative] position in the market . . . which [as the fate of Lorillard shows, it might] never be able to regain." While fully applicable to a failure to follow a price decrease, such a statement is obviously invalid with regard to a price increase (Liggett & Myers' arguments to the contrary notwithstanding). Nonetheless, Liggett & Myers was undoubtedly correct in its belief that "the inertia of custom, plus extensive advertising, tend to assure a well established manufacturer his existing share of the market provided he does not permit his competitors to do anything drastically different from himself." To be sure, in an oligopolistic market situation, "imitation minimizes risk"—the risk of oligopolistic price uncertainties. By the elimination of this risk, the maximization of the dominant firms' joint profits was largely assured.

READING 34

Whenever the front page's biggest headlines are used for economic news, the topic is likely to be either a stock market plunge or a labor strike. But in April, 1962, the major news event was a proposed increase in the price of steel. It was clear from the outset that this was not just any product price, for the drama began with a visit to the White House by the chairman of United States Steel Corporation. What happened after he told the late President Kennedy that his company proposed to increase steel product prices by an average of $6 a ton held the nation's attention for three days. And the debate, about the rights and wrongs on both sides, will continue for a long time to come.

The story can be viewed on a number of levels: as a study in power, as an episode in public relations, as a moment in the fight to maintain reasonably stable prices and minimize an adverse balance of payments, as a critical point in the evolution of government-business relations, or as a case in price leadership in an industry dominated by a few large sellers. We place it here to emphasize the last-named aspect, but, in truth, it cuts across much of our economic life.

Wallace Carroll wrote this as a special correspondent of the *New York Times.* He is editor and publisher of the *Winston-Salem Journal.* He was assisted in the task of fitting together the pieces of this drama by a team of *Times* reporters: Richard E. Mooney, John D. Pomfret, Joseph A. Loftus, Anthony Lewis, E. W. Kenworthy, Peter Braestrup, Jack Raymond, Kenneth Smith, and Austin C. Wehrwein. They admit that the full story may never be written.

Questions to Guide the Reading

What does this drama tell about the interrelationships of Big Government and Big Steel today? One year later, prices in steel were raised selectively and intermittently by some of the producers; does this herald a new approach to pricing and to government? What is the public's stake in both the 1962 and the 1963 events?

In retrospect, what part was played in the collapse of the price hike by the power of the government and what part by the softness of the market for steel?

THE 72-HOUR DRAMA IN STEEL
Wallace Carroll

WASHINGTON, April 22. It was peaceful at the White House on the afternoon of Tuesday, April 10—so peaceful, that the President of the United States thought he might have time for a nap or a little relaxed reading.

Just to be sure, he called his personal secretary, Mrs. Evelyn Lincoln, and asked what the rest of the day would bring.

"You have Mr. Blough at a quarter to six," said Mrs. Lincoln.

From Wallace Carroll, "Steel: A 72-Hour Drama with an All-Star Cast," *New York Times,* April 23, 1962. Reprinted with kind permission of the author and publisher.

"Mr. Blough?" exclaimed the President.

Yes, said Mrs. Lincoln.

There must be a mistake, thought the President. The steel negotiations had been wound up the previous week.

"Get me Kenny O'Donnell," he said.

But there had been no mistake—at least not on the part of Kenneth P. O'Donnell, the President's appointment secretary.

Whether Mr. Blough—Roger I. Blough, chairman of the board of United States Steel Corporation—had made a mistake was a different question.

For when he walked into the President's office two hours later with the news that his company had raised the price of steel, he set off seventy-two hours of activity such as he and his colleagues could not have expected.

During those seventy-two hours, four antitrust investigations of the steel industry were conceived, a bill to roll back the price increases was seriously considered, legislation to impose price and wage controls on the steel industry was discussed, agents of the Federal Bureau of Investigation questioned newspaper men by the dawn's early light, and the Defense Department—biggest buyer in the nation—began to divert purchases away from United States Steel.

Also in those seventy-two hours—and this was far more significant—the Administration maintained its right to look over the shoulders of capital and labor when they came to the bargaining table and its insistence that any agreement they reached would have to respect the national interest.

And in those seventy-two hours, new content and meaning were poured into the magnificent abstraction, "the Presidency," for the historically minded to argue about as long as men remained interested in the affairs of this republic.

A full and entirely accurate account of those seventy-two hours may never be written. The characters were many. They moved so fast that no one will be able to retrace all of what they did.

Understandably, industry participants—facing official investigation now—would not talk much. Nor were Government participants willing to tell all.

Nevertheless, a team of New York Times reporters undertook to piece the tale together while memories were fresh.

Here is what they learned.

Early on that afternoon of April 10, Roger Blough had met with his colleagues of United States Steel's executive committee in the board room on the twentieth floor at 71 Broadway, New York. Three of the twelve members were absent, but Leslie B. Worthington, president of the company, and Robert C. Tyson, chairman of the finance committee, were there.

For several months these men had been giving out hints, largely overlooked in Washington, that the company would have to raise prices to meet increasing costs.

The Kennedy Administration had pressed for no increase in prices last fall, and there had been no increase. It had pressed again for a modest wage contract this year, and a modest contract had been signed a few days earlier. The Administration expected no price increase now.

The company's executive committee reviewed the situation. The sales department had concurred in a recommendation to increase prices by 3½ per cent—about $6 on top of the going average of $170 a ton.

Mr. Blough had taken soundings within the company on the public relations aspects. Everyone realized that the move would not win any popularity prize, but the committee voted unanimously to go ahead.

With the decision made, Mr. Blough took a plane to Washington. Word was telephoned to the White House that he wanted to see the President and had something "important" to say about steel.

A few minutes after 5:45 the President received him in his oval office, motioned him to a seat on a sofa to his right and made himself comfortable in his rocking chair.

With little preliminary, Mr. Blough handed the President a four-page mimeographed press release that was about to be sent to newspaper offices in Pittsburgh and New York.

The President read:

"Pittsburgh, Pa., April 10—For the first time in nearly fours years United States Steel today announced an increase in the general level of its steel prices."

Mr. Kennedy raced through the announcement. Then he summoned Arthur J. Goldberg, the Secretary of Labor. Minutes later Mr. Goldberg reached the President's office from the Labor Department four blocks away.

Grimly, the President gave the paper to Mr. Goldberg and said it had been distributed to the press. Mr. Goldberg skimmed over it and asked Mr. Blough what was the point of the meeting, since the price decision had been made.

Mr. Blough replied that he thought he should personally inform the President as a matter of courtesy. Mr. Goldberg retorted it was hardly a courtesy to announce a decision and confront the President with an accomplished fact.

In the half-hour discussion that followed President Kennedy seems to have kept his temper. But Mr. Goldberg lectured Mr. Blough with some heat. The price increase, the Secretary said, would jeopardize the Government's entire economic policy. It would damage the interests of United States Steel itself. It would undercut responsible collective bargaining. Finally he said, the decision could be viewed only as a double-cross of the President because the company had given no hint of its intentions while the Administration was urging the United Steelworkers of America to moderate its wage demands.

Mr. Blough, a former high school teacher turned lawyer and company executive, defended himself and the company in a quiet voice.

When he had gone President Kennedy called for the three members of his Council of Economic Advisers. Dr. Walter W. Heller, the chairman, a lean and scholarly looking man, came running from his office across the street. Dr. Kermit Gordon followed in three minutes. James Tobin, the third member, hurried back to his office later in the evening.

Into the President's office came Theodore C. Sorensen, the White House special counsel, Mr. O'Donnell and Andrew T. Hatcher, acting press secretary in the absence of Pierre Salinger, who was on vacation.

Now the President, who usually keeps his temper under rein, let go. He felt he had been double-crossed—deliberately. The office of the President had been affronted. The national interest had been flouted.

It was clear that the Administration would fight. No one knew exactly what could be done, but from that moment the awesome power of the Federal Government began to move.

To understand the massive reaction of the Kennedy Administration, a word of background is necessary.

Nothing in the range of domestic economic policy had brought forth a greater effort by the Administration than the restraint it sought to impose on steel prices and wages.

Starting last May the Administration worked on the industry, publicly and privately, not to raise its prices when wages went up in the fall. And when the price line held, the Administration turned its efforts to getting an early and "non-inflationary" wage contract this year.

Above all, the Administration constantly tried to impress on both sides that the national interest was riding on their decisions. A price increase or an inflationary wage settlement, it argued, would set off a new wage-price spiral that would stunt economic growth, keep unemployment high, cut into export sales, weaken the dollar and further aggravate the outflow of gold.

On Friday and Saturday, April 6 and 7, the major steel companies had signed the new contract. President Kennedy had hailed it as "non-inflationary." Privately, some steel leaders agreed with him.

Thus, the President confidently expected that the companies would not increase prices. And the standard had been set, he hoped, for other industries and unions.

This was the background against which the group in the President's office went to work.

By about 8 P.M. some decisions had been reached.

President Kennedy would deliver the first counter-attack at his news conference scheduled for 3:30 the following afternoon.

Messrs. Goldberg, Heller and Sorensen would gather material for the President's statement. Other material of a statistical nature would be prepared in a longer-range effort to prove the price increase was unjustified.

While the discussion was going on, the President called his brother, Robert F. Kennedy, the Attorney General; Secretary of Defense Robert S. McNamara, and the Secretary of the Treasury, Douglas Dillon, who had just arrived in Hobe Sound, Fla., for a short vacation.

At his home on Hillbrook Lane, Senator Estes Kefauver of Tennessee, chairman of the Senate Antitrust Subcommittee, was getting ready to go out for the evening. The phone rang. It was the President. Would Senator Kefauver publicly register "dismay" at the price increase and consider an investigation?

The Senator certainly would. He promised an investigation. So did the Justice Department.

In the President's office, meanwhile, there had been some talk of what could be done to keep other steel companies from raising prices. Most of the discussion centered on the economic rebuttal of the case made by United States Steel.

Mr. Goldberg and Dr. Heller decided to pool resources. Mr. Goldberg called Hyman L. Lewis, chief of the Office of Labor Economics of the Bureau of Labor Statistics, and asked him to assemble a crew.

Mr. Lewis reached three members of the bureau —Peter Henle, special assistant to the Commissioner of Labor Statistics; Arnold E. Chase, chief of the Division of Prices and Cost of Living; and Leon Greenberg, chief of the Productivity Division.

He told them what was wanted and asked them to go to Dr. Heller's office in the old State Department Building.

Dr. Heller who had been working on the problem in his office, hurried off after a few minutes to the German Ambassador's residence on Foxhall Road.

The Ambassador was giving a dinner, a black tie affair, in honor of Prof. Walter Hallstein, president of the European Common Market. The guests were well into the meal when Dr. Heller arrived, looking, as one of the guests remarked, like Banquo's ghost in a tuxedo.

Back at the White House the President had also changed to black tie. The members of Congress and their wives were coming to his annual reception at 9:45.

With the party spread through three rooms, no one could tell how many times Mr. Kennedy slipped out to talk about steel. The President stayed until 12:08 A.M. Then he retired.

By that time, the White House staff, the Council of Economic Advisers and the Departments of Labor, Justice, Defense, Commerce and the Treasury were all at work on the counter-attack.

Wednesday

Midnight had struck when Walter Heller, still in black tie, returned to his office from the German Embassy. With him, also in black tie, came another dinner guest, George W. Ball, Under Secretary of State.

Dr. Heller's two colleagues in the Council of Economic Advisers, Dr. Gordon and Dr. Tobin, were already there. So were the four men from the Bureau of Labor Statistics.

At about 2:45 A.M. the four men from the Bureau of Labor Statistics left the session. Their assignment from then on was to bring up to date a fact book on steel put out by the Eisenhower Administration two years ago.

The idea was to turn it into a kind of "white paper" that would show that the price increase was unjustified.

Toward 4 o'clock Dr. Heller and Dr. Tobin went home for two or three hours' sleep.

As the normal working day began, President Kennedy held a breakfast meeting at the White House with Vice President Johnson; Secretary of State Dean Rusk (who played no part in the steel crisis); Secretary Goldberg; Mr. Sorensen; Myer

Feldman, Mr. Sorensen's deputy; Dr. Heller and Andrew Hatcher.

The meeting lasted an hour and forty-five minutes. Mr. Goldberg and Dr. Heller reported on the night's work. Mr. Sorensen was assigned to draft the President's statement on steel for the news conference. Mr. Goldberg gave him a two-page report from the Bureau of Labor Statistics headed:

"Change in Unit Employment Costs in the Steel Industry 1958 to 1961."

It said in part:

While employment costs per hour of all wage and salaried employes in the basic iron and steel industry rose from 1958 to 1961, there was an equivalent increase in output per man-hour.

As a result, employment costs per unit of steel output in 1961 were essentially the same as in 1958.

The latter sentence was quoted that afternoon in the President's statement.

Secretary of Commerce Luther H. Hodges spent most of the day on the phone to business men around the country.

In Wall Street that morning United States Steel shares opened at 70¾, up 2¾ from the day before. But on Capitol Hill the company's stock was down.

Senator Mike Mansfield, the majority leader, called the price increase "unjustified." Speaker John W. McCormack said the company's action was "shocking," "arrogant," "irresponsible." Senator Hubert H. Humphrey, the Democratic whip, spoke of "an affront to the President."

Senator Albert Gore of Tennessee suggested a law that would empower the courts to prohibit price increases in basic industries such as steel until there had been a "cooling-off period."

Representative Emanuel Celler of Brooklyn, chairman of the House Antitrust subcommittee, scheduled a broad investigation of the steel industry. So did Senator Kefauver.

The pressures on United States Steel were beginning to mount. But now some of the other titans of the industry began to fall in line behind Big Steel.

As the President came out of the White House shortly before noon to go to the airport where he was to welcome the Shah of Iran, he was shown a news bulletin. Bethlehem Steel, second in size only to United States Steel, had announced a price increase.

Others followed in short order—Republic, Jones

and Laughlin, Youngstown and Wheeling. And Inland, Kaiser and Colorado Fuel & Iron said they were "studying" the situation.

When he faced the newsmen and television cameras at 3:30, President Kennedy spoke with cold fury. The price increase, he said, was a "wholly unjustifiable and irresponsible defiance of the public interest." The steel men had shown "utter contempt" for their fellow citizens.

He spoke approvingly of the proposed investigations. But what did he hope to accomplish that might still save the Administration's broad economic program?

In his conference statement the President had seemed to hold out no hope that the price increases could be rolled back. If the increases held, what imminent comfort could there be in possible antitrust decrees that would take three years to come from the courts?

Actually, the possibility of making United States Steel retract the increase had been considered early in the consultation.

Drs. Heller and Gordon, and possibly some of the other economists, had argued that the principal thrust of the Administration's effort should be to convince one or two significant producers to hold out. In a market such as steel, they said, the high-priced sellers would have to come down if the others did not go up.

This suggested a line of strategy that probably proved decisive.

As one member of the Big Twelve after another raised prices, only Armco, Inland, Kaiser, C F & I and McLouth remained holding the line. These five hold-outs represented 14 per cent of total industry capacity, or 17 per cent of the capacity of the Big Twelve.

Everything pointed to Inland as the key to the situation.

Inland Steel Corporation with headquarters in Chicago is a highly efficient producer. It could make a profit at lower prices than those of some of the bigger companies. And any company that sold in the Midwest, such as United States Steel, would feel Inland's price competition.

Moreover, there was a tradition of public service at Inland. Clarence B. Randall, a former chairman of the board, had served both the Eisenhower and Kennedy Administrations. (But he played no part in this crisis.)

Joseph Leopold Block, Inland's present chairman, who was in Japan at the moment, had been a member of President Kennedy's Labor-Management Advisory Committee.

At 7:45 that Wednesday morning, Philip D. Block, Jr., vice chairman of Inland, was called to the telephone in his apartment at 1540 North Lake Shore Drive in Chicago.

"Hello, P. D.," said Edward Gudeman, Under Secretary of Commerce, a former schoolmate and friend of Mr. Block's, calling from Washington.

"What do you think of this price increase of United States Steel's?"

Mr. Block said he had been surprised.

"I didn't ask P. D. what Inland might do," said Mr. Gudeman several days later. "I didn't want them to feel that the Administration was putting them on the spot. I just wanted him to know how we felt and to ask his consideration."

Inland officials agreed to consider. They said they had not been coaxed or threatened by any of the officials who called them.

The approach, which seems to have developed rather spontaneously in many of the calls that were made to business men, was to ask their opinion, state the Government's viewpoint, and leave it at that.

But there also were calls with a more pointed aim—to steel users, asking them to call their steel friends and perhaps even issue public statements.

Another call to Inland was made by Henry H. Fowler, Under Secretary of the Treasury and Acting Secretary in Mr. Dillon's absence.

After Mr. Kennedy's afternoon news conference Mr. Fowler called John F. Smith, Jr., Inland's president. Like other Treasury officials who telephoned other business men, Mr. Fowler talked about the effect of a steel price increase on imports and exports and the further pressure it would place on the balance of payments.

A third call went to Inland that day. It was from Secretary Goldberg to Leigh B. Block, vice president for purchasing.

Both Inland and Government officials insist that there was no call from the White House or from any Government office to Joseph Block in Japan.

Though no concrete assurance was asked or volunteered in these conversations, the Administration gathered assurance that Inland would hold the line for at least another day or two.

Next came Armco, sixth largest in the nation. Walter Heller had a line into that company. So did others. Calls were made. And through these channels the Administration learned that Armco was holding off for the time being, but there would be no public announcement one way or the other.

Meanwhile, Mr. Gudeman had called a friend

in the upper reaches of the Kaiser Company. Secretary McNamara had called a number of friends, one of them at Allegheny-Ludlum, a large manufacturer of stainless.

How many calls were made by President Kennedy himself cannot be told. But some time during all the activity he talked to Edgar Kaiser, chairman of Kaiser Steel, in California.

According to one official who was deeply involved in all this effort, the over-all objective was to line up companies representing 18 per cent of the nation's capacity. If this could be done, according to friendly sources in the steel industry, these companies with their lower prices soon would be doing 25 per cent of the business. Then Big Steel would have to yield.

Parallel with this "divide-and-conquer" maneuver, the effort moved forward on the antitrust line.

During the morning someone had spotted in the newspapers a statement attributed to Edmund F. Martin, president of Bethlehem Steel. Speaking to reporters on Tuesday after a stockholders' meeting in Wilmington, Del., Mr. Martin was quoted as having said:

"There shouldn't be any price rise. We shouldn't do anything to increase our costs if we are to survive. We have more competition both domestically and from foreign firms."

If Mr. Martin had opposed a price rise on Tuesday, before United States Steel announced its increase, and if Bethlehem raised its prices on Wednesday after that announcement, his statement might prove useful in antitrust proceedings. It could be used to support a Government argument that United States Steel, because of its bigness, exercised an undue influence over other steel producers.

At about 6 o'clock Wednesday evening, according to officials of the Justice Department, Attorney General Kennedy ordered the Federal Bureau of Investigation to find out exactly what Martin had said.

At about this same time, Paul Rand Dixon, chairman of the Federal Trade Commission, told reporters that his agency had begun an informal investigation to determine whether the steel companies had violated a consent decree of June 15, 1951.

That decree bound the industry to refrain from collusive price fixing or maintaining identical delivered prices. It provided penalties running up to $5,000 a day.

Meanwhile, more calls were going out from Washington.

The Democratic National Committee called many of the Democratic Governors and asked them to do two things:

First, to make statements supporting the President and, second, to ask steel producers in their states to hold the price line.

Among those called were David L. Lawrence of Pennsylvania, Richard J. Hughes of New Jersey and Edmund G. Brown of California. But the National Committee said nothing in its own name. The smell of "politics" was not to be allowed to contaminate the Administration's efforts.

Another call was made by Robert V. Roosa, an Under Secretary of the Treasury, to Henry Alexander, chairman of Morgan Guaranty Trust Company in New York. Morgan is represented on United States Steel's board of directors and is widely considered one of the most powerful influences within the company.

Thus by nightfall on Wednesday—twenty-four hours after Mr. Blough's call on the President—the Administration was pressing forward on four lines of action:

First, the rallying of public opinion behind the President and against the companies.

Second, divide-and-conquer operation within the steel industry.

Third, antitrust pressure from the Justice Department, the Federal Trade Commission, the Senate and the House.

Fourth, the mobilization of friendly forces within the business world to put additional pressure on the companies.

That night at the White House the Kennedys gave a state dinner for the visiting Shah and his Empress.

When the guests had gone, the President put in a call to Tucson, Ariz. It came through at 12:15 A.M.

Thursday

Archibald Cox, the Solicitor General, had left by plane on Wednesday afternoon for Tucson, where he was to make two speeches to the Arizona Bar.

On arriving at his hotel that night, he received a message to call the President. When he called he was asked what suggestions did he have for rolling back steel prices?

Mr. Cox had been chairman of the Wage Stabilization Board during the Korean War and had worked with young Senator Kennedy on statements about steel prices and strikes of the past.

After the call, Mr. Cox stayed up all night, thinking and making notes, mostly about legislation. From past experience Mr. Cox had concluded that the antitrust laws could not cope with the steel problem and that special legislation would be necessary.

Mr. Cox made his two speeches, flew back to Washington and stayed up most of that night working on the legislative draft.

But Mr. Cox was not the only one at work on the steel problem in the early hours of Thursday.

At 3 A.M. Lee Linder, a reporter in the Philadelphia bureau of the Associated Press, was awakened by a phone call. It was the F.B.I. At first Mr. Linder thought he was being fooled. Then he determined that the call was genuine. The agents asked him a question or two and then told him:

"We are coming right out to see you."

Mr. Linder had been at the stockholders' meeting of Bethlehem Steel in Wilmington on Tuesday and had quoted Mr. Martin about the undesirability of a price increase. Bethlehem Steel later called the quotation incorrect.

The agents were checking on that quotation. Mr. Linder said later that he had given them the same report he had written for the Associated Press.

At 6:30 A.M. James L. Parks Jr. of The Wilmington Evening Journal arrived at his office. Two F.B.I. agents were waiting for him. He had talked to Mr. Martin after the meeting, together with Mr. Linder and John Lawrence of The Wall Street Journal. Later in the day the Federal agents interviewed Mr. Lawrence.

This descent of the F.B.I. on the newsmen was the most criticized incident in the seventy-two frenzied hours.

Republicans, who had kept an embarrassed silence up to this point, pounced on this F.B.I. episode. Representative William E. Miller of upstate New York, chairman of the Republican National Committee, compared it to the "knock on the door" techniques of Hitler's Gestapo.

In Chicago, as the day progressed, Philip Block and two other high officials of Inland reached a decision: prices would not be raised. They called Joseph Block in Kyoto. He concurred and they agreed to call a directors' meeting to ratify their decision the next morning.

No announcement was to be made until the morning and no one in Washington was told.

Back in Washington, the President was holding an early meeting in the Cabinet Room at the White House.

Roger Blough was scheduled to hold a televised news conference in New York at 3:30 that afternoon. The White House meeting decided that the Administration should put in a speedy rebuttal to his case for United States Steel.

Secretary Hodges had long-scheduled engagements that day in Philadelphia and New York. It was decided that he would hold a news conference in New York at 5 P.M. and try to rebut Mr. Blough point by point.

At noon or earlier on Thursday President Kennedy phoned Clark Clifford, a Washington lawyer who had first come to national prominence as counsel for President Truman.

Secretary Goldberg, said the President, knew the officers of United States Steel very well and could, of course, talk to them on behalf of the Administration. But Mr. Goldberg, he went on, was known to the steel men mainly as an adversary.

For years he had been the counsel for the steel workers' union and one of their chief strategists in negotiations with the company. In view of this would Mr. Clifford, familiar as he was with the outlook of corporation executives through his law work, join Mr. Goldberg in speaking to United States Steel?

Supports President. Mr. Clifford agreed, flew to New York and met Mr. Blough. He presented himself as a friend of the disputants, but he made clear that he was in 100 per cent agreement with the President. His purpose, he said, was to see if a tragic mistake could be rectified. The mistake, he left no doubt, was on the company's side.

For fourteen months, he continued, President Kennedy and Mr. Goldberg had worked for healthy conditions in the steel industry. They had tried to create an atmosphere of cooperation in the hope of protecting the national interest. Now all this was gone.

The President, he went on, believed there had been a dozen or more occasions when the company's leaders could easily have told him that despite all he had done they might have to raise prices. But they never had told him. The President, to put it bluntly, felt double-crossed.

What Mr. Blough said in reply could not be learned. But he indicated at the end that he would welcome further talks and he hoped Mr. Clifford would participate in them. Mr. Clifford returned to Washington the same day.

The Blough news conference was held in the ground floor auditorium at 71 Broadway.

"Let me say respectfully," Mr. Blough began, "that we have no wish to add acrimony or misunderstanding."

On several occasions, he said, he had made it clear that United States Steel was in a cost-price torque that could not be tolerated forever, that a company without profits is a company that cannot modernize, and that the price increase would add "almost negligibly" to the cost of other products—$10.64 for the steel in a standard automobile, 3 cents for a toaster.

One question and answer in the fifty-eight-minute session caught the ears of people in Washington: Could United States Steel hold its new price if Armco and Inland stood pat?

"It would definitely affect us," conceded Mr. Blough. "I don't know how long we could maintain our position."

A half-hour after Mr. Blough finished, Secretary Hodges held his news conference in the Empire State Building.

But the words that probably hit Big Steel the hardest came that day from two Pennsylvania Republicans—Representatives William W. Scranton, the party's candidate for Governor, and James E. Van Zandt, the candidate for Senator.

"The increase at this time," they wired Mr. Blough, "is wrong—wrong for Pennsylvania, wrong for America, wrong for the free world. The increase surely will set off another round of inflation. It will hurt people most who can least afford to be hurt."

Meanwhile, Justice Department agents appeared at the headquarters of United States Steel, Bethlehem, Jones & Laughlin and other companies and served subpoenas for documents bearing on the price increase and other matters.

And at 7 P.M. Attorney General Kennedy announced that the Justice Department had ordered a grand jury investigation of the increase.

By that time, President and Mrs. Kennedy were getting ready for another state dinner with the Shah and Empress—this time at the Iranian Embassy.

Friday

The first big news of the day came from Kyoto, Japan. Joseph Block, Inland's chairman, had told a reporter for the Chicago Daily News:

"We do not feel that an advance in steel prices at this time would be in the national interest."

That news heartened the Administration but it did not stop planning or operations. Nor did Inland's official announcement from Chicago at 10:08 A.M., Washington time, that it would hold the price line.

At 10:15 Solicitor General Cox met in Mr. Sorensen's office with representatives of the Treasury, Commerce and Labor Departments, Budget Bureau and Council of Economic Advisers.

The discussion was on emergency wage-price legislation of three broad kinds:

First, ad hoc legislation limited to the current steel situation; second, permanent legislation imposing some mechanism on wages and prices in the steel industry alone, and third, permanent legislation for steel and other basic industries, setting up "fact-finding" procedures.

At 11:45 Secretary McNamara said at his news conference that the Defense Department had ordered defense contractors to shift steel purchases to companies that had not raised prices. Later in the day the department awarded to the Lukens Steel Company, which had not raised prices, a contract for more than $5,000,000 worth of a special armor plate for Polaris-missile submarines.

At 12:15 President Kennedy and most of the Thursday group met again in the Cabinet Room. It was estimated at that time that the price line was being held on 16 per cent of the nation's steel capacity.

Inland had announced. Armco had decided to hold but not announce. Kaiser's announcement came in while the meeting was on. This might be enough to force the bigger companies down again, but the sentiment of the meeting was that the retreat would not come soon.

Accordingly, preparations continued for a long struggle. Lists of directors of the companies that were holding the line were distributed, and each man present was asked to call men he knew.

Notably absent from this meeting was Secretary Goldberg. He was on his way to New York with Mr. Clifford in a Military Air Transport plane.

A secret rendezvous had been arranged with Mr. Blough and some of the other leaders of United States Steel at the Carlyle Hotel.

At this meeting, as in Mr. Clifford's talk with Mr. Blough on the previous day, no demands or threats or promises came from the Government side.

The discussion seems to have been a general one about what lay ahead. The outlook, said Mr. Clifford, was "abysmal."

United States Steel, he contended, had failed to weigh the consequences of its action. If it held this position, its interest and those of the industry would inevitably be damaged, and the nation as a whole would suffer.

While the talk was going on, Mr. Blough was called to the phone. Then Mr. Goldberg was called. Each received the same message. Bethlehem Steel had rescinded the price increase—the news had come through at 3:20 P.M.

President Kennedy heard the news while flying to Norfolk for a week-end with the fleet. It was unexpected.

The Administration had made no special effort with Bethlehem. To this day, officials here are uncertain what did it.

Among other things, Bethlehem's officials were struck by the Inland and Kaiser announcement that morning. Inland posed direct competition to Bethlehem's sales in the Midwest—the largest steel market—and Kaiser posed it on the West Coast.

Further, special questions were raised by the Pentagon's order to defense industries to shift their steel buying to mills that did not raise prices. What did this mean for Bethlehem's vast operations as a ship builder?

Whatever the compelling factors were, Bethlehem's decision brought the end of the battle clearly in sight. The competitive situation was such that United States Steel's executive committee was not called into session to reverse its action of the previous Tuesday. The company's officers acted on their own.

The big capitulation came at 5:28. A secretary in the White House press office was checking the Associated Press news ticker. And there was the announcement—United States Steel had pulled back the price increase.

Mr. Hatcher gave the news to the President as he came off the nuclear submarine, Thomas A. Edison, in Norfolk.

It was just seventy-two hours since Roger Blough had dropped in on Mr. Kennedy.

READING 35

How much competition do we need and want in the American economy? And what does competition look like in any event? We may well change our answers to these questions from one period to another, but we are unlikely to be able to avoid them so long as the economy remains free and vital.

This article by the editors of *Fortune* magazine is now more than a decade old. But it continues to serve as a useful starting point for analysis of selected issues in antitrust policy. Here, in capsule form, are some of the most challenging views held in 1952 about the nature of competition. Some (see Schumpeter, for example, page 246) come in for more detailed discussion later in this section; others stand alone here, while playing their parts in building up a concept of that competition which is not perfect but is at least workable.

Questions to Guide the Reading

How does "the new competition" differ from the old? Wherein does it promise more or less in the way of consumer benefits? Does this "new competition" call for different policing from the old?

Is "countervailing power" essential to make competition workable today? Can we expect countervailing power to arise wherever it is most needed?

Do the tests proposed by Griffin at the end of the article provide useful guideposts for changing our antitrust policies? Would they lead to an optimum amount of competition?

THE NEW COMPETITION
Fortune

Here is a nation that is the home and sanctuary of free competitive enterprise, distinguished from all other nations for such determined adherence to the principles of competition that it has written them into the law of the land with constitutional force. Virtually every American businessman, manager or owner, big or small, producer or distributor, uses the word "competition" habitually and usually sincerely in describing American capitalism. So do his employees, and so do editors, journalists, and even labor leaders.

But here also is a nation about whose competitiveness many "objective" and professional observers are very dubious. Certainly the country's economists, the men whose job it is to describe, analyze, and interpret the economy, do not talk of competition as businessmen do. Many seem to deny that the word competition has much relevance in the twentieth-century U.S.A.

In his *American Capitalism,* Harvard's J. K. Galbraith makes what is perhaps the most sweeping statement so far. He says in effect that there is no competition in the classic sense, and hasn't been for years. Real competition has all but disappeared and oligopoly, or a few big sellers—the "Big Three," "Big Four," and so forth—dominate American markets. The economy is workable because big concentrations of industrial power almost automatically beget "countervailing power"—other concentrations of power organized against one another—which tends to prevent abuse. But the time has come, says Dr. Galbraith, to call an economic fact an economic fact, and to cast out "this preoccupation with competition."

The paradoxes of modern American capitalism are not lost on "realistic" Europeans. Probably few things amuse the sophisticated French businessman and the cynical German industrialist more than the "romantic" American attempts to demonopolize the Continent. The British, too, are amused. Only last December 15, the London *Economist* chaffed the "evangelical" American businessmen for preaching competition and practicing something else. The Kremlin, of course, harps endlessly on its old, well-worn theme that *all* American business is monopolistic.

If the concept of competition has no relevance today, why does the American businessman stubbornly insist that competition is the heart of the enterprise system? Is he hypocritical or merely naive? Is it possible, on the other hand, that he is right? For the good of the national psyche, for the honor of the national reputation—and last but not least for intelligent administration of the antitrust law—it is time to try to resolve this great paradox of the new American capitalism.

The paradox arises in the fact that American capitalism in the past fifty or sixty years has experienced a profound transformation. It *is* a new capitalism, and the period of change coincides with the rise of the big modern corporation with large aggregations of capital and nationwide markets. This corporation changed the pattern of the critical producing areas of the economy from one of many sellers to one of few sellers and more recently to few buyers. The corporation, moreover, is usually run by paid managers who, in the long-term interest of their company, are forced to be responsible not only to stockholders but to employees and to consumers.

One result of this change is that the word competition no longer means what it once did. American business today, and particularly Big Business, is practicing a new kind of competition. This competition is not *Fortune's* invention. It has been developing for more than fifty years, and although it is belittled by many economists, a growing number of respected ones have espoused it. And most businessmen have a very good idea indeed of what it is.

They know for one thing that the "new competition" has been a stunning success, especially when measured in terms of delivering a standard of living to the consumer. Could "classic" competition have done any better? As businessmen see it, that's a fair question, the only question. They ask to be judged by results, not by theory. If they tend to grow apoplectic when they are discussed in learned papers as "monopolists" or "oligopolists," it is because they *know* the U.S. is competitive.

As buyers and sellers, businessmen recognize this new competition in terms of such things as prices that respond to market pressures, products that are constantly being improved, and choice for the buyers. They apply such standards pragmatically, not only because they are unfamiliar with formal economic thought but because they know all too well how markets change with industries, products, companies, regions, and from year to year or even month to month. This approach is more or less what the new competition amounts to. It is also more or less what modern economists think of when they talk about "workable" competition. M. A. Adelman of M. I. T., for instance, suggests that workable competition exists when noncollusive rivalry occurs with a sufficient number of alternatives open to both buyer and seller.

What causes the great paradox is that most of the economists and experts who have until recently shaped the accepted notions of competition do not describe it that way. Competition to them is a way of life that can be defined fairly rigidly. They conceive of competition in terms of the grand old original or classic model of Adam Smith and his followers.

The grand old model

Now this model is based on a great and wise principle, verified by the experience of man through the ages and back into the abyss of time —the principle that the peoples of the earth, if they know what's good for them, should never trust their welfare to the discretion of a powerful few. Thus competition is free society's main safeguard against economic injustice. It drives people to produce more rather than less because it enables them to make more money by producing more to sell for less. It tends to make the best use of resources. It is both a regulator and a spur, and its ultimate beneficiaries are people as consumers.

On these general truths the early British economists reared an ideal superstructure. Its chief characteristic was a market with many sellers turning out practically the same product, and with no seller large enough to have any power to control prices. Competition was assumed to occur by price alone; supply and demand, the impersonal forces of the market, "the invisible hand," automatically regulated the price of everything, including the price of labor. Everybody got no more or less than he deserved, and resources were used with maximum efficiency.

The model was natural and just. It was infinitely superior to socialism in that it recognized the validity of individual incentive. Because it was so comprehensive and fundamental, it became the academic model. When pedagogues expounded capitalism to their pupils, they expounded it in terms of the classic model.

But like many great concepts it was a model of perfection rather than of reality, even in its time. It was set up when no one wielded great economic power. Although the concept of the market and the law of supply and demand retained their validity, the notion that competition was effective only when many sellers competed by price alone gradually lost relevance.

Even in the U.S., the only nation that continued to take the model seriously in the twentieth century, the ideal of many sellers went by the board. Large companies grew up swiftly, both by internal growth and by acquisition and merger. The U.S. antitrust laws, of course, were inspired by and partly based on the classic model. But they at first punished only clear conspiracies and accomplished monopolies. And although the Clayton and its subsidiary acts were passed to *prevent* monopoly by catching it in its "incipiency," confusion and irresolution prevented the new law from being effective until the middle 1930's, and even then it did not reform the economy in its image. It could do nothing about the prorationing of the state commissions, which in effect decides the level of the world's oil prices. It could do relatively little about the price "leadership" of big companies—the judgment of the leader, who posts prices in response to his "feeling" about the market, replaces the impersonal forces of the classic market.

The law, finally, could do nothing about the rise of Big Little Business, Big Agriculture, and Big Labor, which proceeded to use political means to gain what Big Business had gained by political and economic means. They not only emulated but outdid Big Business. All three carried their war to the citadel itself, amending the antitrust laws to exempt themselves from many if not most of the effects of price competition.

The classic economists realized that their model was not working well; the last of the great classicists, Alfred Marshall, made due allowances for the fact that competition in practice was bound to be imperfect. The classicists nevertheless went on preaching and teaching orthodox theory because they believed and still believe it provides them with valid principles for measuring a free, competitive society. Let the U.S. strive for perfect competition, they say in effect, and it will be likely to remain tolerably competitive.

The pragmatic standard

The new competition is an approach, not a model: it cannot be, or certainly hasn't been, rigidly defined. It does not cast aside the classic model. It simply retains the basic principles and discards as much of the model as is necessary to make it consistent with reality. It has no use for collusion, monopoly, or deliberate restraints of trade. But it puts the consumer's interest ahead of theory, and shuns perfect competition for the sake of perfect competition. It makes allowance for the fact that the American economy has delivered to people the benefits that perfect competition was calculated to give.

Therefore it does not hold that business, to bring maximum benefit to consumers, must necessarily consist of many small sellers competing by price alone. It does not hold that the rivalry of a few large sellers necessarily means economic injustice. And it does not necessarily think of competition as the impersonal, pervasive force of the classic model, but grants it can be, in the words of Michigan's Clare Griffin, "conscious and personal." It corresponds roughly to the businessman's pragmatic description of competition. And in terms of such a concept, the businessman who talks sincerely of our competitive way of life is right. Just look at our economy today.

To begin with, that economy is too complex to encompass with a few generalizations. It is a matter of considerable doubt, for example, whether a relatively few large companies—"the oligopolists"—do "rule" the nation's prices and markets. Professor George Stigler of the University of Chicago is an outstanding classicist, and certainly cannot be accused of partiality to Big Business. But even he estimates that only 20 per cent of the industries he was able to classify with inadequate data were, in 1939, represented by what he defines as unregulated monopoly or oligopoly. It is his thesis that competition, even judged by the classic model, has been increasing, not decreasing, over the years.

Professor Clair Wilcox of Swarthmore also challenges easy assumptions about oligopoly, but from the standpoint that most figures on concentration are irrelevant. "Meaningful conclusions as to the structure of markets," he insists with considerable plausibility, "are not to be obtained until someone devises a product classification that groups goods according to the readiness with which one can be substituted for another."

Therefore, he denounces the habit of judging the whole economy in terms of manufacturing, which after all accounts for less than two-fifths of unregulated, non-banking private enterprise. Breaking down the consumer's expenditures, by categories, he finds strong evidence that "oligopoly" does not dominate the market.

Mr. Wilcox's emphasis on the consumer is much to the point. The consumer has an immense choice of goods and prices; even in the wilderness he has the mail-order catalogue. American retailing is often highly competitive by almost any standard, sometimes almost by that of the classic model.

Not only do retailers compete briskly, they force manufacturers that supply them to price their products competitively. This is an example of what Mr. Galbraith terms "countervailing power"—the idea that big sellers cannot control markets if buyers are strong enough; nor buyers if sellers are strong enough. Sears, Roebuck and the A & P can buy almost anything at the lowest market prices because they buy so much—just as the motor industry is able to buy steel at a competitive price because it is a big buyer, and labor unions can sell their members' services at good prices because they are so well organized.

Countervailing power, however, is plainly not a substitute for competition, as Mr. Galbraith seems to imply it is. Without a concept of competition translated into public policy, this power can be a monopolistic force—as it is in Europe, and indeed as it is for the American labor unions that wield power *as* power because they are exempt from antitrust. But countervailing power, plus the competitive principle, does result in delivering to the consumer the benefits that classic competition was presumed to bring.

Not classic but effective

Many manufacturers, of course, need no direct pressure to be competitive. Certainly most makers of new consumer products don't. The frozen-orange-juice industry is compelled by circumstances beyond its control to be so competitive it hurts badly. And, of course, garment manufacturers must compete incessantly or go out of business. They do not gang up to fix production or prices. None dominates the market. Their marginal costs often equal—and sometimes exceed—their prices. What keeps them from being an example of classic competition is David Dubinsky and his ILGWU, which has insulated garment workers from the wage market.

The consumer today certainly enjoys a competitive market in appliances, radios, and television sets. Most are made by a fair number of manufacturers, none of whom can control the market, at least not for very long. These durables are today easy to get into (and to fail in, too). Prices are flexible at the retail level, which is where price counts. And they are flexible at the retail level because manufacturers allow for price competition when they set the markup.

Only two years ago, remember, manufacturers were assuring people that they would never again be able to buy a first-line, eight-foot refrigerator for less than $250 or a sixteen-inch television set for less than $350. Today they are both selling at about $150. It is certainly hard to describe as monopolistic, and therefore antisocial, an economy whose refrigerator industry has sold the astonishing number of 48 million units since 1940; whose radio industry has sold the even more astonishing number of 188 million units since 1922; whose television industry has sold some 18 million units in five years. The competition that made this possible may not have been classically perfect, but who will deny that it has been effective?

This kind of competition, moreover, does not seem destined to wither away but to increase as the nation's productivity increases and the nation's selling apparatus is pressed to get rid of the goods. Buying or countervailing power will surely come into greater play. Retailers will press manufacturers for better buys; manufacturers will press suppliers for cheaper raw materials and components.

Thus the chances are good, unless retailers gang up and legislate sweeping fair-trade laws, that the consumer will continue to buy most of his soft and durable goods, accounting for perhaps 25 per cent of his expenditures, as cheaply as he could were they made and sold under the classic model. (At least no one can demonstrate otherwise.) And although many farm prices are exempt from market forces, the competition of the food chains will doubtless continue to give the consumer a good break on the 30 per cent or so of his income that he spends on food.

The "oligopolists"

Now what about Big Business itself—the "oligopolistic" unregulated industries like autos, steel, chemicals, cigarettes, rubber, oil, tin cans, and so forth—wherein a few big sellers are said to rule the markets? To begin with, none is describable as a true monopoly. Their prices usually respond to the market; prices may be "sticky" at times but they do move. These industries offer a choice to the buyer (and seller), and they are constantly improving the quality of their products. Many are subject to countervailing power. And all are subject to the pressure of public opinion.

By classic theory, of course, they are presumed to get a higher price for goods than "perfect" competitors. Prices no longer "rule" them; they "rule" prices. But thanks to the American preoccupation with competition, this phenomenon is often inconsequential even when it is true.

Price leadership occasionally takes the form of "dominant firm" leadership—i.e., one or two firms hold the price umbrella steady, regardless of market conditions. Such instances can be—and are—dealt with by antitrust law. But price leadership often is evidence of competition of the new kind. It can be observed as the "barometric" leadership practiced in the oil and rayon industries. "The leader bears the onus of formally recognizing market conditions," an oil-industry spokesman describes it. Eugene Holman, president of the Jersey Co., explains it further: "You paste your price on a wall, but you can't be sure it'll stick." Sometimes the leader's prices don't stick. In 1947, after President Truman's plea to keep prices steady, Esso Standard tried to hold the line as smart public relations. But it could not hold the line, at least for very long.

Rule or ruin

Another demonstration of big business' ability to "rule" prices was offered by the motor and steel industries, which after the war held prices considerably below the point where market forces alone would have carried them. The classic argument is that prices should be left to find their own level, not only to encourage more production but to ration what is available "by the purse." But letting prices find their own level, with the restrictions then prevailing, probably would not have resulted in an appreciably greater production. And rationing by the purse, which is theoretically the best way to ration anything, would have created a storm of angry protests from consumers (as the auto dealers' practice of rationing by the purse in fact did).

The motor industry, indeed, could argue without double talk that genuine *competitive* considerations dictated that prices be held. The fundamental purpose of competition after all is not to throw the economy into a tailspin, but to make it function naturally, to dispense economic justice to the consumer. Classic price competition in motorcars after the war might have meant a precipitous rise followed by an equally precipitous drop, and then perhaps by serious economic disruptions and certainly by economic injustice. The restraint of the motor industry thus seems justified from the short-term view of a competitor seeking public approval and the long-term view of an industry cast in a workably competitive mold.

Whether big business is bigger than it needs to be for efficiency and technical progress is a proposition that can be argued endlessly, but there is little doubt that without modern "oligopoly" much of our immense technical progress would not have occurred. Modern research and development not only demand a lot of money, which big companies have; the prospect of making unusually good or "monopoly" profits from research and development before competitors get in the field is what drives big companies to do the research and development.

Thus .it can be argued that this incentive, which results from product or "quality" competition, brings society more benefits than classic price competition would have. If the chemical industry, for example, had cut prices to the bone as soon as costs declined, it today might be charging more for its products than it is.

Certainly "quality" and service competition indulged in by big companies cannot be summarily dismissed, as it is in strict classic theory, as a wasteful if cheap substitute for price competition. The plain fact, verified by anyone who compares consumer goods of thirty years ago with those of today, is that quality competition has given him more for his money.

The utility of luxury

And the plain fact, verified every day by anyone who travels anywhere, eats or drinks in any save the meanest places, or buys anything at retail, is that much service competition is not wasteful unless anything remotely "luxurious" is defined as wasteful. Free delivery and other amenities may add nothing to the national stock of goods. But in a nation whose rising standard of living is measured in terms of rising services, they are an important part of life.

Even in capital-goods industries, anything but an example of classic competition, much real competition is evident as service competition. A small specialty steel company, for example, may quote the same prices as the big companies. But it goes to considerable trouble and expense in tailoring shapes and preparing metal content to the special needs of its customers.

And what about big-business advertising and selling? Many economists say they are economically wasteful methods of bolstering monopoly position and thus excluding potential competitors by differentiating between goods that in fact have little difference. "We may assume," writes Arthur Burns in his *Decline of Competition,*

"that sales pressure by one or more firms in an industry has no effect on total demand—it merely shifts demand from one seller to another. . . ."

This might be true in a threadbare society hardly managing to keep body and soul together. It might also be true in a model society inhabited by clairvoyant manufacturers who always make the right things and by consumers who promptly buy up everything as soon as it is produced. But in this realm of comparative plenty, most people have more money than they need for subsistence, and are "optional" and therefore arbitrary and erratic spenders. Advertising and selling provide the only means of persuading them. Advertising and selling may provide an important means of keeping over-all consumption up to production, thus helping to prevent oversaving and the consequent deflation.

Power and self-restraint

Modern American capitalism, finally, exhibits a kind of long-term drive to behave as if it were competitive even when it is not driven by countervailing power or the impersonal forces of classic competition. It is a fact that businesses often tend to go on expanding sales whether profits are immediately maximized or not. As M. A. Adelman says of the A & P, it tries not for the largest possible profit over a planned period but for the best possible position at the end of it. "They recognize," says economist J. M. Clark, "that it is bad business to sacrifice future growth to an exorbitant rate of present profit, even if the curves on paper would permit it."

One reason it does so is that it understands the advantages of adjusting itself to public opinion and the moral climate of the times. Big business is more and more run by professional men whose primary aim is to keep their companies strong, and who therefore cannot exploit the rest of the country. The American manager "is part of a group that enjoys power only so long as it does not abuse it—in other words, precisely so long as it does not exercise power the way men and groups of men used to [exercise it]."

The "creative destruction"

Another reason companies take the long view is that they sense or understand that in the U.S. economy no one's place is secure. Research and a free-money market have seen to that. Well-heeled companies, no longer beholden to Wall

Street, plow back their earnings and constantly look for new things to get into. No company is safe in a field that is too green, uncrowded, or technically backward. General Motors is not only the largest auto maker; it is the largest refrigerator maker; and because the locomotive industry fell behind the times, G. M.'s Electro-Motive Division is now the largest locomotive maker. Crosley is not only a large refrigerator maker but a large television maker. "Anybody today can make anything," one manufacturer puts it, and it's not much of an exaggeration.

Industrial research, furthermore, is providing hundreds of new products that can substitute for older ones—nylon for silk, aluminum for steel and copper, plastics for leather, wood, metals, etc. The laboratory, today, is the great creator of competition.

No one's place is secure, finally, because the consumer has a great many choices and enough money to indulge the luxury of making them. Thus autos compete with fur coats, television sets with furniture, food with gasoline, and so on all down the line. Any manufacturer who wants to achieve volume must sell at a price that overcomes the competitive pressure of the other dissimilar goods.

On such facts the late Joseph Schumpeter based his notion of the "creative destruction" of capitalism. He argued that actual competition is perhaps less important than the threatened competition of the new technology, the new market, the new product. In the long run, he said, this threat "may enforce behavior very similar to the competitive pattern. It disciplines before it attacks. The businessman feels himself to be in a competitive situation even if he is alone in the field." In the short run Schumpeter noted what we already have digressed upon: precisely because corporations can look forward to good profits for a while, they risk big money for research and technological progress.

Such analysis has been attacked as a plea for letting well enough alone and giving up the fight for a competitive economy—and it is probably true that the country will not stay competitive by itself. But this argument would be valid only if the antitrust laws were not very effective.

"The brooding omnipresence"

Taking everything together, one of the most important reasons why the U.S. economy is competitive is the "contradictory," "impotent," and yet on the whole profoundly effective body of antitrust laws. They were inspired by and based on the classic model, and their contradictions and failures are those of the model itself. They have won comparatively few victories, and some of these, like the basing-point, Alcoa, and Morton Salt decisions, raise as many difficult questions as they answer.

But the law's greatest achievement is not what it has done, but what its "brooding omnipresence" has induced business to do voluntarily. As the saying goes, it has made the ghost of Senator Sherman an ex officio member of every board of directors in the land. No businessman of consequence makes price, employment, advertising, acquisition, or expansion policies without considering whether or not they will violate the law. "I can't even write to a friend in a competing company," laments one company economist, "and ask him any information pertaining to the business, even if it has appeared in print."

And even when the businessman thinks the "law an ass," he usually does not doubt the basic merit of a law. Although now and then he is genuinely baffled and harassed by the law, he usually knows very well when he is deliberately exploring its twilight zones.

Thus the law has made the businessman think always in terms of competition. It has imparted to business a drive, a color, a concern for an ideal that has helped make the U.S. economy different from other economies. Every so often an M.P. or British businessman gets up and thanks God publicly that British business has been spared the frightfulness of antitrust persecution. When a British equipment manufacturer bids on a job he promptly and dutifully notifies all his competitors. If they think his bid too high or too low, they straighten the matter out with him, but they are proud of the fact they never let him down.

Doubtless some American manufacturers would like to do business that way. Few people are naive enough to believe they don't sometimes succeed in doing so. But such occurrences are not the rule, and nobody openly boasts of them. The law is a valiant attempt to extend the Anglo-Saxon common code, the source and measure of the liberties of the English-speaking people, into the realm of business. Few acts of idealism have ever turned out so well.

The economic approach

A good case can be made for tightening up some parts of antitrust law and enforcing it more vigorously. But an even better case can be made for the proposition that the law applies the classic model too literally. In general, it lacks an economic approach to what are essentially economic problems.

The concept of the New Competition—"workable" competition—provides not a hard-and-fast definition but an approach to the problem of keeping competition effective. The job of formulating new policies is not easy. But it is not impossible.

Dr. Galbraith, for example, suggests a plausible rule of thumb: let the government encourage countervailing power when that power opposes existing market power, let it even create countervailing power where it is needed; and let it attack market power that is opposed by no countervailing power. As Michael Hoffman of the New York *Times* remarks, that is pretty much what antitrust does now. But Dr. Galbraith's suggestion has merit, and might well be studied by lawyers, prosecutors, judges, and analysts of antitrust policy.

Another and more carefully worked out guide is offered by Clare Griffin in his *An Economic Approach to Antitrust Problems,* published by the American Enterprise Association. He details five economic performance tests that he thinks should be used in deciding when to prosecute, how to determine penalties, what to legislate, and how to judge. The tests: (1) Is the company or industry efficient? (2) Is it progressive? (3) Does it show a reasonable and socially useful profit pattern—i.e., are its profits the reward of efficiency and progress rather than the result of artificial advantages? (4) Does it allow as much freedom of entry as is consistent with the business? (5) Is it well suited for defense?

Such tests place a heavy responsibility on the discretionary powers of the authorities, and may assume more intelligence and all-around judgment than the authorities possess. But the tests are apt and carefully thought out, and should not be overlooked. They or similar economic tests will have to be applied if antitrust law is to shape competition to benefit the people whom the creators of the classic model themselves intended it to benefit: the consumers.

READING 36

Scratch any one among us and the chances are that he will speak his praise of competition. But a hard look at ourselves and at our fellow voters demonstrates a wide range of issues on which we have compromised the methods of competition with those of a more controlled order. A mere cataloguing of the places where we have modified competition may serve little purpose; but probing inquiry into why we made each modification and what it cost us may help us to see the multiple goals of a society and the "grayness" of what might otherwise appear as a black and white world around us.

Charles Phillips, president of Bates College, has prepared a forceful reminder of our ambiguities toward competition. And he has made an eloquent plea for more, not less, of what we profess to believe in.

Questions to Guide the Reading

What pattern is there in the departures we have made in public policies from classic competition? What does this pattern suggest about the future challenges to an aggressively competitive economy?

Does the competition for which Phillips calls necessarily go well beyond the sort of "workable competition" described in the preceding article from *Fortune*? How might his concept of desirable competition be implemented?

COMPETITION? YES, BUT . . .
Charles Phillips

To ask an American businessman—whether he be grocer, baker, or candlestick maker—if he believes in competition is almost like asking for a sock on the nose. *Of course,* he believes in competition—and he raises his voice to add emphasis to his answer.

But, after he has cooled off a bit from your question, you may find that he has his own definition of competition. For example, let's walk with him down the street toward the grocery store of which he is the proprietor. Across the way in a window of one of his competitors is a large sign: "Sugar, X cents per pound." You call it to his attention and at once his brow knits. "That's unfair competition," he says. "That so-and-so has cut his price again to attract *my* customers." I remind him that he believes in competition. "Why, yes," he replies, "but not unfair and ruthless competition." And, if you then ask him, "But why is it unfair for a competitor to cut his price?" he will explode, "Why, any darn fool knows that it is unfair to sell sugar for X cents. You can't make any money at that price. There ought to be a law in this state against such practices."

We are for freedom, but

I wonder if the reaction of our friend, the grocer, does not illustrate a simple truth which can be expressed in the short but incomplete sentence: "We all like competition, but. . . ."

We all like competition since we know it is essential for our type of economy, and we like the freedoms which our economy gives to each of us—the freedom to enter or withdraw from any specific field or career; freedom to set our own prices; yes, even freedom to undersell somebody else and take business away from him.

But . . . all too often when a competitor really acts like a competitor and does something which hurts us—cuts a price, sells harder, improves quality—it becomes "unfair competition" and we run to our trade association, our resources, or the government for protection.

Of course, you think I am exaggerating the situation, and to a degree I am; but perhaps less than you think. Let's take a little look around this distribution world of ours.

We might begin by a little historical excursion in the retail field. If we go back to the turn of the present century, we find that small country merchants were going through the mail-order scare. Following the lead of Montgomery Ward Company and Sears, Roebuck & Company, mail-order firms were springing up in many parts of our country. To the small country retailer, this newer form of retailing was unfair. It did not employ salespeople. It did not involve the operation of a retail store. It could purchase in huge quantities. For these and other reasons, the local merchant was undersold and he objected to this result. Obviously, such competition was unfair! In a number of communities, "trade at home" clubs were organized while some local retailers organized mail-order catalogue burning parties.

Unfair, they say

Along about the same time, the "unfair" competition of the department store was also growing. As a matter of fact, by 1895 the department store had developed to such an extent that a group of retailers meeting in convention, "after an exciting debate," passed a resolution condemning this form of retailing, as it would "result in oppression of the public by suppressing competition [note the word "suppressing"] and causing the consumer in the end to pay higher prices and ultimately create a monopoly . . . and, further, that it [would] close to thousands of energetic young men who lack great capital the avenue of business which they should find open to them." Once again, the bogey of unfair competition had reared its ugly head. Yet, it is probably not being cynical to remark that what these retailers really were opposed to was the fact that the department store was a formidable competitor.

What happened in the late Twenties and early Thirties in the chain store field is known from personal experience to practically all of us attending this Conference today. Based on charges that the chains were monopolistic; that they used such unfair practices as loss leaders; that they were a detriment to community life because of their absentee ownership, unfairness to local

From Charles Phillips, *Competition? Yes, But . . .* (Foundation for Economic Education, Irvington-on-Hudson, New York). Reprinted with kind permission of the author and publisher. The article was originally published by the Boston Conference on Distribution.

bankers, failure to pay their fair proportion of taxes; and that they were unfair to their employees through long hours, low wages, and offering little chance of advancement, smaller retailers spent much time, effort, and money in attacking this new method of unfair competition. Customers were urged to curtail their purchases at chains. The Robinson-Patman Act was sponsored, the misnamed Fair Trade laws[1] were encouraged, and in over twenty states special taxes discriminating against the chains were enacted.

We all like competition, but. . . .

Of course, this excursion into retail history belongs to the past, and you may ask: Is anything like this going on at the present time? The answer is "yes"—and in practically every area of business. Let's note a few illustrations.

Pick up the trade paper of today, and you will discover that discount houses are a form of unfair competition. All over the country, they are rapidly springing up on the basis of underselling the so-called established retailer, which means, and I now quote the executive secretary of the National Association of Retail Druggists, that they are trying to destroy "every established retailer in the United States . . . by unfair competition. . . ." And he goes on with two sentences which might well have been lifted verbatim from dozens of speeches made against the chain store twenty-five years ago.

> Unless the discount house is effectively curbed . . . there will inevitably be anarchy in the market place. The American public must ask itself whether it wishes to sacrifice the legitimate retailers who make outstanding contributions to our economic and community life and who are the backbone of our mass distribution system.

Discount houses are even pointed to as being unfair to the consumer because, after all, they do not offer him all the services of the established retailer. Incidentally, whether the customer wants those services or not is rarely considered when this argument is advanced.

Solution by elimination

And, what do the established retailers offer as a solution to the discount house? Is it an honest effort on their part to meet this new competitive factor by reducing their own margins

[1] EDITORS' NOTE: In 1963, the new form in which fair-trade laws appeared in Congressional debate was an intensive drive to pass "quality-stabilization" laws.

and prices—which, if history proves anything, *must* be the way to meet it in the long run? In a few instances, the answer is yes. To illustrate, here is a refreshing statement from the chairman of the board of Sears, Roebuck & Company, Theodore Houser, who says:

> I have no patience with people who say that there ought to be some way to stop the discount house. The important thing is to bring down the price to the consumer. If the discount house can do that, good. It's Sears' job to get in there and pitch.

But Houser's statement is really the exception which proves the rule. The majority of established retailers act as if they think the answer is *more* Fair Trade—despite the fact that it is the wide margins set by Fair Trade which are playing an important role in encouraging the growth of the discount house. Consequently, they clamor for the manufacturer to cut off the flow of merchandise to the price cutter and to enforce his Fair Trade contracts. In brief, they say: Let's not meet competition; let's have someone eliminate it for us.

Another form of what some of today's retailers refer to as unfair competition can be discovered by talking with a downtown merchant in any city where one or more major outlying shopping centers have been developed. "Here I am, a well-established retailer," he will tell you. "I have been in this location for thirty years, and I have always given good service to the public. Now, some real estate operator has come along and developed a shopping center five miles outside of this community, and *my* customers are driving out there where they have ample room to park and where they can shop during the evening. In view of all I've done for this community, I don't think it is fair."

Or, again, talk with the president of one of today's drug chains. Twenty-five years ago *his* organization was the culprit. At that time, *he* was the unfair competitor—the price cutter—but, today, he finds that the supermarket has added a drug section and is underselling him. Whereas he opposed resale price maintenance laws twenty-five years ago, today he is one of their strong advocates. His own definition of unfair competition has shifted rapidly, depending upon who is being undersold. Incidentally, this same shift in opinion is becoming evident among the executives of the older and well-established food chains, and the leading trade paper in this area is now an advocate of Fair Trade.

Make competition illegal

We see another aspect of the Fair Trade fight in New Jersey. Here—as elsewhere—the supermarkets began to sell packaged medicines at reduced prices. The regular druggists' reaction was not to meet competition in the market place, but to try for a court ruling to prevent sales of packaged medicines in stores not having registered pharmacists. This method of fighting competition is catching: It has also appeared in Minnesota, California, and other states.

We all like competition, but. . . .

Or, again, consider the so-called plight of the automobile dealer in 1955. For a number of years, he was riding the gravy train. Cars were hard to get; he was in a sellers' market and he made money. But, late in 1953, it became apparent that a shift was occurring; and by 1954, it was clear that the tide was out. The sellers' market turned into a buyers' market.

Many dealers who had grown up in the industry during its easy selling days and had never been trained for the "hard sell" suddenly found themselves in trouble. Their profit margin disappeared; they went into the "red." Some of them began to appear in Dun & Bradstreet's failure statistics. Of course, said the dealers, it was all the manufacturer's fault. As the dealers put it: "The real trouble is that auto-makers are producing more cars than dealers can sell," and they urged their resources to reduce their production. Oh, the dealers would admit that they might have had some part to play in the situation, since some of them were bootlegging cars—selling them to so-called illegitimate dealers who in turn would sell them at reduced prices. To check such so-called unfair competition, the National Automobile Dealers Association even asked the United States Justice Department to come to the dealers' rescue and prohibit bootlegging!

But, we do not have to limit ourselves to illustrations from what we normally consider the retail field. Did you follow the ten-month strike of Local 15 of the United Hatters and Millinery Workers International Union against the Hat Corporation of America? The strike started in July of 1953, brought on basically by the Union's demand that the company sign a contract containing a clause that would prohibit it from opening new plants outside of the Norwalk area and from transferring work now done in Norwalk to any outside plant.

What the Union wanted was a limit on competition. It did not want its members to compete with workers in some other area where Hat Cor-poration might establish a factory. Fortunately, after ten months, the Union lost its fight. It is worth contemplating, however, what would have happened had a similar strike been won when the United States was still located on the East Coast only. Obviously, it would still be located on the East Coast only; and equally obviously, its standard of living today would be far below what it now is.

Agriculture and exports

Then, of course, there is the farmer—the so-called individualist, the man who stands on his own feet, and, as the politician puts it, "is the backbone of the nation." Here, of course, is someone who believes in competition. Yes, he does, but again there comes that but—and the but in his case is a big one, so big that through powerful lobbies he has forced through Congress price support laws which give him protection far in excess of even that provided for the retailer through Fair Trade.

In the foreign trade area, we can find this same attitude. A Randall Commission was appointed; and in January, 1955, it came up with a program which could be described by the phrase, "more trade, less aid." For a time, it seemed as if practically everyone in the country was in agreement that this slogan would be a good one to put into practice. It looked as if we were going to make progress in minimizing some of our tariff barriers which limit competition and result in lower standards of living both here and abroad. Yet, when a specific program to accomplish these ends was proposed last March, many of those who, at their trade association meetings, are warm advocates of competition, suddenly found that there were certain wage cost differentials which led them to oppose lower tariffs "as posing a grave threat to the domestic economy." As they warmed up to their subject, they pointed out that lower tariffs would throw American workers out of jobs, curtail purchasing power, and send us into a depression. The fact that domestic difficulties in specific areas would be far more than offset by benefits in other areas is something with which they were not concerned.

We all believe in competition, but. . . .

I can even illustrate this attitude in the field of education—college education at that. Throughout the United States, colleges use scholarships to capture students—and I use the word "capture" deliberately. Sometimes we want them for their I.Q., sometimes for their A.P. (athletic prowess) and sometimes for both. At my college, of course (or president Jones' college if he is the one doing the talking), we limit these scholarships to students who are in serious financial need; but, unfortunately (that is the word used by college presidents when several of them gather together in a room to discuss the situation), there are a few colleges which use scholarships as an unfair method of price-cutting. Don't you think, their conversation continues, our regional association can do something about this?

Even educators like competition, but. . . .

Unfair competition vs. keen competition

Now, as I conclude, let me be sure that I am not misunderstood as to the point I am trying to make. Please do not think I am saying there is no such thing as unfair competition. When a competitor resorts to false and misleading advertising, engages in misbranding, and makes false and disparaging statements against competitors or their products, he is engaging in practices which all of us would denounce.

What I am saying is this: Much of what we daily refer to as unfair competition is really just keen competition. It is the kind of competition that is essential to our type of economic system. If we want to maintain the freedoms which our system gives us—to enter businesses of our choice, to produce the merchandise we please, to set our own prices—then we must accept the competition which is essential to that kind of an economy. We must not always look to our trade association or our government to protect us from the actions of our competitors.

I would make this positive suggestion. Let us spend more time—in our offices, stores, conferences, and trade association meetings—improving our operations and less time trying to curb our competitors. Not only will individual companies be better off, but so will society. If America wants to continue its long-time development toward a rising standard of living, we need to encourage more, not less, competition.

When Stuyvesant Fish was president of the Illinois Central Railroad, there walked into his office one morning an Irishman, hat on and pipe in mouth, who said:

"I want a pass to St. Louis."

"Who are you?" asked President Fish, somewhat startled.

"I'm Pat Casey, one of your switchmen."

Mr. Fish, thinking it was a good chance to impart a lesson in etiquette, said, "Now, Pat, I'm not going to say that I will refuse your request, but there are certain forms a man should observe in asking a favor. You should knock at the door; and when I say 'Come in' you should enter and, taking off your hat and removing your pipe from your mouth, you should say, 'Are you President Fish?' I would say, 'I am. Who are you?' Then you should say, 'I am Pat Casey, one of your switchmen.' Then I would say, 'What can I do for you?' Then you would tell me, and the matter would be settled. Now you go out and come in again and see if you can't do better."

So the switchman went out. About two hours later there was a knock on the door and president Fish said, "Come in." In came Pat Casey with his hat off and pipe out of his mouth.

"Good morning," he said, "are you President Fish of the Illinois Central Railroad?"

"I am. Who are you?"

"I am Pat Casey, one of your switchmen."

"Well Mr. Casey, what can I do for you?"

"You can go to hell. I got a job and a pass on the Wabash."

Pat Casey might have spent the rest of his life cursing president Fish and voting for congressmen who pledged themselves to work for the removal of Fish as the president of the Illinois Central Railroad. Instead, he exercised his ingenuity and got a job and a pass on the Wabash. Rather than spending our time cursing our competitors and making efforts to limit their competitive activities, some of us need to get a job and a pass on the Wabash.

READING 37

An earlier selection (page 202) told of price leadership in an industry of few sellers. Stability was maintained in the cigarette industry without overt collusion. But, the law notwithstanding, producers in some industries have participated in direct but secret conspiracies to bring price stability into their businesses. Few recent instances have been as dramatic as the one involving some of the nation's largest manufacturers of electrical equipment. Here were big names and big stakes caught up in an economic drama that produced both angry finger-pointing and quieter soul-searching in and out of the business world.

John Brooks, novelist and free-lance writer on business subjects, goes well beyond the traditional economist's approach to this famous law case. The economic issues are here, but so too are the moral issues and above all the communications issues raised by this critical and puzzling chapter in our business history.

Questions to Guide the Reading

What light does the case throw on the difficulties in maintaining stability in oligopolistic markets in the absence of direct collusion? From the public point of view, are the results here substantially different from those to be expected under conditions of legal and effective price leadership?

What are our most effective defenses against a recurrence of this type of conspiracy?

COMMUNICATION AND COLLUSION: THE CASE OF THE ELECTRICAL INDUSTRY
John Brooks

Among the greatest problems facing American industry today, one may learn by talking with any of a large number of industrialists who are not known to be especially given to pontificating, is "the problem of communication." This preoccupation with the difficulty of getting a thought out of one head and into another is something the industrialists share with a substantial number of intellectuals and creative writers, more and more of whom seem inclined to regard communication, or the lack of it, as one of the greatest problems not just of industry but of humanity. (A few avant-garde writers and artists have given the importance of communication a backhanded boost by flatly and unequivocally proclaiming themselves to be against it.) As far as the industrialists are concerned, I admit that in the course of hearing them invoke the word "communication"—often in an almost mystical way—over the past few years I have had a lot of trouble figuring out exactly what they meant. The general thesis is clear enough; namely, that everything would be all right, first, if they could get through to each other within their own organizations, and, second, if they, or their organizations, could get through to everybody else. What has puzzled me is how and why, in this

day when the foundations sponsor one study of communication after another, individuals and organizations fail so consistently to express themselves understandably, or how and why their listeners fail to grasp what they hear.

Recently, I acquired a two-volume publication of the United States Government Printing Office entitled *Hearings Before the Subcommittee on Antitrust and Monopoly of the Committee on the Judiciary, United States Senate, Eighty-seventh Congress, First Session, Pursuant to S. Res. 52,* and after a fairly diligent perusal of its 1,459 pages I think I begin to see what the industrialists are talking about. The hearings, conducted in April, May, and June, 1961, under the chairmanship of Senator Estes Kefauver, of Tennessee, had to do with the now famous price-fixing and bid-rigging conspiracies in the electrical-manufacturing industry, which had already resulted, the previous February, in the imposition by a federal judge in Philadelphia of fines totaling $1,924,500 on twenty-nine firms and forty-five of their employees, and also of thirty-day prison sentences on seven of the employees. Since there had been no public presentation of evidence, all the defendants having pleaded either guilty or no defense, and since the records of

From John Brooks, *The Fate of the Edsel and Other Business Adventures* (Harper & Row, New York, 1962). Copyright © 1962 by John Brooks. Originally appeared in *The New Yorker*, and reprinted with kind permission of the author and publishers.

the grand juries that indicted them were secret, the public had had little opportunity to hear about the details of the violations, and Senator Kefauver felt that the whole matter needed a good airing. The transcript shows that it got one, and what the airing revealed—at least within the biggest company involved—was a breakdown in intramural communication so drastic as to make the building of the Tower of Babel seem a triumph of organizational rapport.

In a series of indictments brought by the government in the United States District Court in Philadelphia between February and October, 1960, the twenty-nine companies and their executives were charged with having repeatedly violated Section 1 of the Sherman Act of 1890, which declares illegal "every contract, combination in the form of trust or otherwise, or conspiracy, in restraint of trade or commerce among the several States, or with foreign nations." (The Sherman Act was the instrument used in the celebrated trust-busting activities of Theodore Roosevelt, and along with the Clayton Act of 1914 it has served as the government's weapon against cartels and monopolies ever since.) The violations, the government alleged, were committed in connection with the sale of large and expensive pieces of apparatus of a variety that is required chiefly by public and private electric-utility companies (power transformers, switchgear assemblies, and turbine-generator units, among many others), and were the outcome of a series of meetings attended by executives of the supposedly competing companies—beginning at least as early as 1956 and continuing into 1959 —at which noncompetitive price levels were agreed upon, nominally sealed bids on individual contracts were rigged in advance, and each company was allocated a certain percentage of the available business. The government further alleged that, in an effort to preserve the secrecy of these meetings, the executives had resorted to such devices as referring to their companies by code numbers in their correspondence, making telephone calls from public booths or from their homes rather than from their offices, and doctoring the expense accounts covering their get-togethers to conceal the fact that they had all been in a certain city on a certain day. But their stratagems did not prevail. The federals, forcefully led by Robert A. Bicks, then head of the Antitrust Division of the Department of Justice, succeeded in exposing them, with considerable help from some of the conspirators themselves, who, after an employee of a small conspirator

company saw fit to spill the beans in the early fall of 1959, flocked to turn state's evidence.

The economic and social significance of the whole affair may be demonstrated clearly enough by citing just a few figures. In an average year, a total of more than one and three-quarter billion dollars is spent to purchase machines of the sort in question, nearly a fourth of it by federal, state, and local governments (which, of course, means the taxpayers), and most of the rest by private utility companies (which are inclined to pass along any rise in the cost of their equipment to the public in the form of rate increases). To take a specific example of the kind of money involved in an individual transaction, the list price of a 500,000-kilowatt turbine-generator—a monstrous device for producing electric power from steam power—may be something like sixteen million dollars. Actually, manufacturers have sometimes cut their prices by as much as 25 percent in order to make a sale, and therefore, if everything is aboveboard, it may be possible to buy the machine at a saving of four million dollars; if representatives of the companies making such generators hold a single meeting and agree to fix prices, they may, in effect, increase the cost to the customer by the four million. And in the end, the customer is almost sure to be the public.

In presenting the indictments in Philadelphia, Bicks stated that, considered collectively, they revealed "a pattern of violations which can fairly be said to range among the most serious, the most flagrant, the most pervasive that have ever marked any basic American industry." Just before imposing the sentences, Judge J. Cullen Ganey went even further; in his view, the violations constituted "a shocking indictment of a vast section of our economy, for what is really at stake here is the survival of . . . the free-enterprise system." The prison sentences showed that he meant it; although there had been many successful prosecutions for violation of the Sherman Act during the seven decades since its passage, it was rare indeed for executives to be jailed. Not surprisingly, therefore, the case kicked up quite a ruckus in the press. The *New Republic*, to be sure, complained that the newspapers and magazines were intentionally playing down "the biggest business scandal in decades," but the charge did not seem to have much foundation. Considering such things as the public's apathy toward switchgear, the woeful bloodlessness of criminal cases involving antitrust laws, and the relatively few details of the conspiracies that had emerged, the press in general gave the story a good deal of space, and even the *Wall Street Journal* and *Fortune* ran uncompromising and highly informative accounts of the debacle; here and there, in fact, one could detect signs of a revival of the spirit of old-time anti-business journalism as it existed back in the thirties. After all, what could be more exhilarating than to see several dignified, impeccably tailored, and highly paid executives of a few of the nation's most respected corporations being trooped off to jail like common pickpockets? It was certainly the biggest moment for business-baiters since 1938, when Richard Whitney, the president of the New York Stock Exchange at the time, was put behind bars for speculating with his customers' money. Some called it the biggest since Teapot Dome.

To top it all off, there was a prevalent suspicion of hypocrisy in the very highest places. Neither the chairman of the board nor the president of General Electric, the largest of the corporate defendants, had been caught in the government's dragnet, and the same was true of Westinghouse Electric, the second-largest; these four ultimate bosses let it be known that they had been entirely ignorant of what had been going on within their commands right up to the time the first testimony on the subject was given to the Justice Department. Many people, however, were not satisfied by these disclaimers, and, instead, took the position that the defendant executives were men in the middle, who had broken the law only in response either to actual orders or to a corporate climate favoring price-fixing, and who were now being allowed to suffer for the sins of their superiors. Among the unsatisfied was Judge Ganey himself, who said at the time of the sentencing, "One would be most naïve indeed to believe that these violations of the law, so long persisted in, affecting so large a segment of the industry, and finally, involving so many millions upon millions of dollars, were facts unknown to those responsible for the conduct of the corporation. . . . I am convinced that in the great number of these defendants' cases, they were torn between conscience and approved corporate policy, with the rewarding objectives of promotion, comfortable security, and large salaries."

The public naturally wanted a ringleader, an archconspirator, and it appeared to find what it wanted in General Electric, which—to the acute consternation of the men endeavoring to guide its destinies from company headquarters, at 570 Lexington Avenue, New York City—got the lion's share of attention both in the press and in the Subcommittee hearings. With some 300,000 employees, and sales averaging some four billion dollars a year over the past ten years, it was not only far and away the biggest of the twenty-nine accused companies but, judged on the basis of sales in 1959, the fifth-biggest company in the country. It also drew a higher total of fines ($437,500) than any other company, and saw more of its executives sent to jail (three, with eight others receiving suspended sentences). Furthermore, as if to intensify in this hour of crisis the horror and shock of true believers—and the glee of scoffers—its highest-ranking executives had for years tried to represent it to the public as a paragon of successful virtue by issuing encomiums to the free competitive system, the very system that the price-fixing meetings were set up to mock. In 1959, shortly after the government's investigation of the violations had been brought to the attention of G.E.'s policymakers, the company demoted and cut the pay of those of its executives who admitted that they had been involved; one vice-president, for example, was informed that instead of the $127,000 a year he had been getting he would now get $40,000. (He had scarcely adjusted himself to that blow when Judge Ganey fined him four thousand dollars and sent him to prison for thirty days, and shortly after he regained his freedom, General Electric eased him out entirely.) The G.E. policy of imposing penalties of its own on these employees, regardless of what punishment the court might prescribe, was not adopted by Westinghouse, which waited until the judge had disposed of the case and then decided that the fines and prison sentences he had handed out to its stable of offenders were chastisement enough, and did not itself penalize them at all. Some people saw this attitude as evidence that Westinghouse was condoning the conspiracies, but others regarded it as a commendable, if tacit, admission that management at the highest level in the conniving companies was responsible—morally, at least—for the whole mess and was therefore in no position to discipline its erring employees. In the view of these people, G.E.'s haste to penalize the acknowledged culprits on its payroll strongly suggested that the firm was trying to save its own skin by throwing a few luckless employees to the wolves, or—as Senator Philip A. Hart, of Michigan, put it, more pungently, during the hearings—"to do a Pontius Pilate operation."

Embattled days at 570 Lexington Avenue! After years of cloaking the company in the mantle of a wise and benevolent corporate institution, the public-relations people at G.E. headquarters were faced with the ugly choice of representing its role in the price-fixing affair as that of either a fool or a knave. They tended strongly toward "fool." Judge Ganey, by his statement that he assumed the conspiracies to have been not only condoned but approved by the top brass and the company as a whole, clearly chose "knave." But his analysis may or may not have been the right one, and after reading the Kefauver Subcommittee testimony I have come to the melancholy conclusion that the truth will very likely never be known. For, as the testimony shows, the clear waters of moral responsibility at G.E. became hopelessly muddied by a struggle to communicate—a struggle so confused that in some cases, it would now appear, if one of the big bosses at G.E. *had* ordered a subordinate to break the law, the message would somehow have been garbled in its reception, and if the subordinate *had* informed the boss that he was holding conspiratorial meetings with competitors, the boss might well have been under the impression that the subordinate was gossiping idly about lawn parties or pinochle sessions. Specifically, it would appear that a subordinate who received a direct oral order from his boss had to figure out whether it meant what it seemed to or the exact opposite, while the boss, in conversing with a subordinate had to figure out whether he should take what the man *told* him at face value or should attempt to translate it out of a secret code to which he was by no means sure he had the key. That was the problem in a nutshell, and I state it here thus baldly as a suggestion for any potential beneficiary of a foundation who may be casting about for a suitable project on which to draw up a prospectus.

For the past eight years or so, G.E. has had a company rule called Directive Policy 20.5, which reads, in part, "No employee shall enter into any understanding, agreement, plan or scheme, expressed or implied, formal or informal, with any competitor, in regard to prices, terms or conditions of sale, production, distribution, territories, or customers; nor exchange or discuss with a competitor prices, terms or conditions of sale, or any other competitive information." In effect, this rule is simply an injunction to G.E.'s personnel to obey the federal antitrust laws, except that it is somewhat more concrete and comprehensive in the matter of price than they are. It is almost impossible for executives with jurisdiction over pricing policies at G.E. to be unaware of 20.5, or even hazy about it, because to make sure that new executives are acquainted with it and to refresh the memories of old ones, the company formally reissues and distributes it at intervals, and all such executives are asked to sign their names to it as an earnest that they are currently complying with it and intend to keep on doing so. The trouble—at least during the period covered by the court action, and apparently for a long time before that as well—was that some people at G.E., including some of those who regularly signed 20.5, simply did not believe that it was to be taken seriously. They assumed that 20.5 was mere window dressing; that it was on the books solely to provide legal protection for the company and for the higher-ups; that meeting illegally with competitors was recognized and accepted as standard practice within the company; and that often when a ranking executive ordered a subordinate executive to comply with 20.5, he was actually ordering him to violate it. Illogical as it might seem, this last assumption becomes comprehensible in the light of the fact that, for a time, when some executives orally conveyed, or reconveyed, the order, they were apparently in the habit of accompanying it with an unmistakable wink. In May of 1948, for example, there was a meeting of G.E. sales managers during which the custom of winking was openly discussed. Robert Paxton, an upper-level G.E. executive who later became the company's president, addressed the meeting and delivered the usual admonition about antitrust violations, whereupon William S. Ginn, then a sales executive in the transformer division, under Paxton's authority, startled him by saying, "I didn't see you wink." Paxton replied firmly, "There was no wink. We mean it, and these are the orders." Asked by Senator Kefauver how long he had been aware that orders issued at G.E. were sometimes accompanied by winks, Paxton replied that he had first observed the practice way back in 1935, when his boss had given him an instruction along with a wink or its equivalent, and that when, some time later, the significance of the gesture dawned on him, he had become so incensed that he had with difficulty restrained himself from jeopardizing his career by punching the boss in the nose. Paxton went on to say that his objections to the practice of winking had been so strong as to earn him a reputation in the company for being an antiwink man, and that he, for his part, had never winked.

Although Paxton would seem to have left little doubt as to how he intended his winkless order of 1948 to be interpreted, its meaning failed to get through to Ginn, for not long after it was issued, he went out and fixed prices to a fare-thee-well. (Obviously, it takes more than one company to make a price-fixing agreement, but all the testimony tends to indicate that it was G.E. that generally set the pattern for the rest of the industry in such matters.) Thirteen years later, Ginn—fresh from a few weeks in jail, and fresh out of a $135,000-a-year job—appeared before the Subcommittee to account for, among other things, his strange response to the winkless order. He had disregarded it, he said, because he had received a contrary order from two of his other superiors in the G.E. chain of command, Henry V. B. Erben and Francis Fairman, and in explaining why he had heeded their order rather than Paxton's he introduced the fascinating concept of degrees of communication—another theme for a foundation grantee to get his teeth into. Erben and Fairman, Ginn said, had been more articulate, persuasive, and forceful in issuing their order than Paxton had been in issuing his; Fairman, especially, Ginn stressed, had proved to be "a great communicator, a great philosopher, and, frankly, a great believer in stability of prices." Both Erben and Fairman had dismissed Paxton as naïve, Ginn testified, and, in further summary of how he had been led astray, he said that "the people who were advocating the Devil were able to sell me better than the philosophers that were selling the Lord."

It would be helpful to have at hand a report from Erben and Fairman themselves on the communication techniques that enabled them to prevail over Paxton, but unfortunately neither of these philosophers could testify before the Subcommittee, because by the time of the hearings both of them were dead. Paxton, who was available, was described in Ginn's testimony as having been at all times one of the philosopher-salesmen on the side of the Lord. "I can clarify Mr. Paxton by saying Mr. Paxton came closer to being an Adam Smith advocate than any businessman I have met in America," Ginn declared. Still, in 1950, when Ginn admitted to Paxton in casual conversation that he had "compromised himself" in respect to antitrust matters, Paxton merely told him that he was a damned

fool, and did not report the confession to anyone else in the company. Testifying as to why he did not, Paxton said that when the conversation occurred he was no longer Ginn's boss and that, in the light of his personal ethics, repeating such an admission by a man not under his authority would be "gossip" and "talebearing."

Meanwhile, Ginn, no longer answerable to Paxton, was meeting with competitors at frequent intervals and moving steadily up the corporate ladder. In November, 1954, he was made general manager of the transformer division, whose headquarters were in Pittsfield, Massachusetts—a job that put him in line for a vice-presidency. At the time of Ginn's shift, Ralph J. Cordiner, who has been chairman of the board of General Electric since 1949, called him down to New York for the express purpose of enjoining him to comply strictly and undeviatingly with Directive Policy 20.5. Cordiner communicated this idea so successfully that it was clear enough to Ginn at the moment, but it remained so only as long as it took him, after leaving the chairman, to walk to Erben's office. There his comprehension of what he had just heard became clouded. Erben, who was head of G.E.'s distribution group, ranked directly below Cordiner and directly above Ginn, and, according to Ginn's testimony, no sooner were they alone in his office than he countermanded Cordiner's injunction, saying, "Now, keep on doing the way that you have been doing, but just be sensible about it and use your head on the subject." Erben's extraordinary communicative prowess again carried the day, and Ginn continued to meet with competitors. "I knew Mr. Cordiner could fire me," he told Senator Kefauver, "but also I knew I was working for Mr. Erben."

At the end of 1954, Paxton took over Erben's job and thereby became Ginn's boss again. Ginn went right on meeting with competitors, but, since he was aware that Paxton disapproved of the practice, didn't tell him about it. Moreover, he testified, within a month or two he had become convinced that he could not afford to discontinue attending the meetings under any circumstances, for in January, 1955, the entire electrical-equipment industry became embroiled in a drastic price war—known as the "white sale," because of its timing and the bargains it afforded to buyers—in which the erstwhile amiable competitors began fiercely undercutting one another. Such a manifestation of free enterprise was, of course, exactly what the intercompany conspiracies were intended to prevent, but just at that time the supply of electrical apparatus so greatly exceeded the demand that first a few of the conspirators and then more and more began breaking the agreements they themselves had made. In dealing with the situation as best he could, Ginn said, he "used the philosophies that had been taught me previously"—by which he meant that he continued to conduct price-fixing meetings, in the hope that at least *some* of the agreements made at them would be honored. As for Paxton, in Ginn's opinion that philosopher was not only ignorant of the meetings but so constant in his devotion to the concept of free and aggressive competition that he actually enjoyed the price war, disastrous though it was to everybody's profits. (In his own testimony, Paxton vigorously denied that he had enjoyed it.)

Within a year or so, the electrical-equipment industry took an upturn, and in January, 1957, Ginn, having ridden out the storm relatively well, got his vice-presidency. At the same time, he was transferred to Schenectady, to become general manager of G.E.'s turbine-generator division, and Cordiner again called him into headquarters and gave him a lecture on 20.5. Such lectures were getting to be a routine with Cordiner; every time a new employee was assigned to a strategic managerial post, or an old employee was promoted to such a post, the lucky fellow could be reasonably certain that he would be summoned to the chairman's office to hear a rendition of the austere creed. In his book *The Heart of Japan*, Alexander Campbell reports that a large Japanese electrical concern has drawn up a list of seven company commandments (for example, "Be courteous and sincere!"), and that each morning, in each of its thirty factories, the workers are required to stand at attention and recite these in unison, and then to sing the company song ("For ever-increasing production/Love your work, give your all!"). Cordiner did not require his subordinates to recite or sing 20.5—as far as is known, he never even had it set to music—but from the number of times men like Ginn had it read to them or otherwise recalled to their attention, they must have come to know it well enough to chant it, improvising a tune as they went along.

This time, Cordiner's message not only made an impression on Ginn's mind but stuck there in unadulterated form. Ginn, according to his testimony, became a reformed executive and dropped his price-fixing habits overnight. However, it appears that his sudden conversion cannot be attributed wholly to Cordiner's powers of communication, or even to the drip-drip-drip effect of repetition, for it was to a considerable extent pragmatic in character, like the conversion of Henry VIII to Protestantism. He reformed, Ginn explained to the Subcommittee, because his "air cover was gone."

"Your what was gone?" Senator Kefauver asked.

"My air cover was gone," replied Ginn. "I mean I had lost my air cover. Mr. Erben wasn't around any more, and all of my colleagues had gone, and I was now working directly for Mr. Paxton, knowing his feelings on the matter. . . . Any philosophy that I had grown up with before in the past was now out the window."

If Erben, who had not been Ginn's boss since late in 1954, had been the source of his air cover, Ginn must have been without its protection for over two years, but, presumably, in the excitement of the price war he had failed to notice its absence. However that may have been, here he now was, a man suddenly shorn not only of his air cover but of his philosophy. Swiftly filling the latter void with a whole new set of principles, he circulated copies of 20.5 among his department managers in the turbine-generator division and topped this off by energetically adopting what he called a "leprosy policy"; that is, he advised his subordinates to avoid even casual social contacts with their counterparts in competing companies, because "once the relationships are established, I have come to the conclusion after many years of hard experience that the relationships tend to spread and the hanky-panky begins to get going." But now fate played a cruel trick on Ginn, and, all unknowing, he landed in the very position that Paxton and Cordiner had been in for years—that of a philosopher vainly endeavoring to sell the Lord to a flock that declined to buy his message and was, in fact, systematically engaging in the hanky-panky its leader had warned it against. Specifically, during the whole of 1957 and 1958 and the first part of 1959 two of Ginn's subordinates were piously signing 20.5 with one hand and, with the other, briskly drawing up price-fixing agreements at a whole series of meetings—in New York; Philadelphia; Chicago; Hot Springs, Virginia; and Skytop, Pennsylvania, to name a few of their gathering places.

It appears that Ginn had not been able to impart much of his shining new philosophy to others, and that at the root of his difficulty lay that old jinx, the problem of communicating.

Asked at the hearings how his subordinates could possibly have gone so far astray, he replied,

> I have got to admit that I made a communication error. I didn't sell this thing to the boys well enough. . . . The price is so important in the complete running of a business that, philosophically, we have got to sell people not only just the fact that it is against the law, but . . . that it shouldn't be done for many, many reasons. But it has got to be a philosophical approach and a communication approach. . . . Even though . . . I had told my associates not to do this, some of the boys did get off the reservation. . . . I have to admit to myself here an area of a failure in communications . . . which I am perfectly willing to accept my part of the responsibility for.

In earnestly striving to analyze the cause of the failure, Ginn said, he had reached the conclusion that merely issuing directives, no matter how frequently, was not enough; what was needed was "a complete philosophy, a complete understanding, a complete breakdown of barriers between people, if we are going to get some understanding and really live and manage these companies within the philosophies that they should be managed in."

Senator Hart permitted himself to comment, "You can communicate until you are dead and gone, but if the point you are communicating about, even though it be a law of the land, strikes your audience as something that is just a folklore . . . you will never sell the package."

Ginn ruefully conceded that that was true.

The concept of degrees of communication was further developed, by implication, in the testimony of another defendant, Frank E. Stehlik, who had been general manager of the G.E. low-voltage-switchgear department from May, 1956, to February, 1960. (As all but a tiny minority of the users of electricity are contentedly unaware, switchgear serves to control and protect apparatus used in the generation, conversion, transmission, and distribution of electrical energy, and around $125 million worth of it is sold annually in the United States.) Stehlik received some of his business guidance in the conventional form of orders, oral and written, and some—perhaps just as much, to judge by his testimony —through a less intellectual, more visceral medium of communication that he called "impacts." Apparently, when something happened within the company that made an impression on him, he would consult a sort of internal metaphysical voltmeter to ascertain the force of the jolt that

he had received, and, from the reading he got, would attempt to gauge the true drift of company policy. For example, he testified that during 1956, 1957, and most of 1958 he believed that G.E. was frankly and fully in favor of complying with 20.5. But then, in the autumn of 1958, George E. Burens, Stehlik's immediate superior, told him that he, Burens, had been directed by Paxton, who by then was president of G.E., to have lunch with Max Scott, president of the I-T-E Circuit Breaker Company, an important competitor in the switchgear market. Paxton said in his own testimony that while he had indeed asked Burens to have lunch with Scott, he had instructed him categorically not to talk about prices, but apparently Burens did not mention this caveat to Stehlik; in any event, the disclosure that the high command had told Burens to lunch with an archrival, Stehlik testified, "had a heavy impact on me." Asked to amplify this, he said, "There are a great many impacts that influence me in my thinking as to the true attitude of the company, and that was one of them." As the impacts, great and small, piled up, their cumulative effect finally communicated to Stehlik that he had been wrong in supposing the company had any real respect for 20.5. Accordingly, when, late in 1958, Stehlik was ordered by Burens to begin holding price meetings with the competitors, he was not in the least surprised.

Stehlik's compliance with Burens' order ultimately brought on a whole new series of impacts, of a much more crudely communicative sort. In February, 1960, General Electric cut his annual pay from $70,000 to $26,000 for violating 20.5; a year later Judge Ganey gave him a three-thousand-dollar fine and a suspended thirty-day jail sentence for violating the Sherman Act; and about a month after *that* G.E. asked for, and got, his resignation. Indeed, during his last years with the firm Stehlik seems to have received almost as many lacerating impacts as a Raymond Chandler hero. But testimony given at the hearings by L. B. Gezon, manager of the marketing section of the low-voltage-switchgear department, indicated that Stehlik, again like a Chandler hero, was capable of dishing out blunt impacts as well as taking them. Gezon, who was directly under Stehlik in the line of command, told the Subcommittee that although he had taken part in price-fixing meetings prior to April, 1956, when Stehlik became his boss, he did not subsequently engage in any antitrust violations until late 1958, and that he did so then only as the result of an impact that bore none of the subtlety noted by Stehlik in his early experience with this phenomenon. The impact came directly from Stehlik, who, it seems, left nothing to chance in communicating with his subordinates. In Gezon's words, Stehlik told him "to resume the meetings; that company policy was unchanged; the risk was just as great as it ever had been; and that if our activities were discovered, I personally would be dismissed or disciplined [by the company], as well as punished by the government." So Gezon was left with three choices: to quit, to disobey the direct order of his superior (in which case, he thought, "they might have found somebody else to do my job"), or to obey the order, and thereby violate the antitrust laws, with no immunity against the possible consequences. In short, his alternatives were comparable to those faced by an international spy.

Although Gezon did resume the meetings, he was not indicted, possibly because he had been a relatively minor price-fixer. General Electric, for its part, demoted him but did not require him to resign. Yet it would be a mistake to assume that Gezon was relatively untouched by his experience. Asked by Senator Kefauver if he did not think that Stehlik's order had placed him in an intolerable position, he replied that it had not struck him that way at the time. Asked whether he thought it unjust that he had suffered demotion for carrying out the order of a superior, he replied, "I personally don't consider it so." To judge by his answers, the impact on Gezon's heart and mind would seem to have been heavy indeed.

The other side of the communication problem —the difficulty that a superior is likely to encounter in understanding what a subordinate tells him—is graphically illustrated by the testimony of Raymond W. Smith, who was general manager of G.E.'s transformer division from the beginning of 1957 until late in 1959, and of Arthur F. Vinson, who in October, 1957, was appointed vice-president in charge of G.E.'s apparatus group, and also a member of the company's executive committee. Smith's job was the one Ginn had held for the previous two years, and when Vinson got *his* job, he became Smith's immediate boss. Smith's highest pay during the period in question was roughly $100,000 a year, while Vinson reached a basic salary of $110,000 and also got a variable bonus, ranging from $45,000 to $100,000. Smith testified that on January 1, 1957, the very day he took charge of the transformer division—and a holiday, at that—he met with Chairman Cordiner and Executive Vice-

President Paxton, and Cordiner gave him the familiar admonition about living up to 20.5. However, later that year, the competitive going got so rough that transformers were selling at discounts of as much as 35 percent, and Smith decided on his own hook that the time had come to begin negotiating with rival firms in the hope of stabilizing the market. He felt that he was justified in doing this, he said, because he was convinced that both in company circles and in the whole industry negotiations of this kind were "the order of the day."

By the time Vinson became his superior, in October, Smith was regularly attending price-fixing meetings, and he felt that he ought to let his new boss know what he was doing. Accordingly, he told the Subcommittee, on two or three occasions when the two men found themselves alone together in the normal course of business, he said to Vinson, "I had a meeting with the clan this morning." Counsel for the Subcommittee asked Smith whether he had ever put the matter more bluntly—whether, for example, he had ever said anything like "We're meeting with competitors to fix prices. We're going to have a little conspiracy here and I don't want it to get out." Smith replied that he had never said anything remotely like that—had done nothing more than make remarks on the order of "I had a meeting with the clan this morning." He did not elaborate on why he did not speak with greater directness, but two logical possibilities present themselves. Perhaps he hoped that he could keep Vinson informed about the situation and at the same time protect him from the risk of becoming an accomplice. Or perhaps he had no such intention, and was simply expressing himself in the oblique, colloquial way that characterized much of his speaking. (Paxton, a close friend of Smith's, had once complained to Smith that he was "given to being somewhat cryptic" in his remarks.) Anyhow, Vinson, according to his own testimony, had flatly misunderstood what Smith meant; indeed, he could not recall ever hearing Smith use the expression "meeting of the clan," although he did recall his saying things like "Well, I am going to take this new plan on transformers and show it to the boys." Vinson testified that he had thought the "boys" meant the G.E. district sales people and the company's customers, and that the "new plan" was a new marketing plan; he said that it had come as a rude shock to him to learn—a couple of years later, after the case had broken—that in speaking of the "boys" and the "new plan," Smith had been referring to competitors and a price-fixing scheme. "I think Mr. Smith is a sincere man," Vinson testified. "I am sure Mr. Smith . . . thought he was telling me that he was going to one of these meetings. This meant nothing to me."

Smith, on the other hand, was confident that his meaning had got through to Vinson. "I never got the impression that he misunderstood me," he insisted to the Subcommittee. Questioning Vinson later, Kefauver asked whether an executive in his position, with thirty-odd years' experience in the electrical industry, could possibly be so naïve as to misunderstand a subordinate on such a substantive matter as grasping who the "boys" were. "I don't think it is too naïve," replied Vinson. "We have a lot of boys. . . . I may be naïve, but I am certainly telling the truth, and in this kind of thing I am sure I am naïve."

SENATOR KEFAUVER: Mr. Vinson, you wouldn't be a vice-president at $200,000 a year if you were naïve.

MR. VINSON: I think I could well get there by being naïve in this area. It might help.

Here, in a different field altogether, the communication problem again comes to the fore. Was Vinson really saying to Kefauver what he seemed to be saying—that naïveté about antitrust violations might be a help to a man in getting and holding a $200,000-a-year job at General Electric? It seems unlikely. And yet what else could he have meant? Whatever the answer, neither the federal antitrust men nor the Senate investigators were able to prove that Smith succeeded in his attempts to communicate to Vinson the fact that he was engaging in price-fixing. And, lacking such proof, they were unable to establish what they gave every appearance of going all out to establish if they could: namely, that at least some one man at the pinnacle of G.E.'s management—some member of the sacred executive committee itself—was implicated. Actually, when the story of the conspiracies first became known, Vinson not only concurred in a company decision to punish Smith by drastically demoting him but personally informed him of the decision—two acts that, if he had grasped Smith's meaning back in 1957, would have denoted a remarkable degree of cynicism and hypocrisy. (Smith, by the way, rather than accept the demotion, quit General Electric and, after being fined three thousand dollars and given a suspended thirty-day prison sentence by Judge Ganey, found a job elsewhere, at ten thousand dollars a year.)

This was not Vinson's only brush with the case. He was also among those named in one of the grand jury indictments that precipitated the court action, this time in connection not with his comprehension of Smith's jargon but with the conspiracy in the switchgear department. On this aspect of the case, four switchgear executives—Burens, Stehlik, Clarence E. Burke, and H. Frank Hentschel—testified before the grand jury (and later before the Subcommittee) that at some time in July, August, or September of 1958 (none of them could establish the precise date) Vinson had had lunch with them in Dining Room B of G.E.'s switchgear works in Philadelphia, and that during the meal he had instructed them to hold price meetings with competitors. As a result of this order, they said, a meeting attended by representatives of G.E., Westinghouse, the Allis-Chalmers Manufacturing Company, the Federal Pacific Electric Company, and the I-T-E Circuit Breaker Company was held at the Hotel Traymore in Atlantic City on November 9, 1958, at which sales of switchgear to federal, state, and municipal agencies were divvied up, with General Electric to get 39 percent of the business, Westinghouse 35 percent, I-T-E 11 percent, Allis-Chalmers 8 percent, and Federal Pacific Electric 7 percent. At subsequent meetings, agreement was reached on allocating sales of switchgear to private buyers as well, and an elaborate formula was worked out whereby the privilege of submitting the lowest bid to prospective customers was rotated among the conspiring companies at two-week intervals. Because of its periodic nature, this was called the phase-of-the-moon formula—a designation that in due time led to the following lyrical exchange between the Subcommittee and L. W. Long, an executive of Allis-Chalmers:

SENATOR KEFAUVER: Who were the phasers-of-the-mooners—phase-of-the-mooners?

MR. LONG: As it developed, this so-called phase-of-the-moon operation was carried out at a level below me, I think referred to as a working group. . . .

MR. FERRALL [counsel for the Subcommittee]: Did they ever report to you about it?

MR. LONG: Phase of the moon? No.

Vinson told the Justice Department prosecutors, and repeated to the Subcommittee, that he had not known about the Traymore meeting, the phase-of-the-mooners, or the existence of the conspiracy itself until the case broke; as for the lunch in Dining Room B, he insisted that it had never taken place. On this point, Burens, Stehlik, Burke, and Hentschel submitted to lie-detector tests, administered by the F.B.I., and passed them. Vinson refused to take a lie-detector test, at first explaining that he was acting on advice of counsel and against his personal inclination, and later, after hearing how the four men had fared, arguing that if the machine had not pronounced them liars, it couldn't be any good. It was established that on only eight business days during July, August, and September had Burens, Burke, Stehlik, and Hentschel all been together in the Philadelphia plant at the lunch hour, and Vinson produced some of his expense accounts, which, he pointed out to the Justice Department, showed that he had been elsewhere on each of those days. Confronted with this evidence, the Justice Department dropped its case against Vinson, and he has stayed on as a vice-president of General Electric. Nothing that the Subcommittee elicited from him cast any substantive doubt on the defense that had impressed the government prosecutors.

Thus, the uppermost echelon at G.E. came through unscathed; the record showed that participation in the conspiracy went fairly far down in the organization but not all the way to the top. Gezon, everybody agreed, had followed orders from Stehlik, and Stehlik had followed orders from Burens, but that was the end of the trail, because although Burens said he had followed orders from Vinson, Vinson denied it and made the denial stick. The government, at the end of its investigation, stated in court that it could not prove, and did not claim, that either Chairman Cordiner or President Paxton had authorized, or even known about, the conspiracies, and thereby officially ruled out the possibility that they had resorted to at least a figurative wink. Later, Paxton and Cordiner showed up in Washington to testify before the Subcommittee, and its interrogators were similarly unable to establish that they had ever indulged in any variety of winking.

After being described by Ginn as General Electric's stubbornest and most dedicated advocate of free competition, Paxton explained to the Subcommittee that his thinking on the subject had been influenced not directly by Adam Smith but, rather, by way of a former G.E. boss he had worked under—the late Gerard Swope. Swope, Paxton testified, had always believed firmly that the ultimate goal of business was to produce more goods for more people at lower cost. "I bought that then, I buy it now," said Paxton. "I think it is the most marvelous statement of economic

philosophy that any industrialist has ever expressed." In the course of his testimony, Paxton had an explanation, philosophical or otherwise, of each of the several situations related to price-fixing in which his name had earlier been mentioned. For instance, it had been brought out that in 1956 or 1957 a young man named Jerry Page, a minor employee in G.E.'s switchgear division, had written directly to Cordiner alleging that the switchgear divisions of G.E. and of several competitor companies were involved in a conspiracy in which information about prices was exchanged by means of a secret code based on different colors of letter paper. Cordiner had turned the matter over to Paxton with orders that he get to the bottom of it, and Paxton had thereupon conducted an investigation that led him to conclude that the color-code conspiracy was "wholly a hallucination on the part of this boy." In arriving at that conclusion, Paxton had apparently been right, although it later came out that there had been a conspiracy in the switchgear division during 1956 and 1957; this, however, was a rather conventional one, based simply on price-fixing meetings, rather than on anything so gaudy as a color code. Page could not be called to testify because of ill health.

Paxton conceded that there had been some occasions when he "must have been pretty damn dumb." (Dumb or not, for his services as the company's president he was, of course, remunerated on a considerably grander scale than Vinson —receiving a basic annual salary of $125,000, plus annual incentive compensation of about $175,000, plus stock options designed to enable him to collect much more, at the comparatively low tax rate on capital gains, if General Electric's stock should go up.) As for Paxton's attitude toward company communications, he emerges as a pessimist on this score. Upon being asked at the hearings to comment on the Smith-Vinson conversations of 1957, he said that, knowing Smith, he just could not "cast the man in the role of a liar," and went on:

When I was younger, I used to play a good deal of bridge. We played about fifty rubbers of bridge, four of us, every winter, and I think we probably played some rather good bridge. If you gentlemen are bridge players, you know that there is a code of signals that is exchanged between partners as the game progresses. It is a stylized form of playing. . . . Now, as I think about this—and I was particularly impressed when I read Smith's testimony when he talked about a "meeting of the clan" or "meeting of the boys"—I began to think that there must have been a stylized method of communication between these people who were dealing with competition. Now, Smith could say, "I told Vinson what I was doing," and Vinson wouldn't have the foggiest idea what was being told to him, and both men could testify under oath, one saying yes and the other man saying no, and both be telling the truth. . . . [They] wouldn't be on the same wavelength. [They] wouldn't have the same meanings. I think, I believe now that these men did think that they were telling the truth, but they weren't communicating between each other with understanding.

Here, certainly, is the gloomiest possible analysis of the communications problem.

Chairman Cordiner's status, it appears from his testimony, was approximately that of the Boston Cabots in the celebrated jingle. His services to the company, for which he was recompensed in truly handsome style (with, for 1960, a salary of just over $280,000, plus contingent deferred income of about $120,000, plus stock options potentially worth hundreds of thousands more), were indubitably many and valuable, but they were performed on such an exalted level that, at least in antitrust matters, he does not seem to have been able to have any earthly communication at all. When he emphatically told the Subcommittee that at no time had he had so much as an inkling of the network of conspiracies, it could be deduced that his was a case not of faulty communication but of no communication. He did not speak to the Subcommittee of philosophy or philosophers, as Ginn and Paxton had done, but from his past record of ordering reissues of 20.5 and of peppering his speeches and public statements with praise of free enterprise, it seems clear that he was *un philosophe sans le savoir*—and one on the side of selling the Lord, since no evidence was adduced to suggest that he was given to winking in any form. Kefauver ran through a long list of antitrust violations of which General Electric had been accused over the past half-century, asking Cordiner, who joined the company in 1922, how much he knew about each of them; usually, he replied that he had known about them only after the fact. In commenting on Ginn's testimony that Erben had countermanded Cordiner's direct order in 1954, Cordiner said that he had read it with "great alarm" and "great wonderment," since Erben had always indicated to him "an intense competitive spirit," rather than any disposition to be friendly with rival companies.

Throughout his testimony, Cordiner used the curious expression "be responsive to." If, for instance, Kefauver inadvertently asked the same question twice, Cordiner would say, "I was responsive to that a moment ago," or if Kefauver interrupted him, as he often did, Cordiner would ask politely, "May I be responsive?" This, too, offers a small lead for a foundation grantee, who might want to look into the distinction between being responsive (a passive state) and answering (an act), and their relative effectiveness in the process of communication.

Summing up his position on the case as a whole, in reply to a question of Kefauver's about whether he thought that G.E. had incurred "corporate disgrace," Cordiner said, "No, I am not going to be responsive and say that General Electric had corporate disgrace. I am going to say that we are deeply grieved and concerned. . . . I am not proud of it."

Chairman Cordiner, then, had been able to fairly deafen his subordinate officers with lectures on compliance with the rules of the company and the laws of the country, but he had not been able to get all those officers to comply with either, and President Paxton could muse thoughtfully on how it was that two of his subordinates who had given radically different accounts of a conversation between them could be not liars but merely poor communicators. Philosophy seems to have reached a high point at G.E., and communication a low one. If executives could just learn to understand one another, most of the witnesses said or implied, the problem of antitrust violations would be solved. But perhaps the problem is cultural as well as technical, and has something to do with a loss of personal identity that comes from working in a huge organization. The cartoonist Jules Feiffer, contemplating the communication problem in a nonindustrial context, has said, "Actually, the breakdown is between the person and himself. If you're not able to communicate successfully between yourself and yourself, how are you supposed to make it with the strangers outside?" Suppose, purely as a hypothesis, that the owner of a company who orders his subordinates to obey the antitrust laws has such poor communication with himself that he does not really know whether he wants the order to be complied with or not. If his order is disobeyed, the resulting price-fixing may benefit his company's coffers; if it is obeyed, then he has done the right thing. In the first instance, he is not personally implicated in any wrongdoing, while in the second he is positively involved in *right*doing. What, after all, can he lose? It is perhaps reasonable to suppose that such an executive might communicate his uncertainty more force-fully than his order. Possibly yet another foundation grantee should have a look at the reverse of communication failure, where he might discover that messages the sender does not even realize he is sending sometimes turn out to have got across only too effectively.

Meanwhile, in the first year after the Subcommittee concluded its investigation, the defendant companies were by no means allowed to forget their transgressions. The law permits customers who can prove that they have paid artificially high prices as a result of antitrust violations to sue for damages—in most cases, triple damages—and suits running into many millions of dollars soon began piling up. (By January, 1962, they had piled up so high that Chief Justice Warren set up a special panel of federal judges to plan how they should all be handled.) Needless to say, Cordiner was not allowed to forget about the matter, either; indeed, it would be surprising if he was allowed a chance to think about much else, for, in addition to the suits, he had to contend with active efforts by a minority group of stockholders to unseat him. Paxton retired as president in April, 1961, because of ill health dating back at least to the previous January, when he underwent a major operation. As for the executives who pleaded guilty and were fined or imprisoned, most of those who had been employed by companies other than G.E. remained with them, either in their old jobs or in similar ones. Of those who had been employed by G.E., none remained there. Some retired permanently from business, others settled for comparatively small jobs, and a few landed big ones—most spectacularly Ginn, who in June, 1961, became president of Baldwin-Lima-Hamilton, manufacturers of heavy machinery. And as for the future of price-fixing in the electrical industry, it seems safe to say that what with the Justice Department, Judge Ganey, Senator Kefauver, and the triple-damage suits, the impact on the philosophers who guide corporate policy has been such that they, and even their subordinates, are likely to try to hew scrupulously to the line for quite some time. Quite a different question, however, is whether they have made any headway in their ability to communicate.

READING 38

Very different issues from those posed in the last reading arise where two independent producers propose to merge. In the case of alleged collusion, the court's task is to determine whether or not the collusion did in fact occur; if it did, then the law has been broken. But in the case of a merger, the issues are judgmental ones where reasonable men may reasonably differ; it is seldom crystal clear whether the merger will aid or reduce competition and hence whether the law condones or condemns it.

Big Steel makes big news. (See "The 72-Hour Drama in Steel," page 210.) So, when Bethlehem Steel and Youngstown Sheet & Tube announced in 1956 that they planned to unite to offer more effective competition in the steel industry, governmental eyebrows were raised. An antitrust suit was filed in court to prevent the merger, and the legal skirmish began. Two years and 20,000 pages of materials later, the government obtained the injunction which it had sought. The merger proposal died, and each company went on with its own independent expansion plans.

The U.S. District Court for the Southern District of New York, in which the decision below was rendered, is the setting for many of the most complex and important law cases in the country. Judge Edward Weinfeld had had eight years of service on this distinguished Manhattan-based court when he was called upon to hear the Bethlehem-Youngstown merger case.

Questions to Guide the Reading

What tests should we apply in deciding whether any proposed merger should be forbidden? What meaning, for example, should be given to the test cited in the

Clayton Act which prohibits mergers that *"substantially* lessen competition, or tend to create a monopoly"?

Are we to use different tests in deciding whether a proposed merger may proceed and whether an existing giant should be broken up? Is the effect of the court's decision here to say to Bethlehem and Youngstown that they may not do what United States Steel had done at an earlier date in melting a number of independent producers into the industry's dominant firm? If so, is this equitable?

Who is protected by the court decision here: The consumers of steel? United States Steel? Other producers?

MERGERS AND COMPETITION: THE CASE OF THE STEEL INDUSTRY
U.S. District Court, Southern District of New York

It is clear that the acquisition of Youngstown, by Bethlehem, would violate Section 7 in that in each of the relevant markets considered the effect may be substantially to lessen competition or to tend to create a monopoly.

The proposed merger would eliminate the present substantial competition between Bethlehem and Youngstown in substantial relevant markets. It would eliminate substantial potential competition between them. It would eliminate a substantial independent alternative source of supply for all steel consumers. It would eliminate Youngstown as a vital source of supply for independent fabricators who are in competition with Bethlehem in the sale of certain fabricated steel products. It would eliminate Youngstown as a substantial buyer of certain fabricated steel products.

One final matter remains to be considered. The defendants urge earnestly that in considering the impact on competition of the proposed merger the court take into account what they point to as its beneficial aspects. Any lessening of competition resulting from the merger should be balanced, they say, against the benefits which would accrue from Bethlehem's plan to expand the Youngstown plants thus creating new steel capacity in an existing deficit area and enhancing the power of the merged company to give United States Steel more effective and vigorous competition than Bethlehem and Youngstown can now give separately.

We pass for the moment the question of whether or not this contention is anything more than an expression of good intention and high purpose.

The substance of their argument is: the steel mills in and around the Chicago area lack sufficient plant capacity to satisfy demand in that area, especially for heavy structural shapes and plates; these have been in critical short supply for years and the lag has been supplied by distant steel producers at excessive freight costs and premium prices. The defendants contend that the situation will become more acute in the years ahead and that the shortage has already resulted in new steel-consuming industries locating their plants in other regions of the country—a "kind of chain reaction [which] is a wasteful drag on the country's economic resources." The defendants say a remedy is sorely needed "and that the merger will unquestionably provide that remedy." In essence this summarizes their justification for the merger.

A major purpose of Section 7 is to ward off the anticompetitive effects of increases "in the level of economic concentration resulting from corporate mergers and acquisitions." Both the Senate and House Committee reports emphasized the deep concern of the Congress with the continued trend toward concentration of economic power through mergers and acquisitions. An immediate result of the proposed merger would be increased concentration of power in the No. 2 colossus of the steel industry by its absorption of No. 6—another giant.

The merger would substantially increase concentration in the nation-wide market for all the products of the iron and steel industry when viewed in terms of blast furnace capacity and production, ingot capacity and production, shipments of total finished steel products and ship-

From *United States v. Bethlehem Steel Corporation and Youngstown Sheet & Tube Company* (U.S. District Court, S.D.N.Y., November 20, 1958).

ments of "common finished steel products." In terms of each of these four guides the percentage of the market represented by Bethlehem is approximately 15 per cent and that by Youngstown about 5 per cent. The proposed merger would thus involve approximately 20 per cent of the nation-wide market for all the products of the iron and steel industry.

At present the two largest companies, United States Steel and Bethlehem, own 45 per cent of ingot capacity. If Bethlehem were to acquire Youngstown the Big 2 would have 50 per cent. At present United States Steel with approximately 30 per cent of the industry capacity exercises price leadership and sets the price pattern for the industry. Bethlehem, as well as all other steel producers, follows the prices set by United States Steel. Bethlehem even follows in the instance of products of which it is the largest producer. Against this pattern of price behavior in an oligopoly framework, it is apparent that an additional increase in concentration amounting to 5 per cent would be a further detriment to competition.

In sum, the merger of Bethlehem and Youngstown would bring together the second and sixth largest integrated steel companies with 23,000,000 and 6,500,000 tons of ingot capacity, respectively, giving Bethlehem almost 21 per cent of the industry capacity. This would add substantially to concentration in an already highly concentrated industry and reduce unduly the already limited number of integrated steel companies. The merger would increase concentration in the hands of the Big 4 and the next three companies to United States Steel by 4.6 percentage points.

Adding 5 per cent to Bethlehem's 16 per cent of industry capacity would not only intensify the existing concentration in the industry as a whole but would increase unduly the concentrated power in the Big 12 as against the reduced number of an already severely limited group. Instead of twelve producers controlling 83 per cent of total industry capacity there would be only eleven; instead of the Big 2 controlling 45 per cent as against the present ten with their 38 per cent, they would control 50 per cent as against the remaining nine with 33 per cent. There would be a stronger Bethlehem to contend with. There would be an even more powerful Big 2 to contend with. It is clearly the kind of further concentration in an oligopoly framework. That Congress was concerned with. "Tend to create a monopoly" clearly includes aggravation of an existing oligopoly situation.

These considerations compel the conclusion that the merger offends the statute, and that in end result there is more than a reasonable probability that it would substantially lessen competition and tend to create a monopoly. But apart from the adverse consequence of increased concentration of economic power, other factors even more directly establish that there would, in fact and in immediate terms, be a substantial lessening of competition—the elimination of actual and direct competition between the defendants.

The fact that Bethlehem has maintained the position it has achieved through mergers clearly indicates that the elimination of Youngstown's share of the market as an independent factor in competition would in all probability be permanent. The prospect of a new entrant to replace an absorbed Youngstown, either in terms of capital investment or experience, is, in the light of the history of this industry, practically nil. Since 1935 only two new integrated steel companies have been established in the iron and steel industry, Kaiser Steel Corporation and Lone Star Steel Company. Both companies entered the iron and steel industry with substantial Government assistance and together account for only 1.6 per cent of total industry ingot capacity.

More than one-fifth of both Bethlehem's and Youngstown's sales of cold rolled sheets throughout the country in 1955 were delivered to common customers in Michigan and Ohio—principally to the leading automobile manufacturers, General Motors, Chrysler and Ford. These shipments amounted to 898,000 tons representing 5.9 per cent of total industry shipments throughout the nation. The substantiality of these shipments is manifest when it is seen that 898,000 tons is greater than the capacity of all but seven of the twenty-one companies producing cold rolled sheets in the United States and is greater than the total capacity for cold rolled sheets of such companies as Ford, Inland, Wheeling, Detroit and McLouth. Youngstown, which would be eliminated as an independent supplier to these customers, accounted for 263,000 of the 898,000 tons.

The defendants, recognizing the force of this situation, suggest that the automobile companies, giants in another giant industry, are each so powerful that they are able to fend for themselves to meet any problem posed by the elimination of Youngstown as a substantial and independent source of supply—in the language of the defendants the automobile companies with their tremendous bargaining power "have many alternative sources of supply and can easily hold such sources in line by playing one off against another."

However, the automobile companies in their efforts to adjust to the merger may well deprive smaller consumers, requiring the same steel products, of their sources of supply.

Moreover, the Congress in its efforts to preserve the free-enterprise system and the benefits to flow to the nation and to the consuming public did not, in enacting the antitrust laws, intend to give free play to the balancing power of gigantic enterprises and leave the less powerful purchaser helpless. What the Congress sought to preserve was a social and economic order not dependent on the power of a few to take care of themselves.

What is planned under the proposed merger is an expansion of the ingot capacity of Youngstown's two existing plants, one at Chicago and the other at Youngstown, by 2,588,000 tons, and a new plate mill and a new structural shape mill at Youngstown's Chicago plant with combined capacity of 1,176,000 tons. The plan also provides for a modernization program which would increase capacity to roll certain products at the Chicago and Youngstown plants. This part of the plan is unrelated to the structural shape and plate program.

It is undoubtedly easier and cheaper to acquire and develop existing plant capacity than to build entirely anew. Each defendant in urging the merger takes a dim view of its ability to undertake, on its own, a program to meet the existing and anticipated demand for heavy structural shapes and plates in the Chicago area.

Youngstown claims it is without the know-how, the experienced personnel or the requisite capital to enter into the structural shape and plate business. Bethlehem, acknowledging it has the know-how and the experience in that field, contends that the construction of an entirely new fully integrated plant in the Chicago area of 2,500,000 tons of ingot capacity is not economically feasible. It estimates that such a new plant would cost $750,000,000 (or $300 per ton of ingot capacity) as compared to $358,000,000 (or $135 per ton ingot capacity) for expansion of Youngstown's existing plants under the plan outlined above. Bethlehem also rules out as uneconomical the construction of a new plant in the Chicago area limited to structural shape and plate mills.

The defendants' apprehensions, which, of course, involve matters of business judgment and, in a sense, matters of preference, are not persuasive in the light of their prior activities and history, their financial resources, their growth and demonstrated capacity through the years to meet the challenge of a constantly growing economy.

Over the decades Bethlehem has grown through mergers and acquisitions; it has grown internally; it has not only maintained but bettered its position in a highly concentrated industry; it has never lacked the financial resources or the effective means required to expand and keep pace with the increased demands of our national economy.

From an ingot capacity of 212,800 tons in 1905 Bethelehem's capacity reached 23,000,000 by Jan. 1, 1958. During the nine year period from Jan. 1, 1948 to Jan. 1, 1957, it expanded its ingot capacity from 13,800,000 tons to 20,500,000 tons, an increase of 6,700,000 tons of 48.6 per cent. Over the five year period from 1953 to 1958 the percentage increase was 30.7 per cent.

The fact is that within one year of the commencement of this action to enjoin the merger, Bethlehem increased its steel capacity by 2,500,000 tons. The significance of this increase is apparent when it is noted that as of Jan. 1, 1957, there were in the United States eighty-four companies with steel ingot capacity, of which seventy-five had a total capacity of less than 2,500,000 tons.

Youngstown no less than Bethlehem has demonstrated ability to keep pace with the demands of our growing economy. Youngstown expanded from an ingot capacity of 806,400 tons in 1906 to 6,500,000 tons by Jan. 1, 1958. During the nine year period from Jan. 1, 1948 to Jan. 1, 1957 it expanded its ingot capacity from 4,002,000 tons to 6,240,000—an increase of 2,238,000 or 55.9 per cent. Over the five year period from 1953 to 1958 its ingot capacity grew 31.4 per cent.

Youngstown, too, has been a vigorous factor in the steel industry. Its position as No. 6 casts it in the role of one of the giants of that mammoth industry. Through the years it has carried on a regular expansion program. In 1955, without regard to the merger, it projected a comprehensive future development plan, part of which has already been put into effect.

During the 10-year period, 1947–56, Youngstown made capital expenditures of $53,000,000.

A fact not to be overlooked—indeed one to be underscored—is that no adverse factor justifies Youngstown's participation in the proposed merger. Indeed for a number of years the return on its invested capital was greater than that earned by either United States Steel or Bethlehem. No financial stringency, present or threatened, justifies its absorption by Bethlehem.

The Court is not persuaded that the proposed merger is the only way in which the supply of plates and shapes in the Chicago area can be expanded. Other steel producers are capable of meeting the challenge. In fact both United States Steel and Inland are in the process of expanding their capacities in the Chicago area for structural shapes and United States Steel is also expanding its capacity for plates in that area.

In essence, the defendants are maintaining that a proposed capacity increase of 1,176,000 tons in the Chicago area for plates and structural shapes counter-balances a merger between companies which produced over 24,000,000 tons of ingots and shipped almost 15,500,000 tons of a great variety of finished steel products in 1955. It has already been noted that hot rolled sheets, cold rolled sheets and hot rolled bars are the three most important products of the iron and steel industry and that Bethlehem and Youngstown are substantial and important factors in the production of these key products.

Plates and structural shapes are substantially less important in terms of tonnage than hot and cold rolled sheets and hot rolled bars. Assuming the relevance of the argument, the defendants have failed to establish counter-balancing benefits to offset the substantial lessening of competition which would result from the merger.

Not only do the facts fail to support the defendants' contention, but the argument does not hold up as a matter of law. If the merger offends the statute in any relevant market then good motives and even demonstrable benefits are irrelevant and afford no defense. Section 7 "is violated whether or not actual restraints or monopolies, or the substantial lessening of competition have occurred or are intended."

The antitrust laws articulate the policy formulated by Congress. The significance and objectives of the Clayton Act and the 1950 amendment are well documented. In approving the policy embodied in these acts, Congress rejected the alleged advantages of size in favor of the preservation of a competitive system. The consideration to be accorded to benefits of one kind or another in one section or another of the country which may flow from a merger involving a substantial lessening of competition is a matter properly to be urged upon Congress. It is outside the province of the Court. The simple test under Section 7 is whether or not the merger may substantially lessen competition "in any line of commerce in any section of the country."

Any alleged benefit to the steel consumer in the Chicago district because of reduced freight charges and an increased supply cannot, under the law, be bought at the expense of other consumers of numerous other steel products where the effects of the merger violate the act. A merger may have a different impact in different markets—but if the proscribed effect is visited on one or more relevant markets then it matters not what the claimed benefits may be elsewhere.

And for that matter, with respect to oil field equipment and supplies, as separate lines of commerce, the contention itself is by its own terms unavailing. Amended Section 7 as stated in the committee reports ". . . is intended [to prohibit] acquisitions which substantially lessen competition, as well as those which tend to create a monopoly . . . if they have the specified effect in any line of commerce, whether or not that line of commerce is a large part of the business of any of the corporations involved in the acquisition. . . . The purpose of the bill is to protect competition in each line of commerce in each section of the country."

The merger offers an incipient threat of setting into motion a chain of reaction of further mergers by the other but less powerful companies in the steel industry. If there is logic to the defendants' contention that their joinder is justified to enable them, in their own language, to offer "challenging competition to United States Steel . . . which exercises dominant influence over competitive conditions in the steel industry . . ." then the remaining large producers in the "Big Twelve" could with equal logic urge that they, too, be permitted to join forces and to concentrate their economic resources in order to give more effective competition to the enhanced "Big Two"; and so we reach a point of more intense concentration in an industry already highly concentrated—indeed we head in the direction of triopoly.

Congress in seeking to halt the growing tendency to increased concentration of power in various industries was fully aware of the arguments in support of the supposed advantages of size and the claim of greater efficiency and lower cost to the ultimate consumer. It made no distinction between good mergers and bad mergers. It condemned all which came within the reach of the prohibition of Section 7. The function of the Court is to carry out declared Congressional policy. "Though our preference were for monopoly and against competition, we should 'guard against the danger of sliding unconsciously from the narrow confines of law into the more spacious domain of policy'." The Court must take the statute as written.

The proposed merger runs afoul of the prohibition of the statute in so many directions that to permit it, is to render Section 7 sterile. To say that the elimination of Youngstown would not result in "a significant reduction in the vigor of competition" in the steel industry is, in the light of its history, to disregard experience.

The Court concludes that there is a reasonable probability that the merger of Bethlehem and Youngstown would, in violation of Section 7, substantially lessen competition and tend to create a monopoly in:

(1) the iron and steel industry,
(2) hot rolled sheets,
(3) cold rolled sheets and
(4) hot rolled bars, in

(a) the United States as a whole,
(b) the northeast quadrant of the United States
(c) Michigan, Ohio, Pennsylvania and New York,
(d) Michigan and Ohio,
(e) Michigan, and
(f) Ohio
(5) buttweld pipe,
(6) electricweld pipe,
(7) seamless pipe,
(8) oil field equipment,
(9) oil field equipment and supplies,
(10) tin plate,
(11) track spikes, and
(12) wire rope, in
(a) the United States as a whole.

Submit decree within ten days, in accordance with the foregoing and the further enumerated findings of fact and conclusions of law filed herewith, enjoining the proposed merger as violative of Section 7 of the Clayton Act.

READING 39

Conventional views of competition in our economy tend to look at the practices of different firms in the same industry or product market. This is the view underlying the court decision in the Bethlehem-Youngstown case, for example. (See page 241.)

But one of the most challenging views on markets has been that which looked beyond an industry or a product to the end use and found competition in the whole process of innovations to meet that end need through new products or processes. That view represents an effective capstone to all the earlier readings in this section; it makes it abundantly clear that, just as competition is dynamic, so too is our understanding of its workings.

Joseph Schumpeter, late professor of economics at Harvard University, is the major name associated with this view. Here he argues that certain of the most criticized aspects of capitalism are in fact essential features in its record of progress. The literature of economics has few pieces to stand alongside the work of Schumpeter.

Questions to Guide the Reading

Is the Schumpeter view of competition at odds with or complementary to the view of, say, Slichter (page 171)?

Are there important prerequisites for the process of "creative destruction" to be operative? Are those conditions met with in all or most of the American economy?

What are the implications of the Schumpeter view for current antitrust policy in the United States?

CAPITALISM AND ECONOMIC PROGRESS
Joseph A. Schumpeter

We have a considerable body of statistical data descriptive of a rate of "progress" [under capitalism] that has been admired even by very critical minds. On the other hand, we have a body of facts about the structure of the economic system and about the way it functioned. We wish to know whether that type of economy was favorable, irrelevant, or unfavorable to the performance we observe.

Profits vs. welfare?

Unlike the class of feudal lords, the commercial and industrial bourgeoisie rose by business success. Bourgeois society has been cast in a purely economic mold. Prizes and penalties are measured in pecuniary terms. Going up and going down means making and losing money. This, of course, nobody can deny. But I wish to add that, within its own frame, that social arrangement is, or at all events was, singularly effective. The promises of wealth and the threats of destitution that it holds out, it redeems with ruthless promptitude. Wherever the bourgeois way of life asserts itself sufficiently to dim the beacons of other social worlds, these promises are strong enough to attract the large majority of supernormal brains and to identify success with business success. They are not proffered at random; yet there is a sufficiently enticing admixture of chance: the game is not like roulette, it is more like poker. Spectacular prizes much greater than would have been necessary to call forth the particular effort are thrown to a small minority of winners, thus propelling much more efficaciously than a more equal and more "just" distribution would, the activity of that large majority of businessmen who receive in return very modest compensation or nothing or less than nothing, and yet do their utmost because they have the big prizes before their eyes and overrate their chances of doing equally well. Similarly, the threats are addressed to incompetence. But though the incompetent men and the obsolete methods are in fact eliminated, sometimes very promptly, sometimes with a lag, failure also threatens or actually overtakes many an able man, thus whipping up *everyone*,

again much more efficaciously than a more equal and more "just" system of penalties would. Finally, both business success and business failure are ideally precise. Neither can be talked away.

In most cases the man who rises first *into* the business class and then *within* it is also an able businessman and he is likely to rise exactly as far as his ability goes. This fact, so often obscured by the auto-therapeutic effort of the unsuccessful to deny it, is much more important than anything that can be gleaned from the pure theory of the capitalist machine.

But is not all that we might be tempted to infer from "maximum performance of an optimally selected group" invalidated by the further fact that it aims at maximizing profits instead of welfare? Outside of the bourgeois stratum, this has of course always been the popular opinion. Economists have sometimes fought and sometimes espoused it.

The so-called classical economists disliked many things about the social institutions of their epoch and about the way those institutions worked. They fought the landed interest and approved of social reforms—factory legislation in particular—that were not all on the lines of *laissez faire*. But they were quite convinced that within the institutional framework of capitalism, the manufacturer's and the trader's self-interest made for maximum performance in the interest of all. Confronted with the problem we are discussing, they would have had little hesitation in attributing the observed rate of increase in total output to relatively unfettered enterprise and the profit motive.

It is exceedingly difficult, at this hour of the day, to do justice to these views. They were of course the typical views of the English bourgeois class, and bourgeois blinkers are in evidence on almost every page the classical authors wrote. No less in evidence are blinkers of another kind: the classics reasoned in terms of a particular historical situation which they uncritically idealized and from which they uncritically generalized. Most of them, moreover, seem to have argued exclusively in terms of the English interests and problems of their time. This is the reason why, in

From Joseph A. Schumpeter, *Capitalism, Socialism, and Democracy* (Harper & Brothers, New York, 1942), pp. 73–92. Reprinted with kind permission of Mrs. Joseph A. Schumpeter and the publisher.

other lands and at other times, people disliked their economics, frequently to the point of not even caring to understand it. But it will not do to dismiss their teaching on these grounds. A prejudiced man may yet be speaking the truth. Propositions developed from special cases may yet be generally valid. And the enemies and successors of the classics had and have only different but not fewer blinkers and preconceptions; they envisaged and envisage different but not less special cases.

From the standpoint of the economic analyst, the chief merit of the classics consists in their dispelling, along with many other gross errors, the naïve idea that economic activity in capitalist society, because it turns on the profit motive, must by virtue of that fact alone necessarily run counter to the interests of consumers.

This later analysis we will take in two strides—as much of it, that is, as we need in order to clarify our problem. Historically, the first will carry us into the first decade of this century, the second will cover some of the postwar developments of scientific economics. Frankly I do not know how much good this will do the non-professional reader; like every other branch of our knowledge, economics, as its analytic engine improves, moves fatally away from that happy stage in which all problems, methods, and results could be made accessible to every educated person without special training. I will, however, do my best.

The profit motive under perfect competition

The first stride may be associated with two great names revered to this day by numberless disciples—so far at least as the latter do not think it bad form to express reverence for anything or anybody, which many of them obviously do—Alfred Marshall and Knut Wicksell. Their theoretical structure has little in common with that of the classics, but it conserves the classic proposition that in the case of perfect competition the profit interest of the producer tends to maximize production. It even supplies almost satisfactory proof. It can be shown that firms which cannot by their own individual action exert any influence upon the price of their products or of the factors of production they employ will expand their output until they reach the point at which the additional cost that must be incurred in order to produce another small increment of product (marginal cost) just equals the price they can

get for that increment. And this can be shown to be as much as it is in general "socially desirable" to produce. Where this is so, there exists a state of equilibrium in which all outputs are at their maximum and all factors fully employed. This case is usually referred to as perfect competition.

The profit motive under monopolistic competition

Let us take the second stride. The classics recognized cases of "monopoly," and Adam Smith himself carefully noticed the prevalence of devices to restrict competition and all the differences in flexibility of prices resulting therefrom. But they looked upon those cases as exceptions and, moreover, as exceptions that could and would be done away with in time. If we look more closely at the conditions that must be fulfilled in order to produce perfect competition, we realize immediately that outside of agricultural mass production there cannot be many instances of it. A farmer supplies his cotton or wheat in fact under those conditions: from his standpoint the ruling prices of cotton or wheat are data, though very variable ones, and not being able to influence them by his individual action he simply adapts his output; since all farmers do the same, prices and quantities will in the end be adjusted as the theory of perfect competition requires. But this is not so even with many agricultural products—with ducks, sausages, vegetables and many dairy products for instance. And as regards practically all the finished products and services of industry and trade, it is clear that every grocer, every filling station, every manufacturer of gloves or shaving cream or handsaws has a small and precarious market of his own which he tries to build up and to keep by price strategy, quality strategy, "product differentiation," and advertising. Thus we get a completely different pattern which there seems to be no reason to expect to yield the results of perfect competition. In these cases we speak of Monopolistic Competition. Their theory has been one of the major contributions to [recent] economics.

There remains a wide field of substantially homogeneous products such as steel ingots, cement, cotton gray goods and the like—in which the conditions for the emergence of monopolistic competition do not seem to prevail. This is so. But in general, similar results follow for that field inasmuch as the greater part of it is covered by largest-scale firms which, either individually or in concert, are able to manipulate prices even without differentiating products—the case of Oligopoly.

As soon as the prevalence of monopolistic competition or of oligopoly or of combinations of the two is recognized, many of the propositions which economists used to teach with the utmost confidence become either inapplicable or much more difficult to prove. The "beneficial" competition of the classic type seems likely to be replaced by "predatory" or "cutthroat" competition or simply by struggles for control in the financial sphere. These things are so many sources of social waste, and there are many others such as the costs of advertising campaigns, the suppression of new methods of production (buying up of patents in order not to use them) and so on. And most important of all: under the conditions envisaged, equilibrium no longer guarantees either full employment or maximum output in the sense of the theory of perfect competition. It *may* exist without full employment; it is *bound* to exist, so it seems, at a level of output below that maximum mark, because profit-conserving strategy, impossible in conditions of perfect competition, now not only becomes possible but imposes itself.

Well, does not this bear out what the man in the street (unless a businessman himself) always thought on the subject of private business? Has not modern analysis completely refuted the classical doctrine and justified the popular view? Is it not quite true after all, that there is little parallelism between producing for profit and producing for the consumer and that private enterprise is little more than a device to curtail production in order to extort profits which then are correctly described as tolls and ransoms?

These conclusions are in fact almost completely false. Yet they follow from observations that are almost completely true. But economists and popular writers have once more run away with some fragments of reality they happened to grasp. These fragments themselves were mostly seen correctly. But no conclusions about capitalist reality as a whole follow from such fragmentary analyses.

Most important of all, the modern standard of life of the masses evolved during the period of relatively unfettered "big business." If we list the items that enter the modern workman's budget and from 1899 on observe the course of their prices not in terms of money but in terms of the hours of labor that will buy them—i.e., each year's money prices divided by each year's hourly wage rates—we cannot fail to be struck by the rate of the advance which, considering the spectacular improvement in qualities, seems to have been greater and not smaller than it ever was before. If we economists were given less to wishful thinking and more to the observation of facts, doubts would immediately arise as to the realistic virtues of a theory that would have led us to expect a very different result. Nor is this all. As soon as we go into details and inquire into the individual items in which progress was most conspicuous, the trail leads not to the doors of those firms that work under conditions of comparatively free competition but precisely to the doors of the large concerns—which, as in the case of agricultural machinery, also account for much of the progress in the competitive sector—and a shocking suspicion dawns upon us that big business may have had more to do with creating that standard of life than with keeping it down.

The process of creative destruction

The essential point to grasp is that in dealing with capitalism we are dealing with an evolutionary process. It may seem strange that anyone can fail to see so obvious a fact which moreover was long ago emphasized by Karl Marx.

Capitalism is by nature a form or method of economic change and not only never is but never can be stationary. And this evolutionary character of the capitalist process is not merely due to the fact that economic life goes on in a social and natural environment which changes. Nor is this evolutionary character due to a quasi-automatic increase in population and capital or to the vagaries of monetary systems. The fundamental impulse that sets and keeps the capitalist engine in motion comes from the new consumers' goods, the new methods of production or transportation, the new markets, the new forms of industrial organization that capitalist enterprise creates.

The contents of the laborer's budget, say from 1760 to 1940, did not simply grow on unchanging lines but they underwent a process of qualitative change. Similarly, the history of the productive apparatus of a typical farm, from the beginnings of the rationalization of crop rotation, plowing and fattening to the mechanized thing of today—linking up with elevators and railroads—is a history of revolutions. So is the history of the productive apparatus of the iron and steel industry from the charcoal furnace to to our own type of furnace, or the history of the apparatus of power production from the overshot water wheel to the modern power plant, or the history of transportation from the mailcoach to the airplane. The opening up of new markets, foreign or domestic, and the organizational development from the craft shop and factory to such concerns as U.S. Steel illustrate the same process of industrial mutation—if I may use that biological term—that incessantly revolutionizes the economic structure *from within,* incessantly destroying the old one, incessantly creating a new one. This process of Creative Destruction is the essential fact about capitalism. It is what capitalism consists in and what every capitalist concern has got to live in.

Since we are dealing with a process whose every element takes considerable time in revealing its true features and ultimate effects, there is no point in appraising the performance of the process [as] of a given point of time; we must judge its performance over time, as it unfolds through decades or centuries. A system that at *every point* of time fully utilizes its possibilities to the best advantage may yet in the long run be inferior to a system that does so at *no* given point of time, because the latter's failure to do so may be a condition for the level or speed of long-run performance.

Second, since we are dealing with an organic process, every piece of business strategy acquires its true significance only against the background of that process and within the situation created by it. It must be seen in its role in the perennial gale of creative destruction; it cannot be understood irrespective of it or, in fact, on the hypothesis that there is a perennial lull.

But economists look at the behavior of an oligopolist industry—an industry which consists of a few big firms—and observe the well-known moves and countermoves within it that seem to aim at nothing but high prices and restrictions of output. They accept the data of the momentary situation as if there were no past or future to it and think that they have understood what there is to understand if they interpret the behavior of those firms by means of the principle of maximizing profits with reference to those data. In other words, the problem that is usually being visualized is how capitalism administers existing structures, whereas the relevant problem is how it creates and destroys them.

In capitalist reality as distinguished from its textbook picture, competition which counts [is] the competition from the new commodity, the new technology, the new source of supply, the new type of organization (the large-scale unit of control for instance)—competition which commands a decisive cost or quality advantage and which strikes not at the margins of the profits and the outputs of the existing firms but at their foundations and their very lives. This kind of competition is so much more important that it becomes a matter of comparative indifference whether competition in the ordinary sense functions more or less promptly; the powerful lever that in the long run expands output and brings down prices is in any case made of other stuff.

It is hardly necessary to point out that competition of the kind we now have in mind acts not only when in being but also when it is merely an ever-present threat. It disciplines before it attacks. The businessman feels himself to be in a competitive situation even if he is alone in his field. In many cases, though not in all, this will in the long run enforce behavior very similar to the perfectly competitive pattern.

Many theorists take the opposite view which is best conveyed by an example. Let us assume that there is a certain number of retailers in a neighborhood who try to improve their relative position by service and "atmosphere" but avoid price competition and stick as to methods to the local tradition—a picture of stagnating routine. As others drift into the trade that quasi-equilibrium is indeed upset, but in a manner that does not benefit their customers. The economic space around each of the shops having been narrowed, their owners will no longer be able to make a living and they will try to mend the case by raising prices in tacit agreement. This will further reduce their sales and so, by successive pyramiding, a situation will evolve in which increasing potential supply will be attended by increasing instead of decreasing prices and by decreasing instead of increasing sales.

Such cases do occur, and it is right and proper to work them out. But as the practical instances usually given show, they are fringe-end cases to be found mainly in the sectors furthest removed from all that is most characteristic of capitalist activity. Moreover, they are transient by nature. In the case of retail trade the competition that matters arises not from additional shops of the same type, but from the department store, the chain store, the mail-order house and the supermarket which are bound to destroy those pyramids sooner or later. Now a theoretical construction which neglects this essential element of the case neglects all that is most typically capitalist about it; even if correct in logic as well as in fact, it is like *Hamlet* without the Danish prince.

Monopolistic practices

Both as a fact and as a threat, the impact of new things considerably reduces the long-run scope and importance of practices that aim, through restricting output, at conserving established positions and at maximizing the profits accruing from them. We must now recognize the further fact that restrictive practices of this kind, as far as they are effective, acquire a new significance in the perennial gale of creative destruction, a significance which they would not have in a stationary state or in a state of slow and balanced growth. In either of these cases restrictive strategy would produce no result other than an increase in profits at the expense of buyers. But in the process of creative destruction, restrictive practices may do much to steady the ship and to alleviate temporary difficulties. This is in fact a very familiar argument which always turns up in times of depression and, as everyone knows, has become very popular with governments and their economic advisers—witness the NRA. While it has been so much misused and so faultily acted upon that most economists heartily despise it, those same advisers who are responsible for this invariably fail to see its much more general rationale.

Practically any investment entails, as a necessary complement of entrepreneurial action, certain safeguarding activities such as insuring or hedging. Long-range investing under rapidly changing conditions, especially under conditions that change or may change at any moment under the impact of new commodities and technologies, is like shooting at a target that is not only indistinct but moving—and moving jerkily at that. Hence it becomes necessary to resort to such protecting devices as patents or temporary secrecy of process. But these protecting devices which most economists accept as normal elements of rational management are only special cases of a larger class comprising many others which most economists condemn although they do not differ fundamentally from the recognized ones.

If for instance a war risk is insurable, nobody objects to a firm's collecting the cost of this insurance from the buyers of its products. But that risk is no less an element in long-run costs if there are no facilities for insuring against it, in

which case a price strategy aiming at the same end will seem to involve unnecessary restriction and to be productive of excess profits. Similarly, if a patent cannot be secured or would not, if secured, effectively protect, other means may have to be used in order to justify the investment. Among them are a price policy that will make it possible to write off more quickly than would otherwise be rational. Again, means may have to be devised in order to tie prospective customers to the investing firm.

In analyzing such business strategy [as] of a given point of time, the investigating economist or government agent sees price policies that seem to him predatory and restrictions of output that seem to him synonymous with loss of opportunities to produce. He does not see that restrictions of this type are, in the conditions of the perennial gale, incidents, often unavoidable incidents, of a long-run process of expansion which they protect rather than impede. There is no more of paradox in this than there is in saying that motorcars are traveling faster than they otherwise would *because* they are provided with brakes.

This stands out most clearly in the case of those sectors of the economy which at any time happen to embody the impact of new things and methods on the existing industrial structure. The best way of getting a vivid and realistic idea of industrial strategy is indeed to visualize the behavior of new concerns or industries that introduce new commodities or processes (such as the aluminum industry) or else reorganize a part or the whole of an industry (such as, for instance, the old Standard Oil Company).

As we have seen, such concerns are aggressors by nature and wield the really effective weapon of competition. Their intrusion can only in the rarest of cases fail to improve total output in quantity or quality, both through the new method itself—even if at no time used to full advantage—and through the pressure it exerts on the preexisting firms. On the one hand, largest-scale plans could in many cases not materialize at all if it were not known from the outset that competition will be discouraged by heavy capital requirements or lack of experience. Even the securing of advantages that run counter to the public's sense of fair play—railroad rebates— move, as far as long-run effects on total output alone are envisaged, into a different light; they *may* be methods for removing obstacles that the institution of private property puts in the path of progress. In a socialist society that would be no less necessary. They would have to be secured by order of the central authority.

On the other hand, enterprise would in most cases be impossible if it were not known from the outset that exceptionally favorable situations are likely to arise which if exploited by price, quality and quantity manipulation will produce profits adequate to tide over exceptionally unfavorable situations. Again this requires strategy that in the short run is often restrictive. In the majority of cases, however, it is so successful as to yield profits far above what is necessary in order to induce the corresponding investment. These cases then provide the baits that lure capital on to untried trails. Their presence explains in part how it is possible for so large a section of the capitalist world to work for nothing: in the midst of the prosperous twenties just about half of the business corporations in the United States were run at a loss, at zero profits, or at profits which, if they had been foreseen, would have been inadequate to call forth the effort and expenditure involved.

All this is of course nothing but the tritest common sense. But it is being overlooked with a persistence so stubborn as sometimes to raise the question of sincerity. And it follows that, within the process of creative destruction, there is another side to industrial self-organization than that which these theorists are contemplating. "Restraints of trade" of the cartel type as well as those which merely consist in tacit understandings about price competition may be effective remedies under conditions of depression. As

far as they are, they may in the end produce not only steadier but also greater expansion of total output than could be secured by an entirely uncontrolled onward rush that cannot fail to be studded with catastrophes.

Even as now extended, however, our argument does not cover all cases of restrictive or regulating strategy, many of which no doubt have that injurious effect on the long-run development of output which is uncritically attributed to all of them. And even in the cases our argument does cover, the net effect is a question of the way in which industry regulates itself in each individual case. It is certainly as conceivable that an all-pervading cartel system might sabotage all progress as it is that it might realize, with smaller social and private costs, all that perfect competition is supposed to realize. This is why our argument does not amount to a case against state regulation. It does show that there is no general case for indiscriminate "trust-busting" or for the prosecution of everything that qualifies as a restraint of trade. Rational as distinguished from vindictive regulation by public authority turns out to be an extremely delicate problem which not every government agency, particularly when in full cry against big business, can be trusted to solve. But our argument, framed to refute a prevalent *theory* and the inferences drawn therefrom about the relation between modern capitalism and the development of total output, yields another outlook on facts and another principle by which to interpret them. For our purpose that is enough.

Part 4

INCOME DISTRIBUTION AMONG PRODUCTIVE FACTORS

What accounts for the share of income going to the use of land? One classic answer to this question came from one of the towering figures in the history of economic thought, David Ricardo (1772–1823). Son of a merchant-banker and himself a phenomenal success in business and the stock market, Ricardo brought a gloomier view to British economics than his predecessor, Adam Smith, had done.

This brief excerpt offers the fundamental logic of Ricardo's answer to the rent question. In this view, rent is the return paid to the landlord for the original, indestructible powers of the soil. Land is fixed in quantity, but varies in quality, since the less productive land is brought into use by an expanding population, and extra return necessarily accrues from farming on the best lands. This extra return goes not to the laborer, nor to the capitalists, but rather to the landlords who are the beneficiaries of the land distribution system.

The argument here is historically important for two reasons. It gave rise to the school of thought, most often associated with Henry George in the United States, that wanted to place all of society's taxes on the landlords to offset their gains from rent. And it represented an early model of abstract, elegant, but somewhat difficult reasoning in economics.

Questions to Guide the Reading

How does the concept of rent here compare with the current usage of the term when a tenant pays rent to his landlord or a driver rents a car from an agency?

Building on the Ricardian argument, followers of Henry George argue that taxes placed on land to recover for society the extra returns from more desirable land will not have any disincentive effect. A man cannot, for example, withdraw his land from the market without suffering zero returns. Is this argument valid, and does it support the wisdom of moving to heavier reliance on land taxes today rather than on buildings, machinery, or labor?

ON RENT
David Ricardo

Definition

Rent is that portion of the produce of the earth, which is paid to the landlord for the use of the original and indestructible powers of the soil.

It is often, however, confounded with the interest and profit of capital and, in popular language, the term is applied to whatever is annually paid by a farmer to his landlord. If, of two adjoining farms of the same extent, and of the same natural fertility, one had all the conveniences of farming buildings, and, besides, were properly drained and manured, and advanta-geously divided by hedges, fences, and walls, while the other had none of these advantages, more remuneration would naturally be paid for the use of one, than for the use of the other; yet in both cases this remuneration would be called rent. But it is evident, that a portion only of the money annually to be paid for the improved farm, would be given for the original and indestructible powers of the soil; the other portion would be paid for the use of the capital which had been employed in ameliorating the quality of the land, and in erecting buildings. In the future, then, whenever I speak of the rent

From David Ricardo, *Principles of Political Economy and Taxation* (George Bell and Sons, London, 1891, 3d edition).

of land, I wish to be understood as speaking of that compensation, which is paid to the owner of land for the use of its original and indestructible powers.

Land scarcity and rent

On the first settling of a country, in which there is an abundance of rich and fertile land, a very small proportion of which is required to be cultivated for the support of the actual population, or indeed can be cultivated with the capital which the population can command, there will be no rent; for no one would pay for the use of land, when there was an abundant quantity not yet appropriated, and, therefore, at the disposal of whosoever might choose to cultivate it.

On the common principles of supply and demand, no rent could be paid for such land, for the reason stated why nothing is given for the use of air and water, or for any other of the gifts of nature which exist in boundless quantity. In the same manner the brewer, the distiller, the dyer, make incessant use of the air and water for the production of their commodities; but as the supply is boundless, they bear no price. If all land had the same properties, if it were unlimited in quantity, and uniform in quality, no charge could be made for its use, unless where it possessed peculiar advantages of situation.

It is only, then, because land is not unlimited in quantity and uniform in quality, and because in the progress of population, land of an inferior quality, or less advantageously situated, is called into cultivation, that rent is ever paid for the use of it. When in the progress of society, land of the second degree of fertility is taken into cultivation, rent immediately commences on that of the first quality, and the amount of that rent will depend on the difference in the quality of those two portions of land.

When land of the third quality is taken into cultivation, rent immediately commences on the second, and it is regulated as before, by the difference in their productive powers. At the same time, the rent of the first quality will rise, for that must always be above the rent of the second, by the difference between the produce which they yield with a given quantity of capital and labour. With every step in the progress of population, which shall oblige a country to have recourse to land of a worse quality, to enable it to raise its supply of food, rent, on all the more fertile land, will rise.

Diminishing returns

It often, and, indeed, commonly happens, that before No. 2, 3, 4, or 5, or the inferior lands are cultivated, capital can be employed more productively on those lands which are already in cultivation. It may perhaps be found, that by doubling the original capital employed on No. 1, though the produce will not be doubled, it may be increased by [more than] what could be obtained by employing the same capital on land No. 3.

If, then, good land existed in a quantity much more abundant than the production of food for an increasing population required, or if capital could be indefinitely employed without a diminished return on the old land, there could be no rise of rent; for rent invariably proceeds from the employment of an additional quantity of labour with a proportionally less return.

Rent not price determining

The most fertile, and most favourably situated, land will be first cultivated, and the exchangeable value of its produce will be adjusted in the same manner as the exchangeable value of all other commodities, by the total quantity of labour necessary in various forms from first to last, to produce it, and bring it to market. When land of an inferior quality is taken into cultivation, the exchangeable value of raw produce will rise, because more labour is required to produce it.

The reason then, why raw produce rises in comparative value, is because more labour is employed in the production of the last portion obtained, and not because a rent is paid to the landlord. The value of corn is regulated by the quantity of labour bestowed on its production on that quality of land, or with that portion of capital, which pays no rent. Corn is not high because a rent is paid, but a rent is paid because corn is high; and it has been justly observed, that no reduction would take place in the price of corn, although landlords should forego the whole of their rent. Such a measure would only enable some farmers to live like gentlemen, but would not diminish the quantity of labour necessary to raise raw produce on the least productive land in cultivation.

If the high price of corn were the effect, and not the cause of rent, price would be proportionally influenced as rents were high or low, and rent would be a component part of price. But that corn which is produced by the greatest quantity of labour is the regulator of the price of corn; and rent does not and cannot enter in the least degree as a component part of its price.

READING 41

In the wealthiest society that the world has seen, there are still substantial numbers of Americans who live in extreme poverty. Many of these people are so far out of sight of their fellow countrymen in the normal day's work that it is easy to skip over them in songs of praise for the affluent society.

Paul Jacobs of the Fund for the Republic brings skills from earlier days in the labor movement and in journalism to the task of describing one large segment of America's poor. The migratory workers on whom he reports have special problems that prolong their position at the bottom of the income ladder. But, because these families move across the land as the seasons change, those problems are not on anyone's doorstep long enough to arouse much concerted effort, public or private, in attacking them.

Questions to Guide the Reading

To what extent are the problems described here inevitable in an industry with such seasonal demands for unskilled labor? Can the farmers who employ these workers reasonably be expected to make substantial improvements in their working conditions?

What public policies might be best suited to improving the lot of the migratory workers? Who should bear the costs of such policies?

THE FORGOTTEN PEOPLE
Paul Jacobs

Item—A picker was badly hurt in a collision while being transported in a truck. He was eleven years old, and had been working fifty-four hours a week.

Item—The cattle feeder was walking alongside a tractor when it suddenly backed up and crushed his foot beneath the tread. He was nine years old.

Item—He was shoveling grain into a moving auger and suddenly he slipped and his foot was caught in the auger. When they pulled him loose, his foot was completely mangled. He was fourteen years old.

None of these children was "helping out" on the family farm. All three were illegally employed as farm workers during 1957 in California, as were 124 other persons under sixteen years who were injured. One-third of these children, some of whom were permanently disabled, were employed in violation of state labor laws. Many others were employed in violation of Federal child-labor laws and state school-attendance laws. But in 1957 only one California farmer was prosecuted for violating state labor laws.

California is the only state that compiles statistics on injuries to young farm workers, and

From Paul Jacobs, "The Forgotten People," *The Reporter,* January 22, 1959. Reprinted with kind permission of the author and publisher.

so it is known there, at least, that from 1950 to 1957 more than a thousand children under sixteen years were seriously injured in farm accidents. Since no other state collects such statistics, it is impossible even to estimate how many children in the entire country suffer the same fate. All that is known is that the number of children illegally employed by farmers has been rising for the past few years. "Agriculture," said former U.S. Secretary of Labor James P. Mitchell, "violates the child labor provision more than any other industry."

Except in a very few states, agricultural workers are still not even covered by workmen's compensation laws. This in spite of the fact that farming has the third highest fatality rate of any industry in the United States, exceeded only by mining and construction.

Neither are agricultural workers covered by Federal minimum wage or maximum hours legislation. At a time when the minimum wage is $1.25 an hour, the average farm worker's hourly pay is sixty-eight cents, as compared to $2.79 an hour for the construction industry or even $1.05 an hour in laundries, whose workers are one of the lowest-paid nonagricultural groups in the nation. All adult farm workers are now supposed, by law, to receive certain benefits of the Social Security System for which both they and their employers make payments. But it is common knowledge that a great many farm employers ignore the law—a state of affairs the Social Security Administration is well aware of but incapable of doing anything about.

But it is not just farm-labor laws or Social Security regulations that are violated by farmers. In Oregon there are farm-labor contractors who supplement their already large incomes by selling marijuana and supplying prostitutes to farm workers as well as by getting commissions from liquor and food sold at jacked-up-prices. In New York, investigation of forty farm-labor camps revealed that only three kept the payroll records required by law.

A mean and ugly survival

In agriculture, the relations between workers and employers often seem to be a mean and ugly survival from an almost forgotten era. Employing at all times seven hundred thousand workers and sometimes more than two million, agriculture has successfully resisted the social and economic progress achieved through legislation and unionization by other millions of workers in industry. For a variety of reasons, agriculture, even though it is a major segment of the American economy, is still given an almost blanket exemption from modes of conduct now considered essential to a civilized society. Economically and politically unorganized, farm workers can do little on their own to help themselves. They possess neither the economic power to wrest better conditions from their employers nor the political influence to exert pressure upon legislators. They are the unorganized debris of an organizational society. They are indeed the forgotten people—forgotten by the labor movement, by the urban liberals, by almost everybody except a small band of men and women who have devoted their lives and meager resources to fighting what must often seem a hopeless battle.

Even when a law is passed, usually over the opposition of the farmers, giving farm workers a few minimal protections, it is chronically and matter-of-factly violated by farm employers, usually with no penalty involved even when they are caught. Most state legislatures are still dominated politically by the agricultural interests, and these same interests have a disproportionate influence in Congress. There are, moreover, still some farmers and farm organizations that fight off any regulation of farm workers' conditions just as bitterly and almost in the identical language they used in *The Grapes of Wrath*.

Investigating violations of the California state law dealing with illegal employment of minors is the responsibility of the state labor commissioner. Lacking an adequate staff, and with its main attention directed, almost inevitably, toward industrial workers, the commission has conducted such investigations haphazardly and indifferently. When questioned about an accident involving a fifteen-year-old boy whose toes were fractured in another auger accident, the labor commissioner's office stated:

> Inasmuch as this accident occurred at a location distant from any of the Division's offices, and for a considerable period of time there was no other Division business in the area, this matter was handled by sending the employer full information relative to child labor laws, together with a written warning.

There is not, in fact, very much the state labor commissioner can do, no matter how zealous he may be. "What jury of farmers will convict another farmer illegally employing minors when so many of them do it?" asks an official in the commissioner's office. "And, before we can get a conviction, we have to find a local district attorney who is willing to file a complaint. This is not easy either, in a farm area."

The migrant streams

The hired farm work force in the United States is composed of three main groups: regular workers, seasonally employed workers, and the foreign farmhands, mostly Mexicans brought in under a special program approved by Congress. The seven hundred thousand regular hired workers, those employed for more than 150 days a year by one employer, are almost all male; they take care of livestock, repair buildings, maintain equipment, drive tractors, and generally work without supervision. Frequently they live on or near the farm where they are employed. About half of this group are hired by the largest farms; forty-eight per cent of them are working for farms of more than 1,900 acres.

The million seasonal farm workers normally work less than 150 days in a year, and they work for more than one employer. They do work that can be completed in a short time and are usually paid by the day, hour, or piece. They clear land, lay fertilizer, chop, weed, and do the harvest work—cutting, picking, packing, and toting. Forty-eight per cent of all hired seasonal workers were employed on the two largest groups of cotton and fruit-and-nut farms in Texas, California, Arkansas, Mississippi, Louisiana, Tennessee, and North Carolina.

The seasonal farm workers split into two main groups: the larger group of local day-haul employees who may go out with a different farmer each day and are picked up by truck from a central employment point; and the much smaller number of migrants, mostly employed by labor contractors in the South and West and by crew leaders in the East. The contractors or crew leaders take the migrants from farm to farm along the migrant stream. They set a flat price with the farmers for the harvesting work, they paying the workers from their own pockets, or else they get a commission from the farmer for each worker supplied. The lush financial rewards open to an unscrupulous labor contractor are obviously tempting, and there has been a sharp increase in the number of people with criminal records who have applied for contractors' licenses in California.

There are six major streams of migratory workers:

(1) The one on the Atlantic Coast is made up of about 60,000 workers, most of whom are Negro, supplemented by workers from Puerto Rico and Mexican-Americans.

(2) The sugar-beet stream starts in Texas and goes up into the North Central and Mountain States. This group, too, consists of about 60,000 workers, almost all Mexican-Americans.

(3) The wheat and small-grain harvest migrants also come up from Texas, generally as combine teams, and work north to Montana and North Dakota. About 30,000 men, also of Mexican descent, do this work.

(4) About 80,000 workers of Mexican descent plus Negroes harvest cotton, starting out from Texas with one group moving off into the Mississippi Delta and a bigger one going westward into New Mexico, Arizona, and southern California.

(5) From Oklahoma, Arkansas, and western Tennessee, about 30,000 people of early American stock move north and west during the harvest season, picking fruit and tomatoes.

(6) Finally, there are about 120,000 workers, of all backgrounds, working in the Western States, up and down the Pacific coast.

In addition to the 380,000 American migrant workers, about half a million foreign farm laborers are brought into the United States each year. Most of these are the "braceros" from Mexico, who more and more are replacing the seasonal American workers, both local and migrant.

The average yearly income for all farm workers in 1958 was only $1,250, including all nonfarm cash income and roughly $200 for prerequisites. Farm workers, in fact, only receive twice as much pay now as they did in 1933, even though farm productivity has gone up nearly threefold since then. In some farm work, like the picking of cotton, the real value of the wages paid to the farm workers has actually declined since 1943.

It is because farm workers have such a low income level that so many of their children work alongside them in the fields. The money earned by the children is essential to keep the family on even a bare below-subsistence level. And so the children grow up badly educated because local schools are reluctant to take them as pupils, sickly because medical facilities are not easily available to them.

Why does this large group of people continue in farm work? Primarily because no other work is open to them. The minority groups among them find that much industrial employment is closed to them, while the white workers are generally unskilled and are ill adapted to urban life. The kind of lives they lead incapacitates them—and their children—for leading any other. And so they go on living as regular farmhands in shabby houses on the fringes of agricultural communities or on the farms, the migrants in tents, barracks, and occasionally decent camps.

All night in a truck

These men, women, and children are utterly exhausted after working long hours in the field. Many of the children suffer from chronic diarrhea. They get horribly cramped, traveling long distances without sleep in broken-down trucks. And if some growers had their way, the trucks would never stop for rest. When the Interstate Commerce Commission held a hearing in May, 1957, to consider setting up safety regulations to govern interstate transportation of farm workers, it was informed by S. H. Butler of the Green Giant Company, Dayton, Wisconsin:

> We feel that the requirement banning travel from 8:00 P.M. to 6:00 A.M. would work a hardship on the laborers being transported as well as upon employers. It has been our experience that these trucks can complete the trip from Texas to Washington in from fifty to sixty hours, with stops only for meals, gasoline, and general "stretching." The men seem to arrive in good physical condition and with a good mental attitude.

At the same 1957 ICC hearing, the Tri-State Packers Association, Inc., of Easton, Maryland, protested a proposal that trucks carrying farm workers be required to have seats.

> The floors of the truck in which the persons are transported are normally covered with bedding or sacks of clothing which provide a more suitable resting place than would seats of the type suggested by the Commission—the requirement that seats be provided appears to be extremely undesirable. It is unsatisfactory as a safety measure for the reason that if seats are not provided, the transients will sit or lie on bedding or clothing and they would be in far less danger in the event of a sudden stop than would be true if they were sitting on wooden benches. In addition, these trucks are used to haul produce to the processor—it would be practically impossible to attach the seats securely and still use the vehicle to haul produce.

But a lack of seats did not act "as a safety measure" for the forty-one American men, women, and child farm workers jammed into the eight-by-fifteen-foot back of a dilapidated one-and-a-half-ton truck that pulled out from the side of a North Carolina highway on June 6, 1957, directly into the path of a ten-ton tractor-trailer. Seconds later, after a grinding crash, twenty broken and mutilated bodies were strewn over the highway. Of the forty-one who had been crammed together in that tiny space without seats, only five were unhurt.

Just as on the national level some powerful farm organizations bitterly—and usually successfully—resist any Federal regulation that affects them (except increased subsidies, of course), so too on the state level is the farm worker left unprotected. The prospects for including farm workers under the compensation acts are "bleak," writes Harold Katz, an authority on workmen's compensation law, "since farm organizations, which have traditionally opposed such coverage, exert considerable influence in our state legislatures."

The extent of the influence of farm organizations on state legislatures can easily be seen even in a state like California, where farm workers are somewhat better off than in many other states. A California state law provides that an illegally employed minor who suffers an accident while working shall receive an additional fifty per cent increased payment in workmen's compensation, paid by the employer—unless the employer is a farmer. In that case, the penalty payment is not made.

Why this exception? State officials shrug. "It's the farm lobby in Sacramento," they say. "That lobby has lots of power."

Sixteen cents an hour

There is no question that agricultural employers have a special difficulty in that they require large numbers of farm workers for short periods of time, lest an entire crop be lost. But if farm wages go up, will food prices necessarily follow? It is clear that the relation is not so simple as that: the labor cost is only one factor in the unstable price structure of those agricultural products that call for the use of migrant labor, and generally not the most important one. Even after a crop is harvested, especially if it be fruits and vegetables, the market price depends to an extraordinary extent upon factors over which the grower has had little control: the weather's effect upon the crop's quality, its size, its availability, and the fickle public taste. In Florida in 1958, a freeze hit the orange crop. Thousands of farm workers, both local and migrant, faced such critical unemployment that the National Council of Churches appealed to the President to establish a state of emergency. But their employers, the Florida growers, made handsome profits because the freeze put oranges in short supply and the frost-bitten fruit could be marketed as "fair" frozen orange juice at a high price per can.

So too with other fruit and vegetable crops. Melon growers in California's Imperial Valley can make or lose fortunes overnight. But becoming a millionaire or a pauper does not depend on the wages paid the melon pickers; rather it depends on the quality of the melons and the time that they reach the market.

In the face of this enormously complicated problem, much of organized agriculture insists on keeping farm wages down. The farm employers' attitude was neatly summed up by a Texas congressman, himself a farmer: "I think the employers, everyone, would protest the twenty-cent minimum wage. Or a ten-cent minimum wage or any other minimum wage." As a matter of fact, Texas growers are accustomed to paying their farm workers sixteen cents an hour for a sixty-hour week.

The payment of substandard wages is justified by farm employers on the uncertainty of their profits. But while their employees are penalized in advance because of the growers' possible unknown financial loss, the farmers do not make any additional payments to their workers if the crop does bring in a large profit. The workers' wages remain the same — abysmally low — no matter what profit the farmer makes. No department-store owner expects to lower the pay of a saleswoman if a dress has to be marked down in price because it doesn't sell, but farmers successfully demand that *their* workers run all the risks of the market place without receiving any of its benefits.

So too with coverage of farm workers under state compensation laws. Farm organizations bitterly resist paying for such coverage, still relying on the fiction that all American farmers are "small," not able to afford insurance. Even if this were true—which it is not, since the great majority of farm workers are employed by the

very largest and most profitable farms—what difference would it make? Small industrial employers must be covered by insurance as well as by wage and hour laws. Extending such coverage to small industrial operations was difficult, but it was done. No one would deny that protecting farm workers by law will also be difficult, but it too can be accomplished if farm organizations can somehow be convinced that arrogant refusals even to discuss the matter are not substitutes for social responsibility.

There is in particular one group of large farmers, associated with the American Farm Bureau Federation, that generally opposes any Federal or state regulations affecting employer-worker relationships, while at the same time it attempts to represent itself as speaking for the overwhelming majority of all farmers.

The 1,600,000 Farm Bureau Federation membership includes not just farmers but bankers, grocers, hardware merchants, filling-station operators, and a variety of other businessmen in rural communities, all of whom display their membership placards in store windows. And among the farmers, the Farm Bureau represents the half million biggest and richest who employ seven-tenths of the hired labor. It is these who are leading the fight against Federal regulation. "Minimum wages would result in limiting the employment of inefficient workers and would seriously limit the income of the average to superior workers," states one Farm Bureau official, while another demands that the Department of Labor "cease forcing users of Mexican national labor to furnish housing to Mexican national laborers that includes standards more rigorous than those usually provided domestic agricultural labor."

A child's day

The net result is that, in 1959, Federal protection and supervision are almost completely denied the American farm worker.

A migrant's children may either have to work in the fields or stay unattended in a filthy camp. Not many communities have adequate child-care centers for the children of migrant farm workers. "There are very few facilities available to migrant mothers for day-care of their children," states a report of the Florida State Board of Health. "Much publicity is given to those maintained by church groups, but in all fairness it must be said that they are too few and too expensive to be available to many migrants."

For the nonmigrant seasonal farm workers, life is not very much better. They too frequently work for contractors on a day-haul basis. In a typical Florida farm household, the eleven-year-old daughter of the family was absent from school forty-one days out of eighty-five because the mother had to work and could not afford to pay a day-care center's fees for her three children under six. A Board of Health report of her activities for one week reads as follows:

Sunday: picked six baskets of beans, earned $3.60. Monday: no work available in Belle Glade; paid $.50 for her transportation by truck to "the coast," where the crop was poor. Picked three baskets, earned $1.80. Tuesday: rained, no work. Wednesday: picked four baskets of beans, earned $2.40. No more work available that day. Thursday: picked five baskets of beans, earned $3.00; transportation cost $.50. Friday: picked eight baskets of beans (in eleven hours in the field), earned $4.80. Saturday: "chopped" peppers in the field for twelve hours, earned $6.00.

The total earnings for the week (less transportation costs) with which to support herself and her four children were $20.60.

Children of school age were involved somewhat differently in a revealing incident that occurred in September, 1955, when there was a shortage of prune pickers in the Santa Clara County, California, area because, stated the California Department of Employment, there was a "loss of students, housewives leaving to enter children in schools, and men drafted to fight forest fires." According to state law, children cannot be employed during school hours. The opening dates for schools throughout the country were therefore postponed a week, "at the request of ranchers in the area," according to one of the local newspapers. As a result of this postponement, approximately 34,000 school children went to school a week late because the ranchers in the area needed, again according to the employment department report, 250 prune pickers.

There are some signs of hope in this hitherto grim situation. For too many years, the farm-labor problem has been almost solely the concern of a few groups like the National Council on Agricultural Life and Labor and the National Sharecroppers Fund, whose yearly money-raising appeals are wearily opened and rather indifferently put aside. For too many years, the priests, nuns, and laymen associated with the Catholic Council for the Spanish Speaking and the National Catholic Rural Life Conference have shouldered their great burden without much help. For too many years, the representatives of the American Friends Service Committee have had to appar alone before state and national legislative committees. For too many years, union leaders, with a few exceptions, have either ignored farm workers or considered them political and economic pawns, useful only as sacrifices for larger stakes. But recently there has been a widening public interest in the problem. The governors of some states, among them Pennsylvania and Oregon, have set up special committees of farm groups and prominent farmers. There seems to be a revival of the instincts for social compassion and indignation—qualities recently absent from our society, perhaps because it is so difficult for the prosperous majority to identify itself with a destitute minority.

READING 42

One observer of the American labor scene has commented that trade unionism is the "conservative movement of our times." Certainly the socialist principles and ideology that dominate much of the European labor movement are weak in the United States. Nevertheless, trade unions have experienced a long history of opposition or of mere grudging acceptance in this country.

Many of the widely held reservations about unions seem to turn upon the assumptions one makes about what the world would be like in the absence of organized labor groups. Would it be a world of a harmony of interests between management and workers, or would it be a world of unmitigated class warfare? Would it be a world of a highly competitive, efficient, and impersonal market mechanisms, a world of unilateral and unchecked management decisions, or a world of sweeping government controls?

Max Ways, assistant managing editor of *Fortune* magazine, reviews some of these questions in the context of the contemporary American labor-management scene, marked as it is by a relatively stable union membership and by an apparently increasing hostility toward labor disputes. He views the overriding labor issue of the day as the problem of adapting our work processes to rapid technological change in the presence of some natural worker resistances and in the absence of completely rational management control. Here then is an exercise in weighing life in a unionized economy not against some Utopian ideal but against some practical twentieth-century alternatives.

These views did not sit well with all employers. Their appearance in one of the nation's leading business publications brought a sharp retort by W. Maxey Jarman, chairman of the GENESCO Corporation, Nashville, Tennessee. Mr. Jarman's comment is reproduced below.

Questions to Guide the Reading

What seem to have been the main determinants of union growth in the United States? Will union membership increase, decrease, or stay about the same in the years ahead? Must the unions grow in membership and in outlook to fulfill the functions which Mr. Ways finds valuable?

In what ways is collective bargaining likely to be a spur to greater technological efficiency? In what ways does it put a drag on technological change?

LABOR UNIONS ARE WORTH THE PRICE
Max Ways
Comment by W. Maxey Jarman

"We have no ultimate ends. We are going on from day to day. We are fighting only for immediate objects. . . ." Adolph Strasser, head of the Cigar Makers' Union, to a U.S. Senate committee in 1873.

Right now and in the years ahead American labor leaders are sure to need all their resilience and their inventive resource. For a mighty wave of denunciation is rolling in upon the unions. Indignation over strikes rose in vehemence through 1962 and especially in early 1963, when a longshoremen's strike posed a major economic threat, and a strike and lockout of New York newspapers exasperated nerve centers of U.S. opinion.

After these disputes were settled, few people noticed that an extraordinary degree of labor peace prevailed, however insecurely, throughout the nation. Instead, there was an acute awareness of other strike dangers ahead. Americans seemed convinced that the burden of strikes was

increasing, although the standard statistical indicators suggested the contrary. In 1962 time lost in strikes was only one-sixth of 1 percent of time worked, doubtless less than the cost of the common cold or the common hangover. (See Figure 1.) But merely correcting the statistical picture was not going to assuage the indignation; the public (or significant parts of it) had lowered its boiling point on strikes. Therein lay grave danger to the unions—and to others.

The widespread demand that strikes be replaced, at least in essential industries, by "some better way" shies away from the question: *what* better way? Representatives of management and labor avoid strikes in hundreds of contracts signed every month, but unless the strike remains as a possibility no genuine collective bargaining can occur. When George Meany says, "Strikes are part of the American way of life," he is not exulting in labor's power to disrupt, but rather expressing awareness that there are no known

From Max Ways, "Labor Unions Are Worth the Price," *Fortune*, May, 1963. The comment is from the Letters to *Fortune* section of this magazine of June, 1963. Reprinted with kind permission of the authors and publisher. Copyright, 1963, Time Inc.

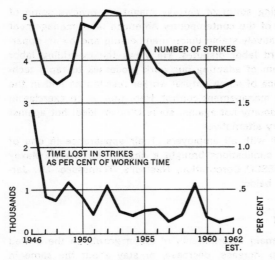

Fig. 1 The unions' failure in the postwar period to organize a larger part of their potential membership is not necessarily a symptom of weak leadership. Historically, union growth has come in spurts. An impressive percentage gain came between 1897 and 1904 when union membership rose from 450,000 to over two million. In the World War I period, the 2,700,000 members of 1914 almost doubled to five million in 1920, representing nearly 18 per cent of all nonagricultural workers, a proportion that was not exceeded until 1937. The onset of the depression sent membership all the way down to 2,700,000, or 11.5 per cent of its potential, in 1933. In 1945 the unions had 14,300,000 members, over 35 per cent of potential; the 1960 figures were 17 million and 31.5 per cent.

Damage done by strikes is difficult to measure. In these two standard indicators, the bottom curve counts time lost only in companies actually struck, but in many strikes additional losses are suffered by suppliers or customers of the struck plants. On the other hand, "time lost in strikes" often overstates the damage; a short strike in the steel industry, for example, may not reduce annual production because extra production before and after strikes compensates for the loss. It is often said that as the economy becomes more interdependent, the indirect effects of strikes become more serious. But some economists doubt this on the ground that in a more highly developed economy there are more alternative sources for the goods or services withheld by strikes.

alternatives to collective bargaining that would not do far more damage to the American system. All the foreseeable substitutes involve, directly or indirectly, massive extension of government power to fix wages and other conditions of labor. Although collective bargaining as it is now practiced in the U.S. does involve many serious departures from an ideal market system, it is a lot closer and more responsive to markets than any system of government intervention could be.

Yet today's labor leaders are haunted men; what haunts them is not some ghost from the past but the uncertainties of the U.S. industrial prospect. "Automation" is the center of their daily practical problems. Their attitudes toward the present period of rapid technological and organizational change are formed within a profound ambivalence they share with the men and women they represent and with Americans generally. All demand the fruits of progress and at the same time resist such painful changes as the breaking up of work patterns, the discarding of skills, the shifting of relative wage rates, and the loss, however temporary, of jobs.

The top leaders of American unions are too smart to oversimplify the problem as one lesser labor leader does: "Look. You can't stop progress in this country. I tell the bosses that and I tell the men that. You can't stop progress. *You can only slow it down.*" The vast majority of American labor leaders say—and honestly believe—that technological advance should move faster. Few of them think they know "the" answer to the problem of how to speed progress and at the same time cushion the painful impact of change. Just now, their public answer is a shorter work week to reduce unemployment, but this is less a practical goal than a symbolic way of calling attention to the insecurity that dogs the men they represent. The unions' more practical and less visible answer is an infinitely complex edifice of arrangements, worked out industry by industry, company by company, and craft by craft, by which they seek—sometimes clumsily and outrageously but sometimes with brilliant ingenuity —to adjust the economic facts of a progressive technology to the social and psychological fact of man's profound resistance to being changed by forces outside himself, or pushed around, or treated as a thing.

Teeming with innovation

The effort toward giving union members a sense of participation in the control of their working life is and always has been at the heart of American unionism. Accelerated technological change increases the pressure from below on the leaders to provide the protection workers want; at the same time it increases the danger that the steps the unions take to fulfill their function will exact too great a price from the U.S. economy.

This dilemma—and not the cost of strikes—is today's and tomorrow's real "labor problem," and much union energy in recent years has been directed toward dealing with the difficulties posed by the pressures of rapid industrial change. To handle this task unions themselves have had to change, to improvise new devices in dealing with employers, with one another, and with their own members. Although accused of stagnation, the unions are, in fact, teeming with innovation and efforts towards internal improvement.

The Steelworkers, for example, is not a model union; some of its old friends complain that the fire and enthusiasm of its early years have been frozen into a bureaucracy. But bureaucracy can be another name for competent, function-alized administration, and this union has con-structed working channels of two-way communi-cation running from the plant floor to the top of a vast (900,000-member) structure. It does much of its bargaining on a national basis, yet it is able to handle effectively the host of indi-vidual grievances that arise in their plants. This is no small achievement. Many British unions that bargain nationally have lost touch with the shop stewards, who often disrupt production by acting independently of the national body; on the Continent national unions have, in general, even less top-to-bottom structure than in Britain. In consequence, workers' specific grievances, in-stead of being resolved within a contractual framework, melt into an ugly lump of politicized class grievance against the bosses and the system.

The Steelworkers and management are now trying to remove a wide range of issues from the pressures of deadline negotiations. The Hu-man Relations Committee is a year-round joint study group investigating such questions as sen-iority and work rules. These matters can be of immense importance to individual workers, but, unless the rules are knowledgeably and carefully written, they can impose inefficiencies that cost much more than the benefits are worth. It's too early to say whether steel's Human Relations Committee will do any real good, but at least a sane and novel approach has been made. More interesting is the recent agreement worked out

between the Steelworkers and Kaiser Steel Corp. Groups of Kaiser workers now receiving incentive pay may vote to give this up (each getting a substantial lump-sum payment for a transitional period); these workers and all others will receive a third of cost savings Kaiser makes by auto-mation or in any other way; to minimize the displacement of workers that may result from cost cutting, workers will be protected by new job-security provisions and strengthened seniority rules. None of the authors of this plan hails it as "the" answer for industry in general or even for the whole steel industry. It is to be a four-year experiment in one company where manage-ment and workers, apparently, are acutely aware of the need for cutting costs in the face of com-petition, while giving the workers as much pro-tection as possible.

Walter Reuther's United Automobile Work-ers is another union that can hardly be accused of stagnation either in collective bargaining or in efforts to improve the quality of its internal organization. For years the U.A.W. has vainly proposed to the automobile companies that joint study groups be set up in advance of negotia-tions. In 1963 for the first time the automobile companies seem interested in exploring the plan. Meanwhile, in the way it runs its own affairs the U.A.W. has made a novel approach to the protection of individual members aggrieved by union decisions. Such cases are bound to occur where unions are large, their contracts and pro-cedures complex, their staffs expert, and their officers possessed of the self-confidence that comes with experience in which the rank and file cannot share. Reuther, than whom there is no more self-confident man, is proud these days of having established in the U.A.W. a "supreme court" of seven eminent men, not members of the union, who can decide appeals by aggrieved members against U.A.W. organs or officers, in-cluding Reuther. This "court" has heard 122 cases, and its existence is said to have had a substantial effect in making U.A.W. leaders at all levels more careful of the rights of dissidents.

When the plumbers go starry-eyed

The four biggest unions in the U.S.—the out-cast Teamsters, the Steelworkers, the U.A.W., and the Machinists—account for a highly sig-nificant quarter of all organized workers, and these four are all exceedingly lively unions. But the vigor and change reach further down. Even the unions of the building trades, usually the prime example of reactionary, restrictive "business unionism," show signs of effort toward internal improvement. In recent years they have reduced the damage done by interunion conflict over job jurisdiction.

The plumbers' union, not in the past a progress-minded group, has responded to the challenge of changing technology by operating one of the best training programs of any union. Purdue University helped to train instructors. Scores of locals have set up their own classrooms. Journeymen as well as apprentices are the students. Not long ago the union's president, Peter T. Schoemann, presented diplomas to a group of trainees whose average age was sixty. "What are you old birds going to school for?" asked Schoemann, who is sixty-nine. He was told, "We got tired of holding the pipe while the young men made the weld. Now we've learned to make the weld and they can hold the pipe." Strictly "selfish," of course—but the kind of motivation that built a great nation.

Heart of the training program is lavishly illustrated textbooks that cost several hundred thousand dollars to develop. Union leaders hold out the pipe fitters' manual, inviting the awe and admiration usually reserved for the *Book of Kells*. When the plumbers go all starry-eyed about a training book, it is certain that not all sense of progress has disappeared from the American labor movement.

Why unions aren't growing

Management will be deluded if it accepts the widespread opinion that the unions' failure to increase their proportion of the total work force is a sign of weakness. Membership figures must be read against the background of union history and in the framework of present U.S. employment trends.

In the first place, the labor movement—unlike the telephone business and the diaper-wash industry—is not comfortably pinned to the population curve. Membership in American unions has always advanced in sprints and these sprints are connected more with broad changes in U.S. life than with the quality or energy of labor leadership. (See Figure 2.) The biggest numerical gains, in fact, have been associated with wartime or postwar labor shortages. In terms of percentage of the labor force, the unions have done better at holding their World War II gains than they did in the years after 1920. American unionism since 1945 has passed through searing vicissitudes—struggles in some unions over Communism, the effects of the Taft-Hartley law, the McClellan investigation—without any substantial exodus of members.

Moreover, U.S. unions have been working against a tide: production workers, among whom unionism has always been strongest, have been declining in proportion to the total work force. Some liberal intellectuals, in their present anti-union mood, will not accept this excuse for union "stagnation"; they demand that unions make more strenuous efforts to break out of their old strongholds and organize the unskilled (especially Negroes) and the growing number of white-collar workers. But in both categories the obstacles to union progress are too deep-seated to be overcome by mere improvement of union leadership or a surge of union organizing "energy."

Before the mid-Thirties unskilled industrial workers were mainly white—and unions made little headway in organizing them. Many unskilled production workers—along with skilled and semiskilled—were enrolled during the rapid progress of industrial unionism from 1936 to 1945. But this still left outside of unions many unskilled workers in the service trades, which are now expanding, and in numerous pockets of employment not accessible to industrial union-

Fig. 2   Organized Labor's Long Advance Has Been Uneven.

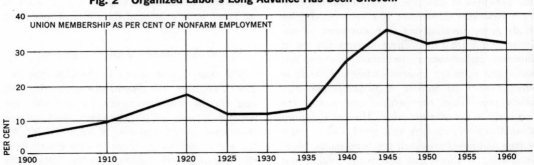

ism. These unskilled workers today have a high proportion of Negroes, Puerto Ricans, and Mexicans, but race is not among the main reasons why more are not organized. Unskilled workers are so easy to replace that they have little inherent bargaining power—the stuff unionism can mobilize and make more effective, but which it cannot create. Moreover, service workers, rarely concentrated in large groups, tend to be harder to organize than factory workers.

In some quarters the idea seems to be that the 1,750,000 Negroes now in unions could be multiplied if labor leaders took a much stronger stand in championing Negro rights and aspirations. In fact, union leadership has a good recent record of anti-discrimination—a record that has undeniably hurt union organizing drives among southern white workers. Whatever may be the ethical merits of the case for even stronger union policies favoring underprivileged groups, there is little chance that adoption of such policies would result in a big net gain in union membership. Those at the bottom of the social escalator may "need" unionism most, but unionism has been most effective within a middle band of workers who have substantial pre-union bargaining power.

Why the white-collars are unorganized

Above the middle band lies the unions' other area of frustration, the white-collar workers, of whom less than 15 percent are unionized. Market demand for white-collar workers has been stronger than for production workers. Just before, during, and just after World War II, however, production workers apparently were closing the pay-and-working-condition gap between themselves and the white-collars. This overtaking movement has ceased, and the white-collars may be drawing away again.

Many of the fringe benefits (e.g., sick pay, vacations) on which blue-collar unions are now concentrating have for years been standard in much white-collar employment. The main white-collar advantage—and the one that makes this group hard to unionize—is continuity of job, "the annual wage." Hourly paid production workers, subject to layoff at management discretion, are less reluctant than white-collar workers to interrupt their pay by striking. Where a very high proportion of a white-collar group has been organized (e.g., actors) there is often a background of discontinuous employment. The upper levels of white-collar workers have one other pertinent advantage over production workers: a

measure of built-in control over the pace and pattern of their own work. Managers usually don't need a union to tell them that "over-bossing" of technicians results in lost efficiency.

The majority of white-collar workers are not likely to be organized unless there are major shifts in the terms of their employment. Such shifts may appear. Years ago, when white-collars were a small minority in most businesses, it was easy to provide them with continuous employment; today the growing proportion of white-collar workers represents in many companies a cost rigidity that is hard to take when business is slack. If management tries to meet this difficulty with white-collar layoffs, or if office automation is too rapid, or if white-collar jobs become overbossed, there may be huge union gains among this group. But in the absence of such changes it is hard to believe that a mere stepping up of union "energy" is going to organize millions of workers who have, without unions, an increasing market power already superior to that of unionized production workers.

In sum, the odds are that in the near future total union membership will not increase or decline sharply.

What does unionism cost?

The present wave of anti-union feeling raises again the question of what effect unions have on the economy. In such an appraisal there are some bear traps for the unwary. The two groups that sound off most loudly about the effect of unions are labor leaders and labor baiters; they tend to agree with each other in rating the impact of unionism very high. The labor leader gives unions credit for a generation of rapid gains by workers, and the labor baiter says almost the same thing when he fixes upon unions the chief blame for rising costs and prices. The truth seems to be that the economic impact of unions is not so great as either group asserts.

In a remarkably clear, concise, and balanced new book, *The Economics of Trade Unions,* Albert Rees of the University of Chicago, working from a number of detailed studies, has arrived at some sophisticated opinions about the cost of unions. One way of getting at the wage effect is to compare the wage rates of union members with those of unorganized employees doing comparable tasks. Rees's educated guess is that the over-all difference at any point in time amounts to between 10 and 15 percent. In some industries that are almost completely organized, unions reach periods when they are unable to raise the relative wages of workers at all. An example is the Amalgamated Clothing Workers, once one of the most effective unions. Since the war it has been stymied, and the usual cries have been raised of tired, old leadership. But the Amalgamated had excellent leadership in depth, and it is hardly plausible that the sudden lowering in the union's effectiveness is traceable mainly to leadership. The explanation, according to Rees, is that market factors heavily condition union effectiveness. In the men's clothing field, the postwar market has been soft and many employers are in trouble. In such a situation, even the strongest union must choose between scaling down its wage demands or accepting greater unemployment among its members.

Following the late Henry C. Simons and others, Rees believes that union action in raising wages tends to decrease employment opportunities. (Even where the number of jobs increases, the expansion of employment is slower than it would have been if wage rates had not been pressed upward by union action.) Usually, unemployment in an industry acts as a brake on wage demands. The great exception to this for years has been the United Mine Workers, which forced up wage rates while making no effort to slow the mechanization that was spurred by rising labor costs. The number of coal miners declined from about 450,000 in 1947 to 119,000, while hourly earnings almost doubled.

Rees says that it cannot be proved that unions measurably increase "the workers' share" of total income at the expense of the owners of capital. Union gains are probably paid for by other workers or consumers. On the other hand, Rees defends unions against the charge that they are solely or mainly responsible for "cost-push inflation." Unions can aggravate inflationary dangers arising from monetary or other causes, but their "push" on costs becomes inflationary only when wrong policies are pursued elsewhere in the economy.

The chief cost of unions is not strike losses or cost-push, but the distortions and rigidities that unionism introduces into the market system. Rees says: "If the union is viewed solely in terms of its effect on the economy, it must in my opinion be considered an obstacle to the optimum performance of our economic system."

He has, however, more to say. Although he is an economist, Rees knows that life is not an exercise in economics. American unions rose not in response to an economic theory, but as a complex institutional form of expressing the complex reactions of workers to the pressures of industrial society. "By giving workers protection against arbitrary treatment by employers, by acting as their representative in politics, and by reinforcing their hope of continuous future gain, unions have helped to assure that the basic values of our society are widely diffused and that our disagreements on political and economic issues take place within a broad framework of agreement." He notes that American manual workers are committed to the preservation of a political democracy and a free-enterprise economy and that they are not, "as in many other democracies, constantly . . . attempting to replace it with something radically different." Rees concludes: "The economic losses imposed by unions are not too high a price to pay" for the psychological, social, and political benefits.

What about "the right to manage"?

Even if this judgment is true about the past and present, what are the prospects? Are the future costs imposed by unions on the economy likely to become "too high"?

In recent years direct union pressure on wage rates has slowed down a bit. But a great deal of present labor activity and conflict is on fronts other than wages; most of these issues are connected with adjustments to technological change; many of them involve the possibility of high economic loss by union infringement on management's "right to manage."

While this danger is real, the actual picture is more complex and more balanced than is generally supposed. In the first place, unions in many industries have had the effect of speeding up the pace of technological improvements. One railroad executive put it this way: "If it wasn't for those damn unions, we'd be using as many man-hours to do every job as we did twenty years ago. Every time they get an increase, we have to get off our duffs and find a cheaper way to do things."

This quote represents an important hidden truth about "the right to manage." If it is assumed that complete managerial control exists prior to any union infringement on management power, then every concession to unions in the form of work rules and other limitations represents a diminution of management power. Examination of the masses of these limitations that have been written in the last fifty years—and are still being written—might lead to the conclusion that management is gradually being pushed into a corner where it has less and less control of the enterprises for which it is legally responsible. But anybody who observes the American business scene knows that picture to be false; management has, in fact, a greater degree of control than it had fifty years ago, and its control increases year by year.

The explanation lies in the falsity of the original assumption that "complete management" preceded union interference. Complete management, the total subjection of action to rational control, never exists. Whether confusion be attributed to original sin or to the undomesticated Freudian id, the truth is that in human affairs, individual or group, the segment of unmanaged activity exceeds the segment of managed activity. (Saints and the Bell Telephone System may be exceptions to this rule.) Masters never exercise complete rational control over slaves, nor parents over children, nor any man over himself, nor managers over a work process.

For example, the imposition by unions of seniority rules in layoffs seems to be an encroachment on the right to manage. But before the unions interfered, the selection of the particular individuals to lay off was often not really a management decision (i.e., it was not worked out rationally in terms of the interest of the enterprise). Foremen and supervisors, unguided by policy from above, selected by favoritism or at random the workers to be retained or laid off. Nobody in his right mind would argue that seniority was the most efficient or economically rational way of selecting workers for continuous employment or for promotion. But in many cases what seniority rules replaced was not rational management but merely power exercised in a way that seemed unfair and arbitrary to workers. It seemed so because that's what it was.

The struggle over the control of labor is not simply management vs. unions. The older struggle is that of management vs. chaos, or unmanagement. Unions make it a three-cornered fight. Nobody can promise that union encroachments upon "the right to manage" will not advance faster than management's ability to win from chaos new frontiers of rational control. In industries where that has happened the costs of unionism may be disastrous. But the general record of a hundred years of unionism indicates that—so far—union power and management effectiveness have *both* advanced together.

Featherbeds for sale

When they encroach upon the right to manage, American unions are not trying to take over enterprises; they are trying to restrict or cushion change or to give the workers a sense that some power over the job is in their hands. Since American unions are themselves immersed in market psychology, every union encroachment has a price at which it may be traded for some other potential union advantage.

A most remarkable example of this occurred on the West Coast in 1961. For thirty years Harry Bridges had built up a fantastically restrictive set of work rules. Unneeded men were required for all sorts of specific jobs around the docks. When Bridges was asked what these supernumeraries should be called, his cynical humor answered: "Witnesses." The burden was becoming so intolerable to employers that they "bought" all the restrictive work rules in a single package in return for large employer payments into a special fund that will make possible earlier retirement and larger pensions for longshoremen. The agreement endangered some hundreds of dock-worker jobs, but these were held by "B-men" without voting rights in Bridges' union. The employers have obtained, at a price, a free hand to improve productivity on the West Coast wharves.

What Bridges did in a wholesale deal, other unions do all the time on a retail basis. Much has been heard lately about the printers' insistence on "setting bogus" or "dead horse." But it is less widely known that "dead horse" is often stored up, unset, on the spike and then traded off at the end of a contract term for small additions to wage or other concessions. After the east-coast longshoremen's strike was settled in February, there was a sudden flare-up on a Manhattan pier, where an employer had introduced an unusual distribution of the work gang between the pier, the deck, and the hold. The workers considered this a violation of an agreement to maintain local work patterns unchanged; apparently they had it in mind that the right to change the pattern could be "sold" in some future negotiation. Union officials had to tell them that on this particular pier the right had already been conceded to the shipowner.

The proliferation of specific work rules in American union contracts is not paralleled in other industrial countries—but the actual situation in other countries is not necessarily better from management's point of view. British managers are conscious of worker resistance to automation and change even though that resistance has not been embodied in specific contractual provisions. One result is that the hidden worker resistance in Britain is used by managers to reinforce their own inertia, with the consequence that the pace of industrial change in Britain is slower than in the U.S. One rogue whale of a shipowner in New York holds that the slowness of technological change on the waterfront there is attributable mainly to the inertia of shipowners, who for decades were dealing with a weak and racket-ridden union. Now that the east-coast longshoremen are somewhat stronger they may make wage and other bargaining gains; squeezed, the shipowners may be forced into cost-cutting improvements.

The U.S. practice of writing specific rules into contracts at least exposes the featherbedding to view where it can be argued about, bargained about, and sometimes traded off. It is somewhat more difficult for management to deal with the deep-seated worker resistance, which surfaces only in unofficial slowdowns and general foot-dragging.

Exegesis on the famous word "more"

The extreme untidiness, the messiness, of collective bargaining in the U.S. is apparent on all sides. One union is deciding to stress wages while another decides to de-emphasize wages and stress security; or the same union reverses its emphasis from one year to another. But these shifting decisions do not express mere whim; they are responses to changing conditions in various industries, and changing fears and desires of particular groups of workers. So untidy, so shifting, so relative is the American labor scene that it *must* be deeply involved in the most untidy, shifting, and relative of all human institutions, the market.

This involvement is no accident but the development of the character that Samuel Gompers imprinted on American unions as boldly as his signature, which adorns the charters that hang in Washington union offices. For Gompers' great invention was the word "more" as a description of what the unions wanted. Usually this word is recalled as an example of the unions' unappeasable voracity; but in its original context and its long-range effect its significance is different. On New York's East Side when Gompers was young, a hundred ideologies of labor competed with one another. His predecessor as head of the Cigar

Makers, Adolph Strasser, rebelled against the belief that unions should be considered instruments for gaining utopian goals. In 1873, testifying before a U.S. Senate committee, Strasser was asked, "What are your ultimate ends?" And he answered: "We have no ultimate ends. We are going on from day to day. We are fighting only for immediate objects—objects that can be realized in a few years." Gompers, accepting the thought, boiled it down to "more, now."

Thereby the U.S. labor movement committed itself to the U.S. market system. Again and again ideologues, many of them Marxists, have tried vainly to turn American unions from their "purposeless" pursuit, their concentration on responding to immediate pressures and on improvement within a short perspective of a few years. Gompers' "more" was a non-utopian acceptance of limits rather than an arrogant demand. He didn't want to get to an ideal society; where he wanted the workers to go was merely ahead.

Anybody who wants to understand the labor movement had better start with the object itself in all its historical complexity and the multiple contradictions and defects of its present position. He had better not start with a preconceived notion of what a labor movement, considered as an instrument for attaining the ideal society, ought to be. An example of the latter approach is the complaint of a liberal intellectual, disillusioned with unions, who declared that government intervention must increase because "collective bargaining has failed to solve the labor problem." Indeed, it has failed—and in a free society there can never be any "solution" to the labor problem, the price problem, the investment problem, or the woman problem.

Why government should stay out

Accepting unions and collective bargaining with their inherent and ineradicable defects does not imply accepting all present union practices or pressures. Such acceptance does not preclude further legislation cutting back the degree to which government influence is thrown on the side of unions. To say that unions in general "are worth the price" is not to say that the union shop is inviolable or that the restrictive practices of the stagehands' union are worth what they cost. The future of collective bargaining, moreover, depends as much upon employer resistance to excessive union demands as it depends upon employer concessions to reasonable demands. What is "excessive" and what is "reasonable" can be determined only company by company, and year by year. The terms on which labor is performed—in their impermanence, complexity, particularity, and susceptibility to market pressures—are *prices*. Terms of this sort are not appropriate subjects for government action, because the basic mode of government action is law, which is supposed to be stable, uniform, and general.

When raw wage rates were the main subject of collective bargaining, it was hard enough to imagine how a government in peacetime might set wages. But it is infinitely harder now that the emphasis in bargaining has shifted to the more complex and particular field of arrangements for cushioning the social impact of rapid technological change. If a government imposed, say, the Kaiser plan on one company, it might be tempted to impose it on others where specific conditions were different. Or else government would abandon its appropriate mode of action—legality—and would decide each labor case on its particular circumstances; that way lies the corruption of constitutional government, a more serious matter than the inefficiencies of collective bargaining. Even assuming—and this is quite a large assumption—that any given Administration would be evenhanded in its treatment of management and labor, the more fundamental objection to government intervention remains: the difficulty of determining labor prices by legal machinery.

The devil we know

The Kennedy Administration certainly does not *want* to take over the role now performed by collective bargaining. But an impatient public opinion, goaded by the Administration's own activism, could come to consider as "inevitable" massive government intervention in labor disputes. In fact, such a trend is probable unless the President resolves to hold intervention to an absolute minimum. Reflecting on his own experience and not speaking in criticism of his successors, former Secretary of Labor James Mitchell has said that it is always easier for a government official to intervene than not to intervene in major labor disputes. When those telegrams from governors begin to arrive in Washington, when the congressional delegations troop to the Labor Department and the White House, when the editorials scream that the government must "do something" to end a strike—it's hard not to say, "We'll look into it and see what we can do." Looking leads to judgment, and judgment to government pressure for specific terms of settlement. Soon no real

bargaining occurs anywhere because one side or the other thinks it will get a better break in Washington than in a test of bargaining strength.

The American labor movement today is certainly no worse than it ever was, and a strong case can be made that it is getting better. Unions and techniques of collective bargaining may not improve fast enough to meet the challenge of the years ahead. The same doubt can be cast on management—and on government. Unions are not only the devil we know, but they are also institutions that fit this society far better than would government regulation of the terms of labor.

The above article drew the following letter to the editor from a corporation executive.

To the Editors:

I am shocked at "Labor Unions are Worth the Price."

For a supposedly responsible business publication to white-wash the union situation at a time that it seemed we might be getting some sentiment for reform is almost inconceivable.

To point out how ridiculous some points are is almost an impossible job, because so many are so obviously biased from a labor union viewpoint. To quote George Meany as saying that "strikes are a part of the American way of life" and therefore good is ridiculous. By the same token, thirty years ago we could have said that bank runs are a part of the American way of life and actually they only affect a small percentage of the total number of banks and therefore why bother about them.

To say that "management has a greater degree of control of business than it had fifty years ago" makes no sense whatsoever.

To say that "no better way than strikes has been suggested for settling labor disputes" is also ridiculous. Responsible people throughout the country have made many suggestions. Other countries have adopted systems that have certainly been an improvement over what we have in this country. To give labor unions the unbridled power, exempting them from all kinds of laws, and put them in the position they now have, and then come out and say that this is a good thing is certainly too much to swallow. To let labor unions be in the position where they can disregard the welfare of the public and hold up the entire country, as the Teamsters Union could do now, is almost unthinkable. To permit the disregard of common law and justice that goes on with union activity, and intimidation of individual workers, is certainly not the mark of an enlightened society.

To try to paint a picture that the cost of labor unions is a very small cost makes no sense. The cost of labor unions in intangible ways, in the stint system, in the restraint of progress, in the backward kind of political power that they have used, add up to an enormous cost.

W. MAXEY JARMAN
Chairman of the Corporation
Genesco
Nashville, Tennessee

READING 43

Have the unions which were discussed in the previous selection had much of an impact on the level of wages in the United States? To raise the question is to sound hopelessly naïve to those who look at the statistics on wage changes since 1940 and then immediately damn or credit the unions that grew strong in those same decades.

But the question turns out to be one of the more complex ones in interpreting past and present. A man who has been warned about the fallacy of *"post hoc, ergo propter hoc"* will demand more evidence on the unions' impact than the mere facts that these unions pounded on the bargaining table and marched away with better contracts time after time. He will, at a minimum, try to answer the question, "What would have happened in the absence of unions, but in the presence of all the other factors, including long periods of relatively full employment, that marked the post-1940 years?"

Clark Kerr, president of the University of California and one of the top labor economists in the country, offers no support here for those who want a simple black or white answer on the unions' impact. His article is marked by the restraint and skepticism that characterize sound social science in an emotion-laden area.

Questions to Guide the Reading

What factors may help to account for the wide variety of conclusions reached by competent economists on the unions' impact? How might one proceed to a further testing of whether Kerr's conclusions on this impact are generally sound?

What light do these conclusions shed upon the wisdom of proposals for revising labor's position under the Taft-Hartley Act and the Federal antitrust laws? What other impacts of strong unions must be taken into account in public policy?

THE IMPACT OF UNIONS ON THE LEVEL OF WAGES
Clark Kerr

Inflation and industrialization have marched together for the past two centuries. Rising prices and growing industrial output have characterized much of the economic history of this period, with the notable exception of the second half of the nineteenth century. While they have marched together, they have not marched closely and evenly in step until the past few years. The alternations of war and peace and prosperity and depression have variously affected the course of both inflation and industrialization. The pace of both has been subject to great variations.

From Clark Kerr, "The Impact of Unions on the Level of Wages," in The American Assembly, *Wages, Prices, Profits and Productivity* (Columbia University Press, New York, 1959), pp. 91–108. Reprinted with kind permission of the author and publisher.

Since World War II, on the other hand, the years have been marked in Western Europe and North America by more nearly constant rather than sporadic inflation and industrialization. And, while a decade and a half constitutes a great deal less than an everlasting trend, a spectre is haunting Western capitalism—the spectre of constant inflation. Many, although not all, of the powers of society have been allied to exorcise this spectre—government officials and editorial writers, monetary authorities and economists, financiers and ministers—but it still exists.

It is a real spectre though it is not new and it need not make society tremble. It is a real spectre because constant inflation could become constantly greater inflation; because it redistributes income often in an inequitable fashion; and because policies to combat it may also combat progress.

Constant inflation presumably should have a constant source. Several new or relatively new developments have accompanied constant inflation and are, consequently, the most likely causes. One of these is the growth of the trade union movement and of its power over the wage-setting process. But it is not the only companion. Other companions have been governmental commitments to full employment, policies and practices leading to unbalanced budgets and low interest rates, rapid industrial expansion, new supply conditions in labor markets and new patterns of mobility and immobility, and new mechanisms for price control by private agencies; and several of these companions are closely related to each other.

The question here is the responsibility of one of these companions—the trade union—for constant inflation. This is not an easy question to answer, partly because of the intermingling of ideology and group self-interest with analysis in so much of the discussion, but particularly because with so many things happening it is almost impossible to state precisely the force of any one development by itself. For example, what would be the effect of the trade union if there were no industrial growth or if there were no administered prices to go along with administered wages? Consequently, reliance must be placed on individual judgments rather than any universally accepted analysis; and judgments have differed.

The split jury

The jury which has sat most constantly on this case has been composed of economists; and al-

most any conceivable verdict can be obtained by picking almost any conceivable economist.[1] To illustrate:

To *Lindblom*[2] the union is a "monopoly" and also a "body politic." As a body politic, under the urging of political pressures, it uses its monopoly power to force wages higher and higher. This leads to "unemployment or inflation" and, with government guarantee of full employment, to inflation. As a result, "unionism and the private enterprise system are incompatible."

To *Chamberlain*[3] the unions introduce a "monopoly element" into the labor market and, whether or not they try to maximize the wage bill, they do try to get "more" and this leads to "wage-push inflation." "Unions today do have too much economic power."

To *The Economist*[4] the real cost of trade unions is not so much the loss in productivity per man-hour they cause but rather that they turn full production into full inflation; and to avoid the latter, the former must also be forgone. This is one of the great economic tragedies of our age and our type of society.

To *Hicks*[5] the "Labour Standard" has replaced the Gold Standard. Governments will adjust their policies to maintain full employment at whatever wage levels the unions choose to set; and price levels follow along. But the unions, or at least British unions, may not be so unreasonable that this "Labour Standard" is much more "dangerous" than other monetary systems.

To *Lerner*[6] the problem is not "wage-cost inflation" alone but "seller's inflation." For there is also "profit inflation" as well as "wage inflation," and it is very difficult and even impossible to untangle the two. Wherever there are administered prices and administered wages, and they

[1] For a summary of the recent literature see G. H. Hildebrand, "The Economic Effects of Unionism," in *A Decade of Industrial Relations Research* (Harper & Row, Publishers, Incorporated, New York, 1958).

[2] Charles E. Lindblom, *Unions and Capitalism* (Yale University Press, New Haven, Conn., 1949).

[3] Edward H. Chamberlain, "The Economic Analysis of Labor Union Power," in *Labor Unions and Public Policy* (American Enterprise Association, 1958).

[4] August 2, 1958.

[5] J. R. Hicks, "Economic Foundations of Wage Policy," *Economic Journal*, September, 1955.

[6] A. P. Lerner, "Inflationary Depression and the Regulation of Administered Prices," in United States Joint Economic Committee, *The Relationship of Prices to Economic Stability and Growth,* March 21, 1958.

seem to be nearly everywhere, "seller's inflation" is a possibility, and it must be dealt with as a unitary phenomenon.

To *Slichter*[7] the unions are only one of several causes of inflation, and the others include the reduced availability of new sources of labor and the policy of government; but they are a significant cause. He concludes that, between 1933 and 1953, unions pushed up the general wage level "at least 25 cents per hour and probably more." This is one-fifth of the total increase that occurred during that period.

To *Reynolds*[8] "collective bargaining does not have as much impact on the money-wage level as has sometimes been suggested. My judgment would be that between 1945 and 1955 the money-wage level rose little, if any, more than it would have risen under nonunion conditions."

To *Morton*[9] unions are a minor factor affecting inflation and may retard it as well as augment it: retard it in a boom period; increase it in certain industries, where government regulation relates prices to costs, like public utilities and railroads.

To *Friedman*[10] unions have both a "rigidity effect" and "upward-pressing effect." The former holds down wage levels in a period of expansion; the latter forces them up in a period of stability. The two largely offset each other; but, of the two, the rigidity effect may be the more important under recent circumstances.

To *Boulding*[11] it is a certainty "that the main effect of unionism is to hold down wages and to prevent them from rising faster than they otherwise would. . . . Unions are the opiate of the people under capitalism. That is why you have got to have them."

From the destroyer of "private enterprise" to the "opiate of the people," from the source of disastrous inflation to a bulwark of price stability, from a powerful monopoly to a minor or even negative force—the judgments vary. Economics is not yet a science; but economists are certainly free thinkers.

As a very part-time economist, I should like to

[7] Sumner H. Slichter, "Big Unions and Inflation," *American Economic Review Proceedings,* May, 1954.
[8] Lloyd G. Reynolds in *New Concepts in Wage Determination* (McGraw-Hill Book Company, New York, 1957).
[9] Walter A. Morton, "Trade Unionism, Full Employment and Inflation," *American Economic Review,* March, 1950.
[10] Milton Friedman, in David McCord Wright (ed.), *Impact of the Union* (Harcourt, Brace & World, Inc., 1951).
[11] Kenneth E. Boulding, in *ibid.,* p. 245.

suggest that all of them are right and all of them are wrong. All of them are right to the extent that they suggest that some kinds of unions could have the suggested effects under some kinds of circumstances. All of them are wrong, to the extent they suggest (and some of them do not) that their conclusions are the universal rule. The only universal rule is that there are all kinds of unions operating under all kinds of circumstances and they can have all kinds of effects. But it should also be added that kinds and circumstances and effects can be related—at least to a certain degree. Truth is more likely to emerge from studying the impacts of the unions, than "the impact of the union."

Types, circumstances and impacts

Types. When talking about unions, it is helpful to specify the kind of union one is talking about. In terms of their approaches to price stability, unions can be broadly divided into the following general types.

Agent of the state. The "agent of the state" union as in Russia or China is the willing tool of the national administration. It serves its policies. It has no policies of its own. It is a weapon of social discipline, and the only variation of which it is capable is in the degree of its effectiveness.

Partner in social control. Some unions serve as "partners in social control." They may be formal partners, as they have been in Holland, assuming joint public responsibility for the economic welfare of the nation; or they may be informal partners, as they have been in Germany, almost equally committed with the government to reasonably full employment and reasonable price stability at the same time. In Britain and in the Scandinavian countries, the unions have served as such informal partners when Labor or Social Democratic parties were in power. Here again there can be degrees of effectiveness as "social partner."

Sectional bargainer. The union, as "sectional bargainer," is concerned not with the national impacts of its actions but with the consequences for its members and for its industry or segment of an industry. Its responsibility is relatively narrowly defined. The United States and Canada are representative of this type of unionism. The "sectional bargainer" union may be found in two major phases—(*a*) a state of excitement and (*b*) a state of normality. A state of excitement is most likely to exist in a new union, a union subject to the challenge of a rival union or a union undergoing internal political upheaval; and bargaining is likely to be much more aggressive in a state of excitement than in a state of normality.

Class bargainer. The union, as "class bargainer," endeavors to get a "fair share," which usually means a larger share, of the national income for labor as a whole. It is usually matched by other "class bargainers," as in France, who seek "fair shares" for agricultural producers, the commercial classes, the civil servants, and so forth; and the total of these "shares" is almost certain to add up to more than the national output of goods and services. The "class bargainer" union usually has or develops a class ideology.

Enemy of the system. The "enemy of the system" union is devoted to the destruction of the surrounding economic and political structure. Among its techniques are the sabotage of production and the encouragement of excessive consumption aspirations. Such unions have been really effective only when a society is in the process of disintegration.

These above types suggest more uniformity and stability than is the actuality. Some societies have mixtures at any one moment of time—as in France with Communist, Socialist and Catholic unions. In some societies, the union movement shifts from one "type" or policy to another. The "agent of the state" union will remain an "agent of the state" so long as the state needs an agent. But the "social partner" union may be a partner only when the nation faces an emergency or when a government it favors is in power and then turn to a "sectional" or "class" approach under other circumstances. The "enemy of the system" union may in non-revolutionary periods follow a "class bargainer" policy instead of open full-scale opposition, or even be a particularly belligerent, "sectional bargainer."

Theoretically, it might be expected that unions, from the top of this list to the bottom, would vary from strong supporters of stability to effective agents of instability.

Circumstances and impacts

Unions, of whatever type, operate within an environment, and their potential impacts on the general level of money wages may be almost as much related to the environment as to their type. Among the environmental situations with which we shall treat are those relating to the policies of other institutions (government and employers), to employment conditions, and to labor market conditions.

The standard for comparison will be "what would otherwise have happened" had there been no union; and this nobody really knows. The standard will not be the absolute increase in money wages; for unions may sometimes do most when they seem to do the least, and do least when they seem to do the most. For example, in a depression a union may hold up wages which would otherwise go down and we can say they "raised the level"; while in a boom period they may belatedly negotiate a substantial wage increase which would have come earlier under nonunion conditions through the operation of market forces, and we can say they "reduced the level."

We shall consider first the policies of other institutions. Guaranteed full employment places the unions in an advantageous position, and two types of unions—"enemy of the system" and "class bargainer"—are in a particularly good position to take advantage of it. Administered prices by employers create a special opportunity for the "sectional bargainer" union, for administered wages can be passed on through administered prices and turn up in administered inflation. With pattern bargaining, high settlements in an area of "administered prices" are likely to be imitated in other areas and thus spread the high "key" settlement. When the government is fearful of strikes and enters the collective bargaining arena to settle disputes, this again creates a favorable environmental situation for each of the three types of unions just mentioned. However, were the government to undertake a critical public review of wage settlements, this would have the opposite effect, and the "sectional bargainer" and particularly the "social partner" unions would be sensitive to such review. Government wage controls create an unfavorable condition for union impact on the general level of money wages and especially for the "social partner" union; the "agent of the state" union is, of course, always subject to wage controls.

In terms of employment conditions, unions probably have the greatest upward impact on money wages in a depression, when their attachment to past levels and the lags inherent in collectively bargained wages work toward stability. Next, in the downswing, particularly the early phases, they may not only be able to hold wage levels but actually increase them, contrary to "normal" tendencies. In a period of stable full employment, union pressure may well keep **wages**

Table 1 Factors Relating to Union Impact on General Level of Money Wages

	Type of Union	Policies of Other Institutions	Employment Conditions	Labor Market Conditions
Raise level	"Enemy of the system"	"Guaranteed" full employment	Depression	
				New recruits
	"Class bargainer"		Downswing	
		Administered prices		
	"Sectional bargainer"		Stable full employment	
(As compared with what would otherwise prevail)		Government settlements to avoid strikes		
	a. State of excitement			
	b. State of normality		Upswing	
		Government review of wage settlements	"Overly full" employment	Immobile labor force
	"Partners in social control"			
Reduce level		Government wage control		
	"Agent of the state"			

rising at some "standard" rate, say 5 per cent a year, when under other circumstances they would have risen more slowly. In an upswing, particularly its later stages, and in "overly full" employment, however, unions with their term agreements and formal approaches may cause a lag behind the adjustments which would otherwise occur. A general rule might be: the smaller the wage adjustment, the greater the true impact of the union; and the greater the wage increase, the lesser the real impact.

Labor market conditions may also relate to union impact. In a period of rapid accessions to the labor force—women, migrants from rural areas, young people—the unions can protect wages from the depressing effects. But when a labor force has become immobile, due to pensions or seniority rules or excessively specialized training or for other reasons, the union may reduce the upward impact on wages of this immobility. In the absence of unions, employers would tend to respond to individual scarcity situations with selective adjustments; and the impacts of these would spread. Unions, with their more formal wage relationships, tend to dampen this tendency and force employers to make other adjustments than the bidding up of individual classes of skills. This may possibly serve to lower, somewhat, the general level of money wages.

Putting together the variety of types of unions and the variety of environmental settings results in a variety of potential effects. Unions raise the general level of money wages greatly; or perhaps only a little. Unions reduce the general level of money wages substantially; or perhaps only a little. Or perhaps they have no effect at all. It all depends. And it all depends on type and circumstance, as the summary table suggests (see Table 1).

The variety of experience

Experience is different from experiment. There have been no conscious experiments, and in the nature of the case there cannot be, through which a determination could be made with accuracy of the impact of the union on the general level of money wages. There is only experience; and the knowable reality from this experience is little more than conjecture. To speak with full assurance in this area is to speak from prejudice or from ignorance or both. Yet some things can be said.

Possible tests

There are at least three ways in which one might try to test the impact of the union.

1. *How have union wages risen as compared to non-union?* One might find here the true impact of the union not only on inter-industry and

inter-occupational differentials but also on the general level of money-wages.

But union and non-union wages are not in water-tight compartments and what happens to one set of wages may affect the other. If it were found that union wages went up only as fast as non-union wages, this might mean the unions had no impact; however, it might only mean that non-union wages were playing "follow-the-leader" and thus that the unions were having an even greater effect on the general level of money wages. Also, if union wages were found to be going up faster, this might imply the unions did have an impact; but it might only reflect the fact that the wages of unionized manual workers, under the impact of broadly available educational opportunities and the breakdown of class lines, were rising faster than those of non-unionized white collar workers who had come into relatively greater supply—the important comparison might be manual and non-manual, not union and non-union.

2. *How has recent history, when strong unions existed, compared with earlier history when there were fewer unions?* Here again it might be discovered how the introduction of unionism has affected the course of the general level of money wages.

But the statistics, on any really comparable basis, do not go very far back. And if they did, it would still be true that more has happened in the course of intervening events than the rise of a union movement. Even adjusting for the amount of unemployment, there is still the question of what effect the expectation of generally lower rates of unemployment would have had on the behavior of employers in any event. Also, since employers, whenever they can, tend to share their profits one way or another with their workers, what would have been the effect of administered prices even without administered wages? And what has been the consequence of the drying up of the old sources of cheap labor on the general level of money wages?

3. *How has labor's share of national income behaved?* If there is evidence that the unions have really "squeezed" profits below their "normal" levels, then it might be said the unions were pushing wages up against profits and thus against prices.

But labor's share is one of the mysteries of economic analysis. And it is also affected by other developments than union pressure alone. There may be implications to be drawn from the analysis but little or no proof.

With all their imperfections, these are possible tests and their application to the actual course of events should give us some indications of how much and under what circumstances unions have had an impact on the general level of money wages.

Actual tests

The application of actual or presumed facts to our problem is fraught with a number of perils, some of which have been mentioned earlier. However, their application may indicate a reasonable range of answers to our questions.

The United States. (1) The various studies which have been made of the course of union and non-union wages offer no clear conclusions. Their results depend, to a substantial extent, on the dates taken for the studies and the definitions used. It may be fair to conclude, nevertheless, that, except for periods of active new unionism (as 1936–37) and for situations with a closed shop (building trades), there is little evidence of a definite upward push by unions on wages.

(2) The history of wage movements in the United States provides some additional evidence. Real compensation per man-hour dropped less from 1931 to 1932 (less than 2 per cent) when unions had strong influence in a few industries than from 1893 to 1894 (3 per cent) or 1920 to 1921 (3 per cent). Compensation in the 1931 to 1932 period held steadier, as compared with consumer prices, than in the two earlier periods, possibly, in part, because of union influence.

Money wages held much steadier in 1944 to 1945 than in 1917 to 1918. In 1944 to 1945, wage controls were in effect by government as against 1917 to 1918, when there was great freedom in wage adjustments. But it should also be noted that the unions in 1944 to 1945 accepted and even cooperated in the imposition of wage controls, and also that the contractual mechanisms which had grown up since 1917 to 1918 helped make it possible to exercise control over the great mass of wage rates that comprise our national wage structure.

In 1936 to 1937, with new and rival unionism, money wages and real wages jumped much more rapidly than one would normally expect in a period marked with as much unemployment as then existed.

Taking two longer periods, 1900 to 1910 and 1947 to 1957, both eras of quite sustained growth, it is noticeable that money wages rose faster than productivity in both periods. From 1900 to 1910, wages rose by one-third and productivity by one-fourth; from 1947 to 1957, by one-half and by one-third. It would appear that there may be an inflationary tendency, with wages rising faster than productivity, in a period of sustained growth under both largely non-union and largely union conditions. However, the excess gains of wages over productivity were somewhat greater in the second period and this may be due, in part, to unionism. Wages rose roughly one-third faster than productivity in the earlier period and one-half faster in the later period.

(3) Labor's share of national income has tended to be quite constant in the long run after adjusting for changes in the proportion of wage earners and in the inter-industry mix. But there have been occasions when the profit share has been "squeezed" and the wage share increased and, perhaps, partly due to union pressure on wages. These have been periods of depression (1931 to 1934 and 1938), periods when prices were held by price controls or the slower movement of administered prices in an inflationary period (1944 to 1947) and, most interestingly, a period of sustained full employment without substantial inflation, as in 1954–1957.

Perhaps it could then be said that wages were really "pushing" on profits and thus on prices under these three circumstances. When there is no change in the profit share, it is harder to say who or what is "pushing" or "pulling"; and, when the profit share is rising, it would seem to indicate a "pull" rather than a "push." "Wage inflation," or wage pressure on the price level without inflation, would seem most likely to have occurred when labor's share had risen above "normal."

Great Britain. (1) A recent study in Great Britain, by A. W. Phillips, relating wage increases to volume of unemployment, shows some interesting parallels and variations. Working with three periods, 1861 to 1913, 1913 to 1948, and 1948 to 1957, the first marked by relatively weak and the latter two by relatively strong unionization, Phillips found a very close correspondence between the related behavior of money wages and unemployment. The 1913 to 1948 period particularly followed the expectations based on the 1861 to 1913 period with only one major exception. Money wages went up faster in the years 1935 to 1937, a time of active union revival after the

depression and also of rising food prices, than the general relation of money wage changes to the volume of unemployment would suggest. Taking the years 1948 to 1957, the "wage restraint" period of Trades Union Congress policy showed a lower than "normal" wage advance, but the years immediately following the end of the policy were noted for an unusually rapid increase, although they were also years of a rapid rise in import prices. As compared with the United States, lower levels of unemployment were found to be associated with the same wage behavior. For example, wages and productivity have seemed to march hand in hand with 2.5 per cent unemployment in Great Britain rather than 5 per cent in the United States.

(2) British experience also shows the importance of the divergence between actual rates and nominal rates—the rates paid in fact and those provided for by collective agreements and other formal documents. This divergence, or "wage drift," varies from one situation to another, but it was particularly great during periods of wage restraint, World War II and 1948 to 1950. Actual rates drifted away from control through local action of employers and unions.

(3) The history of labor's share in Great Britain suggests no different general conclusions than does the history for the United States. Wages have squeezed profits when product markets were "hard" but not when they were "soft."

Western Europe. A review of postwar experience in selected Western European countries, including for the sake of comparisons the United Kingdom and the United States, is instructive (See Table 2). France, with its "class bargainer" approach and the type of economy associated with it, has witnessed the greatest increase in the general level of money wages in manufacturing. Italy, however, with a somewhat similar approach, has had a relatively small increase. This emphasizes the point that other things are happening to an economy aside from union action. In Italy, over this period, unemployment has averaged 9 per cent, while it has been at quite low (but unmeasured) levels in France. Norway, Sweden, and the United Kingdom have all undertaken "responsible" wage policies during part of the postwar period, and when responsibility was most in practice, up to 1950 and the Korean War, wage increases may have been slowed down a bit; but their records are not much different from that of the United States, where no such policy was

Table 2 Indices of Hourly Money Earnings in Manufacturing in Selected Countries, 1946–57 (1950 = 100)

	1946	1947	1948	1949	1950	1951	1952	1953	1954	1955	1956	1957
France	37	53	81	91	100	128	148	152	162	174	187	202
Italy	..	71	94	99	100	110	115	118	122	129	138	
Norway	79	87	92	94	100	114	127	133	140	148	159	169
Sweden	74	85	93	96	100	121	144	150	156	168	183	
United Kingdom	79	87	93	96	100	110	118	125	132	143	155	165
Germany	70	73	82	94	100	113	122	127	130	139	152	166
Holland	81	87	92	92	100	108	110	113	132	136	150	
United States	74	84	92	95	100	108	114	120	123	130	135	141

SOURCES: *International Labor Review, Statistical Supplements;* and United Nations *Statistical Yearbooks.*

in effect. In fact it was in Sweden during this early postwar period that the term "wage drift" was invented.

Holland and Germany have had stronger policies of wage restraint in the postwar period, for the sake of the restoration of their economies, but wages have gone up only somewhat less than in Norway and the United Kingdom, and more than in Italy. In Germany, wage restraint was particularly in force from 1949 (after currency reform) to 1955 with some apparent effect, but this was also a period of great absorption of refugees into the economy. In Germany, with wage restraint by the unions, a "wage drift" began to show up in pronounced form by 1954 particularly in the metal-working industries of North Rhine–Westphalia. And it might be noted that a "wage drift" above contract rates becomes increasingly embarrassing to unions and undermines a wage restraint policy.

Finally, the United States, without wage restraint and with a sectional bargaining approach, has demonstrated a comparatively high degree of wage stability, as Table 2 shows.

Russia. Russian statistics on a comparable basis are not readily available. However, some comparisons can be made. From 1948 to 1952 money wages are said to have risen 8 per cent in Russia as against 24 per cent in the United States; and from 1953 to 1956 the figures are 7 per cent and 12.5 per cent. Also, it should be noted, productivity, as an offsetting force, has been rising faster in Russia (though it is at a much lower absolute level) than in the United States. But even in Russia, with an "agent of the state" union movement and authoritarian control, money wages have been rising; and price rates have been particularly resistant to controls.

Observations

The record, inadequate as it is, does permit some conclusions.

1. The "class bargainer" (or "enemy of the state") union movement, in the type of economy in which it develops, may well add to inflationary wage pressures.

2. The "agent of the state" union movement, in the type of system where it finds its natural habitat, is compatible with a comparatively slow rate of increase in the general level of money wages.

3. The "partner in social control" union movement may join in keeping wage increases somewhat below their normal levels for relatively short periods of time. But the "wage drift" and the internal pressures which develop under a wage-restraint policy make it unlikely that this effect will be long lasting. The results of wage restraint have been modest at best, although useful under the circumstances where they have been applied.

4. The "sectional bargainer" union movement presents a more mixed situation. When in a state of excitement, as around 1937 in both the United States and Great Britain, it may push wages up beyond "normal." In a depression, it may well hold them somewhat higher than they otherwise would be. At the plateau of a period of prosperity or in the early downswing, it may continue rates of wage increases experienced in the recent and more favorable past into the new situation. But in the upswing or a period of demand inflation, it may actually retard wage increases.

Generally, the "sectional bargainer" union movement will probably lead to a steadier advance of the general wage level, neither as fast nor as slow as might otherwise occur. Also through pattern bargaining, wage increases may be spread more uniformly and more broadly throughout the economy than under non-union conditions. Thus the total long-term effect is likely to be moderately inflationary; for the postwar period in the United States a net impact (after allowance for the influence of other factors) on the price level of somewhat less than one-half of one per cent as compared with "normal" or non-union conditions.

The real question might be why, as compared with the havoc it might wreak as seen by Lindblom, it has had so little effect? The answer must lie, in part, in the general reasonableness of the unions and their leaders in the context of the type of society in which they evolve; and thus in the nature of this kind of union as an institution.

In fact, two reversals of common statements come closer to illuminating the truth. Instead of asking why unions have so much inflationary effect, it might be more pertinent to ask why, as "monopolies," they have so little. Instead of accusing unions of an effective upward pressure on wage levels in a period of expansion and inflation, it would be more pertinent to make the accusation about them in periods of depression and deflation. The wrong question is asked; and the wrong accusation made.

5. The volume of unemployment is closely related to changes in the general level of money wages. In general, the level of employment must be considered the most important single factor. Its influence is over and beyond that of the trade union.

6. A period of expansion in a capitalist economy is normally a period of some inflation. Expansion and inflation are common travelling companions, whether a union movement travels with them or not.

7. Government wage controls can have an effect in holding down wage levels, perhaps more in the short run than in the long run, except in an authoritarian economy like the Russian.

8. Administered prices most certainly can make it easier to pass on administered wages without affecting profits.

The type of union and the character of the environment together determine the impact of the union on the general level of money wages. To view either one alone is to view but part of the scene. Taken together, in Western capitalism, the combination has probably become a somewhat more inflationary one than in earlier times.

The union has often become more insensitive to the pressure of unemployment because of seniority rules protecting its older members and unemployment compensation for its newer members; but offsetting this has been the general growth in reasonableness and a sense of responsibility. The major changes are in the environment which is more permissive—full or more nearly full employment, the spread of administered prices and the drying up of pools of readily available labor.

If the unions secure greater wage increases than in the past, it is not so much because they want "more, more and more," which they do, but rather because it is easier to get "more, more and more." The environment is more conducive, rather than the unions more insatiable. The source of the trouble, to the extent there is trouble, is more that there is less pressure on the wage fixers than that the wage fixers are less sensitive to it; is more that there is less power in the environment and less that there is more power in the unions.

If remedies are to be sought, they would seem to lie, first, in strengthening the pressure of the environment toward stability and, second, in making unions more sensitive to that pressure.

Remedies

In considering remedies, in the context of the American economy, it may be well to contemplate these four points:

(1) Some inflation may be a normal cost of growth;

(2) The United States has had a comparatively good record on inflation in the postwar years;

(3) Some mild inflationary pressures are inherent in the kind of unionism which evolves out of American society;

(4) Certain "solutions" are not compatible with the character of this society—"agent of the state" unionism, or even "social partner" unionism, or permanent unemployment in excess (and possibly substantially in excess) of 6 per cent, or, probably, permanent wage (and price) controls by government.

Within the context of our society, however, several things may be possible:

1. To begin with, it would not be wise to guarantee full employment, particularly sector

by sector, regardless of wage and price behavior. There should be some costs to irresponsible actions.

2. Next, administered prices are not fully socially accepted and their more unreasonable excesses should be discouraged by all reasonably available means, including anti-trust action and freer trade.

3. Industries of great pattern-setting importance or otherwise crucial to the economy should be made subject to *ex post* and *ad hoc* impartial fact-finding review of their wage bargains (and price policies) to acquaint the public with their consequences. This is one way to mobilize public opinion to bring pressure for stability on the private wage and price fixers.

4. The government should not enter industrial disputes with a "peace-at-any-price" approach except in a true national emergency.

5. All available action should be taken to increase the total supply of labor, for example, by providing part-time jobs for housewives and older persons, and to improve the mobility and adaptability of the labor force.

6. Unions should be open to all qualified workers. At the same time, rival unionism and great internal union instability should be avoided since the conflicts arising from them usually find their solution, in part, in wage increases.

These are reasonable means and only reasonable results should be expected from them. We are living in an age marked by uneven but rapid economic growth, by a commitment to more-or-less full employment, by an exhaustion of earlier available sources of new accessions to the industrial labor force, by the great advancement of group initiative and group control over the economy, by the substantial freedom of individuals and groups from the imposed power of the state, and by mild inflation. Remedies for the last phenomenon must be seen in the light of the other phenomena which surround it. All things are not possible in all situations; and one thing which is not possible in this situation is full price stability and the wage levels which are consistent with it. The most successful case of wage control in an industrialized nation in the postwar period is also the most repugnant.

READING 44

There are many economists who are less sanguine than Clark Kerr, author of the previous article, about the power of unions in our economy. One of the most articulate of those who fear union power greatly is Edward H. Chamberlin of Harvard University. Here he presents the case that a number of immunities of unions under Federal law give labor leaders excessive opportunities to push wages up too fast, to coerce neutrals, and to interfere with the healthy functioning of competitive pressures.

Questions to Guide the Reading

Chamberlin argues that excessive power in today's unions does not stem from collective bargaining *per se*. Would collective bargaining itself be affected if his proposals for curbing union power were adopted? Would the unions' ability to play the role called for in the earlier article by Max Ways (page 262) be impaired by a lessening of union power?

To what extent does the union power which Chamberlin fears come from the labor market itself? From the existence of high levels of employment? From disorganization or shortsightedness on management's part? From the political climate of the nation?

CAN UNION POWER BE CURBED?
Edward H. Chamberlin

Professor Sumner H. Slichter has pointed out that we live not, as we used to think, in a capitalistic society but in a laboristic one. Certainly most of us have a time lag in our thinking, and the economist's distrust of power has not yet been transferred in any substantial degree to labor. But I do believe that such a transfer is in process. Indeed, the most disturbing thing to my mind is not so much that people are unaware of the significance of this growth in labor union power but that so many seem to think that nothing can be done about it. I do not believe that anything in the field of social policy is inevitable, and we ought to stop saying that it is, however great the difficulties to be overcome.

The belief that nothing can be done about labor union power reduces to the belief that nothing *will* be done about it. This kind of fatalism is particularly evident with respect to the inflationary problem. Creeping inflation, we are told, is inevitable—all we can do is to accept it and learn to live with it.

Now the doctrine that inflation is inevitable is very closely linked with a particular kind of inflation, namely the cost-push type. We know a great deal about how to control inflation of the demand-pull variety by well-established monetary and fiscal techniques. No one believes that such inflation is inevitable, though it may approach inevitability in wartime. If the war years are omitted, prices have risen very little in the United States over the last hundred and fifty years. Years of rising prices have been fewer than those of falling or stable prices, and many of these latter have been years of prosperity.

Inflation of the cost-push variety is held to be inevitable partly because the conventional methods of control are not effective against it. For many reasons, the upward pressure on wages exerted by individual unions is strikingly insensitive to fiscal and credit restraints. And so, when one limits his thinking to fiscal and monetary measures, it is easy to conclude either that nothing can stop the upward cost push or that it can be stopped only at an unacceptable social cost of rising unemployment and lost production. By holding demand in check, the economy is indeed slackened, cost increases are harder to pass on,

employer resistance to wage demands is increased, strikes are harder to win, and wage demands are correspondingly reduced. And so economists like to speculate on how high unemployment must go before it begins to act as a brake on wage demands. The great mistake, I think, is in trying to control wage-push inflation by methods which are inappropriate for the job.

It becomes necessary to go back and ask a very simple and fundamental question: What is the source of the problem? If it is excessive power in the hands of labor, the most obvious way to seek a remedy would be to reduce the power, and this is in fact the gist of my proposal. An alternative proposal would be to strengthen management by such devices, for example, as the pooling arrangement among airlines which has recently received so much publicity. Perhaps we might have some of both. But strangely enough I have found in discussing these matters that many who are horrified at the thought of weakening unions have no objection whatever to strengthening management. They would prefer to equalize power at a higher level, for bigger and better struggles, whereas I should prefer a measure of disarmament.

Inflation is only one aspect of the general problem. The basis of labor union power is similar to that of any monopoly power—control of a market through collective action—but with the superimposition of decisive elements unique to the labor market.

The monopoly problem is simply one of maximum gain, both by the suppression of internal competition and by closing the path of entry to any from outside who would by their participation tend to break down the monopoly. This is precisely the method of monopoly in both the industrial and the labor areas. The striking difference between them is that monopoly in industry has been recognized as a matter of public concern for a long time and has been subjected, with at least partial success, to a program of regulation; whereas labor monopoly, hidden by the attractive phrase "collective bargaining," has hardly been recognized, let alone brought under control.

The control of monopoly generally involves the application of some standard of fairness, and in industry this standard has usually been found by

From Edward H. Chamberlin, "Can Union Power Be Curbed?" *Atlantic Monthly,* June, 1959. Reprinted with kind permission of the author and publisher.

a reference to competitive markets. Two procedures in applying the competitive criterion have been developed. In the case of public utilities and certain forms of transportation, monopoly is permitted and subjected to direct regulation. Here the lack of alternatives open to the consumer is recognized by imposing the obligation of service on the company. Here too, public commissions, subject to court review, regulate rates and earnings in accord with principles designed to bring about a rough correspondence between earnings in the regulated and in the competitive sectors of the economy, with allowance for such special factors as stability of income, risk, and so forth.

For the great bulk of the industrial area which remains, the attempt is made to preserve competition by forbidding agreements in restraint of trade, forbidding mergers under certain conditions, and outlawing certain specific practices which are regarded as detrimental to healthy competition. The expectation seems to be that enough competition can be preserved to give the public at least a reasonable protection against the abuses of concentrated private power and against the consequences of government regimentation.

The success of these policies may be questioned; I think everyone would agree that there is room for improvement. We get perspective on the policy, however, by comparing the prevailing spirit of American industry with that of Continental Europe, where cartelization is generally accepted and where, since agreements in restraint of trade are not forbidden, all manner of informal and tacit agreements and a generally restrictive mentality dominate the picture. I once heard the contrast put in this form: If a European retailer has an item on his shelf for some months without its being sold, he is likely to raise the price because of the cost he has incurred in keeping it for that time; the American retailer, on the contrary, will lower the price so as to get rid of it and make room for something else. The notion of not engaging too vigorously in price competition is a universal phenomenon in some degree, but a willingness to gain business at a rival's expense is fairly well developed in the United States, and I think the antitrust laws in this country are an important part of the reason why this is so.

Concentration of economic power in the labor field is paradoxically very great, partly because few people are aware of it. It is hidden because the gains which are made, say in terms of wages or so-called fringe benefits, are made immediately, speaking from the employer instead of from the public.

There is a common belief that higher wages come out of profits; and this is often superficially the case as a short-run proposition. Yet such a belief is in direct conflict with a fundamental long-run principle of economics as hoary and as generally respectable as the famous law of supply and demand, namely, the law of cost: that prices tend to conform to cost of production, including a normal allowance for profits. The principle is a rough one, and it ought to be elaborated if space permitted, especially as to the *amount* of profit which it includes. But there is no reason to expect wage increases, any more than increases in the cost of raw materials, to be met out of profits; both are paid in the end by the public in the form of higher prices.

Through the law of costs, the power of labor to raise money wages, and so indirectly to raise prices, is fundamentally no different from the power of business to raise prices directly. Monopoly wages, like monopoly prices, are paid in the end by the public; and it is for this reason that there is exactly as much public interest involved in the regulation of monopoly in the labor field as in the field of industry.

Now the problem of industrial monopoly power, even at those times in history when it has been of the greatest public concern, has never been associated with inflation. How is it therefore that such an association is made in the labor field? There are several reasons for this: the practice of wage settlements over wide areas on a pattern basis, so that one increase means many more; the institution of the annual wage increase, augmented by the growing practice of embodying it in long-term contracts; competition among labor leaders to outdo their rivals—and we must include competition from employers in nonunionized areas to do even better, so as to avoid unionization; and finally the fact that wages are more important than profits as an element in prices. The role of union power in cost inflation would seem to indicate that the control of this general inflationary force may be achieved only by putting a damper on thousands of individual wage and price increases.

How then to hold them in check? The decisive elements unique to the labor market which are mainly responsible for the fact that labor has too much power are not a part of collective bargaining per se. They are accretions of power which have developed partly through specific exemptions by Congress and through court interpretations, partly through a failure to understand the problem, but mostly through an uncritical public indulgence which can only be explained by a confused belief that since the labor cause is good, the more power in the hands of labor the better. As a practical matter, it seems to me that progress could be made in reducing union power by attacking directly those accretions which clearly rest upon privileges and immunities of laborers as compared with other citizens, and which it is therefore reasonable and fair to correct on the simple ground of equal treatment for all.

A recent booklet entitled *The Legal Immunities of Labor Unions* by Dean Emeritus Roscoe Pound of the Harvard University Law School analyzes an impressive list of such immunities. They are treated under the headings of torts (civil wrongs), contracts, restraint of trade, duties of public service, the right to work, racketeering, centralized power, and irresponsibility. Legal immunities are related to economic power, and each such immunity therefore contributes its bit to wage-push inflation. Certainly the appeal of equal treatment for all is a strong one in a democracy. Why should it not apply in this area?

On the more purely economic front, the power accretions are startling. The practice of making a deal with the teamsters to "honor" a picket line has nothing to do with free speech, as the Supreme Court seems to think it has because it involves picketing, and it has nothing to do with collective bargaining. It is simply a power gadget to deprive an employer not only of the services of his own workers who are on strike but of all other goods and services as well. The old legal principle that a service of such vital public necessity as transportation must not be closed or obstructed clearly corresponds to the economic realities. Yet it has not been adapted to developments of recent decades in the transportation field. Most firms in modern times are heavily if not totally dependent for their existence on private trucking. In fact, the teamsters derive most of their power not from the racketeering with which they are ridden but from their control over transportation, including the freedom with which they can choke off this vital service from any specific business enterprise they please.

The threat of potential violence and intimidation through the device of the picket line are powerful factors—so powerful, in fact, that nowadays a firm rarely attempts any operations at all if a strike has been called, although it would be within its legal rights to do so. For all practical purposes the alternative of making a bargain with anyone other than the union has been removed. Even the attempts in the 1959 bus strike in Massachusetts

to run a few buses operated by supervisors for school children were successfully blocked by masses of pickets surrounding the buses. Boycotts, hot cargo rules, refusals to work with nonunion labor or on materials produced by nonunion labor or by the wrong union are used with impunity to close the channels of trade and commerce. These and other privileges and immunities which tremendously augment union monopoly power are unique to the labor market.

Many of these developments are a logical conclusion of what seems to be the overriding principle that a union's economic power must not be compromised. In the further matter of agreements and alliances, for instance, anything is legal so long as only labor groups are involved. No—there is one qualification of mock seriousness. A union may restrain trade as much as it pleases and combine with others against other unions, against nonunion laborers, against some particular employer, or against the general public, provided only—in the quaint language of the Hutcheson decision—it is acting in its own self-interest.

I have seen a statement by an important labor leader before the Joint Economic Committee of Congress to the effect that even to raise the question of whether unions have too much power is to question their very right to exist. This is the union point of view, and it seems to be widespread. Yet what could be more absurd? Has anyone ever held that to reduce and regulate monopoly power in the business area was to question the right of business to exist?

We need only to make the distinction between collective bargaining and the application of further pressures, to make clear that such pressures may be reduced as the public interest and ordinary fairness require, without imperiling the existence of unions. Should a union be allowed to strangle a business economically by arranging with the teamsters to cut off its transportation? It seems to me we might as well ask if a physically strong customer in a retail shop should be allowed to twist the arm of the shopkeeper in order to drive a better bargain with him.

I suggest as a good general rule that no employer should have brought against him pressures exerted by anyone other than his own employees.[1] To implement such a principle fully may seem too much to hope for, but it should not be overlooked

[1] EDITORS' NOTE: Since this was written, some tightening up of the restrictions on union power over third parties was passed by Congress in the Landrum-Griffin Act of 1959.

that there is an opening wedge in the outlawing of the secondary boycott by Congress in the Taft-Hartley Act. It remains, after closing some of the loopholes which have developed in this prohibition, to make progress in applying the general principle more widely. There seems every reason to think that the questions of alliances in the labor field, interunion relationships, and the extent of single-union control are as much a matter of public concern and of regulation as are intercorporate relationships and agreements in industry.

A national policy of encouraging collective bargaining, adopted in the middle thirties in the belief that labor's bargaining power was weak and needed to be strengthened, has encouraged not merely collective bargaining but the development of a wide power complex. The careless view that labor must have enough power to win may have been understandable when labor was the underdog. But pilots who can close down airlines in negotiating for top salaries of well over $20,000 a year are not underdogs. And when a few hundred workers in New York who merely deliver newspapers after they have been produced can deprive ten million readers of printed news and inflict losses, not only on their employers but on a whole community, estimated at $50 million, it seems clear that the time has come for a re-evaluation of where the power now lies.

As this article is being written (1959), the fast-approaching crisis in the steel industry provides an example on a national scale of where the power lies. However one may judge the demands of the steel workers and wage-price relationships in the industry, the simple fact remains that the nation will be offered its choice between a long-drawn-out strike which would deal a heavy blow to economic recovery or an inflationary increase in costs. Indeed, it may very well get both.

The increase in wages (or fringe benefits) will be inflationary for two reasons: 1) whether at once or after an interval, steel prices will be higher, and so will the prices of all things made of steel; 2) less obvious but much more important, an increase in steel wages (already among the highest) must be followed by other wage increases. This is so because of the pattern phenomenon: if steel workers get more, inexorable pressures are created to bring other wages in the whole structure into line. So the wage-price spiral works not only vertically from wages to prices but horizontally from wages to other wages, and especially so when a key industry like steel is involved. With these considerations in mind, the question of whether or not certain steel companies could increase wages without raising their own prices (whatever the answer) recedes into proper perspective.

The choice between a disastrous closing down of the steel industry and another round of inflation is indeed a hard one, and if unions had less power other alternatives with a measure of concern for the public interest might have a hearing.

Unions have achieved their present position largely through public indulgence, and if the public becomes less indulgent, union power can be curbed. What is needed is a general awakening to the real nature of the problem. In its fundamentals monopoly power is the same whether used by laborers or by businessmen, and it has the same adverse effect on the rest of society, with an inflationary influence to be added in the case of labor. It has been subjected to regulation in business; how much longer will it go unregulated in the labor area? Will the rest of society continue to accept the principle that a labor union's freedom in the pursuit of its own self-interest shall be unrestrained?

READING 45

Few public policy proposals have been tossed about more frequently and yet casually than the call for putting unions under the antitrust laws. This reading points to the instantaneous surface appeal of this idea: if corporations are covered, why should unions be exempt? Thus, a recent survey by the Chase Manhattan Bank of 321 academic economists found 56 per cent of them favoring the application of antitrust laws to labor's activities. Many of them may have come to this conclusion for reasons similar to those maintained in the previous article by Chamberlin.

But the burden of this article is that we ought to take a longer, harder look at the matter before we rush into action. Frederic Meyers of the University of

California at Los Angeles raises a number of doubts about what the proposals mean, what effect they might have, and what all this has to do with the matter of inflation.

Questions to Guide the Reading

Are there specific legal remedies on which both Chamberlin (see page 281) and Meyers might agree for dealing with aspects of labor power where most men are in agreement that abuse of power now exists? Or are these two positions completely divergent?

One proposal on labor power that crops up from time to time is that unions should be forbidden by law to represent the employees of more than one employer; thus, we would have far more unions than we now have, but each would be smaller. Is this a useful clarification of the vague idea of putting "unions under the antitrust laws" to which Meyers objects? What would the effects of such a law be?

ANTI·TRUST LAWS FOR THE UNIONS?
Frederic Meyers

"Labor legislation" is a perennial subject for Congressional investigation and recommendation, action by state legislatures, debate, name-calling, and general emotional upheaval. No one denies that relationships between unions and management are so fraught with a public interest that they should be the subject of public regulation. At least in this area we have by common consent abandoned our historic slogan that that government is best which governs least. So far as I know John L. Lewis is the only recent protagonist of this classic view.

But regulation should be reasonably directed at the social problem it seeks to solve. We pass laws to accomplish some more or less specific social objective, and, presumably, the law is passed with such reasonably sufficient understanding of the behavior to be regulated that we can expect to achieve the end in view.

I think it is unfortunately true that in the field of labor, we have often tended to legislate by slogan, rather than with an intelligent understanding of the nature of a problem and of solutions appropriate to it. The examples are almost innumerable. The original Taft-Hartley Act's provision for elections to authorize a union to demand union security provisions was predicated on the supposition that many union members resented being prisoners in membership by reason of union shop arrangements of which they disapproved. The provision was repealed in haste and embarrassment when the procedure served only to demonstrate that almost everyone who worked in an organized establishment believed in the union shop. The provision had in fact an effect opposite to that intended: it no doubt resulted in more union shops rather than fewer. I am sure that the predictions of both protagonists and opponents of "right-to-work" legislation as to its probable effects were way wide of the mark. The "national emergency" provisions of the Taft-Hartley Act have become almost wholly a dead letter because brief experience demonstrated very clearly that the provisions, and especially the so-called "last offer ballot," served no useful purpose in averting dangerous strikes, and may even have made some situations worse. The War Labor Disputes Act, in its strike vote provisions, was another example of a remedy inappropriate to the problem.

It seems to me that this is true also of the often advanced proposals to put labor under the anti-trust laws. Such proposals illustrate to me the worst futilities of two approaches to which we seem prone: legislation by slogan, and equity by analogy. The slogan that we ought to put labor under the anti-trust laws is defended by the surface equity of the statement that because

From Frederic Meyers, "Unions, Anti-trust Laws and Inflation," *California Management Review*, Vol. 1, No. 4, Summer, 1959. Reprinted with kind permission of the author and publisher. Copyright, 1959, by the Regents of the University of California.

business is subject to the anti-trust laws, labor in all equity ought also to be.

It is rarely specified precisely what is meant by a proposal to put labor under the anti-trust laws. If what is meant is what appears on the surface, that is, to apply the language of the Sherman and Clayton Acts to trade unions and their activities, it probably comes near to being as meaningless a proposal as any recently advanced. As any businessman knows, the language of these statutes, deceptively simple on their face, is subject to most diverse constructions, and the courts have had a great deal of difficulty in applying that statutory language to the real world of business enterprise. If we were facing the problem of their application to labor unions and their activities, one would be hard put to predict what might happen.

But let it not be forgotten that for more than forty years, labor unions were subject to the anti-trust laws, as the language of the statutes was constructed by a Supreme Court not notably sympathetic, in majority, to trade unionism. I think a review of the leading cases involving allegations of union violations of the anti-trust laws between, say, 1890 and the passage of the Norris-LaGuardia Act in 1932, and perhaps later, would reveal that virtually all of the successful prosecutions involved activities which have, since 1947, been unlawful under the Taft-Hartley Act. Strikes in pursuit of a closed shop and secondary boycotts are, of course, the clear situations.

The present status of certain kinds of organizational picketing is in doubt.

The only major area of union action which seems now to be permissible but which was limited under the anti-trust laws is that of appeals to remote consumers to boycott. I think it can fairly be said that, substantively speaking, unions are now forbidden almost everything they were forbidden in the period of application of the anti-trust laws, and a good deal more besides. There are of course some differences in the remedies, but they are not important. While, after the Clayton Act, a private person might seek injunctive relief, the mandatory features of the injunctive provisions of Taft-Hartley remove any significant differences. Under Taft-Hartley, punitive damages are not available, but unions are rather more easily reached for damages. Furthermore, damage suits were even rarer under the anti-trust laws than they have been under Taft-Hartley.

Unions, then, are already under the anti-trust laws in the same sense that they were when courts made no distinctions between business and union "restraints of trade." Whether to make unions subject to the anti-trust laws, then, is a false issue: the use of a slogan which has no meaning.

If there is a problem lying somewhere behind this slogan, it is successfully obscured by the slogan itself, for by applying the "anti-trust" laws we could accomplish no more than has already been accomplished. I do sense, however, that some of us feel that unions have grown somehow too strong, that they constitute dangerous "monopolies," and that something ought to be done about it. To the less discerning, "putting labor under the anti-trust laws" seems the appropriate solution, since these laws outlaw monopoly, don't they?

The real question, however, is whether or not unions in their present or immediately prospective state of growth are such dangerous aggregations of power that some *appropriate* restriction should be found. I underline "appropriate" for, if I am right in the preceding discussion, legislating a reversal of the Hutcheson case, in which the Court held that for most purposes unions were not to be subject to the Sherman and Clayton prohibitions, would not be a solution to this problem.

One circumstance should be made clear at the outset—that if unions are dangerous aggregations of economic power, that power rests on rather different bases than the kind of power to which the Sherman Act was initially and primarily directed. A business monopoly of a product or service rests on the right of property in the good or service monopolized. That right of property, at least until it was modified by the passage of the anti-trust statutes, carried with it complete control over the decision to release to or withhold the good or service from the market, and the unimpaired right to name the price at which it was to be sold if at all.

If unions do monopolize anything, it is labor services. Certainly the relation between a union and that which it "monopolizes" is quite different from the relation between a business monopoly and that which it monopolizes. There is no right of property of the labor union in the services of its members. In fact, legally and in many ways practically speaking, collective bargaining is not concerned with arriving at a contract of sale and purchase. A union's power is moderated in a fundamental way unlike any threat to the power of a business monopoly: its dependence upon the continued attachment of its members, and their independent need for continued income. The reality of this threat is made clear by the at-least-occasional instances of lost strikes, and successful decertification elections. Imagine a business monopoly which would lose its power if its products, say ingots of metal, should vote that they don't any longer want to be sold by the monopolist!

Let us, however, not make the mistake that is so often made, of assuming that the loyalty of most union members to their unions is tenuous and that their attachment depends largely on coercion. This is simply and demonstrably not so, and the view that it is has led us down many of the legislative blind alleys mentioned at the beginning of this discussion. Indeed, more often than not, where the loyalties of members to a union waver it is because they feel the union has been insufficiently aggressive in raising wages. Most Teamsters remain loyal to Jimmie Hoffa and the Union, despite evidences of improper practice, not because Hoffa has underpriced their services but because he has done an astonishingly good job in meeting their very high wage expectations.

Nevertheless, in a showdown, because of the fundamentally different relationships between a union and its members as compared with a business monopoly and its product, a union's power is limited by the willingness of its members to take the risks they may be called upon to take—the possibility always exists that they will sell their services independently of the union.

Let us return to the objectives of anti-trust legislation. Presumably we approve such laws as they apply to business enterprise because we wish to relieve ourselves of the burden of monopoly prices and reduction in output consequent upon monopoly pricing policies. Considering the differences in the bases of power, can we reasonably conclude that unions exercise such power on the "price" of their "product" (wages) and its "output" (employment) that measures somehow parallel to anti-trust legislation need to be taken to protect ourselves against its exercise?

The main complaints about the impact of unions on wages that might warrant measures parallel to business anti-monopoly legislation seem to center on the allegedly inflationary effect of money wages which, under union pressures, advance more rapidly than the appropriate measure of productivity.

It is, of course, true that we have had a rather modest "inflation" in the post-war period. But what is it that we object to about inflation? No one would care at all if all prices and all incomes doubled all of a sudden. Everyone would be equally well or badly off.

This, of course, has not happened in the course of the current inflation. Price, wage, and income movements have come unevenly. But the gross result has not been any considerable distortion of income distributions. The relative shares of wages and property incomes in national income have not changed markedly. And, stable price levels are no guarantee against changes in these relative shares. Personal distribution of income has not been greatly altered, and, if it has changed at all, except during the very sharp Korean War inflation, it has been in the direction of improving the relative position of the low income groups—the widows and orphans.

True, it has taken some governmental action to protect those groups least able to protect themselves. We have increased old age and survivor benefits, by Congressional action, not only for future but also for current beneficiaries. State old age pension programs, and other state-federal programs such as aid-to-dependent children have been adjusted to meet rising living costs. But these actions have been taken under affirmative political pressures of the labor movement, and often against the bitter opposition of those who, in other forums, weep bitterly over the fate of these people in inflation.

Of course the incomes of the widows, orphans, and pensioners have been protected against inflation, not only by government action, but also by the renegotiation of private pension and benefit plans, often benefitting current benefit receivers. And for these people, as well as the low income wage earner, assets such as liquid savings and government bond holdings are negligible—in 1958, 45 per cent of spending units held liquid assets of under $200, and they may lose perhaps $3.00 per annum in real value of liquid assets through recent rates of price advance. Part, all, or even larger amounts of this may be offset by gain in declining value of their debt. But a day's lost wages through unemployment, if this is the price of price stability, is much more costly than the depreciation of real value of their assets.

There is another problem worthy of significant mention. I have implicitly assumed for the purposes of this paper, though it is not wholly evident, that wage increases brought about by union power are a significant cause of the rising price level, or rather, that if the power of unions to raise wages were somewhat impaired, prices would not rise.

The connection between rising union power, money wages, and prices is not so precise that one can measure the tolerable rate of wage increases. Further, the connection between any proposed legislative impairment of union power and its effect on the rate of wage change is even less precise and predictable.

The limits of the desired result are, I think, very close. Instead of a rate of price increase of 2 to 3 per cent per year, we wish a rate of zero. But I think it clear that an error on the low side would be disastrous. Any wage policy which resulted in sagging prices would almost certainly be much worse than one which results in upward drifting prices. It would be much more likely to lead to deferred investment, underemployment, and economic instability.

It cannot possibly be argued that we can predict the wage and price consequences of the impairment of union power within these necessary limits of tolerance. If we were faced with a 10 or 15 per cent increase in prices per year, clearly resulting from wage increases of this order of magnitude, we could with confidence act legislatively on union strength as a remedy. But the dangers of attempting such fine adjustments with such blunt and indirect tools are simply not worth the risk.

In sum, I take the heretical view that the degree and kind of inflation we have had has at least been better than the degree and kind of price stability to which we were once accustomed. Its allegedly undesirable effects disappear under the search for them, and the values of underlying economic stability, even at the cost of some upward drift of prices, seem, at least to me, to appear more and more evident.

Under this kind of examination, it seems to me that the economic rationale for impairing the power of unions to raise wages disappears. Certainly the danger, if there is one, is not clear and even its presence is doubtful.

There still remains what seems to me to be essentially an equitable, rather than an economic, argument. It runs something like this: admitted that the effect of trade union action has not been such as to alter the gross forms of income distribution—either as between wages and other shares, or as concerns the general shape of the distribution of personal income. But it has "distorted" patterns within these gross distributions. Some, e.g., unskilled and semi-skilled workers relative to skilled, or plumbers relative to school teachers, have gained or lost. It is undoubtedly true that in many ways the structure of wages and incomes is, internally, different than it would have been had we had neither as effective unions nor rising price levels. Whether these differences are "distortions" depends upon one's views, fundamentally, of equity. Over-enthusiastic job evaluation fans to the contrary, no one can tell what is the "right" relationship between the wages of a tool and die maker and an assembly line worker in an auto plant. And, indeed, this very case illustrates the way in which the special relation between a union and its members itself limits its power—the threat that tool and die makers might withdraw from UAW induced that union to reconsider its policy as to wage structures.

In respect to this kind of wage relationship, it is sometimes said that the giant employer, e.g., General Motors, can handle the big union, but the small employer can't. Such a statement is often made by the same person who argues against "industry-wide bargaining," and insists upon fractionizing bargaining units. The recent situation in the Los Angeles retail food industry illustrates both the inconsistency between these positions and the answer to the policy suggestion. The publicity attendant upon a strike in one market and lockout in many others spotlighted the "distortion" of wages in this area, at least the unusual relation between the wages of retail store clerks and other wages in Los Angeles. It is a case example of the ability of a strong union by whipsawing, to get remarkably good bargains for its members from relatively small employers. And the Los Angeles Food Employers Council has, I suspect, found the answer, by itself insisting upon a single bargain for many employers. I would maintain the position that outlawing multi-employer bargaining would increase, rather than decrease, the kind of distortion most people who complain about it have in mind. And, I think, the Wagner Act objective of greater uniformity (equity?) within and between industries has, on the whole, been better served with strong unions than without them. Furthermore, the Taft-Hartley Act contains a provision, prohibiting a union from coercing an employer in the selection of his bargaining representatives, which might well be used to prevent a union from forcing unwilling employers into multi-employer bargaining. This provision has become almost a dead letter.

My position is not that unions are some kind

of sacred cow, immune from regulation in the public interest. I can think of several kinds of union practices, particularly those relating to the internal affairs of unions and the protection of the rights of the individual members, which I think warrant appropriate legislative remedy. But it seems to me that the cry for impairment of the general economic power of unions is wrong, and even dangerous; certainly the antitrust remedy is vain.

READING 46

In a market price system, economic profits (and also economic losses) perform the basic function of directing business enterprise into those activities that are in greatest demand, as determined by dollar votes in the marketplace. High profits attract business and resources, and low profits or losses repel them. Men may disagree on just what level of profit is necessary to fulfill this basic function, but the function itself remains at the core of the enterprise system.

For all of this, misunderstandings and even suspicions about profits are widespread. John D. Harper, president of the Aluminum Company of America, argues here that the key role of the profit incentive must be more deeply appreciated in the United States today, and that profits must reach more adequate levels if we are to stimulate greater economic expansion.

Questions to Guide the Reading

How does one determine what is an "adequate" rate of profit?

Does the fact that "inadequate profits and unemployment go hand in hand" indicate which is cause and which is effect in this situation?

What are the roots of suspicions about the profit motive, and what practical difference do those suspicions make?

THE ESSENTIAL ROLE OF PROFITS
John D. Harper

Despite apparent prosperity, the climate for economic growth in our country—and for free enterprise itself—has been showing signs of potential trouble for some time. Production capacity for which there is no present demand, relatively high unemployment, and U.S. products becoming less competitive in world markets—these are some of the indications. This situation cannot go on for long if we wish to have adequate growth, high productivity and enough jobs for a growing work force.

At the root of the problem, in my judgment, is our widespread failure to understand the nature of our economic system. I am particularly concerned about our repeated failure to capitalize on the power of *profit incentive* to induce productive effort, investment and innovation. While not a cure-all, this incentive *is* the *key* to economic growth. Through its ability to stimulate human effort, we have achieved a more abundant way of life for a greater number of people than was even dreamed of a century ago. If we want to maintain and increase our high standard of living—both in the material and cultural sense—it is essential that the importance of the profit incentive be reaffirmed and encouraged by all sectors of the economy—by individuals as well as by government.

From John D. Harper, "Profitless Prosperity: A Dangerous Illusion," Address at Annual Public Interest Luncheon, Dallas Management Association, May 23, 1963. Reprinted with kind permission of the author.

Yet, today many of us look with suspicion on the profit motive, and—for no apparent reason—are either nibbling away at it or seem to want to do away with it entirely. Can it be that the individual effort, initiative and discipline—which are still fundamental to our personal security now and in the future—are losing their place in our lives as we come to rely more and more on the government? Are we so comfortable and well fed that we are becoming "fat" and complacent?

Prosperity without profits?

Whatever the reasons may be, it is evident that increasing numbers of Americans seem to want the benefits of the free-enterprise economic system without first putting forth the effort to earn the profits that make possible an ever higher standard of living. What many of us seem to want is prosperity without profits.

But "profitless prosperity"—for ordinary human beings in a free society, at any rate—is an impossible condition in the long run. We can have growth and prosperity only as long as the potential for profit is adequate. Profitless prosperity is not a goal that can be won by some kind of compromise. It is an illusion. Furthermore, it is a *dangerous illusion*. If we are to have a public policy of prosperity without profit, this means that we must embrace a new economic and political philosophy—one in which state control and dictatorial power replace our free choice in the market place—and I firmly believe that this is not what Americans, including those in labor and management, really want.

Evidence of the problem

We do not have to look very far to see what small regard we have for the profit incentive today. We have a national tax structure that is antiprofit in many respects, and therefore, anti-incentive to build and grow. We continue to push employment costs up faster than productivity gains and market conditions warrant; and since intense world competition rules out general price increases, part of such higher costs must come out of profits, leaving less available for investment and growth. Business depreciation allowances are kept below levels required to recover at inflated prices the original cost of worn-out equipment, so the difference again must come out of profits. And all the while, the nation keeps piling up huge government spending deficits—regardless of the political party in office—that can only further weaken the purchasing power of all money, including profit dollars.

But, say the critics of modern business, total profits are increasing. And in dollar terms, that is true. In 1962, for example, corporate profits after taxes in the U.S. reached a new high of $26 billion. What the critics conveniently overlook is the fact that the increase in business profits in recent years has not been proportional to the overall growth of the nation's economy—and that at present, profits are below the level needed to stimulate adequate economic expansion.

That profits are the key to future prosperity and fuller employment is apparent from our experience during the past five years. Consumers have been spending at record rates each year, and so have our national, state and local governments. Economic growth, however, has remained sluggish, with unemployment at uncomfortably high levels. The one factor that has not increased sufficiently is gross private domestic investment—which represents primarily capital outlays by businessmen. Such investment must improve substantially if fuller employment is to be achieved. All other attempts by government to promote prosperity have generally failed to produce the desired results.

But for business investment to increase, there must be an *adequate incentive to invest*—that is, an expected rate of return commensurate with the risks of business enterprise. Yet, profits now provide a rate of return on invested capital which is only slightly above what an investor can earn on an insured, risk-free savings account and which is actually below the return on the tax-exempt security.

The "price" of poor profits

What all this means is this: A large and growing economy requires proportionately larger profits to provide the incentive for new, job-creating investment. In other words, inadequate profits and unemployment go hand in hand. This relationship is easily demonstrated by a quick look at our recent economic history.

For this purpose, we can use Gross National Product (i.e., the dollar value of the nation's total output of goods and services) as a convenient measure of the size of the over-all economy. Corporate profits considered as a per cent of Gross National Product—or GNP—reveal a significant relationship to unemployment. In 1929, for example, the last year of prosperity and reasonably full employment in the period following World War I, corporate profits were roughly 8% of GNP. A year later, the beginning of ten years of large-scale unemployment and economic distress, the percentage had slipped to below 3% and did not get far above that level throughout the Thirties.

Following World War II, corporate profits as a per cent of GNP again reached the 7% to 8% range in the late Forties, and unemployment was again relatively low. Although the ratio of profits to the size of the economy has fluctuated since, the general trend has been down—and unemployment is too high. In 1962 for example, the ratio was less than 5%, and 1963 holds little promise of being much better—because profits today are caught in a severe cost-price squeeze for which there is no immediate, simple solution.

What this record clearly says to anyone willing to consider the real need for business profits is this: (1) If we really wanted to get this country moving, corporate profits last year should have been well over $40 billion—or at the very least, 7% of GNP—instead of only $26 billion; and (2) It is no accident that the recent downtrend in profits related to the size of the economy has been accompanied by an uptrend in the level of unemployment that now threatens to become chronic.

The implications of this trend should give every thoughtful citizen of this country reason for concern. The American philosopher George Santayana put it this way: "Those who do not remember the past are condemned to repeat it." Without making any rash predictions, it seems self-evident to me that our country cannot wisely permit present trends to continue. To do so would be to open the door to a two-fold threat to our way of life.

A two-fold threat

First of all, declining profits and rising unemployment are sure roads to economic stagnation and—if they persist for long—can lead to widespread human hardship. This is a particularly sobering thought today in view of the great changes that have occurred in our economic structure in recent years. We now have a complex, highly interdependent society. The effects of severe economic distress will not be cushioned nearly as much today as in the past by the resilience and self-sufficiency of a farm-based, rural economy.

And this circumstance leads to a related and potentially even more serious threat. As everyone must know by now, we have grown increasingly dependent on a large and powerful central government. We have gradually become more and more receptive to the theory of the "Welfare State," even though much of it runs counter not only to our traditions but to our common sense as well. Much of it, in fact, borders on outright socialism—only we don't like to use that word. This process of undermining individual initiative and freedom is made less painful by taking away only one small, seemingly insignificant segment at a time.

We rationalize increased economic aid and intervention by government *even in a period of prosperity* by saying that "times have changed," that these actions are designed by well-intentioned men in the "public interest"—that is, what they consider to be the public interest.

The danger of "Welfarism," however, is that it encourages the drift to more and more authority concentrated in the hands of a relatively few in government. Simultaneously, it undermines private initiative and responsibility, and conditions us to rely on government to solve our problems. These two processes open the door to the exploitation of actual or potential economic distress by those who seek power over the lives of others, as they interpret what is best for the public from the viewpoint of their own private political philosophy. They attempt to dictate choice rather than rely on the operation of a free market. They use political tactics to perpetuate themselves in office by playing on the apathy of voters who lack a sound, mature political and economic background. When these power-seekers get a foot in one door, freedom slowly but surely—a little bit at a time—goes out the other. The pages of history are full of examples.

The work of the power-seekers is aided in times of economic difficulty—in times of growing unemployment—by the simple fact that hardship makes a man less inclined to be concerned about the ultimate consequences of his decisions. He grasps at straws. His urgent economic needs increase his willingness to sacrifice the long-range future benefits of freedom and moral integrity for the immediate though temporary illusion of unearned "security" and "something for nothing." We should not forget that Hitler won the support of Germany's youth by promising them food, clothing and economic security—and the only price was giving up individual freedom of choice.

So, without debating just how far government should properly extend its influence, we are brought back to the thought I advanced in the beginning: Profitless prosperity is a dangerous illusion. It is dangerous because its false promise invites economic consequences that set the stage for the undermining of our most prized possession—individual freedom.

The underlying cause

In searching for reasons why profitable enterprise in America does not receive the support it needs and deserves, it is easy to focus on symptoms rather than actual causes. There is growing recognition, for example, that our national tax and labor policies are contributing factors. But these public policies and attitudes, in turn, are only political manifestations of more basic, underlying misconceptions and lack of understanding of our economic system.

America today presents the paradox of a country which owes much of its greatness to one remarkably simple economic concept—the profit incentive—which invests very little money, time or energy in an effort to understand, preserve and improve it. We appear eager to rely on all manner of panaceas that have failed repeatedly in the past rather than accept the challenges—and responsibilities—of the only approach that has ever proved successful as a way of *voluntarily* inducing useful, productive economic activity. Not only that, but many of us seem to regard another man's honest, reasonable profit with distrust and envy.

Responsibility of businessmen

I, for one, am willing to admit that when businessmen make public statements about profits, they tend all too often to speak only of their own problems or in terms only they and others with a specific interest in business practice are likely to understand. This is a perfectly natural failing, I suppose, and one that is characteristic of many other groups with specialized interests.

At the same time, this tendency has probably done the public a great disservice by reinforcing a feeling of suspicion in those who do not understand the "lingo" and who feel—however erroneously—that they are somehow being excluded from the "profit circle." It does little good to talk continually in terms of job-creating funds, adequate return on investment, retained earnings for new facilities and the like, if the man listening is an employee who is already convinced that the profit dollars of a business can only be acquired at his expense.

These same individuals are not going to be much impressed by the fact that the collected wisdom of man's history is full of references to the desirability of profitable enterprise. Oriental proverbs and Biblical passages such as the parable of the talents may appear to have little bearing on what seems to be going on in today's company or plant.

Nor will much be accomplished by citing the fact that at least two modern-day American presidents have strongly endorsed the need for profits: Dwight D. Eisenhower said—"When shallow critics denounce the profit motive inherent in our system of private enterprise, they ignore the fact that it is an economic support of every human right we possess and without it, all rights would soon disappear." John F. Kennedy said—" . . . in a free enterprise system there can be no prosperity without profits." And to these could be added a long list of educators, economists, labor leaders, writers, philosophers and others.

Still, as long as enough people believe that their efforts to earn a living are being exploited by "those at the top"—and opponents of our way of life work hard to cultivate this notion—the message will not get through. These same people will then be inclined to vote for any kind of policy—tax, labor, welfare and so on—that, on the surface at least, seems to be *for* them and *against* profit-makers. And such alien ideas as "soaking the rich," the "rob-Peter-to-pay-Paul" process of redistributing income, and the "right" to unearned "security"—all of which are the stock in trade of power-seekers—will have a strong appeal for those who do not comprehend the true role of profits in our economic system. It is this social and political threat even more than our future economic well-being that adds urgency to the problem.

Role of profit incentive

Profit incentive is the "spark plug" that generates economic activity through the expectation of a return—or profit—commensurate with the risks involved. It is the only workable alternative to a society based on fear and compulsion. But it is more than an alternative. It not only provides a *voluntary* way of motivating people to take action—to take worthwhile business risks—but it also induces a high level of efficiency and innovation in order to maximize the profit potential. When allowed to function properly, it also automatically provides employment for a growing work force. Today's profit provides the *means*—and the only lasting means—of creating new jobs; the expectation of future profit provides the *incentive* to do so by stimulating the required new investment.

Added to these advantages, profit incentive freed of political interference serves as a built-in guide to an efficient and socially useful allocation of the nation's total resources—including human effort, land and productive facilities. In the process, it provides a completely objective means of evaluating economic performance. And, when disciplined by effective competition, this same unfettered profit incentive acts to limit excesses in the production system: If profits become too attractive, more producers enter the field and profit margins are forced down; if profits are too low, the inefficient producers are weeded out and profits return to adequate elevels.

Profits and the individual

With all these unique, proven advantages, you would think that the American profit system would be the easiest thing in the world to keep functioning properly. And yet, this clearly is not the case—and strengthening and improving it is not going to be an easy job.

I do not pretend to know all the reasons why this situation has developed. But a major one, I think, is simply that more and more individuals in today's highly organized society are no longer directly involved in—and stimulated by—the profit-making process. The development of mass-production and mass-distribution techniques—along with resultant job specialization—has, in a sense, made this unavoidable. It has also generated two basic problems.

First, of course, is that the further a man gets away from the risk-taking aspect of any enterprise, the more he tends to lose sight of the key role of profits. In an older and simpler day, it was easy to understand the benefits of an economic system where a man running his own business could end up with a few dollars of profit as a direct result of putting forth more effort and initiative. Those extra dollars enabled him

to buy additional tools, hire more help, and perhaps to invest in other new or growing ventures—thereby helping to create a higher standard of living.

It is far more difficult, however, for today's mass-production worker—and even the so-called organization man—to comprehend and accept the less direct but basically identical process, whereby the extra dollars a company has after paying all costs are used to fulfill the same functions—to invest in new tools and facilities, to hire additional employees and thereby create a better and more abundant life for more people.

It is but a short step from the failure to see this process for what it really is, to a belief that profits are just "gravy," part of which the individual helped produce and therefore belong to him, but which are not shared with him.

This erroneous belief, which is more common than many of us realize, leads quite naturally to a second problem. The more a man feels he has no direct stake in profits, the less he is interested in protecting or improving them—whether this involves trying new ideas, displaying initiative or simply taking care to eliminate waste and inefficiency. Consequently, his personal incentives today seem to be based on a desire for a kind of "job security" that no longer is related to profitability—even though profitability, of course, remains the only source of *real* security in a voluntary, highly industrialized society.

As a result of this trend—as well as others I do not have time to discuss—the true nature of our economic system has been distorted from the original concept based on reward for successful risk-taking into a system where we somehow think that the "reward" can be "guaranteed"—where we have the *illusion* of unearned "security." This is a disturbing development and, as you know, has been reinforced by recent trends in labor negotiations.

Young people today in particular seem to pride themselves on avoiding business risks. They want a "sure thing" to start with—and a good retirement program, too. They seem not to comprehend—or show any interest in—the fact that ours is a profit *and* loss system; that profit is the *earned* reward for successfully managing to avoid the ever-present possibility of loss; that profit must be adequate to make up for the probability that there will be some losses; and that without the successful risk-takers—and a business and political climate that encourages them—there is no real security for any of us.

It gives me no pleasure to point out these signs

of a serious threat to profit incentive in our society. I sincerely wish that circumstances were such that I would not feel it necessary to talk about them. And I regret that I have no easy answers to leave with you.

I would be doing you a disservice, though, if I closed without saying I am encouraged by certain indications that a trend toward greater economic awareness and understanding may be under way. Business managers are showing increased interest in promoting economic education. The current Administration has stated publicly that adequate profits are essential to economic growth, although how well these words will be translated into needed changes remains to be seen. I think it is true that people are slowly becoming aware that disappearing profits mean disappearing jobs —that the best assurance of job security is being a well-informed, productive member of a profit-making enterprise. There also appears to be growing demand throughout the country for greater fiscal responsibility in government, for a growth-oriented tax structure and for appropriate limitations on unrestrained union power.

The dangerous illusion of profitless prosperity feeds on ignorance, indifference and procrastination. The dynamic power of the profit incentive must be restored . . . and the time is now.

READING 47

Do corporate profits, as now reported, truly reflect the financial state of American business, or are there other measures that may provide a better insight into business finance as well as the state of the total economy? And what significance should we attach to the fact that profits before taxes have been rising more slowly than Gross National Product in recent years?

Peter L. Bernstein, investment counselor and lecturer on economics at the New School for Social Research, argues here that things are seldom what they seem. Much of the "profit squeeze" of recent years, he asserts, is due to increased depreciation allowances. Looking at corporate cash flows (profits after taxes, plus depreciation allowances), Bernstein holds that they have been sufficient to permit increased dividend payments and still meet new plant and equipment expenditures in recent years. The article calls for careful reading and for caution in the use of some familiar statistics.

Questions to Guide the Reading

How does "depreciation" differ from most other business costs? Can depreciation allowances be used to reduce book profits indefinitely?

Under what conditions might a "profit squeeze" lead to increased investment and efficiency and under what conditions might it lead to reduced business investment? Can the essential role of profits, as defined by John Harper of Alcoa in the previous reading, be met if the true state of the economy is as Bernstein sees it?

DOES THE "PROFIT SQUEEZE" HURT?
Peter L. Bernstein

Even though 1962 set an all-time record for corporate profits—about $26 billion after taxes— businessmen were clearly dissatisfied with the results. Complaints about the hard sell, price competition and rising costs were just as frequent and audible as in years when earnings were lower. A typical comment came from one chemical company executive who summed it all up by saying,

From Peter L. Bernstein, "Does the 'Profit Squeeze' Hurt?" *The Nation*, Feb. 2, 1963, pp. 94–97. The figures used in conjunction with this article have been taken from the AFL-CIO's article, "Exploding the 'Profit Squeeze' Myth," *The American Federationist*, June, 1962, pp. 1–8. Reproduced with kind permission of the author and publishers.

"Sure, they're new highs, but they're not the kind of highs to reflect the full effort thrown into them."

Complaints about the profit squeeze have been coming along in such profusion and regularity as to give the appearance of a chronic ailment of American business. If so, this is serious. But how valid is the evidence of deteriorating corporate earning power? Even more important, to what extent is the lagging trend in profits causing a similarly sluggish performance by the economy in general and business capital investment in particular?

An impressive array of statistics can be gathered to show that the profit squeeze is a matter of genuine concern. For example, although Gross National Product—that is, the nation's total output of goods and services—has increased by 120 per cent since the early postwar years of 1947–49, corporate profits before taxes are up only 67 per cent. This lag has become increasingly noticeable in recent years: profits have risen only 11 per cent since 1955, while GNP has climbed about 40 per cent.

A more accurate indication of these trends shows up in the share of corporate output (as contrasted with total output) that has been left over for profits. In 1929, profits before taxes amounted to 19 per cent of corporate gross product; by 1948, the profit share had risen to a little over 21 per cent, as profits expanded faster than output. But by 1957, the profit share was down to 16.5 per cent of corporate gross product, while this past year less than 16 per cent was left over for the owner of corporate business.

While the costs and expenses represented by the earnings of the other factors of production are determined by contract and therefore *must* be paid out by businessmen, profits are a residual item that amount to no more than whatever happens to be left over after everyone else has been paid off. No wonder, then, that the businessman feels jilted by the course of economic events when he sees his sales rising, his employees, creditors, landlord and government agencies all receiving more dollars from him, while the last line on his profit and loss statement stubbornly refuses to follow along the upward path.

Nevertheless, although the squeeze on profits appears to be genuine enough, additional evidence is available to suggest that its intensity has been exaggerated.

In the first place, the stability of corporate earning power in the postwar period has been impressive. This means that the *average* level of profits has been higher than it might have been if profit trends had been more volatile. While profits before taxes dropped from $9.6 billion in 1929 to a loss figure of $3.0 billion only three years later, and while they fell by about a third during the recession of 1937–38, the sharpest *postwar* decline was only 20 per cent (1949). In fact—and this is important in view of the increasing frequency of business complaints about inadequate earning power—the decline in profits during the most recent recession (1960–61) was so brief and so shallow that earnings of $46.1 billion before taxes for the year 1961 as a whole were above 1960's showing and were exceeded only by 1959's record of $46.8 billion.

Second, profits have been repressed much more by competitive pressures on selling prices, due to excess capacity and inadequate demand, than by rising costs. On the contrary, business firms have done an extraordinarily impressive job of controlling their cost structure. Manufacturing production, for example, has clearly risen faster than wage and salary disbursements. Labor costs per unit of output moved downward all during 1962 and had, in fact, been moving in that direction ever since the early part of 1961. At the end of 1962, this ratio was at the lowest point it had reached in more than five years. This was in sharp contrast to normal experience, for labor costs usually move upward much faster than production in the latter stages of business expansion.

Third, the proof of every pudding is in the eating, and corporate stockholders surely have no grounds for complaint: dividends have been rising steadily for fifteen years. The contrast with prewar experience is significant here, too. In 1933, dividends were little more than a third of what they had been in 1929; the drop from 1937 to 1938 amounted to 32 per cent; the 1929 level of dividend payments set a record that was not surpassed for seventeen years.

Ever since 1946, however, dividends have risen every year (except for a negligible decline of 2 per cent during the Korean War under the impact of the excess-profits tax). In fact, dividends have risen at a rate that exceeds the rate of increase in compensation of employees. (See Figure 1.) Dividend payments ($16 billion in 1962) had doubled in thirteen years and tripled since the end of the war. In contrast to total profits, the share of corporate output going to dividends has increased since 1957.

The real villain of the piece is a technical bookkeeping gadget known as depreciation. Since this is something that most laymen don't really understand, its impact has been minimized or

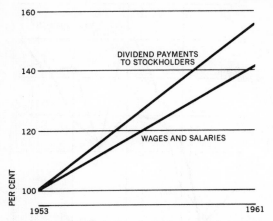

Fig. 1 Percentage Increase in Total Dividend Payments and Total Wage and Salary Payments, 1953–1961. Reproduced in *American Federationist*, June, 1962, p. 3, with the following observation: "Dividend payments increased about 57 per cent between 1953 and 1961 while total wage and salary payments increased only 41 per cent." (Source: U.S. Department of Commerce.)

sales revenues after it has paid all of its out-of-pocket expenses, such as wages, salaries, purchases of parts and materials from other firms, rent, interest and taxes. Cash flow, in brief, is nothing more than net profits plus depreciation.

It is important to remember that depreciation is a cost of production, just like wages or interest. Therefore, the larger the depreciation accrual, the smaller the profits. But the smaller the profits, the smaller the income taxes and the smaller the taxes, the larger the cash flow. And the larger the cash flow, the greater the amount available for dividends and corporate expansion! In short, the larger the depreciation accrual, the more the owners of the company will benefit (and the greater the loss to the government or the greater the burden on other taxpayers who have no capital goods to depreciate on their books).

When we focus our attention on the depreciation item in the corporate earnings statistics, a dramatic picture emerges. Depreciation accruals have doubled since 1953 and tripled since 1948; corporate profits after taxes are up only 45 per cent since 1953 and less than 60 per cent since

rationalized to an extent that disguises its central role in this entire argument about corporate earning power.

Depreciation is an accounting concept to show how much plant and equipment a business firm has used up in the process of producing goods and services during some given period of time. Of course, payment for factories and other capital goods is made when the equipment is acquired. However, since the equipment will provide a stream of productive services over an extended period of time, it would be inaccurate to charge off the entire cost against the output of the year in which it is installed. On the contrary, a portion of the original cost is charged off each year that the equipment helps to produce goods and services for sale, as a contribution to the costs of that year's production. In every sense of the word, depreciation is a proper cost of doing business—it reflects the capital equipment used up in the process of production in the same way that wages reflect the labor power that is used up.

Its impact on the firm, however, is fundamentally different. Wages are a drain on cash—they must be paid out to the employees. Depreciation, on the other hand, is not an out-of-pocket expense—it merely takes account of cash that had been laid out some time in the past when the equipment was originally acquired. This is why we talk about "cash flow," which is the amount of money left over to the business firm from its

Fig. 2 Corporate Depreciation Allowances, After-tax Profits, and Cash Flow 1947–1962. Reproduced in *American Federationist*, June, 1962, p. 5, with the following observation: "The flow of spendable cash to corporations has been high and rising. From $23.5 billion in 1947, the cash-flow rose to $30.1 billion in 1953—up 28 per cent. Between 1953 and 1960, the flow of spendable cash to corporations rose 59 per cent —from $30.1 billion to $48 billion. This year, 1962, the cash-flow is expected to increase about 12.5 per cent to approximately $54 billion." (Source: U.S. Department of Commerce.)

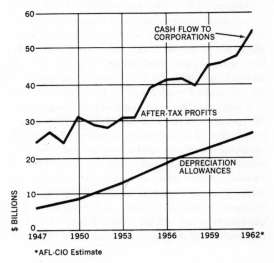

*AFL-CIO Estimate

1948. In 1962, depreciation charges were almost as large as corporate profits after taxes; in 1949, depreciation had been less than a third of net profits. (See Figure 2.)

This puts the picture in quite a different light. We saw earlier that the profits share of corporate gross product had shrunk steadily and significantly since the war. But if we take corporate cash flow, we find that its share of corporate gross product is approximately the same as it was in 1948 and exactly the same as it was in 1957. (Incidentally, the share of compensation of employees was 63.3 per cent in 1929, 64.0 per cent in 1948, 65.2 per cent in 1957 and 64.0 per cent in 1962, so the cause of the profit squeeze can hardly be found here.) In brief, the declining share of profits is really accounted for by the rising volume of depreciation accruals.

This sharp rise in depreciation comes from a variety of causes. One is the obvious increase in the quantity of capital goods at work in our economy as capacity has expanded over the year: depreciation is directly related to the value of the capital investment of business firms. Furthermore, new capital goods have tended to cost more dollars than the old equipment they replace (although the new equipment is frequently so much more efficient and productive that capital costs *per unit of output* have actually been declining). Finally, but by no means least, revisions in the tax laws have permitted business firms to write off their capital goods at a faster rate than had previously been allowable.

Laws adopted during World War II and during the Korean War, the tax bills of 1954 and 1962 and the recently liberalized regulations of the Internal Revenue Bureau have had a substantial effect on depreciation practices. The result, of course, is lower reported earnings and correspondingly lower tax liabilities. According to a recent analysis by the Commerce Department, corporate profits before taxes in 1962 were about $6–$7 billion lower than they would have been without these legal changes. This is no small matter: the saving in income taxes was equal to 20 per cent of total dividend payments in 1962.

While many businessmen complain about both the profit squeeze *and* about depreciation accruals that are inadequate to cover the cost of replacing worn or obsolete equipment, the statistics suggest no real pressure on corporate finances. Cash flow available to corporations after dividend payments to stockholders has approximately equaled plant and equipment expenditures since 1958. (See Figure 3.) For manufacturing corporations alone, this has been

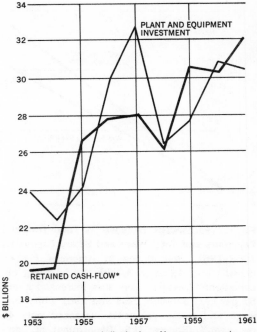

Fig. 3 **Corporate Cash Flow and Capital Investment, 1953–1961.** Reproduced in *American Federationist,* **June, 1962, p. 6, with the following observation: "Corporations have been able to finance almost all their plant and equipment investment in recent years from their own internal financial resources—with very little dependence on bank loans, new bond issues or the floating of new stock." (Source: U.S. Department of Commerce.)**

the case for almost ten years. Net new issues of corporate securities show no rising trend and little or no real variations over a period of six years. Indeed, the generosity of management in dividend payments to stockholders is proof that plenty of money is available to finance corporate needs.

One further point in this connection is worth making. A major cause of the profit squeeze has been the excess productive capacity plaguing most industries since the capital-spending binge of 1955–57 expanded output capabilities so far beyond current needs. This hurts because managements want to recoup investments even though plant equipment lies idle—and also because excess capacity leads to price wars (or inability to raise prices) as firms struggle against one another for additional volume.

Businessmen have tried two ways to work their way out of this tangle. One has been to attempt to raise prices even under conditions where supply clearly exceeds demand (the steel fracas of last spring being the most notorious but by no means the only example). The second has been the incessant campaign for a reduction in corporate income taxes, even though a corresponding reduction in government spending could mean a loss of business for many companies.

Both of these campaigns have been designed to make somebody else—customers or other taxpayers—pay for the idle and excess capacity. But it is questionable whether serious management errors in the almost helter-skelter over-expansion of plant capacity during the mid-1950s should be paid for by anyone except the stockholders of the companies in which the mistakes were made. This is the essential principle of a free-enterprise system: the race is to the fastest, while the community has no responsibility for the success or failure of any individual producer. Those who are most vocal in defense of our economic system might do well to consider the extent to which they are presently violating its most fundamental and traditional philosophies.

The real issue is the amount of harm that the profit squeeze is doing to the economy. Here the matter is moot. The evidence is by no means conclusive that the profit squeeze has caused the inadequate rate of economic growth of the past five years or that, in particular, it is responsible for the subnormal portion of our total output that we are now allocating to the accumulation of productive capital goods.

High profits are neither a necessary stimulus nor a prerequisite for an increase in capital outlays. The capital-goods boom of 1955–57 was not preceded by any great bulge in profits. Even though the excess-profits tax was taken off the books in 1954, net profits after taxes in that year were 7 per cent below 1953 and, with the exception of 1949, were lower than in any year since 1946. Yet, virtually out of the blue, corporate expenditures for plant and equipment rose almost 50 per cent between 1954 and 1957. One could as well argue that the splurge in capital spending contributed to the boom and therefore to the 40 per cent expansion in corporate profits in that three-year period, as to take the more conventional view that the rise in corporate earnings stimulated the increase in capital investment.

In any case, the boom hit a climax in 1957 and has been followed ever since by a generally flat trend in business investment and by a marked slow-down in our rate of economic growth. Yet trends in business spending for plant and equipment have perhaps been better than one might

have expected. Instead of the usual collapse in investment that has always followed overheated periods of expansion, outlays for plant and equipment have held at a relatively high level and have been consistently above expenditures for any year prior to 1956. Indeed, the modest decline in this sector during the recession of 1960–61 was less than half as great as it had been during the brief business setback of 1957–58.

What we see, in effect, is the competitive free-enterprise system operating at its very best. The influence of competition within a generally expansionary economic environment has encouraged—one might more accurately say forced—businessmen to spend substantial sums on modernization and cost reduction. Thus, capital spending has been maintained *despite* the prevalence of excess capacity, *despite* a discouraging pattern of growth in demand and *despite* the lag in profits.

The point can be made even more forcefully. The extraordinary ease with which profits could be realized during the free-spending and goods-hungry atmosphere of the early postwar and Korean period led to a capital-spending spree far beyond the necessities of the time. The maladjustments and excesses of that spending spree are still with us: they are at the root of much of our current troubles. But as profits have been harder to come by, businessmen have been forced to maintain their capital outlays in order to keep their costs down and to stay competitive with other firms.

As a result, costs per unit of output have been held in check. We have snuffed out most of the cost-push inflation that plagued us so persistently in previous years. If one of the primary advantages of a free-enterprise competitive system is to deliver the goods at the lowest possible cost, the experience of recent years shows that what is taught in theory can indeed be true in practice. If profits were there for the taking, our cost structure would be far more inflated.

The real problem is that profits are by no means the only symptom of our economy's substandard performance. The profit squeeze is no more important than the employment squeeze, for, like profits, the level of employment has lagged behind the level of production, and unemployment has become an increasingly serious burden.

The fault lies with lack of adequate demand to justify maximum use of our physical productive facilities and of our labor force. Regardless of current profit rates, businessmen would make many more new investments if they believed the customers were there to buy the additional output. But if demand is sluggish, no businessman will risk funds in new ventures that may never pay out.

What all of this adds up to is that the profit squeeze is neither so intense as it has been described nor so disturbing as many have tried to paint it. It has, in fact, pushed costs down to a level where we can look forward to a significant upward surge in profits when business activity in general shows clearer signs of vigor. Lack of sufficient demand due to inadequate purchasing power at low-income levels, and a repressive tax structure at all points of the economy (together with the deflationary influence of economy-minded Congressmen), explain both the pressure on profits and the subdued levels of business investment.

If high profits always led to high levels of business investment, no boom would ever come to an end. The opposite is also true. The stimulus to businessmen's expenditures on plant and equipment comes from anticipation and hopes for higher *future* profits; otherwise we would never have worked our way up out of recession.

READING 48

The bridges between economics and psychology are infrequently built and still more rarely crossed. Yet the whole issue of income distribution with which this section of readings has been concerned involves some fundamental assumptions about men's motivations. Differential returns on labor or on capital have been assumed to act in a free economy as signals to men to allocate their productive resources in one direction or another so as to maximize their returns.

We conclude the section with a provocative and widely discussed challenge to the economists by one of America's leading social scientists, Professor Herbert A. Simon of Carnegie Institute of Technology. Psychologist, political scientist, and economist all in one, Simon asks whether the profit-maximizing assumption is a valid and useful one, and suggests that we have only begun to learn about economic behavior.

Questions to Guide the Reading

Might a parallel case to Simon's case on profit maximization be made about workers' interests in wage-income maximization? Do the actions of trade unions in collective bargaining help to support or refute an hypothesis that workers do not seek to maximize wages?

How much of the analysis contained in today's economic textbooks might be affected by widespread acceptance of Simon's position? Does this position force a redefinition of what economics is all about?

DO FIRMS MAXIMIZE?
Herbert A. Simon

The economist's traditional lack of concern with individual behavior stems from two considerations. First, he assumes that the economic actor is rational, and hence he makes strong predictions about human behavior without performing the hard work of observing people. Second, he often assumes competition, which carries with it the implication that only the rational survive. Thus, the classical economic theory of markets with perfect competition and rational agents is

From Herbert A. Simon, "Theories of Decision-making in Economics and Behavioral Science," *American Economic Review*, Vol. XLIX, No. 3, June, 1959, pp. 254–280. Reprinted with kind permission of the author and publishers.

deductive theory that requires almost no contact with empirical data once its assumptions are accepted.

Undoubtedly there is an area of human behavior that fits these assumptions to a reasonable approximation, where the classical theory with its assumptions of rationality is a powerful and useful tool. Without denying the existence of this area, or its importance, I may observe that it fails to include some of the central problems of conflict and dynamics with which economics has become more and more concerned. A metaphor will help to show the reason for this failure.

Suppose we were pouring some viscous liquid —molasses—into a bowl of very irregular shape. What would we need in order to make a theory of the form the molasses would take in the bowl? How much would we have to know about the properties of molasses to predict its behavior under the circumstances? If the bowl were held motionless, and if we wanted only to predict behavior in equilibrium, we would have to know little, indeed, about molasses. The single essential assumption would be that the molasses, under the force of gravity, would minimize the height of its center of gravity. With this assumption, which would apply as well to any other liquid, and a complete knowledge of the environment— in this case the shape of the bowl—the equilibrium is completely determined. Just so, the equilibrium behavior of a perfectly adapting organism depends only on its goal and its environment; it is otherwise completely independent of the internal properties of the organism.

If the bowl into which we are pouring the molasses were jiggled rapidly, or if we wanted to know about the behavior before equilibrium was reached, prediction would require much more information. It would require, in particular, more information about the properties of molasses: its viscosity, the rapidity with which it "adapted" itself to the containing vessel and moved towards its "goal" of lowering its center of gravity. Likewise, to predict the short-run behavior of an adaptive organism, or its behavior in a complex and rapidly changing environment, it is not enough to know its goals. We must know also a great deal about its internal structure and particularly its mechanisms of adaptation.

If, to carry the metaphor a step farther, new forces, in addition to gravitational force, were brought to bear on the liquid, we would have to know still more about it even to predict behavior in equilibrium. Now its tendency to lower its center of gravity might be countered by a force to minimize an electrical or magnetic potential operating in some lateral direction. We would have to know its relative susceptibility to gravitational and electrical or magnetic force to determine its equilibrium position. Similarly, in an organism having a multiplicity of goals, or afflicted with some kind of internal goal conflict, behavior could be predicted only from information about the relative strengths of the several goals and the ways in which the adaptive processes responded to them.

The goals of firms

Just as the central assumption in the theory of consumption is that the consumer strives to maximize his utility, so the crucial assumption in the theory of the firm is that the entrepreneur strives to maximize his residual share—his profit. Attacks on this hypothesis have been frequent. We may classify the most important of these as follows:

(a) The theory leaves ambiguous whether it is short-run or long-run profit that is to be maximized.

(b) The entrepreneur may obtain all kinds of "psychic income" from the firm, quite apart from monetary rewards. If he is to maximize his utility, then, he will sometimes balance a loss of profits against an increase in psychic income. But if we allow "psychic income," the criterion of profit maximization loses all of its definiteness.

(c) The entrepreneur may not care to maximize, but may simply want to earn a return that he regards as satisfactory. By sophistry and an adept use of the concept of psychic income, the notion of seeking a satisfactory return can be translated into utility maximizing but not in any operational way. We shall see in a moment that "satisfactory profits" is a concept more meaningfully related to the psychological notion of aspiration levels than to maximization.

(d) It is often observed that under modern conditions the equity owners and the active managers of an enterprise are separate and distinct groups of people, so that the latter may not be motivated to maximize profits.

(e) Where there is imperfect competition among firms, maximizing is an ambiguous goal, for what action is optimal for one firm depends on the actions of the other firms.

In the present paper we shall deal only with the third of these five issues.

"Satisficing" versus maximizing

The notion of satiation plays no role in classical economic theory, while it enters rather prominently into the treatment of motivation in psychology. In most psychological theories the motive to act stems from *drives,* and action terminates when the drive is satisfied. Moreover, the conditions for satisfying a drive are not necessarily fixed, but may be specified by an aspiration level that itself adjusts upward or downward on the basis of experience.

If we seek to explain business behavior in the terms of this theory, we must expect the firm's goals to be not maximizing profit, but attaining a certain level or rate of profit, holding a certain share of the market or a certain level of sales. Firms would try to "satisfice" rather than to maximize.

It has sometimes been argued that the distinction between satisficing and maximizing is not important to economic theory. For in the first place, the psychological evidence on individual behavior shows that aspirations tend to adjust to the attainable. Hence in the long run, the argument runs, the level of aspiration and the attainable maximum will be very close together. Second, even if some firms satisficed, they would gradually lose out to the maximizing firms, which would make larger profits and grow more rapidly than the others.

These are, of course, precisely the arguments of our molasses metaphor, and we may answer them in the same way that we answered them earlier. The economic environment of the firm is complex, and it changes rapidly; there is no a priori reason to assume the attainment of long-run equilibrium. Indeed, the empirical evidence on the distribution of firms by size suggests that the observed regularities in size distribution stem from the statistical equilibrium of a population of adaptive systems rather than the static equilibrium of a population of maximizers.

Models of satisficing behavior are richer than models of maximizing behavior, because they treat not only of equilibrium but of the method of reaching it as well. Psychological studies of the formation and change of aspiration levels support propositions of the following kinds.

(a) When performance falls short of the level of aspiration, search behavior (particularly search for new alternatives of action) is induced.

(b) At the same time, the level of aspiration begins to adjust itself downward until goals reach levels that are practically attainable.

(c) If the two mechanisms just listed operate too slowly to adapt aspirations to performance, emotional behavior—apathy or aggression, for example—will replace rational adaptive behavior.

The aspiration level defines a natural zero point in the scale of utility—whereas in most classical theories the zero point is arbitrary. When the firm has alternatives open to it that are at or above its aspiration level, the theory predicts that it will choose the best of those known to be available. When none of the available alternatives satisfies current aspirations, the theory predicts qualitatively different behavior: in the short run, search behavior and the revision of targets; in the longer run, what we have called above emotional behavior, and what the psychologist would be inclined to call neurosis. (Lest this last term appear fanciful I should like to call attention to the phenomena of panic and broken morale, which are well known to observers of the stock market and of organizations but which have no reasonable interpretation in classical utility theory. I may also mention that psychologists use the theory described here in a straightforward way to produce experimental neurosis in animal and human subjects.)

Economic implications

It has sometimes been argued that, however realistic the classical theory of the firm as a profit maximizer, it is an adequate theory for purposes of normative economics.

The theory of the firm is important for welfare economics—e.g., for determining under what circumstances the behavior of the firm will lead to efficient allocation of resources. The satisficing model vitiates all the conclusions about resource allocation that are derivable from the maximizing model when perfect competition is assumed. Similarly, a dynamic theory of firm sizes has quite different implications for public policies dealing with concentration than a theory that assumes firms to be in static equilibrium. Hence, welfare economists are justified in adhering to the classical theory only if:

(a) the theory is empirically correct as a description of the decision-making process; or

(b) it is safe to assume that the system operates in the neighborhood of the static equilibrium.

What evidence we have mostly contradicts both assumptions.

Conclusion

In exploring the areas in which economics has common interests with the other behavioral sciences, we have been guided by the molasses metaphor elaborated above. In simple, slow-moving situations, where the actor has a single, operational goal, the assumption of maximization relieves us of any need to construct a detailed picture of economic man or his processes of adaptation. As the complexity of the environment increases, or its speed of change, we need to know more and more about the mechanisms and processes that economic man uses to relate himself to that environment and achieve his goals.

How closely we wish to interweave economics with psychology depends, then, both on the range of questions we wish to answer and on our assessment of how far we may trust the assumption of static equilibrium as approximations. In considerable part, the demand for a fuller picture of economic man has been coming from the profession of economics itself, as new areas of theory and application have emerged in which complexity and change are central facts. The needs of normative economics and management science for a fuller theory of the firm have led to a number of attempts to understand the actual processes of making business decisions. In both these areas, notions of adaptive and satisficing behavior, drawn largely from psychology, are challenging sharply the classical picture of the maximizing entrepreneur.

The very complexity that has made a theory of the decision-making process essential has made its construction exceedingly difficult. It seemed almost utopian to suppose that we could put together a model of adaptive man that would compare in completeness with the simple model of classical economic man. The sketchiness and incompleteness of the newer proposals has been urged as a compelling reason for clinging to the older theories, however inadequate they are admitted to be.

The modern digital computer has changed the situation radically. It provides us with a tool of research—for formulating and testing theories—whose power is commensurate with the complexity of the phenomena we seek to understand. Although the use of computers to build theories of human behavior is very recent, it has already led to concrete results in the simulation of higher mental processes. As economics finds it more and more necessary to understand and explain disequilibrium as well as equilibrium, it will find an increasing use for this new tool and for communication with its sister sciences of psychology and sociology.

Part 5

THE UNITED STATES IN THE WORLD ECONOMY

The advantages of specialization and division of labor have long been recognized and praised as one of the main benefits of an exchange economy. Yet, men and nations often adopt different views concerning the benefits of trade when the specialization and exchange take place across international boundaries.

Adam Smith (1723–1790), who is widely regarded as the father of modern economics, was one of the first to note this dichotomy in our thinking. *The Wealth of Nations,* which was published in 1776, not only spelled out the advantages of specialization and exchange, but it also contained a stinging rebuke of many of the interferences with which trade was burdened during his time. Here, as elsewhere in this classic, the heart of the argument was an attack on state interference with the natural working of a free-market system. Smith's famous reference to the "invisible hand," which guided profit-seeking individuals to promote the general welfare in competitive markets, is contained in this passage on the cost to a nation of protecting the domestic market for domestic producers. The two possible exceptions which he offers here to his general principles have become common defenses of those manufacturers who believe in free trade— for others.

Questions to Guide the Reading

How are the costs of protection distributed relative to the benefits of protection? Why then might there be greater pressure for import restrictions than for trade liberalization?

How many of our existing trade barriers can be justified by Smith's two exceptions to his free-trade principles? What other arguments are there in favor of restrictions on foreign imports? How would Smith react to these arguments?

RESTRAINTS ON FOREIGN IMPORTS
Adam Smith

By restraining, either by high duties, or by absolute prohibitions, the importation of such goods from foreign countries as can be produced at home, the monopoly of the home market is more or less secured to the domestic industry employed in producing them. Thus the prohibition of importing either live cattle or salt provisions from foreign countries secures to the graziers of Great Britain the monopoly of the home market for butcher's meat. The high duties upon the importation of corn, which in times of moderate plenty amount to a prohibition, give a like advantage to the growers of that commodity. The prohibition of the importation of foreign woollens is equally favourable to the woollen manufacturers. The silk manufacture, though altogether employed upon foreign materials, has lately obtained the same advantage. The linen manufac-

ture has not yet obtained it, but is making great strides towards it. Many other sorts of manufacturers have, in the same manner, obtained in Great Britain, either altogether, or very nearly a monopoly against their countrymen. The variety of goods of which the importation into Great Britain is prohibited, either absolutely, or under certain circumstances, greatly exceeds what can easily be suspected by those who are not well acquainted with the laws of the customs.

That this monopoly of the home-market frequently gives great encouragement to that particular species of industry which enjoys it, and frequently turns towards that employment a greater share of both the labour and stock of the society than would otherwise have gone to it, cannot be doubted. But whether it tends either to increase the general industry of the society, or

From Adam Smith, *The Wealth of Nations,* Book IV, Chap. II.

to give it the most advantageous direction, is not, perhaps, altogether so evident.

The general industry of the society never can exceed what the capital of the society can employ. As the number of workmen that can be kept in employment by any particular person must bear a certain proportion to his capital, so the number of those that can be continually employed by all the members of a great society must bear a certain proportion to the whole capital of that society, and never can exceed that proportion. No regulation of commerce can increase the quantity of industry in any society beyond what its capital can maintain. It can only divert a part of it into a direction into which it might not otherwise have gone; and it is by no means certain that this artificial direction is likely to be more advantageous to the society than that into which it would have gone of its own accord.

Every individual is continually exerting himself to find out the most advantageous employment for whatever capital he can command. It is his own advantage, indeed, and not that of the society, which he has in view. But the study of his own advantage naturally, or rather necessarily leads him to prefer that employment which is most advantageous to the society.

First, every individual endeavours to employ his capital as near home as he can, and consequently as much as he can in the support of domestic industry; provided always that he can thereby obtain the ordinary, or not a great deal less than the ordinary profits of stock.

Secondly, every individual who employs his capital in the support of domestic industry, necessarily endeavours so to direct that industry, that its produce may be of the greatest possible value.

The produce of industry is what it adds to the subject or materials upon which it is employed. In proportion as the value of this produce is great or small, so will likewise be the profits of the employer. But it is only for the sake of profit that any man employs a capital in the support of industry; and he will always, therefore, endeavour to employ it in the support of that industry of which the produce is likely to be of the greatest value, or to exchange for the greatest quantity either of money or of other goods.

The invisible hand

But the annual revenue of every society is always precisely equal to the exchangeable value of the whole annual produce of its industry, or rather is precisely the same thing with that exchangeable value. As every individual, therefore, endeavours as much as he can both to employ his capital in the support of domestic industry, and so to direct that industry that its produce may be of the greatest value; every individual necessarily labours to render the annual revenue of the society as great as he can. He generally, indeed, neither intends to promote the public interest, nor knows how much he is promoting it. By preferring the support of domestic to that of foreign industry, he intends only his own security; and by directing that industry in such a manner as its produce may be of the greatest value, he intends only his own gain, and he is in this, as in many other cases, led by an *invisible hand* to promote an end which was no part of his intention. Nor is it always the worse for the society that it was no part of it. By pursuing his own interest he frequently promotes that of the society more effectually than when he really intends to promote it. I have never known much good done by those who affected to trade for the public good. It is an affectation, indeed, not very common among merchants, and very few words need be employed in dissuading them from it.

What is the species of domestic industry which his capital can employ, and of which the produce is likely to be of the greatest value, every individual, it is evident, can, in his local situation, judge much better than any statesman or lawgiver can do for him. The statesman, who should attempt to direct private people in what manner they ought to employ their capitals, would not only load himself with a most unnecessary attention, but assume an authority which could safely be trusted, not only to no single person, but to no council or senate whatever, and which would nowhere be so dangerous as in the hands of a man who had folly and presumption enough to fancy himself fit to exercise it.

To give the monopoly of the home-market to the produce of domestic industry, in any particular art or manufacture, is in some measure to direct private people in what manner they ought to employ their capitals, and must, in almost all cases, be either a useless or a hurtful regulation. If the produce of domestic can be brought there as cheap as that of foreign industry, the regulation is evidently useless. If it cannot, it must generally be hurtful. It is the maxim of every prudent master of a family, never to attempt to make at home what it will cost him more to make than to buy. The taylor does not attempt to make his own shoes, but buys them of the shoemaker. The shoemaker does not attempt to **make** his own clothes, but employs a taylor. The farmer attempts to make neither the one nor the other, but employs those different artificers. All of them find it for their interest to employ their whole industry in a way in which they have some advantage over their neighbours, and to purchase with a part of its produce, or what is the same thing, with the price of a part of it, whatever else they have occasion for.

What is prudence in the conduct of every private family, can scarce be folly in that of a great kingdom. If a foreign country can supply us with a commodity cheaper than we ourselves can make it, better buy it of them with some part of the produce of our own industry, employed in a way in which we have some advantage. The general industry of the country, being always in proportion to the capital which employs it, will not thereby be diminished, no more than that of the above-mentioned artificers; but only left to find out the way in which it can be employed with the greatest advantage. It is certainly not employed to the greatest advantage, when it is thus directed towards an object which it can buy cheaper than it can make. The value of its annual produce is certainly more or less diminished, when it is thus turned away from producing commodities evidently of more value than the commodity which it is directed to produce. According to the supposition, that commodity could be purchased from foreign countries cheaper than it can be made at home. It could, therefore, have been purchased with a part only of the commodities, or, what is the same thing, with a part only of the price of the commodities, which the industry employed by an equal capital would have produced at home, had it been left to follow its natural course. The industry of the country, therefore, is thus turned away from a more, to a less advantageous employment, and the exchangeable value of its annual produce, instead of being increased, according to the intention of the lawgiver, must necessarily be diminished by every such regulation.

By means of such regulations, indeed, a particular manufacture may sometimes be acquired sooner than it could have been otherwise, and after a certain time may be made at home as cheap or cheaper than in the foreign country. But though the industry of the society may be thus carried with advantage into a particular channel sooner than it could have been otherwise, it will by no means follow that the sum total, either of its industry, or of its revenue, can ever be augmented by any such regulation. The industry of the society can augment only in pro-

portion as its capital augments, and its capital can augment only in proportion to what can be gradually saved out of its revenue. But the immediate effect of every such regulation is to diminish its revenue, and what diminishes its revenue is certainly not very likely to augment its capital faster than it would have augmented of its own accord, had both capital and industry been left to find out their natural employments.

Though for want of such regulations the society should never acquire the proposed manufacture, it would not, upon that account, necessarily be the poorer in any one period of its duration. In every period of its duration its whole capital and industry might still have been employed, though upon different objects, in the manner that was most advantageous at the time. In every period its revenue might have been the greatest which its capital could afford, and both capital and revenue might have been augmenting with the greatest possible rapidity.

The natural advantages which one country has over another in producing particular commodities are sometimes so great, that it is acknowledged by all the world to be in vain to struggle with them. By means of glasses, hotbeds, and hotwalls, very good grapes can be raised in Scotland, and very good wine too can be made of them at about thirty times the expence for which at least equally good can be bought from foreign countries. Would it be a reasonable law to prohibit the importation of all foreign wines, merely to encourage the making of claret and burgundy in Scotland? But if there would be a manifest absurdity in turning towards any employment, thirty times more of the capital and industry of the country than would be necessary to purchase from foreign countries an equal quantity of the commodities wanted, there must be an absurdity, though not altogether so glaring, yet exactly of the same kind, in turning towards any such employment a thirtieth, or even a three hundredth part more of either. Whether the advantages which one country has over another, be natural or acquired, is in this respect of no consequence. As long as the one country has those advantages, and the other wants them, it will always be more advantageous for the latter, rather to buy of the former than to make. It is an acquired advantage only, which one artificer has over his neighbour, who exercises another trade; and yet they both find it more advantageous to buy of one another, than to make what does not belong to their particular trades.

Merchants and manufacturers are the people who derive the greatest advantage from this monopoly of the home-market. The prohibition of the importation of foreign cattle, and of salt provisions, together with the high duties upon foreign corn, which in times of moderate plenty amount to a prohibition, are not near so advantageous to the graziers and farmers of Great Britain, as other regulations of the same kind are to its merchants and manufacturers. Manufactures, those of the finer kind especially, are more easily transported from one country to another than corn or cattle. It is in the fetching and carrying manufactures, accordingly, that foreign trade is chiefly employed. In manufactures, a very small advantage will enable foreigners to undersell our own workmen, even in the home market. It will require a very great one to enable them to do so in the rude produce of the soil. If the free importation of foreign manufactures were permitted, several of the home manufactures would probably suffer, and some of them, perhaps, go to ruin altogether, and a considerable part of the stock and industry at present employed in them, would be forced to find out some other employment. But the freest importation of the rude produce of the soil could have no such effect upon the agriculture of the country.

Country gentlemen and farmers are, to their great honour, of all people, the least subject to the wretched spirit of monopoly. The undertaker of a great manufactory is sometimes alarmed if another work of the same kind is established within twenty miles of him. The Dutch undertaker of the woollen manufacture at Abbeville stipulated, that no work of the same kind should be established within thirty leagues of that city. Farmers and country gentlemen, on the contrary, are generally disposed rather to promote than to obstruct the cultivation and improvement of their neighbours' farms and estates. They have no secrets, such as those of the greater part of manufacturers, but are generally rather fond of communicating to their neighbours, and of extending as far as possible any new practice which they have found to be advantageous.

Country gentlemen and farmers, dispersed in different parts of the country, cannot so easily combine as merchants and manufacturers, who being collected into towns, and accustomed to that exclusive corporation spirit which prevails in them, naturally endeavour to obtain against all their countrymen, the same exclusive privilege which they generally possess against the inhabitants of their respective towns. They accordingly seem to have been the original inventors of those restraints upon the importation of foreign goods, which secure to them the monopoly of the home-market. It was probably in imitation of them, and to put themselves upon a level with those who, they found, were disposed to oppress them, that the country gentlemen and farmers of Great Britain so far forgot the generosity which is natural to their station, as to demand the exclusive privilege of supplying their countrymen with corn and butcher's-meat. They did not perhaps take time to consider, how much less their interest could be affected by the freedom of trade, than that of the people whose example they followed.

To prohibit by a perpetual law the importation of foreign corn and cattle, is in reality to enact, that the population and industry of the country shall at no time exceed what the rude produce of its own soil can maintain.

There seem, however, to be two cases in which it will generally be advantageous to lay some burden upon foreign, for the encouragement of domestic industry.

The first, is, when some particular sort of industry is necessary for the defence of the country. The defence of Great Britain, for example, depends very much upon the number of its sailors and shipping. The act of navigation, therefore, very properly endeavours to give the sailors and shipping of Great Britain the monopoly of the trade of their own country, in some cases, by absolute prohibitions, and in others by heavy burdens upon the shipping of foreign countries. The following are the principal dispositions of this act.

First, all ships, of which the owners, masters, and three-fourths of the mariners are not British subjects, are prohibited, upon pain of forfeiting ship and cargo, from trading to the British settlements and plantations, or from being employed in the coasting trade of Great Britain.

Secondly, a great variety of the most bulky articles of importation can be brought into Great Britain only, either in such ships as are above described, or in ships of the country where those goods are produced, and of which the owners, masters, and three-fourths of the mariners, are of that particular country; and when imported even in ships of this latter kind, they are subject to double aliens duty. If imported in ships of any other country, the penalty is forfeiture of ship and goods. When this act was made, the Dutch were, what they still are, the great carriers of Europe, and by this regulation they were entirely excluded from being the carriers to Great Britain, or from importing to us the goods of any other European country.

Thirdly, a great variety of the most bulky articles of importation are prohibited from being imported, even in British ships, from any country but that in which they are produced; under pain of forfeiting ship and cargo. This regulation too was probably intended against the Dutch. Holland was then, as now, the great emporium for all European goods, and by this regulation, British ships were hindered from loading in Holland the goods of any other European country.

Fourthly, salt fish of all kinds, whale-fins, whale-bone, oil, and blubber, not caught by and cured on board British vessels, when imported into Great Britain, are subjected to double aliens duty. The Dutch, as they are still the principal, were then the only fishers in Europe that attempted to supply foreign nations with fish. By this regulation, a very heavy burden was laid upon their supplying Great Britain.

When the act of navigation was made, though England and Holland were not actually at war, the most violent animosity subsisted between the two nations. It had begun during the government of the long parliament, which first framed this act, and it broke out soon after in the Dutch wars during that of the Protector and of Charles the Second. It is not impossible, therefore, that some of the regulations of this famous act may have proceeded from national animosity. They are as wise, however, as if they had all been dictated by the most deliberate wisdom. National animosity at that particular time aimed at the very same object which the most deliberate wisdom would have recommended, the diminution of the naval power of Holland, the only naval power which could endanger the security of England.

The act of navigation is not favourable to foreign commerce, or to the growth of that opulence which can arise from it. The interest of a nation in its commercial relations to foreign nations is, like that of a merchant with regard to the different people with which he deals, to buy as cheap and to sell as dear as possible. But it will be most likely to buy cheap, when by the most perfect freedom of trade it encourages all nations to bring to it the goods which it has occasion to purchase; and, for the same reason, it will be most likely to sell dear, when its markets are thus filled with the greatest number of buyers. The act of navigation, it is true, lays no burden upon foreign ships that come to export the produce of British industry. Even the ancient aliens duty, which used to be paid upon all goods exported as well as imported, has, by several subsequent acts, been taken off from the greater part of the articles of exportation. But if foreigners, either by prohibitions or high duties, are hindered from coming to sell, they cannot always afford to come to buy; because coming without a cargo, they must lose the freight from their own country to Great Britain. By diminishing the number of sellers, therefore, we necessarily diminish that of buyers, and are thus likely not only to buy foreign goods dearer, but to sell our own cheaper, than if there was a more perfect freedom of trade. As defence, however, is of much more importance than opulence, the act of navigation is, perhaps, the wisest of all the commercial regulations of England.

The second case, in which it will generally be advantageous to lay some burden upon foreign for the encouragement of domestic industry, is, when some tax is imposed at home upon the produce of the latter. In this case, it seems reasonable that an equal tax should be imposed upon the like produce of the former. This would not give the monopoly of the home market to domestic industry, nor turn towards a particular employment a greater share of the stock and labour of the country, than what would naturally go to it. It would only hinder any part of what would naturally go to it from being turned away by the tax, into a less natural direction, and would leave the competition between foreign and domestic industry, after the tax, as nearly as possible upon the same footing as before it.

READING 50

Adam Smith's thoughts on protectionism in the previous reading employed the direct method of attack. Famous as that excerpt has become, it has had to share the spotlight with a very different form of attack from a French popularizer of classical economic thought. Frederic Bastiat (1801–1850) fought with the weapons of satire and wit, and the results were often devastating. In his *Economic Sophisms* he deliberately took the protectionists' case somewhat further than they intended to go and, in so doing, made the whole case teeter.

Questions to Guide the Reading

How closely do the arguments which Bastiat builds into this petition correspond to the most frequently used arguments for tariffs today?

How might the protectionists argue in response to this satire? Does the free-trade case lend itself equally well to this treatment?

PETITION OF THE CANDLEMAKERS—1845
Frederic Bastiat

To the Honorable Members of the Chamber of Deputies:

GENTLEMEN,—You are in the right way: you reject abstract theories; abundance, cheapness, concerns you little. You are entirely occupied with the interest of the producer, whom you are anxious to free from foreign competition. In a word, you wish to secure the *national market* to *national labor.*

We come now to offer you an admirable opportunity for the application of your—what shall we say—your theory? No, nothing is more deceiving than theory;—your doctrine? your system? your principle? But you do not like doctrines; you hold systems in horror; and, as for principles, you declare that there are no such things in political economy. We will say, then, your practice; your practice without theory, and without principle.

We are subjected to the intolerable competition of a foreign rival, who enjoys, it would seem, such superior facilities for the production of light, that he is enabled to *inundate* our *national market* at so exceedingly reduced a price, that, the moment he makes his appearance, he draws off all custom for us; and thus an important branch of French industry, with all its innumerable ramifications, is suddenly reduced to a state of complete stagnation. This rival is no other than the sun.

Our petition is, that it would please your honorable body to pass a law whereby shall be directed the shutting up of all windows, dormers, skylights, shutters, curtains, in a word, all openings, holes, chinks, and fissures through which the light of the sun is used to penetrate into our dwellings, to the prejudice of the profitable manufactures which we flatter ourselves we have been enabled to bestow upon the country; which country cannot, therefore, without ingratitude, leave us now to struggle unprotected through so unequal a contest.

We foresee your objections, gentlemen; but there is not one that you can oppose to us which you will not be obliged to gather from the works of the partisans of free trade. We dare challenge you to pronounce one word against our petition, which is not equally opposed to your own practice and the principle which guides your policy.

Do you tell us, that if we gain by this protection, France will not gain because the consumer must pay the price of it?

We answer you: You have no longer any right to cite the interest of the consumer. For whenever this has been found to compete with that of the producer, you have invariably sacrificed the first. You have done this to *encourage labor,* to *increase the demand for labor.* The same reason should now induce you to act in the same manner.

You have yourselves already answered the objection. When you were told, "The consumer is interested in the free introduction of iron, coal, corn, wheat, cloths, etc.," your answer was, "Yes, but the producer is interested in their exclusion." Thus, also, if the consumer is interested in the admission of light, we, the producers, pray for its interdiction.

You have also said, "The producer and the consumer are one. If the manufacturer gains by protection, he will cause the agriculturist to gain also; if agriculture prospers, it opens a market for manufactured goods." Thus we, if you confer upon us the monopoly of furnishing light during the day, will as a first consequence buy large quantities of tallow, coals, oil, resin, wax, alcohol, silver, iron, bronze, crystal, for the supply of our business; and then we and our numerous contractors having become rich our consumption will be great, and will become a means of contributing to the comfort and competency of the workers in every branch of national labor.

Will you say that the light of the sun is a

From Frederic Bastiat, *Economic Sophisms* (G. P. Putnam's Sons, New York, 1922), pp. 60–65.

gratuitous gift, and that to repulse gifts is to repulse riches under pretense of encouraging the means of obtaining them?

Take care,—you carry the death blow to your own policy. Remember that hitherto you have always repulsed foreign produce *because* it was an approach to a gratuitous gift, and *the more in proportion* as this approach was more close. You have, in obeying the wishes of other monopolists, acted only from a *half-motive;* to grant our petition there is a much *fuller inducement.*

Labor and nature concur in different proportions, according to country and climate, in every article of production. The portion of nature is always gratuitous. If a Lisbon orange can be sold at half the price of a Parisian one, it is because a natural and gratuitous heat does for the one what the other only obtains from an artificial and consequently expensive one. When, therefore, we purchase a Portuguese orange, we may say that we obtain it half

gratuitously and half by the right of labor; in other words, at *half price* compared with those of Paris.

Now it is precisely on account of this *demi-gratuity* (excuse the word) that you argue in favor of exclusion. How, you say, could national labor sustain the competition of foreign labor, when the first has everything to do, and the last is rid of half the trouble, the sun taking the rest of the business upon himself? If then the *demi-gratuity* can determine you to check competition, on what principle can the *entire gratuity* be alleged as a reason for admitting it? Choose, but be consistent. And does it not argue the greatest inconsistency to check as you do the importation of coal, iron, cheese, and goods of foreign manufacture, merely because and even in proportion as their price approaches *zero,* while at the same time you freely admit, and without limitation, the light of the sun, whose price is during the whole day at *zero?*

READING 51

Some 106 years after Frederic Bastiat published his satirical petition to the French National Assembly, a real-world group of candlemakers offered their serious petition to the Finance Committee of the United States Senate. They were silent on the subject of the sun, but they did argue vigorously, though briefly, on some other grounds for modern-day protectionism.

Questions to Guide the Reading

How does foreign competition in candles differ from, say, new domestic competition in its impact on our economy?

What criteria should our government use to decide whether or not a particular product ought to be given tariff protection?

Assuming that society feels some sort of obligation to a domestic industry being harmed by foreign competition, are there remedies other than those advocated here that might better fulfill this obligation?

PETITION OF THE CANDLEMAKERS—1951
Congressional Hearings

February 27, 1951
Re: Extension of the Trade Agreements Act, H.R. 1612

Chairman, Senate Finance Committee, United States Senate, Washington, D.C.

Sir: This brief is filed in behalf of the candle manufacturers in the United States in protest

against an extension of the Trade Agreement Act of 1934 as amended by the House of Representatives, H.R. 1612. In spite of our brief presented in opposition to tariff cuts (which are a matter of record and available to your committee) we have been given the maximum reduction possible up to this point.

The facts upon which we have based our pre-

From *Trade Agreements Extension Act of 1951: Hearings before the Committee on Finance, United States Senate, 82nd Congress, 1st Session, on H.R. 1612* (1951), pp. 149–150.

vious briefs are as important and as pertinent as they were when first presented. Rather than take the time of the committee by repetition of the entire argument we are listing the facts (all of which we have previously substantiated) in the hope that this time we will reach some one who has the understanding to interpret these facts intelligently and the power to act in the light of those facts.

1. An industry stemming from Colonial times.
2. A product required in national defense to such an extent as to utilize the full capacity of the industry.
3. High essentiality of labor and materials under war conditions.
4. An overcapacity of more than five to one.
5. Increased labor costs of 25 percent from 1946–50 with labor rates well above those prevailing in competitive countries.
6. A decline in sales of 17.45 percent since 1946.
7. A 63 percent increase in number of manufacturers since 1933.
8. With plants operating one shift, present production well above demand.
9. Full impacts of currency devaluations, abnormal conditions, pending legislation in countries not yet felt in our markets.

The record of imports for last year has shown a steady increase through the first 11 months from 12 countries, most of whom have not supplied candles to the United States for many years if ever. These are the countries mentioned in our earlier briefs from whom we feared this type of low-cost-labor competition. As a result of current untenable conditions one of the oldest

manufacturers—representing a substantial percentage of the total candle business—had been forced to close and demolish its plant.

It is evident that the purposes of the act outlined in the preamble are not being fulfilled: "Overcoming domestic unemployment," "increasing purchasing power of the American public," "maintaining a better relationship among various branches of American agriculture, industry, mining and commerce." This country should forgo the trade agreement policy until normal times return during which the benefits or ill effects of this act can be given a fair test. The expanded economy resulting from World War II has precluded any normal business operations and because of the Korean war we are still in an abnormal economy.

Competent legal opinion has proven that the entire act is illegal and unconstitutional.

We are requesting outright repeal of the act at this time. Failing that, we ask that any extension at least carry with it the following recent provisions of the House amendments as well as incorporate the points outlined above.

1. Tie in reductions with parity price levels.
2. Reinstate the peril points empowering the Tariff Commission to fix a point below which the tariff on any item cannot be cut.
3. Reinstate the right of judicial review of grievances and arbitrary decisions which may be imposed upon the citizens by the negotiators.
4. End all tariff concessions to communist countries.

Respectfully submitted.
   The Candle Manufacturing Industry
   by H. R. Farker

READING 52

In his comparatively short tenure as President of the United States, one of John F. Kennedy's major battles and victories was the passage of the Trade Expansion Act (H.R. 9900) of 1962. The principal purposes of this legislation were (1) to give the President increased powers to negotiate reciprocal tariff cuts with other nations and (2) to provide adjustment assistance to those Americans hurt by rising imports as a result of freer international trade. The lengthy debates preceding action on the proposals saw a number of new converts to the side of lower tariffs since Congress last reviewed our trade policies. But the protectionist side of the debate was still vigorously presented and careful political maneuvering was necessary to steer the act through the final passage.

Here are excerpts from four of the witnesses who testified before the House Ways and Means Committee in the spring of 1962. The first two are from opponents and the next two from supporters of H.R. 9900. Each contains a number of implicit assumptions that should afford the reader a chance to test his economic understanding on some real-world arguments.

Questions to Guide the Reading

What does each speaker see as the role for public policy in (1) preserving competition and (2) preserving competitors? What part does the "law of comparative advantage" play in each statement? What would each position here imply about the type of economy that we might expect to have ten years hence if that position were adopted as our policy?

Each speaker here succeeds in identifying his position with the national interest. Is there a clear-cut national interest in foreign trade policy that transcends the self-interest of the individual who happens to have the floor at the moment? If so, how is it to be determined?

THE DEBATE ON TRADE EXPANSION—1962
Congressional Hearings

A. Statement of O. R. Strackbein, Chairman, Nationwide Committee on Import-Export Policy

The present trade proposal as embodied in H.R. 9900 represents a sharp departure from the tariff legislation since the first Trade Agreements Act was passed in 1934.

It is very important, therefore, to mark the principal departures so that they may be considered on their merits.

Those of us who have been in close contact with the trade program are keenly aware of the numerous solemn statements made by Presidents, Secretaries of State, and other Cabinet officials, from Messrs. Roosevelt and Hull on through 25 years, asserting that it was not the intention of the trade program to injure or jeopardize domestic industry. A great virtue was made of the care and caution by which the tariff would be reduced. The approach was to be one item at a time.

If errors were made, and this was conceivable because it was even then foreseen that the State Department was not infallible, or if unforeseen developments should result in injury, there was a remedy in the escape clause. Mr. William L. Clayton, former Under Secretary of State, and recently once more articulate in this field, referred to the escape clause as a sure and prompt remedy and yielded to no one in his strong defense of the principle that domestic industry was not to be injured or "sold down the river" by the trade program.

Now, as stated above, the principle of "no injury" is to be abandoned as a cornerstone. It it to be replaced by a species of adjustment assistance that would make industries and workers wards of the Government and create a dependence on the Government that in turn would greatly enhance the power of the Government.

Also to be abandoned is the item-by-item approach to tariff reduction.

This too was cited by sundry high officials who testified on previous occasions as one of the merits of the program. Numerous quotations from the printed records could be adduced. It was understood then and should be understood now that tariffs should be tailored to the competitive situation of each item. A particular rate no more fits all products than a suit of clothes of one size would fit all men. In years past one of the prime motives in setting up a Tariff Commission was to assure a more scientific tariff, i.e., one that was made to reflect the different competitive conditions of different industries.

This concept would be set aside in this bill by calling for tariff reductions in broad categories of goods. The innocent would be slaughtered along with the guilty, so to speak.

These two departures from previous strongly

From *Hearings before the Committee on Ways and Means, House of Representatives, 87th Congress, 2d Session, on H.R. 9900* (U.S. Government Printing Office, Washington, 1962), Parts II and III, pp. 1312–21, 1656–59, 1969–71, 2062–67.

held positions are not the only ones. Another would be abandonment of the peril-point procedure, which was indeed a part of the caution to be exercised, and substitution of adjustment aid for the escape clause. This reflects abandonment of the no-injury principle which was heavily relied on as a means of persuading both Congress and the public that the trade program was both reasonable and at the same time did not smack of hostility to domestic industry, nor represented a zealous, blind and doctrinaire attachment to the free-trade philosophy.

Yet another departure reflected in the bill is found in the extreme concentration of power in the President, which in effect means the State Department and its subsidiaries in the Commerce and Labor Departments. The existing act had already gone far afield from the constitutional mandate that Congress was to regulate our foreign commerce and to make the tariff, but the proposed new act would go much farther.

H.R. 9900 proposes by lowering trade barriers to stimulate the economic growth of the United States, maintain and enlarge foreign markets for the products of U.S. industry and agriculture, provide lower prices to the American people on a greater variety of goods, and also to strengthen the economic and political relations with the European Economic Community, and so forth. Finally it is to counter economic penetration by international communism.

In place of the no-injury policy we are offered "adjustment assistance" after the damage has been done. It would bestow on imports the right of eminent domain, that is, the power to push domestic industries to one side and onto the ash heap.

Such a competitive effect is justified principally on three grounds. One is that the domestic industry must be inefficient if it cannot compete with imports. This is in reality a libel of our industries. The coal industry cannot compete with imported residual fuel oil even though it is the most efficient in the world and doubled its output per man-hour since 1950. Our agriculture cannot compete with imports: as note the highly restrictive import quotas on wheat and wheat flour and cotton. Yet our agriculture is the most efficient in the world. Our steel industry is among the most efficient in the world. Yet imports have exceeded the export tonnage in the past 2 years.

Another justification for injurious imports is the lower prices they provide consumers. However, consumers who are the beneficiaries of our economic system are not entitled to bargains at its expense. If they want a high-wage, high-profit, and full-employment economy and generally high standards they must be willing to pay for them. They cannot expect to chisel at the foundations and find bargains at the expense of those who in turn support the bargain hunters. Sweatshops in this country formerly were able to undersell competitors and thus to benefit the consumers; but we legislated them out of business by minimum wage and maximum hour laws. We also killed child labor which was cheap labor.

Moreover, domestic competition itself is expected to function in a manner to assure fair prices. If it does not do so that is where we should look rather than to an imported whip with which to scourge our struggling industries.

The third plea rests on the vague theory of international harmony through trade. Yet it must be clear that competitive trade has caused more international ill will and conflict than any other economic factor.

The use of trade as a political weapon in international diplomacy is a very dubious instrument, as economic warfare demonstrates. Nevertheless that is what is suggested in our proposed adjustment to the Common Market.

Our problem is not enlargement of trade. It is part of our problem. It is not the central problem. It is rather the one of adjustment to a fast-moving technology that is now international. The problem of employment is in the forefront and it is in the light of this that we must shape our trade policy or we will be forced later to do so.

H.R. 9900 would aggravate our problem; not alleviate it. It goes in the wrong direction.

Our industry, agriculture, and labor have become exposed to a form of foreign competition that they cannot meet and yet sustain the income, the tax, and the employment and wage base necessary to national progress.

The argument that our high economic plateau is not vulnerable to imports on the grounds that we are so much more productive per man-hour than our competitors is obsolescent and running out of time.

If it is the intent of H.R. 9900 to draw a tight ceiling over our wages, a ceiling to be breached only at the price of becoming or remaining noncompetitive, then it should be passed. If it is the intent to hold our wage level in status quo until the wages of other countries catch up this bill should be passed. If, however, that is the intent it should be announced to the public.

If that is not the intent, and if the bill should nevertheless be passed, we will confront very important segments of our industry and agriculture with market prospects so dismal that the growth and employment expansion that we need will die in the seed. These segments will in no wise be confined to the so-called marginal or inefficient industries. The retarding effect will strike just as readily at our leading mass-production industries as steel, electrical equipment, office machinery, and so forth.

It is said that we can meet this challenge, that indeed we need the challenge, that we have become fat and lazy and unimaginative. What we need is to be prodded to do our best. What we need is vision and vigor and energy and imagination to take vast leaps ahead. So be it. Perhaps we are guilty as charged. Perhaps we need stinging challenges. Perhaps we need to seize the angels of efficiency by the forelock and flock with them into the promised land.

Let us mechanize and automate and leave the pedestrian Europeans and Japanese behind.

Unfortunately there is now a jagged gravel in our shoe. Improved technology has a tempo that gallops out ahead of our powers of adjustment. The latter are slow, painful, and very pedestrian. The more we try to hurry to be imperative the more the gravel cuts into the flesh.

Let us not in our pride of technology overlook the clear and simple fact that we no longer have a monopoly of high productivity; that the people of other countries have been caught up in its fire and that in the mobility of our capital across national boundaries we ourselves are disseminating our so-called know-how far and wide wherever we can find a willing royalty payer or wherever we can invest profitably.

To this there can be no objection and it would work very well if we stood on the same economic and competitive level as our competitors; but we live in an economic split-level world. No matter how much we might wish that this were not true it is nonetheless based on centuries of compartmental development and represents a very stubborn fact.

These levels will not be bridged without a cataclysm if proper safeguards are not provided.

These safeguards should not be of the kind proposed in the bill but should be in the form of preventive measures and remedies rather than

defeat and retreat. That is why we should retain the essence of the peril-point system and provide for a better and surer escape clause.

The great error of the times is to equate greater efficiency and productivity with growth on the one hand and overlooking the fortunes of employment on the other.

The very notion that all we need to do in this country to remain competitive with imports or to achieve that state or to be competitive in exports is to increase our productivity, actually represents an obstacle to a clear understanding of the problem.

A twin notion, equally fallacious, would put its trust in exports as a source of employment expansion. Exports, to be sure, are desirable and we need them, but the contribution to employment from that source beyond present levels must be somewhat minuscule. Since rising exports can be achieved only as a result of rising imports, unless we wish to pay for the exports, as we are doing to a considerable extent even now, even this small contribution may not be made.

Many of these imports would be competitive in character and would kill more actual and prospective jobs than the increased exports would create. They would prevent new jobs from developing as they would if the domestic industry had a better competitive outlook vis-à-vis imports.

What is needed as an antidote to chronic unemployment and assurance that the more than a million additional workers who come on the scene each year and the more than a million displaced by automation can be employed, is an investment climate that will induce expansion in this country and avoid substitution of foreign investment for domestic investment.

This requires a bright enough domestic market outlook for rising production to encourage expansion. It means removal of the heavy threat of low-cost imports that hangs like a dark cloud over market prospects. In turn this calls for judicious use of tariffs and quotas or a combination of them to preserve a specific share of a potentially growing market for our own producers.

B. Statement of B. C. Deuschle, President, Shears, Scissors & Manicure Implement Manufacturers Association

The association respectfully wishes to record with this committee its strong opposition to H.R.

9900 in its present form. This bill could destroy industries such as ours and add to the unemployment problem.

During the past 15 years representatives of our association have appeared before this committee and other congressional committees, the Committee for Reciprocity Information and the Tariff Commission, to present our views on the impact of imported scissors and shears on our domestic industry.

We have never requested or suggested that a complete embargo be placed on the import of scissors and shears. All that we have asked for and desire is a fair competitive opportunity, not an advantage.

To date we have not obtained relief in any form.

We believe that H.R. 9900 would make matters worse. H.R. 9900 provides for new Presidential authority to reduce or eliminate duties. We realize that title III of H.R. 9900 provides for adjustment assistance, but the criteria are general and too much is left to the discretion of the President in granting assistance.

Injury or threat of injury as it is written into our present escape clause cannot be properly defined. When 42 manufacturers out of 50 cease manufacturing and go out of business within 12 years as a direct or indirect result of excessive imports, and the Tariff Commission as well as the President decide that there is no injury or threat of injury, something should be done.

Imports of shears and scissors valued over $1.75 per dozen import value have reached the proportion that they represent 95 percent of domestic production of scissors and shears in this category.

We realize that the domestic scissor and shear industry with its 1,000-plus employees accounts for only a fraction of 1 percent of the gross national product, but we see this as no justification for letting the industry be completely destroyed by imports produced with low-cost labor.

The workers in the domestic scissor and shear industry do not want to become wards of the State; they want to use their skills, which have taken years to develop. These workers are not interested in retraining; over many years they have developed a skill they are proud of and want to continue the work they are happy doing.

If the scissors and shears imported during 1961 had been manufactured in the United States, it would have provided over 2 million man-hours of factory work, or full-time employment for over 1,000 American employees.

Domestic manufacturers of scissors and shears have modernized and automated their operations in an effort to meet foreign competition. But foreign manufacturers also have modern equipment and with their lower wage rates are underselling domestic firms in the U.S. market at today's rate of duty.

H.R. 9900 would give the President unrestricted authority to reduce duties and thereby further reduce the cost of imported scissors and shears in our market. Under the provisions of this bill, scissors and shears would be buried in a category with many other items and the duty cut 50 percent.

This would mean a reduction of at least 20 cents per pair at the retail level for scissors and shears now being retailed at $1 to $1.29 per pair.

If this is permitted, we do not need a crystal ball to see the results. There are only eight domestic firms now remaining of the 50 operating in the United States prior to the 50 percent reduction in import duty during 1950–51.

These few remaining manufacturers would be forced to close their doors and discharge their employees. The United States would then become wholly dependent on imported scissors and shears.

We cannot understand how it could be in the national interest to permit such a loss. We would lose the skills of the employees and management of the industry as well as the capital investment in production equipment. In the event of a national emergency and imports cutoff, the United States would be without a source of scissors and shears, basic tools for many industries and trades essential to our defense.

The scissor and shear industry is one of the oldest in the world. The skill was brought to the United States from Germany at a time when the United States needed new industry and a scissor and shear industry in particular.

Scissors and shears of all sizes and types are used in every school, retail establishment, office, factory, hospital, and home in the United States. Scissors cannot be classified as a luxury, gimmick, or novelty.

Scissors are used to separate us from our mothers at birth; to cut our toenails; to trim the leather in our shoes; to cut and trim the materials used in every piece of clothing that we wear.

They are used to cut our fingernails, to trim our mustaches, the hair in our ears and nose, and to cut the hair on our heads—even down to the end of the road when our best suit or dress is cut down the back so that the undertaker can dress us for the last ride. Scissors are truly used from birth to death. They are essential to our health, education, and general welfare.

I ask you gentlemen, is this an industry that should be permitted to become extinct in this country?

C. Statement of A. B. Sparboe, Vice President of the Pillsbury Co. and a Director of the Chamber of Commerce of the United States

The national Chamber of Commerce strongly supports the principles of H.R. 9900, which would continue and expand the President's authority to reduce tariffs on a reciprocal basis within the scope that Congress will clearly define and establish.

Mutually beneficial trade raises standards of living by providing more goods at less real cost. The United States has a vital stake in promoting measures to achieve a relaxation of discriminatory and restrictive trade practices throughout the world. Such practices include exchange controls, quotas, preferential or discriminatory treatment, subsidies, and other devices.

The current problem involves balancing the longrun advantage of greater international specialization of human and other resources against the shortrun adjustment pains to producers hurt by foreign competition.

These are among the considerations inherent in problems facing the United States in its efforts to maintain and expand foreign markets and to accelerate economic growth of the United States.

Congress should, of course, set international trade policy. It is not practical for Congress to attempt to set rates on the multiplicity of products moving in international trade today.

Therefore, it is imperative that the President be given the tools within the intent of Congress with which to bargain effectively with the European Economic Community and other countries, to meet the intensified Communist trade offensive, and to work in concert with other free nations in finding markets for developing nations.

Let it be noted that there is good reason for the sense of drama that attends the American debate on this proposed legislation. Perhaps no other measure in the current Congress is more compelling in its effect and influence on our own economic growth and well-being and on the future course of the free world.

Forces of change throughout the world are powerful. Failure to develop foreign trade policy in line with changing forces could only mean retardation, or worse, a backward step which could cost the United States its role of leadership in the world today.

This must not happen. The American people have a responsibility in their own self-interest to see and comprehend the broad frame of the problems—to study and understand the constructive measures in this program.

While U.S. industry faces the discipline of foreign competition as never before—the benefits which will accrue to the United States are many.

International Communist conspiracy is reaching out treacherous hands for the new nations of the world—some of which are ill-prepared for the responsibilities they must assume in the community of nations. These new nations must have the help of the free world to establish healthy trading relationships.

Japan—our second best customer and to whom we sell over half a billion dollars a year more in goods than we buy from her—must not be forced into the nearby Communist camp.

This legislation provides ways and means whereby these problems can be worked out in concert with other free world nations.

It is unfortunate that many Americans view the trade agreements program as a one-way proposition—a tariff cutting program whereby we give away our substance and gain nothing. The fallacy of such a view is amply revealed by the results of tariff negotiations recently concluded in Geneva.

According to official reports, other countries have made greater concessions than the United States on the recent reciprocal negotiations for new concessions as well as compensatory negotiations.

The expanding European Economic Community, with growing incomes and latent demand for many consumer items offers market potentials for U.S. goods which are almost unlimited. We must be prepared to bargain for freer access to this great market, and we must permit them to pay for our exports with their goods.

In the present world situation, it is necessary to lower trade barriers. This is the first principle of trade expansion, but it should be done gradually in order to allow ample time for the adjustment that may be required.

Bargaining authority. To achieve these objectives, the chamber supports the two main grants of bargaining authority provided for under the proposed Trade Expansion Act of 1962, H.R. 9900:

1. Authority to reduce in gradual stages by as much as 50 percent present duties on certain items by categories of products; and

2. Authority to eliminate gradually tariffs on certain items in which the United States and the European Economic Community supply 80 percent of the world's trade.

Such negotiating authority by the President should be approved for a period of 5 years—until June 30, 1967, as the bill provides. Considering the lengthy process of preparation and negotiation of major tariff agreements, any shorter period of extension could lead to inefficient and ineffective conduct of the program.

Guarantee reciprocity. It must be stressed that any reductions of trade barriers on our part should be accompanied by comparable or appropriate elimination of restrictions on the part of other nations.

The President in his trade message to Congress on January 25, 1962, said:

We mean to see to it that all reductions and concessions are reciprocal—and that the access we gain is not limited by the use of quotas or other restrictive devices.

Congress should provide in the law that reciprocity be assured as negotiations progress under the terms prescribed.

Staging requirements. A vital feature of a program of this character is the staging requirement —the provision that major concessions take effect gradually in stages stretched over at least a 5-year period.

Since, as noted previously, the preparation and negotiation of major tariff agreements is a lengthy process requiring at least a year in most cases, it would appear that American industry would have at least 6 years for necessary adjustment and accommodation to any reductions which might be made.

Protection for domestic industries. While pursuing means for promoting the growth and cohesiveness of the community of free nations, the United States must afford reasonable protection for U.S. industry and agriculture.

Such protection can and should be achieved through an effectively administered escape clause.

Determination of injury due to imports should be judged in the light of the national interest, including national security considerations.

The chamber supports the administration's proposal for "appropriate and tested forms" of assistance for workers, companies, and industries injured by import competition. However, aid to displaced employees should be administered by the States and should not exceed in amount or duration the benefits provided by State unemployment compensation laws.

This recommendation is not to be construed as discriminatory against workers vis-à-vis companies or industries. On the other hand, it would be discriminatory to provide greater allowances for workers displaced by reason of imports than for workers displaced for other reasons.

Role of imports. Often industries which may be hurt by increased imports are those which are having other difficulties. Although imports may be a factor, changes in consumer tastes, technological developments, and other factors also figure in the problem.

The value of imports to a nation's economy is too often overlooked. The essence of the principle of comparative advantage is that any nation can only hurt itself by excluding imports which can be obtained at lower real cost from abroad than at home.

The real gain from foreign trade to a nation as a whole consists of its imports. We stress the significance of exports to the balance-of-payments problem. This is important. But exports also earn foreign exchange with which we pay for imports —by far the greatest volume of which consists of materials required to keep our own economy producing at a high level.

It follows that the better the bargain we get in the export-import exchange, the better off we are, and it is the consumer who gains the most.

It should be realized, also, in measuring competitive advantage, that wages alone are not a complete measure of the ability to compete. The unit costs of production include all elements of costs—wages, taxes, capital charges, personnel costs, managerial costs, distribution costs, overhead costs, and so on.

D. Statement of Edwin A. Locke, President, Union Tank Car Co., Chicago, Ill.

Perhaps I should say at the start that the company which I represent has a substantial stake in foreign trade through a number of its divisions, and that during the past few years I have often gone to Europe and Asia specifically to deal with problems of foreign trade and investment. I should hope, however, that what I have to say far transcends the interests of my company.

To come directly to my main point: As I understand it, the opposition to the bill before you grows largely out of the fear that if additional elements of foreign competition are allowed to enter the American market, there will be dislocations in American business and employment. The presumption is that these dislocations resulting from foreign competition will be greater and more painful than the bruises that our companies now inflict on each other in their everyday struggle in the market, and which are regarded as normal.

Gentlemen, I submit that a degree of dislocation, a shaking up, will be beneficial to the economy. Business in this country could well do with the kind of stimulation that increased foreign competition would provide. Instead of fearing new competition in the American market, we ought to welcome it.

To see how much new competition can do to stimulate businesses and nations to a new surge of achievement, one need only look at the Common Market countries of Western Europe. One of the big reasons for the success of the Common Market is the charge of renewed purpose now felt by businessmen over there as a direct result of the great broadening of their competitive field.

I have the word of representative European businessmen that this challenge was exactly what was needed to generate a new constructive drive. Confronted with new opportunity and new challenge, they found resources within themselves that they had forgotten they had. They began accomplishing things that they never knew could be accomplished. And the result is the most spectacular broad-scale economic development of our time.

Gentlemen, I believe that stimulation such as would be provided by increased foreign competition and new market opportunities is exactly what business in this country needs. Our economy shows soft spots. It makes me think of a champion athlete who has been taking it a little easy. Getting back into topnotch condition may be a painful process, but it is the only way by which we can tap our reserves of power and maintain leadership in the world of tomorrow.

What I am trying to say is that economic dislocation, kept within limits, can have a powerful constructive aspect. This is not to contest the desirability of giving Government aid to those who are clearly and seriously damaged by foreign competition. The provisions of the present bill for this purpose seem to me humane, wise, and workable.

But the Nation would be a heavy loser if the aid given to businesses which experienced some dislocation weakened their will to adjust and compete in the changed conditions which will confront them. It would be most unfortunate if the assistance contemplated in this bill were carried in practice to the point where it reduced the stimulating force of the new challenge, to the point where men lost the incentive to help themselves, to the point where Government programing became a substitute for personal initiative.

The risk that the country would take in reducing tariffs reciprocally in my opinion is minor. American industry is resilient enough and strong enough to meet almost any kind of competition from abroad. Fear of cheap foreign production seems to me to be exaggerated.

I have seen relatively high priced American products become well established in foreign markets, because our companies are able to give customers advantages that they often cannot obtain from foreign suppliers, a sustained level of high quality, prompt and regular delivery, good service, promotional assistance, modern styling.

These factors are potent enough in world competition so that today, in Japan, for all their low costs and low prices, some Japanese industries have begun to demand and receive protection against American exports to their country.

Actually, the price advantage is with us on many items, especially products of advanced technology that we turn out at relatively low cost, owing to mass production for our large internal market. And with respect to low-cost competition from other countries, their advantage is by no means necessarily permanent or conclusive or even as large as many people think.

Europe and Japan, too, have problems of increasing costs. Their wage rates are rising rapidly. They are having to pay more for power, transportation, capital, and management. In general, higher costs are pushing up their prices for many products.

If we can hold our costs down in this country, as on the whole we have managed to do in the last 4 years, there is good reason to believe that the foreign price advantage will be a diminishing factor.

Other long-range forces are also working for

us. One of them is this country's long tradition of competitive business. In contrast to the cartel habits of Europe, our business has always been free to expand and take risks, and each expanding company has stepped hard on the toes of others.

Most companies in this country have at one time or another had valuable experience in trading competitive punches. Once they realize they are in a fight, they know how to bring production costs and distribution costs down. They know how to meet a competitive threat by improving their products and services. They are far ahead of business in any other country when it comes to merchandising.

It has been by withstanding and absorbing the shocks of competition that our businessmen have continually pressed forward to ever larger achievements. This is a tradition that will stand us in good stead as we come to grips with international competition on a world scale.

I know that there are elements in business, as in labor, who wish to retain the peril-point clause of the old reciprocal trade legislation even though it might defeat the purpose of the present bill. Surely the first peril point to be considered is that at which this Nation now stands. The lower growth of our economy in recent years is a clear sign for all to read. In the Common Market, on the other hand, a tremendous growth cycle is just getting underway. Production there is increasing at a rate much greater than ours. And as additional countries in Europe join the Common Market, we can expect to see a still more powerful upward trend.

Europe has begun to challenge our future economic leadership. The fact that this challenge comes from nations friendly to us does not lessen its significance. The peril is real, and I can conceive of only one way to meet it. That is to create the conditions essential to another major expansion of our economy.

I would expect the passage of this bill to excite and exhilarate businessmen throughout the country, as preparations for more foreign trade produce a surge of additional capital expenditures and employment.

I would expect the new law operating over the next few years to make both management and labor work more closely together in their common interest.

I would expect to see the development of a new breed of executives, qualified for world-scale operation—men with the imagination, courage, psychological insights and facility in languages to grapple with the great diversity of new problems that will have to be faced in production, marketing, and finance.

Many a business, I believe, would need to reappraise its goals and set new standards of performance in order to be part of the forward movement. I would hope to see the Government cooperate with business in working out improved international principles and laws governing foreign trade, and in providing adequate term financing for exports of capital goods.

To sum up, gentlemen, it seems to me that the question before you is not only whether this bill should become law. It is, in effect, whether or not the United States has the resources of will and energy to adjust itself swiftly to the realities of the economic revolution which the space age is bringing to the world.

The time has come when we must either reduce economic barriers and trade increasingly with the rest of the free world or be prepared to see our friends in Europe and Asia move away from us and ahead of us.

READING 53

In any discussion of America's new competition in home and foreign markets, the name of Japan looms very large. The dynamic thrust of Japanese industry in high-quality but relatively low-priced products has forced a major reassessment of our trade relations. Discrimination against Japan and protectionism by Japan have both come up for more searching examination.

This reading gives us the unusual opportunity of seeing what two key business groups—one American and one Japanese—are saying about trade between these two industrial powers. The editing here, which is solely the responsibility of the editors of this book, consists of taking paragraphs from the American report by the Committee for Economic Development (see earlier readings on pages 104 and 125), and setting alongside them relevant paragraphs from a parallel report by Keizai Doyukai, the Japanese equivalent of our C.E.D. (Where the right-hand column is blank in the following pages, it means that no parallel paragraph was found in the Japanese statement.) The language requires close study to detect both the areas of agreement and the areas of disagreement, for the diplomatic style of writing occasionally masks key points.

To aid the American reader, a few essential background facts about the Japanese economy introduce the discussion.

Questions to Guide the Reading

What light do these parallel statements shed on the stickiest points which might emerge in any U.S.-Japan conference on further trade liberalization? What in turn are the pressures that might most effectively overcome those sticky points in such a conference?

The United States has a favorable balance of trade with Japan at this time. Is this likely to continue if the recommendations of the two businessmen's groups are followed?

THE UNITED STATES AND JAPAN
Committee for Economic Development and Keizai Doyukai

Some background data on Japan

1. *General statistics*
   Population, 1961 .... 94.3 million
       Annual growth rate, 1950–60, in population 2.1%
   Labor force, 1961 .... 44.9 million
   Employment, 1961 .... 44.6 million
   Economic indices for 1961:
       (1955 = 100)

Agricultural production 110	Output per employee 166
Capital goods production 548	Gross national product 181
Non-durable consumer goods ... 162	GNP per capita 171
Durable consumer goods 705	Personal consumption per capita .. 142

2. *Comparative national incomes, 1961*

	Total National Income (Billions of U.S. $)	National Income per Capita (U.S. $)
United States	$428	$2,714
United Kingdom	60	1,143
West Germany	60	1,069
France	47	1,022
Italy	27	558
Japan	38	399

From *Japan in the Free World Economy* (Committee for Economic Development, New York, 1963). Reprinted with kind permission of the C.E.D.

3. *Exporting and importing*
   (*a*) *Exports of manufactures*

	1953		1961	
	Value of Exports (Billions of U.S. $)	% of World Exports of Manufactures	Value of Exports (Billions of U.S. $)	% of World Exports of Manufactures
United States	$7.2	25.9	$11.3	20.6
United Kingdom	5.9	21.2	8.7	15.8
West Germany	3.7	13.3	11.2	20.4
France	2.5	9.0	5.2	9.5
Italy	.9	3.3	3.1	5.7
Japan	1.1	3.8	3.8	6.9

(*b*) *Japan's trade contacts, 1961*

	% of Japan's Exports Destined for this Country/Area	% of Japan's Imports Secured from this Country/Area
United States	25.2	36.1
Canada	2.8	4.6
Latin America	6.0	6.4
Europe	12.8	10.0
Asia	36.9	25.7
Australia	2.4	7.8
USSR/Red China	1.9	3.0
All other	12.0	6.4

RECOMMENDATIONS ON JAPAN IN THE WORLD ECONOMY

AN AMERICAN VIEW (Committee for Economic Development)

A JAPANESE VIEW (Keizai Doyukai—Japan Committee for Economic Development)

1. An end to discrimination against Japan

Non-discrimination is a basic principle of international trade in the free world. This principle is concretely embodied in "the most favored nation" rule by which a country undertakes to extend to all other countries (subject to limited exceptions) the terms of trade extended to its most favored trade partner. This rule has a long history. It is now incorporated in the General Agreement on Tariffs and Trade to which Japan, the United States, the Western European countries and most other free world countries are parties.

Nevertheless Japan is denied most-favored nation treatment in her trade with many other parties to GATT, principally those in Western Europe, and Japan is the only party to GATT so treated on a substantial scale.

In most cases this discrimination has been carried out by the application against Japan of Article 35 of the General Agreement.[1] Nineteen countries have at some time invoked Article 35 against Japan and thirteen still do.

Present discrimination against Japan, whether or not based on Article 35 of GATT, should be abolished and most-favored nation treatment should be granted to her.

A certain gradualness may be justified in the removal of these discriminations, to avoid hardship in some cases. But the discriminations are so offensive to the basic principles of the free economy that they should be removed as promptly as possible and the countries now practicing discrimination should accept responsibility for the domestic measures needed to assist adjustment of the resulting imports.

By far the greatest challenge for Japan today, in the midst of changes and continuing problems, is to become an equal partner in the free world economy and for this purpose do its best to further its economic development by increasing its volume of mutual trade with all other countries.

Japan in the past has fallen somewhat behind the West in its efforts to liberalize foreign trade and exchange and capital transactions. This was based upon Japan's deep concern that its economy had not quite developed as compared with the highly industrialized countries in the West. While this concern still remains among many Japanese businessmen, it does not deter our determination to translate the principles of free trade into practice.

Import liberalization already put into practice has put Japan under stronger pressure to increase its exports rapidly. However, exports of cotton goods, sundries and other labor-intensive products in which Japan has a competitive advantage unfortunately have been held down by various restrictive measures imposed by the West.

It is our oft-repeated wish that all the member nations of GATT abolish their discriminatory restrictions against Japanese exports promptly. We realize, however, that they, too, may face many problems as they remove controls over their economic relations with Japan, and therefore we are fully cognizant of the need for a certain period of adjustment. But this period should be kept to a minimum. It is strongly hoped that the industrial countries of the West will stop invoking Article 35 of the GATT in their relations with Japan.

2. Relaxation and removal of voluntary quotas

The United States does not directly deny Japan most-favored nation treatment. But the United States has been a prime mover in the use of the second major form of discrimination against Japanese trade.

This is the voluntary quota, by which Japan keeps its export sales of particular goods lower than they would otherwise be.

[1] This Article permits parties to the GATT to withhold most-favored nation treatment from new signatories if they wish to do so.

AN AMERICAN VIEW (continued)

The use of voluntary quotas grew out of rapid increases — concentrated in a few products — in Japanese exports to the United States of cotton textiles in the early 1950's. These imports raised demands for protection.

The first use of a "voluntary quota" soon followed, in 1955. Since then, the two governments have been on almost continuous consultation on voluntary quota arrangements. At the end of 1961, the Japanese had adopted voluntary export quotas on their sales of 25 products in the U.S. market. These quotas affect 25 to 35 per cent of Japan's exports to the United States. A few of the quotas were adopted as a means of limiting competition among Japanese importers in the U.S. and thus of sustaining prices and profits of Japanese producers.

The "voluntariness" of voluntary quotas does not change their basic character as quantitative restrictions on imports of particular goods from particular countries.

We recognize that some producers and workers in the United States and Europe are now enjoying the protection of these quotas. Termination of these quotas should be phased out over a sufficient period to avoid serious hardship to these protected interests. Affected firms and workers should be eligible for adjustment assistance of the kind now provided in the United States and other countries. Voluntary quotas and other quantitative restrictions on imports to the United States and to Europe should be relaxed and removed together, so that the immediate impact of freer imports will not be concentrated in one country. But the basic objective should be to eliminate voluntary quotas on an orderly schedule over a reasonable period of time.

A JAPANESE VIEW (continued)

3. Japanese elimination of quantitative restraints on imports

Japan alone among the industrial countries of the free world still uses a system of exchange licensing to control the amount of her imports. Under this system, a license must be obtained from the government to import any items on a list of imports subject to license control. Japan justifies continued use of this policy on the ground that she feels herself to be peculiarly exposed to balance of payments difficulties.

In 1959 Japan adopted a policy to remove these restrictions. Commodities which accounted for 90 per cent of Japanese imports were to be free of exchange license control by April, 1963. This will not mean that items still under control would account for only 10 per cent of Japanese imports

As a member of the family of industrialized nations, Japan considers it its duty to move forward in the direction of further trade liberalization. Of course, we are aware that Japan may suffer temporary difficulties, as the "cold wind blows into a greenhouse." But we are equally confident that such temporary difficulties can be overcome internally without transferring them to the shoulders of foreign manufacturers.

On the basis of such beliefs, Japan has been liberalizing its foreign trade and exchange rather rapidly. The liberalization program carried out thus far by the government has not on the whole caused too serious a confusion in the domestic market, because the items freed from the import

AN AMERICAN VIEW (continued)

if there were no control. It will mean that the items under control composed only 10 per cent of Japanese imports in 1960, and this number is low in part because imports of these items were limited by controls.

Controls have tended to be retained on the items that were most competitive, imports of which would rise if controls were eliminated. Moreover, some items freed of exchange licensing controls are still subject to quantitative controls.

Japan does not have persistent large balance of payments deficits that justify use of exchange controls. Her tendency to cyclical balance of payments deficits can be managed, as it largely has been, by domestic financial policy. We believe that Japan should eliminate her exchange controls and other quantitative restrictions on imports. In this case, as in others where we recommend trade liberalization, we recognize the need for orderly timing. But we believe that Japan can proceed more rapidly in this direction than it has been doing.

A JAPANESE VIEW (continued)

control, it must be conceded, have been either industrial raw materials or manufactures in which Japan has been highly competitive in the international market.

The situation is different however, with regard to those items scheduled for future liberalization, such as petroleum products and machinery. Liberalization of oil imports, depending on how it is done, may mean a serious blow to the coal industry which is already in a crisis as a result of the so-called energy revolution. Similarly, removal of the import control over machinery may exert serious influences on the future development of now developing industries such as automobile, electronic computer and large-sized electric generator manufacturing.

Increased imports raise no serious problem in the Japanese economy as long as they are paid for by increased exports, and as the government takes appropriate measures to alleviate any hardship on particular industries affected. Chances of increasing Japan's exports, therefore, hinge upon the possibility of import liberalization in those countries, including the United States and Western European nations, with which Japan trades.

4. General tariff reductions

Aside from these, "special" restrictions imposed by Japan and by other countries impede trade between Japan and the rest of the world. We believe that these tariffs should be substantially reduced in a process of bargaining in which at least the United States, Western Europe, Canada, Australia and Japan would participate.

We hope that the authority given the President by the Trade Expansion Act of 1962 will be used in bargaining for a reduction in Japanese tariffs and of U.S. and European tariffs on items of which Japan is a major exporter.

Western tariffs of particular interest to Japan will be substantially reduced only if Japan is prepared to reduce tariffs of special interest to the West. Participation of Japan in this process may be impeded by the traditional Japanese view of her foreign trade as essentially a means of obtaining raw materials that she doesn't produce at all and only as a last resort certain highly special manufactures. However the benefits to Japan of being both an importer and exporter of manufactures, as other industrial countries are, would be large and we hope they will be recognized.

In all countries, fear of hardship to domestic industry is an obstacle to reduction of tariffs. In the West this fear is likely to be intensified with

Japan is keenly interested in increasing its volume of trade with the Western European countries as well as with the United States and other countries. In its trade relations with Europe and the United States, however, Japan is in the same position as some developing countries—exporting such light industry products as canned fish, ceramics, whale oil and textiles, while importing heavy and chemical industry products. This is partly because Japan has not quite reached the stage of industrialization as arrived at by the advanced European and North American countries. We believe it is partly due also to the discriminatory restrictive measures imposed by the West on a large number of Japanese products.

Instead of now forming a pan-Pacific economic community or an Asian Common Market as proposed by some at home and abroad, we should concentrate our efforts as the stated objectives of the U.S. Trade Expansion Act indicate, on promoting free trade among all the countries in the world by removing trade barriers and showing great opportunities and benefits in the increased interchange of capital, technology and human resources as well as commodities.

AN AMERICAN VIEW (continued)

respect to Japan by a misunderstanding of the significance of low Japanese wage rates. Low Japanese wage rates are not a source of danger or injury to her actual or potential customers. A sudden expansion of imports from any source *may* cause hardship to domestic producers, but such a sudden expansion is not more likely to come from a "low wage" country than from a higher wage country. What is important for the possibility of a great upsurge of imports is the total supply and cost situation of the potential exporter, not just the wage level.

The possibility of hardship to domestic industry does call for a timing of tariff reductions that is adapted to the situations of particular industries. We believe that it will almost always be possible to achieve some tariff reduction without real hardship if a reasonable period is allowed.

We strongly urge that the advanced countries of the free world seize the opportunity lying before them to increase their efficiency, growth and solidarity by substantially reducing their tariffs. Japan's participation in giving and receiving tariff concessions is essential to the idea that there is a "free world."

A JAPANESE VIEW (continued)

5. *United States government procurement in Japan*

Before 1961 the United States government made substantial purchases of goods in Japan to be used in the United States economic and military aid programs, particularly in Asia, because Japan was the cheapest source of supply. Beginning in 1961 the United States reduced these purchases, in Japan as elsewhere abroad, as one step to control the U.S. balance of payments deficit by reducing the outflow of dollars.

Reduction of offshore procurement is an acceptable method of dealing with the U.S. balance of payments only if it is regarded as a purely temporary measure. But in general the principle that we, and others, will be best off if we buy from the cheapest source of supply is no less valid for the U.S. government than for U.S. private citizens. We recommend that the United States should resume worldwide procurement as soon as the balance of payments position permits.

6. *Japan's trade with Sino-Soviet bloc*

Japan has in recent years been exchanging trade missions with Russia, the East European communist countries, and with Red China. Japanese trade with bloc countries is still very small, but it is growing. In theory, at least, Japan can see

Japan, pressed as she has always been by the need to expand its trade with the rest of the world, is keenly interested in increasing its commercial transactions with the Soviet Union and other socialist nations, including Red China. All

AN AMERICAN VIEW (continued)

in the need of the communist countries for capital goods, and in the possible supplies from communist countries of raw materials that Japan needs, a basis for large-scale Japanese-bloc trade.

The practical outlook, however, is not for any large increase in the near future. According to what has become known of bloc offers to the Japanese, the bloc countries have been able to promise Japan only limited amounts of raw materials. Japan has no strong interest in making substantial exports to the communist countries on credit. These two conditions appear to limit the possibilities for Japanese-bloc trade, under present conditions, to fairly small amounts. However, Japan appears to be anxious to exploit fully the present possibilities of trade with the bloc, and to widen them if feasible.

Japan embargoes the shipment of military and strategic goods to bloc countries, in line with general free world policy.

The free world needs a new set of principles that will be followed by all members in trade with the Sino-Soviet bloc. In the absence of such principles there are two important things to say about Japan's position.

First, Japan's trade with the bloc is now much smaller than that of several West European countries. Thus, the problem of trade with the bloc is not primarily a Japanese problem.

Second, the tendency of Japan to seek Sino-Soviet Bloc trade will be influenced by the terms of her economic relations with the West. The importance of avoiding the possibility of Japanese dependence on trade with the bloc is yet another reason for liberalizing trade relations between Japan and the West.

A JAPANESE VIEW (continued)

the countries in the socialist bloc have shown increasing interest in purchasing from Japan steel pipes, steel vessels, precision machinery and other heavy industry products; and in return offering to Japan crude oil, lumber and other industrial raw materials Japan needs for its further economic development.

However, trade with the socialist bloc countries is based on a barter system whereby Japan can export just enough goods to cover its imports from them within a certain time period, usually one year, and the bloc tends to request Japan to provide long-term credit. Moreover, the variety of goods they can export to Japan and import from Japan is limited for strategic or other reasons. For these reasons, it is safe to estimate that no appreciable increase in Japan's trade with the socialist bloc countries can be expected in the immediate future.

Trade with the socialist countries is also subject to political considerations, and transactions on a purely commercial basis are rather few. We believe that Japan should view its trade with the socialist bloc in the same way that other Western countries do.

7. Japanese removal of barriers to foreign investment

Japanese protectionism has come to include major restraints upon foreign investment in Japan. This has deprived Japan of some useful foreign exchange. More importantly however, it has tended to protect Japanese businesses from the competition of foreign ideas and business practices, and has limited the direct benefit to the Japanese economy that would come from introduction of specialized managerial and technical know-how.

The Japanese have sought, instead, foreign loans, secured through the sale abroad of Japanese government and other bonds. The foreign investor who was interested in a simple portfolio

Japan has maintained for one reason or another various restrictions on the inflow of capital from abroad. We believe that from the standpoint of its national interest Japan should reverse this restrictive policy on foreign capital and encourage capital inflow into Japanese industries.

In liberalizing the capital inflow from abroad, however, a few questions should be considered. First, there is the question of how liberalization should proceed and of its timing. Second, there is a question of preference of one form of capital inflow relative to another. Advanced countries seem to have provisions regulating outflow rather than inflow of capital and the movement of short-

AN AMERICAN VIEW (continued)

or equity investment in Japanese shares has been discouraged by restrictions on his right to sell the shares and repatriate his investment. The waiting period for withdrawal of capital invested in shares has recently been reduced from two years to six months.

A more important problem, however, relates to direct investment by foreign firms. Advance permission to such firms to repatriate capital has apparently been granted chiefly where the investment involved advance technology the Japanese authorities regarded as highly desirable and where the technology could not be otherwise obtained. Generally, the Japanese have preferred to obtain technology through licensing or management contract arrangements.

But the matter of repatriation of capital is in practice less important than the right to enter, to stay, and to grow with the Japanese economy without undue restriction. To an excessive extent, Japanese government approvals required by an enterprise have been subject to the condition that the foreign firm go into partnership with a Japanese firm in setting up a jointly-owned subsidiary.

In some cases the difficulty encountered by foreign enterprises in establishing themselves in Japan has caused them to invest in other nearby places such as Hong Kong or Formosa. Thus Japanese businesses have not escaped the competition of foreign enterprise but Japan has missed the advantage of having the investment in its own country.

We regard Japan's hesitancy to permit entry of foreign enterprise in its economy as a major deficiency of Japanese foreign economic policy, and as a major obstacle to the full inclusion of Japan as a partner in the free world economic system. We recommend that Japan dismantle its barriers to equity investment in Japan by foreign firms, and that it permit foreign investors freedom to establish wholly owned and managed branches in Japan comparable to the freedom which Japanese investors enjoy in the United States.

A JAPANESE VIEW (continued)

term rather than long-term capital. There is also an inevitable presentiment among Japanese businessmen that too rapid an enforcement of capital liberalization by the Japanese government might invite a certain amount of confusion in the Japanese economy and in the industries affected.

It is strongly hoped that not only the government but also Japanese industrialists themselves will take appropriate measures to solve problems arising in the process of removing the existing barriers to the movement of foreign capital in and out of Japan.

A final word

Incorporated as an equal partner in the Free World, Japan has much to contribute and much to gain, not only in economic efficiency but also in movement towards a less divided, less fearful and freer world. If she is shut off from that status by Western neglect and insularism at home, no one can tell in what direction Japan's dynamism may move the course of history.

Anxious for a healthy and steady development of world economy, we Japanese industrialists earnestly desire to play an important role as an equal partner in promoting the principles of free trade among all nations. For this purpose, Japan is now making its utmost effort to move forward in its liberalization program on foreign trade, exchange and capital transactions and to expand its finan-

AN AMERICAN VIEW (continued)

There now exists, in the fluid state of international economic policy an unusual opportunity to develop much closer economic ties between Japan and the West based on the principle of reciprocal advantages. By taking this opportunity while it is available, the trading partners will not only serve mutual interests but at the same time will contribute to the political and economic strength of the entire free world community.

A JAPANESE VIEW (continued)

cial and technical assistance to developing countries.

We earnestly hope that the nations of the free world, mindful of the many difficulties Japan is confronted with, will lend their helping hands in furthering Japan's high rate of economic growth so that Japan can become a full-fledged equal partner with the advanced Western nations.

READING 54

The United States is liberally sprinkled with men and women who, if they do not actually embrace economics, at least admit that demand and supply, the Gross National Product, and bank books are not in and of themselves terrifying. But doubts and confusion mount when "foreign exchange" enters the discussion. Dollars, rupees, pounds, lira, rubles—the head swims at the thought of selling them back and forth. Yet much of the confusion can disappear if the reader will work his way through a systematic discussion that treats the foreign exchange market just like any other market bringing buyers and sellers together. And in both markets a key to understanding is to realize that demand and supply are understood only when the forces back of them are identified.

Here, the Federal Reserve Bank of Philadelphia offers a layman's guide to this unusual market. The exposition is a useful supplement to shorter textbook treatises.

Questions to Guide the Reading

What circumstances might account for sudden, sharp changes in one of the major foreign exchange rates in the United States market?

What advantages and disadvantages would flow from permitting more freely fluctuating exchange rates in the world? Can there be restraints on these movements without distorting basic economic signals?

THE FOREIGN EXCHANGE MARKET
Federal Reserve Bank of Philadelphia

"What is the quote on Canadian dollars? I am expecting payment in Canadian dollars in about 60 days; do you think the rate will hold or should I sell for 60 days future delivery?" Other customers inquire as to the current quotation on sterling, French francs, and other foreign currencies. This type of conversation is repeated many times every day in the foreign department of a large commercial bank.

Many business firms and individuals are interested in foreign exchange rates (the prices of foreign currencies), and rates are quoted in the financial section of most large metropolitan papers. Changes in foreign exchange rates may decrease (or increase) the number of dollars received by exporters, owners of foreign investments, and others receiving payment in foreign currencies. They may increase (or decrease) the cost of imports, a trip abroad, and other transactions calling for payment in foreign currencies.

From "The Foreign Exchange Market," *Business Review* (Federal Reserve Bank of Philadelphia), July, 1962, pp. 3–9. Reprinted with permission of the bank.

Payment in international transactions involves exchanging one country's currency for that of another. Foreign exchange markets provide the facilities for such exchanges—for the purchase and sale of foreign currencies.

This article deals with the foreign exchange market in the United States and some of the factors influencing foreign exchange rates.

The nature of the market

A foreign exchange market is similar to any other market in that it has stock-in-trade, buyers and sellers, and facilities for bringing buyers and sellers together.

Institutional structure. The foreign exchange market is not an organized market such as a stock or commodity exchange. There is no single trading place where orders are executed. It is an over-the-counter market similar to that for Government securities, and transactions are executed over the telephone.

The core of the market in the United States consists of a relatively small number of commercial banks and agencies of foreign banks in New York City. Some of the larger banks in other financial centers buy and sell foreign exchange and maintain positions in some of the major foreign currencies. The bulk of the foreign exchange business, however, is handled by a dozen or so large New York City commercial banks.

The larger banks with active foreign departments maintain deposit balances abroad in the principal foreign currencies and have skilled foreign exchange traders who do the actual buying and selling of foreign exchange. In rendering services to their customers, these banks are constantly engaging in transactions which add to their foreign currency deposits abroad. They buy bills of exchange from business firms, purchase travelers' checks payable in foreign currencies, and buy dividend warrants and bond coupons from United States investors owning foreign securities. Sometimes United States banks sell dollars to foreign banks wanting to build up their deposit balances in the United States. Other foreign exchange transactions with customers tend to draw down their deposit balances abroad. They may sell drafts payable in foreign currencies to importers and to United States investors making payment for foreign securities. Purchases and sales of a foreign currency seldom completely offset each other, with the result that a bank's

position may increase one day and decline the next.

Banks dealing in foreign exchange want to maintain working balances in foreign currencies sufficient for day-to-day operations, but try to avoid excess balances because of the risk of fluctuations in foreign exchange rates. Frequent adjustments in foreign exchange positions are therefore necessary.

A bank may turn to other United States banks to dispose of an excess or cover a shortage in a foreign currency; however, banks do not deal directly with each other. Instead, they deal with foreign exchange brokers whose primary function is to put banks and other foreign exchange dealers with excess positions in touch with those with shortages. The broker receives a small commission for his service of bringing buyers and sellers together. He does not buy and sell as a principal.

United States banks and other foreign exchange dealers may also use foreign exchange markets abroad to adjust their positions. A bank with too much sterling may request its London correspondent to sell sterling for dollars. This may be the most convenient method of adjustment, especially near the close of the business day or if there is little demand here for sterling. If, on the other hand, a United States bank runs short of sterling it may buy sterling from or through its foreign correspondent.

A United States bank may adjust its foreign exchange position through swap transactions with a foreign correspondent, the United States bank crediting the account of its foreign correspondent in dollars and the foreign correspondent crediting the United States bank with an equivalent amount in foreign currency. Under current practices of adjusting positions, a demand for foreign currencies in the United States may soon show up in the form of an increased supply of dollars abroad; or a demand for dollars abroad may result in an increased supply of foreign currencies in the United States.

Smaller banks, which do not maintain balances abroad, can still meet the foreign exchange needs of their customers. Such banks may acquire and dispose of foreign exchange for their customers through city correspondents which do participate directly in foreign exchange markets. Through correspondent relationships, the bulk of foreign exchange transactions is funneled to a few large banks which maintain foreign balances and deal directly with banks abroad.

Settlement between United States banks and

foreign banks is now made mainly by debits and credits to deposit accounts. The dollar has become the most widely used currency in international transactions, and New York City has become the leading international money center. Consequently, foreign banks that deal actively in the major currencies maintain deposits in New York City banks, and large United States banks with an active foreign exchange business maintain deposits abroad in the principal foreign currencies.

Stock-in-trade. A frequent question is, what is actually bought and sold? The answer is foreign currencies or claims payable in foreign currencies, commonly referred to in the market as foreign exchange.

The bulk of the volume consists in the transfer of deposits in foreign currencies from one owner to another, such as sterling deposits in London banks or franc deposits in French banks. Deposit transfers are authorized by cable and by mail. Checks, drafts, and coupons payable in foreign currencies are also bought and sold in foreign exchange markets.

There are some transactions in foreign coins and paper money. Tourists going abroad sometimes buy small quantities of foreign coins and currency to use upon arrival pending such time as they may conveniently cash a traveler's check. But the volume of transactions in foreign coins and currency is small.

Sources of demand and supply. The fact that a large part of our exports and imports is invoiced and paid in dollars means that a large part of the foreign exchange transactions involved in our foreign trade bypasses the United States market. The exchange of foreign currencies for dollars is made mostly in foreign exchange markets abroad rather than in the United States.

The supply of foreign exchange offered for sale in the United States market comes from several sources. Payment for some of our exports is still by means of drafts drawn on foreign banks and payable in foreign currencies. Such drafts are sold to United States banks or other foreign exchange dealers. Drafts payable in foreign currencies are sometimes drawn in payment of securities sold abroad and by United States companies remitting interest, dividends, and profits from overseas branches and subsidiaries. Foreign tourists and visitors in the United States may cash travelers' checks payable in foreign currencies or draw drafts in foreign currencies under letters of credit. Speculators may sell foreign exchange purchased previously and, of course, United States banks which maintain balances in foreign currencies abroad also sell foreign exchange to meet demands of their customers.

Basically, the demand for foreign exchange comes from those needing to make payment abroad. American importers buy drafts to pay for goods invoiced in foreign currencies. This is still a common method of payment in certain commodities, such as rubber, jute, and tin, which are often invoiced in sterling, and imports of Swiss watches which are usually invoiced in Swiss francs. Other sources of demand in the United States for foreign exchange are investors desiring to pay for securities purchased abroad; United States companies remitting interest, dividends, and profits on funds borrowed from abroad; American tourists traveling abroad; agencies of foreign banks desiring to return funds previously transferred here; and speculators who buy foreign currencies expecting to sell them later at a higher price.

The mechanics of making payment should not obscure the fact that, except for unilateral transfers, international transactions result in the exchange of one currency for another. United States payments abroad supply dollars to foreigners— they result in the conversion of dollars into foreign currencies or transfer the ownership of dollars to foreigners. Receipts from abroad (foreign payments to the United States) result in an increase in foreign balances owned by Americans or a reduction of dollar deposits owned by foreigners. Therefore, a net deficit in the United States balance of payments tends to build up deposits owned by foreigners in United States banks; a net surplus tends to build up our deposits abroad in foreign currencies.

Foreign exchange rates. Foreign exchange rates are prices—prices of foreign currencies expressed in terms of a country's own money.

A foreign exchange rate reflects demand and supply forces in the market for a particular foreign currency. Rates fluctuate, often during the course of a business day as the demand-supply relationship shifts. An increased demand for sterling may cause the price to rise, say, from $2.80 to $2.81; or an increase in supply in the New York market might lower the price from $2.80 to $2.79.

Wide fluctuations in foreign exchange rates increase risk, and discourage trade and international financial transactions. To illustrate: a jump in the price of sterling from $2.80 to $3.00 would tend to raise the cost of imports from England even though commodity prices there remained the same. A United States importer contracting to buy English goods totaling 100,000 pounds sterling would have to pay $300,000 instead of $280,000. The English importer, on the other hand, would find United States goods cheaper in that he could get $3.00 worth for a pound sterling instead of $2.80.

Countries belonging to the International Monetary Fund agree to maintain market rates within a range of 1 per cent above and 1 per cent below the established par values of their currencies. Some countries maintain market rates of their currencies within even narrower limits. The par value of sterling is $2.80 and the upper and lower limits are fixed at $2.82 and $2.78. The fact that most countries belong to the I.M.F. and have agreed to stabilize the value of their currency means that most foreign exchange rates fluctuate only within narrow limits.

Forward exchange

The major foreign currencies can be purchased and sold for future as well as immediate ("spot") delivery. Futures transactions are commonly referred to as forward exchange. The forward exchange market is similar to the futures market for commodities. Foreign currencies can be bought and sold for delivery at a specified future date and at a price agreed upon when the contract is made. Purchases and sales of major foreign currencies for delivery in 30, 60, 90 days, and even up to six months are common in the United States market. Occasionally, futures transactions for longer terms are negotiated, but foreign exchange dealers enter into such contracts only when they can arrange to hedge their position.

Uses of the forward market. The forward exchange market makes it possible for those engaging in international transactions to protect themselves against the risk of exchange-rate fluctuations. To illustrate: an importer may contract to buy goods from an English exporter for 1,000 pounds sterling which at the current rate of exchange would amount to $2,800; if, however, the price of sterling has gone up by the time the goods arrive and payment is to be made, the cost will be more than the importer anticipated. When he contracts to buy the goods he could

protect himself against the exchange-rate risk by buying at the current forward rate 1,000 pounds sterling for delivery at the time he is to make payment for the goods. An exporter who has priced his goods in a foreign currency to yield a certain number of dollars may likewise find his dollar proceeds reduced because of a drop in the price of the foreign currency. He can protect himself by selling this foreign currency for future delivery or, in the terminology of the market, by selling forward exchange.

An exporter may not be able to determine in advance the exact date his goods will be shipped and therefore when he will have his foreign draft for sale. Importers also are often unable to determine the day on which they will need to make payment abroad. Because of such uncertainties, foreign exchange dealers enter into forward contracts giving the seller or buyer the option of offering or taking delivery on his future contract at any time within a period of one or two weeks. Rates on option contracts are likely to be a shade above or below comparable futures maturing on a fixed date.

Commercial banks and other foreign exchange dealers use the forward market to hedge their positions in foreign currencies. If a bank buys 100,000 pounds sterling in the spot market, it can cover its position by selling sterling forward. If the price of sterling rises, and spot and forward rates move together, the gain on holdings of 100,000 pounds sterling would offset the loss on the forward transaction. If, on the other hand, the price declines, the gain on the forward transaction would offset a loss on its sterling holdings acquired at a higher price. Dealers also use the spot market to hedge their position in forward contracts.

Speculators use the forward exchange market not to hedge against the risk of exchange-rate fluctuations but to profit from them. A speculator would buy forward exchange when he expects the rate to rise, hoping to sell the currency or at least close out his forward contract at a profit. He would sell for future delivery (sell short) if he expects the price to fall. If the price does decline, he can acquire the currency for delivery at less than his selling price. Willingness of speculators to take risk makes it possible for others to cover their risk in the forward market.

Relation between spot and forward rates. Unless the spread between spot and forward rates for a foreign currency is about equal to the difference in comparable interest rates in the United

States and the foreign country, there is an inducement to shift funds to take advantage of the higher rates. For example, if the spot price of sterling is $2.81 and three-month forward sterling is $2.79, the discount on forward sterling is equivalent to 2.85 per cent interest at an annual rate.[1] If the current yield on three-month Treasury bills is 3 per cent and the yield on three-month British Treasury bills is 5.85 per cent, the cost of hedging by selling 90-day forward sterling (2.85 per cent) absorbs the difference in yield. A United States investor who covers his exchange risk would find the net return on British bills the same as that on United States bills. A 6 per cent yield, however, on three-month British bills would enable a United States investor to cover his foreign exchange risk and get .15 per cent higher return on British bills. Under these circumstances, United States investors could obtain a higher net return on British bills, and short-term funds would likely flow from the United States to England.

An outflow of funds to take advantage of the higher net return on British bills would tend to eliminate the profit opportunity. As already indicated, a United States purchaser of British bills would buy spot sterling to pay for the bills and sell 90-day forward sterling to cover his exchange risk. The resulting increased demand for spot delivery and increased supply of forward sterling would widen the spread between the two rates

[1] $\dfrac{\$2.81 - \$2.79}{\$2.81} \times 4 = 2.85\%$ at an annual rate.

and increase the cost of hedging an investment in British Treasury bills. The outflow of short-term funds would tend to raise interest rates here and lower them in England. Thus, interest-arbitrage transactions narrow the differential in interest rates and widen the spread between spot and forward rates.

Conclusions

Foreign exchange markets are an integral part of the modern world economy. There is no single monetary unit that is generally acceptable in international transactions. As a result, settlement of such transactions usually requires exchanging one nation's currency for another's. Foreign exchange markets, in which foreign currencies may conveniently be bought and sold, promote trade and financial transactions among countries.

Even though foreign exchange markets facilitate settlement, they do not alter the basic fact that international transactions are essentially an exchange of goods and services. Countries with balance-of-payments surpluses tend to accumulate deposit balances in countries with deficits. In effect, the surplus countries are exchanging goods, services, or capital for deposits in foreign banks, or other foreign short-term assets. Foreign deposits and short-term investments, however, are not of value in themselves. They are of real value only to the extent they meet a need for working balances and monetary reserves, or can later be used to acquire goods and services.

READING 55

It was not long ago that such objectives of the American economy as growth and stability could be discussed without much reference to our balance-of-payments position. But, by the late 1950s, this was no longer so. Today, talk about such issues as tax cuts, tariff cuts, and changes in the money supply soon wanders inevitably into the pressing problem of the balance of payments.

Here the Federal Reserve Bank of St. Louis tells in comprehensive survey fashion how that problem came about. The story underscores the dynamic nature of the world in which we live. It cannot be read then as mere current events; its meaning is surely that our future policies will have to adjust to still other dramatic changes that will arise.

Questions to Guide the Reading

What are the chief changes in world markets from 1946 to the present that explain why the United States went from surpluses to deficits in its balance of payments?

The focus here is on exposition, not on analysis of the impact of the events. But are there insights in the article on how the current balance-of-payments problem might have been minimized consistent with realizing other goals of our economy at home and abroad?

THE BALANCE OF PAYMENTS IN PERSPECTIVE
Federal Reserve Bank of St. Louis

The prospect of a 1963 deficit in the U.S. balance of payments, no smaller, and perhaps considerably larger than the $2.2 billion deficit of 1962, has sharpened public discussion, both here and abroad, of factors affecting the U.S. balance of payments. Some economic writers insist that large U.S. payments deficits will continue in the absence of such drastic measures as direct restrictions on imports, severely restrictive monetary policy, devaluation, or flexible exchange rates. Others, pointing to the improvement in our payments situation since 1960 (1960 deficit, $3.9 billion; 1961 deficit, $2.4 billion; 1962 deficit, $2.2 billion), argue that the current policies of promoting exports, guarding against inflation, and reducing the net payments burden of Government military and aid expenditures will in time solve the problem of continuing deficits.

The purpose of this article is to review the more distinctive aspects of the U.S. payments situation within the context of the international payments system and the changing pattern of international reserves from 1946 to 1962. This article examines the elements of strength and weakness in our external position as we attempt to reduce our balance-of-payments deficit. It notes that the key role of the dollar in the international financial mechanism is an important factor influencing the nature of the policies adopted or rejected by the United States. It also notes that the choice of actions to strengthen our balance-of-payments position is influenced by our preference for relatively free markets.

Changing patterns of international reserves, 1946–1962: from dollar shortage to dollar glut

Period, 1946–49. The United States entered the postwar period with gold reserves of $20.1 billion, about 60 per cent of the world's monetary or official gold reserves. The rest of the world, using both gold and dollars as official reserves, held $13.2 billion in gold and $4.2 billion in dollar balances. This reserve total of $17.4 billion, although substantial in the aggregate, represented the sum of many small reserve positions distributed throughout the world (Table 1).

The dominant feature of the international payments situation in this period was the one-sided strength of the United States. With the United States virtually the sole source of supply for many industrial goods needed by a war-torn world, the distribution of reserves was grossly inadequate to cope with the payments imbalances which developed in the early years of the postwar period, 1946–49. To finance their relief and reconstruction needs, foreign countries dipped into their official reserves by selling gold and liquidating dollar balances in the amount of $7 billion during this four-year period.

The total reserves loss of foreign nations during this period would probably have been even larger had it not been for the aid rendered by the United States. Final deliveries under relief and rehabilitation programs inaugurated during the war were continued by the U.S. in this period. In 1946 this country made a special loan of $3.75 billion to the United Kingdom. Export-Import Bank loans were also used to finance the heavy purchases of U.S. goods. In 1948 the Marshall Plan for European Recovery was put into operation. Despite the large aid payments and loans which averaged $5.5 billion a year, net of repayments, the U.S. balance of payments was in surplus through these four years (Table 1). For the entire period the U.S. surplus amounted to $7 billion. This surplus was "settled" by a decline of $1.8 billion in U.S. liquid liabilities to foreigners and by sales of gold to the U.S. amounting to $5.2 billion. At the end of 1949 we had $24.6 billion in gold reserves and only $2.9 billion in dollar liabilities to foreign official institutions (Table 1).

From "The U.S. Balance of Payments," *Federal Reserve Bank of St. Louis Review,* July, 1963, pp. 5–11. Reprinted with kind permission of the bank.

Table 1   U.S. Balance of Payments, 1946–62 (in billions of dollars)

Period	Payments* (1)	Receipts* (2)	Surplus (+) Deficit (−) (3)	Liquid Liabilities Decrease (−) Increase (+) (4)	U.S. Gold Losses (+) Gains (−) (5)
1946	−13.7	+14.9	+ 1.3	−0.6	−0.6
1947	−16.1	+20.7	+ 4.6	−1.7	−2.9
1948	−16.8	+17.8	+ 1.0	+0.5	−1.5
1949	−16.4	+16.6	+ 0.2	−0.0†	−0.2
1946–49			+ 7.0	−1.8	−5.2
1950	−17.5	+14.0	− 3.6	+1.8	+1.7
1951	−19.8	+19.5	− 0.3	+0.4	−0.1
1952	−19.8	+18.8	− 1.0	+1.4	−0.4
1953	−19.6	+17.5	− 2.2	+1.0	+1.2
1954	−19.7	+18.2	− 1.6	+1.3	+0.3
1955	−21.8	+20.7	− 1.1	+1.1	+0.0†
1956	−25.7	+24.8	− 0.9	+1.2	−0.3
1950–56			−10.7	+8.2	+2.5
1957	−27.6	+28.1	+ 0.5	+0.3	−0.8
1958	−27.1	+23.6	− 3.5	+1.3	+2.3
1959	−28.5	+24.8	− 3.7	+3.0	+0.7
1960	−31.9	+28.0	− 3.9	+2.2	+1.7
1961	−32.7	+30.3	− 2.4	+1.7	+0.7‡
1962	−34.3	+32.1	− 2.2	+1.3	+0.9
1958–62			−15.7	+9.4	+6.3

* Includes net unrecorded transactions.
† Less than $50 million.
‡ Beginning with the first quarter of 1961, net of change in convertible currencies held by U.S. monetary authorities.
NOTE: Detail may not add to totals due to rounding.
SOURCE: U.S. Department of Commerce. 1946 to 1961 data, *Balance of Payments Statistical Supplement*, Revised Edition. 1962 data, *Survey of Current Business*, June 1963.

The U.S. aid programs enabled foreign countries to rebuild their economies at a much faster pace than would have been possible had those countries been forced to rely solely on their limited export earnings to finance imports.

A significant feature of this period, at least up to the last quarter of 1949, was that the par values of most currencies were admittedly too high relative to their internal purchasing power. Foreign nations had experienced varying degrees of inflation during the war period but most currency parities remained unchanged from the levels maintained during the war. Although the Bretton Woods Agreement provided for changes in par values to reflect changes in price levels, few important countries changed their currency parities in the first few years after the war. Overvalued currencies—coupled with stringent exchange con-

trols—probably improved the "terms of trade" of foreign countries, enabling them to obtain essential imports for rebuilding their productive capacities at a lower real cost than would have been possible otherwise.

As foreign economic recovery proceeded and improved the ability of foreign countries to export, their overvalued currencies became a a competitive burden, hurting their exports. Furthermore, as the need for devaluation became more apparent, payments difficulties of foreign nations were aggravated by hedging and speculative capital flows which occurred despite exchange controls.

In September 1949 leading foreign countries with the approval of the International Monetary Fund devalued as follows: United Kingdom, along with most members of its Commonwealth group, and also Sweden, Norway, Denmark, and the Netherlands, 30.5 per cent; France, 22 per cent; West Germany, 20.6 per cent; Canada, 9 per cent; Italy, 8 per cent; and Belgium, 12.3 per cent.

In 1950 the United States moved from a surplus to a deficit position—an excess of payments over receipts of $3.5 billion for the single year. The United States continued her deficit position through 1956 with annual deficits averaging $1.5 billion for the entire period. The cumulative deficit for these seven years amounted to $10.7 billion, financed by a transfer of gold to foreign ownership of $2.5 billion and a rise in liquid liabilities to foreigners of $8.2 billion (Table 1).

The balance-of-payments deficits incurred by the United States during this period occasioned very little concern; they appeared to be largely "artificial" in that foreign countries discriminated severely against U.S. goods. Most observers continued to refer to the United States as a "surplus" country and seemed to feel that the rest of the world was doomed to struggle for scarce dollars.

The deficits served an important purpose in enabling other industrial countries to rebuild their monetary reserves to the point where they were able to relax some of their exchange restrictions and to consider the possibilities of a return to full currency convertibility. The United States, in the meantime, had lost little of her large gold reserves, financing her deficits by increasing

Table 2   Output Per Man-hour, Hourly Earnings, and Labor Costs in Manufacturing, Selected Countries (1953 = 100)

Item	1953	1954	1955	1956	1957	1958	1959	1960	1961
United States:									
Output per man-hour	100	99	106	107	107	109	117	120	124
Hourly earnings	100	102	107	112	118	121	126	130	133
Labor costs	100	103	101	105	110	111	107	108	107
Belgium:									
Output per man-hour	100	109	117	122	126	127	133	139	143
Hourly earnings	100	103	106	115	125	131	133	138	143
Labor costs	100	94	91	94	99	103	100	99	100
France:									
Output per man-hour	100	108	115	121	133	145	149	154	165
Hourly earnings	100	108	116	130	137	132	119	129	139
Labor costs	100	100	101	107	103	91	80	84	84
Germany:									
Output per man-hour	100	105	112	115	122	129	138	148	152
Hourly earnings	100	102	109	119	129	138	145	160	184
Labor costs	100	97	97	103	106	107	105	108	121
Italy:									
Output per man-hour	100	106	115	123	130	138	152	163	167
Hourly earnings	100	104	109	117	123	128	131	137	147
Labor costs	100	98	95	95	95	93	86	84	88
Japan:									
Output per man-hour	100	107	113	119	128	123	150	173	197
Hourly earnings	100	106	109	120	126	125	136	148	162
Labor costs	100	100	96	100	98	102	91	85	82
United Kingdom:									
Output per man-hour	100	104	108	108	110	112	116	122	122
Hourly earnings	100	107	116	124	133	137	142	155	164
Labor costs	100	103	108	115	121	122	123	127	133

SOURCE: Bela Balassa, "Recent Developments in the Competitiveness of American Industry and Prospects for the Future," *Factors Affecting the United States Balance of Payments,* Joint Economic Committee, 1962, p. 36.

her dollar liabilities. At this point, the international payments system appeared to be running smoothly.

Factors contributing to U.S. deficits in the early years of this period included the impact of the 1949 devaluations, the sharp rise in U.S. imports induced by the Korean hostilities, a doubling of the annual rate of private capital outflow, a substantial increase in military expenditures abroad, and a continuation of large Government grants through 1951.

Although the merchandise trade surplus increased over its 1950 volume, it continued at a level considerably below that maintained in the period 1946–49. With the growing competitive strength of the European economies aided by devaluation, by sharply rising productivity, by relatively stable labor costs per unit of output (Table 2), and by continuing restrictions on imports of American goods, it is not surprising that U.S. exports did not increase more substantially. At the same time U.S. payments abroad for services (including military purchases) were increasing sharply, rising from a level of $4 billion in 1951 to $7 billion in 1956 (Table 3, Col. 5).

Payments surplus 1957. The closing of the Suez Canal in the autumn of 1956, coming near the end of a worldwide capital investment boom period, was accompanied by several shocks to the international payments system.

The political uncertainties arising from the Suez crisis led to a heavy volume of imports by European nations and Japan and added to the exchange difficulties of these countries during the 1956–57 period. As foreign nations turned to the United States for heavy shipments of crude oil, petroleum products, and other basic commodities, U.S. exports rose to a record high of $19.4 billion (Table 3, Col. 1). This surge in exports during the first half of 1957 provided a trade surplus of $6.1 billion and a U.S. balance-of-payments surplus of $0.5 billion.

The deficits of 1958–62: dollar glut. Beginning in 1958, the United States has had a steady sequence of large balance-of-payments deficits, averaging $3.1 billion for the five-year period 1958–62. The U.S. was able to finance more than half its cumulative 1958–62 deficit of nearly $16 billion by incurring liabilities to foreigners in the amount of $9.4 billion (Table 1). The balance was settled by the transfer of $6.3 billion of gold to foreign ownership.

A study of the distribution of the increased dollar liabilities to foreigners shows that, in this period 1958–62, foreign monetary authorities added about $4 billion to their liquid assets in the United States, raising their total holdings to more than $12 billion. Holdings of the International Monetary Fund rose by $2 billion, private holdings increased by more than $2 billion, while holdings of nonmonetary international institutions increased by more than $1 billion.

What factors contributed to the higher level of deficits in this period? While it may be tempting to single out a particular item—too few exports, too many imports, too much foreign aid, etc.—this procedure is unsound. Various types of transactions are closely linked to one another, and a policy-induced change in one component may lead to a partially offsetting change in another component. In fact during this recent period nearly all of the Government and capital account items showed larger "net outflows" (Table 2). These larger outflows were only partly offset by a larger average surplus balance of goods and services. Military expenditures averaged $3.1 billion as compared with a $2.1 billion average for the period 1950–56. Private capital outflow averaged $3.2 billion compared with a $1.4 billion average in the earlier period. The average of recorded short-term capital outflow was up $500 million, while the average long-term capital outflow increased by $1.3 billion. Moreover, net payments on unrecorded transactions have averaged $700 million during the last three years. Previously, the unrecorded transactions led to net receipts rather than net payments. Finally, foreign aid, net of ordinary repayments, has averaged $300 million more per year than in the period 1950–56.

During this recent period the surplus balance on goods and services (excluding military transactions) averaged about $6.0 billion as compared with an average surplus balance of $4.2 billion during the years 1950–56 (Table 3, Col. 14). Since 1960, the trade surplus has been running at the relatively substantial rate of $4.8 billion a year which is considerably larger than the average of $2.5 billion maintained in the 1950–56 period (Table 3, Col. 3).

The U.S. deficits of the 1958–62 period destroyed the general concern over an underlying world dollar shortage which had lingered on even through the period, 1950–56, when the United States was incurring persistent deficits. The large U.S. deficits of the last five years have convinced all observers, here and abroad, of the necessity for reducing the growth of dollar liabilities to

Table 3 U.S. Balance of Goods and Services (in millions of dollars)

Period	Merchandise* Exports (1)	Merchandise* Imports (2)	Merchandise* Balance (3)	Services Exports (4)	Services Imports Total (5)	Services Imports Military (6)	Services Imports Other (7)	Services Balance (8)	Total Goods and Services Exports (9)	Total Goods and Services Imports (10)	Total Goods and Services Balance (11)	Total Goods and Services (Excluding Military Transactions) Exports (12)	... Imports (13)	... Balance (14)	Period
1946	+11,707	− 5,073	+ 6,634	+3,028	−1,918	− 493	−1,425	+1,110	+14,735	− 6,991	+ 7,744	+14,735	− 6,498	+ 8,237	1946
1947	+16,015	− 5,979	+10,036	+3,722	−2,229	− 455	−1,774	+1,493	+19,737	− 8,208	+11,529	+19,737	− 7,753	+11,984	1947
1948	+13,193	− 7,563	+ 5,630	+3,596	−2,786	− 799	−1,987	+ 810	+16,789	−10,349	+ 6,440	+16,789	− 9,550	+ 7,239	1948
1949	+12,149	− 6,879	+ 5,270	+3,621	−2,742	− 621	−2,121	+ 879	+15,770	− 9,621	+ 6,149	+15,770	− 9,000	+ 6,770	1949
1950	+10,117	− 9,108	+ 1,009	+3,690	−2,920	− 576	−2,344	+ 770	+13,807	−12,028	+ 1,779	+13,807	−11,452	+ 2,355	1950
1951	+14,123	−11,202	+ 2,921	+4,621	−3,871	−1,270	−2,601	+ 750	+18,744	−15,073	+ 3,671	+18,744	−13,803	+ 4,941	1951
1952	+13,319	−10,838	+ 2,481	+4,673	−4,928	−2,054	−2,874	− 255	+17,992	−15,766	+ 2,226	+17,992	−13,712	+ 4,280	1952
1953	+12,281	−10,990	+ 1,291	+4,666	−5,571	−2,615	−2,956	− 905	+16,947	−16,561	+ 386	+16,755	−13,946	+ 2,809	1953
1954	+12,799	−10,354	+ 2,445	+4,960	−5,577	−2,642	−2,935	− 617	+17,759	−15,931	+ 1,828	+17,577	−13,289	+ 4,288	1954
1955	+14,280	−11,527	+ 2,753	+5,524	−6,268	−2,901	−3,367	− 744	+19,804	−17,795	+ 2,009	+19,604	−14,894	+ 4,710	1955
1956	+17,379	−12,804	+ 4,575	+6,216	−6,824	−2,949	−3,875	− 608	+23,595	−19,628	+ 3,967	+23,434	−16,679	+ 6,755	1956
1957	+19,390	−13,291	+ 6,099	+7,091	−7,461	−3,216	−4,245	− 370	+26,481	−20,752	+ 5,729	+26,106	−17,536	+ 8,570	1957
1958	+16,264	−12,952	+ 3,312	+6,803	−7,909	−3,435	−4,474	−1,106	+23,067	−20,861	+ 2,209	+22,767	−17,426	+ 5,341	1958
1959	+16,282	−15,310	+ 972	+7,194	−8,032	−3,107	−4,925	− 838	+23,476	−23,342	+ 134	+23,174	−20,235	+ 2,939	1959
1960	+19,459	−14,723	+ 4,736	+7,515	−8,482	−3,048	−5,434	− 967	+26,974	−23,205	+ 3,769	+26,639	−20,157	+ 6,482	1960
1961	+19,913	−14,497	+ 5,416	+8,398	−8,370	−2,934	−5,436	+ 28	+28,311	−22,867	+ 5,444	+27,909	−19,933	+ 7,976	1961
1962	+20,479	−16,145	+ 4,334	+9,311	−8,819	−3,028	−5,791	+ 492	+29,790	−24,964	+ 4,826	+29,130	−21,936	+ 7,194	1962

* Excludes military transfers under grant.

SOURCE: U.S. Department of Commerce. 1946 to 1961 data, *Balance of Payments Statistical Supplement*, Revised Edition. 1962 data, *Survey of Current Business*, June 1963.

foreign nations, particularly the growth in foreign official dollar reserves in the face of declining U.S. gold reserves.

The basis for official concern is that foreign countries hold about $12 billion of their international reserves[1] in the form of dollar claims which they can use to buy gold from the U.S. Treasury; moreover, under present circumstances, these potential claims on our gold stock could be rapidly enlarged through the conversion of foreign private dollar balances and dollar balances owned by U.S. residents into foreign currencies. The substantial decline in the U.S. gold stock during the last 5 years has spurred United States policy efforts to reduce payments deficits and to

joint in international actions to moderate short-term capital movements and to cushion the shocks of large changes in foreign official reserves.

Disruptive movements of liquid capital were one of the features of the period 1958–62. International mobility of short-term capital is a useful adjunct to world trade and finance and has been one of the long-standing objectives of the IMF. But in an environment of serious payments imbalances and uncertainties over the stability of par values speculative capital movements intensify reserve swings—causing large losses for the countries experiencing outflows and excessive accumulations for those gaining capital.

READING 56

The problem which was described in the preceding selection necessarily has commanded the attention of many groups. One of the more succinct and still comprehensive statements on what might be done about the problem is this one from the United States Chamber of Commerce. It was submitted to the President of the United States by the Chamber in July of 1962. The checklist of proposals at the end offers a good testing ground for one's understanding of what the balance-of-payments problem is all about.

Questions to Guide the Reading

To what extent is the balance-of-payments problem, as it is viewed by the Chamber of Commerce, open to solutions that do not seriously impede our ability to solve other problems (e.g., unemployment) in the economy?

How would each of the proposals at the end of the reading be expected to affect the items in our balance of payments?

RIGHTING THE BALANCE OF PAYMENTS
United States Chamber of Commerce

We can and we must meet the problem posed by the deficit in our international balance of payments. The problem is a serious one for two reasons:

First, there is in the current balance of payments situation a threat to existing monetary arrangements, here and in the world generally.

[1] Excludes U.S. libabilities to the International Monetary Fund.

Gold losses of the magnitude experienced in recent years cannot long be sustained even though the reserves of our monetary system are large. Persistence of such losses and any prolonged accumulation at recent rates of foreign short-term claims against the dollar pose a threat to continued acceptance of the dollar as a reserve currency and thus endanger the entire free world structure of international liquidity, payments and trade. A crisis of confidence in the dollar would deal a serious blow

From "The United States Balance of Payments Situation," Chamber of Commerce of the United States, Washington, July 30, 1962. Reprinted with permission of the Chamber.

to the position of the United States as leader of the free world and would dangerously restrict its flexibility of movement.

There is a second aspect of the problem which is of equal concern. This is a danger that, in concern over its gravity, steps may be taken and measures adopted the abiding effect of which will be to compromise or abridge the essential principles of the kind of international economic community we have sought to foster and have invested billions of dollars to achieve.

The balance of payments situation in which we find ourselves is thus serious, and urgently so, but it does not follow that it is immediately critical or that it is unmanageable.

That the situation is not immediately critical is chiefly due to two circumstances. The first is that this country's international liquidity position —defined as its gold stock and holdings of convertible currencies plus the world's willingness to accept and hold dollar assets—is not critically impaired. The second is that a number of steps have been taken, typically in concert with other nations, to supplement the resources and facilities that would, in the event of emerging crisis, be available to this country's monetary authorities.

We here refer to the operations of the Treasury and the Federal Reserve in the international money market, and to increased multilateral cooperation through the Basle Group, the gold pool, and International Monetary Fund. These measures are to be commended. They add to our strength and assurance as we deal with the fundamental problem of improving the long-range competitive position of the United States in the world economy, and they have in them a basis for strengthening the international financial structure.

We have said further that the balance of payments situation is not unmanageable.

That situation is not the result of a sudden reversal in the balance of our international accounts; it comes instead from a substantial increase of an imbalance that had prevailed for the greater part of a decade. This substantial increase of imbalance was, furthermore, contemporaneous with the re-emergence after a long lapse of years of something approximating an international competitive system. Productive capacities, particularly those of Europe, had been restored and had become competitive with our own. No longer were we in the position of being the world's one certain source of supply for most manufactured goods. Equally important was the reconstitution of the world's monetary system on a basis of external convertibility, which had the effect of exposing the dollar to international pressures not experienced for over a generation.

In short, the problem that confronts us is not that of repairing a disrupted American economy but of adjusting it to a world competitive order— *the kind of order that we have worked ever since World War II to achieve.*

There appear to the Committee to be reasons for believing that the required process of adjustment can be realized and that, in particular, it can and must be realized without resort to unwise expedients, such as, for example, control of capital movement or foreign exchange.

The process of international adjustment to an emergent world competitive system will in some part take place in other countries, as indeed it is already beginning to do. The rapid rate of growth in Western Europe and Japan is leading to relatively rapid increases in wages and, to a measurable extent, in prices as well. These changes will undoubtedly have the effect of helping in some measure to restore equilibrium to the international payments situation.

It appears reasonable to expect countries experiencing sustained surpluses on balance of payments to embrace policies appropriate to their creditor position. Nevertheless, the task of the United States is inescapable, and can neither be avoided nor deferred. *It is mandatory that the United States economy maintain and improve its competitive position, and that we comply fully with our responsibilities as the world's banker and custodian of the key international currency.*

The nation's task, as it is defined by these observations, appears to require two directions for action. The first is to settle upon what is to be the United States economy's role within the world economy and the second is to ensure that the United States economy is adequately competitive to fulfill that role.

The role of the United States in the world economy

A primary consideration here is the magnitude of outlay for military expenditures abroad and economic aid to developing countries for which our economy must make provision in the form of an excess of exports over imports of goods and services. These items are sometimes said to be the seat of our present serious problem, and it is inescapable that the greater their amount the more rigorously competitive must our economy become.

Military expenditures and economic aid are

here considered apart from private capital flows for two reasons. In the first place, their size, and indeed the fact that they exist at all, is not primarily determined by economic forces, as are international capital movements. In the second place, these are outlays that, bearing as they do on the general interests of an Atlantic community now substantially restored to economic health, can be more equitably shared than would have been possible ten or even five years ago. It is the view of the Committee that the encouragingly productive efforts of recent years to secure the sharing of these outlays must be pursued with unremitting vigor.

The role of the U.S. economy within the world economy so far as private capital is concerned is a different matter.

It is the conviction of this Committee that the United States must be preserved as a free and unrestricted market for capital funds, whichever may be the direction—in or out—of the flow of such funds. For one thing, it is seriously to be doubted that the integrity of the dollar as a reserve currency can be maintained unless the market for capital be free. But beyond this is the evident fact that private investments abroad are today a substantial source of international income to an economy seriously in need of it. The unimpeded flow of such productive investment funds is thus essential to the United States if we are to take advantage of the opportunities which will prevail in an expanding international economy. If foreign investment is discouraged, an important and rising long-term source of revenue from abroad will be seriously impaired to the detriment of the country's future balance of payments position.

If freedom of capital movement is thus to be preserved, as we believe is required, then it follows that we must, as the occasion demands, adopt and adhere to monetary and fiscal policies consistent with our role in the world economy. If interest rates in the United States are too low in relation to the rates at which funds can be effectively placed or borrowed abroad, either our rates must rise or foreign rates must decline. At this time, it seems obvious that interest rates in the United States must be allowed to rise. Flexible interest rates are an essential part of the balance of payments adjustment mechanism. While it is of utmost importance that interest rate flexibility be accepted in the other major countries also, the United States cannot avoid this same discipline if we are to retain the dollar as a key unit of international exchange.

Finally, this Committee believes that there is no justification for a change in the dollar price of gold, and that such a change, if effected, would make no useful contribution to the solution of our balance of payments problem.

Maintaining the competitiveness of the U.S. economy

It is imperative that every present action be shaped to the pattern of the kind of economy that can be a continuing viable part of the competitive world economy that is now emergent. Restriction, for example, of investment abroad for the sake of relief from today's pressures would be as short-sighted as restriction of commodity imports. The sustained strength of the U.S. payments position on commercial account provides substantial basis for faith that our economy has the resourcefulness to maintain its place in a competitive world order, provided only that we are prepared to abide by the rules of such an order.

The first requisite of such an order is that the private sector of the American economy be made able to produce a current balance of goods and services that, after provision for its investment abroad, is adequate to cover our outlays for military expenditure and foreign aid. The second requisite is that this end be realized within the context of a commercial policy exemplified so far as commodity trade is concerned by the tariff proposals in Title II of the Trade Expansion Act of 1962.

To be made competitive in the degree required by the obligations of military assistance and foreign aid, two types of action are required.

The first is that we must hold the line so far as costs are concerned. This is a minimum requirement, because, while we are presently competitive in the sense that our economy continues to provide an export balance on current account, we are not competitive enough to provide the balance required of us. Holding the line on costs requires forthright rejection of inflationary monetary and fiscal policies.

This is not only a minimum requirement, it is imperative. The situation in which, as far as the balance of payments is concerned, we find ourselves is so serious that we cannot afford to lose ground. Indeed, it is the conviction of this Committee that, with due allowance for essential defense requirements, the balance of payments situation is so pressing that until the required improvement has been registered in the U.S. position within the world competitive order, any other objectives of national fiscal and credit policy must be subordinated to this one. The Committee does not believe that this objective is inconsistent with, but rather that it is prerequisite to, sustained full employment and economic growth. In fact, a U.S. economy that is a continuing viable part of the competitive world economy has its own contribution to make to the attainment of these domestic objectives as well.

The second requirement is that policy must be directed to increasing the effectiveness of the American economy both in supplying commodities in the world market and in the provision of income from services, including tourist expenditures in the United States and, conspicuously, the growth of earnings from investments abroad.

Taxation of foreign source income should be compatible with the vital objective of obtaining a maximum penetration of the world market. It should preserve flexibility for American business operations overseas in covering multiple markets, and should permit re-investment of earnings and expansion of effort in all free-world markets. Tax proposals which would reduce U.S. competitive capabilities in foreign markets should not be adopted.

Other policies affecting our competitive ability to supply goods in the world market include tax revisions appropriate to the stimulation of investment both at home and abroad. It is the opinion of the Committee that each such revision should be made the occasion for careful and discriminating review of government expenditure, in order to minimize the net impact on the government's budgetary position. Continued deficit financing can produce neither confidence nor sound progress. It is essential too to encourage U.S. firms to compete more actively abroad. In this latter respect, we particularly endorse the Trade Promotion Program of the Department of Commerce, the Export Credit Insurance Program of the Export-Import Bank, and the continuing efforts of the responsible agencies to abate and remove all remaining restraints upon the movement of U.S. products into foreign markets.

Our future balance of payments position will be determined primarily by just one thing: the ability of American business to compete successfully and adequately in all markets of the free world.

IN SUMMARY, this Committee recommends the following policy guidelines for dealing with the balance of payments situation:

1. Continued efforts to develop multilateral cooperation for strengthening the international financial structure.

2. Reassessment of U.S. unilateral governmental transfers and military expenditures abroad, to eliminate unnecessary drains wherever possible.

3. Increased efforts to persuade our major allies to shoulder a greater share of the common burden of free-world defense and aid to the developing areas.

4. Rejection of any move in the direction of limitation of the United States as a capital market.

5. Adoption of an interest rate policy sufficiently flexible to bring U.S. rates into line with those of our major trading partners whenever necessary.

6. Maintenance of the present dollar price of gold.

7. Forthright rejection of inflationary monetary and fiscal policies.

8. Increasing efforts along the lines set forth in Title II of the Trade Expansion Act to reduce tariffs and other barriers to world trade.

9. Reduction and revision of United States tax schedules appropriate to the stimulation of investment both at home and abroad.

10. Continued encouragement of U.S. firms to compete more actively abroad.

READING 57

How can the 1¼ billion people who live in the world's poorest countries move toward a higher standard of living?

Mr. Khrushchev professes to see a wave of the future in communism. Americans sometimes seem to be looking for a wave of the future in democratic capitalism. But this article, which introduces a unit on our relations with the world's underdeveloped countries, makes it seem that, far from there being any one wave in sight, the future is likely to find a wide range of economic systems across the globe. Africa presents an interesting case study here. Whatever homogeneity there may be to the outsider disappears when a closer look is taken at how newly independent nations are feeling their distinctive ways toward development.

Arnold Rivkin was director of the African Economic and Political Development Project at M.I.T. from 1957 to 1962. His quick survey of Africa provides valuable background reading for the discussions which follow it.

Questions to Guide the Reading

What are the most critical choices that these African nations must face? To what extent do their political goals help or hinder their economic growth?

What considerations should enter into an American decision about which of these countries should be aided directly in their growth? Which of our actions might enhance growth in an environment of freedom and which might turn out to impede it?

AFRICAN PATHS TO DEVELOPMENT
Arnold Rivkin

The economies of Africa's emerging nations are varied and diverse. They range from the self-styled "Arab socialism" of the United Arab Republic and the "African socialism" of Guinea, Mali and Ghana, through the "democratic socialism" of Senegal and the mixed economies of Liberia and the Ivory Coast to the relatively free economy of Nigeria, with its large, expanding and active private sector.

The newly independent African states have thus chosen, or are in the process of choosing, a wide variety of economic systems. The economies of all the new nations, however, in actuality contain an admixture of public and private ownership, of voluntary performance and public regulation, of incentives and coercion, of rewards and penalties.

The choice in Africa has not been between capitalism and socialism, as Communists claim. Rather it has been a choice between an economy which seeks to decentralize decision making and encourage individual initiative, and an economy which seeks to centralize decision making in government hands and discourage the individual entrepreneur. There are obviously many gradations and variants of each type of economy, and many of these are now evolving in Africa.

More often than not, nations which have decentralized economies and give scope to individual initiative also possess a democratic system of government based on broad popular participation. They recognize a legal opposition; individual and minority rights are safeguarded by law, which is administered by an independent judiciary. In Africa, Nigeria is almost the sole example of a state attempting to develop a mixed economy in a democratic environment.

On the other hand, nations whose economies are centrally directed and give little scope to private initiative usually have an authoritarian-oriented political system, whether of the left or right. In Africa, Guinea, Mali, Ghana and the United Arab Republic have leftist authoritarian regimes and highly centralized "African socialist" or "Arab socialist" economies. Africa also has variants of rightist authoritarian-oriented governments with more or less centralized state-directed economies. Some of the former French Equatorial African territories, such as the Central African Republic, would fall into this category.

Senegal and Tunisia, for their part, have one-party political systems which permit more extensive individual and civil rights than the leftist authoritarian-oriented states such as Guinea and Ghana. The "democratic socialism" of Tunisia and Senegal allows much larger scope for private participation and initiative, especially in the agricultural and commercial sectors, than the systems of Guinea or Ghana. In Liberia and the Ivory Coast there are one-party political systems which

From Arnold Rivkin, "African Paths to Development," *Challenge*, April, 1963, pp. 27–30. Reprinted with kind permission of the publisher.

lean toward the right. Both nations have mixed economies, which allow freer individual expression and more initiative than the right authoritarian political system of, say, the Central African Republic.

Notwithstanding the diversity of economic systems evolving in Africa, there are certain underlying similarities which help explain the magnitude of the public sector, the seeming predilection for authoritarian-type development techniques and the frequent usage of socialist jargon. These factors both limit the growth of strong private sectors and enhance government participation in the African economies.

First, we shall consider the factors which inhibit the growth of private enterprise. Throughout Africa there is a drastic shortage of entrepreneurs. Nigeria is one of the few countries that has a fairly large and growing indigenous group of entrepreneurs. Income in Africa is usually spent or hoarded. It is seldom invested in productive enterprises except real estate, construction and possibly commerce.

In addition to the absence of an entrepreneurial class, there is an acute shortage of indigenous capital. With very few exceptions, annual per capita incomes in African countries usually run between $75 and $150. These conditions obviously do not encourage significant private saving. Banking and savings institutions, which were almost nonexistent in most areas, have been developed only recently along with an internal money market.

Most new African states are only well known to the former colonial powers which ruled them. Thus upon gaining independence the new nations are able to obtain loans and investment capital only from their former rulers.

The African areas which acquired independence peacefully and without undue conflict with the colonial power which ruled them have found it easier to attract loans and private investments, though perhaps on a somewhat more limited scale than in earlier times. This is true of Nigeria, Sierra Leone, the Ivory Coast, Togo, Gabon and Mauritania, all of which have continued to receive private capital from abroad. In some cases new investment capital has come from the United States, West Germany, Japan or Israel.

The experience of nations which won independence after a violent or difficult struggle has been quite different. The flow of private capital from the former colonial power has tended to diminish, and existing investments were sometimes withdrawn. Under such circumstances private capital from other nations has also tended to steer clear of the new state. Experiences of Morocco, Tunisia and Algeria all illustrate what happens when nations win independence after a violent or difficult struggle. Private foreign investment actually ceased to flow into all three countries for a period of time and even now remains small.

Irrespective of whether the transition to independence has been difficult or easy, no great upsurge of private foreign investment has occurred except in mining and oil exploitation. In fact, many of the new states, having been disappointed in their expectations and baffled by their failure to attract private investment from abroad, have turned with renewed zeal to the creation of public development corporations and banks.

The general African tendency toward authoritarian government has also inhibited the development of vigorous private sectors and has reinforced the trend toward public participation and control of the national economies. If new states centralize political power, it becomes difficult, or even impossible, for them to allow the development of strong indigenous groups possessing economic power and private wealth outside the one-party apparatus and independent of it. Such a development would imperil the exclusive concentration of power in the hands of the monolithic party. The government, for the same reasons, also finds it necessary to control the trade unions. This pattern has increasingly emerged in many of the new states, particularly those with authoritarian regimes.

All African states without exception are strenuously seeking to enhance their national status. This drive for "economic independence" is more a reflection of a state of mind than a precise economic doctrine. Time and again utterances of African political leaders, party platforms and political slogans have proclaimed that the goal of national and Pan-African economic policy was to achieve economic independence or, conversely, to uproot neocolonialist influences.

In practice, this mood lends support to the public sector and encourages occasional nationalizations of private enterprises deemed crucial to a country striving for economic independence. Frequently this means that the state takes over an airline, shipping line or a railroad. Sometimes it means that the state purchases wholesale or retail distribution enterprises or nationalizes a mining company. But this in turn may frighten away potential private foreign investors.

There are also a good many common African structural problems which tend to enhance the government's role in the productive sectors of the economy. For the present and the foreseeable future it is essential that Africa concentrate on developing the vitally important agricultural sector, explore and tap mineral resources, build an adequate transportation system and develop the human skills indispensable to a modern economy. Public initiative, participation and investment are essential if these ends are to be attained.

Agricultural research, farm credit, technical aid and education, irrigation projects, and disease and insect control are, by their very nature, government activities. Even so, farmers and nomads who are only now emerging from a subsistence economy are unable to take full advantage of the existing programs. Geological and topographical surveys and explorations also belong to the sphere of government activities. Even in oil prospecting, where private companies are usually prepared to foot the bill, the governments of some of the new states feel impelled to become at least minority partners. As a consequence, some governments even want to share the exploration costs in order to protect their national interests and enhance their potential share of the profits.

In the underdeveloped African countries the construction and operation of transportation systems has long been a governmental function. Furthermore, private capital has shown little interest in investing in road building, port development, air transport and railroads in Africa. Only in West African states such as Nigeria and Ghana has considerable private capital been invested in trucking and passenger road transportation.

Finally, in Africa, as elsewhere, developing human skills through the expansion and improvement of primary, secondary, technical, vocational and higher education is mainly a public function. Even the considerable missionary activity, which provided teachers and financing for school construction during the colonial period and the early years of independence, is becoming increasingly unacceptable to the governments of the new states. The urge to Africanize the educational structures, revamp the curricula and substitute African instructors and administrators for Europeans wherever possible, has, in one African country after another, led to a reduction in the role of private missionary schools and the level of their financial contribution.

In addition, in Ghana and Guinea, and to some extent in many other states, the desire to use the schools to teach citizenship, build na-

tionalist feeling and inculcate certain political views has led to increasing government control of the educational systems. And in some states, such as the Sudan, private missionary schools and teachers have been forced out because of religious considerations.

Thus the African governments, in launching ambitious development plans, have felt impelled to assume a leading role in developing their nations' resources, expanding transportation facilities, power and telecommunications, and training manpower cadres. When we consider that the respective governments have undertaken all these multifarious activities, that indigenous private investment is minimal and that private foreign capital faces great problems, we can readily see why most African states have economies in which the public sector is predominant. Even in the less authoritarian states government participation in the productive sectors of the economies is larger than it might otherwise be.

In all African states, however, private investment is permitted some scope. In Ghana, Guinea and Mali the area is narrow, notably for the reasons already discussed, but also because the African socialist doctrine demands that foreign investment be confined to major government-sponsored projects, such as the Volta River power, bauxite and aluminum development in Ghana, and the bauxite mining and alumina fabrication projects in Guinea.

In Liberia, and many other countries, the area for private investment is relatively wide, although the government frequently requires public participation. In Nigeria, as we have said, private initiative is given broader scope than anywhere else in Africa. But even there the government insists on significant public participation in such enterprises as new oil refineries. In other instances, Nigeria requires only nominal or no public participation at all.

Of what significance are the multiple African approaches to economic development insofar as U.S. policy is concerned?

First, the U.S. must make a basic decision about the role, the emphasis and the extent of aid it wants to expend in Africa as compared to other underdeveloped regions of the world, such as Latin America and South Asia. In recent years Africa has begun to make a major claim on American foreign assistance resources. The U.S. has been drawn into the seemingly endless Congo crises, the consortium financing of the Volta River project as well as the economic development problems of such promising nations as Nigeria and Tunisia. For a complexity of reasons the U.S. has extended loans and grants to a variety of countries ranging from Somalia to Guinea, and from Algeria to Uganda.

Second, the U.S. will have to decide how much of its aid should go to countries trying to develop in a relatively democratic environment and how much should go to those adopting increasingly authoritarian practices. Which emphasis will best serve the U.S. national interest? Should priority be given countries which have soundly based development plans and have themselves shown a capacity to bring them to fruition, or should aid be extended to countries whether or not they are able to make maximum use of it so as to keep them from becoming dependent on Communist bloc assistance?

Third, nations which possess a large public sector will require a great deal of external aid. This will affect not only the size and shape of U.S. aid programs, but also U.S. aid policy. Should the United States assist publicly owned industrial and agricultural enterprises?

Fourth, the U.S. must decide how to deal with the trade problems evolving in Africa. The chief elements of the current trade picture are the association of 18 African states with the European Economic Community, Soviet aid and trade in Africa and the competition with Latin American countries which produce the same commodities (coffee, sugar, cocoa).

The success of African nations in achieving economic growth and political stability will depend in large measure on the development choices they make. If they choose badly, they will stagnate and will be afflicted by political instability, and this in turn will create problems for the U.S. Conversely, if their economies expand and they achieve stability the U.S. will benefit.

The United States is thus vitally interested in the kind of economies the African nations are constructing, all the more so since an intimate relationship exists between the economic and political structures of the emerging countries. Consequently, we must use our aid program and the influence which stems from it to channel African economic development into a democratic framework before it is too late.

READING 58

The United States was itself a recipient of "foreign aid" in the sense of large foreign investments, principally private, over the first century of our independence. But neither this experience nor any other nation's experience was of much help to us in implementing the aid programs that began after World War II. Their size, their complexity, and their closer links to government made these programs fresh learning grounds. One of their first lessons was that humanitarianism, while essential, was scarcely enough to make aid effective.

Barbara Ward Jackson, an astute British observer of international economic developments, raises some of the contemporary issues about foreign aid. In the context of a vigorous defense of such aid programs and of some of the most widely accepted priorities for growth, she still conveys a sense of urgency about reexamining our experience to date.

Questions to Guide the Reading

If the West were to develop a long-term strategy for foreign aid, what would need to be the basic ingredients of such a strategy to give it a reasonable chance for success in the economic world of those developing countries and in the political world at home?

What are the key assumptions made by Lady Jackson on the ways that poor nations may eventually become richer ones? How do those assumptions apply to the ways in which the American economy grew?

FOREIGN AID: STRATEGY OR STOPGAP?
Barbara Ward Jackson

What are programs of economic assistance *for*? After a dozen years of them, the question still has to be asked. Otherwise how can their effectiveness be judged? Clearly, there is no consensus. For some they are tools to stop Communism, for others to propagate Western ideas, for still others to defend Western interests. All these factors certainly enter in but they do not explain why or how such programs can have these effects. In fact, as critics are quick to point out, some assistance programs do not. Countries can swallow aid like blotting paper and at the end of the process are no more pro-Western, anti-Communist or secure and stable than they were at the start.

Here, however, may be the beginnings of an answer. The most fundamental of all Western—and, indeed, of all human—interests is the preservation of peace. Communism is a danger primarily because it is aggressive and expansive. When it is not—as in Jugoslavia or Poland—it can be lived with. But profound internal instability in the modern world *is* a danger to peace. States in the grip of ferment and disorder tend to become—as Cuba has done—a point of polarization in the cold war between East and West. They recreate the risk of conflict which was inherent in Balkan instability before 1914, the risk that rival power systems will seek to flow into any vacuum brought about by local collapse and, in the process, will collide with each other in fatal conflict.

In this large context of peace and war, the fundamental aim of economic assistance is, therefore, to build up stability in unstable states. This cannot be done by piecemeal patching up, by casual subsidies and handouts. The most successful of all programs of economic aid so far—the Marshall Plan—clearly illustrates the need for change in depth. If the nations of Western Europe had simply been restored to where they were before the Second World War, they would inevitably have repeated yet again their melancholy inter-war cycle of economic isolationism and national rivalry. It was American's insistence upon a joint solution of their problems that opened the era of technical modernization, supranationalism and interdependence. What has saved Europe has been not the reconstruction of the old order but the bold projection of a new.

The same vision and daring are needed in the infinitely more complex pursuit of stability among the extra-European peoples. We live in an age of maximum instability. Its general driving force is the modification of all techniques and institutions by reason, science and technology. But the particular context of our day has been formed by two hundred years of history during which the nations around the North Atlantic Ocean made the first transition to the wealth and power locked up in modern technology, and used their dominance to establish colonial control or economic dependence among the pretechnical societies elsewhere. This era is ending as the last of the colonies receives political independence. But its economic and social inheritance is still intact; it is also essentially unstable. Most of the new states emerging from the old tutelage lack inner coherence. And the general economic relationships between them and the developed states do not work well and threaten to grow worse.

Action, therefore, is needed at two levels—to complete the modernization of the local economies and to devise a world system that fosters the necessary change. The starting point is, obviously, the post-colonial inheritance as it stands today. One should be wary of generalizations. Nations as various as India and Mexico on the threshold of full modernization, or Chad and Niger barely emerging from nomadic life, tend to be lumped together as "underdeveloped" and "developing." Development policies, to be effective, have to be based not on generalities but on detailed analysis of the community which is to be aided. The West's increasing acceptance of the need for "country plans" is a fruitful recognition of how specific the problems of development are likely to be.

Yet one can discern a broad pattern of "semi-modernization." In the last 150 years, the modernized states of the North Atlantic have broken up the static stability of traditional society—in Asia, in Africa, in feudal South America. They came in to search for raw materials—minerals, rubber, coffee, tea—and established small modernized export sectors. To these they attached their "infrastructure" of roads, railways and great coastal cities through which the materials flowed out to the West—and Western manufactures flowed back.

This Western incursion did not stimulate or provide much local saving. Mines and plantations were often foreign-owned. Even when peasant farmers or local magnates produced the materials, most peasants quickly spent their earnings on Western consumer goods, while many magnates banked their profits abroad. As a result, little capital flowed back into the local economy—and without capital there is no growth, save in the single category of population. Food production remained unimproved. Industry did not develop. Such enclaves of industrial activity as Bombay state or Minaes Geraes led to no larger developments. Revenue did not rise. Governments therefore could not afford expensive yet crucial services such as wider education. Only a small elite received some modern instruction—through the missionaries or the private enterprise of wealthy parents. Yet even so small a breach in the old stability undermined it. With the new goods came new ideas—sovereignty, nationalism, above all, equality between nations, equality within the state.

Nor was this ferment simply a factor of internal change. As the twentieth century advanced, profound political and economic changes in the world increased the tension. Anti-colonial agitation spread; Communist propaganda fanned it. The West endured a shattering slump. Export prices of primary products remained profoundly depressed and investment fell. Worse than that, the Atlantic world showed signs of shifting, by way of synthetics and substitutes, to a state of providing a permanently smaller stimulus to the less developed economies.

Such, then, is the anatomy of semi-moderniza-tion. Developed export sectors, the infrastructure they require, the beginnings of modern educa-tion—all these set in motion a passionate ferment through the vision they give of a wider and more commodious life. But the stark daily realities are of poverty, illiteracy, stagnant agriculture, mar-ginal industry and a world economic system which offers no way out of the impasse. There is enough change to excite the desire for more, not enough to create it. And if anyone under-estimates the instability bred in such communi-ties, it is salutary to remember that Communism made its European and Asian breakthroughs in two countries—Russia and China—where, in spite

of a profound and secular culture, there had appeared many of the characteristics of semi-modernization—export sectors greatly dependent on foreign capital, only the beginnings of indus-try, a stagnant countryside, education mainly for the elite, an intelligentsia torn between the desire for modernity and despair at the obstacles in its way. Nor, for all its urbanization and sophisti-cation, was Batista's Cuba lacking in these char-acteristics of partial and discordant modernity.

Communism can be seen in this context to be not the culmination of the modern revolution based on capital and technology but rather a phenomenon of an early stage in the process. The Atlantic world has passed far beyond its blocks and frustrations. But the emerging continents today are nearer to Russia in 1914 than to the United States or the Common Market in 1962.

II

The essential task of economic assistance is, therefore, to correct and complete the old lop-sided structure. Within the developing countries, it is a question of extending the colonial infra-structure, expanding education beyond a small elite, raising savings and channeling them into dynamic farming and growing industry where more savings can be secured by higher produc-tivity. Thus the cycle of sustained growth can be set in motion. At the international level, the task is above all to restore a world-wide economy which stimulates and does not depress the pos-sibilities of local development.

These are statements of high generality. For-tunately, in the last ten years, governments have begun to learn to fill in some of the details. The starting point is a progressive attempt to increase the flow of domestic capital. By general agree-ment it must rise to at least 15 percent of na-tional income if sustained growth is to be secured. Such an increase does not happen easily or naturally in post-colonial economies. A strategy of saving must be worked out. Hence the new importance placed on the formulation of country plans. Ten years ago, most plans were no more than the shopping lists of government depart-ments. Today, their aim is at the very least to give a full picture of the economy, to lay down the forms of investment most likely to accelerate growth and to devise a financial strategy for raising the necessary capital and channeling it into the right enterprises. The sophistication of these plans varies, naturally, with the scale of information and the reliability of statistical sources. Some countries—the Ivory Coast, for instance—have to be content at this stage to extrapolate plans from small sample surveys of typical regions. At the other end of the scale, such plans as India's Third Plan are based upon all the data of a modern state.

At the core of the plan is the government's strategy for saving. The aim, in every country, is to keep resources rising in balance with a more ambitious scale of spending. It is a tricky balance. Slam on taxes and forced savings too violently and there are, as in Ghana and British Guiana, strikes and riots and immense discouragement to private and foreign investors. Proceed too cautiously and inflation takes over, as in Brazil. There are no general rules for either the techniques or the scale of saving. But one generalization seems permissible. Governments can hardly be said to be seriously bent on development unless they are willing to raise the level of taxation to some 20 percent of national income. The figure is not impossibly high. Typical Asian landlord-usurers took 50 percent and more of the peasant's crop and charged him several hundred percent on his loans. It is simply that governments are not used to taxing, nor the rich to being taxed. It is, however, also true that a relatively high level of taxation can discourage investment if the plan relies to any extent—as most do—on local and particularly on foreign private enterprise. To this difficulty we shall have to return.

Where should the new resources go? To infrastructure, clearly—to fill in the gaps of the old pattern geared only to exports; and it is perhaps relevant to note that most developing governments underestimate the need for power and transport once growth begins in earnest. India's bottlenecks in its Third Plan are largely due to this. Yet the "infrastructure" of trained minds is even more important than railways or transmission lines. And in this vital field of education, it is very easy to get the balance wrong. Western and Eastern Nigeria have learned what happens if primary education is made very nearly universal before rural life has been improved enough to attract the school-leavers, or urban employment expanded to absorb them as they stream into the cities.

For this reason a new emphasis is appearing on the need to plan investment in manpower in such a way that it fits into the general pattern of investment in the economy. The Ashby Report for Nigeria is the first model of an attempt to produce trained minds and match them with the opportunities that will be available. Manpower budgeting is certain to be increasingly used in planning for development, the more so since education should not be understood narrowly. In the broadest sense of training, it is essential to the two key sectors in all strategies of development—modernized agriculture and growing industry.

Undoubtedly static farming is the toughest obstacle to overcome. If export crops are to be produced at decreasing cost and food production is to begin to expand adequately, the farmer's thinking has to be changed; yet his environment does not change. On land he and his fathers have cultivated for generations as shifting African cultivators or depressed and indebted tenants, he has to learn to use fertilizer, better seed, more efficient tools, better techniques of planting. Only the most intensive farm extension services are likely to make an impact on his mind, and their effectiveness is in any case determined by two further conditions: Are they themselves well organized? And are the basic structures of land tenure such that the farmer has any real inducement to change?

It is not often, at present, that both conditions are fulfilled. The order, the planning, the sheer business efficiency that go, say, into the building of a dam abruptly vanish when it is a question of the water the dam provides. Peasant settlements are not ready, plans for land use do not exist, and where there are villages established, better seed is left out in the rain and fertilizers arrive when the crops are half grown. In Pakistan, the government hopes to improve the efficiency of its agricultural services by setting up a new statutory body, an Agricultural Corporation, with direct responsibility to get supply lines clear down to the villages. In India, "special project areas" are being tried to secure a concentration of efficient effort. Without a breakthrough here, the farmer will not change.

Nor will he if he stands to gain no material benefits by the change. For this, he requires a rather larger scale of operation and freedom from too many middlemen. Where, as in large parts of Africa and east of the Andes, land is available, the need is for new land settlements combining, as in Western Nigeria or the cotton estates of Sudan's Gezira, individual ownership with general managerial supervision and a cooperative structure. But where no more land can be opened up, there is no alternative to drastic land reform, establishing the peasant as owner on the land he has formerly tilled as sharecropper or tenant, and backing him with a full cooperative apparatus. Japan, with its intensive farming and developing cooperatives, is the model here.

The farmer produced by these reforms not only provides enough surplus food for the cities; he can also afford to buy the products the cities begin to manufacture. This is the essential link between modernized agriculture and growth in every other sector. All through the developing world today, agriculture is tending to lose its Cinderella status and to become the first preoccupation of governments and planners. Yet this sensible shift of emphasis does not make industrialization any less essential. All developing countries need to break from their total dependence on primary exports. All are, by definition, under-industrialized. The problem is to pick the right types of activity. Preliminary surveys such as the short, brilliant study undertaken for the Gold Coast (now Ghana) by Dr. Arthur Lewis in 1954 can usually indicate where the processing of local materials and import-substitution—the "beer, boots and bricks" stage—can most usefully begin. The possibilities are as diverse as the resources that are available locally. In fact, only one generalization is possible. The universal test for all enterprise, public or private, must be its ability to operate at a profit. No doubt pioneer industries need reasonable tariff protection and other forms of government support to offset inexperience and the lack of an industrial environment. There is little hope of building up an internal market in depth without such assistance. But profits must be made or the melancholy process of *dis*investment sets in. It is not enough to plan to build an industry. There must be a formal check on subsequent performance.

Profits imply above all a managerial competence and it is at this point that government planners tend to be most interested in the possibilities of investment for foreign firms. True, the capital they bring in is indispensable since virtually all developing countries have balance-of-payments problems and not one can hope to finance out of its own export income the foreign-exchange element in its plans for development. But even more dire than the scarcity of capital is the lack of industrial skills at every level, especially at the crucial level of management. The period of extreme dependence on outside skills can, however, be drastically shortened if the foreign firms are prepared to undertake imaginative programs of training. Such schemes undoubtedly increase the acceptability of foreign enterprise.

Yet there is an unsolved dilemma here. Massive foreign investment may hasten development; equally, however, local nationalist resentment will grow if a large part of the new industrial sector emerges—as it did in Cuba and could in Nigeria—under foreign control of one kind or another. A number of compromises are being explored—joint ventures, management contracts, local government participation, agreed schedules for the transfer of shares to local investors. But the difficulties remain—between local desire for a measure of control and foreign distrust of local intervention, particularly by government.

There is no escaping the problem. Foreign capital is an essential element in all industrialization since under-industrialized countries lack, by definition, the tools and machines for growth. And at this point, we begin to confront the developing nations' critical shortages of foreign exchange and the need to build a world-wide economic system which fosters growth in the developing world and/does not tend, in its casual unplanned way, to inhibit development.

Today, such a system does not exist. The workings of the world economy do not at present naturally provide sufficient access to the currencies of the developed, industrialized West. Western investment has always tended to go to other developed lands. The trend has not changed. If investment in oil is subtracted, the flow of private capital remains quite inadequate. When government grants and loans of all kinds are added, the flow today may reach between $7.8 and $8.7 billion a year—the O.E.C.D. figure. Yet, according to United Nations estimates, if over a billion developing peoples are to stay ahead of their exploding population and increase their rate of growth from 2 or 3 percent to 5 or 6 percent a year, capital coming in from outside should amount annually to some $10 to $12 billion. These are only broad orders of magnitude. The real gaps can be measured only plan by plan. But no one denies the gap. Nor does anyone maintain that the developing nations themselves, by increasing their trade with developing countries, can fill in the gap themselves.

Here the current system works wholly against them. The golden days for development in the last decade have had little to do with aid. They were sparked by the boom in world commodity prices after the Korean war. Then such lands as India and Nigeria financed their entire developmental expenditure. Today no poor nation can do so. The reason is not simply that the plans are bigger. In country after country in the last five years, the effect of economic aid has been very largely nullified by the steady fall in what the nations could earn by their primary exports and as steady a rise in the price of manufactures they import.

Nor is it simply a matter of unfavorable price levels. There is hardly a facet of Western trading policy that does not entail some disadvantage to the developing nations. The relative share of Atlantic income spent on raw materials produced elsewhere is still declining. A developing nation's first alternatives to primary exports—cheap textiles and semi-processed goods—are limited by Western quotas and differential tariffs. In some countries, such tropical products as coffee and tea have to pay internal duties as well. The picture is one of universal discouragement.

To counter this contraction, the United Nations seeks a ten-point recovery in primary prices and a 2 percent growth in the poorer nations' share of the world market—conditions they enjoyed in the 1950s. The aims are modest enough but the means of achieving them are more complex. One possibility lies in securing world-wide commodity agreements which fix prices and export quotas. Another aims at maintaining income by giving primary producers more generous drawing rights on the International Monetary Fund. There are suggestions that the developed nations should take off all internal taxes on tropical products and permit "one-way free trade" in them. They might also "vacate" certain fields—some kinds of cheap textiles, for instance, or competitive products such as soya bean or beet sugar—in favor of increased imports. In short, policies are available. What is unsure is the political will to adopt them.

III

With this question of the will to bring about the needed changes, we reach the tough political core of the assistance effort. At least three-quarters of the processes of modernization can be accomplished only by the recipients themselves. Yet bitter experience in the last ten years has shown that some kinds of society can do nothing with aid but waste it. When presidents fly in by air pink Italian marble for their bathrooms, when aid dollars turn up in discreet private accounts in Swiss banks, what is to be done?

In theory, the path is clear. No government is worth supporting unless it is prepared to undertake the two or three key policies needed to set growth in motion. But in practice such governments often do not appear or cannot be coaxed into activity. After a century of Western control or at least predominant influence, nearly all developing governments react strongly, even violently, against attempts at direct Western political guidance. It represents precisely the tutelage from which they are trying to escape. In some areas, the reaction goes further. It does not take much insight to see that some of the necessary steps toward modernization imply radical social change. Mass education, land reform, wider taxation—all these break up the traditional patterns of authority. Can leaders be persuaded to reform themselves out of power? Is it not more likely that they will simply resist all changes in the name, say, of anti-Communism?

These risks vary from continent to continent. Broadly speaking, ex-colonial governments are less conservative and immobile than those which have kept a nominal independence—Iran, for instance, or Thailand or Latin American countries. Colonial societies have tended to go through some kind of social upheaval during the struggle for independence and the new leaders usually represent a more or less clear break with the conservative past. In Asia, it is a supreme piece of good fortune for the West that the Indian sub-continent is largely governed by men who emerged at the time of independence as moderate reformers; it would be little short of tragic if Western irritation over some Indian leaders and some Indian postures in international affairs led to a lessening of sustained support for the Indian Plan under which over one-third of the people in the developing world are being coaxed and prodded toward effective modernization.

In Africa, too, the new leaders have little commitment to a conservative, tribal past. All are eager for modernization, especially for the widest development of education. The most frequent problem is lack of skill and experience, and, next to it, waste. Frenchmen call Africa *l'Afrique des princes*, and it is astonishing how much savings can be swallowed up by the "personality cult" or disappear into the pockets of ministers who stand at the center of a vortex of grasping tribal kin.

The worst deadlocks seem to arise in Latin America. Many of the rulers remain profoundly conservative—no recent colonial upheaval has widened their ranks. They enjoy friendly links with local American business interests. Neither group is precisely passionate for reform. Moreover, opinion in the United States—especially in Congress—inclines much more to conservative orthodoxy than does opinion in Europe where virtually the entire gamut of political upheaval has been traversed in the last 30 years. If a Modibo Keita in Mali announces the founding of a socialist state and starts excluding Frenchmen from the country's commerce, the French—having drawn realistic conclusions from their catastrophic withdrawal from Guinea—send as ambassador the man who knows most and feels most warmly about Mali to keep tempers sweet, to ensure Mali's continued association with France's franc zone and to let it be known that there is substantial aid to come. Such flexibility is difficult to achieve in America's relations with South America. The politician who makes life more difficult for local businessmen—including Americans—and so inspires Congressmen to reach for their appropriations axe may be the only man ready to break the deadlock of feudal farming and of industry restricted by lack of purchasing power and lack of skills. Leaders like Señor Betancourt who are at once reformers and moderates cannot be conjured up at will. The choice may well lie between reformers verging on left-wing extremism and leaders—often army leaders —all too ready to suppress Communism and every flicker of reform as well.

What can be done? It is at this point that Western governments have to remind themselves of what they are really trying to do—to build viable states capable of cooperating in a viable world order. They have to remember, too, that they are not operating solely in terms of immediate conflicts, failures and successes but are attempting, over time, to produce profound modifications in the social order. To prop up, on any terms, a regime which will neither analyze its economy nor take the crucial steps to set it in motion can do no more than stave off and finally aggravate revolutionary upheaval. The reason why Latin America is more unstable now than it was five years ago has something to do with Fidel Castro. But it has much more to do with five years of declining export prices, general economic stagnation and perhaps 15,000,000 extra mouths to feed.

In some particular situations, subventions may be necessary—to counteract a bad harvest, to maintain a local army or check incipient guerrilla fighting, to tide over a balance-of-payments crisis. But—as the Alliance for Progress attempts to recognize—these grants should have nothing to do with economic assistance. Funds given as foreign aid have to be given within a framework that at least aims at a strategy for growth. Governments with no plans for popular and technical education, with no policy for raising taxes toward the needed 20 percent of national income, with no ardor for land reform, with no general strategy for fostering savings and channeling them into productive investment—such governments are simply incapable of becoming valid partners in a serious effort of economic aid. Generous assistance must wait upon a change of heart and plan. The judgment may seem harsh. But what other way is there of convincing hesitant leaders that the reforms needed for growth, far from being window dressing, are the preconditions of assistance?

The refusal to give aid can, moreover, be somewhat sweetened. If the local government is simply not technically competent to produce an effective plan, it can be given time, temporary financial assistance and the help of planning experts to put a program into shape. Such experts can and should be drawn in part from international agencies and from the country or continent in which the plan is being carried out. Under the Alliance for Progress, "Nine Wise Men"—all Latin Americans—are empowered to check the feasibility of its programs. India has declared that it would be ready to accept a World Bank audit of its use of aid in return for sustained commitments. The U.N. Special Fund has found it possible to lessen local extravagance on the plea that its funds are collected from rich and poor nations alike.

This greater use of local and international expertise is not simply a manoeuvre designed to increase political acceptability. Western governments and their experts simply do not yet know the answers to a large number of the problems thrown up by social blocks and inhibitions lying in the way of modernization. If they intervene in dogmatic detail, they not only madden local opinion; they are probably wrong as well. Far closer consultation with local opinion, more joint research work in Western and local universities, more field work by joint teams—all these are needed not as sops to local opinion but as essential guarantees of success.

Yet the most persuasive pressure is likely to come not from the negative side of refusing aid where reform is lacking but from the positive side of aid generously given when conditions are favorable. So far, this "demonstration effect" is missing. If the West seriously intended to coax the laggards along by carrots as well as sticks, the scale of Western commitments to India's Third Plan would not have been allowed to seem certain in 1961 and dubious again in 1962.

Nigeria would not be wondering, six months after the publication of a sensible six year plan, whether, in addition to the $250 million pledged by the United States, any more of the $950 million it needs from abroad will in fact be available. Yet the experience of France suggests that aid on a really massive scale has its effects. The $300 million made available each year for some 25 million people in French West Africa have given each local government elbowroom, offered inducements to stern anti-colonialists to keep their links with Paris and preserved a framework of community comfortable enough even to tempt runaways like Sékou Touré. The policy is not cheap. But it cannot be said, so far, to have failed.

The maintenance and extension of generous programs of aid would ease the Western task in yet another way. Among new politicians in ex-colonial lands, among young firebrands in backward, caste-ridden societies, among the rising intelligentsia of the developing continents, the reaction to the West is all too often one of resentment and suspicion. It reflects a recent past in which the "new men" chiefly discern dependence and exploitation. So far, this image has not been effectively dimmed. If, however, the aid programs continue, if pressure for reform is sustained and the officials who administer assistance are not identified with the old order but look intelligently and devotedly toward new relationships, these facts cannot fail to have a vital political impact. In spite of all the cries of "neo-colonialism," the impact is felt already. Less certain is whether it will be maintained long enough —and boldly enough—for the full political harvest to be reaped.

IV

Do the Western powers really intend to develop an imaginative long-term strategy? The evidence seems rather contradictory. True, one can point to a number of promising signs that the Western effort is becoming more accepted and institutionalized. The funds available to the International Monetary Fund and to the World Bank have been doubled and the International Development Authority has been set up to provide less bankable loans. The United States agency for aid has been reorganized to make it more capable of undertaking sustained programs and Congress has given the Administration some latitude in aid-giving on a longer basis. France and Germany have Ministries of Coöperation,

Britain a Department of Technical Coöperation. There is also more coördination—with the Alliance for Progress, under the Treaty of Rome with its common European Fund for Development, through the Atlantic-wide Organization for Economic Cooperation and Development with its Development Assistance Committee, through the United Nations Decade of Development.

Why, then, should one hesitate? The chief reason for concern is the fact that behind a good deal of governmental rhetoric and some solid governmental spending, the shape of a genuine Western strategy for aid and development remains very hazy. In other words, the second great task of world modernization—to provide a viable international framework for the developing nations—still hangs fire. If one takes three key issues in assistance—manpower, capital and trade—it is still impossible to discern anything like a clear and interrelated structure of policies.

To begin with manpower, development planning implies the availability of development planners. A start has been made in certain universities and international agencies to train them, but they are still so scarce that their lack has become a bottleneck to advance under the Alliance for Progress. There are also few firm plans—apart from France's effort and that of the small but valuable Peace Corps—for providing the massive number of teachers needed to carry out modernization, especially in Africa.

The capital contribution made by the West is difficult to establish. No one has yet agreed on a yardstick to separate aid proper from ordinary commercial lending. But of the Western governments, only France and the United States have certainly fulfilled the aid target of 1 percent of national income. Even including all forms of capital, the annual flow is still too small by between $2 and $3 billion a year. Moreover, unbalanced contributions to foreign aid are one more factor of disequilibrium in the West's balance of payments and could inhibit the most generous of the donors—the United States.

But it is over the issue of trade that one has most completely the sense of a blank in Western strategy. Only in the last year or so has the realization become more general that almost every aspect of Western trade policy discriminates *against* the developing world, and just as Western minds began to focus on this fact, the debate has become engulfed in the passionate issue of Britain's entry into the Common Market and of the trading relations which might evolve in an eventual Atlantic partnership. Here the division of policy does not lie between the developing and the developed nations. On both sides there are leaders who wish to continue the exclusive, preferential arrangements which tie Western Europe's ex-colonies in Africa to the Common Market. Equally, other governments, rich and poor alike, follow America in seeking to open the fabulous demand of the Six to the trade of all developing nations, keeping Western tariffs to the lowest level—or where possible to zero—encouraging local industrialization and compensating those who lose preferences by means of generous aid and world-wide commodity agreements. In this, there is indeed the outline of a general strategy. But it is not yet clear whether European governments or their partners in Africa are prepared to break with a preferential past.

Behind the delays and tepidities of Western governments lies the indifference or the ignorance of Western electorates. Few voters feel a natural passion for voting themselves into taxes in order to assist foreigners. In Britain, aid is barely discussed. In France, some voters listen to the journalist Raymond Cartier when he demands that aid money be spent not at Dakar but in the Dordogne. And the reactions in the United States Congress betray a gathering impatience which must in some measure reflect the prejudice and muddle of opinion outside.

Given this political context, efforts to persuade and enlighten the electorates of the West have to be intensified. The passage of time has not lessened the force of any of the old arguments. Enlightened self-interest among the trading nations of the West is still involved in any policy which systematically expands the economies and purchasing power of millions who, today, do not enter the market at all. In fact, the argument may now be stronger since, in the Western world, there are signs on all sides that Atlantic demand is near to saturation and new markets and new needs have to be opened up to keep the vast industrial system in trim.

There is equally no change in the argument that the alternatives to assistance are all worse. Aid may not absolutely ensure progress. But there is no "may" and "might" about the unchecked regression of unaided, unreformed economies toward anarchy and collapse. Aid, therefore, in the most literal sense, remains an essential instrument in Western security.

Above all, nothing has modified the argument which should be decisive for peoples who still like to boast of their Christian and humane inheritance and contrast their performance with the evils of "godless Communism." In the last decade, the national income of the Atlantic powers has grown by at least 3 percent a year. In the next decade, it is their declared intention to add to it another $500 billion. During this same period, the people of the poorer countries are barely keeping pace. In some areas, there has been a sharp decline. Given this contrast, no Western nation can plead inability. The issue is quite simply an issue of moral will. One may be forgiven for doubting whether the rich man's professions of idealism or religion have the faintest validity so long as the world's homeless are not sheltered and the hungry are not fed.

READING 59

The 1950s and, even more so, the early 1960s have seen most peoples of the world caught up in talk about change. Age-old poverty is not disappearing rapidly, but there is a new feeling over most of the globe that something can and should be done about that poverty here and now. This very determination is itself destabilizing, for now it is obvious that the will to grow has outstripped the knowledge about how to do so.

Calvin B. Hoover, professor of economics at Duke University, feels that the time has come for sober second thoughts on what can be done to meet rising expectations. He offers a challenge in particular to some of the current assumptions about what socioeconomic reforms can contribute to the growth process. The article should be read alongside the earlier piece by Barbara Ward Jackson (page 348).

Questions to Guide the Reading

What are the essential characteristics of capitalistic and socialistic growth processes? Do they offer basically different prescriptions for growth?

What do Hoover's arguments suggest about the likelihood that satisfactory growth can take place in the midst of democratic political institutions? Can a government subject to effective challenge from a rival party afford both to restrain expectations and to take the necessary painful steps to promote growth?

RISING EXPECTATIONS MUST BE POSTPONED
Calvin B. Hoover

Maximum rate of economic growth through industrialization is now the universal goal of under-developed countries. Where these countries have recently attained their independence, as in Africa and Asia, the new national governments have held out the prospect of immediate improvement in standards of living as a consequence of the end of colonial exploitation. In Latin America, political leaders have offered to the masses a program of reform through redistribution of wealth and income, to be brought about by the overthrow of reactionary, dictatorial governments, which is to produce concurrently an increase in the economic productivity of agriculture and industry. In Africa and Asia, as well as in Latin America, it is taken for granted that socioeconomic reforms will facilitate increased industrialization, so heavily depended upon to bring about the maximum annual rate of economic growth.

The formation of the capital required for this industrialization, however, depends upon restriction of consumption through limitations of wage increases, peasant incomes and nonproductive governmental expenditures. Entrepreneurial abilities and favorable expectations must also exist if the capital saved is to be invested productively or indeed if the saving is to continue. If private entrepreneurial abilities are not exercised because favorable expectations do not exist, the investment function may alternatively be carried on by the state.

The restriction of consumption, just as has been true under Western capitalism, is nevertheless an absolute necessity, regardless of the organizational implementation of the investment function. Yet no government of any underdeveloped country would today be willing to depend upon the historical process by which the capital formation requisite to industrialization took place in the advanced countries of the West.

This unwillingness to repeat the experience of the West reflects the repudiation in most underdeveloped countries of the economic system of capitalism under which industrialization took place in the advanced countries. Thus the parliament of India, while accepting the existence of private enterprise in some sectors for an indefinite period, has nevertheless proclaimed its adherence to socialism as the economic system toward which progress is envisaged. Egypt, Algeria and Ghana, as well as most other formerly colonial countries of Africa, have proclaimed their repudiation of capitalism.

Indeed, Pakistan represents almost the only exception to the explicit or implicit repudiation of capitalism among formerly colonial countries in Africa and Asia. Among Latin American countries, which long ago threw off colonial rule but which are still underdeveloped, political instability, together with the current anticapitalist popular movements under Communist agitation, has retarded the development of modern capitalistic institutions and hence the traditional process of capital accumulation.

By the historic process through which capital accumulation took place during industrialization in the West, the increase in national income was not made available at once to the industrial workers who would have consumed it, but instead was largely vested in the bourgeoisie. The standard of living of the new industrial proletariat could rise only slowly during the early stages of capitalism in the West if sufficient capital to per-

From Calvin B. Hoover, " 'Rising Expectations' Must Be Postponed," *Challenge*, November, 1963, pp. 14–17. Reprinted with kind permission of the author and publishers. Originally published in the *Virginia Quarterly Review*, this article is also to be published as a chapter in *Growth for What*, edited by John Hallowell (Duke University Press).

mit industrialization was to be available to entre-preneurs. The capital accumulation essential to support industrialization in Western Europe was a process requiring some two or three centuries.

It is not only that there is no sign that the governments of the emerging nations of Africa and Asia are willing to depend upon the historic process of capital accumulation. There is appar-ently little realization that if the capitalistic proc-ess of capital accumulation is not to operate, *some other system which will insure the with-holding of income from the masses will have to be adopted.*

Withholding income from consumption for capi-tal accumulation is rendered more difficult by the "revolution of rising expectations." The belief that capital for industrialization can be obtained either by grants and loans from the United States, or from Soviet Russia, or from both, likewise inhibits realization of the necessity for limiting consumption of the masses. There is no possi-bility whatever that this aid could be large enough to obviate obtaining much the larger portion of the required capital funds out of domestic sources. The very real danger is that economic aid from the more industrially advanced countries will come to be depended upon as part of consumer income and may even inhibit domestic saving and investment in underdeveloped countries.

This failure to recognize the nature and neces-sity of capital accumulation is the more para-doxical since the leadership of the new nations is so generally influenced by Marxist doctrine. Marxist doctrine held that socialism could come into existence only as the successor to a capitalism which had already provided the essential eco-nomic resources through accumulation out of sur-plus value withheld from labor. Lenin had indeed amended Marx to explain how socialism might be set up in Russia in spite of its being one of the less industrialized countries.

It was Stalin, however, who through the col-lectivization of agriculture and the policy of con-centrating on heavy industry and holding the production of consumption goods to a minimum effectively withheld income from the masses. Since the Soviet leadership has, however, not admitted outright that capital for industrialization was ob-tained by this authoritarian mass withholding, it is not surprising that the Marxist-influenced leaders of the new nations have refused to rec-ognize the process of capital accumulation for what it must be under any economic system, namely, the withholding of income from con-sumption and its devotion to investment.

From the Communist point of view, a decline in productivity, or indeed economic chaos, simply hastens the end of capitalism. It is time enough, after capitalism has been overthrown, to see to it that land is not allowed to pass into the hands of individual peasants, or to reassemble peasant holdings into collective farms if temporary par-celing out of land has had to be permitted. This is the process which has gone on under Castro in Cuba. There is, indeed, a certain logic in it. As the Soviet writer S. S. Sergheev has put it in re-spect to the Soviet economic system, "All private farming contains in itself the seed of capitalist reincarnation." Even disregarding their ideologi-cal opposition to peasant ownership of land, the communists are in no doubt about the probable economic results of fragmentation of landhold-ings below optimum size.

Similarly, after a Communist takeover, there is no hesitancy about reducing real wages of workers in order to obtain capital funds for in-dustrialization, although this may be camouflaged in various ways, once more precisely as in Castro's Cuba. From the Communist point of view, this is quite logical. Although the reduction in real wages is never admitted, its actuality is justified in terms of "sacrifices willingly undertaken by the workers to build up the workers' society, at the behest of the workers' state." This, indeed, differs from the historic process of capital forma-tion under capitalism, where the capital funds accumulated by withholding from the workers become the property of capitalists for their con-sumption or for further investment.

Under a Soviet type of economic system, the capital funds accumulated are at the disposal of the "New Class" which rules the state, likewise for further investment, to the extent it is so de-cided. In contrast to the capitalist system, the workers in a Soviet type of economic system have no means of influencing investment decisions through collective bargaining, through the capital or goods markets, or through the election of par-liamentary representatives. The "New Class" sim-ply rules the state through its monopoly of all instruments of coercion and propaganda and makes decisions with respect to wage rates, con-sumption levels, and amounts and directions of capital investment and its own compensation.

In Africa, the large landholdings which have been in the hands of white settlers, as in the case of the French *colons* in Algeria and the British settlers in Kenya, are bound to be taken over by the newly decolonialized government if they are not simply seized by the indigenous inhabitants of the area. The income which formerly went to the white settlers, if it could be sequestered by the new governments and used for investment in agriculture and industry, would constitute a partial substitute for the traditional process of capital accumulation.

A decline in production is, however, likely to be the result of fragmentation of these large holdings. A shrinkage in the income which the government could otherwise obtain from taxation would be the probable result, not only from the decline in productivity, but from the decline in the surplus income above comsumption available as a source of taxation. The owners of the small holdings will increase their consumption wherever possible unless incentives for saving can be created. It sometimes seems that only the free market or something approaching an oriental despotism can withhold income from farmers once they have had political power.

Only in Egypt, among the countries which have been decolonialized, does the problem of providing funds for industrialization out of the income from industries themselves yet exist. Here a rather complicated process of partial but substantial confiscation of large industrial holdings, both foreign and domestic, has taken place. It is not yet clear whether a simple redistribution of wealth among larger numbers of persons is intended, or whether the objective is to retain governmental ownership of the confiscated shares of industrial corporations. As in the case of land, however, the government must resist the temptation to disburse too much of the industrial product to workers in industry if funds for taxes and capital for industry are to be available.

Since the free market of the capitalistic economic system cannot be counted upon in the emerging nations to facilitate the task of restraining the income of peasant producers and of workers employed in such industries as may come into existence, the state must do so. But it is likely to be difficult for a democratically controlled state apparatus to take the unpopular decisions necessary and to implement them.

In detail, the kind of decision which must be taken involves, for example, denying to the growers of a particular crop, say cocoa, rubber or cotton, the full value of the foreign exchange which is received from the exports of the crop. This has indeed been done in West Africa, but it is naturally not a popular policy with the growers of these commodities. As another example, it involves denying to the laborers in copper

mines the opportunity to use their collective bargaining power to retain for themselves the full value of the output of the mines. The absence of some sort of free enterprise market economy to aid in restricting wages, peasant incomes and consumption in general, places upon the state the necessity for taking this first step in making resources available for capital investment.

The provision of potential capital funds for investment to facilitate economic development will be useless if there does not exist either an operable political system or economic organization adequate for the investment of these potential capital funds. If the funds withheld from consumption are dissipated through political corruption, through proliferation of the state bureaucracy and an unnecessarily high standard of living for the "New Class," or through general ineptness, they are, of course, not available as a source of capital.

Even if political stability and integrity exist, then state enterprises would have to be set up to carry out investment of funds withheld from consumption, if private or corporate enterprise is not to be encouraged to do so.

That these difficulties of carrying out the processes of withholding income from consumption and providing for its investment are likely to set the stage for the establishment of the totalitarian state and a personal dictatorship is illustrated by the case of Ghana. Almost total suppression of personal liberty and the development of a "cult of personality," in which the adulation of Nkrumah surpasses, in revolting phraseology, the sycophancy of the regime of Stalin in Soviet Russia if it has not yet attained its bloodiness, now characterize the totalitarian state in Ghana. It is by no means clear, however, that the creation of a dictatorship has solved the most critical problems of capital saving and investment in that country.

In Latin America, the conflict between socioeconomic reform and the accumulation of capital for industrialization has taken even more complex forms than in the case of the underdeveloped countries of Africa and Asia. It is an article of faith among intellectuals in the United States that economic progress in Latin America depends upon economic reform. The credo further runs that economic reform is blocked by the political power of reactionary landlords and capitalists. By economic reform is meant, in the first instance, redistribution of wealth and income.

The government of the United States, indeed, insists on most of these socioeconomic reforms as a prerequisite for extending economic aid under the Alliance for Progress. The position of the United States government is that unless the tax resources of the countries to be aided are fully exploited, it is unreasonable to expect its own taxpayers to provide economic aid. This means that upper income receivers in Latin American countries should, through progressive tax rates, be required to pay as high rates of taxes as do those of the United States.

There can be no doubt that if rates of taxation on upper incomes were raised, if these taxes were actually collected, and if tax receipts were used to pay for more and better schools, road construction and other productivity-promoting activities of government, an increased rate of economic growth would be promoted thereby. There can likewise be no doubt that from a social standpoint measures to decrease the inequality of distribution of wealth and income would be desirable if these could be taken without a net loss in productivity.

It is true that under the most favorable circumstances and the most effective administration, these socioeconomic reforms would even facilitate the capital formation essential to economic growth. Unfortunately, there can be no guarantee that the victory of a party with proclaimed radical goals will increase total tax receipts from upper income groups, since measures to increase the wages of workers or to bring about redistribution of landholdings may limit or diminish production. The mistake of liberals in the United States is to assume that since redistribution of income in Latin America is desirable, almost any overt act in this direction, at least if it is not directly attributable to the Communists, will increase economic productivity.

In Chile, for example, the money wages of copper miners are already some four times the national industrial average. In addition, there are very substantial fringe benefits, including hospitalization on a lavish scale. In this case, increasing the wages of copper miners would certainly diminish investment in the copper industry and reduce the real income of other workers in Chile. Indeed, both the Anaconda and Kennecott copper companies have already cut back their investment programs drastically.

Likewise, land redistribution in Chile could be carried out without reducing production only on the basis of a most carefully administered and necessarily complex system. It is not impossible to work out plans or to administer a land redistribution program in the face of these problems,

as land redistribution in postwar Italy has demonstrated. It is difficult to do so without setting up an administrative bureaucracy which would absorb the rental values formerly going to the landlords, as the Italian experience also indicates.

Such difficulties need not and should not prevent carrying out programs of redistribution of wealth and income in Latin America. Legislation which would authorize a small beginning was passed in 1962 in Chile. A small beginning has actually been made in Colombia on the basis of legislation passed several years ago. It must be recognized that these reforms cannot be counted upon in their early stages to facilitate economic growth.

The kind of financial reform necessary to prevent runaway inflation, whether due to "cost-push" wage inflation, speculation or simply to printing press inflation, is a very different kind of economic reform from that advocated by liberals in the United States and radical leaders in Latin America. Unfortunately, economic reform which simply involves measures intended to redistribute wealth and income and to make economic growth possible will often be in conflict, and it is vital that this be recognized.

President Betancourt has demonstrated in Venezuela that it is possible to devise an economic program in which measures for social reform and for economic growth can be made reasonably compatible. His experience demonstrates also the extremes to which Communists and rightists will go to frustrate such a program. This is likely to be true in the case of such programs in the other countries of Latin America as well.

Countries which are presently underdeveloped now have the opportunity to abridge drastically the time required by the countries of Europe to acquire both the techniques and the capital required for industrialization. Underdeveloped countries can now import the techniques of advanced industrial countries instead of having to develop the techniques themselves. This transfer of technique is further very greatly facilitated by financial economic aid and technical assistance furnished gratis or at low rates by the already industrialized countries. None of the already industrialized countries had this special form of assistance from other countries.

There is also evidence that the ratio between population and natural resources is no longer so determinative in productivity as was formerly true. This development by no means eliminates the hazards of the "population explosion," but it does afford the possibility of developing economic viability if the rate of population increase can be kept within bounds.

Since in the industrialized countries of the West some 70 to 80 per cent of value added in production represents labor costs, if underdeveloped countries can keep wage rates down so that this percentage is smaller, they can become competitive on international markets. They must become internationally competitive if they are to be able to pay for imports of capital equipment and the most essential consumer goods. This is to say that in underdeveloped countries with high ratios of population to natural and capital resources, their chief resource is cheap labor. If labor costs per unit of product rise faster than labor productivity, this resource is dissipated.

In the underdeveloped countries the problems of restricting the power of the various economic groups and subgroups to seize more income for themselves than can be permitted—if economic growth is to take place—differ only in degree and in detail from those of the industrially more advanced countries such as the United States, the United Kingdom or France. In these countries problems of restricting inflation, securing adequate rates of economic growth, preventing unacceptable levels of unemployment and the like also turn on the still unsolved problems of how to limit or control the economic and political power of particular economic groups.

This involves finding supplements to or a partial substitute for the free market which used to perform this function. One could wish nostalgically that the restoration of the free market could be recommended both to developed and underdeveloped countries as the sovereign solution for these problems. The retention of as much of the free market mechanism as possible is still to be recommended. However, the phrase "as much as possible" identifies this recommendation for what it is, an attitude and not a program.

While the underdeveloped countries are struggling with these problems, it is essential that the task of their governments should not be made more difficult by our promoting the revolution of rising expectations or pretending that socioeconomic reforms always promote economic growth.

READING 60

The United States foreign aid programs have frequently had a rough time in Congress. Some of the opposition has had more hysteria and politics than careful economic analysis in it. But there have also been sober economic criticisms, most often from those who fear the growing influence of government in economic life at home and who do not want to see a similar pattern repeated, on a grander scale, in the newly independent nations.

Milton Friedman of the University of Chicago is a leader among the spokesmen for more use of free-market mechanisms here and abroad. His concern in the foreign field begins with that same acceptance of the desirability of more rapid growth in the underdeveloped countries which characterizes the pro-foreign aid camp; but, from that position, his path diverges from the philosophy which has won the support, however tenuous, of a succession of Congresses.

Questions to Guide the Reading

Are there substantial elements in our aid programs which, far from striking at the extension of market mechanisms abroad, actually enhance the strength of those mechanisms? Are there critical places both abroad and at home where market mechanisms are unsatisfactory to do the job at hand?

Do the underdeveloped countries face a "bread or freedom" choice? If faster short-run growth should be possible under centralized government with little or no democracy, what are the prospects that free-market mechanisms and democratic institutions may prove acceptable in the developing nations?

AN ALTERNATIVE TO AID
Milton Friedman

There is a tendency to describe any program in terms that will make it sound good and popular.

We speak, for example, of whether the United States Government should engage in economic aid. What economic aid in this context means is something very specific. It means subsidies by the United States Government to foreign governments, to foreign groups. The question is whether the kind of action we have engaged in under the title of foreign aid does promote either our interest or the interest of the peoples to whom the so-called aid is granted.

I think most of us believe that it is in the interests of the United States that the poorer countries of the world—the so-called underdeveloped or lesser developed countries of the world—have an opportunity to improve their own well-being, to embark on a program of economic expansion and growth, to establish strong, democratic, free governments. It is in our interest that these ends be achieved. In this I agree wholly with the people who are in favor of foreign aid.

Where I differ from them is in their belief that the way to achieve these ends is by grants of money, or funds, or technical assistance from our Government to other governments. The notion that this is the way to achieve the ends generally is simply taken for granted.

The fundamental objection to our foreign aid program is that rather than assisting the foreign countries to develop more rapidly economically, to develop a free economy or a free society, it is working in exactly the other direction. The foreign aid program in the long run will tend, I would argue, to strengthen governments in the foreign countries relative to the private sector, to promote centralized planning and socialist methods of control, and to reduce the strength and the force of the free enterprise sector, political democracy and freedom. I want to go into some of the reasons why this is so. But before doing this, however, it is worthwhile to look at experience.

Philippine experience

I suppose the oldest example of a foreign aid program at which we can look is the Philippine Islands. We do not call this a foreign aid program but in essence this is what it was. The Philippine Islands were freed after we had them 50 years. During the course of that time, we spent a lot of money there; we devoted a lot of know-how to them. What was the result? The Philippine Islands' national income tripled, and the Philippine Islands' population tripled. The average income per person in the Philippine Islands at the end of 50 years of American stewardship was not far from where it was at the beginning.

We have a closer example of the effects of a foreign aid program. It is a much more dramatic and striking one—the famous island 90 miles from our shore. We have been engaged in foreign aid to Cuba for a long time; there is no other way to regard our sugar subsidy to Cuba. We have been buying sugar from Cuba at two cents a pound more than we pay the rest of the world. This was a foreign aid subsidy.

We have other examples where we have had formal foreign aid programs since a few years after the end of the war, originally in the form of the Marshall Plan which went to Europe, more recently in the form of economic aid to a very large number of countries spread throughout the world. Suppose you were to ask, as I have done at times, people in the foreign aid program, the ICA (I want to make it clear that I am not prejudiced against them at all. Some of my best friends work for the ICA. In fact, I have worked for them myself.)—"how have your programs been going? Where have you been successful? In what countries of the world has American economic aid stimulated growth?" You will, for the most part, get an embarrassed silence.

Why is it that foreign subsidies do not promote our major objective of strengthening economically the underdeveloped countries of the world or of helping them toward free, democratic governments? So far as the direct political effect of foreign aid is concerned, almost everyone—including almost all proponents of foreign aid—agree that it is adverse to the objectives we want to achieve. Because our foreign aid involves our giving money from our Government to another government, this strengthens the other government at the expense of the private sector.

From Milton Friedman, "An Alternative to Aid," *Wall Street Journal*, April 30, 1962. Reprinted with kind permission of the author and publisher.

The necessary condition

It is perfectly clear from history that there has never been a politically free society unless the bulk of its activities were organized through the private market known as free enterprise; there is no exception to this—there has never been a society, as far as I know, which has been economically centralized and politically free at the same time. This does not mean that economic freedom and free enterprise is in itself enough to guarantee political freedom, for societies have existed that have been economically free but politically very far from free. What I am saying is something else; economic freedom and reliance on the market system is a necessary, but not alone a sufficient, condition for political freedom. On the political side it is clear that the grants to a foreign government strengthen that government at the expense of the private sector, promote socialism, and thus are adverse to freedom.

Those proponents of foreign aid who grant this regard it as only a temporary phenomenon, a cross which must be borne. On the other hand, they say: The underdeveloped nations are determined to develop and grow and they are going to do it one way or another. There is no chance at all for political freedom and democracy unless they can grow. Therefore, we must endure the temporary cost of strengthening their governments in order to achieve the objective of promoting their economic growth so that in the course of time a solid economic foundation for a democratic and free society can be built. In this manner the argument is economic, even on the political side.

The belief that subsidies to foreign governments promote economic development rests fundamentally on three propositions which have become a widely accepted view about the process of economic growth. The three propositions are: First, the availability of capital—money, resources to get machinery, factories, and the like—is the key to economic development. Second, the underdeveloped countries of the world are too poor to provide the capital for themselves and therefore it must come from outside. Third, in these countries, centralized control is needed in order to promote development.

I want to consider each of the propositions in turn because each seems to me a misleading half truth. Let us start with the first proposition: That capital is the key to economic development. There is no doubt that other things being the same, the more capital the better. Capital is important. It is nice to have the wherewithal to build machines, factories and so forth. But how capital contributes to a nation's well-being and growth depends a great deal on how it is used. The pyramids of Egypt involved enormous capital formation and capital expenditures. I do not think anyone would maintain that the pyramids of Egypt contributed in any significant way to the economic growth of ancient Egypt.

One of the important things about capital made available to governments on a gift basis from another government is that it is very likely to be used for such monuments. There is hardly an underdeveloped country in the world today that does not have an underdeveloped airline. It is a sign of a modern nation that it has an airway, so every government in every nation is determined to have a modern airway.

We could go down the line in case after case but I think I have said enough to make my main point clear. While capital is important for economic development, it is not by itself a guarantee of economic development. It can be wasted. Much depends on how it is used and the important thing to consider is that the kind of capital made available is very likely to be misused. It is likely to be misused and wasted for two reasons. First, because it goes to a government and government's interests are not the same as the interests of the masses of the people in the country. The government interests are the interests of getting prestige, of monument building. Second, because of the natural tendency to treat things that you get for nothing as if they are worth nothing.

In addition, the capital made available to government is not a net gain of capital because it induces government to follow policies which will discourage other sources of capital. In the first place, when governments obtain capital from abroad, they tend to follow internal policies which discourage internal savings. They tend to follow policies of governmental control, of governmental domination of industry, of controls on private groups. Governments tend also to adopt policies which discourage the inflow of capital from abroad.

Providing capital

A second point that is made is that these underdeveloped countries are too poor to provide the capital for themselves; therefore, it must be made available from the outside. Well, let me point out first that outside capital can be made available in other forms. The United States, in the course of its development, obtained lots of capital from the outside, but it obtained it in the form of interest-bearing loans. It paid interest on the loans and it paid the loans, so this is no argument for gifts.

It is obvious that a poor country can provide its own savings, or else no country could ever have developed. All countries were once poor. Where did the first country get its assistance? Actually, if the conditions are right for economic development, there will be no shortage of capital. No matter how low its level of living, every country is in a position to accumulate capital if its people have the incentive, the drive, and the desire to make some part of it available.

The third argument is that you need a governmentally centralized, controlled and planned program of economic development. This again is a half-truth. It is certainly true that government plays a very important role in economic development. It must establish law and order to protect private property, enforce contracts, provide a stable money and do many things such as providing roads, facilities and the like. But this is a far cry from saying that what is needed for economic development is centralized government control over industry or over the use of capital. On the contrary, this is a hindrance to economic development.

What is the real problem of development in these countries? What is needed are change, flexibility and a set of institutions which will make it possible to take advantage of new developments and to disregard those that do not work. We all know the characteristics of government control. A major one is that it induces rigidity. It is very difficult for government to recognize its mistakes. It might well be that in underdeveloped countries at the present time governments might be just as good as private individuals in choosing what plant to put up or even in running them. But there would, nonetheless, be a decisive difference in that a private plant can go broke and government enterprises are very unlikely to go broke. If government makes a mistake that mistake will be subsidized by taxes or it will be supported by import duties.

I think I can illustrate some of these points that I have been making and show how widespread are the beliefs that underlie them by quoting a couple of remarks from a report given some years ago to a special committee of the Senate which was studying foreign aid programs. This is a report prepared at Massachusetts Institute of Technology. One of the authors was Walt Rostow (now a high Government official).

The report considered what criterion to use to determine whether a country should have more or less foreign aid. The criterion given was whether the country was making an additional national effort toward economic development. How do we know this? Well, said the report, there are two rules of thumb. One, and I quote: "One index that national effort is being mobilized for development is the launching of measures to capture a good fraction of increase in income for the purpose of further investment." The second index, and I quote again: "Another measure of national effort is the degree to which a country's leaders have worked out an over-all development program."

The striking thing about those criteria is that under them the United States of America would never have qualified. At no time in the course of the history of the United States have we had measures to capture a good part of increase in income for the purpose of further investment. Individuals have been free to invest or not.

What these standards involve is a centralized governmental collectivist technique of growth. The only countries that can satisfy these criteria in the modern world are the Communist countries behind the iron curtain. And interestingly enough, they have not succeeded in raising the standard of living of their people either.

So what our foreign aid program involves is essentially accepting the premises of the system against which we are fighting. We are engaged in an ideological war with a hostile ideology. The way to win that war is not to accept the premises of that ideology.

What we ought to do is to practice what we preach. We have been going around preaching the virtues of free enterprise, of free competition in a free market. What have we been doing? We've been practicing the opposite, not only through our foreign aid program, but also at home. We tell other countries: Use the market; we tell our farmers, look to Washington. We tell other countries, don't try to be self-sustained; try to develop valuable industries that can compete on the international market, and then what do we do? We impose import quotas on oil, we impose tariffs on goods that come in, we dump agricultural products abroad and impose quotas on their import at home. The rest of the world listens to what we say and they think "now there is a fine bunch of hypocrites" and they are right.

Produce and sell

Contemplate the effect in the world on our international economic position and our international political position if, instead of foreign aid grants, we said to the rest of the world: Within the course of the next five years we are going to tear down our trade barriers, open our ports, eliminate all import and export controls and have a free market. Under those circumstances, we would say to other nations: "Here you are, here is your opportunity: if you can really produce and really increase your ouput, you can sell here."

I think it is easy to underestimate the importance of promoting our ideas in the world, our moving in this direction. I happen to be a free trader and I think that we would benefit at home from free trade because it would enable us to use our own resources better, to get things where they are cheap. But leave that aside for the moment. I want to talk from the international point of view about the alternative of free trade as opposed to the sort of foreign aid now being proposed.

In the first place, our tariffs and the tariffs which they induce in other countries tend to inhibit the process of foreign investment, although it is true that some investment is encouraged by it. If India puts up a tariff so that automobiles cannot be imported, then an automobile plant may be established in India, and this encourages private investment. But from a world point of view that private investment is wasted; it is being used to produce in India what could be produced more cheaply here or somewhere else.

Knitting the world together

But more important than this, I think, is the extent to which trade is a carrier of culture. What is it that knit the world together in the 19th Century, that produced a greater degree of movement? More than anything else, it was unquestionably the British free trade policy. If you go abroad in country after country and ask: "Where does the United States influence come from?", the answer is that it does not come from the United States Information Service; it does not come from the missions of VIPs who go abroad to see what foreign aid projects can be used. The American influence abroad comes from Coca-Cola, from Singer Sewing Machines, and the other great American industries which spread their goods and services abroad.

Now I cannot, of course, hope to outline this sort of a program completely. I have set it up and discussed the free trade alternative in order to show the difference between a program which is based on our beliefs and a program which is based on the beliefs we are fighting.

And the main conclusion I would like to leave is that in examining our so-called foreign aid program and our program of grants from one government to another, we recognize the extent to which this is based on the premises to which we are opposed. I suggest we take another look and ask ourselves, ought we not to be playing from our strength, from the belief in freedom that has enabled us to develop our society. Is that not the direction in which we ought to try to spread American influence rather than through grants of money abroad?

Part 6

AMERICA'S UNFINISHED BUSINESS

Much of the excitement of being a participant in the American economy comes from a sense that whatever has happened to date is not nearly good enough for tomorrow. Hence, our economic system must prove itself again and again—not only by its remarkable past record, but by its ability to make meaningful dents in wholly new sets of problems and by its continuing ability to deal with persistent problems out of the past.

Here, one of America's most distinguished economists, Arthur F. Burns of Columbia University and the National Bureau of Economic Research, who served as chairman of President Eisenhower's Council of Economic Advisers from 1953 through 1956, surveys some of our economy's continuing challenges and opportunities against the background of its achievements to date.

Questions to Guide the Reading

In what ways do the problems discussed here differ from some of our problems in the past? In what ways do they differ from those faced by other countries in the world today?

Are there any ways in which our contemporary problems are less pressing than some of those we have faced in the past? Are there any ways in which they are more urgent?

What implications does this reading carry for the types of problems which we are likely to have high on our agenda of unfinished business in 1970?

OUR UNFINISHED BUSINESS
Arthur F. Burns

The outstanding social achievement of our times has been the expansion of economic opportunity in our country. We had great prosperity during the 1920's, but the fruits of that prosperity were not shared widely enough. We carried out major social reforms during the 1930's, but in the best year of that decade close to eight million men and women were unemployed. We practically eliminated unemployment during the 1940's, but a huge part of people's savings was simultaneously wiped out by inflation. Poverty, unemployment, unstable money—each of these has been a great destroyer of opportunity through the ages. These obstacles to progress appear smaller as we face the tasks of the future.

Let me cite a few facts on the spread of economic opportunity and well-being. First, jobs have been generally plentiful in recent years. Opportunities for useful work have increased for women as well as men, for the elderly as well as the young, even for the physically handicapped.

Second, a progressive shift has been under way from low-paid and unskilled occupations to well-paid and more interesting work. The professional, scientific, and managerial group is growing rapidly and already accounts for over a fifth of the nation's work force.

Third, small and independent businesses continue to be an important gateway of economic opportunity, despite the giant corporations that seem at times to surround us. Over four and a half million independent concerns are presently engaged in various types of business and their number is growing. Indeed, there are more business firms today, both absolutely and in relation to the size of the nation's work force, than there were ten, twenty, or thirty years ago.

From Arthur F. Burns, "An Economist's View of Our Unfinished Business," *The Reporter*, November 24, 1960. Reprinted with kind permission of the author and publisher.

Fourth, our progressively rising national income is being shared widely. The ownership of a good home, an automobile, a refrigerator, an electric washer, a television set, has become the rule rather than the exception in American family life.

Fifth, the disruptive forces of the business cycle have at last been brought under moderately good control. The recessions of the past twenty years were merely pauses in the general advance of prosperity. Not only that, but their impact on the lives of individuals has been blunted through unemployment insurance, the growth of pensions, flexible taxes, better corporate management, a sounder banking system, and a somewhat nicer adjustment of governmental policies to the needs of the economy.

Sixth, the pace of inflation has been materially checked in the past few years. In consequence, we may have greater assurance that the savings accumulated through our bank accounts, savings bonds, insurance policies, and pension funds will remain intact for meeting life's contingencies and opportunities.

These extensions of economic opportunity are a moral as well as an economic achievement. Far from being an isolated development, they are merely the most recent installment in a long history of progress. Amidst all the conflicts, exuberance, and turbulence of history, one fact that repeatedly stands out is our determination to seek progress by expanding freedom and opportunity. Can there be any doubt that individual liberty and equal opportunity are and must remain our basic ideals? I do not think that many of us want merely to live in peace, have a steady job, and enjoy an abundance of bread, automobiles, or symphonies. We value and want all that, but we value still more the practice of freedom. We want to remain free to choose our occupations, to live where we see fit, to worship God as our conscience dictates, to speak our minds without fear, to choose as our governing officials those who we think can serve us best, to work for ourselves or for employers of our own choosing, and to spend or to save or to invest as we think proper.

This is the great message of freedom and opportunity which America first gave to the world and which Communism is now challenging aggressively. If our message is ultimately to triumph, we must diligently practice its principles. It is characteristic of freedom and opportunity that they can evolve and expand indefinitely, and that is why a free society will always find new things

to do. In today's troubled world the two tasks that seem most urgent are, first, to continue aiding the poorer nations whose peoples are restlessly seeking improvement and, second, to make a greater effort to draw into the stream of progress those who have been left behind by its onrush in our own land.

Those left behind

Despite the high level of employment in recent times, substantial unemployment has persisted in some communities in different parts of our country. The problem posed by these depressed areas is not new, as anyone familiar with ghost towns that were once thriving centers of commerce realizes. A progressive economy such as ours will always be characterized by uneven development of its parts, and it would be folly to ignore this truth. However, the very advances and improvements I have mentioned are encouraging the American people to apply more exacting standards to the performance of our economy. As we have become concerned about local pockets of unemployment, the belief has grown that these communities must not be left to their own devices and that both the Federal and state governments can do more to enable them to help themselves than has yet been attempted.

We can expect extensive experimentation in the future with retraining programs for workers, technical assistance to local groups in devising plans for rehabilitating their economy, and schemes for financing industrial projects that promise to improve a community's long-range economic outlook. These social innovations should be welcomed. Wisely administered, they will serve to ease the harsh adjustments that are often forced on people by a changing economic environment. At the same time we will need to be on our guard that the efforts of government are not carried to the point of weakening the spirit of adventure, initiative, and self-reliance on which both our free society and our economic prosperity ultimately rest.

A more difficult and more serious problem than the chronic unemployment in a few of our cities is the ineffectiveness of human effort in many of our rural areas. Here we find numerous families struggling on farms that are too small or too poor for efficient operation. Here we find inadequate skills on the part of people and inadequate opportunities for off-farm employment. The remaining poverty in America largely centers in these areas.

Whether governmental price supports have proved an advantage or a hindrance for farmers as a class may be debated, but it is plain that they have done little for the marginal farmer. Nor can much be expected of schemes of this type in the future. The most constructive way of aiding low-income families in farming areas is to attack the causes of their trouble, which center around their low productivity. This cannot be accomplished quickly, since it will be necessary to improve the skills of these people and, more important still, their children's education. It will be necessary also to raise their standards of health and nutrition, to improve the sanitary conditions under which they live, to devise credit arrangements suited to their needs, to enlarge or create opportunities for obtaining off-farm jobs in their communities, and to develop better means of conveying information about jobs in distant places. These reforms can be carried out most effectively through local initiative, both private and public. The Federal government can, however, be very helpful in stimulating and coordinating the local efforts. The Rural Development Program, which was established on these general principles a few years ago, is so full of promise for the future that it deserves to be pursued with a greater sense of urgency.

The economic position of the small businessman also requires thoughtful attention. During the past generation certain basic changes in our economic environment—in particular rising taxes, the accelerating pace of technology, and the spread of national advertising—have complicated the problems of organization, survival, and growth of smaller businesses. Small firms have always had little or no access to the public markets for capital. In the past, however, they were able to expand their plant, equipment, and markets by plowing profits back into their businesses. The extent to which that can be done nowadays is severely limited by the heavy burdens of taxation. We must recognize and be prepared to deal with this and other restrictions on the opportunities of small businesses, so that they may be able in time to challenge the primacy of old-established and often oversized firms.

But surely the most pressing of all our domestic needs is to enlarge the economic opportunities of colored citizens. Despite the great progress of the Negro during the past century, political discrimination has continued on an extensive scale throughout the South and economic discrimination to some degree has persisted prac-

tically everywhere. The consequence is that Negroes are still mainly engaged in unskilled occupations, that their productivity and incomes continue to be relatively low, that many of them remain jobless even when employers find cause to complain about labor shortages, that their children are often denied the opportunity to develop their capacity for a useful and dignified life, that the growth of our entire economy is held back, and—worst of all—that Americans as a people are burdened with an uneasy conscience.

It is proper that we do what we can to remedy the depressed status of the Negro through new legislation. What we need most, however, is a broader and more persistent educational effort. All too often we think of education exclusively in terms of formal schooling in English, mathematics, science, and other academic disciplines. But education involves also training in citizenship, in ethics, and in personal manners. It involves, besides, vocational training, vocational guidance, and practical assistance to employers or employees who may harbor fanciful notions about the capabilities of this or that group of people. The job of educating ourselves sufficiently to overcome racial prejudice will not be accomplished rapidly under the best of circumstances, but we will make faster progress if we recognize that reform of our laws cannot be the end of the quest for equal opportunity for the Negro.

They are watching us

An enlargement of the economic opportunities of the Negro, of marginal farmers, of small businesses, and of the few areas suffering from chronic unemployment should bring great advantages to our country. If we go about these tasks with practical understanding, we will improve the general welfare, broaden the base of our future prosperity, and invigorate our children's faith in institutions that advance freedom and widespread opportunity. But these are not the only advantages. What happens in America is nowadays of great concern also to the nations of Latin America, Asia, Africa, in fact everywhere. Modern science and technology have made all these people—hundreds of millions of them inadequately fed and poorly informed—our neighbors. Having recently heard echoes of a better life, they are now stirring restlessly to achieve it, although they commonly lack the means or the knowledge to do so. Our historic message of freedom and opportunity will mean more to people abroad than it has of late, if we practice it with greater vigor in handling our international relations as well as the problems at home.

We are accustomed to thinking of international relations as being exclusively the business of governments, but that of course is not true. Private citizens always play a role, and their role is apt to be more fundamental than that of government officials.

Over a great part of our history we held out a hand of welcome to immigrants. The many millions who swarmed to our shores were preponderantly of European stock; but people came here from every corner of the world seeking adventure, economic opportunity, personal freedom, religious tolerance. Some immigrants broke their ties with the Old World, but many maintained them by sending money, food, clothing, and messages to their relatives or friends back home. When a letter from America arrived in a European village or town, it was often passed from hand to hand and soon the entire community knew its contents. Remembering the men or women who had written, people were well disposed to believe what they heard or read. Of course, not all immigrants liked everything about America; they said so and sometimes proved it by returning to their native land. But the great majority stayed, participated in building and adorning the New World, prospered as the rest of us prospered, kept their distant kinsmen informed of their doings, and in the process did far more to spread America's message of freedom and opportunity than our official ambassadors ever accomplished or could accomplish. Largely as a result of such unplanned efforts, America became known the world over as the land of freedom, equality, opportunity, abundance, and —as popular exaggeration would have it—a land in which even ordinary men could perform miracles.

I believe that we lost something very precious when we gradually permitted the tensions in our society to tempt us into an immigration policy that, besides becoming severely restrictive, loudly professes that some races or peoples are superior to others.

Of late, financial grants and easy loans to other nations have assumed a large role in our foreign policy, but there is a limit to what dollars can accomplish in human affairs—as every individual discovers sooner or later in working out his personal adjustments. Nothing can match the warmth or understanding evoked by a willingness to share the joys and sorrows of life with others, and we must learn to give larger expression to this human principle in handling our international affairs. Although there is no prospect of returning to our earlier immigration policy, which served so powerfully to promote understanding of our national objectives and way of life, we need not lose time in raising the present quotas, which are unreasonably low, or in removing their offensive accent of discrimination. We surely need to devote far more effort than we now do to the study of foreign languages and foreign cultures and we need to use this knowledge actively—by traveling, studying, and doing business abroad, by corresponding with foreign citizens and encouraging our children to do so, by joining with our townsmen to enable foreigners to visit our communities, by welcoming them and other visitors to our homes, and in such other ways as will appeal to thoughtful men and women who want to do their part, as private citizens, in bettering international understanding.

But private efforts to promote international good will cannot suffice in a world that has suddenly shrunk as a result of the marvelous discoveries and applications of science. The enormous disparities of wealth, income, and education among the nations are now exposed to everyone's view, and therefore raise moral as well as political problems. Suppose that we awoke one morning and found that our own homes had become surrounded during the night by shacks filled with hungry, superstitious, and illiterate men who had come to stay. Is it not likely that we would begin to wonder about our personal security or the permanence of our prosperity? But if these fears were quieted in the course of the day by the discovery that our new and unwished neighbors seemed on the whole to be law-abiding citizens, would not our hearts soon respond to their misery? Would not practical sense lead us, besides donating what we could from our pantries, to take common counsel on the best ways of helping them to find useful jobs, obtain medical care and also some sort of schooling, so that they could in time become resourceful and productive members of our community? And would we not see that some of these needs, such as schooling, could be met more swiftly and more securely through our local government than through voluntary efforts?

I think that in this paradigm I have expressed the essence of the problem of foreign economic aid in our time. The seriousness of the problem is intensified by the menace of Communism, but the problem would be grave enough without it. As the world's principal architect of personal freedom and opportunity, to say nothing of being the richest of nations, the United States neither can nor should want to avoid carrying the major responsibility for assisting, through public as well as private means, the poor and underdeveloped nations.

We must keep in mind, however, that large-scale governmental economic assistance is a new concept and that we need to keep reviewing our aid programs, so that we may learn how to manage them wisely. I have stressed the importance of education as a means of expanding opportunity for a better life for Americans. The need for schooling at all levels is all the greater in the new and struggling nations. Certainly, one of the greatest obstacles to their development is the scarcity of skilled and professional manpower. We and other well-to-do nations have tried to be helpful, but no nation either can or wants to depend entirely on the outside world for its essential skills. On the other hand, there are limits to the number of native students who can be sent abroad for training. For not only is the cost very heavy, but it has been found that some of the students return home with an education that is not suited to local needs.

Let us suppose, therefore, that our government, duly mindful of the pride as well as the practical needs of other countries, advised each of several of the poorer nations that, if it so wished, we would build for its people a university to train students in engineering, agriculture, medicine, public administration, and other professions, and that we would assist in staffing the faculty only to the extent we were requested to do so. The financial cost to us would not be large, as such things go in our time, and perhaps could be met by redirecting some of the present outlays on economic aid. In any event, the benefits of such a program could repay the cost a thousand times over. Few Americans appreciate the love, respect—indeed, the reverence—for learning that exists even among the poor and illiterate people of other lands. To very many of them a university is a temple in which men come closer to God— a temple that will still be there, distributing its blessings, after they have gone. But the universities of which I speak, besides being noble monuments to international good will, would have the immediate and practical purpose of widening the opportunities of many for a better life. With universities of their own, the poorer nations could in time train the thousands of professional experts they so urgently need.

These reflections on the need for universities, however seriously one may take them, matter less than the generalization to which they point, namely, that the kind of aid we extend to other nations and the way in which we do it are just as vital as the amount of aid. It may be tempting, in view of the embarrassments of our agricultural plenty, to persuade foreign nations to take some foodstuffs off our hands when they would prefer machinery. It may again be tempting, in view of the deficit in our international accounts, to require that foreign credits be spent on goods produced in the United States. Such practices, however, run counter to the principles of freedom which we are trying so earnestly to communicate and to share with other nations. Not only that, but they spread distrust of our motives and can harm our foreign policies.

To be sure, we have our domestic problems, and the two I have just mentioned are serious, but we should be wise enough to seek constructive solutions. In the case of agriculture, if we pursue policies that prevent surpluses from arising in the first place, we will not need to invent ways of pushing them out. And as for our balance-of-payments difficulties, we are likely to do well enough if, besides persuading other prosperous nations to do their part in helping to provide development capital to needy areas, we ourselves cling resolutely to domestic policies that promote reasonable stability of costs and prices. By so doing we will not only stimulate export trade far more effectively than by any "Buy American" arrangements, but we will also provide assurance to foreign governments, banks, and investors that the billions of dollars which they have elected to hold here will remain safe.

If my sketch of current needs and possibilities is anywhere near the mark, our generation can look forward with a sense of exhilaration to the continued enlargement of human freedom and economic opportunity. But as we bend our energies to this high objective, we should bear in mind the teaching of history that monopolies, pockets of special privilege, even governmental tyrannies can grow out of misguided efforts to enlarge opportunities for a good life. These misadventures of the human spirit should not diminish our zeal for improvement, but they should lead us to support our idealism and compassion with economic statesmanship.

A disciplined idealism

Let us proceed then with vigor to devise or improve special programs for bringing the lagging parts or groups of our own economy and of the outside world into the stream of progress.

Let us be careful, at the same time, not to underestimate what our government accomplishes through policies that operate with some uniformity over the economy as a whole, as when anti-trust laws are passed to foster open and competitive markets, when tax laws are reformed to stimulate investment in better tools of production, when monetary and fiscal arrangements are adjusted to promote a high level of employment and reasonable stability of the price level, or when tax revenues are spent on research, education, roads, airports, and other investments to enhance the productivity of the private economy. When jobs are readily available and the produc-

tivity of labor is rising, the most powerful of all forces are already operating through the market place to lift low incomes, to increase opportunities, and to spread prosperity. Nor are these effects confined to the domestic economy. As our economy grows, so also will our imports from the less developed nations, and this will mean even more to them than direct economic aid.

When all is said and done, our largest contribution to world progress is likely to be the example of an expanding economy that remains both strong and humane, precisely because our eagerness to enlarge freedom and opportunity is disciplined by economic intelligence.

READING 62

So many definitions of automation abound that a man may well conclude from one reading that this is nothing more than a publicist's name for ordinary technological change, and from another that it represents a new force to make man expendable and the machine supreme. The most careful definitions lie between these two extremes and start with the assumption that automation represents significant breakthroughs in combining familiar automatic materials-handling methods with new electronic equipment capable of (1) processing masses of complex data and (2) discovering and feeding back necessary corrections in the flow process. Much technological change from the past extends the powers of the human body; automation adds to this an extension of the powers of the human mind.

The promise of benefits in automation is as clear as our dependence on higher productivity for higher living standards. But automation may also pose serious problems in the total number of jobs available and in the skills required for those jobs. The fears of men directly threatened by job changes are unlikely to be removed by bland assurances that automation eventually creates more jobs than it destroys; these men will understandably reply, "Show me."

The late President Kennedy created a special 21-man Advisory Committee on Labor-Management Policy. These men from unions, companies, and the public had as one of their assignments a report on automation's most likely benefits and problems. This reading is the heart of their report and their recommendations for minimizing the harm while drawing the maximum good from the new productive processes. Dissenting and supplementary views from individual members are included, but the report still stands as an example of rather broad agreement on a vexing policy issue.

Questions to Guide the Reading

How do the issues posed by automation relate to other issues raised in these readings such as economic stability, economic growth, and international trade?

Which of the Committee's recommendations break new ground and which simply extend existing policies? Are the recommendations adequate or excessive to meet the challenges posed by automation? What difference does it make whether or not most of the proposals are implemented?

THE CHALLENGE OF AUTOMATION
President's Advisory Committee on Labor-Management Policy

Three central propositions have emerged in the Committee's consideration of the significance and impact of automation and other technological advances.

First, automation and technological progress are essential to the general welfare, the economic strength, and the defense of the Nation.

Second, this progress can and must be achieved without the sacrifice of human values and without inequitable cost in terms of individual interests.

Third, the achievement of maximum technological development with adequate safeguards against economic injury to individuals depends upon a combination of private and governmental action, consonant with the principles of the free society.

Automation and technological change have meant much to our country. Today the average worker in the United States works shorter hours, turns out more goods, receives higher wages, and has more energy harnessed and working with him than a worker anywhere else in the world. Increasingly, machines are relieving men of heavy physical labor and of dangerous and repetitive work. Competition in the world markets has been possible against foreign countries whose standards of living are below our own, though this advantage is diminishing. Finally, in a world split by ideological differences, automation and technological change have a tremendous and crucial role to play in maintaining the strength of the free world.

For these reasons, we emphasize at the outset the imperative need for and desirability of automation and technological change. Indeed, increased productivity and fuller utilization of resources are urgently needed to improve our rate of economic growth. They are likewise needed to improve our competitive position in world markets. Failure to advance technologically and to otherwise increase the productivity of our economy would bring on much more serious unemployment and related social problems than any we now face.

It is equally true that the current rate of technological advance has created social problems and that an acceleration of this rate may intensify these problems.

While advancing technology has given rise to new industries and jobs, it has also resulted in employee displacement; and the fact that new work opportunities are eventually created is no comfort or help to the displaced individual who cannot, for one reason or another, secure comparable or any employment. While employment has expanded in some industries, the net effect of rising output per worker, of the growing labor force, and of other factors has been an increase in the volume of unemployment during the past few years—even as total employment has reached new heights.

The impact of technology on agricultural employment has been particularly great. Along with other factors, it has resulted in over 1,600,000 workers—20 percent of the total—leaving the farms since 1950. Yet farm output has increased 28 percent, making available to our people an abundance of food, while there was famine in some of the Communist countries. This increased output enabled this country to be of substantial assistance to needy people elsewhere in the world.

Our purpose, then, is to seek that course of action which will encourage essential progress in the form of automation and technological change, while meeting at the same time the social consequences such change creates.

We recognize that the subject of automation and technological change cannot be dealt with apart from two broader subjects: increased productivity in general, and unemployment.

We note here the basic importance of economic growth to any consideration of the problems—and the opportunities—automation and technological advance present.

Regarding technological advance and unemployment, it is clear that unemployment has resulted from displacement due to automation and technological change. It is impossible, with presently available data, to isolate that portion of present unemployment resulting from these causes. Whether such displacement will be short-run depends to a considerable extent on our ability to anticipate and plan for programs involving technological change and to make better use of vari-

From *Automation: Report of the President's Advisory Committee on Labor-Management Policy* (Government Printing Office, Washington, 1962), pp. 1–9.

ous mechanisms for retraining and relocating workers who find themselves unneeded in their former occupations. We have necessarily given general consideration in this report to some aspects of the broader unemployment problem and to the prospects of more effective use of the work force.

A long stride toward solution of the unemployment problem will be made if we first recognize the nature of the problem. We regard the following factors as important in this connection:

1. The recent rate of economic growth in the United States has been insufficient to reduce unemployment to a tolerable level.

2. The exact extent of unemployment attributable to automation and technological change is unknown, since it is greatly complicated by other factors, such as:

   a. The economic recession of 1960–61.

   b. The unusually high entrance rate into the labor market, caused by the great postwar population increase. In the next 10 years it is expected that there will be a net gain in the labor force of 13½ million workers.

   c. Chronic unemployment in distressed areas.

   d. The effects of the rapid advances which have been made by foreign competitors.

   e. Changing consumption patterns.

   f. The changing nature of jobs which often leaves a gap between job requirements and qualifications of applicants. During the 1950's there was a 58 percent increase in the number of skilled technical and professional workers. Unskilled workers, with only a limited education, found it more difficult to get, or hold, a job. In this connection, the Department of Labor projections indicate that unless steps are taken to reduce the dropout rate among high school students, some 7½ million of those new workers joining the labor force in the 1960's, or more than 30 percent, will not have completed high school, and over 2½ million of them will not even have completed grade school.

   g. Discrimination against workers on the basis of age, sex, race, and creed.

   h. Multiple jobholding by individuals.

   i. The continuing movement of workers away from the farms.

3. Public employment service facilities have been inadequate as well as seriously uneven in their effectiveness with respect to helping workers find new jobs, counseling them as to the kind of jobs which are liable to be available in the future, and advising them as to job prospects in other geographical areas.

4. The mobility of workers is reduced by factors running contrary to the demands of a dynamic society, and an economy in transition.

   a. The nontransferability of pension, seniority, and other accumulated rights may result in an employee's being dependent upon his attachment to a particular job as the sole means of protecting his equities.

   b. Desirable and essential mobility is affected by reluctance to leave home—because of personal ties, or because other members of the family may be working; by the cost of moving and possible losses on local property; and by the insecurity of jobs in a new locality.

5. Educational and informational facilities have been inadequate in that:

   a. The requirements for general education prior to vocational and professional training have not kept pace with the shift in job opportunities.

   b. The required types of vocational and technical training and retraining are often not available, e.g., for workers leaving the farm.

   c. There has been an inadequate liaison among school systems, industry, and government with respect to future job requirements, and in fact there is insufficient information about the nature of such jobs.

   d. There has been inadequate financial support for needy students.

   e. Counseling facilities have been generally inadequate.

6. Proper retraining facilities, and a system of financial support for workers while retraining, have been lacking.

These are some of the relevant circumstances of a society in which automation and technological advance are essential motive forces. The operation of these forces within the social context creates serious displacement problems—not as a necessary price of progress but as the stern consequence of failure to recognize and provide for these problems. We reject the too common assumption that continuing unemployment is an inherent cost of automation.

We believe, rather, that a combination of energetic and responsible private and public action will permit the advancement of automation and technological change without the sacrifice of human values, and that such combined efforts can cope satisfactorily with the total unemployment problem—including whatever part of it may arise from the displacements which result inevitably from the introduction of new devices and processes.

We do not attempt here an exhaustive exploration or enumeration of all the ways and means of achieving maximum technological progress with the minimum of individual disadvantage. Our suggestions can be only representative of a broader set of possibilities. We recognize, furthermore, that the totality of any combination of recommendations must be viewed in the light of such relevant factors as their costs to individual enterprises, their effect on the Federal budget, and their influence on general price levels.

We recommend that serious consideration be given the following measures:

1. Adoption by the government and others of policies which will promote a high rate of economic growth and fuller utilization of resources. A much higher rate of growth is essential and is the best device for reducing unemployment to tolerable levels.

2. Acceptance by government agencies of the responsibility for collecting, collating, and disseminating information with respect to present and future job opportunities and requirements in a rapidly changing society.

3. Cooperation between government and private organizations in the field of education in improving and supporting educational facilities to the end that:

a. New entrants to the labor force will be better qualified to meet the occupational demands of the future;

b. The dropout rate at grade and high school levels will be reduced;

c. Better vocational, technical, and guidance programs will be available;

d. Rural and depressed areas, where surplus workers reside, will be better served;

e. Financial support will be available for deserving and needy students; and

f. There will be a general upgrading in the quality of our education.

4. Acceptance by management of responsibility for taking measures, to the maximum extent practicable, for lessening the impact of technological change, including:

a. Adequate lead time.

b. Open reporting to the employees involved.

c. Cooperation with representatives of the employees to meet the problems involved.

d. Cooperation with public employment services.

e. The timing of changes, to the extent possible, so that potential unemployment will be cushioned by expected expansion of operations and normal attrition in the work force (through separations resulting from retirement, quits, and so forth).

5. Support from both public and private organizations for retraining of workers who have been and will be displaced.

a. Private employers and unions faced with automation or technological changes should make every reasonable effort to enable workers who are being displaced, and who need to be retrained, to qualify for new jobs available with the same employer, and to enjoy a means of support while so engaged.

b. Where it is not possible for the employer to reabsorb displaced workers, appropriately safeguarded public support in the form of subsistence payments should be available to industrial and agricultural workers who qualify for and engage in retraining.

c. Unemployment compensation laws should be liberalized to permit and to encourage retraining.

6. Support from both public and private sources, with due consideration to the circumstances of the enterprise involved, for the displaced worker who is seeking new employment.

a. The duration, coverage, and amount of unemployment compensation, where inadequate, should be increased and made subject to realistic uniform minimum requirements under the Federal-State system.

b. Employer supplementation of public unemployment compensation should be accomplished through severance pay, supplemental unemployment benefits, and similar measures.

c. Attention should be given to provision for the special case of the worker who is displaced during the period when he is approaching retirement. This may appropriately include consideration of provision for early retirement, through private arrangements or social security measures; but alternative possibilities of more constructive temporary uses of such services warrant exploration.

7. Support from both private and public sources to the end that a worker's job equities and security may be protected without impairment of his mobility. This will warrant consideration, taking into account relevant cost factors, of such measures as:

    a. Financial aid in the transfer of employees to other plants in a multiplant system, and protection of existing rights for individuals so transferred.

    b. The use of public funds in order to give financial aid in the transfer of unemployed workers from one area to another where the result will be to provide continuing employment.

    c. The improvement of public and private protection of pension rights.

    d. The recognition by unions, individual employees, and employers of the necessity of adapting seniority and other rules in order to facilitate mobility of workers, while providing protection for the equities of employees.

The Committee notes particularly the need for further study and exploration of this vital area.

8. Vast additional improvement of the public employment service so that it can effectively place, counsel, and relocate workers both locally and across State lines. We note with approval the start which has been made in this direction.

9. Vigorous and unremitting efforts by all segments of the population—including government, employers, unions, and employees—to eliminate discrimination in employment because of race, creed, age, or sex.

10. There are pressing national needs to be met, and an abundance of manpower available to meet these needs. This matching of manpower and national needs, which is part of the vital context of the automation and technological advance problem, will obviously be affected by various broader governmental policies. Reserving fuller consideration of this area for our economic growth report, we nevertheless note here that:

    a. When technological changes or other factors develop particular pockets of unemployment, this becomes an additional reason for the undertaking, particularly at the State and local levels but with Federal assistance where this is necessary, of public development projects for which there is need independent of the employment need itself.

    b. Every effort should be made to maintain on an up-to-date and ready-to-go basis a schedule of needed public development projects, particularly those which could be started most quickly and which would be of short or controllable duration, so that the initiation of such projects can in the future be advanced, and the flow of projects already under way can be speeded up, if the manpower situation warrants this.

    c. If the operation of the economy, including the effect of automation and technological change, creates or leaves an intolerable manpower surplus, consideration should be given to monetary and fiscal measures—including the possibility of appropriate tax reductions—which would give promise of helping alleviate this situation.

    d. Governmental action along the lines suggested here, stimulated in part by the need to meet unemployment situations, would obviously have to take account of other considerations, including particularly the maintenance of national economic stability and security. We simply assert, however, the coordinate importance of stability and growth.

11. The need for goods and services must not be left unfilled, particularly in a time of international crisis. At the same time, high unemployment is intolerable. In the light of our current responsibilities to meet world conditions, and in view of our unmet needs at home, we consider the development of programs directed at the achievement of full employment as being more significant at the present time than the consideration of a general reduction in the hours of work. A reduction in the basic work period has, however, historically been one means of sharing the fruits of technological progress, and there may well develop in the future the necessity and the desirability of shortening the work period, either through collective bargaining or by law or by both methods. In connection with such a development, consideration would necessarily be given to the extent to which purchasing power could be maintained along with a reduced work period.[1]

[1] Mr. Meany, Mr. Dubinsky, Mr. Harrison, Mr. Reuther, and Mr. Keenan are of the view that this paragraph should read as follows:

"The need for goods and services must not be left unfilled particularly in a time of international crisis. At the same time, high unemployment is intolerable. In the light of our current

We affirm our conviction that the infinite promise of automation and technological advance can be realized without loss or cost of human values. America can enjoy the fruits of higher productivity without having to accept, as the inevitable result, serious social consequences growing out of the displacement of workers.

The recommendations made here suggest our view of a broader pattern of possible courses of action which would necessarily have to be adapted to particular circumstances, but which permit the constructive and responsible uses of technology and automation. We see no barriers—except misunderstanding, timidity, and false fear—to the accomplishment of this purpose by a coordination of private and public programs wholly consonant with the essential concepts of the free society.

We assert the necessity of automation and technological development to the maintenance of American standards of living and to the fulfillment of this country's role of leadership in freedom's fight for survival. We assert equally the obligation and the capacity of Americans—as individuals and as a group—to use these new

responsibilities to meet world conditions, and in view of our unmet needs at home, we consider the development of programs directed at the achievement of maximum output and full employment as most significant at the present time. However, if unemployment is not reduced substantially in the near future we will have to resort to a general shortening of the work period through collective bargaining and by law. In connection with such a development, consideration would necessarily be given to the extent to which purchasing power could be maintained along with a reduced work period. A reduction in the basic work period has historically been one means of sharing fruits of technological progress."

Mr. McDonald, Mr. Reuther, and Mr. Keenan comment as follows:

"We agree that, in the light of the considerations stated, the most desirable solution now to the problem of unemployment is the development of programs which will achieve full employment at forty hours per week. Saying that this is the most desirable solution is not, however, the same thing as saying that we have in fact achieved that solution or that we will in fact achieve it in the near future. And only the fact of full employment—not a statement of its desirability—can properly serve as the premise for the statement that the necessity for shortening the work period will only develop 'in the future.' If we fail, as we have so far failed, to achieve the most desirable solution we will have to move more quickly than we are now moving in the direction of shortening the work period."

instruments and methods to enrich the lives of *all* of us.

We see no reason for alarm if out of a greater sense of common purpose we can achieve the good will and the determination to act together.

COMMENT by ARTHUR F. BURNS
President, National Bureau of Economic Research

I find parts of this report highly constructive, particularly the recommendations designed (*a*) to achieve efficient and yet humane management of technological changes, (*b*) to improve the functioning of the labor market, and (*c*) to extend the coverage and otherwise strengthen the unemployment insurance system. Nevertheless, I am troubled by the report as a whole, and I consider it a dubious guide to economic policy.

The reasons for my dissent are as follows:

1. The report fails to identify or to analyze or to assess the quantitative importance of the different causes of unemployment. Nevertheless, it conveys the impression that technological advances are a major, if not the major, cause of recent unemployment. I know of no evidence to support this view, and I deplore anything that adds to the greatly exaggerated fears that many people have of what is loosely called automation.

2. The report suffers from a failure to link its proposed remedies to the causes of unemployment. Thus the report does not mention seasonal unemployment or ways of dealing with it. It does not mention the loss of exports by some industries or the policies needed for coping with this source of unemployment. It does not distinguish cyclical unemployment from other types or indicate how public policy for dealing with recessions should be improved. On the other hand, the report puts heavy emphasis on public works and seems to suggest that this kind of governmental spending is a good remedy for unemployment regardless of its cause. Unhappily, public works are poorly suited for dealing with mild recessions or with local pockets of chronic unemployment.

3. Most recommendations of the report are couched in such vague language that they may mean much or little, depending on how they are interpreted. But if experience is any guide, neither the vagueness of language nor the surrounding qualifications will prevent articulate groups of our society from claiming the authority of this Committee for programs that could prove damaging to our economy. If all or most of the recommendations were implemented fairly

promptly and on a liberal scale, both employer costs of production and governmental outlays would rise substantially. The report passes over lightly the question of how such increases would affect business profits or the Federal budget or the general price level. I find this question very troublesome at the present time. The deterioration of profit margins during the past decade is already a serious obstacle to achieving a high rate of economic growth. The protracted rise of the price level has already put severe pressure on our balance of international payments. This year's projected rise of Federal cash outlays already exceeds the increase of any peacetime year in our history and, the international situation being what it is, military expenditures may soon need to be still larger. In view of these facts, unless great caution is exercised in pursuing programs that raise costs of production or public outlays, we may find that economic growth is curbed, that confidence in the dollar is weakened, and that our international political position is undermined.

4. Apart from these dangers, the report fails to analyze how its recommendations would affect the volume of unemployment itself. The report seems to call not only for liberalizing the unemployment insurance system, but also for extending private supplements to unemployment insurance, for providing public subsistence payments to workers who undergo retraining, for lowering the age at which displaced workers can qualify for social security, and for using public funds to aid unemployed workers in moving to areas where jobs can be found. I deem it a duty to point out that if all these measures were adopted in quick order and on a substantial scale, some individuals who now are outside the labor force will see an advantage in entering it, while there will be others who, having quit or lost their jobs, will be tempted to take more time in settling on new ones. In other words, unless great care and caution are exercised in implementing the Committee's recommendations, the end result may well be the social misfortune of permanently higher unemployment.

5. In large part, the shortcomings of the report are traceable to the pessimistic assumption on which it seems to proceed—namely, that there is a serious possibility that our Nation's economic progress will prove insufficient to provide jobs for all those who are able and eager to work. I have greater faith in our Nation's future. A tremendous expansion of prosperity lies within our

power. The degree to which we attain it will mainly depend, first, on how much work people care to do; second, on how productive they wish to be; third, on how earnestly we pursue public policies to stimulate new, creative, and more efficient economic activities by business enterprises. If the report had started from this broad but fundamental premise, it would have dealt more constructively with the economic and human problem of unemployment.

COMMENT by HENRY FORD II
Chairman, Ford Motor Company

I share wholeheartedly the concern over unemployment expressed in this report, and I applaud this Committee's desire both to speed industrial progress and to spread its human benefits more widely.

Few things are as costly to our Nation, or as crushing to the human spirit, as lack of work for those who are willing and able to work.

Because I hold these views so strongly, I feel compelled to state my belief that this report does not really get to the heart of the matter.

Its major premise is the assumption that automation and technological advance are in and of themselves significant causes of unemployment—an assumption that neither history nor an analysis of current unemployment supports. Technological advance has been with us for many generations. But, popular beliefs to the contrary, technological advance has not been accelerating. Figures from the Bureau of Labor Statistics show, for recent years, an increase in productivity well below the average rate for the postwar period and not much different from the average rate since 1909.

Moreover, the factual evidence strongly indicates that, while automation displaces some individuals from the jobs they have held, its overall effect is to increase income and expand job opportunities. History teaches us that, by and large, workers displaced by technological advance have moved rapidly into other employment, ultimately to better paying jobs. This is why we have had rising personal incomes rather than mass unemployment as new technology has come into use and productivity has increased.

When the economy is prosperous, displaced workers quickly find new employment. This is illustrated by the movement of workers off farms and into industrial employment when times are good, and the slowdown in this movement when times are bad.

The Committee has recognized that the general problem of unemployment is the key problem, but its recommendations are concerned mainly with the important but secondary matters of retraining and mobility. A good employment service and unemployment compensation facilitate the transfer from one job to another, but these measures, even if accompanied by massive retraining, relief, and other social programs, will scarcely make a dent in unemployment when economic conditions are poor.

If, therefore, we would help persons displaced by technological advance, we must focus our attention not on relief or even training—though these, properly conceived and administered, will help—but on creating new jobs for people who seek them and can perform in them.

When wages rise faster than productivity in the economy, costs will rise and then either prices will go up or profits will come down—or both will happen. If profits come down, then incentive to save and to invest savings in new, job-creating plants, enterprises, and industries must suffer. Moreover, unless inflationary measures are taken to support the higher wage, cost, and price levels, demand will not be adequate to maintain production and employment. And, when the integrity of the dollar is at stake, inflationary measures cannot be taken without calamitous results.

We must find ways consistent with a free economy to keep wages and other costs from causing either unemployment or inflation.

I regret that the report does not make this focal problem the primary target of its comments in recommendations. For, when we have found and placed in operation those policies and practices that can keep costs from rising and forcing us into either unemployment or inflation, we will have done much more than could be accomplished by all other measures combined.

The recommendations in this report are concerned mainly with ways of preventing and relieving technological displacement. I personally endorse many of them, and the company with which I am associated has long followed practices similar to many of those recommended in the report.

Nevertheless, I have the following general reservations about the character of the recommendations:

First, they cannot solve the problem of mass unemployment because they are directed primarily at helping people to find jobs—not at the basic need for more jobs.

Second, the massive program of public and private actions called for may have unexpected consequences that the Committee has not been able to evaluate. Indeed, I believe that the knowledge and experience necessary to evaluate this sweeping program do not now exist, and that it is therefore inappropriate and unwise for this Committee to place its stamp of approval upon such a program. For example, greatly expanded Federal assistance could very well destroy incentives that stimulate private economic activity and generate individual initiative.

Third, the endorsement of comprehensive, economy-wide programs in very general terms diverts attention from and complicates the search for carefully selected measures to meet particular problems. For example, I believe that the main result of a large-scale, nationwide program to retrain the unemployed might be to impede the development of useful local programs carefully tailored to existing job opportunities and the needs and abilities of individuals.

In addition to these general reservations, I have misgivings about some of the specific recommendations.

With respect to unemployment compensation, I believe that duration, coverage, and amount of benefits must be increased where they are inadequate. In addition, safeguards to protect against abuses should be strengthened. I do not endorse Federal standards, but believe the States should continue with responsibility for fitting their particular systems to their own conditions and needs.

I agree that in the main the recommendations for improving our school systems are good. In many areas and localities, however, the most urgent need is not more money but greater public concern with what is taught in our schools.

Arbitrarily shortening the workweek in order to decrease unemployment would be a confession of defeat. Not only a poor remedy, it is also a harmful one; for it would retard the growth needed for the safety and welfare of our Nation at this point in its history. We can and should look forward to normal increases in our leisure time, but they must come as our growing economy can afford them and not as expedient solutions to unemployment problems.

In summary, I find some things in this report of which I approve, and much of which I disapprove. Its goal of making certain that high employment accompany technological improvement and increasing efficiency has my full support. However, I believe that the general direction of its recommendations is not well calculated to achieve this goal. I believe, too, that the report's basic assumption concerning the relationship between technological advance and unemployment is in error.

Therefore, I feel it necessary to say, with reluctance, that I cannot concur in the report.

READING 63

For all of its great wealth, the United States is still the home of far more relatively impoverished families than many Americans realize. Changes in living patterns—the movement to suburbia and the daily trips into the city via superhighways—have permitted many of us to escape direct confrontation with lingering poverty in the cities. Rural poverty, in turn, is hidden from the main roads of commerce and tourism.

In the middle of the 1960s, there has been a reawakening to the dimensions of the poverty problem. The national mood has swung from unconcern to all-out involvement in the story. Statistics and plans fly about with abandon, so that it becomes hard to separate what is real from what is fancied or feared. But, through all of the confusion, there appears to be a genuine, growing conviction that so wealthy a society must be able to find ways to lift far more of its people out of destitute conditions.

One of the most significant voices speaking out on poverty is that of the President of the United States. Lyndon B. Johnson had been in office only a few months when he delivered to Congress his "poverty package," a summation of what he believed active government policy might do to help some of the most needy families. With this message, the war on poverty became front-page news.

Questions to Guide the Reading

Does this package of proposals make a sufficiently direct attack on the basic sources of poverty in America? What is new and untried here, and what represents economic policies tried before?

What costs, both direct and hidden, might be associated with the implementation of these proposals? How should judgments be made about whether those costs are worth paying?

THE PRESIDENT'S POVERTY MESSAGE, 1964
Lyndon B. Johnson

We are citizens of the richest and most fortunate nation in the history of the world.

One hundred and eighty years ago we were a small country struggling for survival on the margin of a hostile land.

Today we have established a civilization of free men which spans an entire continent.

With the growth of our country has come opportunity for our people—opportunity to educate our children, to use our energies in productive work, to increase our leisure—opportunity for almost every American to hope that through work and talent he could create a better life for himself and his family.

The path forward has not been an easy one.

But we have never lost sight of our goal: an

From President Lyndon B. Johnson's Message to Congress, March 17, 1964.

America in which every citizen shares all the opportunities of his society, in which every man has a chance to advance his welfare to the limit of his capacities.

We have come a long way toward this goal.

We still have a long way to go.

The distance which remains is the measure of the great unfinished work of our society.

To finish that work I have called for a national war on poverty. Our objective: total victory.

There are millions of Americans—one fifth of our people—who have not shared in the abundance which has been granted to most of us, and to whom the gates of opportunity have been closed.

That does this poverty mean to those who endure it?

It means a daily struggle to secure the necessities for even a meager existence. It means that the abundance, the comforts, the opportunities they see all around them are beyond their grasp.

Worst of all, it means hopelessness for the young.

The young man or woman who grows up without a decent education, in a broken home, in a hostile and squalid environment, in ill health or in the face of racial injustice—that young man or woman is often trapped in a life of poverty.

He does not have the skills demanded by a complex society. He does not know how to acquire those skills. He faces a mounting sense of despair which drains initiative and ambition and energy.

Our tax cut will create millions of new jobs—new exits from poverty.

But we must also strike down all the barriers which keep many from using those exits.

The war on poverty is not a struggle simply to support people, to make them dependent on the generosity of others.

It is a struggle to give people a chance.

It is an effort to allow them to develop and use their capacities, as we have been allowed to develop and use ours, so that they can share, as others share, in the promise of this nation.

We do this, first of all, because it is right that we should.

From the establishment of public education and land grant colleges through agricultural extension and encouragement to industry, we have pursued a goal of a nation with full and increasing opportunities for all its citizens.

The war on poverty is a further step in that pursuit.

We do it also because helping some will increase the prosperity of all.

Our fight against poverty will be an investment in the most valuable of our resources—the skills and strength of our people.

And in the future, as in the past, this investment will return its cost many fold.

If we can raise the annual earnings of 10 million among the poor by only $1,000 we will have added 14 billion dollars a year to our national output. In addition we can make important reductions in public assistance payments which now cost us 4 billion dollars a year, and in the large costs of fighting crime and delinquency, disease and hunger.

This is only part of the story.

Our history has proved that each time we broaden the base of abundance, giving more people the chance to produce and consume, we create new industry, higher production, increased earnings and better income for all.

Giving new opportunity to those who have little will enrich the lives of all the rest.

Because it is right, because it is wise, and because, for the first time in our history, it is possible to conquer poverty, I submit, for the consideration of the Congress and the country, the Economics Opportunity Act of 1964.

This program asks men and women throughout the country to prepare long-range plans for the attack on poverty in their own local communities.

These are not plans prepared in Washington and imposed upon hundreds of different situations.

They are based on the fact that local citizens best understand their own problems, and know best how to deal with those problems.

These plans will be local plans striking at the many unfilled needs which underlie poverty in each community, not just one or two. Their components and emphasis will differ as needs differ.

These plans will be local plans calling upon all the resources available to the community—Federal and state, local and private, human and material.

And when these plans are approved by the Office of Economic Opportunity, the Federal Government will finance up to 90 per cent of the additional cost for the first two years.

The most enduring strength of our nation is the huge reservoir of talent, initiative and leadership which exists at every level of our society.

Through the community action program we call upon this, our greatest strength, to overcome our greatest weakness.

Third, I ask for the authority to recruit and train skilled volunteers for the war against poverty.

Thousands of Americans have volunteered to serve the needs of other lands.

Thousands more want the chance to serve the needs of their own land.

They should have that chance.

Among older people who have retired, as well as among the young, among women as well as men, there are many Americans who are ready to enlist in our war against poverty.

They have skills and dedication. They are badly needed.

If the state requests them, if the community needs and will use them, we will recruit and train them and give them the chance to serve.

Fourth, we intend to create new opportunities for certain hard-hit groups to break out of the pattern of poverty.

Through a new program of loans and guarantees we can provide incentives to those who will employ the unemployed.

Through programs of work and retraining for unemployed fathers and mothers we can help them support their families in dignity while preparing themselves for new work.

Through funds to purchase needed land, organize cooperatives, and create new and adequate family farms we can help those whose life on the land has been a struggle without hope.

Fifth, I do not intend that the war against poverty become a series of uncoordinated and unrelated efforts—that it perish for lack of leadership and direction.

Therefore this bill creates, in the executive office of the President, a new Office of Economic Opportunity. Its director will be my personal chief of staff for the war against poverty. I intend to appoint Sargent Shriver to this post.

He will be directly responsible for these new programs. He will work with and through existing agencies of the Government.

This program—the Economic Opportunity Act—is the foundation of our war against poverty. But it does not stand alone.

For the past three years this Government has advanced a number of new proposals which strike at important areas of need and distress.

I ask the Congress to extend those which are already in action, and to establish those which have already been proposed.

There are programs to help badly distressed areas such as the Area Redevelopment Act, and the legislation now being prepared to help Appalachia.

There are programs to help those without training find a place in today's complex society—such as the Manpower Development Training Act and the Vocational Education Act for Youth.

There are programs to protect those who are specially vulnerable to the ravages of poverty—hospital insurance for the elderly, protection for migrant farm workers, a food stamp program for the needy, coverage for millions not now protected by a minimum wage, new and expanded unemployment benefits for men out of work, a housing and community development bill for those seeking decent homes.

The act does not merely expand old programs or improve what is already being done.

It charts a new course.

It strikes at the causes, not just the consequences of poverty.

It can be a milestone in our one hundred eighty year search for a better life for our people.

This act provides five basic opportunities:

It will give almost half a million underprivileged young Americans the opportunity to develop skills, continue education, and find useful work.

It will give every American community the opportunity to develop a comprehensive plan to fight its own poverty—and help them to carry out their plans.

It will give dedicated Americans the opportunity to enlist as volunteers in the war against poverty.

It will give many workers and farmers the opportunity to break through particular barriers which bar their escape from poverty.

It will give the entire nation the opportunity for a concerted attack on poverty through the establishment, under my direction, of the Office of Economic Opportunity, a national headquarters for the war against poverty.

This is how we propose to create these opportunities.

First, we will give high priority to helping young Americans who lack skills, who have not completed their education or who cannot complete it because they are too poor.

The years of high school and college age are the most critical stage of a young person's life. If they are not helped then, many will be condemned to a life of poverty which they, in turn, will pass on to their children.

I therefore recommend the creation of a job

corps, a work-training program, and a work study program.

A new national job corps will build toward an enlistment of 100,000 young men. They will be drawn from those whose background, health and education make them least fit for useful work.

Those who volunteer will enter more than 100 camps and centers around the country.

Half of these young men will work, in the first year, on special conservation projects to give them education, useful work experience and to enrich the natural resources of the country.

Half of these young men will receive, in the first year, a blend of training, basic education and work experience in job training centers.

These are not simply camps for the underprivileged. They are new educational institutions, comparable in innovation to the land grant colleges. Those who enter them will emerge better qualified to play a productive role in American society.

A new national work-training program operated by the Department of Labor will provide work and training for 200,000 American men and women between the ages of 16 and 21. This will be developed through state and local governments and non-profit agencies.

Hundreds of thousands of young Americans badly need the experience, the income, and the sense of purpose which useful full- or part-time work can bring. For them such work may mean the difference between finishing school or dropping out. Vital community activities from hospitals and playgrounds to libraries and settlement houses are suffering because there are not enough people to staff them.

We are simply bringing these needs together.

A new national work-study program operated by the Department of Health, Education and Welfare will provide Federal funds for part-time jobs for 140,000 young Americans who do not go to college because they cannot afford it.

There is no more senseless waste than the waste of brainpower and skill of those who are kept from college by economic circumstance. Under this program they will, in a great American tradition, be able to work their way through school.

They and the country will be richer for it.

Second, through a new community action program we intend to strike at poverty at its source—in the streets of our cities and on the farms of our countryside, among the very young and the impoverished old.

Finally there are programs which help the entire country, such as aid to education which, by raising the quality of schooling available to every American child, will give a new chance for knowledge to the children of the poor.

I ask immediate action on all these programs.

What you are being asked to consider is not a simple or an easy program. But poverty is not a simple or an easy enemy.

It cannot be driven from the land by a single attack on a single front. Were this so we would have conquered poverty long ago.

Nor can it be conquered by government alone.

For decades American labor and American business, private institutions and private individuals have been engaged in strengthening our economy and offering new opportunities to those in need.

We need their help, their support and their full participation.

Through this program we offer new incentives and new opportunities for cooperation, so that all the energy of our nation, not merely the efforts of government, can be brought to bear on our common enemy.

Today, for the first time in our history, we have the power to strike away the barriers to full participation in our society. Having the power, we have the duty.

The Congress is charged by the Constitution to "provide . . . for the general welfare of the United States." Our present abundance is a measure of its success in fulfilling that duty. Now Congress is being asked to extend that welfare to all our people.

The President of the United States is President of all the people in every section of the country. But this office also holds a special responsibility to the distressed and disinherited, the hungry and the hopeless of this abundant nation.

It is in pursuit of that special responsibility that I submit this message to you today.

The new program I propose is within our means. Its cost of 970 million dollars is 1 per cent of our national budget—and every dollar I am requesting for this program is already included in the budget I sent to Congress in January.

But we cannot measure its importance by its cost.

For it charts an entirely new course of hope for our people.

We are fully aware that this program will not eliminate all the poverty in America in a few months or a few years. Poverty is deeply rooted and its causes are many.

But this program will show the way to new opportunities for millions of our fellow citizens.

It will provide a lever with which we can begin to open the door to our prosperity for those who have been kept outside.

It will also give us the chance to test out weapons, to try our energy and ideas and imagination for the many battles yet to come. As conditions change, and as experience illuminates our difficulties, we will be prepared to modify our strategy.

And this program is much more than a beginning.

Rather it is a commitment. It is a total commitment by this President, and this Congress, and this nation, to pursue victory over the most ancient of mankind's enemies.

On many historic occasions the President has requested from Congress the authority to move against forces which were endangering the well-being of our country.

This is such an occasion.

On similar occasions in the past we have often been called upon to wage war against foreign enemies which threatened our freedom. Today we are asked to declare war on a domestic enemy which threatens the strength of our nation and the welfare of our people.

If we now move forward against this enemy— if we can bring to the challenges of peace the same determination and strength which has brought us victory in war—then this day and this Congress will have won a secure and honorable place in the history of the nation, and the enduring gratitude of generations of Americans yet to come.

READING 64

Inevitably the Administration's proposals for a war on poverty produced some counterproposals and some second thoughts on what could and could not be done for the nation's poorest families. The debate once again raised the basic issue which surrounds all economic policy discussions: How much should government do directly for its citizens?

Harley L. Lutz, emeritus professor of public finance from Princeton University, has been a consistent spokesman for the view that there should be serious limits to government's active intervention in the economy. He accepts the poverty problem as being a real enough one, however much the politicians add to it, but he wants the marketplace to play a bigger role than positive government action in solving the problem on grounds that direct intervention often hurts as much as it helps.

Questions to Guide the Reading

What evidence might support or refute the contention that at least five government policies have acted as serious bars to more rapid increases in employment?

What are the limits on how much a freer market structure might accomplish to give a higher standard of living to the poorest Americans?

LIMITS IN THE WAR ON POVERTY
Harley L. Lutz

"War on Poverty" is a slogan that can reasonably be expected to yield considerable political mileage. No one is in favor of poverty and criticism of a program purporting to deal with it is as risky, politically, as being in favor of sin or against motherhood.

Yet the odds are heavily against complete elimination of poverty by any kind or degree of

From Harley L. Lutz, "Preserving Poverty," *Wall Street Journal*, April 15, 1964. Reprinted with kind permission of the publisher.

Government action. The dramatic announcement of the slogan may carry for some the implication that theretofore poverty had been tolerated but that little serious thought or effort had been given to its amelioration.

The fact is that the whole history of economic progress is a record of the struggle against poverty in the sense of a scarcity or deficiency of goods in relation to needs. Everything that has been done to increase production, from the most primitive tools and implements to today's enormous complex of machines, materials, technology and skills has broadened and strengthened the drive to minimize scarcity.

In a more literal sense, destitution has long been a matter of concern among enlightened people everywhere. It was dealt with at first on a family or clan basis. One of the earliest recorded steps by government was the Elizabethan Poor Law of 1601. Private contributions by individuals, families, and charitable organizations have always provided, however, the bulk of relief from want, but welfare statism has led government to assume an ever-larger role.

The problem of alleviating or of eventually eliminating economic destitution is two-fold: First, production must be further increased, and, second, the incomes of those who are now in want must be raised.

The prerequisites of the first of these conditions—greater production—have been set out by many writers on many occasions. The fundamental requirement is more capital, for production cannot be significantly increased without a greater supply of capital. A bona fide Government attack on poverty must include, therefore, modification of the rules and bureaucratic attitudes which hamper the provision and efficient use of capital.

Given continued increase of production, the second aspect of the problem remains how to raise the incomes of those who are in want. In a money economy, indigence is usually, though not always correctly, indicated by inadequate money income to buy food, clothing, shelter, and other necessaries.

Deficiency of income can be overcome in one of two ways. One way is for the Government to give destitute persons or families enough money to put them above the arbitrarily determined poverty level, and the other way is for Government to do its part to create, or restore, the conditions under which these persons or families can obtain more income through their own efforts.

The Federal Government's way has been mainly to make grants for public assistance, give free food stamps, provide housing at rentals below

cost, lend money in various directions at interest rates below the terms of Treasury borrowing, subsidize its own competition with private taxpayers, and so on. The dimensions of the dependency situation have not been diminished by this over-expanding outflow. Quite as futile has been the progressive tax system, the only justification for which is the equalization of wealth and income. The roadblocks to capital formation and incentives to effort set up by this kind of taxation have done more harm by curtailing job opportunities than any good that might have resulted from taxing the rich to support the poor.

Thus far there has been no announcement of striking new departures from the pattern already established. The proposals made public include youth camps, grants to submarginal farmers, more low-cost housing, more loans to small business, more aid to depressed areas, more Federal aid to education—in short, the same old package tied up with a lot of new red tape.

The attack on poverty by way of gifts, grants, subsidies and other forms of handout is largely self-defeating because this method carries with it no incentive to strive for change of condition or improvement of lot. There will be exceptions, but the general effect of "something for nothing" is demoralizing rather than stimulating.

Since we are dealing here with a program for specific action, the main question involves what, if anything, Government can do to enable individuals and families to become decently self-supporting through their own efforts. As noted above, income-supplementing devices of every sort, from cash handouts and made-work to sharing the wealth, are not a permanent solution.

It is submitted that a bona fide long-range attack on the conditions which may now prevent those able and willing to work from finding employment must include a thorough review and revision of Government policies which operate as bars to employment.

Among the policies that have hindered the employment objective are these:

1. The tax load on the nation's productive resources. Despite the tax rate reductions of the 1964 Act, it is still necessary for a corporation to earn almost two dollars in order to have one dollar after tax for additional investment and/or dividends. Individual incomes through the range where the bulk of the energetic, ambitious, capable persons are found are still relatively discriminated against under the new rate scales.

2. The Federal minimum wage. It tends to limit employment of unskilled persons, particu-

larly among the younger members of the labor force.

3. Government support and protection of union monopoly power. Union discrimination against nonunion workers and indifference to their condition are promoted by this favoritism.

4. Policies of price support, marketing orders, and other devices to protect incomes of producers. Creation of an office of special counselor on consumer affairs is typical of the bureaucratic method of proceeding at a tangent instead of facing an issue directly.

5. Emphasis on handouts. An individual's first obligation is to support himself rather than to assume that he has a vested right to public support.

Educational deficiency is unquestionably an important reason for the inability of some to find employment and of others, even though employed, to earn enough to rise above the poverty level. It would appear, however, that there should be no excuse for inadequate education if the amount of money being spent be the criterion. Public school expenditures as compiled by the Office of Education are given herewith:

Year	School Population (5-17 years)	Expenditures (millions)
1920	27,728,786	$ 1,036
1940	29,805,259	2,344
1960	43,927,801	15,644

Public school expenditures have increased over this entire period, or over any 20-year part of it, at a much faster rate than the school population to be educated. In addition, it is known that the expenditures of private and parochial schools have increased substantially, though the exact amounts are not available. In face of this steadily accelerating effort, why is it that lack of education can be held responsible, to the degree that has been charged, for inability to get and hold jobs and to earn enough income for adequate self-support?

A distinction should be pointed up here between the amount of money being spent as a test of educational efficiency, and the failure of the educational system to do for all pupils what it obviously does for a goodly proportion of them. Some hold that much larger spending will overcome this failure. But additional spending will not make A and B students out of those whose educable potential is not up to this level of achievement. Nor will it necessarily solve the problem of "drop-outs," a matter of growing concern, especially at the high school level.

A final issue of great importance in a fundamental attack on poverty is the increase of population. The ecologists have emphasized the balance of nature, by which they mean, as one writer has put it, "the teamwork and delicate balance between the different forces that keep life functioning on this planet." His reference is to the life-giving cycle of the relationship between plants and animals. The number of people is part of this balance. The level of human life is dependent upon the relation between the number to be supported and the available resources. Wise use of resources, renewable and otherwise, will permit more people to live in comfort. But this cannot be the case for long if the human race were to multiply without limit.

Even before food scarcity should happen, water scarcity could impose a population limit. An ample water supply is the foundation of modern sanitation, without which one of the cruel limitations envisaged by Malthus—pestilence—would come into operation.

No absolute population total can be prescribed for any country. All children born must be protected as persons fully entitled to life, liberty, and the pursuit of happiness. It is in the highest degree cruel and immoral to permit more to be born than can be provided with these essentials on a decent level.

A solution to the problem of poverty must include many elements. And one indispensable ingredient is information as to the importance, and as to the methods, of limiting the world's population.

READING 65

A rapid increase in our school-age population began after World War II and has continued ever since. Total school enrollment in elementary and high schools alone increased from 28 million in 1950 to over 42.5 million by 1960, and current projections indicate that this number might rise to over 53 million by 1970. If college and university enrollments are added to these figures, the totals become

30.3 million in 1950, 46.3 million in 1960, and a projected 60.3 million in 1970.

These developments come at a time when research indicates that investment in human capital has been one of the most significant factors in accounting for the historical growth rate realized in the United States. Thus, increasing strains are placed on our educational institutions as we try to provide both more and better education to the end that all Americans may come closer to realizing their full potential.

Widespread agreement that greater investment in education is a wise move from the viewpoint of both the individual and the society, however, does not resolve some of the nagging questions about how the cost and the benefits of education should be shared. A recent focal point for the debate has been the role that the Federal government should play in this area. A common position among school administrators is that Federal funds are needed to help local and state school systems, but that such funds should have no "strings" attached.

Sidney Sufrin, professor of economics at Syracuse University, reviews this and other issues in the education debate, and takes the provocative position that the problem of our economic capacity to support education is not as pressing as it often appears. Professor Sufrin argues that it is Federal standards rather than Federal funds that are most needed in this area.

Questions to Guide the Reading

What relevance does the adage, "He who pays the piper calls the tune," have in confronting today's educational problems? Can fiscal and curriculum-content issues be separated in discussing American education? Who should have the responsibility for establishing educational standards in American schools?

What factors are relevant in determining a society's "ability to pay" for education?

FINANCING EDUCATION
Sidney Sufrin

Primary and secondary education in the United States has traditionally been the concern of state and local communities. While the federal government has always expressed an interest in the problems of public education, its financial contribution has been marginal.

The amount of state and local educational expenditures is enormous, amounting to somewhere in the neighborhood of five or five and one-half per cent of the gross national product, if expenditures on higher education are included. Even in the realm of higher education, publicly supported institutions spent more than $4.2 billion in 1961 as compared with expenditures of $3.1 billion by private institutions. At the elementary and secondary levels, however, private school expenditures are much less significant.

In 1961, for example, $2.9 billion was spent by private schools compared with $17.1 billion spent for public primary and secondary schools. The $17.1 billion spent for public schools went mainly for current expenditures (77.2 per cent); the remainder was for capital outlay and interest.

Obviously the extent of support for education varies from state to state, not only because of variations in the ability to pay and the number of students to be serviced, but also because of the attitudes of different states toward education.

In the last decade, however, every state has increased its expenditures on education, usually at a faster rate than the increase in its per capita personal income. For example, Mississippi, between 1950–51 and 1960–61, increased its current expenditures per pupil in average daily attendance by more than 142 per cent—the largest increase in the nation—while its per capita income

From Sidney Sufrin, "Where There's a Will," *Challenge*, January, 1963, pp. 27–30. Reprinted with the kind permission of the author and publisher.

in that period rose only 74.2 per cent. New York increased its current expenditures per pupil in average daily attendance by 78.4 per cent, while its per capita income rose only 55 per cent. In only 11 states did the rate of per capita personal income increase more rapidly than the percentage increase in current expenditure per pupil during the 1950s. Thus, current expenditures for education are extremely sensitive to increases in per capita personal income.

Ideally, one should be able to judge state financial efforts in education in the light of the state's ability to pay. Unfortunately, this ideal is not only statistically difficult to the point of impossibility, but even if all of the statistics that one wanted were available, the conceptual and operational frameworks to use these statistics are lacking. The capacity of a state to support education, or any other service, does not depend only upon its income; it also depends upon such considerations as what all the taxes collected are to be used for and on the value (absolute and relative) taxpayers place upon the services in question.

Everyone concerned with education is convinced that education is the most important or at least among the two or three most important public services. But some communities in their own wisdom have decided that roads or hospitals or simply maintaining purchasing power in the hands of consumers is as important, or more important, than increased expenditures on education. The method of raising taxes is also significant because the manner of obtaining revenue can affect the performance of a locality's economy.

At best one can say that the level of a community's educational expenditures reflects the values and attitudes of the citizens of that area. The problem of economic capacity to support education is not as pressing as it often appears. In no instance in the United States is the fraction of personal income taken up in educational taxes so great that a reasonable increase (even 100 per cent) would drastically change the disposable income level of taxpayers.

Federal penetration into primary and secondary education occurs mainly through Public Laws 815 and 874 on the one hand, and the National Defense Education Act on the other.

Public Law 815, which is designed to aid socalled federally impacted areas, provides federal funds for school construction in districts that are excessively burdened because federal activities have brought a heavy student enrollment, or because federal ownership of property in the area has reduced the tax base. In 1962 the federal

government appropriated $55 million to lighten the local school construction burden in these localities. Between 1951 and 1962 more than $1 billion was appropriated for this purpose.

Public Law 874, the companion act to PL 815, provides funds for the maintenance and operation of schools in the impacted areas. Federal payments to eligible districts represent, on the average, only about five per cent of their operating budgets. In 1962, $231.3 million was appropriated under this law.

The National Defense Education Act, originally passed in 1958, was, in part, a legislative response to the first Sputnik shot of the Soviet Union which occurred in the fall of 1957. More importantly, it represents a collection of programs which educators have been discussing for many years.

Insofar as primary and secondary schools are concerned, $47.5 million was appropriated under the NDEA in 1961 as grants to states for the acquisition of equipment to assist the teaching of languages, mathematics and science. A small sum of money was appropriated for the same purpose as loans to private schools ($6.5 million). Another $3.75 million was appropriated in 1961 and in 1962 for improving the supervision and administration of teaching programs in the states. These two programs—the acquisition of equipment for the teaching of languages, mathematics and sciences, and grants to states for the improvement of educational supervision—represent probably the closest relationship of a financial sort between primary and secondary education on the one hand, and the federal government on the other.

In addition to the appropriations outlined above, the NDEA also provided $15 million in grants to the states for improvement of guidance, counseling and testing programs, and $6.5 million for institutes for counseling personnel. The purpose of these programs is to make possible the identification of especially able or gifted students. Additional funds were appropriated for language development and the improvement of educational teaching and training through research grants to colleges and universities.

In general, the grants and contracts to colleges, universities and other institutions which improve the quality of teaching are viewed in the Act as purchases of the services of these institutions. Thus the states and their school systems are not involved directly. Moreover, it is hoped that the teaching levels of the states and the competence of the teachers in their school systems will thereby be improved.

In 1961 somewhere between $60 million and

$70 million was made available to the states for the direct improvement of their teaching and guidance programs. Possibly an equal amount would ultimately redound to the improvement of the primary and secondary school systems through loans to students attending universities (many of whom, of course, will become schoolteachers), language development programs, educational research, etc. The NDEA, however, is, from the viewpoint of dollars spent, miniscule as compared to the school expenditures of the 50 states.

In the first year of the Kennedy Administration, Congress considered but failed to pass a bill calling for massive federal aid to education. In brief, this bill would have provided funds to the states, based inversely upon the incomes of the states and directly upon the number of students in average daily attendance. No question of standards or any other major substantive administrative provision was in the bill, except that the states had to provide accounting evidence that the funds were properly used. The bill, after much bitter debate, was killed and, instead, the National Defense Education Act was extended for two years. The two-year extension was a political stratagem to avoid having to reconsider an education bill in the election year of 1962.

This strategy by the opponents of the education bill prevailed over the valiant attempts of the measure's proponents who hoped to make the measure an election issue in 1962.

Perhaps the major difference between the National Defense Education Act and the federal aid bill backed by the Administration is that the latter provided funds to supplement the existing educational programs of the states, while the former provides funds for specific, in educational jargon, categorical aid—i.e., for mathematics, language and science teaching. This was one bone of contention between proponents and opponents of the two legislative approaches.

At least two other issues, however, must be faced in any educational debate in America. One of these is the belief, held by a very small minority of those who testified on educational matters before the Congress in recent years, that no federal aid is required or, more properly stated, no *additional* federal aid is required. There has been no argument against vocational aid or against so-called impacted areas aid. The opponents simply argued that neither a general act nor a categorical act was necessary. The other issue still unresolved is, of course, the question of aiding parochial schools.

The one issue which *neither* side chose to face

in the whole debate on education was (and is) the question of maintaining certain minimal standards as a condition for receiving federal grants. Yet this is perhaps the most significant problem facing our primary and secondary schools. The essential issue that any educational system must continually face is to define the purpose of education and secure the means to implement it.

The only way that one can talk reasonably about these questions is to set up standards which act both as goals toward which efforts are directed and as yardsticks against which the accomplishments can be measured.

Yet, in the U.S., with its tradition of local and state "control" of education, we have in effect built up a myth that education is somehow a community or, at best, a state concern. This idea prevails despite the fact that we are a migratory people who simply refuse to stay put in a *given* state for any length of time. An additional factor is our well-recognized national, social, political and economic interdependence.

The myth about education being solely a community or state concern goes even further. Both state and local school administrators and members of boards of education fear the encroachment of the federal government. But, at the same time, they fear each other's encroachment. Local school boards often tend to react unfavorably to many of the rules and directives of state administrations. On the other hand, many state administrations doubt the wisdom and ability of local boards.

Since funds to finance schools come in large part from property taxes, local politicians as well as members of school boards are often greatly concerned with problems of assessments and tax rates. Indeed, the enormity of the fiscal problem often seems to overshadow educational questions. In addition, new suburbs require all sorts of public expenditures in addition to school expenditures. The changing pattern of populations within cities, too, requires new expenditures and thus new taxes. Justifiably or not, the local taxpayer feels that he is being crushed by property taxes and, in many cases, by sales taxes.

What has happened, of course, is that as incomes have risen in America, wants have increased even more rapidly. It is difficult, perhaps even meaningless, to compare a sewer system or a new car or a winter vacation with an improvement in a classroom or a better course of instruction for a high school student. As a result, the pressure for a good school system loses its force. It is with this in mind that many educators, indeed probably most educators, support *some* form of federal aid to education.

Of course, federal aid to education implies that the richer states will, through taxes, subsidize the relatively poorer ones. And federal taxes somehow have more of the unavoidable and inevitable about them than do state and local taxes!

The technical question involved is: How will the federal government administer the funds? Here again the question of standards becomes very significant. The Office of Education of the Department of Health, Education and Welfare has up to now been mainly concerned with *distributing* federal funds under the NDEA. Attempts to assist state school administrations and local school bodies to improve their operations have not been extremely successful nor always well received.

The major fault probably lies in the fact that the communications between the Office of Education and the state and local education bodies have not been as good as they might be. In interviews I conducted with state and local officials, I found an almost universal fear of the Office of Education as well as a tendency to question its special competence in assisting state and local bodies to carry out their functions. One cannot but view this as part of the distrust and antagonism which arises, not from any inherent incapacity of the Office of Education, but, rather, from the fear that the Office of Education will encroach upon the authority of the state and/or local educational bodies.

Most of the state and local school administrators who support some form of federal aid to education wish the federal government would merely allot funds to the states and have each state administer its own program. An additional complication is that most teachers feel that the federal government would do well to support *their* particular subject. The administrators object to this, arguing that only the administrator can know how the budget should be allocated over the broad spectrum of courses.

Nevertheless, American tradition has always favored categorical aid. Congress passes laws and puts them into effect through appropriations for quite specific purposes, as our examination of the National Defense Education Act and Public Laws 815 and 874 has shown.

However, the issue in educational circles of categorical vs. general aid seems less sharp than the debate assumes. In the last analysis, all aid

is categorical because once income is budgeted, it is budgeted for specific purposes. The real issue is: Shall the *federal* government determine which particular category or categories, e.g., language, mathematics or social science, it desires to aid, or shall the states make the categorical distinctions using, in part, federal funds, if such are forthcoming? The main issue reverts, of course, to the issue of standards and subject matter. To be sure, school administrators fear that they will be dictated to by the federal government.

But, obviously, if the standards of the nation's schools need improvement, it is clearly within the jurisdiction—legal and political—of the Congress to legislate. Ideally, legislation should be of the sort in which the federal government enunciates general guidelines which are subsequently carried out at the local level. Such a program would certainly not impose a rigid federal curriculum on the localities. The cloth should be cut to fit the needs of the individual communities which, obviously, are different.

The federal government would be assisting local school boards in programs that are in the interest of all the citizens of the United States. This is not an empty phrase because, in truth, New York City or Cleveland suffers when the educational systems of Mississippi or Alabama produce badly trained persons. The migration of labor and the commercial and political interdependence of the United States do not permit us to allow low standards of education in any section of the country. Such an approach does not imply federal control in any sense of the word.

As the demand for more and better education grows—both in terms of the number of students, and in the variety of courses and the complexity of teaching them—the authority and decisions of the local boards and the state departments of education will undoubtedly increase. With federal aid, the role of the federal government also increases.

All the increases will not be of such a nature as to maintain the *relative* significance of the three layers of school administration; but the whole process will grow larger, so that the *absolute* number and significance of decisions at all three levels will increase.

This is a hard point to get across to school administrators. They view the world as somehow static, and any change either increases their position or decreases it. In an expanding universe, elementary and secondary education clearly is expanding, and the administrative roles of all concerned can absolutely increase. But the necessary administrative adjustments become greater and possibly more difficult.

One of the great roles of the federal government in primary and secondary education is to provide leadership, ideas and information to the states and to the local school boards. In the opinion of many educational administrators, the federal government has not done particularly well in this enterprise. Here, then, is a challenge to the U.S. Office of Education, no matter what kind of legislation is eventually approved.

This challenge is much more significant than any particular sum of money that Congress appropriates for school aid. In fact, all things considered, I am inclined to believe that the National Defense Education Act, for all its limitations, can provide a framework for meeting this challenge.

The modernization and recasting of the elementary and secondary school curricula, in the light of modern knowledge and theory, is the most significant task facing American education. The issue is not economic, it is one of will.

READING 66

"Megalopolis," "urban sprawl," and "urban blight" are increasingly common terms in the discussion of our metropolitan areas. With hindsight on our side, it seems strange now that we were so late in recognizing the magnitude of the economic, political, and social problems we share in living and working together in crowded areas. For most Americans, the quality of life is shaped in large part by participation in metropolitan society—yet we persist at key points in thinking of America as a rural society (witness our apportionment in so many state legislatures). The amount of careful thought to the shared economic needs of men in any given metropolitan area remains at a low level, but the picture is beginning to change as the inadequacies of today's institutions to meet today's problems become more apparent.

The Committee for Economic Development's report on metropolitan problems presents a strong challenge from a concerned group of business leaders who want us to see what it is that we are living with in these radically changing subeconomies.

Questions to Guide the Reading

To what degree do differences between private costs and social costs, and between private benefits and social benefits, lie at the root of these metropolitan problems? What is the most appropriate decision-making unit for facing these problems in a highly interdependent urban complex?

What are the proper roles for private agencies and for public agencies in guiding metropolitan growth? How much of an overall plan is needed for such guidance?

GUIDING METROPOLITAN GROWTH
Committee for Economic Development

1. Background. Within the span of a century America has gone through two great changes in its living patterns. In the last quarter of the 19th century and the first quarter of the 20th century we shifted from a predominantly rural to urban society.

The second change in American life during the 20th century is from a basically urban to metropolitan condition. Prior to the metropolitan era cities were centers of industrial and commercial activity. The workers lived in closely built houses and tenements within walking distances of fac-

From *Guiding Metropolitan Growth* (Committee for Economic Development, New York, 1960), pp. 6–24. Reprinted with kind permission of the C.E.D.

tories or of trolley car and subway lines that went out only relatively short distances from the hub. Sanitation problems of this pattern of urban concentration were met by a central public sewer system. There was little question where the city ended and the country began. Outside of city boundaries there were no large population concentrations, and government structure outside these boundaries was designed for a basically rural condition.

The metropolitan area is in effect a new community. Its boundaries often are hard to define. In some instances they change and expand frequently. The area ignores old geographic boundaries, jumping over and around rivers and land masses. It ignores the political lines of districts, villages, towns, cities, counties and states.

The metropolitan area reflects a new kind of society resulting from higher average incomes, the development of new tastes in living standards, and technological means for releasing people from the old patterns. The private automobile has freed many from dependence on local public transportation. The greatly increased use of septic tanks has, temporarily at least, freed dwellers from dependence on a central public sewer system. The location of industrial plants outside the core city has diffused job opportunities throughout a wide area. Suburban shopping centers have changed the marketing pattern.

These tendencies have increased rather than decreased the problems of government. As our population grows and our technology advances, the decisions about the use of land and of public revenue become increasingly complex. The governmental machinery to make these decisions, and the governmental influences on private market decisions, have not kept pace with this complexity. As a result, we are faced with increasing traffic congestion, blight in our central cities, unequal public burdens of suburban expansion, duplication of public facilities, and an inefficient use of public and private resources.

2. Population growth.

Two trends have dominated the long-term growth of population in the United States; an ever-larger proportion of our people live in urban areas; and within urban areas, the suburbs and fringe are growing relatively faster than the central districts. Urbanization of our population has been in process for more than a century. In 1850 only 15 per cent of our people lived in urban places. By 1900 the proportion had risen to 40 per cent and twenty years later passed the half-way mark.

Today two out of three Americans live in urban areas. The growth in urban population—both relatively and in absolute terms—shows no sign of abating. It is a reflection not only of the shift of population from rural to urban areas, but of the tendency of urban populations to expand by natural increase.

Metropolitanism is a 20th century phenomenon. Technological advances, primarily in the field of transportation, have made possible a diffusion of plants, homes and shops in a wide expanse around the older central city. As of June, 1959 the Bureau of the Census recognized 192 standard metropolitan areas—central cities of 50,000 or more together with their contiguous suburban areas. Within these areas, slightly more than half of the population still reside in the central cities, but 80 per cent of the population growth in metropolitan areas since 1950 has been registered in the suburbs and the day is fast approaching when a majority of our metropolitan population will reside outside the central cities.

Where are these trends taking us? An intermediate projection by the Bureau of the Census is for a population of 220 million in 1975, an increase of roughly 40 million over 1960. If metropolitan areas continue to get three-fourths of this national growth, our metropolitan population in 1975 will approximate 140 million persons. Central cities will still hold great concentrations of people—in the aggregate perhaps 60 million. But the balance will have shifted to areas outside present central city boundaries; 80 million people will live in the suburbs and fringes of metropolitan districts.

By the year 2000, only 40 years from now, the population will exceed 300 million according to intermediate estimates of demographers, an increase of 120 million. As many as 100 million of these will be added to the present population of our metropolitan areas.

3. Urbanization.

Two large questions must be examined: First, will the forces making for urbanization be sustained? Second, how will various activities—manufacturing, wholesaling, retailing, business service, home building—be spatially distributed *within* metropolitan areas?

The forces which have transformed the United States into an urban nation within the lifetime of many of us are still ascendant. Barring several events—nuclear war, a national program for dispersal, or a pronounced shift in values—existing urban-metropolitan regions will continue to grow. For such concentrations are evidently necessary to take maximum advantage of technological opportunities that give us a high and rising standard of living. The economies of mass production and distribution which are made possible by large urban markets are widely recognized.

We are perhaps less aware of the importance of external economies of aggregation in urban areas. These are savings available to the individual concern in the form of services or facilities outside the plant and shared with other producers. Among these are middlemen and distributors, bankers, legal experts, accountants, advertising services and market analysts. Also, our transportation facilities, waterworks, sewerage plants and other massive overhead investments, and the availability of research facilities and technicians concentrated in university, library and laboratory yield economies of this type.

Urban growth in the United States has been a cumulative process. The pre-condition for this growth, of course, was a marked rise in productivity on the farm with the introduction of new types of agricultural machinery in the second and third quarters of the 19th century. This not only yielded a surplus to feed large urban populations but released labor to the mills and shops of the city.

Meanwhile, as markets grew, mass production methods in manufacturing became more feasible. The resulting increases in output per worker were reflected in rising income for the community. This in turn made effective new consumer wants. To fill these demands a host of service industries emerged in the fields of recreation, education, personal and medical care. Commerce and industry also required more and different skills and services.

Partially offsetting the economies of urban living are certain "diseconomies" which have required additional services; building inspectors, settlement house workers, laundries, traffic police and window washers.

The growth in urban-type activities is revealed in the changing composition of the nation's labor force over an 80-year period. In 1870 slightly more than half of all gainfully employed workers were engaged in farming; by 1950 the proportion had dropped to one in eight workers.

4. The pattern of development. Within metropolitan regions, we are witnessing a significant redistribution of economic activities from the older central districts to the fringe areas. Home building and industrial plant construction are leading this outward movement; retail trades and household services, warehousing and other industrial services are rapidly adapting to the new patterns of development.

The statistics on home building and retailing since the end of World War II simply confirm our everyday observations. Of 13 million dwelling units erected in nonfarm areas from 1946 through 1958, approximately 11 million, or 85 per cent, have been located outside of central cities.

In retailing, data for the New York region are illustrative of the national trend. Both sales and jobs in retail lines have dropped steadily in the core as a proportion of the New York region over a 25-year period with the outer rings registering the corresponding gains. In 1929 the core area accounted for about 69 per cent of retail employment as well as sales; in 1954 these were down to about 60 and 55 per cent, respectively.

A gradual but unremitting relative decline in manufacturing jobs located in central cities is also discernible. Of total production workers in 48 standard metropolitan areas, 66.5 per cent worked in the central cities of the areas in 1929; in 1954 the ratio was down to 53.6 per cent.

Certain types of activities, however, show little inclination to deconcentrate. Business and governmental services requiring face-to-face relationships or dependent upon a large pool of female labor continue to exercise a strong preference for office space in the core of large metropolitan areas. In eight leading standard metropolitan areas about 80 per cent of all employment in finance, insurance and real estate in 1956 was in the central cities.

Central locations have also retained their hold on manufacturers of unstandardized products and those dependent upon a diversified mix of skills and materials. Among those industries with the highest percentages of employment in the central city were: fur goods, footwear cut stock, printing trade services, millinery, periodicals, and miscellaneous publishing.

Between the business core and the rapidly growing suburbs lies a large expanse of older districts—the "gray areas." In the more compact city of 1920 these areas housed most of our families. Increasingly since 1945, middle-income families with children have been departing for the suburbs; lower-income groups, including substantial numbers of racial minorities, have taken up the slack. But while there are few vacancies, physical deterioration of housing and supporting facilities is much in evidence. The gray areas are experiencing capital consumption and their economic future is in doubt.

What is the shape of things to come in metropolitan areas? In our mixed economy, investment decisions reflect a combination of factors —changes in industrial techniques, consumer preferences, and public policy. With regard to the location of new investment in metropolitan areas, the net effect of these factors in the postwar period has been to encourage a more dispersed pattern of development. For industries dealing in standardized products, the shift to horizontal-line processing in single-story plants has compelled a search for larger sites available only in the outer reaches of the metropolis. At the same time, the clustering of plants in new industrial districts has yielded some of the external economies formerly available mainly in the central city.

The strong desire for lower-density living on the part of families with children has led many to choose a suburban home. Federal policies in the field of mortgage insurance, which have generally favored single-family construction as against apartment developments, have strengthened this outward movement. So, too, have public policies in the fields of highway construction and education. On balance, these and related factors portend a more and more widely dispersed pattern of metropolitan development in the years ahead.

Metropolitan problems

The large-scale breakout of residences, commercial activities and manufacturing from the bounds of the central city has produced a number of major problems. Each part of the metropolitan area is faced with problems peculiar to itself. This diversity may strengthen the feeling of mutual antagonism between city and suburb. The area as a whole, however, faces problems which cannot be dealt with adequately on a piecemeal basis. Yet, so far, few areas have developed institutions which can adequately deal with these problems, and the prevailing antagonism between city and suburb inhibits the development of such institutions.

1. Central city problems. The public service requirements of central cities are shaped by a unique set of pressures. One is the burden of handling a daytime population 30 to 50 per cent greater than the residential population. The continuous decline in use of mass transit facilities is making this task enormously more difficult. Between 1950 and 1958 transit riding in American cities fell from 17.2 billion to 9.7 billion rides

per year, a drop of 43 per cent. More and more people are getting to work or shopping by car.

The principal response of the cities has been to facilitate this shift by building or planning to build expressways to the core district and by adding to the supply of parking space. But discouraged by the growth of congestion, some cities like Washington, D.C. and San Francisco are considering a new emphasis on rapid-transit systems. For central cities, the provision of good access to the central business district can be expected to have a high priority in capital improvement programs in the years ahead.

An historic function which the central city continues to perform is that of reception center for low-income migrants from outside the region. A steady stream of people from the rural South and Puerto Rico has replaced earlier migrations from abroad as the chief source of unskilled and semiskilled labor in urban centers. The majority of these migrants characteristically settle in the central cities.

Thus the cities carry a major share of the responsibility for helping newcomers adapt to an urban environment. It follows that city expenditures for social services, health clinics, welfare agencies and public housing are considerably higher per capita than in suburban areas.

Another major concern of the central cities is the relentless spread of blight and obsolescence both of public and private facilities. In New York City, for example, almost half of the current capital budget is allocated to the replacement of outworn and outmoded public facilities. The prevention of excessive depreciation of private investments such as housing is a responsibility the municipality now shares with private owners.

Blight may afflict residential, commercial or industrial areas. It involves neglect of property by owners and it may result in the development of unsafe and unsanitary conditions. Generally, large areas are afflicted. The law of contiguity, a Gresham's law of land-use whereby poor uses drive out good, prevents private redevelopment in small parcels.

Under favorable circumstances one activity would replace another when it could make better use of the site. But thousands of acres of built-up land in the central cities of our metropolitan areas are underutilized and not filling needed functions. To restore land to sound use, redevelopment of a large acreage is generally required to overcome the impact of bad neighborhood influences.

Private ownership commonly finds it very difficult to redevelop on the scale necessary to establish new dominant uses. Owners of plots in such areas frequently have a price expectation far above market realities; many small plots must be accumulated, a few hold-outs can make the cost inordinately high; and there are large demolition costs. Any major shift in land-use requires a combination of capital, foresight, willingness to risk, and the full cooperation of the local government.

The public interest in restoring land to sound use and generally to a higher tax-paying basis is considerable. Not only does this increase vital functions in parts of the central city, but it also reduces the heavy burden of providing fire protection, police protection, public health facilities, and other services which a seriously blighted area requires.

The development of effective programs to check blight and obsolescence would entail substantial increases in municipal efforts to enforce building and housing codes, relocate displaced tenants, prepare community-wide and neighborhood plans and zoning ordinances, and related activities. Few, if any, cities are yet geared to handle this immense job. Thus, continuous pressure on city budgets may be expected from this field of municipal activity.

While the needs of central cities are growing, their revenue sources are not keeping pace. Property tax income is checked by the exodus of upper and middle-income families and the establishment of retail shopping centers, new factories and "clean" industries such as research laboratories outside the city limits. The resulting squeeze on taxpayers in some cases has sent property taxes so high as to make new private construction almost uneconomic. Without new construction to support and encourage new economic activity, the city finds it increasingly difficult to meet its revenue needs.

2. Suburban needs. With more than 8 out of 10 new homes being erected in suburban communities, it is these places which are feeling the brunt of demand for new schools, water systems, sewage disposal plants, fire stations, streets and utility lines. Each new house in a suburban development requires a package of public services which entail capital outlays ranging in cost from $2,500 to $3,500 or more, depending upon the density of development and degree of utilization.

Thus, capital expenditures run substantially higher in suburban communities than in the cen-

tral city or nonmetropolitan areas. In the New York region, for example, suburbs made capital outlays in 1955 of $68 per capita compared with $44 in the central city and $38 in the nonmetropolitan section. Considering these expenditures, it is no surprise that many communities try to effect their own salvation by screening out moderate-priced housing and forestalling a need for public sewerage systems and other facilities through such devices as two-acre zoning.

For rapidly growing suburbs the good design of neighborhoods that will provide long-term amenities and sound capital values is a problem that can be solved by intelligent local use of planning and zoning. The requirement is local awareness and willingness to use tested techniques. Since most residential construction occurs in new suburbs, they present the easiest and greatest opportunity for steps to provide long-lived improvement at minimum cost. Failure to take these steps now will prove very costly in 10 to 20 years.

3. Area-wide problems. Some services essential to metropolitan living cannot be provided separately by each municipality. The size and geographic extent of the capital investment, the economic forces at work, the nature of the physical environment, or the claims for use by the residents of the area make it almost impossible for communities to provide services or meet these needs separately. Among these are the provision of area-wide transportation systems, the control of air and water pollution, the reservation of open land for outdoor recreation, broad land-use planning, a fair distribution of tax resources, and the stimulation of growth in the economy of the area.

A. Transportation. The transportation of goods and people is basic to the life of a metropolitan area. The most important transportation problem is the movement of people within the area to places of employment and for shopping. Recreational and other personal travel needs are generally adequately met by the facilities provided for the first two purposes.

Historically, public transportation and rail commuter travel developed in our older metropolitan areas before the general use of the automobile. In these areas increased use of private automobiles has put financial strain on mass transit and rail commuter facilities. Some of our newer metropolitan areas have come to rely predominantly or almost exclusively on the private automobile supplemented by bus systems. In all areas increased use of the automobile has posed a serious congestion problem.

In the allocation of land and public revenues to various means of transportation three questions arise:

(1) How shall facilities and travel be divided among highway, transit and rail commuter?

(2) Where shall facilities be located? and

(3) How shall the cost be covered?

In planning for population growth and higher incomes, public agencies need to determine how to strike a balance among programs which expand highways, provide mass transportation or shore up commuter facilities. At some point the additional space required for private automobile travel will so encroach on other land uses that mass transportation will have to be provided, or improved to handle the additional travel.

In some major metropolitan areas rail commuter services transport a significant number of people into the central city daily. Yet the abandonment of commuter lines under the provisions of the Transportation Act of 1958 is forcing more people to turn to the private automobile. A wholesale abandonment of commuter runs by railroads would greatly increase the expenditure and the land required for the highway system.

Commuter lines are suffering financial difficulties, with no easy solution. The property tax on roadbed and terminal facilities used by commuter lines is a competitive burden, for the highways used by alternative forms of travel are tax-free public facilities. But rail commuter facilities share roadbed with rail freight and with long-distance passenger traffic.

Public responsibility for the problems of the commuter railroads is divided among the Federal government, the state governments and the many communities through which the rights-of-way run. As with mass transit systems, the benefits are enjoyed by users, businesses dependent on commuter travel for employees and customers, and the general public.

Transportation networks within metropolitan areas are basic, the capital costs of new construction are high, and the operating costs of rail and mass transportation are heavy. Yet in most metropolitan areas there is no single public agency able to study the relative needs for highway, mass transit, or rail. There is no single body able to allocate costs among users, businesses and the

general tax funds. No authoritative body is able to balance transportation capacity and the traffic-generating uses of land.

Under these circumstances many ills are apparent: undue congestion, duplicated facilities, poor service, financial difficulties, inequitable sharing of burdens, and inadequate anticipation of future needs and costs.

B. Control of air and water pollution. The winds that blow across the Hudson River are no observer of municipal or state boundary lines. Any program to control smoke or other pollution of the air in and around New York obviously must be area-wide. Each metropolitan area has a similar problem. The same holds true for control of the degree of contamination in fresh or salt water bodies in or on the boundaries of metropolitan areas. A river may serve as a source of water supply or as a means of waste disposal. No individual municipality can influence the water flowing into it, or washing its shores, except by cooperative effort with other municipalities, or through an area-wide or state governmental body.

C. Land-use planning and open land. Vacant land on the fringe of metropolitan areas is being absorbed at a rate of approximately one million acres a year. Current investments in housing, shopping centers, plants, streets and public facilities are fixing the environment for two generations or more. But in few, if any, metropolitan areas is the magnitude of this responsibility matched by adequate preparation, planning and land development controls on a metropolitan scale. In consequence, transport facilities, sewerage and water systems and schools have been overtaxed in many areas; commercial ribbon-developments have sprung up alongside metropolitan highways, choking traffic and blighting the countryside.

Equally important, few areas have reserved sufficient space for parks and recreational needs, and rights-of-way have not been set aside for future expressways and utility lines. All too frequently, land only recently developed in the outskirts of a metropolis has had to be purchased for a right-of-way at a price five to ten times as much as the cost of the raw parcels. These costs as well as the uprooting of families and businesses are avoidable through advance planning and acquisition by the government of rights in land.

D. Industrial development. The expansion of income-generating activities is desired by practically all metropolitan areas—both to provide more jobs and to provide an expansion in the tax base. The most important economic activities generally sought are expanded or new manufacturing plants.

The success of local communities in attracting new industry is partly dependent upon the expansion of the national economy and the region's economy, and some factors in industrial location are beyond the control of individual localities. But other influential factors can be controlled within the metropolitan area. Among these are space for industry, traffic, public services, the attractiveness of the community as a place to live, and local taxes.

Allocation of space for industrial use takes place partly through the free workings of the real estate market. It can be strongly influenced by industrial zoning provisions which limit or exclude other uses. Thus the small percentage of land in a metropolitan area which is most suitable for industrial use can be reserved for such use. Where a clear conflict exists between two good uses not easily satisfied by most land, such as waterside industrial and waterside recreation uses, some mechanism for careful decision should exist so that allocation is not made by default.

Taxes in any community in a metropolitan area may become an influence on industrial location when they are excessively high or abnormally low. Abnormally high taxes may be the result of inequitable assessment or of an inefficient local government, but they may also be the result of the community having to carry an undue share of the metropolitan area costs for welfare, for highway maintenance, for mass transit, for schools or for other public purposes.

Abnormally low taxes in some areas may result from an avoidance of responsibilities which are passed on to others to carry; or they may reflect a reluctance to provide positive services in the nature of good schools, recreational facilities and the like. The absence of good public services of this type may reduce a community's attractiveness for new industry.

Recommendations

The heart of our problem is the use of land and of other economic resources, particularly public revenue resources, in our metropolitan areas in the most efficient manner. The use of these resources almost always involves choices among alternatives. The methods by which we make these choices have evolved over a long period of time, and are subject to further modi-

fication. In brief, there are three essential elements:

1) A primary reliance on the private enterprise economy, private initiative and private decision making;

2) A body of government regulation of private activities extending from the allowable uses of property and the rights of property owners to traffic regulations;

3) Direct government decisions regarding provision of public capital investment and services.

The concentration of population in metropolitan areas and the spread of this population and of economic activity outside the limits of the central city have reduced the effectiveness of existing procedures of allocating resources in metropolitan areas.

The Committee recommends four types of action which should lead to the making of better decisions about the use of land, public revenue, time and human effort in our metropolitan areas.

1. Careful studies of the economic base. The Committee believes it important to bear in mind that a metropolitan community is a place for earning a livelihood. The existence of any urban area at a particular place, and its growth or decline, depend on the expansion or contraction of opportunities for employment and investment. If this is understood, a community will usually desire to take the governmental steps which can help maintain and increase such opportunities. Growth or change in employment and private investment may also call for changes in land-use patterns, expansion of highway or other transportation systems, and development of utilities such as water and sewers. The attendant population growth will influence school requirements and other public services.

A fundamental step in meeting the problems of a metropolitan area, then, is systematic and periodic analysis of its economic base. Many areas could benefit from a careful analysis of the economic and demographic forces influencing the volume and pattern of its income-generating activities. Such knowledge is essential to an understanding of the influence of public policy on the retention, expansion or attraction of private investment and employment opportunities. Only with such knowledge is it possible to formulate sound master plans to guide community development, to invest wisely in public improvements, and to make the right decisions about urban renewal. Such knowledge is of great value to businessmen making investment and location decisions within a metropolitan area. In a private enterprise economy an improvement in private economic decisions adds to the public welfare.

Such base studies should cover the entire region and should be carried out on a nonpartisan and objective basis by official planning and development agencies with metropolitan-wide jurisdiction. In the absence of a public agency, these studies might be under the auspices of a special council of local governments in the metropolitan region or a broadly representative non-profit corporation of community leaders.

The Committee believes that this field of inquiry deserves a larger commitment of research and educational resources. The preparation of economic base studies is currently handicapped by a lack of skilled technicians. Systematic procedures for collecting meaningful data about the metropolitan economy are also lacking. These are matters of national importance and should be brought to the attention of the public through a national advisory body.

As a first step, the Committee recommends that the recently-formed Advisory Commission on Intergovernmental Relations appoint a council of recognized scholars, technicians, local officials and business leaders to advise the Commission on objectives and techniques applicable to economic base studies. Existing sources of data for such studies—Federal, state, local and private—should be catalogued and proposals should be made for obtaining any additional data required but not presently available.

2. Recasting urban renewal programs. The value of tangible real estate in our cities is conservatively estimated at more than 500 billion dollars. For this present generation these capital facilities represent a life trust, to be used responsibly and to be conserved and supplemented. But this responsibility is not being adequately met. The spread of blight and obsolescence is visible in most of our urban areas.

Beyond this is the task of conserving and modernizing middle-aged and older residential neighborhoods where the majority of dwellings are not yet substandard. Some indication of the dimensions of this job is the fact that more than half of the national housing inventory is now at least 30 years old. And in addition to residential areas,

there are large sections of commercial and industrial blight found in virtually all our cities.

Estimates of the capital requirements to renew our cities cover a wide range—from 120 billion dollars up. These estimates assume that three-fourths to seven-eighths of the total outlay will take the form of private capital outlay. The government's role is viewed as setting the stage for private development and providing financial assistance only to the extent required to permit the private real estate market to function effectively.

Most of the local activity in the field of slum clearance and urban renewal has taken place under the stimulus of the Housing Acts of 1949 and 1954. The latter act increased the emphasis on slum prevention and encouraged the development of local programs to conserve stable neighborhoods and to rehabilitate deteriorating sections which can still be restored to good living standards.

The Committee believes that a continuation of urban renewal activities is essential. At the same time the Committee believes that a comprehensive review of the programs is required.

The Committee is particularly concerned about the following matters:

(*a*) The need for an effective method of economic analysis of past, current and proposed projects, which would not only provide a comparison of probable costs and benefits, but would also indicate a system of priorities for allocating public funds;

(*b*) The possibility of allocating renewal funds in accordance with metropolitan plans and economic studies rather than on a project-by-project basis;

(*c*) The possibility of further extending Federal aids for the renewal of blighted commercial and industrial areas as well as residential areas;

(*d*) The development of renewal policies and procedures which will minimize the relocation hardship on low-income families living in renewal areas;

(*e*) The possibility of so improving state and local laws and administration—zoning, housing codes and the like—that the private real estate market could more readily prevent blight or improve blighted areas with a minimum of public subsidy. Resale of publicly-acquired sites without write-downs should be thoroughly explored;

(*f*) The need for experimentation with devices for conserving and rehabilitating existing neighborhoods without wholesale razing of all structures in the search for more extensive as well as less costly methods of dealing with blight;

(*g*) The possibility of raising qualitative standards for elements of the workable program, such as more stringent housing code requirements and better enforcement practices;

(*h*) Improving coordination between urban renewal planning and planning for all other related public works, particularly the urban portion of the vast Federal highway program.

Until such an evaluation is completed, the Committee recommends the continuation of present programs with Federal aid maintained at approximately the current level. Some progress is being made and we can learn more with a program in operation than at a dead stop.

The Committee feels that planning for urban renewal should be on an area-wide basis in accordance with metropolitan plans. The subdivision of renewal responsibilities among the many municipalities in metropolitan areas undoubtedly results in the misplacement of public and private facilities and a general misallocation of resources.

The Committee recommends that the Urban Renewal Administration give special preference in financial and administrative assistance to communities where workable programs and renewal planning are carried out on an area-wide basis.

3. Reorganizing government in metropolitan areas.

In a number of areas across the country efforts are underway to equip governments to handle metropolitan-wide problems. These efforts should be encouraged. There is no single formula or pattern of government which is ideal for all metropolitan areas in our country.

The reformulation of American political institutions in metropolitan areas is just beginning to emerge. Whatever the eventual forms, the Committee sees the need for modernizing our governmental structures in metropolitan areas so as to enable them to carry out more efficiently and effectively those public responsibilities which are clearly metropolitan in scope.

There are three basic reasons for advancing this position. First, there are grounds for believing that an integrated approach to area-wide problems such as transportation is, over the long run, more efficient and economical per unit of service provided.

Second, there are a number of problems which are not being met adequately or at all for lack of a metropolitan approach. For example, there are few if any metropolitan areas which have a public policy with regard to the provision of open space for future development and recreational needs.

Third, we believe that these problems are of such mounting importance that sooner or later they will compel governmental action. We think that these governmental policies should be developed and carried out at the level of government closest to home. These matters—transportation, air pollution, and the like—cannot be tackled by small local jurisdictions. A metropolitan level of government could cope with these matters without sacrificing local control.

Failure to establish metropolitan governments with wide powers will lead to a greater loss of self-determination in local affairs through the continuous transfer of responsibility to the state and Federal governments.

In this connection, state governments have a responsibility to study this problem since the local governments are created by the states. Solutions for the problems of metropolitan areas will require the revision of state constitutions as well as legislative and administrative action. Moreover, interstate agreements will be necessary in the case of at least 23 metropolitan areas which extend across state boundaries.

It is encouraging to note that some state governments have recently set up units or study commissions concerned with metropolitan problems. But there is a clear need for wider recognition by the state governments of their responsibility for studying metropolitan problems and developing more uniform laws and permissive legislation for the solution of these problems at the metropolitan level.

The form of metropolitan government organization is a matter for determination within each area. One promising approach is the metropolitan federation under which only the most obvious regional functions are vested in a single government with other duties remaining in the hands of the individual localities. Whatever the formula for unifying responsibility, we should, to the greatest extent possible, preserve institutions which permit direct popular participation in local government.

4. Business leadership and metropolitan growth.

The Committee believes that local business leaders should participate more actively with local officials and other groups in setting goals for their community and guiding metropolitan affairs. Big public decisions lie ahead in each metropolitan area, decisions which will vitally affect opportunities for private employment and private investment. Civic responsibility and enlightened self-interest demand that local business leaders work closely with elected and appointive officials in their communities in reaching public decisions and carrying out public programs. This will become all the more important if new structures of local government are established, as recommended, to embrace metropolitan-wide responsibilities.

There has been a tendency on the part of some businessmen to remain aloof from political affairs and the government decision-making process in their local communities. In part this stems from a reluctance to take time away from their business responsibilities. But more and more businessmen, particularly heads of leading concerns, are finding nonpecuniary rewards in devoting time to civic undertakings.

Another deterrent, the old view that local poli-

tics are dominated by the spoils system, has less validity today, with the extension of civil service systems and the increased prestige of public service. Businessmen should encourage this trend by supporting efforts to attract more qualified people into local elective office and public employment. One way to support this movement is for some businessmen to seek elective office at the local level. Others can participate by accepting appointments as lay members of city planning commissions and advisory boards.

Business leadership can emphasize the importance of establishing community priorities in the use of resources. They should stress the usefulness of factual studies such as economic base analyses. They should urge a metropolitan-wide and long-term point of view in planning for future development and the provision of public facilities. With these guidelines we can begin to transform our local governments into modern institutions equal to their responsibilities.

READING 67

The racial crisis of the 1960s is multidimensional. One critical aspect is in the area of jobs for Negroes in private industry. Many employers, in the North and the South alike, are aware of patterns of economic discrimination that have persisted for a variety of reasons over long years and are convinced that these patterns must now change rapidly. The economic aspects of race relations demand discussion in any unit on unfinished business—but it becomes clear at once that any such discussion cannot stay in the area of pure economics for very long. Inevitably, the debate must carry over into the moral and the social arenas.

Charles E. Silberman, a member of the board of editors of *Fortune* magazine, presents a provocative series of views on the job aspects of race relations. His plea to businessmen to take deliberate, compensatory steps to give Negroes a much better break than they have had in the past stands in contrast to the views of Kyle Haselden in the next reading.

Questions to Guide the Reading

What are the economic costs associated with patterns of discrimination on grounds of race, religion, or nationality? Are there substantial economic gains to be realized from breaking down these patterns?

What considerations must enter any decision by public or private groups in choosing an action program on economic discrimination?

Is a full-employment economy a necessary condition for Negro progress in getting better jobs? Is it a sufficient condition?

MANAGEMENT AND JOBS FOR NEGROES
Charles E. Silberman

The events of the spring and summer of 1963, beginning with the demonstrations in Birmingham in April and May, represent a major watershed in the history of U.S. race relations. Birmingham, and its aftermath in a hundred cities around the country, demonstrated, so that no one could doubt it any longer, the depth of Negro discontent, the extent of Negro anger and hate, and the ease with which it can flare into violence.

The great majority of Negro Americans are still mired in poverty. Until the Birmingham crisis, however, these lower-class Negroes were imprisoned by apathy and despair, and they left the protesting to small, highly disciplined cadres of educated, middle-class Negroes. But when the police dogs were unleashed in Alabama, every Negro in America felt their fangs in the marrow of his bones. The explosion of anger and hatred that resulted broke through the traditional apathy of the poor and created an almost universal desire to act.

The entrance of the poor into the Negro protest movement has profoundly altered its direction and temper. Jobs, not civil rights, will be the key issues; boycotts, sit-ins, and mass picketing, not "moderation," will be the principal weapons; the streets, and not the courts, will be the major forum. Indeed, Negroes of every income level are now eager to demonstrate. They are increasingly intolerant of "moderation," and the poor, in particular, are contemptuous of the doctrine of nonviolence that has dominated the struggle so far.

The Negro rank and file are now bringing pressure to bear on their leaders, instead of the other way around. Indeed, the Negro leaders' position recalls Mahatma Gandhi's famous remark, "There go my people. I must catch them, for I am their leader."

The verge of crisis

Underlying this shift in goals and tactics is the fact that two out of three Negro households earn less than $4,000 a year, and that one Negro male in nine is out of work. This poverty and insecurity are particularly galling to the Negro, who sees the white society that surrounds him grow increasingly affluent while he remains tied to his slum. Contrary to popular impression, Negroes' economic position has actually deteriorated over the last ten years, relative to that of whites. Negroes did make enormous advances during World War II and the boom years that followed, for the shortage of labor drew them into factory and white-collar jobs that had always been barred to them. As a result, Negro income increased 80 percent faster than white income, and the median income of Negro families jumped from only 37 percent of white income in 1939 to 57 percent in 1952. But this escalation came to a halt with the slowdown of the economy after the end of the Korean war. As a result, the median income of Negro families dropped from its high of 57 percent of white income in 1952 to 53 percent in 1962.

The future is even bleaker than the present; it is no exaggeration to say that Negroes are on the verge of a major economic crisis, for the gap is widening between Negro education and training, on the one hand, and the requirements of the labor market, on the other. Automation, new management techniques, and changes in consumer spending patterns are all reducing the demand for unskilled and semiskilled labor and increasing employment in professional, managerial, clerical, and sales jobs, many of which require considerable education and training. These white-collar occupations account for no less than 97 percent of the total increase in employment that has occurred since 1947. The professionalization of the labor force accelerated during the mid-Fifties, and will pick up more momentum in the decade ahead. But Negroes are badly prepared for this change. Three Negro men in five now work in unskilled or semiskilled blue-collar jobs, compared to three out of ten white men, and more than half the Negro men over the age of twenty-five (vs. 21 percent of white men) have had less than a grammar-school education. Small wonder that in northern industrial centers one out of every three Negro workers has suffered unemployment in the last several years, or that in some Negro neighborhoods the unemployment rate may run as high as 40 percent.

But Negroes' lack of education and training

and their concentration in unskilled occupations—conditions produced by past discrimination—do not entirely account for Negro poverty. On the contrary, the Negro unemployment rate is higher than the white rate in *every* major occupational group. Among craftsmen and foremen, for example, Negro unemployment runs to 9.7 percent, compared to 4.8 percent for whites; among clerical workers, 7.1 percent vs. 3.8 percent. While a great many Negroes can't find jobs because they lack the necessary skills, all too many Negroes who do have the education and training are unable to put their skills to work.

Many firms employ Negroes only in a few job classifications. In the South, employment of Negroes is limited by the tradition that Negroes not be permitted to work on an equal status with whites, and that they never be placed in a supervisory position over whites. In the North, exclusion of Negroes from the better jobs stems less from conscious corporate decisions to discriminate than from the conscious or unconscious biases of the personnel officers, the foremen, the executives, i.e., all those involved in hiring and promoting. At the heart of this kind of unconscious discrimination, management consultant John Perry has suggested, is the concept of "place"—i.e., the notion that certain jobs and certain situations are appropriate, others inappropriate, for Negroes. In almost every company, that is to say, whether through accident or choice, tradition has reserved some jobs almost exclusively for Negroes and some almost exclusively for whites ("Negroes wouldn't be happy there"; "Negroes wouldn't fit in there"; "I'm not prejudiced, but my customers might object").

Because discrimination is so endemic, Negro youngsters all too often see no point to finishing high school or going on to advanced training; they drop out at the first opportunity, and they shirk their studies while they are in school. "Education is a difficult enough process under any condition," Dr. Carl Hansen, Superintendent of Schools of Washington, D.C., has explained, "because educational effort is primarily an expression of hope on the part of the student. . . . The Negro pupil is obliged to be more hopeful than the white student. He is asked to have faith and confidence which at the moment he is in school seems unreasonable and unjustifiable."

Jobs are the fulcrum, therefore, on which Negro progress rests, and to which Negro protests will be directed. Businessmen will be in the thick of the fray. Corporations of every sort will be served with demands to hire more Negroes in non-menial positions and to train them for promotion. The pressure to open up job opportunities will encompass every level, from apprentice to foreman to the executive suite, though the emphasis will be on the broad middle range. The pressure will be at least as strong in the North as in the South; more than half the Negroes of the U.S. now live in the cities in the North and West, where they constitute a large and rapidly growing proportion of the population. The methods used will run the entire gamut from polite moral suasion to legal action to boycotts, mass picketing, and sit-ins.

What is involved is an attempt to liquidate, in one generation, the consequences of 250 years of slavery and 100 years of discrimination and neglect. To do so, needless to say, will require difficult and heroic decisions on the part of civic and political as well as business leaders; it will require changes in the behavior of Americans in every walk of life. But businessmen occupy a peculiarly strategic position, and they may, as a result, be called upon to bear more than their proportionate share of the burden of change.

So far, however, business has done little more than react to pressure from Negro groups. The "Plans for Progress" program of the President's Committee on Equal Employment Opportunity provides a perfect case in point. Over 100 corporations have signed Plans for Progress, promising to "undertake a program of affirmative action" to recruit Negroes and train them for employment and promotion. The President's committee has the power to force compliance with the plans, but until very recently it emphasized the virtues of voluntary compliance.

The virtues are hard to find. While total employment of Negroes has increased since the program began, only a few contractors account for the bulk of the increase. Most firms have done very little to redeem their pledges.

The fact that so few firms are carrying out their commitments under the Plans for Progress program does not necessarily imply that the signers are insincere; it does suggest a lack of realism on their part about what they have to do to carry out the program.

"They just don't apply"

Most executives contacted by *Fortune* had heard of the Plans for Progress program, however, and most seemed willing enough to hire more Negroes. The problem, they said, was that qualified Negroes just didn't seem to come around.

Of course they don't; the door has been closed too long. Three hundred and fifty years of exclusion from American society have persuaded Negroes that there's no point in applying, that "the man" (the white man) has stacked things so that Negroes can't get ahead, and that there is, consequently, no use in trying. Hence Negroes will assume that a firm discriminates until they get positive reassurance to the contrary.

Merely adding a "We Are An Equal Employment Opportunity Employer" tag line to a company's want ads, for example, will not persuade Negroes that the way is open to them. "Industry has to do more than just sit and wait for Negroes to come to their doors," J. J. Bricker, personnel vice president of I. B. M., argues. It has to beat the bushes to find them, by recruiting at Negro colleges, high schools, and employment agencies; by advertising in Negro newspapers and over Negro radio stations; and by using the employment services of the National Urban League, which has representatives in sixty-five cities.

A number of factors have conspired to keep Negroes from acquiring the education and skills they need for non-menial jobs:

Negro high-school students in the South are generally offered vocational education only in traditional Negro occupations. In Houston, for example, the sole vocational high school, which is restricted to whites, offers three-year courses in air conditioning and refrigeration mechanics, automotive mechanics, drafting, machine shop, photography, printing, radio, television, and welding. None of these courses are given in the five Negro high schools. As school officials explain it, "It would be wasteful . . . to educate a student for admission to a craft or trade that is not open to him."

Trade unions are equally culpable. In a number of occupations, workers can qualify for employment only by completing an apprenticeship-training program, which is usually controlled by the trade union involved. Negroes have generally been barred from access to apprenticeship programs run by the plumbers, sheet-metal workers, steam fitters, lathers and plasterers, and electricians, among others.

Most important of all, years of slavery and the discrimination that followed destroyed Negroes'

self-confidence, and thereby limited their aspirations and their willingness (and ability) to compete. They are understandably fearful about trying to "make it" in the white world, especially the impersonal world of business.

Are tests necessary?

To end this vicious circle that keeps Negroes untrained and unemployed will require patience and imagination, and, in many cases, a break with corporate tradition. A large merchandising chain, for example, recently asked the National Urban League for help in hiring Negroes for a number of jobs, including store managers. But there was an unintentional catch; the firm required ten years of merchandising experience with the chain as a condition for promotion to manager. Since it had never employed Negroes in merchandising jobs before, the requirement obviously made it impossible for them to qualify for at least another ten years. The Urban League suggested that the firm develop methods for testing managerial ability in a shorter time.

The doctrine of the debt

All this sounds like a demand for special treatment for Negroes, and that is precisely what it is. Negroes are not content with equal opportunity any more; they are demanding preference, or "positive discrimination" in their favor. Negroes liken their position to that of a runner who is kept at the starting line until his opponents in the race are halfway to the finish line; merely "freeing him" to run will not enable him to catch up. More and more Negroes, therefore, are espousing "the doctrine of the debt," which holds that the U.S. owes the Negro something for 250 years of slavery and 100 years of discrimination. "If those who make the decisions in this country are really sincere about closing the gaps," Whitney Young, the brilliant young director of the National Urban League, argues, "they must go further than fine impartiality. We must have, in fact, special consideration if we are to compensate for the scars left by three hundred years of deprivation, which actually represented special consideration of another sort." Hence Young is demanding special priority in employment, suggesting as a precedent the ten-point preference given veterans on civil-service exams after World War II.

The Urban League is proposing that when a

Negro and a white have equal qualifications for a job, the former should be given the preference. Militant Negro organizations are demanding considerably more; they are insisting, in effect, that business firms hire Negroes not because they are qualified but because they are Negroes. And they are developing a good deal of muscle to back up their demands for preferential hiring. The most widely used technique is the boycott, or "selective patronage campaign," as Negroes prefer to call it. "Don't buy where you can't work" campaigns were frequent during the 1930's, but they were sporadic and only occasionally effective. The contemporary use of the weapon began three years ago in Philadelphia. The campaign was organized and directed by a group of Negro ministers (some 400 ministers cooperated) with no formal organization. The ministers' technique is to approach one company at a time, usually a manufacturer or distributor of consumer products for which a number of competing brands are available—e.g., bakeries, dairies, oil companies, supermarket chains. If the company refuses to negotiate with the ministers, it is given an ultimatum to hire a specified number of Negroes in specified job classifications before a given date; if the demands are ignored, a boycott ensues. With 400 ministers using their pulpits to announce the boycott, a substantial portion of the Negro population takes part. All told, the ministers have won concessions from twenty-four firms so far. The technique has spread to Boston, New York, Atlanta, Detroit, and other cities, and is bound to be widely imitated. As the Reverend Ralph Abernathy, Martin Luther King's chief lieutenant, puts it, "Not every Negro is able to go to jail, but every Negro can stop buying a particular brand of bread or milk or gasoline."

Cracking the "power structure"

Now the boycott is being supplemented by the use of mass picketing, which is better suited to industries that do not make any consumer product. In the summer of 1963, for example, a coalition of civil-rights groups picketed construction sites in New York City in an effort to enforce their demand that Negroes make up at least 25 percent of the work force on all governmentally financed construction projects.

Negroes are demanding more than jobs, however. Their leaders are determined that what they refer to as "the power structure" recognize them and negotiate with them—that business and civic leaders, in short, come to the bargaining table not as patrons but as equals. Negroes have long been rankled by the white "power structure's" traditional prerogative of picking the Negro leaders with whom it wants to deal. They are insisting that whites recognize the leaders selected by the Negro community, whoever they may be or however distasteful the whites may find them.

When businessmen (or civic and political leaders), as is their wont, talk to the eight or ten most prosperous or most politically sophisticated Negroes in town, they aren't really talking to the Negroes at all, and they can be badly misled as to the temper and desires of the Negro community.

Negroes' insistence on recognition is more than just a play for power; it is a crucial part of the struggle to overcome the devastation that the past 350 years have wrought on the Negro's personality. The apathy, the aimlessness, the lack of interest in education that characterize the Negro lower classes stem from their sense of dependency and powerlessness — their conviction that "Mr. Charlie" controls everything, and that he's stacked the cards so that Negroes can never win. Negroes must gain a sense of potency if they are to move into the mainstream of American life.

And power has to be taken; the nature of power is such that it can never be received as a gift. Hence when businessmen say they're willing to grant some of the Negro demands, "but not if we're pushed too hard," they're missing the point. Negroes want to achieve their aims by their own efforts, not as a result of white beneficence. Thus, the very militancy and stridency that whites find so upsetting is essential if the Negro is to shuck off his traditional dependency and become truly free and equal, if he is to learn to respect himself, and to be respected by whites.

The years ahead may be harsh and painful but a necessary prelude to the peace that will follow, it is to be hoped. But it would be fatuous to pretend that any set of policies adopted by business and government can bring racial peace within the next few years. For one thing, Negroes' impatience, bitterness, and anger are likely to increase the closer they come to full equality. This is not a quirk of Negro character but a characteristic of all disadvantaged groups: the closer they are to their goals, the harder it is to understand or justify the disparities that remain. Indeed, it is a commonplace of history that revolutions (and the Negro protest movement resembles a revolution in many ways) stem from hope, not despair; from progress, not stalemate. And the nearer to triumph the revolutionaries get, the tougher they usually become. Corporations will find, therefore, that there is no magic formula, no safe and sure way of buying immunity from racial conflict. Indeed, firms that have taken the initiative in employing Negroes may still find themselves the object of attack, perhaps the victim of internecine warfare between competing Negro groups.

Redressing the injuries done to Negroes in the past, moreover, will involve some heavy costs in the present. Granting Negro demands for more jobs, for example, may mean fewer jobs for whites, or at the very least, an end to the monopoly that white employees have thus far enjoyed in many job classifications. Executives can expect to be attacked from both sides, therefore; they will need all the political art they can muster to persuade white employees that "reverse discrimination" is socially necessary and for the greater good. And businessmen may find, to their surprise, that they actually *want* an F.E.P.C. law forbidding all businesses to discriminate in employment or in customer service; such a law would protect them against employees, trade unions, and hostile elements in their communities.

The cost will be high

Efficiency may be lowered by the costs of hiring unqualified Negroes and training them on the job. Even more damage to efficiency may be done by the blow to the morale (and consequently to the productivity) of white employees when firms begin to discriminate in favor of Negroes.

To be sure, no corporation is completely consistent in its adherence to the principle of merit; all kinds of subjective and irrational judgments enter into the selection and promotion of employees. But deliberately departing from the merit principle is something else again, and there is no point in pretending that corporations won't pay a heavy price for doing so. The cost of not discriminating in favor of Negroes, however, will be considerably greater, both to business and to the community at large. "Make no mistake about it, we're going to have to subsidize Negro employment for some time," one industrialist told *Fortune*. "But it will be a lot cheaper to do that than to pay it out in welfare"—or in the cost to the community of racial violence.

It will be far easier to do these things, of course, if the present business expansion continues and the economy returns to full employment. But the question is no longer what to do, but whether there is still time to do it.

READING 68

This brief reading challenges the view set forth by Charles E. Silberman in the previous excerpt that American employers ought to practice some degree of preference toward Negroes to make up for past wrongs. Kyle Haselden's argument, like the Silberman one, necessarily goes beyond the economic arena into moral and social judgments, but this is true of many of the most pressing issues with which economists deal.

Mr. Haselden is managing editor of *The Christian Century* and author of "The Racial Problem in Christian Perspective."

Questions to Guide the Reading

The income gap between Negroes and whites has apparently widened in the past decade. In the absence of compensatory hiring can that gap be closed or even prevented from widening? What are the consequences of maintaining the gap as it now stands?

What is the most effective operational meaning that can be placed on the phrase "equality of employment opportunity," in a society concerned with effective use of all its human resources?

THE CASE AGAINST COMPENSATORY HIRING
Kyle Haselden

In the struggle for racial justice a technique is not valid simply because it annoys the white man or because it promises some temporary advantage to the Negro. It is valid only if it honors the moral ground on which the Negro makes his claim for justice, respects the right of all men to the same justice, preserves in the human relationship values which are equivalents of justice, and promotes rather than prevents the Negro's progress.

The idea of "compensation," which has been suggested as a device to equalize competition between whites and Negroes, fails these crucial tests. By compensation—in the passive rather than the active sense—is meant compensation *for* the Negro rather than *by* the Negro. It has been proposed that the Negro cannot succeed in his search for freedom and equality unless there is an arbitrary—in fact, artificial—removal of the academic, cultural and professional lag forced upon him by over two centuries of slavery and by another of exploitation. It is argued further that the Negroes' years of involuntary, payless servitude established a collectible claim against the descendants of those who enslaved and exploited him.

How can this debt be paid? The proposal is that the Negro be given preference in employment wherever a vacancy occurs, a premium in salary, and a quota system guaranteeing that one-tenth of all people hired by firms, professional enterprises and industries be Negroes. Even though this proposal is obviously unfeasible, what shall we say of it as a theory?

Compensation must be rejected as an equalizer of competition between Negroes and whites for several reasons, all of which rest on the grounds to which the Negro appeals in his demand for freedom and equality.

First, compensation for Negroes is a subtle but pernicious form of racism, It requires that men be dealt with by society on the basis of race and color rather than on the basis of their humanity. It would therefore as a public policy legalize, deepen and perpetuate the abominable racial cleavage which has ostracized and crippled the American Negro. Racism, whoever may be its

temporary beneficiary, should be eliminated from the social order, not confirmed by it.

Second, preferential economic status for Negroes would penalize the living in a futile attempt to collect a debt owed by the dead. The 20th-century white man is no more to blame for the fact that his ancestors bought and held slaves than are 20th-century Negroes for the fact that some of their ancestors captured and sold slaves. This is the ironic tragedy of exploitation. It leaves with the descendants of the exploiters a guilt they cannot cancel and with the descendants of the exploited a debt they cannot collect.

Third, a scheme which gives Negroes preference in employment and a premium in salary would bestow on Negroes the debilitating social status which has for centuries cursed the initiative and enterprise of the white man in the South. Preferred status for the Negro, however much society may owe him a debt, will inevitably destroy in him the initiative and enterprise required of a minority people in a highly competitive society. Slavery corrupts ambition and self-reliance; so, too, does patronizing social status.

Fourth, compensation for Negroes would be unfair to other minorities handicapped by their history or by rapid social and industrial change: Puerto Ricans, Mexican-Americans, migrants of all races, Indians, coal miners and others. Negroes are entirely right in demanding that they be hired, paid and promoted on their merit and in boycotting those enterprises which discriminate on a racial basis. But they are not right in demanding an artificial scheme which is unworkable, racist, destructive of initiative and unfair to other struggling Americans.

Our goal should be parity, not preferment, and there are three things we must do, none of them pleasant, none easy, if we are to attain it.

First, there must be a total, across-the-board desegregation of American society.

Such liberation, however, would leave the Negro still handicapped by centuries of poor schooling and by his long exclusion from most trades and professions. A desegregated society

From Kyle Haselden, "Parity, Not Preference," *New York Times Magazine,* October 6, 1963. Reprinted with kind permission of the author and publisher.

would open to the Negro opportunities which are rightfully his and should be granted to him but for which centuries of neglect and abuse leave many of his race inadequately prepared. Even though all racial bars were removed, most Negroes could not, in a free and impartial society, compete on equal terms with most white people for jobs and preferments.

But this, as we have noted, is a handicap which Negroes share with another one-tenth of the population, whose competitive strength has also been sapped by an unfortunate history or by the entrapping eddies of industrial development.

Our second task, therefore, is to undertake a nationwide crash program for the education, training and employment of the underprivileged, underdeveloped one-fifth of the nation, a domestic Point Four which would give to the employable a fair chance and to the unemployable

qualifying education and training. Such a program would be based not on race but on need. Negroes would of course be the chief beneficiaries of an educational and economic crash program, because of the predominant number of deprived Negroes. But a domestic Point Four program aimed at the needs of *all* the nation's backward peoples would close rather than widen the nation's racial cleavage.

Finally, irritating as it may be, the fact might as well be faced that no immigrant or minority group has ever made its way into the mainstream of American life without studying and working harder and longer than the general population. This is the third task as it now confronts the Negro. The hard historical fact is that self-compensation is essential if he is to escape that social substratum into which a cruel history and an arrogant, avaricious white man have coerced him.

READING 69

What if peace breaks out? Could this economy, where 10 per cent of the Gross National Product is made up of defense expenditures, make smooth adjustments to a world in which armaments and armies played a much smaller role than they now do? The urgency of the question is suggested by a dilemma we face: unless we ask the question soberly and objectively, we run the risk of becoming prisoners of assumptions that the consequences must be disastrous and that we therefore cannot explore with enthusiasm all possibilities for safe disarmament.

The United States Arms Control and Disarmament Agency and the United Nations have both commissioned major studies on the economic impact of sharp cutbacks in defense expenditures. Emile Benoit, professor of economics at Columbia University, has been one of the leaders in this new and critical area of research; he summarizes some of today's conclusions here. The more detailed economic arguments supporting his conclusions are to be found in the Disarmament Agency's Report, "The Economic Impacts of Disarmament" (Government Printing Office, Washington, 1962).

Questions to Guide the Reading

Would the economic effects of disarmament be substantially different in the U.S.A. and the U.S.S.R.? What would each gain economically from disarmament? Is it mandatory that a sharp cutback in government spending on defense be compensated for, to a considerable extent, by increased government spending elsewhere?

Defense expenditures today have some undetermined volume of side effects in research and development work applicable to a peacetime economy as well. Are these side effects worth preserving in themselves? Can this be done in a disarmed world?

CAN WE AFFORD DISARMAMENT?
Emile Benoit

On Dec. 5, 1962, the Economic Committee of the United Nations unanimously approved a joint declaration by the U.S. and the U.S.S.R. urging nations to plan for economic and social adjustments to disarmament. The declaration took favorable note of a detailed study on this subject prepared by a committee of experts, including U.S. and Soviet members, which concluded that economic adjustment to disarmament would pose no unmanageable problems for any country, including the United States.

The basic thinking behind the U.S. concurrence in that conclusion was explained in a report by a panel of American experts—under my chairmanship—called "The Economic Impacts of Disarmament," which was published early in 1962 by the new U.S. Arms Control and Disarmament Agency in Washington. Since this is one of the very few areas in which it has been found possible to achieve full agreement with the Russians, it is well worth while for all Americans to understand the thinking that lies behind this optimistic appraisal—especially since it flies in the face of many popular impressions.

Something less than one-tenth of the output of our economy is now devoted to defense—about $52 billion out of a total production or gross national product (G.N.P.) of $550 billion. A somewhat similar proportion of our employment is now absorbed in defense activities. Out of a total labor force of around 75 million, about 6.5 million people are employed directly or indirectly in defense work—roughly 2.5 million people in defense industry, some 3 million in the armed forces, and over 1 million as civilians in the Department of Defense and related agencies.

The big industrial concentration of defense production is now in the aerospace-electronics-nucleonics complex, which accounts for about four-fifths of all procurement. There is also a heavy geographic concentration of defense plants and installations, making such areas particularly vulnerable to the effects of disarmament. In Kansas, Washington, New Mexico, California and Connecticut, at least 20 to 30 per cent of all those employed in manufacturing work on de-

fense projects. In Alaska, Hawaii, the District of Columbia and Virginia, one-tenth to one-quarter of all income is generated by military pay and allowances, or Defense Department civilian wages and salaries.

For individual communities and areas the problem may be even more acute. In a recent year, 82 per cent of all workers employed in manufacturing in San Diego worked in missiles and aircraft; the corresponding figure was 72 per cent in Wichita, 53 per cent in Seattle, and 27 per cent in the Los Angeles–Long Beach area.

The sudden termination of all this defense activity would obviously create quite a problem. However, we can be almost certain that disarmament will not occur overnight. To set up proper procedures for inspection and the prevention of disarmament treaty violations and aggression, and to man the necessary agencies, will take time—probably a dozen years at the minimum.

Even assuming a production cut-off in the first stage, of bombers, liquid-fuel missiles and other vulnerable strategic delivery vehicles, plus an immediate scaling down of military manpower, defense spending probably would not be reduced by more than $5 billion in any one year, even in the initial period of maximum impact. This would amount to less than 1 per cent of our G.N.P.; by contrast the cutback in 1946 was 30 per cent of our G.N.P., and in 1954, 3 per cent.

We were able to handle these much steeper defense cutbacks without major economic letdowns. To be sure, conditions are different today and our economy may be less resilient, lacking the big backlog of unsatisfied demand for durable goods and housing and the abnormal level of liquid savings created by $180 billion of World War II deficit financing.

Today a cutback of even $5 billion could cause trouble if there were no offsetting increases in other public and private expenditures. It is unlikely, however, that we would allow a downward spiral to develop without some increase in Government spending programs for education, health, housing, roads, or whatever, all of which have been held back because of urgent defense priori-

From Emile Benoit, "Would Disarmament Mean a Depression?" *New York Times Magazine,* April 28, 1963. Reprinted with kind permission of the author and publishers.

SPEEDUP IN GOVERNMENT SPENDING

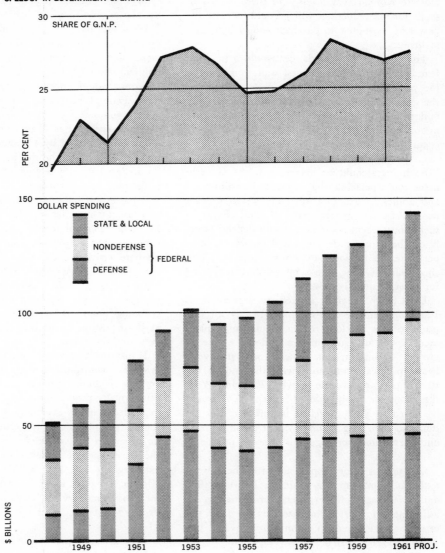

Fig. 1   The bar chart shows how total government spending is divided between defense, other federal outlays, and state and local expenditures. It is noteworthy that in the past several years nondefense spending, federal as well as state and local, has been rising rapidly while defense has been relatively stable. The line chart shows total government spending as a percentage of G.N.P. In 1959 and 1960 the percentage fell somewhat below 1958, when the G.N.P. was low. But government's share turned up again in 1961, giving a powerful stimulus to the economy.

ties. Moreover, we are still taxing ourselves at close to Korean War levels, and there is obvious scope for tax reductions which could increase the power of consumers to purchase and of industries to invest.

The chief depression danger would arise from fear, and hesitation to invest and to spend on the part of business and consumers alarmed at the novel prospect of a long series of deflationary budget cuts over a decade or longer. Pessimism might be heightened if a stock market break occurred at this time.

Such fears could be overcome if the Government could persuade the public of its willingness and ability to generate adequate offsets quickly enough to sustain aggregate demand. Faith in such Government assurances would depend largely on the capacity demonstrated to protect prosperity in the period before disarmament. From this point of view, the time to start preparing for disarmament is now.

Even if we avoid an immediate depression, as I am confident we can, we may still face a tough problem over the long run in keeping unemployment down and sustaining an adequate rate of growth. Failure in this respect could involve a heavy political cost, since with the end of the strictly military struggle between East and West, the economic competition between them would be raised to a new level of importance. Stagnation and mounting unemployment could damage our international prestige and national morale.

Our unsatisfactory experience after the Korean cutbacks points up the problem. Between 1953 and 1960, real defense expenditures, making an adjustment for price increases, dropped 30 per cent—most of the drop coming in 1954. In this same 1953–60 period, the average rate of industrial growth dropped by two-thirds, and the number of unemployed rose by 40 per cent as compared to the preceding 1948–1953 period.

We entirely failed to provide adequate offset programs. At the very time we were cutting real defense spending by 30 per cent, we also cut real Federal non-defense expenditures on goods and services by 30 per cent. And, instead of providing adequate tax cuts, tax rates were kept at close to Korean War levels; by 1960 the Federal Government was collecting 37 per cent more in taxes and other revenues than it had been in 1953.

As a result, in four out of the seven years, 1954 to 1960 inclusive, the Federal Government took more purchasing power away from private consumers and business than it restored to them by its own expenditure and benefit programs.

We would have to steer a quite different course to stay out of trouble in the event of disarmament, and such reorientation would encounter political obstacles. Even in the unlikely event that Congress would approve a doubling of non-defense Federal programs, this would offset only about one-quarter of the probable net cutback in defense expenditures. Tax cuts, though popular, might be restrained by a feeling of moral obligation to use part of the defense savings to reduce the national debt—a feeling which public opinion polls show is quite strong.

A pattern of holding back on new expenditures and tax cuts in order to achieve a budget surplus for debt reduction could cause a good deal of trouble. Cuts in defense contracts have an immediate restrictive effect on the economy even before there is any actual reduction in Government spending. This underscores the crucial importance of replacing defense contracts with new spending programs or tax cuts almost immediately—if possible at the very time that the defense cuts are announced.

If disarmament occurs, the Government's main economic contribution will, therefore, probably consist of maintaining a brisk demand in the economy by prompt and adequate tax cuts and expanded public expenditure programs. There should be no difficulty in finding worthwhile public programs that could be speeded up. Despite the stereotypes of runaway public spending and extravagance, the fact is that on a real basis— allowing for price increases—Federal expenditures for goods and services, other than defense, have declined, not risen, over the years.

Indeed, on a per capita basis, they are now only about half what they were back in 1939. Even if we add in state and local government expenditures, total real government purchases, for other than defense uses, have declined from 16 per cent to 11.5 per cent of gross national expenditures over this period.

Tax cuts in a period of disarmament should be partly permanent and partly temporary and flexible. For the permanent tax cuts, emphasis could well be given to selective cuts in business taxes which would have beneficial indirect effects. For example, reductions in excise taxes would lower the price of travel, entertainment, telephone calls and many goods, thereby helping to stabilize the cost-of-living index and combat inflation. As another example, lowering the tax on business profits used to buy new machinery could stimulate investment and productivity and help us sell more goods abroad.

For the temporary and flexible tax cuts, I suggest "tax holidays." Whenever sufficiently adverse trends in unemployment and expenditure appeared —as defined in advance by Congress—the Treasury Department might request business firms simply to omit the withholding tax on their employes' earnings for one or more payroll periods. The Treasury would also permit the taxpayer a corresponding percentage deduction from taxable income when making out his income-tax statement at the end of the year. This procedure would be a lot simpler from a bookkeeping point of view than giving the President the power to modify the basic tax rate, as he has recently proposed, and would make it quite clear that the tax concession was of a temporary character.

The excellent United Nations study, "Economic and Social Effects of Disarmament," documents in considerable detail the various needs to the satisfaction of which the resources freed by disarmament could be allocated.

The existence of such needs requires little demonstration. Even in our so-called "affluent society," nearly seven million families and single individuals have incomes of $40 a week or under. Our commuter and urban transportation systems, much of our housing, our municipal services generally, our provisions for public health and education, and other public-welfare programs obviously fall far short of the standards which a highly prosperous nation could reasonably expect. And our need to modernize and expand our industrial plant, if only to remain internationally competitive, is becoming a matter of serious concern to well-informed people. Beyond our own shores, the magnitude of the world's needs is appalling.

Thus there can be no question of inadequate "needs" for the resources which disarmament would release; there can only be a question as to how these needs could be endowed with sufficient purchasing power to transform them into effective "economic demands," capable of putting people to work and turning out goods and services. The knowledge of how to do this does exist in modern economics.

Those who doubt the survival capacities of private enterprise should be reassured by the brilliant progress of the European private enterprise economies in recent years, despite substantially lower defense expenditures than in the United States and major defense cuts after Korea.

The European Common Market countries increased their industrial output by 82 per cent between 1953 and 1961—compared with only 20 per cent in the United States. They thus equaled or exceeded the growth rate of the Soviet Union, especially when due account is taken of the Soviet's relatively poor performance in agriculture, housing, transportation and services.

As I suggested in a recent book, "Europe at Sixes and Sevens," Europe's recent growth has outstripped that of the United States not only because of the beginning of the Common Market, but also, and primarily, because of its more expansionary monetary-fiscal policies (especially its avoidance of budget surpluses) which provided a stable framework within which European companies could confidently plan for expanded investment and employment.

What of the "structural problems" of industries, regions, communities and occupational groups which now depend heavily on defense activities, and which would have to make occupational changeovers as a result of disarmament? It is my belief that these problems will be less troublesome than many people fear, providing we succeed in maintaining aggregate demand and opportunities for growth.

American workers are motorized and highly mobile; if new jobs are available they will usually get to them. Similarly, factories are usually willing to retrain and upgrade workers when order books are bulging. Incidentally, an exceptionally high proportion of defense workers are skilled, and even have professional qualifications, while our armed forces are better educated and more highly skilled than the average population.

Some strengthening of public employment services and unemployment compensation systems would, of course, be helpful for such an emergency, as well as the further development of the recently installed program of area readjustment and development, and the worker retraining program now under consideration. Because of the rising cost of such community facilities as housing, schools and hospitals relative to the cost of factories, the case for aiding new industries to enter areas where there are pools of skilled unemployed labor is becoming more persuasive than the case for major Government programs for aiding worker relocation.

In any case, it is clearly unnecessary to plan out in advance just what each factory will make in a post-disarmament situation, and just where each worker will go. Our private enterprise system has great flexibility in guiding a restructuring of productive processes in accordance with the new demands which will emerge, and it is the task of monetary-fiscal policy to assure that the over-all total of such demands will be adequate.

The chief structural problem in my view is not that of merely finding a place where the resources released from the defense program can be deposited; rather, it is the problem of making the best use of the valuable productive potentials of the high-caliber human and physical resources now employed in the defense effort.

This refers particularly to the exceptionally able and smoothly functioning teams of scientists, engineers and management people now working within the framework of the defense program on some of the most difficult scientific and technical problems facing mankind. There are problem areas which urgently require the fresh and creative analysis such teams could provide. Space exploration is perhaps the most dramatic example; research on problems of inspection and controlling disarmament is another.

There are many other such areas where highly organized and dynamic attacks on key problems of broad national and international significance could have very large payoffs. Examples taken more or less at random would include improved urban transportation and commuting systems; a fundamental attack on the related problems of electronic microscopes, cell functioning, aging, cancer and on circulatory and mental diseases.

Other examples—which might contribute particularly to the removal of bottlenecks in world economic development — include unconventional energy sources (nuclear fusion, solar energy, fuel cells, etc.); teaching machines; desalinization of water; population control; climate control; mass batch production of key nutrients in which tropical diets are deficient; and mass production of standardized components for housing, factory construction and production of simple types of machinery.

With this type of reconversion program, we could be much more alive to the positive and constructive aspects of disarmament and could enjoy its economic challenge.

READING 70

The publication of Harvard economist John Kenneth Galbraith's book, *The Affluent Society*, in 1958, touched off one of the liveliest episodes in the continuing debate on the proper role of government in our society. Friends and foes alike turned their attention to the main theme of this book, which argues, in essence, that the private sector of our economy has grown prosperous and overconcerned with material luxuries while our public sector has been deprived of the resources needed for social purposes such as highways, slum clearance, education, and cultural activities.

Note that this is a distinct issue from the one of government spending as a stabilizing force in the economy. (See Readings 24 and 25.) The attention now is upon private versus public spending as alternative ways of allocating the nation's limited resources to meet its unlimited ends. And each type of spending raises certain ethical issues: the private market operates on the ethic of "one dollar, one vote," while public spending operates on the ethic of "one man, one vote."

Questions to Guide the Reading

What guidelines can help us determine whether a particular service might best be performed privately or publicly? Are there effective ways of combining public and private resources in such a way as to minimize the dangers about which *Fortune* is concerned?

How can the efficiency of a dollar spent privately be compared with the efficiency of a dollar spent publicly? Do we have sufficient examples where we can compare the two activities under similar conditions?

THE DANGERS IN BIGGER PUBLIC SPENDING
The Editors of Fortune

The idea that the country is "starving" the public sector of the economy, while spending too much money on luxuries, will undoubtedly echo through the halls of Congress often as it struggles with such current issues as aid to housing, aid to education, and public health insurance.

It goes without saying that the national interest and the general welfare require strong and effective government to care for defense, to maintain internal law and order, to provide a sound and efficient monetary system, and to undertake certain public works. But we believe that the misallocation-of-resources school of thought is mistaken in at least three particulars. In the first place, it is simply not true that the public sector of the American economy is being starved for resources. In the second place, its proponents subtly confuse the discussion by equating "public needs" with government activity and greatly underrate what private enterprise can do in meeting those needs. Finally, the critics have overlooked the basic difference between coercive government activity and private activity, which gives free play to the choices and options of individuals and groups. In the process they have misjudged the nature and functions of government in a free society.

The government's bite

On the first point—relating to the magnitude and growth of government in our lives—it is really extraordinary how the advocates of more spending have tended to play down the revealing statistics. Yet those statistics are there for all who care to read. Government expenditures—federal, state, and local—have dramatically expanded in the last decade. The expansion is even more marked if we take a longer perspective. In the late Twenties, for instance, expenditures by the

federal government ran to only about $2.8 billion, while spending by the states and local communities was $7.7 billion. In 1940 the figures had risen to $9.6 billion and $10.3 billion respectively. But in 1960, cash expenditures of the federal government had soared to $90.9 billion, with the states and local communities spending an additional $40.7 billion, *making a grand total of $131.6 billion.* Meanwhile, of course, national output has also been going up rapidly, but by no means so fast as government outlays. In the late Twenties total government spending ran to about 10.8 per cent of the national product; in 1940 it was 20.8 per cent; last year it was 27.5 per cent, or over one-quarter of our total economic activity.

This mounting burden on the taxpayer has, of course, been in part due to the rise of defense expenditures, which are now running at close to $50 billion. But this is not the whole story. Government outlays have been dramatically rising in most of the nondefense areas that the critics say need attention. Expenditures for highways, for instance, have risen from $1.8 billion in the mid-Twenties to $8.7 billion in the late Fifties. Expenditures for "public welfare and assistance" have gone up thirty times over. Social-insurance benefits, which ran to only $1.2 billion in 1940, ran to $15.9 billion in the late Fifties. In the same span of years outlays for public education rose from $2.8 billion to $16.8 billion, and last year they ran to nearly $18 billion. In addition, some $4 billion is being spent for private schools and colleges. On a per capita basis, the U.S. is spending more on education than any country in the world.

Are we all fools and wastrels?

So it does not appear that the government sector of the economy is exactly starving. But

From "That 'Starved' Public Sector," *Fortune*, August, 1960, pp. 87–89. Reprinted with kind permission of the publishers.

this is not the only point that deserves emphasis. What the advocates of more public spending have forgotten is that all this massive government activity depends on the private economy, and that this economy makes an enormous contribution to "public needs" and to "public purposes" through its production of consumer goods and services and through the process of private investment. To hear the critics talk one might suppose that expenditures for consumption were so much waste. But this is a terrific perversion of the facts. Of total disposable income in 1959— the income left over to individuals after taxes —easily three-quarters went for food, clothing, shelter, and transportation. These are surely "public needs" just as much as are new roads or school buildings. In addition, some $19 billion was spent on medical care, $4 billion went to charity and religious institutions, and $24 billion was set aside in the form of private savings. These savings in turn flowed over into private investment, which provides the economy with new factories and better tools, on which rising living standards and rising real wages depend.

All this does not exactly indicate that the American consumer is a fool or a wastrel—his fondness for tail fins to the contrary notwithstanding. (And even tail-fin cars are now giving way to compacts.) On the contrary, private expenditures in an "affluent society" can in fact greatly reduce the need for government action. The $19 billion that private citizens spent in 1960 for medical care, for instance, is a huge contribution to meeting an obvious social want. Moreover, over 70 per cent of the civilian population now has some form of health insurance. These figures do not foreclose consideration of supplementary government effort. They do indicate that whatever government does in the field of social security is marginal to what private activity accomplishes. And, certainly, if the federal government is now to involve itself in health insurance, the system should be so far as possible on a voluntary rather than a compulsory basis.

Even more in point is the whole problem of urban renewal, which is today engaging so much public attention. According to the critics the great American cities are "rotting away," and so it is proposed that the federal government pour billions into the task of rebuilding them. But this proposal overlooks the fact that money taxed by the federal government is money lost to the states and local communities for carrying on their own functions. More important, cities are renewed by the upkeep of old buildings as much as by the building of new ones, and both jobs depend primarily on private decisions. Governments can help by various financing devices and by taxation policy. But the fundamental task of keeping our cities in order calls for private and local government activity; such cities as Pittsburgh and Philadelphia are striking examples of how civic pride can go to work.

You can take it or leave it

Today there is every reason for encouraging private citizens to take on so-called public jobs in the interests both of economy and of maintaining constitutional principles. The power to tax is also the power to destroy, and at some point there is danger of collectivizing the American economy through the back door. If, for instance, government activity rose from its present 27.5 per cent of the national product to, say, 50 per cent, then it would be evident that the economy had been subtly collectivized without the advocates of statism having fired a shot.

This leads directly to the third gap in the argument of those who advocate more government spending. According to them there is, in the end, no real difference between governmental and private use of resources: "Surely when we act publicly or privately we are the same people." The trouble is that we aren't. There is a world of difference between earning and spending one's own money and having the government spend it for one. When G.M. sells cars on the market, the people can take them or leave them. They exercise free choice and consumer option. But when the government taxes for its expenditures, the case stands otherwise. True, the citizen has had a chance to vote for the government in office, or for the bond issue in question. But this chance for choice occurs only intermittently. Moreover, public expenditures are determined by the bare will of the majority. If 51 per cent of a community vote for more roads, the other 49 per cent must bow to the decision. This is quite different from the kind of continuous choice that guides production and distribution in the competitive economy.

Put more generally, most government action involves *coercion*—outright coercion in the administration of justice, but also coercion through the taxing power. Such coercion is necessary if there is to be any government at all. But precisely because government must have large coercive power the scope of its action requires limitation, and it is the great strength of the U.S. constitutional system that it plainly recognizes this necessity. It is also the great merit of the private-enterprise system that it takes care of the allocation of the bulk of resources, relieves the government of this responsibility, and so makes limited government possible. The two institutions thus complement and reinforce each other, and have together produced our unique political economy.

This whole American system is of course marvelously adaptable, and the lines separating government and private activity are not fixed.

But when pressure groups are everywhere active, and when the legitimate demands for defense and winning the cold war are enormous, the need is to define the limits of government rather than to go whole hog for its expansion. Nor should we allow ourselves to believe that more government spending in all directions is necessarily synonymous with furthering the national purpose. For the national purpose of the U.S. is not the aggrandizement of statist power but the preservation and extension of human liberty under law.

READING 71

In contrast to the views just presented, there are other influential and articulate Americans who hold that our economic problems can be faced and our economic opportunities realized only through a still more active role for government. They see a host of problems that differ either in degree or in form from those found by this nation when it was less populous, less technologically oriented, and less involved in world affairs. And they conclude that the private mechanisms on which we have relied for so many things in the past cannot meet the new challenge alone.

Milton J. Shapp is the former chairman of the board of the Jerrold Electronic Corporation in Philadelphia; he has since thrust himself more heartily into the area of public discussions on key economic and political issues. This paper identifies some of the major myths and misunderstandings that he feels have plagued our whole approach to government's proper role in the economy.

Questions to Guide the Reading

Does Shapp's analogy between business and government provide a reliable and useful way of approaching government's accounts? Where is the analogy weakest and where is it strongest?

Are there reasonable alternatives to substantially higher public expenditures on education and research? What advantage and disadvantages lie in such alternatives?

THE GROWING DEMANDS ON GOVERNMENT
Milton J. Shapp

For years we have talked about the need for introducing modern business techniques into the operation of local, state and federal government. However, we have made but little progress in this direction. Paradoxically, one of the main obstacles has been and still is the violent opposition of many business leaders to changing the fiscal policies and organizational structure of our government to conform with sound business practices.

We must make these changes if we are to attain the rate of national, state, and local economic growth required to provide opportunities

From Milton J. Shapp, "A Plan to Put the Operation of Our Government on a More Business-like Basis," Statement for the White House Regional Conference, Philadelphia, November 17, 1961. (Privately printed.) Reproduced with kind permission of the author.

for full employment and higher standards of living for all of our growing population.

Of outstanding importance, we must drop the time encrusted concept that in preparing government budgets, in effect, cash is treated as our only asset. Because we keep no business-like balance sheet for government fiscal operation, we talk disparagingly about our National Debt of 300 billion dollars but ignore the fact that the government possesses physical assets that perhaps exceed 2000 billion dollars in value.

A balance sheet of a business firm lists many assets of far greater importance to the potential earning power of the company than its cash-on-hand. Money is invested in programs of research to develop new products and in capital equipment with which to produce these items. Raw inventory is purchased, labor hired and trained and goods produced. Marketing programs are developed. The sale of finished inventory creates receivables. These, in turn, convert to cash, and the process repeats itself over and over again. Money is used in business merely as a tool to create and increase wealth.

A business firm normally prepares two separate budgets—one for capital investments and the other for operating expenditures. In addition, as another tool to insure effective fiscal control, most firms compile a cash-flow sheet.

The capital budget deals normally with long term investments needed to insure growth of the company, and often necessitates the borrowing of large sums. In business this is considered good practice if it can be shown that the potential return on investment exceeds its cost. Operating budgets cover current expenses of doing business and must be minimized if the business is to show a profit. The cash-flow sheet simply compares cash-in with cash-out for the period covered. If a company were to consider cash as its only asset, it could never grow; it could never show a real profit. Capital investments made to insure long-term profitable growth would have to be written off each year as ordinary expense rather than depreciated over a period of years in accordance with the usefulness of the capital equipment. To make progress, a business must convert its cash into other assets in order to stimulate the forces of production.

Yet today we ignore this basic principle in handling the fiscal affairs of our government. Actually, state and federal governments and most cities have no budgets in the real sense—only cash flow sheets. If more revenue is collected each year than is paid out, this is called surplus. If more is paid out than collected, this is called a deficit—regardless of whether the money is used for secretarial salaries or invested in new schools, highways, water supply systems, hospitals, airports or other capital improvements vitally needed to increase the wealth potential of our country. *Since budgeting lies at the center of all financial planning, this false concept of measuring only cash-input against output in the preparation of government budgets lies at the very core of our economic illness today.* Until we alter this concept, we can make but little progress in resolving our economic problems.

On the other hand, once we adopt modern business principles in the treatment of governmental budgets (beyond the treatment of some accounts on an accrual basis), new vistas open and practical methods of resolving our economic and social problems become discernible.

To stimulate new growth and new jobs in America, we must use our "liquid assets" in effective programs to increase our total wealth.

If we consider our economy as a public address system, this becomes clearer. A child speaks into a microphone and the voice resounds throughout a large auditorium. The function of an amplifier system is to accept low level signals and transform these into more useful high level signals.

Our capital, properly utilized to stimulate the forces of production, can accomplish the same function for our economy. Relatively small sums spent for research and education can be transformed into tremendous economic wealth when combined with intelligent capital investment, manpower and marketing programs.

Some of these programs involve the public sector of our economy—others the private. *What is of vital importance, especially to the business community, is that unless proper investments are made in the public sector, the return on private investments is not maximized*—industry suffers and employment possibilities are reduced.

This is where the importance of proper government budgeting methods becomes apparent. Since the end of World War II private investments per capita have increased about threefold, but the public sector investment—the combined total of our local, state and federal capital improvement programs—has actually decreased about 2% per capita. Because operating expenses of government for welfare, defense, veterans' payments, etc. have increased substantially, needed capital investments in schools, highways, hospitals, water and sewerage systems, resource development programs (to name but a few) have been curtailed. Thus we are spending an increasingly larger percentage of our government budget for operating expenses and a reduced proportion for capital needs.

As a result, despite the fact that government purchases of goods and services today stimulate our economy to the extent of 20% of our Gross National Product (whereas the pre-war total never exceeded 15%), our economy is sputtering unevenly, and unemployment has hovered close to the 7% mark for almost a year.

Yes, government money is being spent in greater quantities today than ever before in peace time, but because our public sector capital investment program since the war has been insufficient and failed to keep pace with needs, full effectiveness of the tremendous private sector investment program has not been achieved, and the wealth of our nation has not been growing sufficiently to accommodate the requirements of our expanding population.

Where have we failed—and what must we do? Fundamentally, the government must finance those programs of investment that private enterprise cannot undertake, but which are sorely needed to complement and to enhance the private sector investment program.

Education and training

Industry must recognize that government expenditures for education and training should not be considered as an operating expense, but actually as a long-term investment to enhance the value of our greatest single asset—people. Today, business is being penalized doubly for the failure of our educational system to equip people—young and old—with the educational background and/or vocational skills required by modern industry.

Many new industries find it impossible to sustain growth due to lack of trained personnel, while taxes mount ever higher to support those who lack the educational background or vocational skills to find employment. Facilities to match manpower with job skills are woefully lacking.

The surest way to create a welfare state is not to provide the adequate educational system required to make productive and useful citizens of all people within our borders. The City of Philadelphia is spending $4 million a month—$48 million a year—to take care of over 100,000 welfare cases within its city limits. Pennsylvania is spending $150 million a year for welfare. If but a

fraction of this sum was spent to step up education and to expand vocational training and retraining programs, the total demand on our tax dollar would be reduced drastically. The morale of these now unemployable people would be raised greatly if they became productive once again (rather than dependent upon society) and the taxes they would pay would help support the government rather than serve as a drain upon our economy.

Moreover, there are important aspects of national security that have been and will continue to be impaired if we fail to increase our investment in educational facilities.

The Communists — Russian and Chinese — are rapidly expanding their educational systems despite their severe shortage of building materials. Their needs for housing and industrial construction are also very great. Nonetheless, very high priority has been assigned to school, college and laboratory facilities. We have no such handicap. There is no shortage of materials in the United States to build schools. In fact, the reverse is true. We have an excess of building materials and trained construction labor. The difference is that the Communist leaders know that the *future* of mankind is being determined *today* by the education of youth. Too many of us fear the future and prefer to sit on our gold reserves without recognizing that when we are no longer a first rate technological power, our people will be as vulnerable to exploitation and loss of property as were the American Indians and the people of Africa and Asia in the 17th, 18th and 19th centuries, who were either driven from their lands or colonized by others possessing superior technology.

This is the challenge we face. Everything is comparative.

Those of us who are satisfied by the statistics that reveal the number of new school rooms constructed in the United States since 1945, by the increase in the number of teachers, or by the modest expansion of our college campuses should understand that by comparison we are still operating a "propeller driven" educational system—perhaps augmented by "turbo prop jets." In this, the pure jet—the rocket—the missile age—we are lagging behind our competitors.

Our failure to provide an educational system that meets the needs of the times is being measured today by our inability to provide full employment opportunities for our citizens. Tomorrow it will be measured by our inability to survive as a free nation.

Research and development

Both government and industry must increase substantially their outlays for research and development. Our present generation operates the industrial machine made possible by the brain power of yesterday's geniuses—Einstein, Steinmetz, Edison, the Wright Brothers, et al. It is impossible to imagine how many additional industries would be flourishing today — in America and throughout the world — if research effort had been doubled in a period between 1900 and 1950. Whatever the statistics might have shown, it is indisputable that the benefits would have exceeded the cost by a fantastic margin.

As an essential part of this program, the government should establish centers of "pure research" in numerous areas throughout the country. While it is true that basic research is national and even international in scope, it produces direct benefits to regional industries as well.

Consider for a moment the situation that exists in New England today. The shoe and textile industries, upon which the economy of New England formerly was based, have been hard hit by the exodus of plants to other areas of the country and by the flood of imports from abroad. Fortunately, during World War II the government spent large sums of money on research programs at MIT in Cambridge, Massachusetts. Today, as a direct result of this, many hundreds of new electronic and instrumentation companies have taken root around MIT, giving New England an economic rebirth. Within a relatively short period of time, it is anticipated that these new technically oriented industries will absorb the New England work force left idle by the demise of the older industries. In Massachusetts alone almost 50,000 new jobs have been created in the electronics industry since the end of World War II.

If by chance the original radar research contracts had been issued to Carnegie Tech and the University of Pittsburgh instead of MIT in 1941, it is entirely possible that western Pennsylvania would be flourishing today as a major scientific center instead of wallowing in the depths of a recession that finds approximately 9% of its labor force unemployed.

The question arises as to whether basic research programs should be sponsored by government or by private industry. The answer is both, but there are several reasons why federal and state governments must take a leading role and not rely upon private industry to supply major impetus to this project.

First, to be realistic, industry by its very nature will only support programs of research and development that within a reasonable period of time will result in profit. All industry needs, but with the exception of our largest corporations, individual businesses cannot afford to finance long term programs of research designed to derive basic scientific data rather than the direct development of new products or processes.

Further, a private company has a natural tendency to retain the results of any research program within its own organization. This not only negates the primary purpose of obtaining and disseminating basic knowledge broadly to assist all industry, but, conversely, if data obtained by research programs were available only to the companies who could afford to conduct these programs, this would increase the likelihood of our larger corporations becoming more monopolistic in the future.

It is, therefore, in the interest of developing a more competitive economic system that basic research programs should be financed publicly as well as privately and the data made available to all.

Development of national resources

Approximately 35 billion gallons of clean water will be needed each year to support the projected increase of almost one million population during the next decade in Pennsylvania. Most of the water requirement is industrial.

But will the industry that needs the water, supply the funds required to develop this resource? The answer is obvious. This is a responsibility of government.

This is but one of the resources that need development. Nationally, we may one day face a crisis if our supplies of raw materials from overseas (mostly from underdeveloped nations) should be severed as in the case of nickel and chromium.

In considering future economic growth and employment problems within this country; in considering production of aircraft, rockets, missiles and items of military nature, we must give great consideration to the question of what would happen if suddenly America should be shut off from the imported supply of raw materials that are so vital to our prosperity and to the very security of this nation. If the communists should be successful in controlling the output of countries in Latin America, Asia and Africa, upon whom we depend for many of our resources, or if chaos should come to some of these areas as with the

Congo, we will find it difficult to maintain the economic pace that is necessary if our country is to survive.

Samson lost his strength when he lost his hair. Our economic strength would be torn out by the roots if we were cut off from these resources.

This grave problem obviously suggests a national program to develop and husband our natural resources; to develop new uses for low grade materials; and above all, to make our country independent of imported resources (as nearly as possible) in case of emergency.

It adds up to good business, because in the process of developing such a program, new industries will come into being and many present industries will be strengthened.

Marketing

The recent Congressional report on "The Impact of Automation on Employment" revealed that by the end of 1962 the United States will be able to produce as much on its farms and in its factories as it did in April, 1961, with 1,800,000 fewer workers. It becomes imperative that government and industry work together to develop new markets for our products because only through increased sales can there be increased future job opportunities.

Today we can produce more on our farms and in our factories than we consume or sell through present marketing methods. Unfortunately, in industry and in government too often we follow a philosophy of subsidization, cut-backs and quotas, rather than a program of opening new markets as a means of handling this surplus production. A positive business-like approach reveals that great domestic and international markets exist for our farm and industrial output. If we are to reach the national growth rate that is needed to provide full employment to our work force, it is the prime responsibility of management to seek these new markets actively and not be content to profit by raising prices on smaller output.

Only about 14,000 out of the 300,000 manufacturing firms in the United States do any exporting. The Department of Commerce has already taken steps to stimulate export activity by expanding its services both overseas and in the United States. Management of industrial firms should follow this lead and devote more time and effort to the development of important overseas markets.

The adoption of an optimistic view of some of our perplexing problems reveals that enormous markets exist for the sale of many farm and industrial products both domestically and abroad.

For example, we should not be pessimistic about the high costs of rebuilding our decaying urban centers or providing decent living standards for elderly people. Not only must these needs be met, but looking at this optimistically, we should consider the tremendous possibilities that exist for thousands of manufacturing and construction companies supplying the materials needed in rebuilding these blighted areas and also the great new markets for goods and services that will be created when millions of our elderly people are supplied with sufficient funds to enjoy decent standards of living. We should look upon extension of life for our parents as a blessing—not a burden.

Internationally, we should look to the great new markets that can be developed for our products within the emerging nations of the world.

We have surplus food bulging our warehouses costing our taxpayers untold billions for storage. It is ridiculous to think that people should starve in any land for any reason while food rots here.

The emerging nations need help in expanding their own food production and housing facilities. Hundreds of millions of acres of their virgin land is untilled today because access roads are needed to reach the areas, and/or irrigation required to make the soil fertile. Roads, bridges, tractors, bulldozers, pipelines, housing materials, etc. are needed in seemingly limitless quantities. With many of our own factories working at little better than half capacity—with so many of our own people unemployed — we should look at the opportunity to assist these nations as a blessing in disguise — as an opportunity to remove many of our own citizens from relief and welfare rolls and give them productive jobs.

Instead of looking at foreign aid as a giveaway program, we might very well consider this as a long term investment being made by our government to develop future markets for our products. If we succeed in raising living standards in the developing nations, we shall thereby increase the demand for billions of dollars worth of all sorts of products, simultaneously reducing the Communist threat within these areas.

Conclusion

The resolution of our local, state and national economic problems lies in the application of well established business principles to the fiscal management of government. Organization should be streamlined for efficiency. Operating expenses should be minimized, but we should never shirk from making needed public sector investments in wealth producing facilities. Schools, highways, airports, hospitals, colleges, water and sewer systems, programs of basic research and programs to develop national resources—these are the facilities and services needed to develop the economic strength of our country and increase the productivity of our citizens.

These are investment programs that must be maximized by the government and considered as long term capital investments. Such programs should not be considered as expense items in a cash budget. Nor should such capital investments in needed facilities be considered in the light of public works programs merely to lift the economy in times of recession.

A successful growing business firm does not wait until business is bad before it intensifies attempts to develop new products, to train production, sales and executive personnel, or to build new plant facilities. While business is good, expansion programs are pushed. The whole concept of utilizing public works programs to lift the economy and to provide employment during a recession ignores the principle that *capital investment programs must precede effective economic expansion.*

When we finally—as eventually we must—adopt a sensible businesslike fiscal program for managing government finances, then we shall be on the path to correcting the ills of our economic system. Until we do, we shall continue to wallow, blaming everything from taxes to inflation, from automation to featherbedding, without really coming to grips with our basic problem.

READING 72

A number of issues in the 1960s have focused our attention once more on the question of what reliance we shall choose to maintain on free markets in the allocation of resources. Adam Smith would find our economy far removed from the laissez-faire world he defended in *The Wealth of Nations*; but he might have some sympathy for at least some of the forces that have moved us to a re-definition of what we want to do through free markets and what we want to do through more direct intervention. In any event, he could not move through our society without being challenged to ask again what kind of an economy is evolving here.

Adolf Berle, distinguished lawyer, government servant, and author, raises some of the more topical issues in this question. They make it evident that the question can never be fully resolved; there will be new cutting edges to it as each generation faces new specifics in the interrelations of private and public agencies.

Questions to Guide the Reading

What are the yardsticks by which one measures whether a specific market interference by government is, on balance, socially desirable? Do we have appropriate mechanisms now for appraising costs and gains associated with any proposed extension of these interferences?

Is the movement farther and farther away from unrelated markets an inevitable drift? What key variables will determine the rate of any such drift?

HOW FREE SHALL THE FREE SOCIETY BE?
Adolf Berle

Steel prices rose again in 1963—to be followed by another round of contract negotiations between the industry and labor. President Kennedy's close interest in these events throws into relief the persistent question of Government intervention in the price-wage structure.

Factually, the Government controls the prices of goods and services in perhaps half of the American economy. Prices of communications, public utilities, transport and most forms of energy are fixed or influenced by one Government commission or another. The Department of Agriculture maintains prices on most agricultural products. In the defense industries, the Government is the single buyer, and conventional "free market" principles cannot apply. The price of labor in great areas of the economy is set by agreements between the big labor unions and industry. Everyone knows this, has adjusted to it, and the results are tolerable. Even in those industries—steel among them—where no controls exist, the Government "intervenes" from time to time when prices become oppressively or dangerously high or low.

The N.R.A. period of the New Deal was a frank intervention to prevent prices from falling below a tolerable level—but it required setting prices for almost everything. Similarly, when steel prices threatened to skyrocket in 1947–48 owing to short supply, the result was "political intervention." A couple of Senate investigating committees and the Department of Justice took a hand, and President Truman in his inaugural message of 1949 suggested the possibility of taking over the industry.

Less publicized, but not less effective, have been occasional interventions from the administrative side. In some commodities, the Government has maintained large stockpiles — perhaps larger than were necessary — and when prices threatened to rise unduly, it has sometimes released supplies for sale. Similarly when prices threatened to fall, it has been charged that stockpile buying was used to limit or prevent a price slump.

President Kennedy's incursion into the steel-price situation in 1962, therefore, was merely an unusually dramatic instance of intervention that has had plenty of precedents. The incident, however, had one unsuspected secondary effect. It raised the question whether Government intervention in free-market prices should be "institutionalized"—by setting up some regularly constituted form of procedure—or whether such intervention should continue to be left to the chances of political sentiment and the willingness of Government officials to tackle or decline to deal with such problems.

In considering these alternatives, we may as well begin with the fact that America is a political democracy. If the situation is serious, men who are hurt by the rise or fall of free market prices will appeal to the Government. They always have. They may (and usually do) say that they want the Government out of "business," yet when the price-wage structure throws many men out of jobs, prompt pressure is exercised on the Congress and on the Executive to "do something" about it. When prices become so high that consumers consider themselves wronged, they are quick to make their grievances known. Conversely when an industry is going broke because prices are unduly low, it seeks Government action of some kind to relieve the stress.

Theoretically, Americans are staunch adherents of the "free market." Actually, we back the free market just so long as it behaves acceptably and regularly, but raise political hell when it does not. The familiar businessman's joke is that everyone wants a free market—for someone else. In result, the "free market" has become a modified form of statist instrument. It would not continue to exist at all except for the Sherman and Clayton Antitrust Acts, for the steady policing of the Federal Trade Commission, and because of at least one big antitrust case every week.

These measures prevent monopoly. The enforced competition exerts a measure of control on the "up" side. Without this, mergers or cartel arrangements would give uncontrolled market power to the commercially strong. When the price threatens to fall disastrously, competition obviously is not the remedy, but the Government can move in to "stabilize" in a number of ways, and frequently has. Thus, the supply of oil is equated to estimated consumer demand. Imports of cane

From Adolf Berle, "How Free Shall the Free Society Be?" *New York Times Magazine,* June 23, 1963. Reprinted with kind permission of the author and publisher.

sugar are adjusted to estimates of consumption. Quotas for imports of non-ferrous metals are imposed when foreign competition depresses prices. Informally, the system performs acceptably. But it does not cover all major commodities at all times, and price changes may pack a mean wallop under some circumstances.

When the 1963 steel price raise came along, President Kennedy observed that it was difficult, if not impossible, to control prices in a single industry. In this situation, he thought the quite moderate steel-price rise might be left to the "free market." It was, he said, a case where the big units having power to "administer" the price must use restraint.

In the 1963 steel price affair, this worked. But will it—or can it—work at other times or in other situations? Or should we have some sort of an "institution," a commission, court, committee or equivalent with jurisdiction to meet these problems? Obviously the President of the United States cannot be expected personally to attend to these matters save in dramatic cases.

I think there is an intermediate possibility. Americans want the instrument of the free market. Significantly, they want it so that every price shall not become a political issue. A free market insulates government from the headaches of the market place and saves it from the limitless task of examining costs, business administration techniques, profits and business operations in general. Business does that job well; but for governments, it is the most difficult economic task in the world. We found that out in N.R.A. days and again in wartime experience with price administration.

Government regulation also has a deadening, not to say paralytic, effect on business, on production and on the enthusiasm with which Americans go at the job of developing, manufacturing and offering old and new products, and of providing old and new services. That élan has made the American economy the most productive in the world. Instead of controlling prices and profits, the normal American tactic has been to let them run, but to take a good healthy share through taxation. Instead of socializing the productive process, we have, through taxation, virtually socialized a substantial slice of the resulting profits.

Judged by results, the system has worked well. Few, save doctrinaire Socialists, think the free market ought to be abandoned as a first-line method of determining prices.

Experience nevertheless indicates both a desire and a need for a measure of guideline vigilance. This is necessary because the "free market" is no longer the free market of classical theory—if, indeed, such a market ever really existed. A majority of American industries are dominated by big units—often by extremely big units. Two, three, four or perhaps five corporations dominate each industry in an aggregate comprising perhaps two-thirds or so of all American manufacturing. This is called "oligopoly."

Large units have power to "administer" prices —that is, to set price levels which will stick for a considerable period of time. On the wage side, the more powerful trade unions can do the same thing with wages—the system being legalized under the Taft-Hartley and Landrum-Griffin labor relations acts. In both cases, prices or wage levels in any one industry can be set capable of throwing large areas of the rest of the economy out of whack. Prices may be run up, resulting in a cost-push toward inflation, or occasioning distress in other industries. At bottom, the price, wage and production system is one large machine, all parts being pretty closely geared to all other parts.

The two modern factors are the close intermeshing of business processes and the market power of big corporations and big labor. When free-market theory was first developed, meshing was not intense. Corporations of any kind, let alone big ones, were almost nonexistent, as were labor unions. Market power as we know it today was unknown to Adam Smith, to Ricardo, and even in the time of John Stuart Mill. It took the 20th century to develop really "big" business and certainly to permit really big labor organization.

Equally, it took the intense growth of industry and population to push all business and economic elements into a recognizably single system. With the advent of price-and-wage market power, responsibility for the functioning of the machine as a whole has to be located somewhere. In the American economic republic, that responsibility has been placed on the shoulders of the Federal Government by the Employment Act of 1946.

No corporate management and no group of corporations, and certainly no labor union or group of labor unions, has or should have, responsibility for the meshing of the entire machine. The task of each is to look out for its own sectors. The big corporation wants to make profits for its stockholders, to accumulate further reserves of capital for its own use, to retain or enlarge its share of the market and to provide continuous supplies for its customers. Labor unions want as many jobs for their members at as high a pay and with as desirable conditions as they can conveniently get. What the demands of either group may do to the rest of us or to the business economic machine as a whole is not their primary concern.

This is why the Government machinery must evolve toward its next stage—a stage foreshadowed, though not spelled out, by the Employment Act of 1946 and indicated by the unwritten law developing around the Federal Reserve System.

Two agencies of the Government watch the whole picture and all its parts with great care. One of them is the President's Economic Advisory Council. Constituted under the Employment Act of 1946—capstone in the arch of Federal responsibility for American economic conditions—it observes trends and advises the President on measures to effect the statutory policy of the United States to "promote maximum employment, production and purchasing power." Its statistical knowledge is the greatest in the country—in detail as well as in general.

Alongside it is the Federal Reserve Board which also follows the figures, though from the more limited angle of money and credit factors. The Federal Reserve function is indirect—so much so, indeed, that as far as the law goes, it has no responsibility other than to maintain a sound and adequate banking and currency system. Unwritten law and public acceptance have nevertheless assigned to the Federal Reserve a stabilizing function which it has accepted, though its tools are monetary and financial.

From one or the other of these groups—preferably, I suggest, from the Economic Advisory Council—a price-and-wage committee could be set up. Working with the very well-equipped Bureau of Labor Statistics in the Department of Labor, such a group should know better than anyone else the probable effect of any major rise or fall in prices and wages in key commodities and key industries.

It could maintain continuous contact with the representatives of both management and labor in these industries. It could know profit levels and capital requirements. It should have the best possible opinion as to the danger, if any, of inflation, or the possibility of depression. It could, if need

be, make its views public for the guidance of business and labor. In cases of necessity (which should be rare), it might enlist the support of the banking machinery or of other governmental agencies or, on occasion, of the President.

When "restraint" seemed called for, it could say so privately or publicly, and could say why. When the "administered price" power of the large corporations is used to raise prices so as to endanger the general economic welfare, it should be in a position to state that fact. Businessmen, commodity buyers and bankers are sensitive to this sort of thing. Good corporate managers know very well that their prices must correspond to a general healthy level. Similarly, if prices fall unduly for one reason or another, such a committee would know what powers the Federal Government had at its command to stabilize the situation, and could advise on their use.

Such a committee should not often have to invoke government intervention. Persuasion or publicity ought to be adequate to deal with most situations. In extreme cases calling for drastic Federal intervention, it should be able to suggest a reasoned solution rather than a hit-or-miss, shotgun remedy wrought out of distress and compelled by high pressure politics.

Peacetime price-fixing is both difficult and as a general rule undesirable. In any case it is politically impossible at present. I think it is justifiable—and was—in dangerous emergencies like the crash of 1933. In wartime, it is a necessity. Short of such situations, however, the reasoned approach is preferable and ought to work.

Big business and big labor alike know very well that their existence depends on the privileges accorded them by government. The Government permits big corporations, else they would not be there. Statutory law gives specific authority to labor organization and labor unions essential to their position. If their powers are badly used, an act of Congress could eliminate both. In either case, the extremist threatens the group's existence. What is needed, therefore, is a solid realization by both groups that they are part of a great whole, and stand or fall with the welfare of the entire economy.

Part 7

COMPARATIVE ECONOMIC SYSTEMS

This is one of the most famous documents in economic thought, both for those who have read it and for those who have not. The *Communist Manifesto* is, at some points, a classic in propaganda: the language is ringing and the conclusions are black and white with little supporting evidence. It is, at other points, rather turgid prose with a foretaste of the involved arguments that were to follow in *Das Kapital* some years later. But any document with an impact comparable to this one demands serious attention.

Karl Marx (1818–1883) and Friedrich Engels (1820–1895) wrote the *Manifesto* for their colleagues in a secret society, the "League of the Communists." Its publication in 1848 afforded the members an interpretation of the history of the working-class movement, a critique of some existing approaches to solving labor's problems, and a rallying cry to a more revolutionary banner.

Questions to Guide the Reading

What are the major points at which this analysis contrasts with the assumptions we most often make about the driving forces in our economic life?

Much of the Marxian analysis is couched in terms of revolution among industrialized workers. What is there in these ideas that may help to explain why twentieth-century communism has made so many of its converts not in the most highly industrialized nations but in the underdeveloped, agricultural nations?

What are the major charges that a twentieth-century Marxist might level against capitalism?

THE COMMUNIST MANIFESTO
Karl Marx and Friedrich Engels

A spectre is haunting Europe—the spectre of Communism. All the Powers of old Europe have entered into a holy alliance to exorcise this spectre; Pope and Czar, Metternich and Guizot, French Radicals and German police-spies.

Where is the party in opposition that has not been decried as communistic by its opponents in power? Where the Opposition that has not hurled back the branding reproach of Communists against the more advanced opposition parties, as well as against its reactionary adversaries?

Two things result from this fact.

I. Communism is already acknowledged by all European Powers to be itself a Power.

II. It is high time that Communists should openly, in the face of the whole world, publish their views, their aims, their tendencies, and meet this nursery tale of the spectre of Communism with a Manifesto of the party itself.

Bourgeois and proletarians

The history of all hitherto existing society is the history of class struggles.

Freeman and slave, patrician and plebeian, lord and serf, guild-master and journeyman, in a word, oppressor and oppressed, stood in constant opposition to one another, carried on uninterrupted, now hidden, now open fight, a fight that each time ended, either in a revolutionary reconstitution of society at large, or in the common ruin of the contending classes.

The modern bourgeois society that has sprouted from the ruins of feudal society has not done away with class antagonisms. It has but established new classes, new conditions of oppression, new forms of struggle in place of the old ones.

Our epoch, the epoch of the bourgeoisie, possesses, however, this distinctive feature: it has simplified the class antagonisms. Society as a whole is more and more splitting up into two

From Karl Marx and Friedrich Engels, *The Communist Manifesto* (1848).

great hostile camps, into two great classes direct-ly facing each other—Bourgeoisie and Proletariat.

From the serfs of the Middle Ages sprang the chartered burghers of the earliest towns. From these burgesses the first elements of the bour-geoise were developed.

The feudal system of industry, under which industrial production was monopolized by closed guilds, now no longer sufficed for the growing wants of the new market. The manufacturing system took its place. The guildmasters were pushed aside by the manufacturing middle-class; division of labor between the different corporate guilds vanished in the face of division of labor in each single workshop.

Meantime the markets kept ever growing, the demand ever rising. Even manufacture no longer sufficed. Thereupon, steam and machinery revo-lutionized industrial production. The place of manufacture was taken by the giant, Modern In-dustry, the place of the industrial middle-class by industrial millionaires, the leaders of whole industrial armies, the modern bourgeois.

Modern industry has established the world market, for which the discovery of America paved the way. This market has given an im-mense development to commerce, to navigation, to communication by land. This development has, in its turn, reacted on the extension of indus-try; and in proportion as industry, commerce, navigation, railways extended, in the same pro-portion the bourgeoisie developed, increased its capital, and pushed into the background every class handed down from the Middle Ages.

We see, therefore, how the modern bourgeoisie is itself the product of a long course of develop-ment, of a series of revolutions in the modes of production and of exchange.

Each step in the development of the bourgeoisie was accompanied by a corresponding political advance of that class. The bourgeoisie has at last, since the establishment of Modern Industry and of the world-market, conquered for itself, in the modern representative State, exclusive po-litical sway. The executive of the modern State is but a committee for managing the common affairs of the whole bourgeoisie.

The bourgeoisie, historically, has played a most revolutionary part.

The bourgeoisie, whenever it has got the upper hand, has put an end to all feudal, patriarchal, idyllic relations. It has pitilessly torn asunder the motley feudal ties that bound man to his "natural superiors," and has left no other nexus between man and man than naked self-interest, than cal-lous "cash payments." It has drowned the most

heavenly ecstasies of religious fervor, of chivalrous enthusiasm, of Philistine sentimentalism, in the icy water of egotistical calculation. It has re-solved personal worth into exchange value, and in place of the numberless indefeasible chartered freedoms, has set up that single, unconscionable freedom—Free Trade. In one word, for exploita-tion, veiled by religious and political illusions, it has substituted naked, shameless, direct, brutal exploitation.

The bourgeoisie has stripped of its halo every occupation hitherto honored and looked up to with reverent awe. It has converted the physician, the lawyer, the priest, the poet, the man of sci-ence, into its paid wage laborers.

The bourgeoisie has torn away from the family its sentimental veil, and has reduced the family relation to a mere money relation.

The bourgeoisie cannot exist without constantly revolutionizing the instruments of production, and thereby the relations of production, and with them the whole relations of society. Conservation of the old modes of production in unaltered form was, on the contrary, the first condition of exist-ence for all earlier industrial classes. Constant revolutionizing of production, uninterrupted dis-turbance of all social conditions, everlasting un-certainty and agitation distinguish the bourgeois epoch from all earlier ones. All fixed, fast frozen relations, with their train of ancient and venerable prejudices and opinions, are swept away, all new-formed ones become antiquated before they can ossify. All that is solid melts into the air, all that is holy is profaned, and man is at last compelled to face with sober senses his real conditions of life, and his relations with his kind.

The need of a constantly expanding market for its products chases the bourgeoisie over the whole surface of the globe. It must nestle every-where, settle everywhere, establish connections everywhere.

The bourgeoisie, by the rapid improvement of all instruments of production, by the immensely facilitated means of communication, draws all, even the most barbarian nations into civilization. The cheap prices of its commodities are the heavy artillery with which it batters down all Chinese walls, with which it forces the bar-barians' intensely obstinate hatred of foreigners to capitulate. It compels all nations, on pain of extinction, to adopt the bourgeois mode of pro-duction; it compels them to introduce what it calls civilization into their midst, *i.e.,* to become bourgeois themselves. In a word, it creates a world after its own image.

The bourgeoisie, during its rule of scarce one

hundred years, has created more massive and more colossal productive forces than have all preceding generations together. Subjection of Nature's forces to man, machinery, application of chemistry to industry and agriculture, steam-navigation, railways, electric telegraphs, clearing of whole continents for cultivation, canalization of rivers, whole populations conjured out of the ground—what earlier century had even a presentiment that such productive forces slumbered in the lap of social labor?

We see then: the means of production and of exchange, on whose foundation the bourgeoisie built itself up, were generated in feudal society. At a certain stage in the development of these means of production and of exchange, the conditions under which feudal society produced and exchanged, the feudal organization of agriculture and manufacturing industry, in one word, the feudal relations of property became no longer compatible with the already developed productive forces; they became so many fetters. They had to burst asunder; they were burst asunder.

Into their places stepped free competition, accompanied by a social and political constitution adapted to it, and by economical and political sway of the bourgeois class.

A similar movement is going on before our own eyes. Modern bourgeois society with its relations of production, of exchange and of property, a society that has conjured up such gigantic means of production and of exchange, is like the sorcerer, who is no longer able to control the powers of the nether world whom he has called up by his spells. For many a decade past, the history of industry and commerce is but the history of the revolt of modern productive forces against modern conditions of production, against the property relations that are the conditions for the existence of the bourgeoisie and of its rule. It is enough to mention the commercial crises that by their periodical return put on its trial, each time more threateningly, the existence of the entire bourgeois society. In these crises a great part not only of the existing products, but also of the previously created productive forces, are periodically destroyed. In these crises there breaks out an epidemic that, in all earlier epochs, would have seemed an absurdity—the epidemic of overproduction. Society suddenly finds itself put back into a state of momentary barbarism; it appears as if a famine, a universal war of devastation, had cut off the supply of every means of subsistence; industry and commerce seem to be destroyed; and why? Because there is too much civilization, too much means of subsistence,

too much industry, too much commerce. The productive forces at the disposal of society no longer tend to further the development of the conditions of the bourgeois property; on the contrary, they have become too powerful for these conditions by which they are fettered, and as soon as they overcome these fetters they bring disorder into the whole of bourgeois society, endanger the existence of bourgeois property. The conditions of bourgeois society are too narrow to comprise the wealth created by them. And how does the bourgeoisie get over these crises? On the one hand by enforced destruction of a mass of productive forces; on the other, by the conquest of new markets, and by the more thorough exploitation of the old ones. That is to say, by paving the way for more extensive and more destructive crises, and by diminishing the means whereby crises are prevented.

The weapons with which the bourgeoisie felled feudalism to the ground are now turned against the bourgeoisie itself.

But not only has the bourgeoisie forged the weapons that bring death to itself; it has also called into existence the men who are to wield those weapons—the modern working-class—the proletarians.

In proportion as the bourgeoisie, *i.e.*, capital, is developed, in the same proportion is the proletariat, the modern working-class, developed, a class of laborers who live only so long as their labor increases capital. These laborers, who must sell themselves piecemeal, are a commodity, like every other article of commerce, and are consequently exposed to all the vicissitudes of competition, to all the fluctuations of the market.

Owing to the extensive use of machinery and to division of labor, the work of the proletarians has lost all individual character, and, consequently, all charm for the workman. He becomes an appendage of the machine, and it is only the most simple, most monotonous and most easily acquired knack that is required of him. Hence, the cost of production of a workman is restricted almost entirely to the means of subsistence that he requires for his maintenance, and for the propagation of his race. But the price of a commodity, and also of labor, is equal to its cost of production. In proportion, therefore, as the repulsiveness of the work increases, the wage decreases. Nay more, in proportion as the use of machinery and division of labor increases, in the same proportion the burden of toil also increases, whether by prolongation of the working hours, by increase of the work enacted in a given time, or by increased speed of the machinery, etc.

The lower strata of the middle class—the small tradespeople, shopkeepers and retired tradesmen generally, the handicraftsmen and peasants—all these sink gradually into the proletariat, partly because their diminutive capital does not suffice for the scale on which Modern Industry is carried on, and is swamped in the competition with the large capitalists, partly because their specialized skill is rendered worthless by new methods of production. Thus the proletariat is recruited from all classes of the population.

With the development of industry the proletariat not only increases in number; it becomes concentrated in greater masses, its strength grows and it feels that strength more. The various interests and conditions of life within the ranks of the proletariat are more and more equalized, in proportion as machinery obliterates all distinctions of labor, and nearly everywhere reduces wages to the same low level. The growing competition among the bourgeois, and the resulting commercial crisis, make the wages of the workers even more fluctuating. The unceasing improvement of machinery, ever more rapidly developing, makes their livelihood more and more precarious; the collisions between individual workmen and individual bourgeois take more and more the character of collisions between two classes. Thereupon the workers begin to form combinations (Trades' Unions) against the bourgeois; they club together in order to keep up the rate of wages; they found permanent associations in order to make provision beforehand for these occasional revolts. Here and there the contest breaks out into riots.

Now and then the workers are victorious, but only for a time. The real fruit of their battle lies not in the immediate result but in the ever-expanding union of workers. This organization of the proletarians into a class, and consequently into a political party, is continually being upset again by the competition between the workers themselves. But it ever rises up again, stronger, firmer, mightier. It compels legislative recognition of particular interests of the workers by taking advantage of the divisions among the bourgeoisie itself.

Of all the classes that stand face to face with the bourgeoisie today the proletariat alone is a really revolutionary class. The other classes decay and finally disappear in the face of modern industry; the proletariat is its special and essential product.

The lower middle class, the small manufacturer, the shopkeeper, the artisan, the peasant, all these fight against the bourgeoise, to save from extinction their existence as fractions of the middle class. They are therefore not revolutionary, but conservative. Nay, more; they are reactionary, for they try to roll back the wheel of history. If by chance they are revolutionary, they are so only in view of their impending transfer into the proletariat; they thus defend not their present, but their future interests; they desert their own standpoint to place themselves at that of the proletariat.

The "dangerous class," the social scum, that passively rotting mass thrown off by the lowest layers of old society, may, here and there, be swept into the movement by a proletarian revolution; its conditions of life, however, prepare it far more for the part of a bribed tool of reactionary intrigue.

The modern laborer, instead of rising with the progress of industry, sinks deeper and deeper below the conditions of existence of his own class. He becomes a pauper, and pauperism develops more rapidly than population and wealth. And here it becomes evident that the bourgeoisie is unfit any longer to be the ruling class in society, and to impose its conditions of existence upon society as an over-riding law. It is unfit to rule, because it is incompetent to assure an existence to its slave within his slavery, because it cannot help letting him sink into such a state that it has to feed him, instead of being fed by him. Society can no longer live under this bourgeoisie; in other words, its existence is no longer compatible with society. What the bourgeoisie therefore produces, above all, are its own grave diggers. Its fall and the victory of the proletariat are equally inevitable.

Proletarians and Communists

In what relation do the Communists stand to the proletarians as a whole?

The Communists do not form a separate party opposed to other working-class parties.

They have no interests separate and apart from those of the proletariat as a whole.

They do not set up any sectarian principles of their own, by which to shape and mould the proletarian movement.

The Communists are distinguished from the other working class parties by this only: 1. In the national struggles of the proletarians of the different countries, they point out and bring to the front the common interests of the entire proletariat, independently of all nationality. 2. In the various stages of development which the struggle of the working class against the bourgeoisie has to pass through, they always and everywhere represent the interests of the movement as a whole.

The Communists, therefore, are on the one hand, practically, the most advanced and resolute section of the working class parties of every country, that section which pushes forward all others; on the other hand, theoretically, they have over the great mass of the proletariat the advantage of clearly understanding the line of march, the conditions, and the ultimate general results of the proletarian movement.

The immediate aim of the Communists is the same as that of all the other proletarian parties: formation of the proletariat into a class, overthrow of the bourgeois supremacy, conquest of political power by the proletariat.

The theoretical conclusions of the Communists are in no way based on ideas or principles that have been invented or discovered by this or that would-be universal reformer.

They merely express, in general terms, actual relations springing from an existing class struggle, from a historical movement going on under our very eyes.

The distinguishing feature of Communism is not the abolition of property generally, but the abolition of bourgeois property. But modern bourgeois private property is the final and most complete expression of the system of producing and appropriating products that is based on class antagonism, on the exploitation of the many by the few.

In this sense, the theory of the Communists may be summed up in the single sentence: Abolition of private property.

You are horrified at our intending to do away with private property. But in your existing society private property is already done away with for nine-tenths of the population; its existence for the few is solely due to its non-existence in the hands of those nine-tenths. You reproach us, therefore, with intending to do away with a form of property, the necessary condition for whose existence is the non-existence of any property for the immense majority of society.

In one word, you reproach us with intending to do away with your property. Precisely so; that is just what we intend.

From the moment when labor can no longer be converted into capital, money, or rent, into a social power capable of being monopolized, i.e., from the moment when individual property can no longer be transformed into bourgeois property, into capital, from that moment, you say, individuality vanishes.

You must, therefore, confess that by "individual" you mean no other person than the bourgeois, than the middle-class owner of property. This person must, indeed, be swept out of the way and made impossible.

Communism deprives no man of the power to appropriate the products of society: all that it does is to deprive him of the power to subjugate the labor of others by means of such appropriation.

The Communist revolution is the most radical rupture with traditional property relations; no wonder that its development involves the most radical rupture with traditional ideas.

The first step in the revolution by the working class is to raise the proletariat to the position of ruling class, to win the battle of democracy.

The proletariat will use its political supremacy to wrest, by degrees, all capital from the bourgeoisie, to centralize all instruments of production in the hands of the State, i.e., of the proletariat organized as a ruling class; and to increase the total productive forces as rapidly as possible.

In the most advanced countries the following will be pretty generally applicable:

1. Abolition of property in land and application of all rents of land to public purposes.

2. A heavy progressive or graduated income tax.

3. Abolition of all right of inheritance.

4. Confiscation of the property of all emigrants and rebels.

5. Centralization of credit in the hands of the State, by means of a national bank with State capital and an exclusive monopoly.

6. Centralization of the means of communication and transport in the hands of the State.

7. Extension of factories and instruments of production owned by the State; the bringing into cultivation of waste lands, and the improvement of the soil generally in accordance with a common plan.

8. Equal liability of all to labor. Establishment of industrial armies, especially for agriculture.

9. Combination of agriculture with manufacturing industries; gradual abolition of the distinction between town and country by a more equable distribution of the population over the country.

10. Free education for all children in public schools. Abolition of children's factory labor in its present form. Combination of education with industrial production, etc., etc.

When, in the course of development, class distinctions have disappeared, and all production has been concentrated in the hands of a vast association of the whole nation, the public power will lose its political character. Political power, properly so called, is merely the organized power of one class for oppressing another. If the proletariat during its contest with the bourgeoisie is compelled, by the force of circumstances, to organize itself as a class, if, by means of a revolution, it makes itself the ruling class, and, as such, sweeps away by force the old conditions of production, then it will, along with these conditions, have swept away the conditions for the existence of class antagonism, and of classes generally, and will thereby have abolished its own supremacy as a class.

In place of the old bourgeois society, with its classes and class antagonisms, we shall have an association in which the free development of each is the condition for the free development of all.

The Communists everywhere support every revolutionary movement against the existing social and political order of things.

In all these movements they bring to the front, as the leading question in each, the property question, no matter what its degree of development at the time.

Finally, they labor everywhere for the union and agreement of the democratic parties of all countries.

The Communists disdain to conceal their views and aims. They openly declare that their ends can be attained only by the forcible overthrow of all existing social conditions. Let the ruling classes tremble at a Communistic revolution. The proletarians have nothing to lose but their chains. They have a world to win.

Working men of all countries, unite!

READING 74

Few economists can match Karl Marx in the challenge offered to anyone seeking to distill the essence of their thought into one readable article. Marx is as easily misunderstood by his friends as by his critics, both of whom might be surprised by what is *not* in his writings. The present article is an unusually fine summary of Marxian economics. It simplifies and reorders a formidable mass of ideas from a man who was at once scholar-economist and propagandist-revolutionary.

Robert L. Heilbroner's writings on economics appear in numerous magazines; his books have made economics intelligible and exciting for vast audiences. He is a part-time lecturer in the New School for Social Research in New York City. The book from which this chapter is taken is a survey of the ideas of the major figures in economic thought.

Questions to Guide the Reading

What are the most critical assumptions in the Marxian views of history, of "surplus value," and of capitalism's internal problems? Are these assumptions testable ones?

How and to what extent has capitalism in the West refuted Marx's prediction of recurring crises and impending disaster?

MARXIAN ECONOMICS—A SURVEY
Robert L. Heilbroner

The *Manifesto* opened with portentous words: "A spectre is haunting Europe—the spectre of Communism. All the powers of old Europe have entered into a holy alliance to exorcise this spectre: Pope and Tsar, Metternich and Guizot, French Radicals and German police-spies."

The specter certainly existed: 1848 was a year of terror for the old order on the Continent.

From Robert L. Heilbroner, *The Worldly Philosophers* (Simon and Schuster, New York, 1953). Reprinted with kind permission of the author and publishers.

There was a revolutionary fervor in the air and a rumble underfoot. For a moment—for a brief moment—it looked as if the old order might break down. In France the plodding regime of Louis Philippe, the portly middle-class king, wrestled with a crisis and then collapsed; the king abdicated and fled to the security of a Surrey villa, and the workingmen of Paris rose in a wild uncoordinated surge and ran the Red Flag over the Hôtel de Ville. In Belgium a frightened monarch offered to submit his resignation. In Berlin the barricades went up and bullets whistled; in Italy mobs rioted; and in Prague and Vienna popular uprisings imitated Paris by seizing control of the cities.

"The Communists disdain to conceal their views and aims," cried the *Manifesto*. "They openly declare that their ends can be attained only by the forcible overthrow of all existing social relations. Let the ruling classes tremble at a Communist revolution. The proletarians have nothing to lose but their chains. They have a world to win."

The ruling classes did tremble and they saw the threat of communism everywhere. Nor were their fears groundless. In the French foundries the workmen sang radical songs to the accompaniment of blows from their sledge hammers, and Heinrich Heine, the German romantic poet who was touring the factories, reported that "really people in our gentle walk of life can have no idea of the demonic note which runs through these songs."

But despite the clarion words of the *Manifesto,* the demonic note was not a call for a revolution of communism; it was a cry born only of frustration and despair. For all of Europe was in the grip of reaction compared with which conditions in England were positively idyllic. The French government had been characterized by John Stuart Mill as "wholly without the spirit of improvement and . . . wrought almost exclusively through the meaner and more selfish impulses of mankind" and the French had no monopoly on such a dubious claim to fame. As for Germany, well, here it was, the fourth decade of the nineteenth century, and Prussia still had no parliament, no freedom of speech or right of assembly, no liberty of press or trial by jury, and no tolerance for any idea which deviated by a hair's breadth from the antiquated notion of the divine right of kings. Italy was a hodgepodge of anachronistic principalities. Russia under Nicholas I (despite the Tsar's onetime visit to Robert Owen's New Lanark) was characterized by the historian

De Tocqueville as "the cornerstone of despotism in Europe."

Had the despair been channeled and directed, the demonic note might have changed into a truly revolutionary one. But as it was, the uprisings were spontaneous, undisciplined, and aimless; they won initial victories and then, while they were wondering what next to do, the old order rocked invincibly back into place. The revolutionary fervor abated, and where it did not, it was mercilessly crushed. At the price of ten thousand casualties, the Paris mobs were subdued by the National Guard, and Louis Napoleon took over the nation and soon exchanged the Second Republic for the Second Empire. In Belgium the country decided that it had better ask the king to stay after all; he acknowledged the tribute by abolishing the right of assembly. The Viennese and Hungarian crowds were cannonaded from their strongholds, and in Germany a constitutional assembly which had been bravely debating the question of republicanism broke down into factional bickering and then ignominiously offered the country to Frederick William IV of Prussia. Still more ignominiously, that monarch declared that he would accept no crown proffered by the ignoble hands of commoners.

The revolution was over. It had been fierce, bloody, but inconclusive. There were a few new faces in Europe but the policies were much the same.

But to a little group of working-class leaders who had just formed the Communist League, there was no cause for deep despair. True, the revolution for which they had entertained high hopes had petered out and the radical movements pocketed throughout Europe were being more ruthlessly hounded than ever before. But all that could be regarded with a certain equanimity. For according to their understanding of history, the uprisings of 1848 were only the small-scale dress rehearsals of a gigantic production that was scheduled for the future, and of the eventual success of that catastrophic spectacle there could be not a shadow of a doubt.

The league had just published its statement of objectives and called it the *Communist Manifesto*. But for all its slogans and its trenchant phrases, the *Manifesto* had not been written merely to whip up revolutionary sentiment or to add another voice of protest to the clamor of voices that filled the air. The *Manifesto* had something else in mind: a philosophy of history in which a communist revolution was not only desirable but demonstrably *inevitable*. Unlike the

Utopians who also wanted to reorganize society closer to their desires, the Communists did not appeal to men's sympathies or to their addiction to build castles in the air. Rather, they offered men a chance to hitch their destinies to a star and to watch that star move inexorably across the historical zodiac. There was no longer a contest in which one side or the other ought to win for moral or sentimental reasons or because it thought the existing order was outrageous. Instead there was a cold analysis of which side *had* to win, and since that side was the proletariat, their leaders had only to wait. In the end, as necessarily as two and two made four, they could not lose.

The *Manifesto* was a program written for the future. But one thing would have surprised its authors. They were prepared to wait—but not for *seventy* years. They were already scanning Europe for the likeliest incubator of revolt. And they never even cast a glance in the direction of Russia.

The *Manifesto*, as everybody knows, was the brain child of that angry genius, Karl Marx. More accurately, it was the result of collaboration between him and his remarkable companion, compatriot, supporter, and colleague, Friedrich Engels.

They are interesting, and, of course, enormously important men. The trouble is, they are no longer just men; Marx the human being is obscured behind Marx the Figure; and Engels behind the shadow of Marx. If we are to judge by a count of worshipping noses, Marx must be considered a religious figure to rank with Christ or Mohammed, and Engels thus becomes a sort of Saint Peter or a John. In the Marx-Engels Institute in Moscow, scholars have pored over their works with all the idolatry they ridicule in the antireligious museums down the street; but while Marx and Engels are canonized in Russia, they are still crucified in much of the world.

They merit neither treatment, for they were neither saints nor devils. Nor is their work either Scripture or anathema. It belongs in the great line of economic viewpoints which have successively clarified, illuminated, and interpreted the world for us, and like the other great works on the shelf, it is neither without flaw nor devoid of merit. The world has been preoccupied with Marx the Revolutionary. But had Marx not lived there would have been other socialists and other prophets of a new society. The real and lasting impact of Marx and Engels is not their revolutionary activity, none of which bore too much fruit during their own lifetimes. It is with Marx the Economist that capitalism must finally come to grips. For the final imprint he made on history was his prediction that capitalism must inevitably and necessarily collapse. On that prediction, on that "scientific" prognostication, communism has built its edifice.

What was Marx's prognosis for the system that he knew? The answer lies in that enormous work *Das Kapital—Capital*. With Marx's agonizing meticulousness, it is remarkable that the work was ever finished—in a sense it never was. It was eighteen years in process; in 1851 it was to be done "in five weeks"; in 1859 in "six weeks"; in 1865 it was "done"—a huge bundle of virtually illegible manuscripts which took two years to edit into Volume I. When Marx died in 1883 two volumes remained: Engels put out Volume II in 1885 and the third in 1894. The final (fourth) volume did not emerge until 1910.

There are twenty-five hundred pages to read for anyone intrepid enough to make the effort. And what pages! Some deal with the tiniest of technical matters and labor them to a point of mathematical exhaustion; others swirl with passion and anger. This is an economist who has read *every* economist, a German pedant with a passion for footnotes, and an emotional critic who can write that "capital is dead labour, that vampire-like, only lives by sucking living labour" and who tells us that capital came into the world "dripping from head to foot, from every pore, with blood and dirt."

And yet one must not jump to the conclusion that this is merely a biased and irascible text inveighing against the sins of the wicked money-barons. It is shot through with remarks which betray the total involvement of the man with his theoretical adversary, but the great merit of the book, curiously enough, is its utter detachment from all considerations of morality. The book describes with fury, but it analyzes with cold logic. For what Marx has set for his goal is to discover the intrinsic tendencies of the capitalist system, its inner laws of motion, and in so doing, he has eschewed the easy but less convincing means of merely expatiating on its manifest shortcomings. Instead he erects the most rigorous, the purest capitalism imaginable and within this rarefied abstract system, within an imaginary capitalism in which all the obvious defects of real life are removed, he seeks his quarry. For if he can prove that the best of all possible capitalisms is nonetheless headed for certain disaster, it is certainly easy to demonstrate that real capitalism will follow the same path, only quicker.

And so he sets the stage. We enter a world of perfect capitalism: no monopolies, no unions, no special advantages for anyone. It is a world in which every commodity sells at exactly its proper price. And that proper price is its *value*—a tricky word. For the value of a commodity, says Marx (and Smith and Ricardo before him), is the amount of labor it has within itself. If it takes twice as much labor to make hats as shoes, then hats will sell for twice the price of shoes. The labor, of course, need not be direct manual labor; it may be overhead labor which is spread over many commodities or it may be the labor which once went into making a machine and which the machine now slowly passes on to the products it shapes. But no matter what its form, everything is eventually reducible to labor, and all commodities, in this perfect system, will be priced according to the amount of labor, direct or indirect, which they contain.

In this world stand the two great protagonists of the capitalist drama: worker and capitalist— the landlord has by now been relegated to a minor position in society. They are not quite the same protagonists we have met earlier in similar economic tableaux. The worker is no longer the slave to his reproductive urge. He is a free bargaining agent who enters the market to dispose of the one commodity he commands—labor-power—and if he gets a rise in wages he will not be so foolish as to squander it in a self-defeating proliferation of his numbers.

The capitalist faces him in the arena. He is not a bad fellow at heart, although his greed and lust for wealth are caustically described in those chapters which leave the abstract world for a look into 1860 England. But it is worth noting that he is not money-hungry from mere motives of rapacity: he is an owner-entrepreneur engaged in an endless race against his fellow owner-entrepreneurs; he *must* strive for accumulation, for in the competitive environment in which he operates, one accumulates or one gets accumulated.

The stage is set and the characters take their places. But now the first difficulty appears. How, asks Marx, can profits exist in such a situation? If everything sells for its exact value, then who gets an unearned increment? No one dares to raise his price above the competitive one, and

even if one seller managed to gouge a buyer, that buyer would only have less to spend elsewhere in the economy—one man's profit would thus be another man's loss. How can there be profit in the *whole* system if everything exchanges for its honest worth?

It seems like a paradox. Profits are easy to explain if we assume that there are monopolies in the system which need not obey the leveling influences of competition or if we admit that capitalists may pay labor less than it is worth. But Marx will have none of that—this is to be *pure* capitalism which will dig its own grave.

He finds the answer to the dilemma in one commodity which is different from all others. That commodity is labor-power. For the laborer, like the capitalist, sells his product for exactly what it is worth—for its value. And its value, like the value of everything else that is sold, is the amount of labor that goes into it—in this case, the amount of labor that it takes to "make" labor-power. In other words, a laborer's salable energies are worth the amount of socially necessary labor it takes to keep that laborer alive. Smith and Ricardo would have agreed entirely: the true value of a workman is the wage he needs in order to exist. It is his subsistence wage.

So far, so good. But here comes the key to profit. The laborer who contracts to work can only ask for a wage which is his due. What that wage will be depends, as we have seen, on the amount of labor-time it takes to keep a man alive. If it takes six hours of society's labor to maintain a workingman, then (if labor is priced at one dollar an hour), he is "worth" six dollars a day. No more.

But the laborer who gets a job does not contract to work only six hours a day. That would be just long enough to support himself. On the contrary, he agrees to work a full eight-hour, or in Marx's time a ten- or eleven-hour, day. Hence he will produce a full ten or eleven hours' worth of value and he will get paid for only six. His wage will cover his subsistence which is his true "value," but in return he will sell the value which he produces in a full working day. And this is how profit enters the system.

Marx called this layer of unpaid work "surplus value." But it is quite devoid of moral indignation. The worker is only entitled to the *value* of his labor-power. He gets it in full. But meanwhile the capitalist gets the full value of his workers' whole working day, and this is longer than the hours for which he paid. Hence when the capitalist sells his products, he can afford to sell them at *their* true value and still realize a profit. For there is more labor-time embodied in his products than the labor-time for which he was forced to pay.

How can this state of affairs come about? It happens because the capitalists monopolize one thing—access to the means of production themselves. If a worker isn't willing to work a full working day, he doesn't get a job. Like everyone else in the system, a worker has no right and no power to ask for more than his own worth as a commodity. The system is perfectly equitable and yet all workers are cheated, for they are forced to work a longer time than their own self-sustenance demands.

Does this sound strange? Remember that Marx is describing a time when the working day was long—sometimes unendurably long—and when wages were, by and large, little more than it took to keep body and soul together. The idea of surplus value may make little sense in a world where the sweatshop is very largely a thing of the past, but it was not merely a theoretical construct at the time that Marx was writing. One example may suffice: at a Manchester factory in 1862 the average workweek for a period of a month and a half was 84 hours! For the previous 18 months it had been 78½ hours.

But all this is still only the setting for the drama. We have the protagonists, we have their motives, we have the clue to the plot in the discovery of "surplus value." And now the play is set in motion.

All capitalists have profits. But they are all in competition. Hence they try to accumulate and so to expand their scales of output, at the expense of their competitors. But expansion is not so easy. It requires more laborers and to get them the capitalists must bid against each other for the working force. Wages tend to rise. Conversely, surplus value tends to fall. It looks as if the Marxian capitalists will soon be up against the dilemma faced by the capitalists of Adam Smith and David Ricardo—their profits will be eaten away by rising wages.

To Smith and Ricardo the solution to the dilemma lay in the propensity of the working force to increase its numbers with every boost in pay. But Marx has ruled out this possibility. He doesn't argue about it; he simply brands the Malthusian doctrine "a libel on the human race" —after all, the proletariat, which is to be the ruling class of the future, cannot be so short-sighted as to dissipate its gains through mere

unbridled physical appetite. But he rescues his capitalists just the same. For he says that they will meet the threat of rising wages by introducing laborsaving machinery into their plants. That will throw part of the working force back onto the street and there, as an Industrial Reserve Army, it will serve the same function as Malthus' teeming population: it will compete wages right back down to their former "value"— the subsistence level.

But now comes the crucial twist. It seems as though the capitalist has saved the day, for he has prevented wages from rising by creating unemployment through machinery. But not so fast. By the very process through which he hopes to free himself from one horn of the dilemma, he impales himself on the other.

For as he substitutes machines for men, he is simultaneously substituting nonprofitable means of production for profitable ones. Remember that in this never-never world, no one makes a profit by merely sharp bargaining. Whatever a machine will be worth to a capitalist, you can be sure that he paid full value for it. If a machine will yield ten thousand dollars' worth of value over its whole life, our capitalist was charged the full ten thousand dollars in the first place. It is only from his living labor that he can realize a profit, only from the unpaid-for hours of surplus working time. Hence when he reduces the number or proportion of workers, he is killing the goose that laid the golden egg.

And yet, poor fellow, he has to. There is nothing Mephistophelean about his actions. He is only obeying his impulse to accumulate and trying to stay abreast of his competitors. As his wages rise, he *must* introduce laborsaving machinery to cut his costs and rescue his profit margin—if he does not, his neighbor will. But since he must substitute machinery for labor, he must also narrow the base out of which he gleans his profits. It is a kind of Greek drama where men go willy-nilly to their fate, and in which they all unwittingly cooperate to bring about their own destruction.

For now the die is cast. As his profits shrink, each capitalist will redouble his efforts to put new laborsaving, cost-cutting machinery in his factory. It is only by getting a step ahead of the parade that he can hope to make a profit. But since everyone is doing precisely the same thing, the ratio of labor (and hence surplus value) to total output shrinks still further. The rate of profit falls and falls. And now doom lies ahead. Profits are cut to the point at which production is no longer profitable at all. Consumption dwindles as machines displace men and the number of employed fails to keep pace with output. Bankruptcies ensue. There is a scramble to dump goods on the market and in the process smaller firms go under. A capitalist crisis is at hand.

Not forever. As workers are thrown out of work, they are forced to accept subvalue wages. As machinery is dumped, the stronger capitalists can acquire machines for less than their true value. After a time, surplus value reappears. The forward march is taken up again. But it leads to the same catastrophic conclusion: competition for workers; higher wages; labor-displacing machinery; a smaller base for surplus value; still more frenzied competition; collapse. And each collapse is worse than the preceding one. In the periods of crisis, the bigger firms absorb the smaller ones, and when the industrial monsters eventually go down, the wreckage is far greater than when the little enterprises buckle.

And then, one day, the drama ends. Marx's picture of it has all the eloquence of a description of Damnation: "Along with the constantly diminishing number of the magnates of capital, who usurp and monopolize all advantages of this process of transformation, grows the mass of misery, oppression, slavery, degradation, exploitation; but with this too grows the revolt of the working-class, a class always increasing in numbers, and disciplined, united, organized by the very mechanism of the process of capitalist production itself . . . centralization of the means of production and socialization of labour at last reach a point where they become incompatible with their capitalist integument. This integument bursts asunder. The knell of capitalist private property sounds. The expropriators are expropriated."

And so the drama ends in the inevitable overthrow which Marx had envisioned in the dialectic. The system—the *pure* system—breaks down as it works upon itself to squeeze out its own source of energy, surplus value. The breakdown is hastened by the constant instability which arises from the essentially planless nature of the economy, and although there are forces at work which act both to prolong and to hasten its end, its final death struggle is inescapable. And if the pure system is unworkable, what possible hope can there be for the real system, with all its imperfections, monopolies, cutthroat tactics, and heedless profit seeking?

For Adam Smith, the capitalist escalator climbed ever upward, at least as far as the eye could rea-

sonably see. For Ricardo that upward motion was finally stalled by the pressure of mouths on insufficient cropland, which brought a stalemate to progress and a windfall to the fortunate landlord. For Mill the vista was made more reassuring by his discovery that society could distribute its product as it saw fit, regardless of what "economic laws" seemed to dictate. But for Marx even that saving possibility was untenable. For the dialectic told him that the State was only the political ruling organ of the economic rulers, and the thought that it might act as a neutral body, as an impartial third force which might balance the claims of its conflicting members, would have seemed little else but sheer wishful thinking. No, there was no escape from the inner logic, the inexorable development of a system which would not only destroy itself but which, in so doing, would give birth to its successor.

As to what that successor might look like, Marx had little to say. It would be "classless," of course—by which Marx meant that the basis for an economic division of society based on property would be removed once society owned all the means of production of goods. Just how society would "own" its factories; what was meant by "society"; whether there would or could be bitter antagonisms between the managers and the managed, between the political chieftains and the rank and file—none of this did Marx specify. During a transitional period there would be a "dictatorship of the proletariat"; after that, "pure" communism itself.

Marx, it must be kept in mind, was not the architect of communism. That task would fall to his successor, Lenin. *Das Kapital* is the Doomsday Book of capitalism, and in all of Marx there is almost nothing which looks beyond the Day of Judgment to see what lineaments paradise may present.

What are we to make of his apocalyptic argument?

There is an easy way of disposing of the whole thing. Remember that the system is built on value—labor value—and that the key to its demise lies in that special phenomenon called surplus value. But the real world consists not of "values" but of real tangible prices. Marx must show that the world of dollars and cents mirrors, in some approximate fashion, the abstract world that he has created. But in making the transition to a price-world from a value-world, he lands in the most terrible tangle of mathematics. In fact he makes a mistake.

It is not an irreparable mistake and by going

through an even worse tangle of mathematics one can make the Marxist equations come out "right" —one can, that is, explain a correspondence between the prices that really obtain in life and the underlying values in terms of labor-time. But the critics who pointed out the error were hardly interested in setting the scheme aright and their judgment that Marx was "wrong" was taken as final. When the equations were finally justified, no one paid much attention. For regardless of its mathematical purity, the Marxian rigmarole is at best a cumbersome and difficult framework and an unnecessarily laborious method of getting at the required understanding of how capitalism works.

But while we might be tempted to toss the whole analysis to one side because it is awkward and inflexible, to do so would be to overlook its values. Marx, after all, did not strip capitalism down to its barest essentials merely to indulge his bent for abstract argument. He did so because he believed that in the simplicity of a theoretical world the mechanics of the actual world would lie clearly exposed; because he hoped that the very starkness of his model world would highlight tendencies hidden in real life.

And so it did. For all its clumsiness, Marx's model of the capitalist world seemed to *work*, to display a kind of life of its own. Given its basic assumptions—the *mise en scène* of its characters, their motives and their milieu—the situation it presented *changed*, and changed in a way that was foreseeable, precise, and inevitable. We have seen what these changes are: how profits fell, how capitalists sought new machinery, how each boom ended in a crash, how small businesses were absorbed in each debacle by the larger firms. But all this was still within the framework of an abstract world: now Marx applied his findings on paper to the real world about him—the actual world of capitalism, he said, must also display these trends.

He called the trends the "laws of motion" of a capitalist system—the path which capitalism would tread over future time. And the astonishing fact is that almost all these predictions have come true!

For profits *do* tend to fall in an enterprise economy. The insight was not original with Marx, nor do profits fall for the reason he gave—we can dispense with the idea of exploitation contained in the theory of surplus value. But as Adam Smith or Ricardo or Mill pointed out—and as any businessman will vouchsafe—the pressures of competition and rising wages will serve quite as

well. Impregnable monopolies aside (and these are few), profits are both the hallmark of capitalism and its Achilles' heel, for no business can *permanently* maintain its prices much above its costs. There is only one way in which profits can be perpetuated: a business—or an entire economy—must grow.

But growth implies the second prediction of the Marxist model: the ceaseless quest for new techniques. It was no accident that industrial capitalism dates from the Industrial Revolution, for as Marx made clear, technological progress is not merely an accompaniment of capitalism but a vital ingredient. Business *must* innovate, invent, and experiment if it is to survive; the business that rests content on its past achievements is not long for this enterprising world. It is interesting to note that recently one large chemical company announced that sixty per cent of its income came from products that were unknown ten years ago; and although this is an exceptionally inventive industry, the pattern is typical.

The model showed still two more tendencies for capitalism which have also come to pass. We hardly need document the existence of business cycles over the pasty ninety years nor the emergence of giant business enterprise. But we might remark on the daring of Marx's prediction. When *Das Kapital* appeared, bigness was the exception rather than the rule and small enterprise still ruled the roost. To claim that huge firms would come to dominate the business scene was as startling a prediction in 1867 as would be a statement today that fifty years hence America will be a land in which small-scale proprietorships will have displaced giant corporations.

It was, all things considered, an extraordinary bit of foresight. And note this: all these changes, vast and portentous as they were, could not have been unearthed purely by examining the world as it appeared to Marx's eyes. For these are historical changes, slow in their unfolding and stretched out over time; as real, but as unnoticeable, as the growth of a tree. It was only by reducing the world to a microcosm and then by observing that microcosm in its speeded-up life span that this drift of the future could be apprehended.

It was not, of course, exact. Marx thought that profits would not only fall *within* the business cycle, which they do, but that they would display a long downward secular trend; this does not appear to have taken place. Marx did not stop to consider that the economic particles with which he played had feelings and volitions and

COMPARATIVE ECONOMIC SYSTEMS **441**

consciences that could also change and that they would not therefore behave with the imperturbable predictability of the particles under a chemist's microscope. But for all its shortcomings—and it is far from infallible, as we shall see—the Marxist model of how capitalism worked was extraordinarily prophetic.

But everything that Marx had predicted so far, was after all, innocuous. There remained the final prediction of the model; for as the reader will remember, in the end Marx's "pure capitalism" *collapsed*.

Let it be said at the outset that this prediction as well cannot be lightly brushed aside. In Russia and Eastern Europe capitalism has disappeared; in Scandinavia and Britain it has been partially abandoned; in Germany and Italy it drifted into fascism and emerged from its bath of fire in less than perfect health. Indeed, almost everywhere except in the United States capitalism is on the defensive; and while wars, brute political power, exigencies of fate, and the determined efforts of revolutionaries have all contributed their share, the grim truth is that its demise has largely been for the very reason Marx foresaw: it broke down.

Why did it break down? Partly because it developed the instability Marx said it would. A succession of business crises, compounded by a plague of wars, destroyed the faith of the lower and middle classes in the system. But that is not the entire answer—we too have had our wars and depressions, and capitalism here is very much alive. Something else spelled the difference between survival and destruction: European capitalism failed not so much for economic as for *social* reasons.

And Marx predicted this too!

For Marx recognized that the economic difficulties of the system were not insuperable. Although antimonopoly legislation or antibusiness cycle policies were unknown in Marx's day, such activities were not inconceivable: there was nothing inevitable in the *physical* sense about Marx's vision. The Marxist prediction of decay was founded on a conception of capitalism in which it was *socially* impossible for a government to set wrongs aright; intellectually, ideologically, even emotionally impossible. The cure for capitalism's failings would require that a government would have to rise above the interests of one class alone—and that, as Marx's doctrine of historical materialism revealed, was to assume that men could free themselves from the shackles of their immediate economic self-interest.

And it is just this lack of social flexibility, this bondage to shortsighted interest, which weakened European capitalism. For one who has read the works of Marx it is frightening to look back at the grim determination with which so many nations steadfastly hewed to the very course which he insisted would lead to their undoing. It was as if their governments were unconsciously vindicating Marx's prophecy by obstinately doing exactly what he said they would. When in Russia under the Tsars all democratic trade-unionism was ruthlessly stamped out, when in England and Germany monopolies and cartels were officially encouraged, the Marxist dialectic looked balefully prescient indeed. Even today, when one considers that in France or Italy or Greece capitalist governments still cannot collect the taxes they levy on their own business communities, when one inspects the enormous gulf between rich and poor and sees evidence of the indifference of the former for the latter, then one has the uneasy feeling that the psychological stereotypes which Marx cast in his historical drama were all too truly drawn from life.

And it is these very facts which give us the clue as to why capitalism has worked in the United States. We have had our share of reactionaries and revolutionaries. But capitalism here has evolved in a land untouched by the dead hand of aristocratic lineage and age-old class attitudes. Hence we have faced up to the economic problems of capitalism with social attitudes that sprang from a less hardened heritage: attitudes of experiment and adaptation, a healthy disrespect for too much power, public or private, and a social flexibility that has prevented the development of brittle and die-hard class structures.

The result has been a Marxist impossibility. Here is a capitalist government that actually prosecutes monopolies! Here is a nation in which almost no one thinks of himself as a proletarian; upper-class America has sometimes kicked its lower classes around, but it has not *despised* them. Here is a business community in which "public relations" have come to be a paramount concern—in which, that is, business is engaged in explaining and justifying its place in society. How incomprehensible to a Marxist that one of our biggest motor companies should give ninety per cent of its earnings to a philanthropic fund and then divest itself of all control over that fund!

It is in these attitudes that the answer to Marxian analysis lies. Marx was not so much "wrong" in his economic vision as he was wrong in assuming that his psychological and sociological preconceptions were fixed and unalterable. The laws of motion which his model of capitalism revealed may still be visible in American capitalism—indeed, they are—but they are faced with a set of remedies which spring from social attitudes quite beyond his imagination. To Marx, the capitalist class was as incorrigibly chained to the ruthless search for profit as the working class had been, for Malthus, to sex. For Marx, a government was as inevitably a tool of the capitalist class as a revolutionary proletariat was inevitably a product of factory life. There was reason to form such ideas in the dark atmosphere of England in the 1860's—let us not forget that the world Marx knew, economically and politically, was cruel, cold, and doctrinaire. In too much of Europe it never quite lost that unhealthy cast—and the result for European capitalism was catastrophic. But in the New World new attitudes have emerged: the idea of democracy, the idea of an impartial government seeking to reconcile divergent interests, the idea of a class *struggle* without a class *war*. Our government has often been tinctured with class interest; it has rarely been tainted with it. All this would have seemed only a wishful fantasy to Marx.

The fact is that capitalism was capable of developing in almost totally divergent social directions. The tragedy is that for much of the world —and for all of the communist world—the stereotypes with which Marx set his plot into motion, the grasping Manchester millowner and the untractable regimes of 1848, are still taken as true likenesses of capitalism everywhere.

But shorn of its overtones of inevitable doom, the Marxist analysis cannot be disregarded. It remains the gravest, most penetrating examination the capitalist system has ever undergone. It is not an examination conducted along moral lines with headwagging and tongue-clucking over the iniquities of the profit motive—this is the stuff of the Marxist revolutionary but not of the Marxist economist. For all its passion, it is a dispassionate appraisal and it is for this reason that its somber findings must be soberly considered.

To repeat an earlier statement: it is with Karl Marx the Revolutionary that the world has been preoccupied, with Marxism as an intolerant force for the enslavement of free opinion. Certainly that is the immediate battle. And yet it is not with Marx the Revolutionary that capitalism must finally contend. It is with Marx the Economist, Marx the finicky scholar who laboriously sought to prove, through the welter of surface distraction, that the essence of capitalism is *self-destruction*. The answer to Marx lies not so much in pointing out the injustices of communism as in demonstrating that in a social atmosphere of which Marx never dreamed, capitalism can survive and flourish.

Karl Marx pronounced his sentence of doom on capitalism in 1867; the system was diagnosed as the victim of an incurable disease, and although no timetable was given, it was presumed to be close enough to its final death struggle for the next-of-kin—the Communists—to listen avidly for the last gasp that would signal their inheritance of power. Even before the appearance of *Das Kapital,* the deathwatch had begun, and with each bout of speculative fever or each siege of industrial depression, the hopeful drew nearer to the deathbed and told each other that the moment of Final Revolution would now be soon at hand.

But the system did not die. On the contrary, it seemed to emerge from each attack of weakness with renewed strength and to rebound from each crisis with a vigor that dismayed the critics. True, many of the Marxist laws of motion were amply verified by the march of events: big business did grow bigger and recurrent depressions and unemployment did plague society. But along with these confirmations of the prognosis of doom, another highly important and portentously phrased Marxist symptom was remarkable by its absence: the increasing misery of the proletariat.

For Marx had believed that with the protean struggle of the system to maintain itself, the working classes would be relentlessly ground underfoot, and that when the final death throes of capitalism were at hand, their revolutionary tempers would have snapped. With a kind of grim justice, the cruelties of capitalism would have brought into being its own executioner.

And that simply failed to happen. On the contrary, a British Committee on Depression which convened to look into the slump of 1886 reported that "there is no feature in the situation which we have been called upon to examine, as satisfactory as the immense improvement which has taken place in the condition of the working class." And this was not just the patronizing cant of class apologists: conditions were better, enormously better. In 1840, according to the calculations of Arnold Toynbee, the wage of an ordinary laborer came to eight shillings a week, while his family necessaries of life cost him fourteen shillings; he made up the difference by begging, stealing, sending his children to the mills, or simply by drawing in his belt. But by 1875, although necessaries had gone to fifteen shillings and a little over, his wages had nearly drawn abreast. *For the first time* he was making enough to keep body and soul together—a sorry commentary on the past, but certainly a hopeful augury for the future.

And not only had wages gone up, but the very source of surplus value had diminished: hours were far shorter. At the Jarrow Shipyards and the New Castle Chemical Works, for example, the workweek had fallen from sixty-one to fifty-four hours, while even in the sweated textile mills, the stint was reduced to only fifty-seven hours. Indeed the mill-owners complained that their wage costs had risen by better than twenty per cent. But while progress was expensive, it paid intangible dividends. For as conditions ameliorated, the mutterings of 1848 died down. "You cannot get them to talk of politics so long as they are well employed," testified a Staffordshire manufacturer on the attitude of his working force.

Even Marx and Engels had to recognize the trend. "The English proletariat is becoming more and more bourgeois," mourned Engels in a letter to Marx, "so that this most bourgeois of all nations is apparently aiming ultimately at the possession of a bourgeois aristocracy and a bourgeois proletariat *as well as a bourgeoisie*."

Clearly, Marx was premature in his pronouncement of impending doom. For the Faithful, of course, the unexpected turn of events could be swallowed in the comforting knowledge that "inevitable" still meant inevitable, and that a matter of a generation or two came to little in the grand march of history. But for the non-Marxist surveyors of the scene, the great Victorian boom meant something else. The world appeared full of hope and promise and the forebodings of a dissenter like Karl Marx seemed merely the ravings of a discontented radical. Hence the great intellectual bombshell that Marx had prepared went off in almost total silence; instead of a storm of abuse, Marx met the far more crushing ignominy of indifference.

READING 75

The problems of understanding so vast and complex an organism as the Russian economy can only be grasped by putting oneself in the shoes of a Russian who, starting from little knowledge and some deep prejudices, wanted to understand the elements of the American economy. The traps to beware of are all the standard ones in approaching any highly charged subject: accepting facts that are not facts, wishing things were so, failing to relate institutions to the particular environment in which they arose, and thinking in black and white terms. Yet, the entry of the Soviet Union into the front rank of the world's higher industrialized economies betokens a story that Americans must know in spite of all the difficulties in the way of understanding.

A useful starting point in this learning process may be to hear what a Soviet leader selects for stress in talking before an American audience. These are excerpts from a speech made by Premier Nikita Khrushchev of the U.S.S.R. before a Pittsburgh audience during his 1959 tour of the U.S.A. The speech naturally enough tells little about Russia's problems, but it can still afford revealing insights and raise key questions about another way of organizing men's economic activities.

Questions to Guide the Reading

What further factual information would you want on each of the points made by Premier Khrushchev in order to measure Soviet economic performance?

Are the criteria by which Khrushchev evaluates his economy different from those we would use in evaluating our own? (How would an American government, business, or labor leader describe our economy before a Russian audience?) Do these criteria represent fundamentally different values or different economic realities?

THE RUSSIAN ECONOMY
Nikita Khrushchev

While in your country I acquainted myself with the life of the American people insofar as this was possible in such a short time, and I saw and heard much. I am deeply grateful for the warm cordiality and hospitality that were accorded to me as the head of the Soviet Government and to those who accompanied me.

We were strengthened in our conviction that the American people are striving for friendship with our people and love peace and their homeland. The American people have created great wealth and enjoy a high standard of living. Like you, the Soviet people love their homeland, want peace and want to live in friendship with your people as well as with all the people of the world.

Owing to the victory of socialism the people of the Soviet Union have attained great successes, and although we are not yet as rich as you are, we are on the right road toward reaching the highest living standard in the world. This is the objective toward which our people aspire, and it will be attained.

The question of the social and political structure, or, in other words, the question of whether to live under socialism or capitalism, is an internal affair of each nation, and the principle of noninterference by countries in each other's domestic affairs should be strictly adhered to. If all countries are guided by these principles, there will be no particular difficulties in insuring peace among nations.

To live in peace we must get to know each other better. Permit me to tell you, if only briefly, something about our country and the life of our people and their plans for the future. I trust that you will understand me when I say that the impressions I have gained here and even the things I have liked in your country have not shaken my faith that the political, economic and social system in the Soviet Union is the fairest and most progressive.

The Soviet Union is a nation of the working people. We have no capitalists. Our factories and mills belong to the people; all the land in the country, with its wealth, belongs to the people. The farmers till their land collectively, each has an income depending on his work, not on invested capital.

Under socialism, a working man's remunera-tion is determined by the quantity and quality of his work for society. When we in our country expand our production still more and accumulate more wealth, we will go over to the Communist principle of distributing that wealth. Each will work according to his ability and receive according to his needs.

The Constitution of our country is in reality a most Democratic one. It insures universal, equal and direct elections to legislative bodies with secret ballot. It insures the right to work, to study and to rest.

"Those who work enjoy distinction"

Before the Revolution it used to be the case in our country that whoever had capital had position. For the first time in our history we established the just rule in our land that those who work will enjoy distinction in the community.

Consider for example the composition of our highest legislative body—the Supreme Soviet of the U.S.S.R. All in all there were elected 1,378 Deputies to the Supreme Soviet. Out of this number, 366 are women; more than 1,000 Deputies are directly engaged in industrial and agricultural production. These are workers, engineers, collective farmers, agronomists and others.

The rest are statesmen and people prominent in public life, in science, culture, literature and art, teachers and doctors. As you see, there are no capitalists in our country and no representative of them in the Supreme Soviet. Our Government is made up of men who come of the working people.

About myself I can say that my grandfather was an illiterate peasant, a serf—he was the property of a landlord and could be sold or even, as it was often the case, exchanged for cattle. My father was a miner and I, too, worked in a mine as a mechanic. I took part in the civil war and afterward the Soviet Government sent me to study at a worker's school and then at the so-called industrial academy. Now the people have entrusted me with the high post of chairman of the Council of Ministers.

Both of my First Deputies recently visited your country, Anastas Mikoyan and Frol Kozlov. Who are they? Anastas Mikoyan is a carpenter's son,

From Nikita Khrushchev, TV Address to the American People, *New York Times*, September 28, 1959.

while Frol Kozlov is a smith's son and was himself a worker and then an engineer.

Neither capital nor important posts are inherited in our country, and everyone in Soviet society enjoys full freedom.

The only thing we do not have is freedom to exploit the labor of others, to privately own factories and mills, land and banks. We of the older generation started life when our country was a capitalist country. Why do we consider that the socialist way is fairer? For hundreds of years mankind developed in conditions in which the minority appropriated the wealth created by the majority, and always people have sought a better organization of society without exploitation of man by man.

We are grateful to Marx, Engels and Lenin, who blazed the trail to the society, and we have followed it. We have been followed along this road by many nations of Europe and Asia.

The working people, on taking over political power, have put an end in our country to a tendency to acquire wealth at the expense of others. Indeed, human greed is a terrible thing. Has there ever been a case of a millionaire not wanting to become a multi-millionaire?

I want to be understood correctly. It is one thing when a man has a pair of shoes who wants to have another pair or so, when he has a suit and wishes to have several more, and when he has a house and desires to build a better one for himself. This is a legitimate desire, and socialism does not restrict people's tastes or requirements.

But we think it is quite another thing when a man has a factory and wants to have two, or when he owns one mill and wants to get ten.

Clearly, nobody, not even with his whole family and not even if he were to live several lives, could earn a million dollars, let alone a billion by his own work. This can be accomplished only when he appropriates the labor of others. But that runs counter to man's conscience, we think. As you know even in the Bible it is said that when those who sold and bought turned the temple into a house of money lenders and changers, Christ took a scourge and drove them out.

Therefore religious people, if they are guided in accordance with their morals by the principles of world peace and love for their fellow men, should not oppose, we think, the new socialist system, for it is a system asserting the most humane and truly just relations in society.

In order that you should understand why we are so proud of our Soviet country, I must say a few words about our past before the Revolution.

Our people were living very hard lives at that time. Nearly 80 per cent of the population was illiterate. Hunger and disease were taking a toll of millions of lives.

This should make it clear to you why the Soviet people are so glad that their country has in a short space of time become the second industrial power of the world. We have increased our industrial production thirty-sixfold, wiped out illiteracy and are now training almost three times as many engineers as you are, for instance.

Our people would now be even better off if we did not have to spend nearly half of these forty years on wars forced upon us and on post-war economic recovery. Let me remind you that during the war the Nazi invaders destroyed and burned down 1,710 of our urban communities and over 70,000 of our rural communities, leaving about 25,000,000 people homeless. We lost many millions of people and sustained damages estimated at about $500,000,000,000.

If it were not for this terrible devastation and losses, we would probably have already overtaken the United States in production and in living standards.

Our people are now working on a Seven-Year Plan, and under this plan we are to double our industrial production. During this period we are to invest the equivalent of about $750,000,000,000 in the national economy. The United States is at present the richest and economically the most highly developed power. The figures for your country represent the highest ceiling in the capitalist world.

You must bear in mind, however, that the average annual rate of industrial expansion in the Soviet Union is about three to five times higher than in your country, and for this reason within the next ten to twelve years we shall surpass the United States both in physical production and in production per capita of the population, while in agriculture this will be accomplished much earlier.

Large-scale housing construction is going on in our country. I will give you an example.

In the past eight years alone more apartments have been built in Moscow than in its entire 800 years' history before the revolution. Next year the people of Moscow will get apartments whose total floor space will exceed a quarter of all the apartments that there were in our capital before the revolution.

Within the next seven years we are going to build about 15,000,000 apartments in cities and 7,000,000 houses in the countryside. This is just about the same as building fifty new cities like San Francisco.

Another important point is that our rent is the lowest in the world and amounts to only 4 to 5 percent of a family's budget.

We are anxious that there should be more comfortable homes and that Soviet people get more consumer goods of high quality. And our words do not part from our deeds. In the past six years, our agriculture has increased sales of meat to the urban population threefold and milk more than twofold.

In the near future, we're going to abolish—and I repeat, abolish—all taxation of the people—and I think you will appreciate the significance of this step.

Our Communist party, the Soviet Government and our trade unions care for the well-being of all Soviet people.

A Soviet citizen need not worry about such things, for instance, as unemployment. In the Soviet Union it is not the man who seeks the job but the job that seeks the man.

All our children are studying not only high school but college education as well. It's free in the Soviet Union. The students receive scholarships from the state. In general we are giving a great deal of attention to bringing up the children —the young generation. The nursery, kindergarten, schools with full board and then a start in life—such is the prospect for the rising generation.

The merits of the Soviet system are well known. It is the graduates of Soviet schools— scientists, engineers, technicians and workers—who astonished the world with the first earth satellite. We are proud that the Russian words "sputnik"

and "lunnik" are understood all over the world without translation.

Two million teachers and nearly 400,000 doctors look after the Soviet people's need. We take care of our people's health. The sickness rate has vastly diminished in our country while the mortality rate is the lowest in the world. Every industrial and office worker and professional has an annual holiday with pay and the finest palaces, sanitoria, health resorts and rest homes have been turned over for the people to rest in.

Everyone in our country gets free medical treatment. The simplest and most complex medical operation does not mean any expense for the patient.

You sometimes do not understand certain aspects of our way of life. The Soviet citizen similarly does not understand how it can be that in the event of misfortune, when someone is taken severely ill and requires an operation and hospital treatment, this calls for the payment of money. But what if a person hasn't got it! What happens then? Does he have to lay down and die?

When a person is sick and does not work in our country, he continues to draw his salary, and when old age comes, he does not feel redundant —he gets a pension from the state. Farmers get pensions from their cooperative.

You may ask, but surely all is not so fine and smooth in their country? Unfortunately, it isn't. We have our difficulties, our shortcomings and unsolved problems. But I can assure you that the most emphatic and uncompromising critics of these shortcomings are we, the Soviet people ourselves.

READING 76

One question that perplexes a man in a market economy is how Soviet Communism manages to motivate people to want to work at useful tasks. In the market economy, the basic incentive is that men are paid in accordance with the value the marketplace puts upon their contributions of labor, land, or capital. This process is sometimes hindered by imperfections of the market and sometimes softened by public and private actions to ensure at least a minimum income regardless of contribution. But, even with these qualifications, distribution of the nation's products is still used as the lure to get resources, including labor, into those activities that society is most willing to pay for.

Does a communist economy try to use inequalities in distribution for these same purposes? Does it have to rely on force to motivate men? Or has it so changed human drives that men are ready to contribute according to their ability while taking according to their need?

Robert Campbell summarizes the U.S.S.R.'s experience in answering the questions of motivation and distribution. In the process, he adds new insights to our understanding of what planned economies can and cannot do.

Questions to Guide the Reading

How do the "carrot" (as opposed to the "stick") aspects of motivation for U.S.S.R. (1) managers and (2) workers compare with the U.S.A.? To what extent do we have parallel problems in the use of incentives?

How does the resultant distribution system in the U.S.S.R. relate to the theories of Karl Marx as set out in the previous two readings?

INCENTIVES IN THE U.S.S.R.
Robert Campbell

In the Soviet system the people who have the responsibility of carrying out the plan are bureaucrats, employees of the state, and the private profit motive which plays so important a role in the free enterprise economy is absent. In such a situation will people really exert themselves to achieve production goals which planners have set for them? Is there any kind of motivation system that will effectively persuade all these employees to exert themselves to fulfill the plans drawn up by the regime?

Motivation must be examined at two separate levels: (1) at the level of the managerial class, and (2) at the level of the mass of workers actually on the production line. Let us consider first motivation at the level of the managerial class. The number of people involved here is clearly much smaller than the number of production workers, but this relatively small group plays a much more important role than its numbers indicate. This is the group that supervises, innovates, organizes, fights for improved methods, and infuses others with the enthusiasm for effort and progress. In short, these manager-bureaucrats have the same function in the Soviet-type economy as has traditionally been performed by entrepreneurs in the free enterprise economy.

Incentives for the managerial elite

Nature of the Soviet enterprise. In certain respects, the individual Soviet enterprise is not much different from a capitalist corporation. It gets its resources in the first instance as a grant from the state, but subsequently it is to proceed more or less on its own, covering its expenses out of the revenues from sale of its output. The things it produces it sells for money and the things it consumes it pays for in money. It is expected to carry on accounting and to determine its own profit or loss. The director of this enterprise, like the officers of a corporation, is in effect a steward of someone else's property and is held responsible for the operation and conservation of that property. The main difference is that in the Soviet case the steward is responsible to the Soviet state, rather than to a group of private citizens. This stewardship, the responsibility for managing the enterprise to produce as much as possible as efficiently as possible, is what the Russians call the principle of economic accountability, or *khozraschet.*

A second important principle of industrial administration which characterizes the management of the enterprise, and indeed the whole structure from top to bottom, is the principle of *edinonachalie,* which can be translated as "unity of authority." In practice this principle means that there is a clearly specified line of command and assignment of responsibility. The director of an enterprise is held accountable for performance of the enterprise, but at the same time he has authority to direct the affairs of the enterprise commensurate with this responsibility. Likewise both above him and below him are individuals who have clearly defined responsibilities and the authority over those below them necessary to fulfill the responsibility. For instance, within the enter-

From Robert Campbell, *Soviet Economic Power* (Houghton Mifflin Company, 1960). Reprinted with kind permission of the author and publisher.

prise, the manager of a shop or subsidiary department of the enterprise has full authority within his jurisdiction, but at the same time he is held accountable by the director of the enterprise. Likewise, above the director is the chief of the chief administration to whom the plant director is responsible. The chief of the chief administration is in turn subordinate to the minister of the ministry of which he is a part. An analogy with military organization may be helpful here. Any commander has full authority over his unit. He is responsible to his superiors, but all orders downward have to go through him.

Having described this environment the question of motivation can be restated somewhat more specifically with reference to the group of people who hold various positions in this line of command. What implements does each of these commanders have to make his subordinates work hard at the job of fulfilling the plan? We are most interested in the role of enterprise management, but clearly it is also important to ask something about the motivations of people above the manager and about his means for controlling the people subordinate to him. How can the managers in this system be made to shun waste, care about efficiency, take upon themselves the trouble of introducing more efficient methods in their plants, and of trying new forms of organization? Or, thinking back to some of the objectives discussed in previous chapters, what sort of pressure will make the managers try to squeeze more output from their machines, try for greater efficiency in fuel consumption, reduce costs, or speed up the turnover of working capital?

There is certainly good reason to suspect that these desirable results will not come just as a matter of course. The goals of the managers do not necessarily coincide with those of the regime. These economic officials are not working directly for themselves but for the state which is their master. The increased output, the rubles saved from more efficient operation, are not in the first instance for them but for the greater glory of communism. Why should these bureaucrats break their backs so that Stalin can build monuments to himself in Moscow, so that Khrushchev can extend economic aid to Egypt, or so that Russians a generation later should have a thirty-five hour work week? Obviously it is necessary to structure the setting in which the manager works in some way so that he has adequate incentive to do what the regime wants him to do. The solution which the regime has used can be described crudely by the familiar idea of the carrot and the stick, although this simple conception scarcely does justice to the intricacies of the system of both positive and negative incentives which the manager faces.

Material rewards of managers.   First of all successful managers, those who fulfill and overfulfill the plans assigned to them, are well rewarded in material terms. The managers are very well paid and in addition enjoy other perquisites such as a home, the use of an automobile, travel on expense accounts, vacations at resorts, and so on. Many of these rewards are things that money alone cannot buy in the Soviet Union—they come only with certain official positions. But these rewards are dependent on performance, and the size of the manager's income depends on how well he performs. This differentiation of reward is based on the system of bonuses which the manager and his staff receive in addition to their base salaries.

There are two main kinds of bonuses. One is for fulfilling the plan generally and, in addition, there are many specific kinds of bonuses in individual branches of industry based on specific problems of those branches. For instance, in the electric power industry there are specific bonuses for reducing the input of fuel per kilowatt-hour of power generated. In other industries there may be special bonuses for improving the average quality of goods, and so on. The size of the bonuses for fulfillment of the plan varies by branch of industry and by size of firm. Under the schedule for some important branches of industry, the director of an enterprise can earn up to 37 per cent in addition to his base salary just for fulfilling the output plan. In addition he can receive up to 4 per cent of his base salary for every percentage point of overfulfillment of the plan. Thus if he overfulfilled the plan by 10 per cent he would have a bonus of 77 per cent of his base salary, in addition to the base salary. For other branches of industry the rewards are not quite so high and for people lower in the managerial hierarchy of the enterprise the rewards are likewise somewhat smaller. Some idea of the magnitude of rewards that may be received under these schemes is provided by the rule that total bonuses in some industries may not be more than 1.5 times the base salary and in others not more than twice the base salary. Not everyone has such advantageous possibilities for earning bonuses. The scales vary depending on the branch of industry and on the size of plant and on one's position in the management structure of the enterprise.

We have emphasized the material rewards which motivate the managerial elite, because these are probably the ones that work most powerfully in assuring dedicated managerial effort. But the motivation of managers in the Soviet economy is undoubtedly complex, just as in a capitalist corporation. Mixed in with the concern for material success is a host of other motivations and incentives—the desire to serve society, to hold power, to exercise one's initiative and energy in some creative way. To convince oneself that such a system of incentives will draw forth adequate managerial effort, one should think of its similarities to the goals that motivate the "organization men" in American corporations.

Negative sanctions. One distinctive, and to Americans, repellent, feature of the Soviet manager's environment is the extreme harshness of the negative sanctions that may be employed. In the Soviet Union, insecurity is one of the major elements of the managerial environment. Loss of one's job and the perquisites that go with it is certainly a possibility.

Actually, however, that is the least of the evils that can befall responsible people in the Soviet managerial structure. They are held to a very strict accountability for their actions and are often judged arbitrarily. Failure to achieve fulfillment of the planned targets may bring an accusation of criminal negligence, of economic crimes against the state, and the responsible persons could be imprisoned or shot. At the same time, a manager's best efforts to meet the plan targets may lead him afoul of the multitudinous legal prohibitions that circumscribe his freedom of action. For instance, the materials supply system works ineffectively and he may have to resort to illegal means of procuring materials in order to fulfill the plan. As another example, he may have to pay out more wages than planned in order to meet the output goal, but to get the cash from the bank he may have to violate accounting rules or falsify documents.

Many of these legal restraints are not rigorously enforced, but enterprise officials always place themselves in a potentially dangerous position by violating them. Negative sanctions work best if they lurk more or less in the background; making managers excessively insecure defeats the objective of keeping them as productive as possible. Still, such sanctions have been used on a large enough scale and often enough in the past that neither we nor the Soviet managers doubt that they may be used again.

Problems in the administration of incentives

Thus it can be said without cavil that Soviet managers are highly motivated to try to fulfill the plans which are handed down to them. They have every reason to do their best to meet the goals of the plan and to convince their superiors that they are doing a good job. In such a system, however, there inevitably arise two important problems.

1. The first of these has to do with cheating. When the pressures to fulfill the plan are so strong, there is a strong temptation for managers to fulfill the plan by what has been called "simulation." The idea is to achieve the appearance of plan fulfillment if not the substance. A plan can be fulfilled in more than one way. One of the easiest methods is to arrange things beforehand so that one has an easy plan to fulfill. In the process of planning, enterprises propose targets for output, costs, labor force, and capital investment. It is not surprising, therefore, that enterprises look upon this part of the process as an important bargaining situation. They bargain for a small output goal, a generous allocation of materials, as large a labor force as possible. The reason it is possible to carry on such bargaining is that it is very difficult for people at higher levels to know what the performance of an enterprise really should be. Another more blatant form of cheating is to falsify reports of plan fulfillment. A Soviet enterprise reports monthly, quarterly, and annually on its progress in fulfilling its plan. What is to prevent the manager from drawing up a very optimistic report claiming that he has overfulfilled the plan? And if he does, how will his superiors ever find out that the report on plan fulfillment is falsified?

2. The second big problem is one of setting up some system of measuring how successfully a plan is fulfilled. The plan specifies a great many targets the manager is to achieve and in the nature of things the plan is never fulfilled exactly. Therefore those who evaluate plan fulfillment must establish some set of priorities for relating underfulfillment of one goal to overfulfillment of another. As we shall see it is difficult to establish a set of priorities that will always lead the enterprise managers to do the things that are best from the national economic point of view.

Falsification. Let us first discuss the problems of falsification and simulation. How can the regime forestall efforts to obtain an easy plan and the temptation to falsify reported achievements? Essentially the regime has adopted the hardboiled attitude that it is impossible to take at face value the word of people at lower levels and has constructed many separate channels for checking on the performance of managers and for placing pressure on managers to tighten up plans.

One of the distinctive things about the Soviet economy is the great number of agencies that in some way check on or examine in detail the work and reports of enterprises. The most important of these control agencies is the agency which stands immediately above in the administration hierarchy. For most enterprises this is the *glavk*, and for the *glavk* it is the ministry. The *glavk* demands a large volume of statistical and accounting reports from enterprises under its jurisdiction. The very completeness and volume of this reported information by itself makes falsification somewhat difficult. All the different aspects of the performance of a plant are mutually interrelated and falsifying reports on one aspect would require that other parts be falsified as well. There is a variety of internal checks among the different indicators of performance that an enterprise reports, and attempted falsification would run the risk of detection because of these cross-checks. For instance, it is impossible to give the correct report on output and the correct report on labor force and at the same time falsify the report on labor productivity. If the enterprise tried to support the falsified indicator of labor productivity by understating the number of persons employed, it would also have to falsify the report on the amount of wages paid out, and so on in a never-ending chain of interrelated magnitudes. The first thing the superior organ does on receiving a report from an enterprise is to check it for internal consistency. In view of this close examination of internal consistency, the room for maneuver in falsifying reports is extremely limited. Another factor that makes it extremely difficult to falsify reports is that the rules for drawing up statistical reports and for carrying out accounting are prescribed in minute detail from above.

The controls which the superior organ has over the enterprise are well illustrated by the position of the chief bookkeeper in the enterprise. In a number of respects the chief bookkeeper is not subject to the authority of the manager of the enterprise at all, but to the superior organ. Many of the documents associated with transactions of the enterprise require his signature, and he is not supposed to carry out the orders of the manager and indicate his approval if these transactions involve some illegality or falsification. He is offi-cially described as the "eye of the state" within the enterprise and the listing of his functions and responsibilities makes it clear that he is to insure accurate reporting to his boss, the bookkeeping department of the superior organ. Even so, the superior organ does not really trust the reports presented by the enterprise, and it is envisaged in Soviet accounting legislation that an auditor from the central organization will audit the books of every enterprise once a year.

It should not be concluded from all that we have said that reports submitted by Soviet enterprises are never falsified. There are some kinds of falsification which will get by, and careful research into the kinds of falsification that enterprises try to carry off provides interesting insights into the nature of managerial behavior in the Soviet system. But the point is that falsification is a dangerous business and the distortions that one can safely get away with are likely to be relatively minor.

Moreover, the checks performed by the superior organ are only the beginning. There are many other chains of command and information that reach into the enterprise. One of the most important is the *Gosbank*, the "one big bank" which services the whole Soviet economy. It is in a particularly strategic position to check on and control enterprise actions since all the monetary transactions of the enterprise pass through its hands. Generally speaking, Soviet enterprises use very little cash in their transactions. They sell their output to other state organizations and are paid by transfers of bank balances rather than by the exchange of actual cash. Thus the Soviet firm never has much access to cash and makes payments from its bank account by writing orders to the bank authorizing transfers. One of the main functions entrusted to the bank is the duty of checking on the legality of these transactions. Prices must be in accordance with prices fixed by the government, payments must be for purposes specified in the plan, and so on. The one transaction for which the enterprise draws cash from the bank is for payment of its workers, and in this case the bank is supposed to exercise particularly careful control. The bank does not simply hand over whatever money the enterprise says it needs to pay workers, but checks wage payments against the plan and checks the payroll, including the names of payees, to make certain that they are really employed in the enterprise.

The measurement of success. The second big problem in operating this system of incentives involves the choice of appropriate indicators of plan fulfillment. The Russians have a more difficult problem here than American corporations generally do.

In the Soviet economy, the higher level of administrative officials are unable to rely on profit as the most important indicator for evaluating the performance of enterprise directors. Because of distortions in the price system, maximizing profit at the level of the enterprise does not mean maximizing the overall objectives of the regime. Frequently prices are set below cost on certain very badly needed items, while other, less crucially needed items may have prices which allow high profits. If, in such a situation, managers were told that their performance would be judged on the basis of their profits, disequilibrium between supplies and demands would quickly develop. The unreliability of profit as an index of the best action from the point of view of the national economy forces the planners to specify in considerable detail just how enterprise management should operate; the plan which an enterprise receives in the Soviet economy specifies not a single goal, but many separate ones. At the very minimum the plan will indicate the size of the labor force and the volume of wage payments, the amounts of various kinds of materials that will be allocated to the enterprise, a cost budget, the total value of output, and the amount of profit that is to be earned. In most industries the plan will specify a number of indicators in addition to these. All these targets must be specified in the plan. These details cannot be left to the discretion of the enterprise director because they have been painstakingly fitted into the overall system of plans beforehand. Encouraging management to disregard them in favor of maximizing profit would cause endless trouble.

The fact that so many details are laid down complicates the job of the superior organ when it comes to evaluate the fulfillment of the plan as a whole. There is no single indicator of performance which they can compare with a planned target and decide whether or not the plan was fulfilled and to what degree. Plans are never so accurate or the manager's control over his operations so complete that he will just fulfill all the indicators exactly. It usually happens that he will do better than the plan on some of the targets but underfill some others, or at least meet different targets in varying degrees. When this happens, a perplexing problem of evaluation arises for the authorities. What should their reaction be if the output plan is overfulfilled by 10 per cent but the planned wages expenditure has been exceeded by 5 per cent, or what if the plant has produced 20 per cent more of one commodity than the plan specified but 10 per cent less than the planned amount of another? How can these various indexes of performance be balanced off against one another so that it is possible to decide whether or not the plan has been fulfilled and whether or not to hand out the bonuses and other rewards described earlier? Clearly what happens in such a situation is that sooner or later there must emerge some set of priorities which guide the controllers in making their evaluations of plan fulfillment. And once the managers have learned what the set of priorities is, they will take these priorities into account in making their decisions.

The establishment of the correct system of priorities is a tricky business, however. If too much emphasis is given to one goal the managers are likely to pay very little attention to the other goals. For instance, generally speaking, in the thirties very great stress was placed on fulfillment of the output goal, and other aspects of the plan were not considered so important. Managers naturally tried to fulfill the output plan somehow or other, even if it meant exceeding planned costs or violating other parts of the plan. This was not necessarily desirable from the national economic point of view, since in many cases the extra output was more than offset by the waste of resources used in producing it. Since then the emphasis has changed somewhat so that bonuses are not paid for fulfillment of plan unless the cost plan is also adhered to. Ideally the controllers would like to find some system of priorities that would lead managers to do exactly what they want them to. But this is an unattainable goal. The planners can set only a general order of priority, and since situations change and since different managers find themselves in varying situations, the rough system of priorities will always tempt people into some actions that are undesirable from the overall point of view.

Thus we find the following problem arising over and over again in many different contexts in the Soviet economy. Whenever controllers give high priority to one particular goal in their evaluation of plan fulfillment, and make that priority effective through bonuses, enterprise managers will violate other parts of the plan in order to fulfill the high-priority indicator. For instance, in the machine tractor stations (MTS), one of the high-priority indicators has been the reduction of fuel expenditure in tractor work. Fuel is one of the biggest inputs into tractor operation and naturally the controllers wanted to motivate people to reduce fuel expenditure. But because of the high priority of this goal the managers of

MTS did many things that were clearly undesirable and irrational in order to improve this one indicator and get bonuses. They would systematically plow to less than the standard depth, refuse to do for the collective farms those kinds of work that required more fuel, and in other such ways interfere with effective work of the collective farms.

Another interesting illustration of the principle occurred in the electric power industry. Electric power stations themselves consume a certain fraction of the power they produce to run various kinds of machinery in the power station. In the Soviet Union this internal consumption has been higher than it should be, say, by comparison with United States plants. The authorities made reduction in internal consumption a high-priority goal, and bonuses were given for good performance with regard to this indicator. The reaction of managers of electric power plants was rational enough from their own point of view. They replaced electric motors in their plants with steam engines and internal combustion engines in order to reduce their consumption of electric power. But of course such a substitution is not really efficient for the economy as a whole and was not intended when the bonuses for reduction of internal consumption were established. Installation of new machinery involved a waste of investment funds and its operation meant some increase in costs, but since the system of priorities did not place much emphasis on these indicators, the waste was overlooked and managers got their bonuses for being wasteful!

Many problems arise because of the difficulty of finding unambiguous measures for certain kinds of enterprise performance. When the output of some commodity is measured in physical terms (for instance, cement in tons) the enterprise will be tempted to reduce quality for tonnage. A ton of low-quality cement is just as good as a ton of high-grade cement for fulfilling the plan and is easier to produce. This general problem crops up again and again in many different branches of the economy. For instance, one interesting case involved the goal for costs of production in book publishing. Clearly if the plan specified simply cost per book the enterprise would be tempted to produce only small books and to print these in tremendous volume. So the planners instead specified the cost plan in terms of cost per printed page. What the book publishers did then was simply to use larger and larger type, to put wider and wider margins on the pages, and more and more space between the lines. One of the biggest costs in book publishing

is the editorial and typesetting work, and if this is spread over a larger and larger number of pages, there is naturally a reduction in the cost per page. So this indicator had exactly the opposite effect from what was intended. It tempted the book publishers to seek success and earn bonuses by wasting paper and binding materials, rather than by reducing costs and making savings.

Very often these problems can be solved by changing the indicator or by changing the system of priorities, though the system will never work perfectly. When specific problems are solved very often new ones arise. However, it would be wrong to overemphasize these difficulties in the motivation and controlling system. The examples we have discussed are characteristic diseases to which the Soviet system is subject but, like the human organism, it manages to survive. When certain errors become too serious and therefore obvious, a way is found for eliminating them. In its rapid movement forward the Soviet economy is involved in a certain amount of waste motion but it pushes ahead nevertheless.

The conclusion of all this is that the Soviet regime motivates and controls its managerial elite fairly effectively. The material rewards offered for successful managerial activity are great enough to elicit an adequate supply of effort and talent. At the same time the system of control has been arranged so that managers must really perform in order to win these rewards. The regime burdens economic administrative officials with heavy responsibility and has devised moderately effective means for checking on whether or not they fulfill the responsibility.

This is not to say that the system works perfectly. There are ways of evading responsibility, certain aspects of the control system encourage people to engage in actions that are irrational from the national economic point of view, and the operation of the system of checks and controls represents a considerable overhead cost for the economy. But there is no doubt that the Soviet regime has devised a reasonably successful system of motivating its manager-bureaucrats to act like entrepreneur-capitalists If this is hard to believe, think back over the system described and ask whether it is really so much different from the system that motivates most management in the United States. After all, most of the entrepreneurial functions of a capitalist country are performed not by capitalists but by hired managers, people who are really bureaucrats within the structure of the corporation. But although they often have virtually no ownership rights in the corporation and so do not have much personal interest directly in maximizing its profits and efficiency, they still do a good job because they are motivated by the same incentives as are offered to the Soviet managers.

Incentives for the mass of the workers

The second half of the motivation problem concerns the incentives which drive the mass of the workers. Despite the crucial importance of the functions performed by the managerial group we have been considering so far, it is actually a fairly small elite. The thousands of managers are far outnumbered by the millions of production workers who wield the tools and handle the materials and products at the factory bench, in the mines, or on the construction job. Surely the productivity of any economy must depend to a considerable extent on the degree of motivation of these ordinary workers. Unless the worker brings to his job a measure of carefulness, some pride in his work, and a willingness to learn, the capacity of the economy to produce and to progress must surely suffer. Since we have often been presented with the image of the Soviet economy as a sort of vast slave labor camp, we are inclined to picture the Soviet worker as going through the motions of work more out of desperation than out of any positive incentive. Our purpose here is to replace this lifeless stereotype with a more balanced and rounded picture of the pressures and motivations that drive the Soviet worker to do his job well.

Payment according to productivity. The general approach to labor policy is not much different in principle from that regarding the managers. The regime presents highly contrasted possibilities to the Soviet workers. Those who enter certain elite occupations, those who are earnest workers and overfulfill the work norms, those who are willing to acquire new skills and move up the educational ladder will receive much higher rewards than their fellows. On the other hand, those who are unskilled, do not fulfill the work norms, and are generally unproductive will suffer low wages, loss of certain benefits, dismissal, and perhaps even criminal punishment. This general picture can be illustrated with a few details.

First of all, on the positive side, there is great differentiation in the wage rate established for different jobs. At the basis of the wage system in every branch of Soviet industry is a scale which sets out a number of skill classifications corresponding to different responsibilities and degrees of skill. A basic rate of pay is established for each

of these categories. Generally speaking, the differentiation of wages among the skill classifications is greater than would be true in a comparable American plant or industry. For many of these pay scales, the difference between the pay of the person in the highest skill category and that of the person in the lowest is 2.8 times, in others 3.5 times, and there are some industries in which base pay rate of the highest skill category is 4.5 times as high as that of the lowest. Such great differentiation between the highest- and lowest-paid manual workers in a plant is rare in industry in the United States. In addition to this variation within industries, considerable variation between pay scales exists for different industries. Those which the government considers high-priority industries and which require special skills generally have much higher pay scales than does, say, the food industry.

Another aspect of the differentiation of rewards for the production worker lies in the extensive use of the piece-rate system in the Soviet Union. To a far greater extent than in American industry, the Soviet worker is paid on the basis not of how much time he puts in, but by how many units of output he produces. In recent years, about 75 per cent of Soviet industrial workers, for instance, have been paid on a piece-rate basis. The corresponding fraction for American industry would be much smaller. Under the piece-rate system, there will be set for each job a certain hourly or daily norm of output which the worker is supposed to try to fulfill. If he fulfills the norm just 100 per cent, he gets the basic wage specified in the wage scales described above. For exceeding the output norm he will receive a wage higher than that specified in the wage scale. Moreover, in recent years about a third of Russian industrial workers have been paid on the basis of what the Russians call the "progressive piece-rate system." That is, the rate of pay per unit of output goes up as the norm for production is exceeded. For producing more than a certain number of units per hour, the worker will be paid at a successively higher and higher rate, so that if he overfulfills the norm by 10 per cent he may get 20 per cent more income than if he just fulfilled the norm 100 per cent.

Soviet wages are further differentiated according to the unattractiveness of the work. For instance, the government establishes large geographical differentials in wages. In order to get people to work in the far north and in some of the remote eastern areas, wages almost double those in most parts of the Soviet Union are offered. In some other branches of industry there may be differentials for dangerous work, for underground work, and other unattractive features of certain jobs.

Coercive labor discipline.

Positive incentives in the form of monetary rewards for working hard, for entering elite occupations, and for improving one's skills are accompanied in the Soviet Union to an unusual degree by legal forms of labor discipline. There has traditionally been a considerable degree of compulsion in Soviet labor policy. For instance, all Soviet workers carry what are called labor books. The labor book shows the worker's name, his qualifications, the jobs he has held, the pay he has received during his whole working career. When a worker takes a job, he turns his labor book over to his employer, who keeps possession of it as long as the worker is in his employ. Since a worker cannot get a new job without presenting this labor book to his new employer, he must virtually have permission from his old employer to leave his job. The very existence of the labor book deprives the worker of a certain degree of independence and mobility. Moreover, during some periods of Soviet history, the law has provided severe punishments for workers who were late to work, who came to work drunk, or were absent from work. At one point a worker who was twenty minutes late to work might end up with a prison term of two to four months. In other cases workers might be sentenced to forced labor at their regular job. They would work at their regular place of employment but get pay reduced below their usual wage by as much as twenty-five per cent.

The balance between these positive and negative incentives has varied over time. Emphasis on the negative incentives became particularly strong beginning in the late Thirties and during the Second World War. During the Second World War some workers, as for instance railroad workers, were even made subject to martial law and laborers were conscripted and assigned to factories. In recent years, however, the trend has been more and more away from the negative incentives. Some of the repressive labor legislation has been repealed, and in general labor laws have been interpreted more leniently. This is probably a change in the direction of economic rationality. The Russians are recognizing that a relatively free labor market, dominated by positive incentives, is more effective than one characterized by compulsion.

Thus far nothing has been said about the Soviet slave labor camps. During much of the history of the Soviet regime there have existed what the Russians call corrective labor camps, to which persons were sentenced for various kinds of offenses against the regime. No one knows just how many people have been in these camps, but at times prisoners have numbered in the millions. Camps were often located in remote parts of the country, such as Siberia and the far north, and prisoners were used for various economic activities, such as lumbering, building canals, or digging coal in mines above the Arctic Circle. But these camps do not really deserve much attention in a discussion of Soviet labor policy. Their operation is more an aspect of the Soviet totalitarian political system than a considered policy of labor utilization. Such labor is extremely inefficient, and although some good was gotten out of the prisoners, the slave labor camps involved a costly waste of labor, even from the point of view of the regime. This was one of the most hated and feared features of the regime and after the death of Stalin, most of the prisoners were amnestied.

READING 77

International comparisons of growth rates are invariably tricky: the statistics are hard to come by and easy to play with. Yet the vaunted growth of the Russian economy in the last two decades has caused considerable concern in the United States. There are Cassandras and Polyannas alike among the interpreters of the data showing that the Soviet Union is growing at a faster rate than we are.

What does the best recent scholarship suggest on the ability of the Russians to maintain their higher growth rate and to pass us as the world's greatest industrial power? Abram Bergson, professor of economics at Harvard University, is one of the best known of the American economists specializing in Russian affairs.

Questions to Guide the Reading

What are the most reasonable assumptions to make now about the likelihood that (1) the Soviet Union will maintain its current growth rate and (2) the United States will increase its growth rate by either 1 or 2 per cent per annum?

What difference does it make whether the Soviet Union catches up to the United States in Gross National Product by, say, 1985?

THE U.S.S.R.'s GROWTH RACE
Abram Bergson

As the 1962 Cuban episode showed, Khrushchev, in seeking to "bury us," is prepared to vary his tactics as circumstances permit. But in the economic field he has pursued steadfastly the imperative he inherited from Stalin: by outpacing the U.S.A. economically, the U.S.S.R. must eventually supplant us as the world's first industrial power. How are the Russians progressing in their "economic competition" with us? What are their future prospects?

Stalin died March 5, 1953. For the years that followed, through 1961, the Soviet government claims that the U.S.S.R. increased its national income at an average rate of 9.7 per cent a year. Independent Western calculations, however, place the correct figure at somewhere around six per cent, which is still a rapid pace. While it is certainly not unprecedented in Western experience, the Soviet growth rate compares favorably enough with that of the U.S. for recent years— about 2.7 per cent over the last few cycles.

In expanding their output in recent years, the Russians have been able to rely only to a very limited extent on increases in *employment* of labor. Industrial expansion has been achieved principally through increases in *output per worker*. Moreover, available population projections indicate that employment is not apt to increase any more rapidly in the coming years than it has in the recent past. In fact, there is a good chance that the rate of increase will decline. In hourly terms, however, the Soviet government might avoid such a trend if it should decide to postpone the promised reduction in the workweek to 35 hours by 1964–68. It follows that the growth in output will depend, as it has in the recent past, primarily on productivity increases. What are the prospects for such increases?

Any serious appraisal must consider, to begin with, that, because of the limited amount and quality of natural resources, production in the U.S.S.R., as elsewhere, is subject to diminishing returns. While these limitations will be felt throughout the Soviet economy, in the years ahead they are especially apt to be felt in agriculture—for the U.S.S.R. in terms of soil and climate is not nearly as well endowed agriculturally as its great land surface might suggest. The Russians' recent experience in farming is a dramatic reminder of this fact. I refer, in particular, to the already reduced returns on the vast new acreage cultivated during 1955–58. Thus, in Tselinnyi Krai, the heartland of this acreage, even dubious official figures show that the grain harvest, which was not especially high to begin with, has steadily declined. It was 14.3 million tons in 1958, 13.9 million in 1959, 12.9 million in 1960 and 10.3 million in 1961.

Furthermore, in expanding their output lately, the Russians have still been able to borrow new technology from the West and to extend to industry in general borrowed technology which previously had been used only in advanced enterprises. This "advantage of backwardness," however, is no longer as important as it was in the Thirties, and as the Soviet economy continues to advance, its role will decline even further. Of course, the U.S.S.R. now has a large corps of scientists and engineers of its own, one which can even stand comparison with that of the U.S.A. In addition, the Soviet government is devoting large and increasing sums to research. Therefore, as opportunities to profit from foreign technology dwindle, self-generated innovation will be something of an offset.

Closely related to but not the same thing as

From Abram Bergson, "The Great Economic Race," *Challenge,* March, 1963, pp. 4–6. Reprinted with kind permission of the author and publisher.

the state of technology is "economic efficiency." To weigh from this standpoint the impact of the extraordinary changes in economic organization, principles and procedures that have occurred since Stalin is a difficult task. But by all accounts the Soviet planning system still leaves much to be desired with respect to economic efficiency. And the succession of reforms at least attests to the fact that the government is seriously concerned with exploiting such "hidden reserves." Moreover, the government has also seen fit recently to allow Soviet economists a degree of discretion to explore and debate alternative techniques that was unheard of under Stalin. Even branches of "bourgeois" economic theory, such as "input-output analysis" and "linear programing," are no longer beyond the pale.

By implication, even though it is faced with diminishing returns from natural resources and slowing technological progress, the U.S.S.R. may still be able to avoid a reduced rate of productivity increase by raising economic efficiency. In trying to accomplish this through their planning system, however, the Russians will be treading new and as yet unexplored ground, and how much they will be able to achieve still remains to be seen.

As output has expanded, so too has variety, and partly for this reason the task of planning has become more complex. Accordingly, the Russians may have to improve their economic organization even to hold their own with regard to efficiency, to say nothing of raising it.

I have been referring to the efficiency of the economic system generally. In the agricultural sector, chiefly because of the use of the state farm in the execution of the new lands program, the notorious collective farm is no longer as important as it once was, but it is still predominant. And avowedly the government will continue to rely heavily on it in the coming years. When we consider the U.S.S.R.'s adverse natural endowment, we can see that the Soviet collective farm is not quite as inefficient as is often supposed, but future gains in this regard should be modest.

There are indications, however, that the government at long last is preparing the ground for the transformation of the collective into state farms. Among other things, in place of their customary cooperative shares, collective farm members are increasingly being paid a money income of a sort very much like the money wage of state farm employees. Because of differences in capital and quality of land, the comparison of state farm and collective farm productivity is a complex matter. Soviet economists probably are correct, however, in maintaining that the state farm is often superior to the collective farm, particularly in the growing of grain. But to what extent the higher productivity would survive the conversion of the collectives into state farms, especially if the conversion is abrupt, is another matter.

In general, how much progress will be realized regarding agricultural efficiency will depend very much on the prudence and restraint exercised with regard to farm policy and administration. These are qualities which the arbitrary and impatient Soviet government has thus far found it difficult to realize.

One of the principal reasons for the rapid rise of labor productivity in the past has been the authoritarian political control exercised over the volume of capital investment. One must be highly optimistic to suppose that this will not persist.

Indeed, given such control, one might wonder whether through its exercise alone the government could not offset or more than offset any and all forces making for a slowdown in the growth of the economy. But it should be borne in mind that the Soviet stock of fixed capital already is growing at an extraordinary rate—in the Fifties by some 11 per cent per year. Even maintaining this high tempo, to say nothing of increasing it, will be a difficult task. This could not be accomplished merely by maintaining the present share of national income devoted to new capital investment. Rather the government would have to continually raise this share.

While this important fact is still not always understood, it becomes obvious when one considers that capital stock has been growing much more rapidly than output and that this is the chief reason that it has been possible to increase output at a rapid pace to begin with. As we saw, the growth in the employment of labor has only been modest.

Thus, in order for the capital stock to expand as in the past, the share of income going to capital investment would have to rise even if in the future output continued to grow at the past tempo. If output should slow down because of retarding forces elsewhere, the rate of investment would have to rise still more.

This leads to the conclusion that the share of national income available for consumption would have to fall. If the rate of growth of income should be maintained or not decline much, total consumption could still increase, for even a declining share of a growing pie can increase absolutely. There might also be an increase in per capita consumption. But the gains in the latter would have to be modest and no doubt would only seem more so to a people who have waited so long and have lately been led by their government to expect so much as have the Russians.

Thus suppose even that there should be no retarding forces elsewhere, so that with the capital stock growing no more rapidly than before, output should continue in the future to grow at six per cent. If allowance is made for the investment needed currently to assure this continued expansion of the capital stock by 11 per cent, according to a crude calculation, consumption per capita during the Sixties might rise by 2.3 per cent, or $9 to $12 a year, from the 1960 level of, say, $400 per capita. This would be respectable progress, but the result would hardly be the affluence that has been promised. If because of retarding forces elsewhere output should tend to grow less rapidly than six per cent, consumption would increase still less.

In deciding its future investment policy, the Soviet government must consider such possible consequences. As we may judge from the continuing stress on "heavy" compared with "consumer goods" industries, it already has determined to increase further the rate of investment, but how much is a momentous matter which it no doubt will decide currently only in the light of the circumstances of the time.

Reference has been to consumption exclusive of communal services, particularly education and health care. What of the latter items? How these might vary in the future is conjectural, but for purposes of the above calculation they are taken to increase proportionately with national income. Hence, with their inclusion in consumption, this category might grow somewhat more rapidly than was indicated. Actually, under its new program the party has committed itself to expand sharply the scope of communal services in the

coming years. Among other things, housing in time is to be supplied free of charge instead of (as is now done) at a nominal rental. But such rearrangements would be purely financial and could not affect at all the underlying realities of the matter, particularly the total supply of consumer goods and services of all sorts that will be made available.

For purposes of the hypothetical calculation, I also assume that defense outlays will increase proportionately with national income. Should they fail to do so, there would necessarily be additional productive resources available for either consumption or investment, as the government might wish. And resources available for these purposes would only be greater if at long last defense expenditures were curtailed absolutely. In short, for the U.S.S.R., defense outlays are onerous, and it can only gain economically from disarmament. On the record to date, however, there is little basis to suppose that the Soviet government might determine its future policy on disarmament simply on this basis.

In sum, we can hardly foresee with any accuracy the future course of the Soviet economy. But it should be difficult for the Russians in the coming years to maintain the six per cent growth rate in output they have realized since Stalin. Still we must assume that they will continue to outpace the U.S.A., at least for some years to come, but most likely the margin by which they do so will tend to diminish.

At this juncture, prospects for a sharp acceleration of the U.S. growth rate do not seem as bright as they did in November, 1960, but a quickening expansion of the labor force is in prospect. Partly for this reason many U.S. economists feel that in the coming years the U.S. economy might grow by at least 3.5 per cent a year. If this tempo is realized, the margin between the Soviet and U.S. rates of increase will narrow more.

In any event, if the Russians ever are to achieve the economic superiority over the U.S. that they seek, it will not be soon. This emerges clearly enough from the hypothetical projections of national income in the two countries as shown in the preceding table. All figures, including those for the U.S.S.R., are expressed as percentages of the U.S. national income in 1960.

We must not underestimate the Soviet economic challenge, but it is not quite as serious as many in the West have supposed. The threat will be less should we manage to accelerate our own growth above its recent sluggish tempo.

National Income Projections: U.S. and U.S.S.R. (As % of U.S. National Income, 1960)

	U.S. with Annual Increase of		U.S.S.R. with Annual Increase of	
	3.0 Per Cent	4.0 Per Cent	5.0 Per Cent	6.0 Per Cent
1960	100.0	100.0	48.0	48.0
1970	134.4	148.0	78.2	86.0
1980	180.6	219.1	127.3	153.9

READING 78

The idea that communism represents one monolithic approach to economics or politics has been shaken to its roots by the variations among the European communist societies and, above all, by the patterns of events in the People's Republic of China. Moscow and Peking are at odds over the correct interpretation of Karl Marx in today's world; but they also pursue sharply different paths to solve their distinctive problems.

The Communist China case has relevance that goes well beyond the argument that we need to look closely at alternative systems so as to understand our own system better. China's example, if it were to prove successful in lifting large numbers of people out of centuries of poverty, would have appeal for other poor countries gripped by the urgency of new expectations. This article tells in outline form what the Communists faced when they came to power, what they did with their power, and what problems they have encountered. Because the situation is so constantly in flux and because data on the Chinese experience are so hard to come by, this article needs to be read less for specifics on today's China than for an analysis of the overall strategy of a made-in-China brand of communism.

Questions to Guide the Reading

What considerations might communist leaders take into account in deciding upon the relative priorities as between agriculture and industry?

What principal lessons emerge from this account of Chinese experience? To what extent are the problems here unique to communism and to what extent are they inherent in all attempts at rapid economic growth in underdeveloped lands?

THE ECONOMY OF COMMUNIST CHINA
A. Doak Barnett

While political power in Communist China, as in all totalitarian societies, has become an end in itself—in fact, if not in theory—it is also much more than that. It is the tool to shape society into the Communists' image of the millennium, the weapon with which to achieve their vision of China as a powerful, industrialized state. From the start, therefore, the leaders have placed high priority on the need for rapid, planned, state-controlled, economic development and have used their power to this end.

The economy which the Chinese Communists inherited in 1949, however, was not only one of the poorest and least developed of any major nation, it was also in a shambles after years of disunity and war. Both industrial and agricultural production had dropped to low levels. Transport was disrupted. Inflation was rampant.

Economic reconstruction

The Communists' first task, therefore, was to rehabilitate the inherited economy, to get existing farms and factories working again, to repair transport, revive trade and control inflation.

China's first plan was modeled closely on Stalinist experience. Moreover it drew heavily on Soviet technical assistance and depended fundamentally on imports of capital goods from Russia (for which, however, the Chinese have had to pay). "The Soviet Union of today is the China of tomorrow," Peking proclaimed and its first plan, like Stalin's, called for over-all state planning under tight central control, rapid industrialization with a primary focus on heavy industries and high levels of state investment requiring enforced consumer austerity.

From A. Doak Barnett, "Communist China—Continuing Revolution," *Headline Series* (Foreign Policy Association, New York), No. 153, May–June, 1962. Reprinted with kind permission of the author and publishers.

The struggle to achieve daily, weekly, monthly, quarterly and annual production or construction goals soon became a new way of life for millions of Chinese. Prodded to fulfill and overfulfill quotas by the ever-present cadres and the entire party and government apparatus, the Chinese worker entered a new world of "socialist competition," a world obsessed by numbers, figures and statistics, all designed both to demonstrate the inexorable progress of economic growth and to spur each worker to do a little more.

Before long, results began to be visible. Not only did the wheels of existing industries move faster, but also new factories dotted the countryside and new rail lines crisscrossed its open spaces. Factories and mills producing steel, machine tools, chemicals, cement and an impressive range of heavy manufactured goods, from trucks and tractors to generators and electronic equipment, rose not only in the older established centers of foreign-built industry, such as Manchuria, Shanghai and Tientsin, but also in remote cities in central, northwest and southwest China—and even in Inner Mongolia and Sinkiang. These burgeoning symbols of the growth and spread of industrialism in China became the show places for foreign visitors, and to the Chinese Communists themselves they provided reassuring symbols of economic development. These signs of progress were visible, tangible and impressive. The high price paid for them by the masses of Chinese people in overwork, underconsumption and regimentation was not so readily observable.

First plan accomplishments

Without doubt, Communist China was able, during 1953–57, to initiate an extremely significant process of economic growth. After 1953 it was able to build its economy at a rate as high or higher than that achieved by any other important underdeveloped nation—and higher than the rate achieved by the Soviet Union in its early years.

The most spectacular progress during the first plan period was in heavy industries. In some, including steel, the rates of growth suggested that in time Communist China might be able to achieve, in certain key industries most crucial to modern industrial power, output levels comparable to or surpassing those of important industrial nations such as Britain and Japan (only in absolute terms, however; in per capita terms China will long remain far behind).

The rate of total economic growth, measured

in gross national product (GNP), was also extremely impressive during this period. Independent estimates by qualified economists in the West indicate that during 1953–57 the average annual increase in China's GNP may have been 7 or 8 percent, a rate about double India's during the same period (Japan's rate at that time, though, was comparable to China's and probably somewhat higher).

Lag in agriculture

Peking's emphasis on heavy industry was lopsided, however. Agriculture was seriously neglected, especially in the state's investment policies, and a persistent lag in farm output created continuing and growing problems for the regime. The Chinese Communists did foster many projects for irrigation and flood control, and tried to improve agricultural methods in simple ways, but their main response to the problem was to step up efforts to organize and control the peasants—to insure that, come what may, the state would obtain the grain and other farm produce needed to support China's economic plans.

In 1953 Peking established nationwide state control and rationing of grain. From then on it slowly increased the pressures on the peasants to join various types of farm organizations designed to prepare the way for collectivization. And then in 1955–56 came the big push that organized the peasants into roughly three-quarters of a million full-fledged collectives (called "higher state agricultural producers' cooperatives"), carried out with remarkable speed and efficiency.

Shortcomings and shifts in planning

Despite their pride in what had been achieved during the first plan, Peking's leaders began to show increased anxiety and dissatisfaction with economic trends during the final year of the plan. The year 1957 was not a good one and the regime had to cut back in many fields. The new collectives were encountering numerous problems. Per capita consumption actually declined from the level of 1956. The last payment from past Soviet loans was received—it was only $10 million —and there was no indication that more financial aid would be forthcoming to help China pay for needed industrial imports. In addition, China was obligated to repay all past loans and interest. Peking was forced to reduce its over-all budget, and state investments were cut 10 percent below 1956. It appeared, in fact, as if Communist

China's entire development program might be losing momentum.

This was the context in which Peking's leaders pondered new solutions to existing problems. Those who favored a relatively cautious approach lost out. The "radicals" took charge. The approach they dictated called for bold, even reckless, policies based on the premise "it is not technique but man" that counts. To speed up the process of growth, the entire population, male and female, would be mobilized, recharged with ideological fervor and set to work on new tasks developing both agriculture and small-scale industry (the latter to supplement, not replace, continued construction of large-scale modern industry). The important thing would be manpower and morale, not technique or material incentives. This would be a new, unprecedented road to modernization and communism, differing significantly from the Stalinist model which guided China's First Five-Year Plan.

"Great leap forward"

The new policies first began to unfold during the winter of 1957–58. Over 100 million peasants reportedly were set to work on huge state-directed water control projects. In early 1958, "the great leap forward" was officially announced. The original production targets for 1958, and for the entire second plan period, were soon torn to shreds. The regime projected unprecedented growth rates and set literally fantastic targets. A startling new program was pushed to construct small-scale industries throughout rural China—industries using maximum labor and minimum capital. "Back yard steel furnaces" sprouted everywhere. Suddenly, instead of rural underemployment, there was actually a labor shortage in the countryside. City people were sent to the villages to work and everyone was prodded to work harder, but there were too many things for even China's huge population to do.

In the fall of 1958, only a few months after the first experimental commune was established, the entire countryside was quickly communized during a hectic campaign in which the collectives were merged into about 26,000 communes. These new units took over the functions of local government, mobilized and allocated labor like military command posts giving orders for the day, and undertook to manage almost every conceivable activity within their respective areas—not only agriculture, but also local industry, commerce, finance, education and military affairs. A big push was made to promote communal living, partly to make a rapid stride toward the ultimate goals of communism, partly to release more manpower and womanpower for production. Common mess halls, nurseries, old people's homes and service industries were established to release women from household duties.

Everybody was worked to the point of exhaustion. The peasants went into the fields in large organized teams to do "close-planting" and "deep-plowing," agricultural techniques that acquired almost mystic significance. They were assigned by the millions to hundreds of thousands of new rural "factories" (many of them little more than handicraft establishments). The pace of work was accelerated until Communist China's leaders were compelled to caution local cadres to see that people were given time for adequate sleep.

Breakdown of planning

Although Peking provided the motive power behind all of these developments, central planning became almost meaningless for many of the hectic programs in the countryside, and the national statistical system went haywire. This was a guerrilla warfare approach to economic development. Local cadres were like low-level commanders, on their own; higher authorities demanded results, but how the cadres achieved them was largely their problem. They had to do their best and then report the results to the chain of command. Under relentless pressures from above, they did make great efforts—and sent in glowing reports, many of them grossly exaggerated. As a result, Peking was badly misinformed, so much so that at first it published incredible figures indicating that both grain and steel output had more than doubled in 1958 alone. It soon became necessary to backtrack and scale these figures drastically downward.

The great leap continued, at least in the official view, through 1960, but actually the pace began to slacken even during 1959. While some small-scale rural industries were successful, many were so inefficient and wasteful they had to be abandoned. The back yard steel furnaces were a notable failure; most of their output was unusable. Close-planting and deep-plowing proved to be no panacea; in some instances, in fact, their effects were harmful. The lack of effective central planning, or even statistical control, resulted in many serious dislocations and imbalances. The transportation system, overloaded and disorganized, developed crippling bottlenecks. The communes proved unable to plan and administer all of their new responsibilities. Through poor management, labor and resources were allocated in ways which damaged production. The peasants, treated like conscripts in a production army and deprived of almost all material incentives, began to drag their feet. And despite the millions of man-days invested in water control projects, the regime was still unable to control floods and droughts. Old man weather, one of the greatest tyrants of all throughout China's history, struck once again with natural disasters during three successive years, starting in 1959.

Steel versus grain

Looking at the great leap in retrospect, perhaps nothing highlights its successes and failures more clearly than the results achieved in two key commodities—steel and grain. Steel output skyrocketed from 5.35 million tons in 1957 to a claimed 18.45 million in 1960, a phenomenal achievement which seemed to put the regime way ahead of its original plans. By contrast, however, it is estimated by well-qualified Western analysts that although grain output did rise from 185 million tons in 1957 to perhaps 200 or 210 million in 1958 (Peking's claim, even the revised one, of 250 million is-not credible), it then dropped to roughly 190 million in 1959 and in 1960 was probably again close to 185 million. In grain production, therefore, Communist China probably ended its great leap about where it started—but in the meantime China's population had grown by perhaps as much as 30 to 40 million.

Over-all growth, measured in GNP, is more difficult to judge, but independent estimates by Western experts suggest that it too followed a similar pattern. According to one such estimate, Communist China's rate of annual growth in GNP zoomed from about 5 percent in 1957 to 17 or 18 percent in 1958, dropped to roughly 12 percent in 1959, slumped still further to perhaps 4 percent in 1960, and during 1961 was very low indeed.

These facts, trends and problems forced Peking to re-examine its policies and to make a major retreat from the great-leap policies and the communes.

Changes in communes

Since the Chinese Communist party Central Committee meeting of January 1961, the pressure has been relaxed. Prime emphasis, moreover, has

shifted from industry to agriculture. Every effort is now being made to increase agriculture output and to regularize and normalize the economy. The communes, while preserved as administrative units, have been radically changed—at least for the present. Many commune functions, including allocation of labor and distribution of income, have been shifted down to the production brigades (equivalent to the old collectives), and some have been decentralized even further to the small production teams. Numerous steps have been taken to try to restore the morale of individual peasants and create some incentives for them to increase output. Once again peasants have been allocated small private plots for their own use and rural trade fairs have been reopened so they can market the produce of these plots.

Many communal dining halls have been closed down and participation in numerous other communal activities, once compulsory, has now been made voluntary. The number of local commune industries has declined, and allocation of labor and resources to them has been minimized. At the national level, industrialization appears to be marking time. A sizable number of industries closed down during 1961 for varying periods of time, in some cases to service and repair machines suffering from the attrition of years of almost uninterrupted operation, in others because of raw-material shortages. New investment in heavy industrial construction appears to have been drastically cut. Special emphasis is being placed on industries producing goods which support agriculture — fertilizers, tractors and farm tools. Consumer goods industries are being encouraged, but they are also suffering from serious shortages of agricultural raw materials.

Unresolved problems

The events since 1958 clearly demonstrate that there is no miraculous formula for quickly solving the problem of increasing agricultural production in China. The struggle to solve it will be long and arduous. Investment in the rural sector of the economy will have to be increased and farm techniques improved. And the attitudes and feelings of the peasantry cannot be completely overlooked.

The continuing growth of China's population will also be difficult to ignore, as the Chinese Communists have done so far except for one short period toward the end of the first plan period when they briefly pushed birth control. Estimated to be close to 700 million already (specific estimates vary; some are above 700 million, some below), China's population could reach a billion by the 1980's if the present annual increase rate of perhaps 2 percent is not reduced. Conceivably Peking, with its great totalitarian power over people's lives, might be able to accomplish something in birth control if it really tried. But apparently the party does not wish to limit population—and consequently the labor force—at the present stage.

The problem of importing essential capital goods for industrialization has also become increasingly difficult. In 1960 Communist China incurred a deficit of over $300 million in its balance of payments with the Soviet Union. The Russians agreed to give the Chinese five years to pay this off, but an obligation of these dimensions, added to debts already incurred, will impose definite limits on Peking's ability to buy more machines and equipment from the Soviet Union. The need to purchase huge quantities of food from the West—in both 1961 and 1962—has already forced China to cut substantially its imports of industrial goods from Western Europe. Both of these trends portend increased difficulties in obtaining what is needed from abroad for China's continuing industrialization.

Problems such as these will probably make it extremely difficult for the Chinese Communists to get their economic development program into high gear again. Nevertheless one can be sure they will try. They might, in fact, be willing to pay a high price and take substantial risks to re-accelerate their industrialization drive whenever they decide that the time is ripe for a new push.

READING 79

Between the world's several experiments in communism and the American experiment in mixed free enterprise, there are almost as many other patterns of organizing economic activity as there are nations. Perhaps few among these patterns teach fundamentally different lessons from what communism and free enterprise can teach, but there is one in-between stage that needs a closer look. This is the case of broader use of central planning than we employ in the U.S.A. while maintaining more economic and political freedom than in the U.S.S.R. For us in the West, the question about such a mixture is, "Can it be done?" We realize that our own system is a mixed one, but how much of a mixture is possible without destroying freedom itself?

France has been experimenting with broader use of state planning. In this article, Pierre Massé, who is commissioner general of the Plan for Equipment and Productivity in Paris, tells an American audience of businessmen what he finds most interesting in this experiment.

Questions to Guide the Reading

In Reading 60, Professor Friedman argued that there are no known examples of political freedom surviving successfully alongside economic centralization. Is this French case an exception, or does it serve to confirm Friedman's argument?

Is the limited use of planning here something that would be wise or unwise to adopt in the American context? Are we already moving on the road toward planning without necessarily having a Plan?

FRANCE: ARE PLANNING AND FREEDOM COMPATIBLE?

Pierre Massé

Development plans for the French economy are the main products of the organization I serve in, the Commissariat General du Plan which is a branch of the Prime Minister's Office, the equivalent of what would be called here an Agency in the Executive branch of the Federal Government. I think I should first try to give you a feeling of what such a development plan actually is.

Physically, it is a book, about 250 pages long. The first page bears the text of a law. It says something like "The development plan published as an annex to this law is approved as a guide for the economy to follow and as a framework for all investment programs."

The remaining two hundred and forty-nine pages contain the "approved" plan: not a law in itself, but a document approved by a law. It begins with a general assessment of the problems and potentialities of the French economy and of its past achievements, from which are drawn the main lines of development for the period covered; rate of growth of national production, level of employment in agriculture, industry and other, rate of capital formation, forecasts of exports and imports. Then come statements of Government policy intentions; amount of resources to draw from the economy in favor of military expenditures, of foreign aid, of scientific research; allocation of the bulk of resources which remain in the economy, between individual disposable income, welfare benefits, and investment for collective well-being (in schools, hospitals, city planning, etc.); means, fiscal, incentive, and other, by which the State will help the economy reach the set targets.

After this most general part comes one that deals with the conditions to gather in order to be able to pursue the aims first defined; training and allocation of manpower, technological research efforts, balance of foreign trade and payments, savings towards investment, tax structure, counter-cyclical provisions, and many other conditions. And last comes the thickest part of the book; rather detailed chapters describing the expected growth process for each sector of the economy and of the economic or social activities of Government.

There is nothing exceptional, or even rare, about any one of those items. What I believe is interesting is that they are listed together, with reference to a single period of time, and all checked against each other, so as to be mutually consistent.

Any large firm operated on modern lines draws for itself medium and long term programs, in which market forecasts, equipment programs, and all aspects of the firm's policy are made mutually consistent, and ends and means are checked against each other. We really do nothing else, at the level of a whole economy.

I believe that the knowledge of a coherent set of targets and forecasts, aggregate as they be, at the level of the whole economy, is good for anyone who has to make decisions in the economy: investment decisions, production decisions, purchasing decisions, training decisions, decisions in the realm of Government as well as in that of the business firm. All those decisions, and singularly the most costly ones, I mean the ones pertaining to investment, have to face the uncertainty of the economic future of the environment in which they are made.

That uncertainty comes from the speedy and unpredictable character of evolution in many fields. This gap can only be filled by what is known as market surveys. All large firms resort to such studies when they want to establish their manufacturing and investment programs, and many trade associations perform the same service for smaller firms, their members. The steelmaker will make safe his supplies of ore and coke, the quantity of manpower and capital he can enroll; he will study the outlets for steel in different branches such as engineering, transport, power, housing; he will try and inform himself about the plans of his competitors. In other terms, he makes his decisions only after having carefully examined his industrial environment.

But while limiting himself to his own environment, our steelmaker may overlook other fields of activity which are not within his easy reach and yet are likely to react on his own situation. The evolution of farmers' incomes, for instance, depends upon that of the disposable income of certain other groups in the population, also upon foreign trade, and also upon Government meas-

From Pierre Massé, "How Is National Planning Possible and Efficient in a Free Economy?" Address before the Economic Club of Detroit, November 19, 1962. Reprinted with permission of the author and the club.

ures with respect to surplus crops. The sale of tractors closely depends upon farm incomes, and the tractor industry is an important customer of the steel industry. Furthermore his own forecasts are made even more uncertain by the fact that other people's forecasts—his suppliers', his customers', his competitors'—are not made with reference to the same set of hypotheses about the future of the economy in general as his own.

The guiding idea of our planning system consists in providing all those who have to make their own forecasts with a single set of references, and in integrating all the interdependent effects in the national economy into a single prospective economic table. Of course, all this has to be quite aggregate, and the plan is drawn branch by branch, not firm by firm. It makes the general program approximative in its form, but it does promise every branch of activity the possibility of purchasing its supplies and selling its goods, for a few years ahead, on a balanced market. The promise of course is only kept if everybody believes in it and plays the same game. At the level of the individual firm, it acts merely as an incentive, an indication with strong arguments in its favor but no binding powers. Firms are not dispensed from working out their valuations of their own attitude concerning risks. But they can do so much better informed.

Useful as it may be, I do not think our national "market survey" would meet great success if it was made for the people who make the daily decisions in the economy by a specialized group of bureaucrats, or even less if it was made against their views and will. Therefore the whole philosophy of our methods is to have the plan made by those who will have to follow it, not for them or against them.

The most specific task of my office is to organize and coordinate the work of twenty-five planning committees appointed by the Government for the detailed preparation of each plan. Twenty of them deal with a sector of production or a branch of the public services: Agriculture, Transport, Chemicals, Schools and Universities, Equipment of Cities, and so on. They cover every field where any investment takes place. The remaining five deal with general problems: Manpower, Overall Balance and Financing, Research, Productivity, Regional Planning. Each Committee includes, as a rule, officials from the Ministries concerned, personally appointed heads of firms (when the Committee deals with an industry), representatives of business associations and of trade unions, and individual experts.

The committees as such do not meet very often. They usually divide themselves into a number of working parties, each of which covers either a fraction of the Committee's sector, or one of the aspects of the Plan for the whole sector. Such parties must include members of the same broad categories as the Committees do. Usually a few of them come from the Committee itself, and the total force thus mobilized in the process of detailed planning is of about 3,500 persons, a good sample of the influential circles in the French economy.

In fact, the best description of our work is: Planning without Planners, or: Planning by the Planned.

Moreover, it has good sides even from the technical point of view: the quantity and quality of information brought to the common pool by the 3,500 authors of the plan is a priceless complement to the current statistical, economic and technological data. The very process of pooling it all through the planning procedure teaches a lot to all those who take part in it, and enables them to shape a common view of the country's economic development—a view supported by their considerable authority as a group.

And of course the feeling of participation created by such a procedure is quite exciting for each individual involved, and really creates a spirit of common purpose throughout the whole economic system as well as in Government and political circles. This, as we shall see later, largely explains why the plan need not be an imperative one to be much more than a single forecast.

Now I wish to emphasize again what I touched on a moment ago: the plan has nothing to do with a detailed, bureaucratic control of the economy. When I tell you that my staff is 40 persons, I am sure you will realize that I am quite unable to impinge on the free decisions of the hundreds of thousands of people who exert some responsibility, big or small, throughout the economy.

The outcome of all those investigations, the plan itself, uses a division of all economic activity in 28 branches only. Except in a few cases, like railways or electricity, generally nationalized monopolies, there is no immediate connection between the decisions to be made in a firm and the targets shown in the plan for production, investment, employment, etc., in the branch to which the firm belongs.

Freedom of enterprise is not reduced because a lot of knowledge is supplied about the expected future of the branch and of the economy as a whole. On the contrary, endeavor is made easier as some of the uncertainty of the future is dispelled. Competition is not less free because competitors know better the size of the market on which they compete. Certainly our planning process, by bringing people together and showing prospects more clearly, has accelerated the movement towards concentration and specialization in the French industry. But it has never degenerated into restrictive practices before the Common Market came into being, and now of course it couldn't any more, in view of competition from five countries outside the area of the French plan. On the contrary I think it can be validly claimed that our plan, inasmuch as it has contributed to the fairly rapid and regular growth of our industries, and made our business community accustomed to that movement, has weakened the existing tendencies towards restrictions in competition, in innovation, or generally in expansion.

The French economy is one where free enterprise predominates. At the same time it is one where State intervention is now quite frequent, in view of all the responsibility commonly laid on the State in the field of full employment, price stability, economic growth, labor relations, development of depressed areas, and many other problems. Furthermore, the French State is itself, like all other States, a major investor. The total amount of capital formation it supervises, be it in Government agencies, nationalized industries, towns, cities, rural areas, or in the private firms which receive Government grants or loans, is roughly around one-half of total gross capital formation.

I must add that our Government has in its hands a few specific incentives for the implementation of the plan by large private investors. Not only is it much easier to borrow at medium term or to float bonds when the money is to be used along the lines drawn by the plan, but also it is possible to benefit from limited corporate tax exemptions.

All that financial procedure has created the opportunity for close contacts between the managers of most large business firms, who must try to have their investment programs approved by the authorities, and my own staff, who are there to certify the general conformity of a firm's orientation with the plan targets.

Of course there are sometimes discussions about those conformity evaluations, but they seldom create among businessmen the feeling that they are subject to arbitrary treatment by a Government agency. The reason, of course, is that, as I said before, the drafting of the plan has been a joint venture in which they, or other businessmen whom they consider their qualified representatives, have been associated. After sixteen years of experience, this feeling of participation is quite widespread, and accounts for a lot in the successful outcome of our plans.

Another major factor is that, as I emphasized before, the plan is quite a convincing survey of the potentialities of the future years for each branch of the economy. Enlightened self interest suggests that the best course towards business success is to navigate in accordance with such a map of the market.

Anyway the fact is that our plans are executed with a very satisfactory degree of approximation in the industry. Proof of it is that, until now, we have been able to grow fast without either bottlenecks or excess capacities.

Let us come now, very briefly, to a few points of method. I would like to begin with a rough sketch of the planning procedure we use, at least in its present state.

The first phase of a plan's preparation is the drawing up of alternative sketches of development, so as to explore the future possibilities of the economy, and to come to a decision about the best general course to follow during the plan period. The starting point of each sketch is a given structure of final consumption during the last year of the plan period, accompanied by a hypothesis concerning foreign trade and another concerning the level of investment required to carry on expansion along the period. From such data, conventional input-output techniques allow us to set up an economic table for the last year of the period, where the economy is broken down into twenty-eight sectors.

In principle, one may say that the best sketch is the one which considers the maximum growth rate of the economy, while taking into account basic equilibriums: full employment, investment equal to savings, balance of public finance and of foreign payments. For instance, the sketches drawn up at the beginning of 1960 for the present plan period, 1962–65, corresponded to three yearly growth rates of national production: 3%, 4%, 5% and 6%. The 6% variable quickly appeared a little too ambitious because it led to a vulnerable balance of foreign payments. The choice made was 5%, a rate which was increased again up to 5.5% in the following course of the procedure.

The choice I just mentioned, which is made by the Cabinet upon my proposals and after due consultations, is not only about the rate of growth, but also about the basic features of the distribution of the new resources created by expansion.

Once the Cabinet has approved a general sketch, which amounts simultaneously to a statement of policy intentions and to a coherent framework in which to fit the detailed programs of each branch, those detailed programs are elaborated by the planning Committees I described earlier: this is what I call the second phase of the plan's preparation, where those responsible for the actual daily functioning of the economy take over, after the economists and the general policymakers.

In the course of this second phase, basic alterations can be made to the initial sketch, if the know-how of the Committee members suggests a correction to the calculations of the economists: this is what happened lately, when we raised the proposed rate of growth from 5 to 5.5%. And this is where our "general market survey," as I described it earlier, is carried out.

My duty during this second phase is to make sure that coherence is preserved among the various targets proposed by the Committees, and then to present them to the Government and the Parliament in an ultimate synthesis.

Speaking of progress reports, would you allow me, before I conclude, to spend a few minutes on a quick survey of our first three plans. Or should I say more modestly, of the evolution of the French economy since 1946, when we started planning.

The first plan, called "Modernization and Equipment Plan," was prepared by my predecessor whom you probably all have heard of, M. Jean Monnet. It covered a period 1947–52, later extended to 1953. The problem was to transform our productive machinery, which had known decadence before the war, and destruction during it. A bold choice was made, at the expense of a faster increase in the level of life of our harassed people, in favor of priority progress in sectors having a driving influence and providing the means for future overall growth: coal, electricity, steel, cement, transport, farm machinery.

With the powerful support of another Plan: the Marshall Plan, and through a period of great difficulties, social unrest, bitter quarrels, and inflation with all its consequences, the targets set were attained. Production had increased by 75% for electricity, by 150% for steel. No basic shortages were to be feared any more. The economy had recovered a long lost habit of sustained growth.

Then come two plans, covering the periods 1954–57 and 1958–61, which are not any more plans of severe priorities, but plans for a balanced growth. All sectors of productive economy are covered, as well as schools, hospitals and other public equipment. Coherence between them is sought through the newly introduced input-output techniques. More emphasis is put on productivity, efficiency, rationalization, and on external balance and monetary stability. Growth went too fast in 1956, had to be slowed down in 1958–59, and recovered a fast rate in 1960–61. On the average, it was a little over 4% a year for gross internal production, and most of the targets set were thus met.

Balance was maintained in 1954–55, then a deficit started in external trade in 1956, and continued in 1957. In 1958–59 it was restored, not without a devaluation of our currency, and it has been maintained ever since.

The interesting point to make is that in 1960, 1961 and 1962 we have had, for the first time, quick growth: 5.5% a year, and good balance: a small surplus in foreign trade, a comparatively moderate rise in home prices. It is the first time that we demonstrate to ourselves that we can do the two things simultaneously for more than a few months. The continuation of this happy combination is the main target of the present plan.

To conclude this lecture which I am afraid has put some strain on your kind attention, let me say a few words of a problem which, I am sure, has already occurred to your minds as you listened to me: that is, the problem of having a national plan within an international Common Market such as we now have in Western Europe.

Opinions on that matter are far from unanimous inside the Common Market. On the one hand, there are a few powerful voices within our European Economic Community, which would tend to proclaim that the French Plan is all but worthless, and that nothing of the kind is of any interest for the European Community.

On the other hand, our Dutch and Belgian neighbors are embarked on an experience similar to ours, and our other associates watch it with a very positive interest. France, Netherlands, Belgium, and the Commission of the Common Market itself hold the position that some measure of cooperative, liberal, active planning of some sort like the one we practice, is necessary for the future of the Common Market. This has just been strongly emphasized by a memorandum of the Common Market Commission to the Six national governments of the Community, in which European programming is suggested as an essential part of our future common policy. Of course I have nothing I can say about this document as long as neither the Common Market ministers nor my own Government have had time to voice authoritative opinions. But it bears witness of the speed with which such ideas evolve.

We, at any rate, believe that what has been found useful at nationwide scale will be found perhaps even more useful at the scale of a group of nations with problems of coordination, fears of over-equipment, and a general craving for quick growth. Of course we French still believe, perhaps more than ever, in modest beginnings like ours in 1946–47, with efforts concentrated on a few obvious points and without necessarily a preconceived idea of all future developments. Just as we have our plans made together, with bargain and compromise, by all parties concerned, we want to negotiate some empirical first step in European programming with our partners, and now, before some crisis compels us or them to hasty arrangements.

Of course, methods of implementation should remain based on persuasion and stimulation, with in no way curtailing the basic human freedoms, including the right to free enterprise.

READING 80

Where have we been in the American economy? What is this system that we have evolved? And where does it go from here? This article addresses itself to all these questions. It could be read profitably as an introduction to the study of this economy. It can be still more useful as a summing up in which the reader tests his new understanding and judgments against those of two economists who are willing to stand back and look at the broad picture. Here is a picture that is only partly finished. There are no blacks or whites in it. And masses of details are omitted so that a few things, which appeal to these two viewers as critical, stand out in sharper relief. Such a picture has its greatest value when it induces the reader to construct his own overview of the world around him.

Gerhard Colm and Theodore Geiger are senior economists with the National Planning Association, an independent, nonpolitical organization devoted to study and discussion of economic and political issues by leaders in agriculture, business, labor, and the professions.

Questions to Guide the Reading

This system is not one of laissez-faire market economics. Nor is the Russian economy discussed in Readings 75 to 77 one of complete central planning. Where do the two economies today have important points in common and where are there still wide differences between them? Are these differences increasing or decreasing?

What are the most critical choices that this economy must face in the years ahead? Is it inevitable that more active pursuit of one set goal—say, security of employment—must clash with the pursuit of another—say, stability of prices or freedom of individuals to pursue their own ends? How will the choices be made?

THE AMERICAN ECONOMY TODAY AND TOMORROW
Gerhard Colm and Theodore Geiger

The American economic and social system of today has undergone many changes and is substantially different from what it was 25 or 50 years ago. But there has been no sharp break with the past, as in countries which have experienced social revolutions. In the United States, inherited institutions have been adapted to fulfill new functions. Here, the emerging economic and social system confounds the observer who tries to characterize it by using traditional names, such as capitalism or socialism. The American economy does not operate in accord with any of the "pure" laws of laissez-faire capitalism or of socialism. Nevertheless, it operates very effectively—probably more effectively than either of those pure systems could.

Here we attempt to summarize the nature of the American economic system. In a sense, this is an impossible task, because the most characteristic feature of the American system is that it is not fixed, but a living thing, moved by many—and, in part, conflicting—impulses. By looking at some of the characteristics that have made it work in the past, however, it is possible to discern the directions in which the American economy is most likely to move in the future.

American individualism and the role of government

Perhaps the most basic fact in the American economy is that the people working in shops and factories, in offices and laboratories, in homes and on farms, feel that they, as individuals, are an integral part of the American system. Neither business managers nor workers nor government officials are regarded as the sole movers or even the most important factors in the system. Each has his indispensable role to play. Nor is his role one that is imposed by superior authority. Rather, it is evolving, open to criticism, and subject to change.

In their jobs and in their daily life, the American people are striving for their own and their families' happiness. But they are convinced that by seeking their own advancement they are also serving a common purpose—the interests of the community as each one conceives them. These

sometimes conflicting impulses do not lead to anything like "class conflicts." Instead, they are more or less effectively resolved either directly, as in labor-management relations, or indirectly, through the day-to-day political life of the nation. This is possible because the American system is based on a deeply rooted bond by which conflicting interests and aspirations are held together. Although difficult to define, this bond is the essence of American democracy.

The feature of the American economy hardest to comprehend is that it combines individual freedom and initiative with a high degree of organizational management. What might on the surface appear as a basic contradiction in objectives or attitudes is reconciled in the American pattern of life. In spite of the industrialization and urbanization of the past century, some elements of the frontier spirit of an earlier age have survived. This spirit combined a strong sense of self-reliance with a ready willingness to join in cooperative efforts when the need arose. Both attitudes still have their creative places in the American economy. Even in the largest factory or office, the worker never becomes a mere number; he always remains Mr. Smith or Mr. Jones—or more likely, Bill or Bob. This is more than a mere mannerism. It reflects an enduring respect for the individual—which explains, in part, the high productivity of American labor.

This economy emphasizes the absence of dogmatic solutions and the persistence of the spirit of trial and error in which difficulties are tackled as they arise in the light of the relevant facts and real alternatives. One example is the very flexible dividing line between public and private responsibilities. Foreign visitors, who are impressed by the accomplishments of American free enterprise, are often puzzled by the important role which the government plays in agriculture, housing, social security, or economic growth and stabilization. Among Americans, there is lively controversy about the proper function of government, but it is rare to find disagreement among them on this basic principle: In a free enterprise system, the greatest possible degree of reliance must be placed on the individual, but the govern-

From Gerhard Colm and Theodore Geiger, *The Economy of the American People* (National Planning Association, Washington, 1961), Chap. 13. Reprinted with kind permission of the authors and publisher.

ment must take effective action when and where needed in the interest of the general welfare.

Proposals for increases or decreases in the extent of government participation in the economic process usually require legislation, which means that they must survive not only the mutual checks and balances of the legislative and executive processes but often a subsequent review by the judiciary. Moreover, all citizens have the essential democratic right of advocating or opposing governmental policies and programs, and many specific interest groups have formed organizations designed to influence legislative or executive actions in behalf of their constituents. To reduce the possibility that they might misuse their economic power, the Congress has adopted laws regulating the activities of such "lobbying" organizations. Nonetheless, these and other constitutional and organizational arrangements are among the most important ways in which the American democracy ensures a reasonably satisfactory balance between governmental and private decision making in the democratic process.

Without exception, the written constitutions of the Federal and state governments have been premised on the conviction that economic activity is a right of the individual, and that the government can regulate it in the public interest and can undertake economic activities of its own only in specified and limited ways. True, the government's powers and actions in the economic field have grown over the years, particularly in response to the unprecedented conditions of the 20th century. But its role is still only a residual and supporting one, with decentralized private initiative continuing to occupy the center of the stage. Nor is there any disposition on the part of the American people today to make a fundamental change in this relationship.

There is no doubt that Americans still prefer to make their own decisions as managers, as farmers, as workers, and as consumers. They recognize, however, that a complex modern society cannot work without certain regulations. To illustrate, motorists would resent it if someone told them when and where to drive their cars; but, with only a minimum of grumbling, they comply with the system of motor vehicle regulations without which there would be traffic chaos. There may be a great deal of discussion whether more or fewer traffic lights would expedite the flow of traffic, but there is no disagreement in principle that government operated traffic lights are useful and compatible with the self-responsibility and self-reliance of the drivers. So it is with govern-

ment regulation of many important aspects of private activity.

Planning in the American economy

A further source of confusion about the United States is the fact that there is much discussion here about planning even though the American economy is regarded as the opposite of a "planned economy." A planned economy is usually thought of as one in which the major decisions concerning production, investment, and consumption are made by a central authority. An economic plan for a period of years is laid down by the central authority, and the plan must be followed by the managers of production and distribution, who are functionaries of the state. Failure to live up to the plan makes these managers liable to severe punishment. This, indeed, is the very opposite of the American system.

The absence of an authoritative central plan does not mean, however, that there is no room for planning in the American economy. Businessmen today make their investment decisions not merely in response to short-range market fluctuations but, increasingly, in recognition of long-run prospects. Business cannot pursue its objectives, such as the greatest amount of profits over a period of time, without an estimate of future markets for its products; future markets for one group of products can be appraised best in relation to the prospective growth of the economy as a whole. Similar considerations apply to economic decisions by farmers, while labor leaders could not engage in wage strategy and government could not appraise farm, water, and power development, social security, economic stabilization, or national defense programs, without planning each in relation to the potential growth and needs of the economy as a whole.

There may be differences of opinion among planners in business, labor unions, farm organizations, and government as to the exact pace of prospective economic growth, as to the effects of automation and other technological developments, as to the best rate of capital formation relative to consumption, and so on. These differences are subject to debate, and to some extent lead to general controversies which give substance to democratic processes. There is no difference of opinion, however, on the need for each decision maker—whether in business, labor, agriculture, or government—to *plan* his decisions. Nor is there much difference of opinion that the plans of these various decision makers must be brought into reasonable accord with one another, and that the government, through its economic and fiscal policies, has the function of promoting such an accord within the process of balanced economic growth.

Planning is not a monopoly of centrally regulated economies. It is an equally essential factor in an effectively functioning free enterprise and free labor economy with democratic institutions. But the techniques of planning in centrally directed and in free economies are entirely different. A centrally directed economy requires a blueprint, which becomes a set of inflexible directives for the agents of production. In contrast, planning in a democracy enables each farmer or businessman or labor leader or official in an individual government agency to establish his own bench marks for the actions for which he is responsible within a broad framework for the economy as a whole as projected by the government or by qualified private research organizations. Furthermore, the better the economic planning by these private decision makers, the less the need for centralized planning.

Decentralized planning can be greatly aided if general projections of potential economic growth are made inside and outside the government. Such projections can serve as guides for the various decision makers, but it is the decision maker's own responsibility to select the projections which he prefers to use. The necessary degree of consistency among the private and public decisions is in part made possible by the fact that they are all using as a common frame of reference the prospective growth of the economy as a whole. This does not mean that there is or should be unanimity about the precisely desirable rate of economic growth; but rather that, over time, there has been slowly but surely developing a general acceptance of certain standards of economic performance which establish responsibilities and provide guides for action.

The various techniques of planning used in a free enterprise economy cannot be discussed here in detail. We only want to emphasize that while the American economic system knows no central planning, it is an economy with a great deal of both private and public planning. Indeed, such planning is essential to the freedom and efficiency of the American system.

The depression of the 1930s and the growth of the 1960s

A disquieting question may be lurking in the mind of the reader. He may be convinced that the American economic system functions well today. Why then did it not produce the same result during the depression of the 1930s? At that time, certain economists were busy explaining why, under the conditions of American society, economic stagnation had to be expected. In contrast, they recently have been explaining why continued prosperity is an almost innate characteristic of the American economy. What assurance is there that, overnight, America may not be back in a period of stagnation?

This crucial question should be raised; nothing could be so dangerous as to assume that the American economy has become immune to depressions. There are, however, decisive differences between the 1930s and the 1960s. In the 1930s, government action was haphazard, a mixture of reform and recovery measures, and met much skepticism and distrust—particularly in business circles. Now, the economy has certain checks and cushions which have been built into its structure, and which tend to mitigate possible downswings. The government—both the Executive Branch and the Congress—is organized to adopt antidepression measures promptly when needed. Most important is a third factor: The major private groups and the public at large now expect and are prepared to support preventive action by the government. Agreement on this concept of the government's responsibility to take action in case of a downswing or inadequate growth could mean more ready acceptance of needed measures which might run counter to the more immediate or imagined interests of some groups. For these reasons, there is a greatly increased confidence in the economic future which gives the private economy a much improved chance of continuing or resuming economic expansion.

Thus, unlike the 1930s, when fears of continued economic stagnation held sway, the 1960s are looked upon as the threshold of a new age of economic abundance. By mid-century, the United States had gone a long way toward eliminating the economic deficiencies of the "one-third of a nation" which President Roosevelt in his Second Inaugural Address called "ill-housed, ill-clad, ill-nourished." Today, the problems of poverty and economic distress are steadily being overcome. For those that persist, it is only a question of time before the future growth of the economy and the improvement of methods will almost certainly make possible their solution. If war can be avoided, the United States has the possibility of achieving material abundance for all within the next decade or two.

Assuming that America can meet the challenge

of its potentialities, the average family could achieve by 1970 a level of consumption about 30 percent above 1960's standard, and the productive capacity of the country would permit a 60-percent increase in production. Americans would thus be able to meet more adequately the growing responsibilities for preserving and developing natural resources, providing needed community facilities, and improving education, health, and the care of the aged.

But the elimination of poverty and of human suffering caused by economic deprivation would not mean that American society would have solved its major problems. Quite the contrary. We have both achievements and continuing deficiencies in the efforts to maintain balanced economic growth, prevent excessive concentration of power, and mitigate other immediate, but relatively familiar, problems of the American economy. There is growing agreement on these objectives, and as desirable standards of economic behavior are further developed, the methods and techniques for dealing with these problems will improve. There are also problems of more recent origin which only now are beginning to emerge clearly and to acquire urgency. They will require many difficult decisions and actions in the years ahead. For example, there are the as yet only partially understood needs and problems involved in adapting our cities and metropolitan areas, our educational system, and our other social institutions to the consequences of population growth, the expansion of industry, and the advancing conquest of poverty in the United States. Much remains to be done in providing more constructive American leadership and more ample resources for helping to unify the nations of the West, to advance the economic and social evolution of the underdeveloped countries, and to meet the challenge of Communist imperialism. Growing needs will have to be met for the training of people and the provision of facilities for scientific and technical research of all kinds. And the as yet unimaginable potentialities, both for good and for ill, which the exploration of space is opening to the human race will inevitably make larger and larger claims upon U.S. resources and skills in the years to come.

The future quality of life

While America confronts many serious problems of these kinds, it also faces new difficulties of a complex and baffling character which are being created, in large part, by the very advances toward the elimination of poverty which it has been making. These interrelated problems have to do with what might be called the quality of life in an age of quantitative material abundance. As such, they involve not only economic difficulties but increasingly raise social, psychological, and moral questions characteristic of an abundant society. Important among these qualitative problems are the constructive use of increasing leisure time and the strengthening of individual creativity in the face of pressures for conformity and uniformity.

The continuing growth of productivity and intensified spread of automation will mean that Americans can produce vast quantities of goods and services with ever shorter hours of work and with less and less physical strain or drudgery. Judging from the recent past, there is ample evidence that Americans, given the necessary time and money, are prone to pursue vigorously whatever leisure-time activities may interest them personally. We have discussed some of the directions these activities have been taking, and there is no question that there has been a steady and encouraging increase in a wide variety of cultural, recreational, and handicraft activities. For the future, however, Americans may need to develop new forms of constructive activity in order to take full advantage of their growing opportunities for, and greater freedom in, choosing the ways they spend their nonworking hours. The challenge to American society, and particularly to the educational system, is so to develop the interests of Americans that their new-found leisure will find them willing and able to devote themselves to activities which are personally satisfying and socially useful rather than harmful.

The increased danger of conformity and uniformity is the product of the complexity and interdependence of modern industrial economies, accompanied by the pressures created by the growth of population, the efforts to raise living standards, and continuing international tensions. Government agencies, business corporations, trade unions, and even universities and other private institutions have been compelled to increase their size, expand their functions, and rationalize their operations in order to cope effectively with the rigorous and changing conditions of the mid-20th century.

There are, however, characteristics of American society which counteract the tendencies toward greater conformity and uniformity. In the United States, almost everyone belongs to a variety of uncoordinated groups and organizations. The factory or office, the trade union, the church, the political party, the social club, and the neighborhood cultural and sports associations—each has its own claim on the loyalty of members and competes for their participation. In one sense, joining such organizations is itself an expression of conformity with current notions about the desirability of being active in community life. Nonetheless, a strong sense of belonging derived from meaningful participation in a particular church, party, trade union, or professional group frequently strengthens the individual's courage to resist less desirable and more general patterns of conformity. At the same time, such competing loyalties also help to ensure diversity of attitudes and interests, and thereby counteract pressures for excessive uniformity.

American concern about these tendencies can only be understood in the light of the traditional American ideal of individualism. The fate of individual creativity in American society will depend on the countervailing power of increasing awareness of the dangers; the open-minded and experimental attitude of most Americans; the growing sense of social responsibility on the part of business corporations, trade unions, and other large organizations; the universal conviction that government is the servant and not the master of the people; and many other institutions and values. So long as these characteristics of American society persist, there is hope that Americans will sooner or later find new and more effective ways of orchestrating individuality and community in the prospectively more difficult conditions of the coming decades.

Marxist dogma and the American system

A large part of communism's strength is its unquestioned belief in the Marxist dogma. Many of the Marxist views have been subject to revision, but one basic credo is essential for the devotion of its followers. This is that "capitalism" and the allegedy related "colonial imperialism" are doomed and that the communists, despite present difficulties, are riding the wave of the future. They are convinced that they are the vanguard of an army marching in accordance with an already determined world destiny.

The fact that the American system has made great advances in technological and managerial achievements is not denied by the communists. They frankly admit that they can learn, and want to learn, from American accomplishments in this respect. However, they are convinced that the more rapid these achievements in a free enterprise system, the nearer the day of its final collapse. They believe that only the communists can make lasting productive use of technological achievements regardless of where they have originated.

According to Marxism, capitalism is doomed by the necessity of so-called natural laws. The communists contend that this will happen in what seems to them the following logical way:

1. Technological advances make for the superiority of large over small firms.
2. The resulting concentration of capital goes hand in hand with a concentration of wealth and incomes in fewer and fewer hands. This leads to a gradual "proletarianization" of the middle classes and a growing gulf between the few wealthy and the many poor.
3. The inevitable existence of unemployment permits an exploitation of labor and makes for continued impoverishment of the masses.
4. The discrepancy between rising productive power and shrinking mass purchasing power and markets leads to the inescapable doom of capitalism, which can only temporarily be delayed by diverting production into armaments and international imperialistic ventures.

We believe that a survey of the American economy as it actually is refutes this Marxist argument step by step. The Marxist dogma was formulated in the light of the economic history of the 19th century and in answer to a laissez-faire interpretation of those developments. This dogma has no relevance if applied to the present American economy. However, being basic doctrine, it could not be abandoned by the communists.

It is true that technological advances have made for the superiority of large enterprises in some branches of industry, but not in all. Contrary to Marxist dogma, the degree of concentration in industrial capacity and capital has not gone hand in hand with a growing inequality in the distribution of income and wealth. The small and middle-sized enterprises have proved their superiority in many lines of activity. The middle classes have not been proletarianized; on the contrary, the status of what the Marxists love to call "the toiling masses" has been raised so high that they have largely merged into a growing middle class which includes most Americans. The economy of the American people has not resulted in impoverishment but has brought the people—all the people—of the United States to the threshold of abundance. Far from increasing the concentration of personal wealth and incomes in fewer and fewer hands, it has created a broadening of opportunities and more satisfaction for all.

Nor is mass unemployment an inevitable result of technological development. The theoretical insights and practical experiences of the past two decades suggest that a free enterprise society can, if it has the will to do so, prevent large-scale depressions and mass unemployment. The U.S. government is committed to such a policy of maintaining maximum employment, and this commitment is endorsed by both major political parties, by leaders of business, agriculture, and labor, and by the public generally. Continuing efforts are made to improve the techniques for carrying out this commitment.

The threat of economic depressions at home has not forced the American government into a policy of aggression and imperialism. On the contrary, the United States has played a constructive role in the liquidation of colonialism and has used the aid it freely provides as leverage for promoting economic and social development in the under-developed countries of Asia, Africa, and Latin America.

Large-scale armaments are a necessity forced upon the democracies by the exigencies of the world situation; they are a burden, and not an outlet for surplus production. There are a great many desirable tasks—domestic and international—which have had to be postponed until a reduction in armaments becomes possible and releases productive resources for these constructive purposes.

Thus, American experience reveals the fallacies in the apparent logic of the Marxist doctrine. Our belief in the practical and moral worth of the American economic system is based both on this economic experience and on our conviction that what we have called the Jeffersonian concept of individual freedom and self-reliance is deeply ingrained in the human soul. We are convinced that the American system in the long run offers greater promise than any authoritarian system in productive and managerial efficiency; we know that it affords more freedom and self-responsibility than any totalitarian system.

What should the American economic system be called?

How are we to define this American economy which confounds the observer who seeks to classify it in terms of traditional economic concepts?

The American system is capitalistic to the extent that the desire to make a profit by privately owned and conducted activities is one of the major motivating factors of economic growth. It is a system of free enterprise, free labor, and free consumers. The American economy is not capitalistic, however, if capitalism means an arrangement in which the entrepreneur can do as he pleases and in which workers and consumers are exploited and the capitalist reaps the main benefits of economic activity. The American system is not capitalistic if capitalism means a government operating only in the interest of the entrepreneur. Nor is it capitalistic if capitalism is understood as 19th-century laissez-faire.

The American system is not socialistic if socialism is defined as an economy in which all or most factories are owned and operated by the state and the state determines what is to be produced, what new plants are to be built, what wages are to be paid, and so on. The American system is not socialistic if socialism means an arrangement in which the state plays the determining role in economic and social life. But the United States could be called a socialistic society if by that term is implied a system which democratically works out desirable goals and standards of individual freedom, human welfare, and economic security. The American people expect the government both to help the private economy achieve as many of these goals as possible and to undertake those public programs which are needed to accomplish the remainder. Indeed, *in this sense,* the United States is more democratically socialistic than the Communist states!

In the American system, all institutions, public as well as private, are expected to serve the general well-being. In such a system, private enterprise is not an end in itself, but is the most effective form of organization for serving the needs of the people with a minimum of government regulation. In such a system also, the government is not an end in itself but is organized to fulfill the functions which cannot be adequately discharged by private enterprise.

Thus, the American system is neither capitalism nor socialism in the historical meanings of the terms. It cannot be classified under these headings because it is dominated neither by the state nor by private business nor by any other single group. All the institutions—public and private—play their roles with a great deal of self-determination and self-responsibility.

Who, then, is the master who, in the last analysis, provides the yardstick for judging what a responsible performance is? The answer to this crucial question is difficult to give and that is why it is difficult to define the American system precisely. We would probably come closest to the truth by saying that the American economic system serves the national interest of the American people—as expressed through democratic political processes, articulate public opinion, the multiplicity of private groups and organizations, and the attitudes of all Americans as individual consumers.

The "national interest," vague and fluid as the concept may be, has become more tangible than in the past. The advocates of laissez-faire frowned on any attempt to develop economic standards, such as desirable levels of consumption or housing or a desirable rate of economic expansion. If everybody only pursued his own self-interest, they contended, the best possible economic result would follow. Today there are emerging specific ideas about the desirable performance of an economy—jobs for those able and willing to work; avoidance of heavy fluctuations in employment, production, and prices; adequate wages, housing, nutrition, and health services; and a rate of economic growth which uses the advances of science and technology, makes possible the elimination of poverty at home, and supports cooperation in the solution of world problems. It is no longer taken for granted that the unrestrained pursuit of self-interest either by individuals or by organized groups will necessarily lead to the desired results. Individuals and organized groups are expected to pursue their self-interests in a way that will serve the requirements of the national interest.

Only a part of the requirements of the national interest have become crystallized into laws. Some are in the form either of "unwritten laws" and traditions or of the individual choices of men and women who are free to make both political and economic decisions. The general public accepts large enterprises, large unions, and large government as useful institutions, but does not want the political, economic, and social life of the people determined by any one of them. Those in charge of large enterprises or large unions or large government agencies are aware of this attitude and are learning more and more to respect it. Thus, for example, regardless of whether the antitrust laws cover all instances of possible abuse of economic power, the unwritten law does provide a punishment for actions by business corporations which violate the public interest. The punishment may consist of unfavorable publicity, with a possible adverse effect on sales of products or on the recruitment of needed personnel. It may consist of Congressional investigations, and of any other techniques for the expression of disapproval which exist in a democracy. Similarly, dissatisfaction either with inadequate governmental action or with overextension of government power finds prompt expression in election returns.

Thus, the economic system emerging in the United States embodies features of various "pure" economic systems, and promises to provide the capacity for reconciling the needs and values of the individual with the requirements of a complex society and the possibilities of modern technology.

The economy of the American people— is it for export?

We have described the economy of the American people with considerable pride in its accomplishments and in the way it works out its own improvements. But what, if anything, can other countries learn from this American experience? Is the American system, in whole or in part, for export?

The American system has both universal and unique features. On the one hand, it expresses many of the fundamental values and aspirations that are common to all mankind, and it uses economic techniques which are used or could be adapted for use anywhere in the world. On the other hand, the specific institutional embodiments of these values have been much influenced by the particular culture and traditions of the Western society within which they have evolved, and by the limitations and possibilities imposed by a particular geographical environment.

Insofar as other nations seek to achieve the same values of freedom, justice, and welfare as do Americans, they can adapt to their own situations many of the attitudes and techniques which have characterized American pursuit of these objectives. For example, the freedom and diversity of insight and initiative which result from the large measure of decentralized and private decision making in the United States are valued by many other countries. American attitudes toward work and workmanship; toward innovation and enterprise; toward mutual help and cooperation regardless of so-called class differences; toward practical experience, rather than traditional doctrine, as a guide to action—all these are suited to, and in varying degrees are characteristic of, other countries. Similarly, because of their efficiency, American productive techniques and managerial methods are spreading throughout the world under a wide variety of different forms of economic organization.

American experience has a profound significance for other countries particularly in two respects:

1. It shows that rapid economic growth—in contrast to largely futile attempts to redistribute a fixed national income—provides the necessary condition for increasing the economic welfare of all the people and achieving greater social justice in the society.

2. It shows that substantial economic growth can be had without sacrificing individual freedom, initiative, and self-responsibility.

In effect, American society has been achieving an historically unique reconciliation of three partially conflicting human ideals—economic welfare, social justice, and individual freedom. Such a reconciliation can never be complete, but it has gone further in the United States than in most other societies and gives promise of progressing even further in the future. The fact that so substantial a reconciliation can actually be accomplished is certainly a message of great significance to all humanity. Other countries with different cultural and environmental limitations and possibilities may find some of the specific American institutional forms of private enterprise uncongenial to their traditions or irrelevant to their present conditions. In this brief report, we cannot specify the differences in economic organizations which may be warranted between, for example, a highly industrialized country in the Western cultural tradition and a predominantly agrarian country with an entirely different cultural background. Again, owing to rapidly growing populations and rising economic expectations, some densely populated but inadequately developed countries are in a situation in which they must strive to condense into a few decades the amount

of economic development and expansion which the United States took over a century to achieve. In such circumstances, the governments of these countries are likely to assume more initiative and responsibility in economic development than the U.S. government has undertaken.

Thus, it is important to distinguish between those features of the American system which are relevant to the needs and possibilities of other countries and those which are not. Failure to make this distinction is largely responsible for the misunderstandings, both at home and abroad, over the "exportability" of the American economic system. There are some Americans who insist that other countries can make substantial economic progress only if they adopt the specific institutional forms of the American economy as well as its attitudes and techniques. There are Asians and Africans who claim that nothing in the American experience has any relevance for their very different cultures and traditions. Both views are equally erroneous, for neither recognizes that probably the major contribution which the American people have been making in this century to the progress and welfare of mankind is the unique combination of attitudes and techniques they have evolved for achieving high productivity and living standards without sacrifice of freedom and individuality.

It is true that Communist dictatorship also has achieved remarkably rapid economic expansion, high rates of capital formation, and fast technological advances in the Soviet Union and may eventually do so in other Communist countries. However, these have been purchased at the price not only of political and individual freedom but also of forcing productive resources into armaments and industrialization with utter disregard for the welfare of the people. It is our conviction that balanced economic growth can be obtained without resort to terror and injustice, not only in advanced industrialized nations but in all countries.